PHILOLOGY

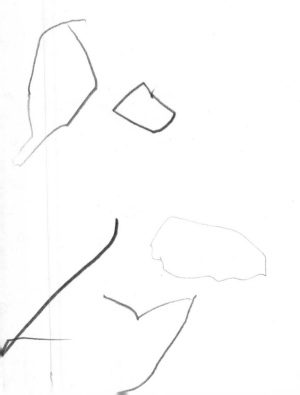

PHILOLOGY

THE FORGOTTEN ORIGINS OF THE
MODERN HUMANITIES

James Turner

PRINCETON UNIVERSITY PRESS
PRINCETON AND OXFORD

press.princeton.edu

Cover design by Faceout Studio, Kara Davison
Cover image © iStock Photo

Endpaper map: *Mare Internum*, from Richard J.A. Talbert, ed.,
The Barrington Atlas of the Greek and Roman World.
© 2000 Princeton University Press.

Fifth cloth printing, and first paperback printing, 2015

Paper ISBN: 978-0-691-16858-6

The Library of Congress has cataloged the cloth edition as follows:

Turner, James, 1946– author.
Philology : the forgotten origins of the modern humanities / James Turner.
pages cm
Includes bibliographical references and index.
ISBN 978–0-691-14564–8 (hardcover : alk. paper)   1. Philology—
History.   2. Historical linguistics.   3. Humanities.   I. Title.
P61.T87 2014
409—dc23

2013035544

British Library Cataloging-in-Publication Data is available

This book has been composed in Minion Pro

Printed on acid-free paper. ∞

Printed in the United States of America

9 10

FOR MY DOKTORKINDER
WITH THANKS FOR ALL THEY TAUGHT ME

CONTENTS

PROLOGUE

In his *Adages* (1500) the great humanist Erasmus of Rotterdam quipped, "The fox knows many things, but the hedgehog one big thing."[1] Might the two animals know the same stuff? Could the hedgehog's one contain the fox's many? The book you are reading began in my growing curiosity about whether humanistic scholarship in the West is ultimately many or one.* I have more to say about how I got curious, but first a few words are in order about what our fox and hedgehog comprehend.

Studia humanitatis—humanistic studies—in one guise or another have for many centuries dwelled at the heart of Western learning.[2] In British, Irish, and North American universities today, the 'humanities' make up a central strand of teaching and research. But their present forms are a modern novelty. The many humanistic disciplines that today's fox knows date only from the nineteenth century. Trace their several origins, and (as the hedgehog realizes) the trail usually leads back to one big, old thing: philology—the multifaceted study of texts, languages, and the phenomenon of language itself.

Philology has fallen on hard times in the English-speaking world (much less so in continental Europe). Many college-educated Americans no longer recognize the word.[3] Those who do often think it means no more than scrutiny of ancient Greek or Roman texts by a nit-picking classicist, while British readers may take it as referring only to technical research into languages and language families. Professors of literature use the term to belittle a simpleminded approach to their subject, mercifully discarded long ago. Indeed, for most of the twentieth century, philology was put down, kicked around, abused, and snickered at, as the archetype of crabbed, dry-as-dust, barren, and by and large pointless academic knowledge. Did I mention mind-numbingly boring? Whenever philology shows its face these days in North America or the British Isles—not often, outside of classics departments or linguistics faculties—it comes coated with the dust of the library and totters along with arthritic creakiness. One would not be startled to see its gaunt torso clad in a frock coat.

---

* Non-European civilizations have their own vigorous traditions of humanistic scholarship; for instance, Confucian erudition in China. These figure in this book only when they affected the Western tradition, such as the impact of the Sanskrit learning of India described in chapter 4.

It used to be chic, dashing, and much ampler in girth. Philology reigned as king of the sciences, the pride of the first great modern universities—those that grew up in Germany in the eighteenth and earlier nineteenth centuries. Philology inspired the most advanced humanistic studies in the United States and the United Kingdom in the decades before 1850 and sent its generative currents through the intellectual life of Europe and America. It meant far more than the study of old texts. *Philology* referred to *all* studies of language, of specific languages, and (to be sure) of texts. Its explorations ranged from the religion of ancient Israel through the lays of medieval troubadours to the tongues of American Indians—and to rampant theorizing about the origin of language itself.

The word *philology* in the nineteenth century covered three distinct modes of research: (1) textual philology (including classical and biblical studies, 'oriental' literatures such as those in Sanskrit and Arabic, and medieval and modern European writings); (2) theories of the origin and nature of language; and (3) comparative study of the structures and historical evolution of languages and of language families. This last inquiry had stunning result: the recovery of a vanished, previously unsuspected language, parent of most tongues of Europe, northern India, and the Iranian plateau.*

These three wide zones of philological scholarship, diverse in subject, shared likeness in method. All three deployed a mode of research that set them apart from the other great nineteenth-century model of knowledge, Newtonian natural science. All philologists believed *history* to be the key to unlocking the different mysteries they sought to solve. Only by understanding the historical origins of texts, of different languages, or of language itself could a scholar adequately explain the object of study. Moreover, all breeds of philologist understood historical research as *comparative* in nature. Only by placing a classical text or the grammar of Sanskrit into multiple comparative contexts could a scholar adequately understand either—by comparing the classical text with other manuscripts and with historical evidence surrounding them; by comparing Sanskrit grammar with similar Indo-European grammars (as well as, at least tacitly, dissimilar grammars of other language families). Furthermore, philologists understood history not only as comparative but also as *genealogical*. They aspired to find historical origins in a very specific sense of the term: to uncover lines of descent leading from an ancestral form through intermediate forms to a contemporary one. Later in this book we shall see how *historicism*, with its insistence on *comparison* and *genealogy*, replicated itself in the DNA of the modern humanities.

Equipped with these powerful tools of investigation, philology animated sundry types of knowledge across the academic countryside. Until the natural sciences usurped its throne in the last third of the nineteenth century, philology supplied probably the most influential model of learning.[4] The immense

---

* This long-lost language is now called Proto-Indo-European.

resonance of philology as a paradigm of knowledge is much less well known today than the parallel influence of natural science, because science won and philology lost. Victors often erase the footprints of the defeated. Ask any modern student of ancient Carthage.

I stumbled on some buried ruins by accident, over thirty years ago. In the early 1980s, I set out to write a life of Charles Eliot Norton. Norton was the most prolific begetter of the humanities at the time when modern American higher education was taking off, the decades after 1870. It made sense to start research for a biography with my subject's parents. The mother, Catharine Eliot Norton, left behind only scraps of correspondence. The father, Andrews Norton, a Bible scholar, supplied a lot more posthumous debris. The trove included notes for his Harvard University lectures on biblical criticism. In perusing these, I learned that a 'conventionalist' theory of language (more about this in chapter 1) undergirded the elder Norton's understanding of the Bible and theology. He even believed that other philosophies of language threatened religious faith. In the 1830s, Andrews Norton got into a public argument with his sometime student Ralph Waldo Emerson over the latter's heterodox religion. In plowing through the printed and private records of their row, I discovered that Emerson's ideas about language frightened and angered Norton as much as his religious doctrines: Emerson's linguistic heresy, Norton insisted, underlay his religious infidelity.

In the spring of 1985 the history department of the University of Michigan invited me to deliver what we in the trade call a job talk. I took the opportunity to decipher further the Norton-Emerson rhubarb by poking around in other American writings about language in the period. I found myself trying to convince my Ann Arbor listeners that a peculiarly American style of linguistic theorizing, now largely forgotten, flourished in Norton's day and might help to explain thinkers as influential as the philosopher Charles Peirce and the anthropologist Lewis Henry Morgan. I got the job, at least. A few years later an acquaintance in Paris found these musings curious enough to publish in a journal there.[5] The ball was rolling.

But Andrews Norton still mattered to me mostly for shaping his son. As biblical critic, Andrews made the Gospels his specialty. To explain such ancient texts, he taught, one had to set them in historical context. Their interpreter needed to know the idioms of the first-century Greek in which the Gospels were written; literary forms then current; the mind-set of Jews of the era and of their Roman rulers; customs governing relations between the sexes and family life; religious practices; economic activities; legal codes; diet—the welter of details that enabled a modern reader to decode the texts as their writers intended. To amass this expertise, the critic had to bring to bear on the Gospels other texts of the era: these cast light on not only linguistic and literary problems but more broadly the culture, specific to its time and place, that formed the Gospels' authors. They could no more escape it than a medieval peasant could escape his culture or Madame de Maintenon hers. And every text of the era revealed *something* about the culture it came from; and so the Gospels helped the scholar to understand other contemporary texts, just as these other texts cast light on the Gospels. Each text might provide a snippet of information that made something clearer in the others. By tacking back and forth between the books of central concern (here the Gospels) and texts surrounding them, the critic re-created, as best he could, the lost world that produced all these texts. He thus made the original meaning of the Gospels clearer to a modern reader. Andrews was, in short, a textual philologist.

Like father, like son. Charles Norton first made his scholarly mark by translating Dante—a task requiring philological skills like those he knew from his father's works. Later in life, he edited seventeenth-century English poetry, another act of philology. But the younger Norton never limited himself to studying texts. He became best known, in fact, as a historian of art—the first professor of that subject in the United States. He also wrote about classical archaeology—and founded the Archaeological Institute of America, which became the major professional group for that new academic discipline. As I tracked his career of innovation in the humanities, it dawned on me that Charles Norton treated Greek temples, medieval cathedrals, and Renaissance paintings all as 'texts.' He put these physical relics of past worlds into their historical contexts, comparing them with other 'texts' of their times (literal and metaphorical) in order to recover their meanings to the people who made them. He then in turn used, for instance, the Parthenon or the cathedral of Siena to throw light on the long-dead cultures that produced these buildings. This man—who more than any other individual became 'founding father' of the modern humanities in the United States—applied the same historicizing, comparative, genealogical philological methods whether he studied poems, buildings, or pictures.[6] And I doubted that Norton was sui generis.

He was not. Historical scholarship is a small world. Colleagues elsewhere knew I was at work on Norton. When organizing conferences, they sometimes solicited papers from me on related topics. So, while writing Norton's biography, I had the chance to test my hunches about the kinship of philology and the modern humanities. Samples excavated from other archives gradually turned my guess into a working hypothesis. When Norton breathed his last in 1999 (for the second time, poor man), I set out to learn how far the fingers of philology extended into modern humanistic learning. By then I did not feel nearly as lonely as in 1985. More and more explorers were detecting traces of philology in various fields of scholarship.

Still, we are only beginning to recover how language study in its heyday formed the skeleton of modern erudition and gave us many disciplines that today make up the humanities and even social sciences. Historians have excavated philology's role in the origins of anthropology, of classics (as distinct from mere teaching of Greek and Latin), of comparative study of religions, of literary scholarship, indeed of certain kinds of legal research. We have also become increasingly aware that two other learned activities, related in topics, method, and attitude, went alongside philology for most of its long history: rhetoric (the art of expressive speaking or writing) and antiquarianism (the study of physical and other relics of the past). Their traces, too, appear in scholarship today.

Yet, despite many fine monographs, no one to date has ventured an overview of the whole process: the birth of the modern humanities in the English-speaking world from the womb of philology. ("English-speaking" is explained in the "Conventions" section.) This book tells that story.

I am far from its ideal narrator. Innocent of Sanskrit, barely acquainted with ancient Greek and Hebrew, feeble in Latin, I am bound to get tangled in vines, to trip over roots while exploring the dense forests of philology—as any specialist will happily point out. My excuse for undertaking the expedition is simple: no one else has. Technical frailties may even prove strengths. Specialized arguments agitating different branches of philology do not distract me. Products of specific philologies interest me less than their digestion by workers in other domains (sometimes as ignorant of the original field as I). I am oriented to the general intellectual history of the last two or three centuries, not to any philological subfield. I am apt, then, to ask questions about broad influence, maybe to see the forest more clearly because my hyperopic vision blurs nearby trees. But I hardly need add that I stand on the shoulders of scholarly forerunners, since the reference notes scream of dependence—though I have also had to hack my own way through little-explored thickets.

Because philology's legacy survives in ways we build knowledge today, the excavation of the philological past becomes an effort at once of historical reconstruction and present-day self-understanding. When we see where our modes of knowing came from, we grasp better their strengths and weaknesses, their acuities and blind spots. I hope that a broad view of the philological heritage will help us to detect these things more easily, to locate ourselves more securely on the map of knowledge, and thereby to improve our future investigations.

The benefits for humanists of knowing our own past hardly need stating. We live with conflicted minds. On one hand, disciplinary walls divide humanistic fields from each other. Historians of the twentieth century rarely read the journal *Twentieth-Century Literature*, and it has been a long time since I saw a colleague in art history scanning the book reviews in the *American Historical Review*. On the other hand, praise of interdisciplinary research is the Hallelujah Chorus of the university these days, and humanistic scholars from different disciplines do collaborate on occasion—sometimes as individuals, sometimes in cross-disciplinary programs like American Studies. The *American Historical Review*, in fact, does from time to time review books about art history, and literature departments house quite a few professors whose books I, a historian, routinely read as 'intellectual history.' The situation is curious. We would understand it better if we knew how it arose. When did 'literature' diverge from 'history,' and in what ways? What genuine differences in method came to separate 'history' from 'art history,' and how much do the two disciplines still overlap? If we humanists grasped more fully how we came to be what we are today, we would better see when and how we can fruitfully work together, as well as what we gain and what we lose by staying apart.

Perhaps less expectedly, social scientists, too, might learn something about themselves from the history of humanistic scholarship. Reflection on it could clarify where they stand in relation to other fields of knowledge. All scholars (historians included) tend to get caught up in internal self-understandings of our disciplines. We all enrich our conceptions of our work by getting out of our skins.

Take political science as an example. It conventionally splits into two broad wings: political theorists and their more empirically inclined colleagues who study such things as comparative politics, politics in different national contexts, international relations. (Some political scientists wear both hats, but the hats still differ.) The first big branch, political theory, comes out of the Western philosophical tradition. For many centuries (going back to Plato) philosophy stood as the self-conscious opposite of philology and its cousin rhetoric—a standoff that ended only in the eighteenth century, if then. (More about this confrontation will come.) Political theory still carries tendencies honed by philosophy's persistent denigration of the mere 'opinion' that philology and rhetoric were alleged to offer. These include a leaning toward seeking general rules or principles and a bias toward prescription rather than description alone. It remains a historical enigma why political theorists are regarded as closer to the humanities than their empirically minded colleagues. As to the latter: among the means that empirical political scientists apply in their sub-fields, one of the most favored is the comparative method—sometimes historical, sometimes not. The use of comparison to highlight similarities and differences in objects of study is very ancient and perhaps universal. But the most numerous, obstinate, thoroughgoing practitioners of comparative method in the West have been philologists—from antiquity right into the modern period when political science formed as a discipline. When political scientists and other social scientists began to make use of the comparative method in the late nineteenth century, they were borrowing from philology: a lineage now masked by the quantitative data commonly compared.

Anthropology, like political science, is a house divided—and infested with philology. As political science has a theoretical and an empirical side, so anthropology has a cultural and a physical side. The line between them is not always clear. Biological anthropologists, working with bones and DNA, plainly inhabit the physical section. Cultural anthropologists just as obviously do not. Linguistic anthropologists focus on an aspect of human cultures, language, that has a physical basis. Archaeologists in anthropology departments, like their peers in classics departments, work with material remains but strive to draw from them cultural meaning. Cultural anthropology teeters very close to the humanities in its methods; and, thanks to historians like Thomas Trautmann and John Burrow, scholars by now recognize its roots in philology. In contrast, archaeologists and linguistic anthropologists today 'look' more like scientists than humanists. Yet, as we shall learn, they, too, ultimately derive from the philological tradition and lines of study associated with it, especially during the period between the Renaissance and 1800.

In short, the bins into which we today sort academic knowledge—at least in the 'humanities' and 'social sciences,' if those labels have coherent meaning—produce unfortunate outcomes. Our categories require ripping apart modes of knowledge and methods of acquiring it that were once connected. Self-awareness about these matters will allow all of us in universities to see more clearly what our disciplines mean, where they tie into each other, how we can most effectively cooperate with each other, and how we can most sensibly and usefully organize knowledge. These are things students, professors, deans, and provosts need to know.

They are also things citizens need to know. Higher education may be perpetually in crisis, but today pressures on it in America and Europe are exceptionally relentless. Some are financial, as state support ebbs and tuition costs surge. Some are economic, as demands rise for colleges and universities to focus on 'practical' fields like science, technology, or business. Some are curricular, as course offerings grow more diffuse and student learning more dubious. Higher education needs reconstruction—from the general-education component, to the structure of specialized programs, to the layout of graduate training, to the configuring of knowledge itself beyond the present disciplinary setup. But rebuilding can only proceed intelligently if we understand how knowledge has evolved over time. Otherwise we will miss important pieces of the puzzle latent in the structure of knowledge today, as well as pieces now so much taken for granted that we overlook them.

We lack much of this needed historical understanding. The history of natural science *is* a mature field. The history of the social sciences is a toddler, the history of the humanities an infant. Look in any well-stocked library; you will find lots of historical monographs on special aspects of individual disciplines all across the map of knowledge. You will find many broad historical surveys of natural science as a whole. You will find a few such books about the social sciences collectively. You will find no general history of the humanities written in English—the sort of work that would show how different humanistic fields of study grew over time, in changing relationship to each other and to other areas of knowledge.

To clearly see connections and disjunctions requires a wide vista of the development of humanistic learning. This book tries to offer one to readers living amid the educational and research institutions of the English-speaking world. To ensure breadth of view, the first four chapters are devoted to the formative 'prehistory' of nineteenth-century philology and its partners rhetoric and antiquarianism, from ancient Greeks to the end of the eighteenth century. But 'the humanities' as *we* know them came into existence only in the nineteenth century; and so the book reaches focus *after* 1800 on the English-speaking lands ringing the north Atlantic. Philology in the nineteenth century pervaded the intellectual life of every country in Europe and the Americas and in Europe's settler colonies elsewhere. But I pay closest attention to England, Scotland, and the United States. (Ireland gets less heed than it might deserve, and Canada barely any, because relevant secondary literature and archives are sparse.) One reason for this focus is personal: my career as historian has centered on the English-speaking north Atlantic. There I can most easily detect connections among different fields of knowledge crucial to this story. But common language and, to some extent, shared history and mutual prejudices linked English-speaking scholars across the Atlantic. They looked more like a quarrelsome clan, with a single family history, than like distantly related tribes.

They shared much with counterparts in France or Chile but also pursued philology and its offshoots in distinctive British and American ways. One revealing instance: many German philologists absorbed the philosophical hermeneutics (theory of interpretation) sketched by Friedrich Schleiermacher. These philosophical concerns stood out in August Boeckh's *Encyclopaedie und Methodologie der philologischen Wissenschaften* (*Encyclopedia and Methods of Philological Scholarship*),* posthumously published in 1877. By then, every American and British classicist knew Boeckh's pathbreaking *Staatshaushaltung der Athener* (1817), translated into English as *The Public Economy of Athens* as early as 1828. Yet his *Encyclopaedie und Methodologie* went untranslated and, as far as I can tell, unread by English-speaking philologists—even those who had, as students in Germany, attended the lectures that made up the book![7] Far more empirically minded than their German colleagues, they left Schleiermacher's theorizing to the theologians.

Still, Anglophone philologists borrowed heavily from foreign work. German universities housed the masters of philological research from the late eighteenth to the start of the twentieth century; English-speaking scholars leaned heavily on German writings and personal contacts, at least from the 1830s, when ability to read German grew more common. German philologists appear often in the following pages, both as background to and as direct influences on English-speaking scholarship. To a lesser extent, so do savants from France and other non-English-speaking lands. But their roles, even when seemingly ever-present (as in the early chapters), are always ancillary to the story of philology and its offspring in the Anglophone north Atlantic.

A further clarification: this book does not concern humanistic *higher education* but rather the humanities as *fields of academic knowledge*. They could inhabit freestanding research institutions as well as colleges and universities—or even live outside any institution. The appearance of a subject in university teaching does testify to a discipline's acknowledged existence, and I cite

---

* You may also see it spelled as Böckh. But, like Johann Wolfgang von Goethe's, Boeckh's name is more commonly rendered (in German as well as English) with an *e* instead of the umlaut; that is how it appears in this book.

such evidence from time to time. But knowledgeable observers on both sides of the Atlantic recognized anthropology as a scholarly discipline well before 1860, even though university courses and faculty appointments in the subject appeared only some twenty years later (save one course offered in Toronto in 1857). Discussions of higher education merely subserve the real topic of this book: the emergence of the humanities as academic disciplines.

Readers who did not specialize in history as undergraduates may find helpful an explanation of chronological labels used, fuzzily, by historians of the West, including me. 'Antiquity' means the period before around the seventh century CE. 'Late antiquity' (a category imported into English from German-language scholarship in 1971) runs from about the fourth century to the end of antiquity. The 'Middle Ages' begin when antiquity ends, around 700 CE, and stop with or just before the Protestant Reformation, shortly after 1500. After that, it's all 'modern'—except that modern history, like antiquity, is divided in two. The 'early modern' period ends with the eighteenth century (classically with the outbreak of the French Revolution in 1789); 'modern' *pur sang* goes from then to now.

One word commonly used in the following pages may also need clearing up: the verb *publish*. A work is *published* when made *public*. With reference to ancient Rome, publication might simply mean that an author gathered acquaintances at home to hear him read a new composition. In the era of manuscripts, a work is also said to be published when made available to be copied for wider circulation: the standard medieval method of publication. But an author might also circulate copies of a manuscript within a small group, intending to keep the work semiprivate. Pretty much the same situation persisted after 1450 when printing made copying books easier. A printed work is not published when it comes off the press, but when it goes on sale or otherwise becomes available for public distribution. A famous example is the Complutensian Polyglot Bible, discussed in chapter 2: the printers had it ready by 1514, but its publication waited for the pope's OK in 1522. In the nineteenth century, scholarly authors with enough money often had a draft work printed to send around for comment; we do the same now, without needing as much money thanks to laser printers and e-mail attachments. In neither case is the work 'published'; in both, the author gives it to selected readers. Perhaps the best-known case of unpublished circulation in American literary history is *The Education of Henry Adams*, privately printed in 1907, not published until Adams's death in 1918, but in between rather widely read. 'Publication' is not always clear-cut.

Translations into English are my own unless otherwise indicated in the reference notes. Italicized words in quotations were emphasized in the original unless otherwise noted. Double quotation marks signal material quoted from another work. Single quotation marks are 'scare quotes,' indicating a term or phrase I have singled out because it needs emphasis, interpretation, or qualification.

Sources appear in endnotes, where author's surname and year of publication lead to the list of works cited. Some endnotes also provide supplementary information for specialists. The footnotes contain explanations or asides that I think might interest all readers. More specialized elaboration of comments in footnotes and sources for them sometimes appear in the endnote for the paragraph.

To avoid blinding readers in a hailstorm of personal names, I have deployed a smaller number of representative figures, sometimes repeatedly.

No reader can feel more keenly than I how much the following pages omit, compress, and simplify. Squeezing inflicted sharpest pangs in the early chapters, where centuries cram into paragraphs. To take but one instance, I barely hint at the rich, tortured relations between Christian biblical philologists and their Jewish counterparts. A book could be written about what Christian scholars learned about their Old Testament from just one medieval rabbi, the famed Talmudic and biblical commentator called Rashi.* In fact, the book *has* been written.[8] Other fascinating swathes of scholarship do not even get a bare hint. You will find no discussion of musicology, of Turkic philology, or of many other flourishing, if smallish, humanistic disciplines. Folklore studies could easily have filled a space between anthropology and literature. Such neglect appeared to me mandatory, however painful. I skim lightly over oceans of erudition because plumbing the depths—or merely dipping down a fathom or two—would stretch this book from a few hundred pages to a few hundred volumes. I offer a *tour d'horizon*, not an encyclopedia.

Some readers may wish for explanations of other choices I have made, in matters including gender-neutral language, dates, geographic names, and the like. These can be found in the section titled "Conventions" immediately following this preface. The rest of you should dive right into the story.

---

* Rashi is the conventional acronym for Rabbi Shlomo Yitzhaki (1040–1105), formed in the same way as (to mention an individual better known to most readers) the nickname Rambam for Maimonides: *Rabbi Moshe ben-Maimon.*

CONVENTIONS

It has in recent years become a convention in works by professional historians to lay out, at least in reference notes, one's agreements and disagreements with other historians. I resist the trend. Experts will see where I stand in
relation to others. Nonexperts will not care. Besides, in a book of this breadth,
marking every specialist quarrel would make the endnotes explode.

The gender-neutral language expected in scholarly works usually goes missing
in this one. Absence stems not from churlishness but from an effort to reflect historical reality. Until the late nineteenth century, the learned people I discuss were
almost all male. This situation may now appear disgraceful, but to call the generic
philologist of 1500 or 1850 'him or her' merely veils the disgrace.

Chronological clarity is essential, yet too many dates fog the windshield.
Mostly, I keep time by giving year of publication when mentioning a book. In
the earlier chapters, which cover long stretches of time, birth and death years
also appear in parentheses for individuals who loom large, as well as for less
prominently featured persons whose place in time may otherwise be unclear.

I translate titles of books in foreign languages unless I believe their approximate meaning obvious to readers. Thus Leone Modena's *I riti degli Ebrei* gets
'Englished' as *The Rites of the Hebrews*, whereas Johannes Buxtorf's *Synagoga
judaica* appears only in Latin.

CE (Common Era) and BCE (before the Common Era) replace the venerable AD (anno Domini, year of the Lord) and BC (before Christ). The older
usages imply that everyone recognizes Jesus as Lord or at least as the central
figure in history. Even Christians who wish this were true know it is not. The
adoption of Christian time reckoning as the international standard has made
it truly 'common,' no longer distinctively Christian. And 'Common Era' is no
recent product of political correctness. It appeared in the title of the great astronomer Johannes Kepler's *Eclogae chronicae* (1615), while the first volume of
Ludovico Muratori's *Annali d'Italia* (1744) began, as its title page proclaimed,
"Dall'Anno primo dell'Era volgare"—from the first year of the common era.
Both as an amateur astronomer and as a teensy historian standing on the
shoulders of giants like Muratori, I happily follow their lead.[1]

Much recent historical writing about philology focuses on its political pen-
umbra: its place in the genealogy of anti-Semitism, for example, or its role in

imperial knowledge systems. I generally avoid such issues. This is not because they do not matter—they matter greatly—but because I have almost nothing to add to what others have already said. Moreover, in my view, such factors usually affected the uses or the topics of philology rather than its methods. (Usually, not always.) These latter, structural matters—'internal' to scholarship— shaped the modern humanistic disciplines and so get my attention.

No universally agreed label exists for those books of the Bible originally written in Hebrew (a few passages in Aramaic). Tanakh or, less commonly, Miqra denotes the version used in Jewish worship.* Christians call their equivalent the 'Old Testament' (a collection differing somewhat for different Christian groups). 'Hebrew Bible,' a modern coinage, often appears in academic writing as a neutral, generic substitute. Because most biblical philologists who appear in this book started from a Christian point of view, I most often use the term *Old Testament*—as they did. On occasions where Old Testament is inapt, I have preferred Hebrew Bible. 'Bible' refers generically to sacred writings honored by all varieties of Christians and Jews without regard to the specific books in the collection.

Some geographic names need elucidation. From 1707 Scotland and England united as 'Great Britain' (the kingdom of England having long, long before absorbed Wales). People sometimes called this new entity the United Kingdom, and at times I do the same. From 1801 until the early twentieth century, this kingdom also integrated the formerly separate kingdom of Ireland (already governed by Great Britain); and 'United Kingdom' became official. (It still is, though now the United Kingdom of Great Britain and *Northern* Ireland.) So from 1801 until about 1920 United Kingdom supplies a label for the entire 'British Isles.'[2] This last term understandably makes Irish people wince when used as shorthand for Britain, Ireland, and the smaller islands of the region. But more recent, neutral labels—Britain and Ireland; the North Atlantic Archipelago—have their own problems. I stick with British Isles but use it sparingly and only when United Kingdom does not apply. Flouting geographic precision, I use North America to mean the United States and Canada and their colonial antecedents, although Mexico inhabits the same continent. Canada did not exist as an entity until the 1840 Act of Union created the United Province of Canada and did not begin to resemble its modern form until the years following confederation in 1867. Likewise, 'Italy' acquired political meaning only in 1861, 'Germany' in 1871. These realities do not stop me from using 'Canada,' 'Italy,' and 'Germany' to mean the respective regions regardless of their political status at the time.

My references to the 'English-speaking' north Atlantic countries may rattle speakers of Scots, Tiwa, Irish, French, or other languages spoken as mother

---

* *Tanakh* is an acronym derived from the Hebrew initials of its three parts: Torah ('the law'), Nebi'im ('the prophets'), and Kethubim ('the writings'). Christians know these as (a) the Pentateuch, (b) the Prophets and historical books, and (c) the poetic and wisdom books. *Miqra* means 'what is recited.'

tongues in North America and (gulp) the British Isles. I use the term *English-speaking* in a sense specific to my subject. Almost all *scholarship* between the later eighteenth and early twentieth centuries in these lands appeared in English. (Before then, Latin provided a medium for erudition—and still did for classicists afterward.) The English-speaking world of *this* book spoke English in *this* sense.

- Taxonomy of specialization

(Isocrates) - Lebonius —— St. John Chrysostom

Acknowledgments

A nyone who undertakes a history of this scope, put together over so many years, amasses debts of gratitude too extensive to confess fully or even to recall exactly. The University of Notre Dame repeatedly gave time off for research and writing as well as liberal funding to use the time efficiently. The former Max-Planck-Institut für Geschichte in Göttingen and the John W. Kluge Center for Scholars at the Library of Congress hospitably housed my research in autumn 2003 and spring 2004, respectively. I owe special thanks to Hartmut Lehmann in Göttingen and Peg Christoff in Washington. The Spencer Foundation and the National Endowment for the Humanities generously supported a year of writing in 2007–8 that produced a first draft of this book. Earhart Foundation with equal generosity made possible a leave in 2011–12 that resulted in the final one.*

The thing more needful even than money and time in writing a book like this one is helpful people. Librarians at the University of Notre Dame and, before that, the University of Michigan bore the brunt of my research. Nancy Mitchell was my cheerful and reliable lifeline to the Notre Dame libraries during the last years of research and writing. I am grateful also to archivists and librarians at the American Philosophical Society Library; Bentley Historical Library, University of Michigan; Bodleian Library, Oxford University; British Library; Cambridge University Library; Center for American History, University of Texas–Austin; Courtauld Institute; DeGolyer Library, Southern Methodist University; Dr. Williams' Library; Edinburgh University Library; Gould Library, Carleton College; Harry Ransom Humanities Research Center, University of Texas–Austin; Eisenhower Library, Johns Hopkins University; Hoole Library, University of Alabama; Houghton Library, Harvard University; Library of Congress; National Library of Scotland; Niedersächsische Staats- und Universitätsbibliothek; Queen's University Belfast; Regenstein Library, University of Chicago; Wren Library, Trinity College Cambridge; Trinity College Dublin; and University College London.

---

* The NEH requires grantees to state, "Any views, findings, conclusions, or recommendations expressed in this publication do not necessarily reflect those of the National Endowment for the Humanities." The same, of course, holds true of other institutions that supported my research.

I learned much from audiences who over the years responded to my developing ideas at the École des Hautes Études en Sciences Sociales (Paris) on multiple occasions; the Library of Congress; Oregon State University; Pazmany Peter University (Budapest); Princeton Theological Seminary; Princeton University; Sogang University (Seoul); and the Universities of Calcutta, Michigan, Notre Dame, and Texas.

My early thoughts about ramifications of philology germinated in talks with Tom Trautmann when we worked together at the University of Michigan between 1984 and 1995. The research assistance of Siobhan Donnelly many years ago at Michigan aided my first investigations. Among scholars who kindly replied when I pestered them for advice were Margaret Abruzzo, Steve Alter, Mary Ellen Brown, Erwin Cook, Tony Grafton, Paul Gutjahr, Sean Harvey, Iván Jaksić, Wolfgang Kullmann, Ulrich Lehner, the late Sabine MacCormack, John McGreevy, Margaret Meserve, Mark Noll, Mike O'Brien, Jon Roberts, Bob Sullivan, the late Frank Turner, and Caroline Winterer. There are surely others whose names I cannot now recall but for whose aid I am nonetheless thankful. Steve Alter, Keith Bradley, Brad Gregory, Iván Jaksić, Sabine MacCormack, John McGreevy, Margaret Meserve, Mark Noll, Jim VanderKam, and John Van Engen read draft chapters and gave helpful advice; Chris Stray supplied very useful comments on a related paper. Caroline Winterer read the full, semifinal version with her sharp eye for style and organization. Tony Grafton and Frank Turner commented shrewdly on an entire first draft.

Both the reader and I owe a large debt to Brian Bendlin for his meticulous editing of the manuscript. The editorial team at Princeton University Press— including Beth Clevenger, Rob Tempio, Maria Lindenfeldar, and Alison Anunzis—shepherded the book into print with care and grace that left me bleating in gratitude. Terri O'Prey carefully oversaw the entire process of production. Peter Dougherty is an editor of extraordinary skill, shrewdness, and even wisdom, except where college football is concerned; and I give thanks that he took this writer in hand.

The untimely deaths of Frank Turner in 2010 and Sabine MacCormack in 2012 were great losses to me and to the republic of letters. This book stands as one among many monuments to their erudition and generosity.

PART I

⤙⚬━━━⚬⤚

FROM THE FIRST PHILOLOGISTS TO 1800

Language and its products enthrall human beings. Our enduring love affair with words should not surprise. After all, the expanding capacity of *Homo sapiens* to use language in ever more intricate ways partly powered our evolution, gave us an edge over other animals, deepened the interdependence basic to humanity. The earliest schools, in Mesopotamia, taught not augury, astrology, or the art of war but how to handle written language. When systematic erudition emerged in ancient civilizations, it often made language its subject. In *Shuo Wen Jie Zi* (121 CE), the Han dynasty scholar Xu Shen invented the strategy of indexing Chinese characters by the root elements they shared, still basic to Chinese dictionaries. But already, some four centuries earlier, in present-day Pakistan, Pāṇini had composed his dauntingly terse grammar, the *Ashtadhyayi*; in it he set out rules covering Sanskrit syntax, morphology, and semantics—arguably the fountainhead of the science of linguistics. Here I can merely nod toward the boundless steppes of philology lying beyond the confines of Western civilization.

This book's more provincial story begins in the Mediterranean basin, with Greek speakers who lived in Pāṇini's era. Some of these Hellenes invented the language-centered instruction that supplied the basis of European schooling for many centuries to come—and in some senses still does. Others of them devised methods for meticulous inquiry into questions more or less related to such education—that is, into problems posed by language. Where did words come from? How do they function together? How does the Greek tongue specifically work? How ought one to interpret *texts*, wherein written words weave intricate nets of meaning? (English *text* and *textile* share the same Latin root, meaning something woven.) How could one keep texts under control when their numbers multiplied vastly? In doing all these things, these teachers and these scholars together midwived the fraternal twins born of language: the practical art of rhetoric and the erudite science of philology (the latter then including grammar, other sorts of linguistic theorizing, and the multisided study of texts).

Neither child enjoyed an untroubled life. When the Roman Empire gobbled up the Hellenic world, it absorbed Greek rhetoric and philology. Learned Romans took great interest in both, honed them, complicated them. But the empire split in two, and its western half soon collapsed into chaotic centuries poisonous to any form of learning. The shards of the western empire eventually re-formed as Latin Christendom (the immediate ancestor of 'Europe'). But its erudite elite had things on its mind other than philology. Not until nearly a thousand years after the disintegration of the western Roman Empire did a shift in intellectual climate—conventionally called the Renaissance—revive philology and rhetoric.

By then, teaching and scholarship had evolved vastly more elaborate institutions. To the old Greeks and Romans, a 'school' was a gaggle of pupils and a teacher who met in any space at hand—even outdoors. And with rare exceptions ancient scholarship went on in the houses of whichever rich, leisured men happened to care about such things. But medieval monasteries and cathedrals birthed schools with an abiding existence; by the late Middle Ages some even got their own buildings. After 1200, universities emerged. These provided homes for erudition, though rarely philological erudition in their early centuries. In the sixteenth and seventeenth centuries, 'academies' began to spread: establishments for advanced learning separate from universities, often patronized by a royal or noble court. After perhaps 1500, improved communication and the new technology of printing increasingly tied together scholars based in universities, academies, or elsewhere—even Jesuit missionaries in China—into an international Republic of Letters.

In this worldwide web of learning, philology and rhetoric stood out. They were often closely allied with an antiquarianism that delighted in material relics of the past—from prehistoric stone monuments to Roman coins. (Scholars in the ancient Mediterranean world had shown this same sensibility.) Early modern philologists still astound with their energy, creativity, and diverse curiosity. Our purposes require looking especially closely, in the later seventeenth and eighteenth centuries, at the heterogeneous stew of British philological erudition. Our true subject, the modern humanities in the English-speaking world, grew right out of it.

1

"CLOISTERED BOOKWORMS, QUARRELING ENDLESSLY IN THE MUSES' BIRD-CAGE"

FROM GREEK ANTIQUITY TO CIRCA 1400

The metaphorical bookworm, like its literal cousin the earthworm, loves to burrow. Imagine several bookworms patiently tunneling down through the roots of each modern Western humanistic discipline until finally coming to the last, most deeply buried tendril. When bookworms reached bottom, they would find themselves together in the ancient Mediterranean world, listening to Greek.

To retrace this journey—to follow upward in time the roots from which the modern Western humanities sprouted millennia later—requires starting where these bookworms ended. Ancient Greeks did not devise 'the humanities' as Europeans and Americans know them; today's notions of humanistic learning in the West lie light-years from Greek thinking. But Greeks did beget the primeval ancestors of today's humanistic scholarship. Greeks began systematic speculation about language; they invented rhetoric; they commenced methodical scrutiny of texts; and out of all these materials they then fabricated grammar. Ancient Greeks gave birth to the European tradition of philology, in the very broad sense used in this book. And philology eventually gave us our humanities.

'Philology' is the only label large enough to cover all such studies of language, languages, and texts. The noun itself (φιλολογία, *philología*) and the parallel adjective first appear in Plato, with meanings as mixed as those of their root λόγος (*lógos*): love of talking, love of argument, love of reason. But the word *philology* soon became associated specifically with the study of language—with reading, rhetoric, literature, textual scholarship. Eratosthenes of Cyrene in the third century BCE may have been first to tag himself φιλόλογος—*philólogos*, 'philologist.' By φιλόλογος he most likely meant, broadly, a learned lover of the written word. Later, Romans would call such an all-round scholar of language and literature *grammaticus* or *criticus*, limiting *philologia* more or less to imaginative literature and its study. Despite such unstable connotations and sometimes awkward fit, *philology* provides the only adequate portmanteau word. Even the rhetorician came close enough in spirit and in matter to fit inside.[1]

To understand more easily the growth of ancient philology requires subdividing it topically, but division risks distortion. Greek philology became possible after Greek speakers engineered their own alphabet from the Phoenicians', perhaps in the ninth century BCE. Most people continued to live lives untouched by the new letters.[2] But, however limited the audience, inquiries into language and texts multiplied during the first several centuries of Greek literacy. Thus came to life an enduring and evolving scholarly curiosity about language and its products. Ensuing studies overlapped or fed into each other so much as to frustrate any attempt to herd them into clearly defined fields. But for clarity one can split ancient philology into four areas: linguistic speculation, rhetoric, textual philology, and grammar—appearing more or less in that order. Such partition does not do violence to the facts, but it serves present convenience more than it reflects ancient practice. That point understood, philology's career can be tracked by starting with Greek creativity, then exploring what Romans and their successors did with Hellenic inventions.

To begin, recall the layout of languages around the ancient Mediterranean. Today Greece comprises the southern Balkan peninsula and nearby islands. But ancient Greek speakers (Hellenes,* they called themselves)—seaborne people and avid colonizers—ranged much farther. In the seventh century BCE, Greek cities already stretched from Sicily and southern Italy, across the Balkan peninsula and the islands of the eastern Mediterranean, along the western coast of Anatolia (modern Turkey), to the shores of the Black Sea. The conquests of Alexander the Great between 336 and 323 made Greek also the lingua franca of an arc of land running from Anatolia through Syria to Egypt. Non-Greek peoples in this 'Hellenistic' world spoke various vernaculars—Armenian, Syriac, Aramaic, Egyptian, and so forth. But Greek supplied the jargon of commerce and government. This dialect was not the Attic Greek of Demosthenes and Plato but a simplified form, suited to practical use as a second language, called κοινή (*koiné*, 'common, shared'). Christians know it as the idiom of the New Testament. 'Classical' Greek—Attic, in particular—persisted in education and high culture, like Latin in medieval and early modern Europe.

Meanwhile a new people, coming out of central Italy, spread a rival language. In a series of wars, Latin-speaking Romans first gained hegemony over most of Italy and then, in the third century BCE, sent armies beyond it. Con-

---

* 'Greeks' comes from the Latin *Graeci*, the Romans' name for the inhabitants of the territory roughly corresponding to modern Greece.

quest proved as bloody and difficult as it was protracted. But by 100 BCE Rome controlled the Iberian Peninsula, much of north Africa, mainland Greece, and chunks of Asia Minor. A hundred years later, Romans not only held sway over lands washed by the Mediterranean. They had also expanded their empire northward to absorb what are now France and the Low Countries (adding England later). Roughly speaking, where the Greek language had already taken hold—in the eastern half of the Mediterranean—it remained the common tongue. Around the western half of the Mediterranean and (to the north) in the continent west of the Rhine, Latin played the role of Greek in the east: the language of business, of administration, of schooling, of the elite.* In the *agora* of Alexandria or Ephesus, a traveler heard Greek; in the *forum* of Hippo or Barcelona, Latin.[3]

GREEK ORIGINS

It may be no accident that Hellenes started philology on its long European career. The ancient Greek language consisted of a cluster of regional dialects: a situation not unusual as such. In Greek, however, unusually clear boundaries divided the dialects. Yet Greek speakers—who could and regularly did talk across dialects—drew a bright line between Greek and other ('barbarian') tongues. Perhaps this diversity-within-unity was what pushed some Greek speakers to ponder language. In any event they did, and their reflection on language and on its written products gave the West philology.[4]

Greek philosophers wondered about the source and nature of language. Pythagoras, in the second half of the sixth century, apparently gave thought to where the names of things came from. Heraclitus of Ephesus, around the century's end, believed that words somehow reflect the inner essence of the things they name. His approximate contemporary Hecataeus of Miletus argued that historical events lurked behind personal names and place-names. Mere scraps survive of such early conjectures. But in the first half of the fourth century Plato's dialogue *Cratylus* staked out three positions distinctly: (1) language is conventional: words mean what they do only because people agree to use them in that way; (2) language is natural: words express the nature of the things they name (or they are meaningless); (3) language is both: words are based on nature but altered by convention. This last position—spoken by Socrates in *Cratylus*—was Plato's own. Words, he believed, arose from efforts to mimic natural objects vocally; but usage changed their forms, and custom fixed their meanings. *Cratylus* features fantastic etymologies, possibly meant as parody. But it also made the first serious stab at analyzing language to sur-

---

* The extent of Greek colonization complicated this picture. Merchants around Roman Massilia (modern Marseilles), originally a Greek foundation, continued to use Greek; and it was spoken in parts of southern Italy into the twentieth century.

vive from the ancient Greek world. Plato and his pupil Aristotle sorted out some basic linguistic concepts that later scholars would develop; for instance, word and sentence, verb and noun phrases, inflection.[5]

Another stream feeding into philology also arose in early Greece—and drenched classical antiquity far more thoroughly than these guesses about the nature and history of language. Hellenes doted on public debate: think of the quarrelsome assemblies in the *Iliad* or of the βουλευτήριον (*bouleutérion*, 'council hall') that today's tourist finds in every ruined Greek city. Small wonder that rhetoric grew into a formal study. Around 500 BCE, Athens put in place political and judicial regimes based on citizen participation. In the wake of these democratic reforms, certain 'sophists' began instructing students how to argue capably in public. (Sophist derives from σοφος—*sophos*, 'wise'—but in early Greek σοφος also meant 'skillful.') To hostile eyes, such newfangled teaching scorned appeal to truth or tradition in favor of the sinister power of manipulating opinion. This alleged amorality brought down on the sophists' heads the wrath of Plato. Paradoxically, Plato's own Socratic dialectic gave a terrifically effective example of rhetoric, though one supposed to reach certainty rather than preference or likelihood. Plato connected dialectic (philosophic argument) to assured knowledge of truth and tied rhetoric to opinion or 'mere' probability. The linkages proved enduring. So did the orientation of rhetoric to civic life. Plato's pupil Aristotle—engrossed by actual politics, unlike Plato—respected rhetoric more than his master had. Where Plato accepted as knowledge only a grasp of universal, timeless essences, Aristotle believed that awareness of particulars and of rough generalizations also qualified as knowledge. Where *dialectic* proceeded from *universally* accepted opinions, he said, *rhetoric* started from *individual* ones. He thus stressed the importance of knowing the facts of a case and reasoning logically from them.[6]

Through the centuries to come, this dichotomy appears again and again, in one form or another: philosophy arrives at universally valid generalizations, whereas philology interprets individual cases. Here lies in embryo the modern distinction between law-seeking ('nomothetic') natural sciences like physics and chemistry and interpretive ('hermeneutic') disciplines like literature and history.

But return now to antiquity, when Aristotle's *Rhetoric* paled in impact beside the writings of Isocrates (436–338). Isocrates did much to rescue the teaching of public discourse from the calumny of his contemporary Plato. Isocrates insisted that speakers must never make "the worse case appear the better"; that oratory should be used only for public good; even that a lofty style would elevate a speaker's morals. The style he taught highlighted composition in balanced periods, equal in length, achieving equilibrium through (in Thomas Conley's words) "parallelism and antithesis at every level from that of diction to that of larger units of composition." If Isocratean style sounds insufferably baroque, think of Edmund Burke or Daniel Webster; and the popularity of Isocrates's instruction may become clearer.[7]

But Isocrates did not really innovate in rhetorical theory; rather, he became vastly influential because he made rhetoric the heart of advanced education. Before him, Greek education—beyond teaching some boys how to read and write—was scattershot. No detailed information survives about Isocrates's own school: just its fame and a few of its elite pupils. Even his extant statements on teaching tell us little except that he stressed deliberative discourse, written as well as spoken. Yet classical Greco-Roman education at its higher level was rhetorical schooling descended from his practices. These spread through the Mediterranean in the wake of Alexander's conquests. Rome, in turn, adopted Hellenistic rhetorical education, implanted it everywhere, and passed it on, much modified, to the Middle Ages. This enduring Isocratean heritage kept rhetoric prominent in the family of *philología*. Rhetoric's relation to philological *scholarship* always proved shakier. A few learned men did explore rhetoric. Many more humdrum schoolmasters only drilled pupils in it.[8]

The first scholars actually to call themselves philologists stood at a distance from rhetoric. They worked in a library rather than in the public square. They devoted their labors to texts rather than to the spoken word. And the texts that most absorbed them were those of Homer.

To understand why requires a digression, backtracking in time from the era of Plato and Isocrates. Ancient Greeks long looked on the *Iliad* and *Odyssey* with unique reverence, much as Jews and Christians view the Bible.* The Homeric epics even seemed storehouses of divine wisdom, masked in allegory. No wonder that, as John Sandys said, from "the days of Solon" onward, "Homer was constantly studied and quoted, and was a favorite theme for allegorizing interpretation and for rationalistic or rhetorical treatment." Yet what did the name Homer mean in the days of the Athenian lawgiver Solon (ca. 638–558 BCE)—and thereafter? Unlettered singers had long entertained Greeks by stitching together tales of the Trojan War and the wanderings of Odysseus. Solon's contemporaries ascribed such epic yarns generically to Homer, a great songster of uncertain date and reality. Some time after the Greeks learned the alphabet (again, soon after 800 BCE), someone committed some of these stories to writing, perhaps first as an aid to oral performance. No one today knows who, where, when, or in what form. One dubious tradition says it happened by order of the Athenian ruler Pisistratus around 550 BCE. Some modern classicists have plumped for a century or two earlier. If Pisistratus did so act, he may have wanted a transcript for use by the rhapsodes who intoned the *Iliad* and *Odyssey* at the Greater Panathenaea, a quadrennial festival. But not until the second century BCE did Homer's poems settle down into the shape known today. The relentless quotation, the varying interpretations, the wish for an authoritative version, all help to explain why textual philology eventually developed.[9]

---

* One biblical critic has argued that New Testament authors consciously imitated Homer; see MacDonald 2000 and 2003.

But philology happened only after books become common enough to pose complex problems. During the fifth century BCE, written works snowballed in prose as well as verse. At the same time, run-of-the-mill terms used to pass moral judgment on oral recitations acquired new, technical meanings; for example, μετρον (*metron*), meaning 'measure' (as in 'due measure'), came to mean poetic 'meter.' These idioms better fitted discussion of written work and eventually provided jargon for critical scholarship. Near the century's end, bookselling appeared as a recognized if rare business. Booksellers imply book manufacturers, turning out multiple copies. Copyists wrote, as had the authors they duplicated, on rectangular papyrus pages pasted together to form long sheets, one page wide; these sheets were rolled up for ease in handling and storage.* A reader would hold one end of the roll in one hand, the other end in the other hand, unscrolling from one side and rolling up from the other as he read. (Or as she read, far less often. Patriarchal though it was, classical antiquity did not utterly deny schooling to girls, especially girls of high caste.) Throughout antiquity, indeed until modern times, books remained the indulgence of an elite; but the tiny elite was growing slightly larger. Once booksellers existed, book collectors appeared. After 400 BCE, more and more references pop up to private libraries. Most at first must have been small, holding more like a dozen than hundreds of scrolls.[10]

Handwritten scrolls, copied by hand, offered boundless chances for error to creep in. Even the most meticulous scribe could slip when lamps guttered or ink smudged. Cicero's gripe to his brother described the stock of many an ancient bookseller: "both written and sold so carelessly." The complaint echoed down through the ages, from Galen in second-century CE Pergamum to Maimonides in twelfth-century Egypt and Chaucer in fourteenth-century London. The more copies of a work, the more mistakes. In works as long and as commonplace as Homer's epics, whole lines vanished or materialized out of thin air. Rhapsodes reciting Homer altered words and even added their own riffs, multiplying the variants circulating in writing. Where religious propriety demanded consistency—recall the declaiming of the *Iliad* at the Greater Panathenaea—unreliable texts shamed a city. During the later fourth century certain plays of Aeschylus, Sophocles, and Euripides were repeatedly performed in Athens during state religious celebrations. The politician Lycurgus mandated, around 330, that official versions of these plays be kept with the public records. One might joke that Lycurgus legislated textual philology and made the Athens record office into the first public library.[11]

The real first public library (so far as anyone knows), and the nursery of textual philology, lay across the Mediterranean. After Alexander the Great's death in 323 BCE, one of his generals made himself king of Egypt as Ptolemy I.

---

* Papyrus—whence 'paper'—is a Nile reed (*Cyperus papyrus*) from which Egyptians formed durable, flexible sheets for writing, exported all over the ancient Mediterranean world. βιβλος, the Greek word for the papyrus plant, got transferred to the scroll made from it. *Biblos* gave us bibliography, bibliophiles, and the Bible.

Cultivated and ambitious, Ptolemy carried a Greek tradition of monarchical literary patronage to spectacular new lengths. Many Greek cities had a Μουσεῖον (*Mouseīon*), a shrine to the Muses, sometimes a center for literary activity. Around 300 Ptolemy set up in Alexandria his own Μουσεῖον (whence our word *museum*). But he really created a new species: a college of scholars and scientists on royal salary engaged in both teaching and research. Ptolemy aimed to challenge Athens as cultural center of the Greek world. For at least the next three reigns (to 205), his successors—confusingly also called Ptolemy—must have shared this ambition. Dogged royal persuasion lured to Alexandria's Museum intellectual stars like Euclid and Eratosthenes (he who computed the earth's circumference). Ptolemy I or more likely his son Ptolemy II added the great Library.* The Ptolemies seemingly planned to amass all Greek texts, from tragedies to cookbooks. By the time the dynasty's final heir, Cleopatra VII, began dispensing her books, along with other favors, to Julius Caesar in 48 BCE, the Library of Alexandria held thousands and thousands of scrolls. The Ptolemies got their manuscripts by sending out agents to buy, by hijacking books from ships docked at Alexandria, and by bald-faced deceit. Ptolemy III supposedly borrowed Athens's official manuscript of plays by Aeschylus, Sophocles, and Euripides—after posting an enormous bond—and then pirated it, sending Athens a copy and forfeiting the bond. (The first library fine?) Such free-spending bibliomania affected the quality of the collection for bad as well as good. Some dealers turned out as dodgy as the third Ptolemy, passing off sloppy copies, even outright forgeries of 'old' manuscripts. (Booksellers in Rome were pulling the same scam three or four centuries later, when the rhetorical teacher Quintilian also groused that they swiped his lectures.) The mushrooming Alexandrian trove contained, too, lots of duplicates, rarely identical in wording.[12]

These quality-control issues posed problems for which the invention of textual philology gave the solution. The Alexandrians around the library were not first to see such predicaments or to handle texts with a scholarly cast of mind. The earliest scroll to survive from ancient Greece was dug up in 1962 in the residue of a funeral pyre, badly singed. This Derveni Papyrus contains a strange, line-by-line, allegorical commentary on passages ascribed to Heraclitus, Homer, and the mythical Orpheus. In form, the exegesis prefigures later literary commentaries. The scroll dates from about 330, but its contents maybe from seventy years earlier. Clearly, the tide of written books swelling from the later fifth century onward had begun to turn attention to problems of texts and their meanings. The poet Antimachus of Colophon (fl. 400) studied Homer's language and prepared the first known 'edition' of Homer; on what basis no one knows. Aristotle's lost work *Homeric Problems* used historical context to clear up puzzles in the text. Aristotle had earlier emended the *Iliad* for his

---

* Our knowledge of the Library of Alexandria and of Hellenistic scholarship in general depends on assertions by later writers: thus there is much uncertainty in what follows.

pupil Alexander (the future Great), though in what way he did so is unknown. Aristotle also compiled a historical catalog of dramatic performances in Athens. Some of his disciples carried on his philological and historical studies. One follower, Demetrius of Phaleron, seems to have advised Ptolemy I in founding the Museum. If so, Demetrius's role may clarify why Alexandrian scholars took up where Aristotle's pupils left off.[13]

In any case, the library's resources let the Alexandrians attack such problems with new methodological sophistication. These Egyptian scholars mixed their own inventions with the haphazard innovations of earlier writers; this menu of techniques created systematic textual philology. The ingenuity of Alexandrian erudition in the third and second centuries still amazes.

The most urgent need was to locate a given needle in the immense haystack. Zenodotus of Ephesus probably served as the first librarian, until about 270. So far as known, he invented the idea of ordering items alphabetically. He likely applied his brainstorm to arranging the scrolls, sorted by author. Based on the collection, the poet and heroic grind Callimachus of Cyrene (ca. 310–240) compiled a survey of all Greek writers, arranged in eight categories, from drama through legislators to miscellaneous. Besides listing authors and titles, Callimachus composed short lives of the writers, analyzed disputed authorship, and supplied the opening words and number of lines in each work (vital for identification, titles being unstable). His toils began to provide systematic data needed to study texts and their transmission, enabling later research.[14]

In Alexandria, such research tackled the second great mess the library faced: the errors infesting its manuscripts. Its agents went after older copies of books, knowing that the more times a book had been copied, the more mistakes it contained. Eventually, this partiality for older manuscripts would become an inbred philological leaning. Immediately, it inspired shady booksellers to the textual equivalent of the modern fraud of 'antiquing' furniture.[15] But even wary buying could not exclude texts where original meanings had grown blurred, where sentences had evaporated, where phrases unknown to the author had crept in. Bringing the books into order meant not just arranging scrolls on shelves but also mending their contents. And emendation, in turn, could trip up on linguistic evolution. The Greek familiar to third-century Alexandrians differed from the Greek written in fifth-century Athens. The language of Homer lay still further off. Imagine a twenty-first-century Texan reading Chaucer.

Homer was most often replicated, ipso facto most corrupt of texts; so Homeric scholarship became the template. Zenodotus, around 275, took on the challenge. With multiple manuscripts of Homer at hand in the library, Zenodotus put together the earliest 'standard editions' of the *Iliad* and *Odyssey*— or of any book. He seemingly based his versions on the crucial principle of comparing manuscripts. (*Collation* is the technical term.) Two of his successors as librarian, Aristophanes of Byzantium (ca. 257–180) and Aristarchus of Samothrace (ca. 216–144), much refined his editing. To decide which words in competing manuscripts were really Homer's required aesthetic as well as linguistic and historical judgments; so assessing the literary qualities of a passage formed as much a part of the philologist's task as deciphering its meaning. What 'edition' meant in Alexandria is unclear. Scholars today lean toward the theory that Zenodotus or Aristarchus chose what he thought the best manuscript and annotated it, rather than writing the text anew as a modern editor would. Many Alexandrian emendations seemed risible to later critics, but the principle of a standardized text based on collation of manuscripts endured. Verses in the oldest surviving Homeric papyri vary widely; soon after the editions of Aristophanes and Aristarchus, extensive variations disappeared.[16]

Zenodotus and his successors forged other durable tools of textual scholarship. One was the line-by-line commentary on a text: a genre already exemplified in the Derveni Papyrus and probably practiced by Aristotle's disciples in Athens. Aristarchus expertly honed it. In his hands the commentary became a book in which a passage from a work under study was followed by careful explication—of its meaning, of rare words in it, of any doubts of its genuineness, and so forth. Aristarchus, too, coined an enduring axiom of such text criticism: that a writer's own words provide the best guide to his meaning. Scholars should resolve linguistic puzzles in a text by checking the same author's usage elsewhere. Aristarchus also embedded in the philological tradition an axiom voiced by Aristotle: the critic must understand a text in relation to the customs of the period that produced it. Philologists should thus gauge passages against social and cultural context as one means of deciding their meaning or even their spuriousness. Eratosthenes of Cyrene (ca. 285–194) pioneered in using historical chronology to resolve textual puzzles. The Alexandrians upgraded yet another inherited implement, the glossary, a book defining uncommon or archaic words in a text. By arranging such words in Zenodotus's newfangled alphabetical order, they created the ancestor of the modern dictionary.[17]

All later textual philologists would face the same challenge as the Alexandrians: how to resolve obscurities and to correct dubious passages in a text— or, put more abstractly, how to move from words on paper to meanings in them. And all later textual philologists would deploy the two fundamental tactics of the Alexandrians in attacking a passage under scrutiny. Look at the rest of the text. What interpretation, what wording fits most closely the author's meaning and language elsewhere? Look at the historical context. What interpretation, what wording makes most sense in terms of social customs, religious usages, legal norms, military practices, family relations, and other habits prevailing when the author wrote?[18] And for a long time to come philologists would assert their conclusions in the Alexandrian form of the commentary, while making tools like glossaries to aid their research.

In his Homer edition, Zenodotus set in motion another innovation. He flagged lines he judged doubtful with a horizontal pen stroke in the left margin. This came to be called an ὀβελός (*óbelos*, 'spit' or 'skewer'; Latinized as *obelus*). The ball Zenodotus started rolling never stopped. We still put tiny marks on pages to guide readers through the maze of words. Succeeding Alexandrian critics dreamed up other marginal signs. These included the *diplē* (>) to signal something worthy of note in Homer (replaced in non-Homeric texts, puzzlingly, by the letter chi [χ]) and the *asteriskos* (*) to mark a wrongly repeated passage in a manuscript. Aristarchus even concocted a sign to object to Zenodotus's deletions. Too arcane for ordinary readers, the system proved a huge boon to scholars. They could now show emendations without altering the words of a manuscript. Absent these editorial symbols and the commentary, we might be stuck today with an *Iliad* warped by even the wackiest of Zenodotus's inspirations. Instead, the slash-and-burn approach that some Alexandrians took to Homer vented harmlessly in editions with *obeli*-littered margins. The most prolific inventor of signs for guiding readers through a scroll was Aristophanes of Byzantium. He not only came up with several new critical symbols but also devised accent marks in use today (acute, grave, and circumflex); these aided nonnative speakers of Greek (the majority in the Hellenistic world) to pronounce correctly words that they read. And he invented other new marks to help such readers know when and how long to pause in a text when reading—the comma, the colon, and the period (or full stop). The first textual philologists gave us punctuation. Any casual museumgoer trying to decode a Roman inscription knows the value of that gift.[19]

Besides their editions, commentaries, and grammars, the philologists of Alexandria—and of other Hellenistic centers of erudition—did much that looks to modern eyes more like history than philology. They wrote scholarly biographies; collected old lore about shrines, gods, heroes, cities, and so forth; copied inscriptions; described monuments; and tried to sort out the chronology of past events and writings. Much that historians now do, these learned men did—though 'history' did not yet mean only past happenings. But (comparing them to earlier Greek historians) Hellenistic philologists did not share the sensibility of a Thucydides, who fixed his eye on war and politics. They look more like Herodotus, with his omnivorous appetite for curious details about this people or that. And yet they did not try to compose organized narratives such as Herodotus had written—and such as a Hellenistic contemporary like Polybius (ca. 200–118) created in his history of Rome. If anything, they preferred to arrange the scattered fragments they excavated from the past into revealing mosaics. We would perhaps label these ancient scholars antiquarians; and their interests do resemble those of the antiquarians who would play a huge role in early modern scholarship. Learned research into such matters as natural wonders or chronology does not, by modern lights, fit well with textual criticism and rhetoric. But to divide such inquiries from philology would warp Hellenistic conceptions of learning. And antiquarian erudition stayed tightly bound to philology as it developed in Rome and then in Europe in later centuries.[20]

The scholars around the library and Museum probably had nothing to do with the best known monument of Alexandrian philology. Under the Ptolemies the city housed a large Jewish community. By and large these Jews, Hellenized in culture, spoke Greek as their mother tongue. Like all Jews, they revered as the scriptural center of their faith the ancient Hebrew writings called Torah—'teaching' or 'law.' (Jews also called the Torah the Five Books of Moses: thus to Greek speakers the 'five scroll-cases,' πεντάτευχος, whence Pentateuch, a term still standard.*) But few Hellenized Jews understood the Hebrew of the Torah—a pickle like that of English-speaking Catholics before the 1960s hearing the Latin Mass. Around the early third century BCE, Jewish scholars in Alexandria translated the Torah into Greek: compare the English missals that those Catholics used to carry to Mass. The work possibly went on under the patronage of Ptolemy II, who would have had his own royal reasons for wanting the law of a subject people in his library. There followed—and maybe preceded—other Greek translations of Hebrew scriptures. Collectively, these came to be called the Septuagint, abbreviated with the Roman numeral LXX (seventy), although the writings under this label varied. (The name and abbreviation come from a tale that seventy-two translators miraculously finished their work in seventy-two days.) These translations found wide use in the Jewish diaspora, until eventually versions reckoned more authentic expelled them. But they survived long enough for early Christians to adopt the Septuagint as their divinely inspired Old Testament. It will reappear soon, along with knotty relations between Jewish and Christian philologists.[21]

But first another new path blazed in Hellenistic philology needs explication. Of the four main strands of ancient philology—language theory, rhetoric, textual criticism, and grammar—the last emerged latest as an independent study. Grammatical issues did crop up in early rhetorical teaching, and stabs at figuring out how pieces of language work go back to at least the fifth century BCE. The sophist Protagoras then stumbled toward the ideas of noun gender and verb mood. Aristotle recognized a notion of verb tense, a few parts of speech, and difference between active and passive verbs. Alexandria's great rival as a hub of scholarship was Pergamum, in present-day western Turkey, site of the *second*-largest library in the Hellenistic world. As with Alexandrian erudition, mere echoes of fragments of Pergamene learning survive. But scholars in and around Pergamum apparently spent more time analyzing language than wrestling with textual problems. Later sources suggest that, as early as the third century BCE, Pergamenes were at work on etymology and phonetics (sidelines in Alexandria) and on grammatical problems. Yet Pergamum was in the lead, not alone. In second-century Alexandria, grammar formed part of Aristarchus's discussions. His methodical dissection of language yielded propositions that might be called grammatical laws, although

* The Pentateuch comprises the books known in English as Genesis, Exodus, Leviticus, Numbers, and Deuteronomy.

perhaps not yet grammar as an autonomous branch of learning separate from textual philology.[22]

Aristarchus's student Dionysius Thrax (ca. 170–90 BCE) may have been the first person to devote a book to grammar. At any rate the Τέχνή γραμματική (*Téchnē grammatikē; Art of Grammar*) was long ascribed to Dionysius. Recent scholars doubt the attribution, while thinking the opening section of the *Téchnē* and its basic system to be Dionysius's. Whoever the author, he (like Aristarchus) melded Alexandrian and Pergamene traditions. The mixing probably mattered. Bypassing an apparent Alexandrian quest for general prescriptive rules, the more empirically minded grammarians of Pergamene seem to have gotten much further than their rivals in breaking down Greek into parts of speech and identifying their inflections. Recognizing how little we really know, one might hazard a guess that Alexandria supplied the broad framework of the *Téchnē* and Pergamum most of its detailed contents. A reconstructed version, some fifty pages in print, covers everything from accents and punctuation, through declensions and conjugations, to relative, personal, and possessive pronouns. The little book remained a standard handbook through the Middle Ages. School grammars today are its great-great-grandchildren.[23]

But in antiquity grammar meant much more than parsing sentences. Dionysius divided grammar into six parts. His pupil Tyrannion separated it, more influentially, into four modes of treating a text: recitation, explanation, emendation, and evaluation. This program boiled down to teaching people how to read, with sophisticated grasp, in a culture of oral reading where voice mattered as well as comprehension. Yet here grammar gains almost the breadth of *philología* itself. And why should it not? What did a refined ancient reader need, besides well-modulated vocal cords? He (again, far less often she) required a scroll purged of errors, mastery of the language written on it, and knowledge of the historical and mythological lore to which the writer referred. Add some arguments about etymology and you have a summary of Hellenistic philology and its associated antiquarian research. Such range suggests how grammar could become the core of secondary schooling, as it did in the Roman world. Rome, not coincidentally, is where Tyrannion settled around 67 BCE. There he made a bundle as a chic teacher. There his four-part division of grammar, adopted by the Roman scholar Varro, became normative—in theory if not in the ordinary schoolmaster's drill.[24]

ROMAN ANNEXATION

By the time Rome's imperial paw finished pinning down the Greek-speaking world, Hellenes like Tyrannion had completed the foundations of 'philology'—in a meaning as broad as its nineteenth-century usage, though far from identical to it. The Romans absorbed Hellenistic *philología* as they soaked up so much else from the Greeks. Centuries before, they had borrowed even their alphabet directly or indirectly from Greek. The first known poet to write in Latin was a Hellene, while the first Roman historian wrote in Greek. By the time of Augustus, the well-educated Roman was bilingual; the rhetorician Quintilian even wanted boys to learn Greek grammar before Latin.[25]

Pergamum first taught Greek philology to Rome. One story credits Crates of Mallus, a Pergamene scholar, with awakening Romans to philology. Visiting Rome around 168 BCE, Crates broke his leg in a sewer. Naturally, he whiled away his convalescence giving philological lectures. Whatever the truth of this adorably academic anecdote, Rome did have close ties to Pergamum—which became even closer when Pergamum's last king, Attalus III, bequeathed it to Rome in 133 BCE. The Pergamenes massively swayed Romans trying to catch up intellectually with the Greek-speaking world. Not until three quarters of a century after Crates's leg healed did a scholarly Roman, Lucius Aelius Stilo (ca. 154–74), import Alexandria's critical symbols and methods: or so it was later said. Stilo went briefly into exile in Rhodes in 100 BCE, and he may have picked up Alexandrian tools from Dionysius Thrax, then teaching on the island. Stilo loyally clung to Pergamene grammar when adopting Alexandrian critical ways. He applied his newfangled criticism to the earliest Latin comedies, those of Plautus (fl. 200 BCE).[26]

Whatever Stilo did in naturalizing Hellenistic philology in Rome paled beside the efforts of his pupil Marcus Terentius Varro (116–27). More than a century after Varro's death, Quintilian called him *vir Romanorum eruditissimus*, the most learned Roman; and Augustine said that Varro read so much that it was hard to believe he had time to write, and wrote so much that it was hard to believe anyone could read all his books. Varro wrote about art, antiquities, agriculture, libraries, as well as literary and linguistic topics. His antiquarianism looked back nostalgically to the supposedly incorrupt life of republican Rome before the civil wars, and a lot of what we know of that earlier Rome comes through him. His philological repute rests chiefly on *De lingua Latina* (*On the Latin Language*)—itself antiquarian in flavor—a mutilated six of whose twenty-five books survive. With his Rome lolling in the intellectual shade of Pergamum, Varro naturally shared its enthrallment with etymologies. A later Roman work also tags him as first to divide rhetoric into its enduring three styles: simple, intermediate, and copious (also termed plain, middle, and grand—a partition, one quickly adds, that scarcely mattered to the greatest Roman master of rhetoric, Quintilian).[27]

Varro's attention to rhetoric hardly surprises given the Roman fixation on oratory. Public speaking played, if anything, an even larger part in Roman than in Greek life; and in Rome all sorts of literature, even poetry, got grouped under rhetoric. Roman writers not only systematized Hellenistic rhetoric but amplified its critical vocabulary. Nothing in Greek came close to the massive, methodical *Institutio oratoria* (ca. 95 CE) of Marcus Fabius Quintilianus (ca. 35–late 90s), famous in later ages simply as Quintilian. The manuals of rhetoric passed down through the Middle Ages to the Renaissance and beyond were Roman: Cicero's early, uncompleted *De inventione* (ca. 90 BCE); the similar but full-blown *Rhetorica ad Herennium* (ca. 85 BCE), studied throughout the Middle Ages under the mistaken belief that Cicero wrote it; and Quintilian's great *Institutio*. (Ironically, medieval teachers preferred the *Inventione* and *Ad Herennium* to Quintilian, which then circulated in truncated form.) Even the fourth-century *Ars grammatica* of Aelius Donatus discusses style and figures of speech.[28]

Yet, as Varro's range suggests, Romans also plundered Greek learning far removed from rhetoric. And such thieves abounded, capturing Hellenistic methods for Roman and Latin topics. Like the Alexandrians, Cornelius Nepos (ca. 110–24 BCE), labored to build up accurate chronologies—but, in his case, of Roman history. Marcus Verrius Flaccus (ca. 55 BCE–20 CE) compiled an Alexandrian-style glossary of unusual or obsolete Latin words, a landmark of ancient lexicography that outdid anything we hear of from Alexandria. Quintus Remmius Palaemon (fl. 35–70 CE) adapted Hellenistic grammar to Latin language and literature. Marcus Valerius Probus (ca. 20–105) used Alexandrian tools in correcting and commenting on Roman authors, including Vergil and Terence. The *Noctes Atticae* (*Attic Nights*) of Aulus Gellius (ca. 125–180) shows us an ancient 'grammatical' work in its widest sense: 398 chapters of textual, linguistic, rhetorical and literary criticism—not to mention history, philosophy, law, and medicine—drawn from Gellius's lifetime of poring over Roman and Greek writers. Gellius went beyond the Alexandrians in inventing, according to Gian Biagio Conte, "the method of comparing point by point the style of a Latin poet with that of his source," a new tool of research in textual philology. Around 400 CE, a grammar teacher in Rome called Servius (full name unknown) turned out a commentary on Vergil larded with irreplaceable antiquarian detail, especially about religion. Servius's work typified a new sort of commentary, first appearing around two hundred years before him: scholia. These provided unbroken observations on a text, verse by verse. They had the colossal advantage of collecting in one place insights of different earlier critics of a text. Scholia in the long run became a normative critical form.[29]

Such learned Romans proved crucial. True, Roman philologists followed paths blazed in that outburst of Alexandrian creativity rather than turning in entirely new directions. But Roman grammarians greatly refined and expanded analysis of language. Roman rhetoricians did the same in their field. Roman textual philologists made Alexandrian methods more sophisticated. Moreover, Alexandrian scholarship barely survives in bits and pieces refracted through later sources (notably quotations in the scholia just mentioned). The Romans were the ones who transmitted philological method, the philological focus on text and context, and the fruits of philological erudition to later ages. Like *De inventione* and *Rhetorica ad Herennium*, the grammars of Donatus (fourth century) and Priscian (fifth or sixth century) became workhorses of medieval schooling.[30]

In one key institution, Roman development and diffusion of Greek invention decided the future of philology. In the last century BCE, the Isocratean ideal of higher education as rhetorical training became pervasive among the Roman elite, with grammar the universal stepping-stone to it. Quintilian's *Institutio*, a manual for teachers and parents that covered education from early childhood to maturity, outdid any Greek educational treatise. (After recovery in its entirety in 1416, it served Renaissance scholars as the warehouse of ancient educational wisdom.) Having learned to read and write, a Roman boy with prosperous parents—in Gaul, Spain, Asia, Africa, or Rome itself—moved to the school of a *grammaticus* and then graduated to teaching by a *rhetor*.* The boy's instruction was solely literary or, better, philological. (His sister's, if she got any, most likely took place informally at home.) From the early empire through the breakdown of Roman power in the west, as Robert Kaster observed, the "grammarian's school was the single most important institution, outside the family, through which the governing classes of the empire perpetuated and extended themselves." This makes sense only when one recalls that *grammar* had a much wider reach than the word now does.[31]

Roman grammar mirrored the rapacious curiosity of the Hellenistic philologists who hatched its progenitor. The teaching of grammar fused into a unified pedagogy textual criticism, analysis of language, and use of antiquarian data and historical writings to illumine works under study. And all the while the *grammatici* sustained the seamless passage onward to rhetoric for the boys they taught. Without question a gap yawned between so hopelessly totalizing an ideal and the sometimes stultifying reality of schooling. The devotion even of erudite graybeards to this all-embracing dream of knowledge ebbed and flowed over the centuries to come.

But again and again the integrative impulse reemerged in philology. In the Renaissance and after, philologists going about their business of emending texts and dissecting language could not keep their hands off antiquarian research and rhetoric. Not only Varro subsumed under grammar the study of history, chronology, antiquities, oratory, and poetry; and not only he insisted that grammar should instill in students the abilities to emend, interpret, and explain texts, as well as skill in reading them out loud.[32]

Varro also wrote a kind of encyclopedia, one of the earliest in Latin, of the *artes liberales*. He divided it into nine books, each devoted to an individual area of study: grammar, dialectic (or logic), rhetoric, geometry, arithmetic, astronomy, music, medicine, and architecture. This list (its membership a little unstable) reappeared in north Africa well over four centuries later—in Augustine and again in an allegory of the marriage of Mercury and Philology by Martianus Capella, both widely read in the Middle Ages. From late antiquity, the liberal arts migrated, via the schools of grammar and rhetoric, into medi-

---

*Recall that 'school' did not imply a dedicated building. In Greek and Roman antiquity, schooling took place in whatever space was available.

eval schooling. There, stripped of medicine and architecture, the now seven liberal arts became the curriculum: the mostly philological *trivium* (grammar, rhetoric, dialectic) and the mathematical *quadrivium* (geometry, arithmetic, astronomy, music). (In antiquity and the Middle Ages, astronomy and music were mathematical sciences, studied theoretically rather than practically.) Fittingly, Martianus Capella made Rhetoric salute Philology with a noisy kiss.[33]

CHRISTIAN ADAPTATIONS

Martianus was a pagan, writing in troubled times to defend and pass on the pagan cultural heritage; his readers mostly were not. In 313 the coemperors Constantine and Licinius had granted Christians freedom of worship; in 380 Theodosius proclaimed Christianity the state cult. Once marginal, still a minority (especially in the countryside), Christians now moved to the center of Roman life.

Imperial sanction mattered a lot to the Christians—and to Roman culture and politics—but not to philological method. Just as Christian bishops pilfered pagan shrines to build churches, even remodeled old temples for new rites, so Christian scholars adopted and adapted pagan literature and erudition. Christians could learn from a commentary on Vergil how to write one on Genesis; and the biblical commentary quickly became as paradigmatic a form for scholarly Christians as the Homeric commentary for the philologists of old Alexandria. Christians embraced Roman schooling, too, if they belonged to the elite that got schooled.[34]

Famously, frictions did arise. Everyone knows of Tertullian's snappish query, "What has Athens to do with Jerusalem?"—and of Jerome's supposed wrestling two centuries later with the luscious siren of Ciceronian eloquence. But Tertullian did as much as any early Christian to fit literary Latin to Christian purposes; and, whatever his vows, Jerome notoriously could not keep his hands off Latin literature.[35]

Early Christians fretted over the dangers of pagan, secular literature; but few wanted to toss out baby and bathwater. Basil of Caesarea opined that pagan literature actually prepared students for Christianity. Augustine wished to pillage the classics of anything useful to Christian teaching and throw away the rest. (So he turned Roman rhetoric to the task of improving Christian preaching.) And yet all through his life Augustine grappled with Vergil, as Sabine MacCormack has shown, "whether by way of imitation, of adaptation, or of contradiction." One fifth-century Roman aristocrat in Gaul kept his Christian books at one end of the library, where ladies sat, his pagan classics at the other, 'male' end. Cassiodorus, who in the sixth century adopted Augustine's more severe precept, found room in it for Martianus Capella, whose pagan allegory he baptized for centuries of medieval readers. Cautiously, Christianity made itself more or less at home with pagan philology.[36]

Yet it also added fresh ingredients. Take for an example the Christian scholar Origen (185–254). He worked first in Alexandria (still a capital of philology) and then in Caesarea in Palestine. Origen started from a background of Neoplatonic and Stoic speculation on language. Wrestling with the Gospel of John, in which λόγος (*lógos*, 'word') figures decisively at the start, he came up with the novel notion that language exists apart from the human voice.[37] His theory matters here not for its substance, but for showing an early Christian engaged creatively with the ruminations of pagan philosophers on language. Curiosity like Origen's linked his pagan predecessors with his Christian successors in the Middle Ages and ultimately his post-Christian heirs beyond: all speculators on the origin and nature of language. This ever-moving tradition of inquiry, from which today's linguistics emerged, drew on past philology at every step—although the starting place (whether Platonic speculation or Priscian's grammar or somewhere else) changed at every stage of the journey as concerns of inquirers shifted and as the past available for mining grew in bulk. The more immediate point is that early Christians did not passively absorb previous study of language and texts in all its varieties; they reshaped it in accord with their distinct needs and problems. Jerusalem had more to do with Athens than Tertullian alleged—and a lot more to do with Alexandria.

Most fatefully for philology, the new religion added a momentous new set of texts to the writings philologists scrutinized. The earliest followers of Jesus were one of several squabbling Jewish sects, and they naturally used Jewish scriptures in their worship. But these 'Christians' (a label quickly slapped on them) soon produced other, Jesus-oriented writings for instruction or use in worship. Their inherited Jewish scriptures came to be known as the Old Testament. In late antiquity, after much dispute over the status of various Christian writings, some of them settled into a second canonical collection called the New Testament. Old and New together comprised not just any book but, for Christians, *the* book.* Homer did not vanish from the face of the earth—for one thing, too many of him were lying around—but he slouched into disgruntled semiretirement. The Bible, its stories telling of the providential action in history of the one God, its teachings key to salvation, was holier than Homer could ever hope to be. And as the handbook of a vigorously missionary faith, the Bible needed translation for the many Christians or potential Christians who did not understand Greek. It equally demanded exegesis: not every passage had a crystal-clear meaning, and those that did might bear more meanings than the obvious one. Christian philologists had a lot of work on their hands.[38]

All true, but far too simple, for the new Christian Bible did not evolve in isolation. Jews—like Greeks, Romans, and other ancient Mediterranean peo-

---

* Or, more accurately, *books* (plural). Singular 'Bible' only emerged later from Latin *biblia*, itself from Greek βίβλια, both plurals. In medieval Latin the neuter plural *biblia* came to be taken as a feminine singular, the two forms being identical in spelling.

ples—had a temple for their rites, where priests sacrificed animals to a god. Jews stood out for having only one god and one temple, in Jerusalem. Even a reader of the Christian Gospels learns how deeply pilgrimage to the temple in Jerusalem mattered to a pious Jew like Jesus. Yet a Jew living in Alexandria or Babylon had a tough haul getting to Jerusalem. Possibly for this reason (no one really knows), buildings for communal prayer and scripture reading as well as secular community activities began to appear among Jewish populations: synagogues. The first clear evidence for them (not yet called synagogues) comes from Egypt in the third century BCE. In these last centuries before the Common Era, teachers learned in interpreting Torah also appeared who became known as rabbis. (The Gospels call Jesus "rabbi.") The synagogue complemented the sacrificial worship in the temple in Jerusalem; indeed, the temple itself may have contained one. But the synagogue could not displace the temple rites: Torah itself so dictated. Then, in 70 CE, crushing a Jewish revolt, Roman legions sacked Jerusalem and destroyed the temple. Jewish sacrificial worship ended, from that moment to the present day.[39]

The destruction of the temple left a vacuum in Jewish life; and the synagogues, as well as the scriptures and the traditions of interpreting them, flowed into it. This process created the rabbinic Judaism that persists to the present day. Rabbinic Judaism did not appear overnight, but neither did Judaism as a 'religion of the book' come from nowhere. In the last centuries before the temple fell, sects proliferated within Judaism. As a result, so did scriptural interpretations and even new scriptures. All Jews accepted as authoritative the five books of the Torah and probably as well (though less weighty) the works now known collectively as the Prophets. (The New Testament thus in a few places refers to 'the law [Torah] and the prophets,' a phrase that occurred earlier in the Dead Sea Scrolls.) But around Pentateuch and Prophets swirled a sea of other texts, their scriptural status disputed. At least one group of Jews revered the book of Jubilees, which appears in no standard Bible today. In the centuries after the temple fell, rabbis strove to bring order to this textual confusion, to define a canon of holy scripture for all Jews. The final component of the Jewish Bible ('the writings') had been agreed no later than about 100 CE, at least among the rabbis. Before 1000 CE the precise *words* of the Hebrew scriptures had been fixed in the Masoretic Text, still used in Jewish worship—and used today also by Christians in translations of their Old Testament.[40]

In the same few centuries after the sack of Jerusalem, Christian leaders engaged in a parallel task—in an eerie, mostly silent pas de deux with the rabbis amid growing Christian hostility to Jews. The Jesus movement attracted a lot of Greek speakers, soon a majority of its members. Thus early Christians adopted as their Bible (eventually to become the Old Testament) the Greek translations of Hebrew scriptures known as the Septuagint, in use among diaspora Jews. Possibly partly for this reason many rabbis distanced themselves from the Septuagint. (Scholars do not agree on how to interpret sketchy and obscure evidence.) Around 130 CE a Jewish convert named Aquila produced a new Greek translation of Hebrew scriptures to replace the Septuagint in Hellenistic synagogues. Aquila came from a Greek-speaking region of Anatolia where Christianity evidently made some of its earliest inroads, so he may have been alert to Christian kidnapping of the Septuagint. Though mostly now lost, his translation seems to have been very literal, very close to the Hebrew original; and apparently many rabbis embraced it with joy. As the rabbis converged on an agreed canon of Hebrew scriptures at the beginning of the Common Era, they excluded some material in the Septuagint—and hence in the Christian Old Testament. Meanwhile, despite Christian venom against Jews, the Christians' own sacred books required them to stay connected philologically to learned rabbis. "The Jews," Augustine said, "are our librarians," the "guardians of our books."[41]

Christian scholars remained tied to pagan predecessors, too. By the time Christianity emerged, Alexandria had become not only a center of Homeric scholarship but also of Neoplatonist philosophizing. The Jewish philosopher Philo of Alexandria (fl. early first century CE) borrowed the allegorical mode of interpretation worked out by Neoplatonic students of Homer; but Philo applied it in commentaries on the Septuagint. A Christian, Clement of Alexandria (ca. 150–215), in turn pirated the method from Philo to vindicate his own religion. From a Christian point of view, the Old Testament—about three quarters of the pages in the Christian Bible—direly needed a rereading. In the Old Testament the Jews played the role of the Chosen People, but Christians believed that God had now pushed the Jews from the stage and made *them* the stars. Within a couple of decades of Jesus's execution, Christian preachers were using a typological interpretation familiar to Jews to show how Jesus fulfilled the Jewish scriptures. The Old Testament thus began to be read as foreshadowing the mission of Jesus and even prophesying Christianity's supersession of Judaism. The symbolic style of reading worked out by students of Homer allowed Clement to fortify and expand this new construal of the Bible. Clement's student Origen—with his own copies of Philo's works—followed his master's example. Clement and Origen's strategy came under fire from other Christians at first, particularly in cities like Antioch, where Jewish traditions remained powerful within the new faith. But Origen's threefold exegesis, moving from the literal meaning of a text to a spiritual meaning cloaked in allegory, would powerfully sway medieval exegetes. Origen also applied more down-to-earth philological tools to understanding the scriptures: history, grammar, and so forth.[42]

Yet the Christian Bible posed problems beyond baptizing its Jewish majority. Stitched together from books written originally in three languages, it also got rendered into yet other languages (unlike, say, the *Iliad*, which usually remained Greek, or the *Aeneid*, a stay-at-home in Latin). This jumble of translations created vexing philological woes. Discrepancies between the Septuagint and the Hebrew text of the rabbis in the early Common Era posed perhaps the most worrisome problem: which was God's word? After moving to Caesarea in Palestine in 231, Origen focused on the question. He brought textual philology to bear on clashes between Hebrew and Greek renderings of the Old Testament (using Alexandrian critical signs in the margins). Origen got along with Jews better than most Christians did. Drawing on rabbinic expertise, he set up an apparatus that exhibited six different versions in parallel columns, his famous *Hexapla*. (He thus prefigured the Polyglot Bibles of early modern Europe, though all but shreds of his work is lost.) Origen never doubted the salience of the Hebrew text for his labors. But he gave it only chronological, not theological, priority. Like many Christians in his day, he believed the *translation* in the Septuagint inspired, a gift of God to upgrade the Jewish scriptures. He perused Hebrew scriptures only to emend manuscripts of the Septuagint.[43]

This seemed massively wrongheaded, a century later, to his philological successor Jerome (347?–419). This scholarly monk also relocated to Palestine, though from the Latin-speaking western Roman Empire. Jerome knew Hebrew better than Origen; and—at risk of getting labeled heretic—he draped himself in Jewish learning. Jerome spurned the Septuagint as derivative. He took the original Hebrew scriptures as the inspired word of God and, therefore, the proper basis for the Christian Bible. (He wasted no time worrying that the *original* Hebrew scrolls were long gone: a kind of problem that did not yet bother scholars, Christian or rabbinic.) In translating Old Testament texts into Latin, Jerome applied philological expertise equal to Origen's. His version won slow acceptance as the common Bible of the Latin church (the 'Vulgate' Old Testament; much of the Vulgate New Testament is his as well).* Clement, Origen, and Jerome were soldiers in a growing corps of Christian scholars putting pagan textual philology to new uses.[44]

Another such scholar overhauled one of the antiquarian pursuits long linked to philology. As mentioned in passing earlier, Hellenistic and Roman philologists struggled to sort out the chronology of long-ago events. They devised techniques to put in order the pasts of their own peoples, such as the Greek dating by Olympiads invented in the third century BCE. But they also tried to integrate the records of different peoples into a universal history. Here 'synchronisms' proved essential: years when the same happening showed up in more than one system of reckoning. Let us say that Babylonian and Egyptian chroniclers both give a date to the same solar eclipse. This known common event links the two different calendars in a relation with each other. You can now figure out which other Babylonian and Egyptian events occurred at the same time—although you still have to deduce the corresponding years in your own calendar. In principle, enough synchronisms allowed a scholar to meld disparate *relative* chronologies into one *absolute* chronology. In practice, ancient evidence was and is very messy—not to mention that Babylonians

---

* *Vulgate* comes from the Latin verb *volgare*, meaning 'to make generally known.'

used two different calendars, Egyptians three, and both tended anyway to date events by regnal years, not calendar years.[45]

Eusebius of Caesarea (ca. 260–339) put the old study of chronology on a new footing: "I have perused diverse histories of the past which the Chaldeans and Assyrians have recorded, which the Egyptians have written in detail, and which the Greeks have narrated as accurately as possible." In the first of the two books of his *Chronicon* (*Chronicle*, ca. 310), he recorded in traditional narrative the results of his labors. But in the second book he did something dramatically new. Eusebius used synchronisms to, well, synchronize his data in tables easy to compare, one each for roughly twenty peoples. The columnar *Hexapla* of his Caesarea forerunner Origen perhaps inspired Eusebius's brainchild.* From the patriarch Abraham up to Eusebius's own times, the *Chronicon* collated year by year all the reigns, battles, biblical events, foundings of cities, floods, legendary exploits, inventions, Jupiter's adulteries (several entries), notable buildings—you name it—that Eusebius could recover. As Anthony Grafton and Megan Williams observed, the work "served until the sixteenth century as the richest single source of information for anyone interested in the history of human culture." And its structure became the model for later chronology. The highly specific, year-by-year format itself forced scholars from Eusebius on to face squarely the knottiest problems of dating. But the *Chronicon* was not Eusebius's only innovation in writing about the past.[46]

In composing historical narratives, he quoted extensively from documents, the first known historian to do so. Eusebius larded both his history of the Christian church (ca. 325) and his unfinished life of the emperor Constantine with excerpts from written records. Perhaps he did so because he saw actual documents as rhetorically more effective in proving the truth of Christianity—the purpose of his history. Later church historians, with similar apologetic agenda, would emulate him in hauling the archives into their narratives. Historians of secular affairs generally did not. Eventually, many centuries later, the creation of the modern discipline of history would pivot on linking archive and narrative: on merging the philologist's zest for texts with the taleteller's love of a good yarn, on yoking the ecclesiastical historian to the civil historian.[47]

Many of the books that Eusebius toiled over looked, in physical form, very unlike the scrolls that Aristarchus and Varro marked up. For centuries, besides using papyrus, writers had scribbled more casually with a stylus on thin rectangles of wood coated with wax. The writer could tie two or more such tablets together with string running through holes drilled along one side. The Romans called this multilayered memo pad a *codex*. They also figured out that using sheets of parchment or papyrus instead of wood made a codex less un-

* It is a useful reminder of parallel traditions of philological erudition in other civilizations that Sima Qian, working at the Han dynasty court of Emperor Wu, made chronological tables of Chinese history structurally similar to Eusebius's some four hundred years before him. See Hardy 1999, 29–35.

wieldy: you stacked a few sheets in a neat pile, folded them down the middle, and sewed them together at the crease. The idea caught on, evolved. Take several such codices; bind them together; and you have space for more than a grocery list. You can write down the *Aeneid*. The name *codex* got transferred from the multitiered notepad to the many-paged tome. The new codex had an edge over scrolls: it was easier to read (turning pages instead of unrolling and rerolling); higher in capacity and thus lower in cost; less of a nuisance to carry around. And (if you had a table to set it on) it left one hand free to scratch flea bites—or to take notes (a boon to philologists). Still, few species show more inertia than the bookworm. The newfangled codex existed in Rome by the late first century CE; but not until around 300 did it equal the scroll in popularity, and only at around 500 did it take over. Just as slowly, papyrus gave way to parchment: more durable, easier to write on both sides of, and manufacturable outside the Nile valley. (Paper displaced parchment for most purposes in the late Middle Ages, ultimately making the printing press practical.) Curiously, from the outset Christians much preferred their writings in codices. Several plausible tales explain why, but scholars only guess.[48]

Just as the novel codex was winning a majority, philology split into two Christian streams. In 330 the emperor Constantine betook himself to an ancient Greek town on the Bosphorus called Byzantium, rebuilt it grandly, made it capital of the Roman Empire, and renamed it New Rome. Other people called it Constantinopolis (Constantinople to us): Constantine's city. The center of gravity of Roman culture shifted from the Latin west to the Greek east. The Roman Empire erratically flourished in the east for several centuries, then hung on for a few more before finally succumbing to the Ottoman Turks in 1453. Modern historians label it the Byzantine Empire after about 600.

In the east, Roman schooling and Roman scholarship persisted, in Greek rather than Latin. The schooling shifted in the Byzantine period to the same sequence of *trivium* and *quadrivium* that prevailed in the medieval west— probably not rigidly followed in either region. (West may have got it from east.) Quantity and quality of scholarship ebbed and flowed with the political and economic fortunes of the empire. But, save at the worst of times, scholarly activity never ceased in Constantinople. From the ninth century onward, scholars did their work in a new 'minuscule' script, leaner and easier to write. Even as the empire wheezed toward its demise, Byzantine philologists produced writings that mattered. Demetrius Triclinius (ca. 1300–?) reworked scholia on a number of authors into helpful new commentaries and snatched from oblivion nine plays of Euripides. Manuel Moschopoulos (ca. 1265–1316) produced an expert edition of Sophocles and a lexicon of the defunct Attic dialect of classical Athens. The latter work descended from another lexicon prepared four centuries earlier by the learned Patriarch Photios (ca. 820–92). On the whole, eastern empire scholarship seems unadventurous, in keeping with a tradition-minded culture.[49]

Byzantine philology mattered to later humanistic scholarship not for dramatic breakthroughs but for saving a lot of texts and scholarly practices otherwise lost. For instance, the stylistic ideas of the second-century rhetorician Hermogenes of Tarsus stayed alive only in Byzantium. In 1426 George of Trebizond brought them to western Europe and sent a fresh breeze through Renaissance literature. And do not forget those nine plays of Euripides that we still have, thanks to Demetrius.[50]

MEDIEVAL SURVIVAL

If the Greek east tended to timidity, the Latin-speaking western half of the empire never rose to that level after the fifth century. It is telling that John Edwin Sandys's venerable *History of Classical Scholarship*, when it reaches the western Middle Ages, becomes no longer a history of scholarship (of critical editions, commentaries, and scholia) but of survival—of where knowledge of ancient texts persisted, of where grammar and rhetoric were still taught.[51] Nonetheless, as begetter of later European philology, the Latin west must command more attention in this book than the sturdier Byzantine Empire.

In the west, 'barbarian' armies ravaged the empire from Italy to Africa, from Gaul to Hispania. So-called barbarians were not necessarily more barbaric than Romans they defeated. Barbarian leaders could be thoroughly Romanized, even well disposed toward erudition. Roman aristocrats, and the grammarians and rhetoricians who schooled their children, could flourish under barbarian rule. The problem was episodic disorder, often extreme. The Roman Empire fell apart in the Latin-speaking world in the late fifth century. In the seventh century the new power of Islam seized the eastern and southern Mediterranean portion of the old empire, from Syria to the Atlantic; early in the next century Muslim armies captured the bulk of the Iberian peninsula as well. In most of the rest of the former western empire, administration decayed; networks of communication frayed; cities shriveled; schools withered; literacy declined.[52]

Scholars strained to keep alight the guttering flame of ancient learning, now mostly in order to illuminate Christian texts. Magnus Aurelius Cassiodorus Senator (ca. 490–585) was one such salvager. A high official when Ostrogoth kings ruled Italy, Cassiodorus finally fled the maelstrom of politics. He founded a monastery on his estate in southern Italy, provided a library, then set his monks to copying books. He himself proved philologist enough to use critical marks to manage manuscripts (not the signs inherited from Alexandria). Around 537, he wrote for his monks—and kept revising for decades—a handbook known in its final form as *Institutiones divinarum et humanarum lectionum* (*Introduction to Divine and Human Reading*). Cassiodorus's *Institutiones* became a stock item in medieval libraries. In it he conserved the erudition of "the secular teachers" to ensure that the scriptures were rightly interpreted and accurately copied: "both in the Bible and in the most learned commentaries [on it] we understand a great deal through figures of speech, through definitions, through grammar, rhetoric, dialectic, arithmetic, music, geometry, and astronomy." Here are Martianus Capella's liberal arts, put to Christian purposes. Cassiodorus listed in what became the traditional order the *trivium* and then *quadrivium* of medieval education. A forerunner of this new way of schooling, his monastery went under in chaos brought by Lombard invaders soon after his death. Its library, scattered, left traces in medieval manuscripts made as far away as northern England.[53]

In the next century, in the temporarily more peaceful setting of Visigothic Spain, Bishop Isidore of Seville (ca. 570–636) more extensively reworked ancient knowledge for the new world. Isidore arranged his *Origines sive Etymologiae* (*Origins or Etymologies*) by the curious device of tracing meanings of terms to their supposed roots (in a sense a faint echo of Pergamene etymology). This encyclopedia amassed in twenty books a hoard of information about education, medicine, law, languages, monsters, metallurgy, ships, building, farm implements: you name it. Isidore's work spread rapidly—remarkable in the seventh century. It became possibly the most vital single adapter of ancient knowledge (educational ideas and philological learning included) to the European world taking shape.[54]

Other signs of a new order appeared. Some monasteries carried on Cassiodorus's program of copying secular as well as religious texts—although others scraped the ink off their classical parchments to write instead the words of the Bible or Church Fathers. ('Palimpsests,' through which a skilled reader can discern an original script under new writing, helped later in recovering ancient texts.) Scholarly churchmen such as Gregory of Tours (ca. 538–94) and Paul the Deacon (ca. 720–99) set histories of new 'barbarian' nations within Romano-Christian frameworks like Eusebius's. In England the historian Bede (ca. 673–735) found access to parts of Vergil, Pliny, Macrobius, and other Roman authors. His critical attitude toward sources, his care for documentation, and his antiquarian interests imply that he also shared ideals of ancient erudition. Besides his famed history of the English church and people, Bede drew up a world chronology like Eusebius's, more tightly bound to biblical and Christian history. He died working on a translation of the Gospel of John into Old English. This last philological project put him very broadly in the lineage of Origen and Jerome. But, unlike them, Bede probably never wondered whether the Latin text he translated needed emendation. Medieval scholars did not usually fret about textual philology when studying the Bible—or secular works. Yet grammar did intrigue Bede and his Anglo-Saxon contemporaries; and in this, too, they foreshadowed later medieval erudition.[55]

A younger, learned Anglo-Saxon, Alcuin of York (ca. 735–804), helped to launch the 'Carolingian Renaissance.' Alcuin became in effect minister of education under the Frankish king Charlemagne (in Latin, Carolus Magnus; hence Carolingian). Charlemagne fostered learning, even sponsored (exceptionally) emendation of the Bible. He and his immediate successors supported scholars in monasteries but also drew learned men to court. The Carolingian Renaissance renewed interest in ancient grammar and in classical writings, although sacred literature almost always took precedence. Almost: the Benedictine abbot Lupus of Ferrières (ca. 805–862), at least, preferred Cicero to theology. Lupus also emended the classical texts he collected by collating manuscripts: a philological routine largely abandoned in the Latin-speaking world. Carolingian chronographers compiled mosaics of historical data as Eusebius had done, but now built to show the new Frankish empire as continuing the Roman one. Much Carolingian energy went into transcribing. Our oldest copies of many classical works date from this period. They were written in Carolingian minuscule, a new hand parallel to the Byzantine minuscule developed about the same time. Easily legible to modern readers, Carolingian minuscule is ancestor of the typefaces printers use today. *Older* scripts may sometimes have tripped up Carolingian copyists. This would explain why they left so many errors for early modern scholars to emend. Charlemagne's courtier Einhard memorialized his monarch in a sometimes elegant Latin biography modeled on Suetonius's life of Augustus. Then a new period of turmoil made this 'renaissance' a false dawn.[56]

Around 1100, calmer social conditions and the spread of cathedral schools nurtured a 'twelfth-century renaissance.' This revival of letters and learning had a poetic and rhetorical flavor, although some of the erudite also pursued literary and textual research as under the Carolingians. Grammarians improved on Priscian's late-antique discussion of language by developing the concepts of subject and predicate. Biblical texts occasionally came under philological scrutiny. Andrew of St. Victor (ca. 1110–75) even consulted rabbis in the neighborhood of his monastery in northern France. Another scholar devised a method to pick out *nova falsitas* (newly introduced error) in liturgical texts. He scoured records of past synods and the like to find precedent; failing to find it, he tossed out the suspect words. Given the state of records, a lot of innocent verbiage must have died on the trash heap. But textual philology did not occupy many people. More typically, the *Didascalicon* of Andrew's teacher Hugh of St. Victor (1096–1141) reworked the seven liberal arts. Hugh abandoned the snippets and summaries used by earlier medieval teachers and required students to read entire speeches or poems in order to grasp them as works of literary art.[57]

Hugh's contemporary Bernard of Chartres (?–ca. 1130) also stressed literary study of major Latin writers, teaching in a pretty standard rhetorical-grammatical mode. John of Salisbury, who studied under Bernard's disciples in the cathedral school at Chartres, told what he had heard of him. The report gives a flavor of the tradition. Bernard would point out, in reading the authors, what was simple and according to rule. On the other hand he would explain grammatical figures, rhetorical embellishment, and sophistical quibbling, as well as the relation of given passages to other studies. . . . The evening exercise, known as the "declination," was so replete with grammatical instruction that if anyone were to take part in it for an entire year, provided he were not a dullard, he would become thoroughly familiar with the [correct] method of speaking and writing. . . . He would also explain the poets and orators who were to serve as models for the boys in their introductory exercises in imitating prose and poetry.

Bernard's fondness for pagan writers upset some people, but prayer pervaded his teaching at Chartres—a Christian edition of the philological, rhetorical education inherited from antiquity.[58]

And thus the philological legacy of antiquity survived, thin and pale. Long after the twelfth-century renaissance went the way of its Carolingian predecessor, throughout the later Middle Ages educated men still read Ovid and Statius, Horace and Vergil, Seneca and Cicero. Some of these authors appeared in school texts alongside grammars adapted from ancient authors. Tales derived from Livy or Vergil circulated in medieval dress. The tradition of chronology also endured, though now localized in monastic or court chronicles (some of which showed skill in sorting out absolute dates). So did 'paradoxography': like the scholars of Alexandria, some medieval writers—frowned on by university philosophers—cataloged startling or bizarre natural phenomena or human artifacts. Above all, the *trivium*, the base of more advanced education, included grammar and rhetoric as well as dialectic. As Marcia Colish stressed, the education of medieval men "saw to it that the trivium was as much a part of their mental equipment as their Christian faith." Whatever the fate of grammatical and rhetorical *scholarship*, not even to speak of textual philology, every educated man had learned grammar and rhetoric as a schoolboy. So philology persisted, even if as a passive, ghostly presence. Yet for two centuries after 1200, Hugh's *Didascalicon* or teaching like Bernard's did look more like relics of a dead past than jewels of a living tradition.[59]

The creation of universities during that period furnished new frameworks for a type of intellectual life averse to philology: the Scholastic program of education and research. A late fruit of the monastic and cathedral schools that preceded universities, Scholasticism made itself at home in the new institutions. Scholasticism privileged dialectic, with its stress on logical abstraction and its filiation with philosophy and theology, over grammar and rhetoric, with their emphasis on textual and literary studies. Thirteenth- and fourteenth-century scholars north of the Alps by and large turned away from the philological and even rhetorical heritage of antiquity to pursue instead its philosophical legacy. "By the mid-thirteenth century," as Daniel Hobbins observed, "the notion of the 'liberal arts' was more symbol than substance, and studying at a university meant studying Aristotle." (Rhetoric remained central in Italian universities.*) True, later medieval scholars did avidly pursue certain kinds of old texts. Around 1150 Adelard of Bath translated into Latin the astronomical tables of the ninth-century Persian mathematician al-Khwarizmi, themselves based on Sanskrit work; Adelard thus brought to Europe previously unknown techniques of Indian astronomy. More famously, the rediscovery during the later twelfth century—again via the Islamic world—of key works by Aristotle made a great stir in Scholastic circles. In fact, the translation of these 'lost' books virtually created mature Scholasticism in the thirteenth century.[60]

But Scholastics pretty well limited their interest in ancient writings to philosophical, scientific, and ethical works—and largely forgot that even such manuscripts raised philological problems. That ancient invention, the learned commentary on an individual text, survived as a standard tool of Scholastic erudition. (Scholars even still read Servius on Vergil.) But Scholastic commentaries neglected the historical and antiquarian material key for Hellenistic and Roman scholars. Not until the Renaissance did philological modes of commentary reemerge.[61] Meanwhile, much of Quintilian's rhetoric lay hidden in forgotten manuscripts. Other classical texts of a literary, historical, or antiquarian nature, scrupulously copied by Carolingian scribes in their lucid minuscule script, likewise gathered dust in monastic libraries. Serious engagement with the philological heritage of antiquity held no appeal for Scholastics. The erudition born in Alexandria went into near hibernation in most of Europe after 1200.

Ancient rhetoric and grammar did carry on a shadow life within Scholasticism. The Scholastic zeal for dialectic sharpened a dichotomy perhaps first clearly asserted by Plato. On one hand, philosophy gave access to assured knowledge, certainty, truth (*scientia*, 'science,' in a medieval meaning very different from our own). On the other hand, rhetoric (and the philology allied with it) offered probability at best and a suspicious-looking resort to mere persuasion. Medieval Scholastics voted for truth and 'science.' But they kept rhetoric and grammar on life support: they absorbed rhetoric into logic; and they approached grammar—the one part of ancient philology many of them admired—as if it *were* dialectic. Early medieval Latin grammars had imitated classical ones, devoted to practical analysis of a single actual language. Starting in the twelfth century, grammars became more philosophical and logical in character, more remote from any actual language. At the same time, old-style rhetoric and grammar remained school subjects, and pedagogical texts used in earlier eras survived—indeed, a brief burst of new grammar books appeared in France and northern Italy in the late twelfth century, incorporating the more logical Scholastic version of the subject.[62]

---

*Education in northern Italian cities had never lost its civic complexion, inherited from Roman schooling. Instruction in rhetoric still prepared students for public life, and this agenda carried over to universities when they developed. This 'Italian difference'—to use Ronald Witt's phrase—mattered a great deal to the rest of Europe at the end of the Middle Ages.

But *schooling* is one thing; *erudition* another. The antiquarian and historical curiosity of Hellenistic and Roman scholars, still lush in Bede, largely withered. Hugh of St. Victor was no slave to dialectic: he wanted his students to study scripture in light of history and geography—that is, philologically. But, to find such contexts, he could direct students to little more than the Latin Fathers and the Bible itself. A century later, Hugh's successors, by squeezing biblical truths through the grid of philosophical analysis, created a totally ahistorical theology that could be studied independent of the sacred text from which it ultimately derived. Scholasticism, its interests directed elsewhere, made an arid landscape for philological learning.[63]

Not an unwatered desert. Medieval dialecticians strove to use words precisely. They even created a 'science of language.' This, at least, is one way to see the well-known debate between realists and nominalists at the heart of medieval philosophy. Did general terms point to something real, like a Platonic form? Or were they purely nominal conventions, convenient for referring to all the individual entities sharing certain traits? Did the species 'horse' denote an actual universal horsiness, or only the myriad of particular horses? This realist-nominalist debate carried forward, in much altered terms, ancient arguments between naturalists and conventionalists about the origin and character of language, echoing the dispute laid out in Plato's *Cratylus*. Moreover, the Scholastics' intensely logical approach to grammar eventually produced, starting from Priscian's late-antique grammar, a *grammatica speculativa* (speculative grammar). This science sought rules common to all languages, assuming that each reflected the real makeup of things. *Grammatica speculativa* faintly echoed some ancient conjectures and built a base for later linguistic theorizing. On the margins of the academic world, too, speculation on language continued. Jewish kabbalist mystics in Spain and Provence believed that language mirrored reality and that manipulating letters therefore yielded esoteric knowledge. Dante studied the splintering of the Romance languages; he sought to shape an Italian vernacular that would restore the primal linkage between words and the objects they name—a return, he believed, to the linguistic bliss of the Garden of Eden.[64]

Even scriptural study—which before and after the Middle Ages seemed a predestined site for textual philology—drifted away from it during the medieval period. In this case, Scholasticism was not the agent. The ancient Christian writers who allegorized the Bible, mimicking the interpreters of Homer, were ultimately responsible. From Augustine up to Aquinas, most Christian readers found several layers of meaning in scriptural passages, with spiritual senses often overwhelming the literal one. For a scholar mining the Bible for theological insight, a preacher using scripture to give moral direction, or a nun reading to deepen her spiritual life, having several strata in the text enriched the Book. Exegetes disagreed about how many distinct types of meaning a passage should bear. The down-to-earth Hugh of St. Victor favored three: literal (historical); allegorical (doctrinal); and tropological (moral)—and, unusual in his day, insisted on the literal as the basis of all readings. More fanciful commentators found as many as seven kinds of meanings. A fourfold exegesis was commonest: literal, allegorical, tropological, and anagogical (mystical). Such construals put a premium on theology, preaching, contemplation. They turned attention away from philological problems.[65]

A rationalizing Scholasticism pulled the reins on fancy. Hugh of St. Victor began the restraint. Thomas Aquinas provided a stronger theoretical basis, as Beryl Smalley noted, by importing into Scholasticism the Aristotelian principle "that substance could only be known through its sensible manifestations." It followed that "the 'spirit' of Scripture" was "not hidden behind or added on to, but expressed by the text." Scholastic pedagogical method pushed in the same direction. In the new universities, lecturers addressed not just a biblical text directly but also collected glosses on that text. To avoid hopeless confusion, teachers had to assume in the text itself, first of all, a straightforward, foundational, literal meaning—though they did allow spiritual modes of reading on top of the primary literal meaning.[66]

Literal exegesis thus came into a certain vogue after perhaps 1300, though still buried under mounds of textual glosses: the inheritance of a long tradition of learned but nonphilological commentary. The Franciscan exegete Nicholas of Lyra (1270–1349) insisted on the primacy of the literal sense when many of his contemporaries still vigorously allegorized. But he included in 'literal' both the original writer's intent and "the prophetic meaning that was to come." For late medieval interpreters like Nicholas, 'literal' did not mean historical in the sense of illuminating the text with ancient context. But sooner or later, under the new regime, biblical scholars *would* need Hebrew and Greek and historical research to do their job well. This literalist turning within Scholastic exegesis gave new energy to textual philology, but very slowly. The handful of philologically-minded students of the Old Testament text in the 1200s—who struggled with Hebrew, consulted erudite rabbis, and scoured manuscripts for variant readings—worked outside the universities. In contrast, just a little later, Nicholas of Lyra's command of Hebrew learning may help to explain his rapid rise at the University of Paris. (He used the same learning to attack Judaism.) In the early 1300s, two church councils and a pope ordered major universities to set up professorships of Greek and oriental languages (Hebrew, Aramaic, and Arabic), probably to support evangelizing. A couple of universities made feeble stabs at obeying, but nothing much happened for another century. Competent candidates were not pouring out of the academic establishment. Biblical philology required the literary and historical learning that Scholasticism had devalued in favor of philosophy and its irrefutable *scientia*.[67]

Philological expertise would take time to recover. Around 1400, hints of movement rustled even through the heartland of Scholastic Europe, north of the Alps. Some French writers tried to compose more elegant Latin, holding up Cicero as their silver-tongued ideal. Those who spent time at the papal court in Avignon developed an ardor for classical texts that reminds one of Lupus of Ferrières. Jean Gerson, chancellor at the University of Paris, proudest citadel of Scholasticism, decried the "great famine of worthy and eloquent historians and poets" afflicting France. He worried that dense, technical theological jargon made no impression on the reading public, even as that public grew in number. He criticized the literary clunkiness of Scholastic writings and called for deeper study of rhetoric—though dialectic held him enough in thrall that he called rhetoric a second kind of logic! In Scholasticism's other premier university, Oxford, around the same time, theologians were growing disenchanted with an excess of logic and showing a new fondness for the ancient Church Fathers. None of this amounted to full-throated philology—Jean Gerson never collated a manuscript—but straws floated in the breeze.[68]

And even the high medieval heritage included tidbits that philology later devoured. After around 1100, government, legal proceedings, trade, and religion all made more and more use of writing, and texts multiplied. In particular, Scholastic method demanded that university teachers and students master authoritative books in detail; and the number of works requiring control ballooned during the thirteenth century, especially as ancient Greek learning preserved by Islamic scholars leached into Latin. The growing 'information overload' needed management: search engines, one might say. So learned men either refined tools inherited from antiquity (such as the encyclopedia), or they invented new ones (such as the alphabetical index to a book). The most widely used index—employed by preachers as well as teachers—was the biblical concordance.* This implement indexed at first the words in the Bible but soon topics, too. When philology eventually revived, its adepts adapted such reference works to their own uses. More substantively, *grammatica speculativa* had offspring in what would later be called linguistics. In the very long run, too, spiritual exegesis of the Bible left its mark on erudition. The grafting of ancient modes of reading Homer onto the Christian scriptures, after a thousand years, had embedded itself deeply in reading practices. Digging beneath the surface of a text to excavate hidden meanings could offer a way of understanding secular books as well.[69]

All this lay dormant. With few notable exceptions, later medieval scholars neglected philology for other interests. Ancient learning eked out a bare existence as the least respected parts of the *trivium*. Yet rhetorical and grammatical erudition, literary and textual criticism, even chronology and antiquarianism, had not vanished. They lay on countless library shelves, in monasteries across Europe, waiting to be discovered anew.

---

* The concordance in turn led to dividing the books of the Bible into our present standardized chapters, to help users find a given word or topic regardless of how a particular manuscript of the Bible was laid out. This Christian invention eventually became standard in Jewish Bibles, too.

2

"A COMPLETE MASTERY OF ANTIQUITY"

RENAISSANCE, REFORMATION, AND BEYOND

No sharp break divided late medieval intellectual life, with its Scholastics who scorned philology, from the Renaissance, with its humanists who gave philology new life. Jean Gerson long personified the supposed aridity of late Scholasticism. Yet Gerson pioneered new literary forms and admired the Latin style of humanists of his era. Italian universities of the fifteenth and sixteenth centuries, once pictured as hostile to humanists, turn out to have welcomed them.[1]

Yet one need not caricature the *dramatis personae* to realize that a new act opened in the northern Italian peninsula during the thirteenth century. There Scholasticism had not seized control of the universities. There self-governing city-states had evolved a civic consciousness alert to ancient Roman writings suited to urban republics. Teachers of rhetoric had shifted focus from preaching to *ars dictaminis*, the art of letter writing; they looked back to antique models, but their literary skill brought present-day jobs as secretaries and chancellors in state offices. Finally, study of Roman law to aid civic governance awoke scholars in places like the University of Bologna to the vigor of antiquity. These circumstances combined to transform intellectual life in urban centers dotting the peninsula north of Rome. The ancient philological and rhetorical heritage again enticed. Italians revived it, then extended it.[2]

ITALIAN HUMANISM

The unlikely revolutionary was a judge in Padua, Lovato dei Lovati (1241–1309). Around him congregated a coterie of admirers of classical antiquity. Lovato's wide reading in ancient Roman writers showed in his own works, ranging from letters in Latin verse to a little essay explaining Seneca's meter (possibly the first such analysis of classical verse since antiquity). Like ancient antiquarians, he loved old inscriptions and other tangible traces of Padua's past. When by chance builders unearthed an early Christian sarcophagus, Lovato declared it to hold the bones of Antenor, mythical Trojan founder of Padua; patriotic Paduans applauded. According to Nicholas Mann, Lovato displayed key traits of emerging humanism: "an appetite for classical texts; a philological concern to correct them and ascertain their meaning; and a desire to imitate them." He also pioneered in hunting rare manuscripts buried in monastic libraries. And in his Latin poetry Lovato mimicked ancient authors. His disciple Albertino Mussato imitated the ancients in another way: he became in 1317 the first individual since the end of antiquity known to celebrate his birthday. Italian humanism was born.[3]

In the next century, Francesco Petrarca (1304–74)—Petrarch in English—turned Lovato's activities into something like a program. Tuscan by birth, raised around the papal court in Avignon, trained in Roman law at Montpellier and Bologna, Petrarch fell under the spell of ancient Latin literature. Famed for vernacular poetry as well as Latin eloquence, Petrarch matters here as philologist. His rhetorical and legal education landed him a job as a papal bureaucrat in Avignon, with access to the riches of the pope's library. Petrarch traveled often on church business—indeed, he spent much of his life in motion before settling near Padua in his last years. In Liège in 1333 he found a manuscript of Cicero's forgotten oration *Pro Archia*. In Paris he came across a copy of the first-century BCE love poems of Propertius. Both texts he emended and annotated. He edited, too, Vergil *and* Servius's commentary on Vergil (correcting errors in Servius). He partly restored the fragmented text of the historian Livy—by collating manuscripts like his ancient predecessors and, when that failed, by conjectural emendation. His ample knowledge of Roman history fed antiquarian studies—of coins, inscriptions, monuments. When he died, he owned more Roman literature than any other private person, some of it his own discoveries. Petrarch personified comprehensive study of Latin classical antiquity, grounded in philology and antiquarianism. He brought back to life the all-embracing ancient 'grammar.'[4]

And he became a model for future humanist scholars. In Petrarch's wake, humanist erudition did three jobs: (1) policing the purity of contemporary writing (i.e., how closely it mirrored an idealized ancient usage); (2) finding, editing, and appraising ancient texts; and (3) pursuing historical and antiquarian research. But not all Italian humanists aspired to erudition. Most cared more about rhetoric than learning, while a Neoplatonist like Marsilio Ficino (1433–99) bypassed the historical concreteness of philology in search of abstract universals. Only a minority practiced scholarship of Petrarch's sort.[5]

Among those who did, study of ancient buildings and statues paralleled scrutiny of old manuscripts. Petrarch wandered Rome with Giovanni Colonna, admiring its ruins. Their rambles commonly ended at the Baths of Diocletian, where, he remembered, "our conversation often turned on history."

Petrarch's sensibility took more methodical form in later generations. Poggio Bracciolini (1380–1459) tried to date the ancient gates of Rome by inspecting construction materials and inscriptions. *Roma instaurata* (*Rome Restored*, 1447) by Flavio Biondo worked on a grander scale. Examining old books, archives, inscriptions, and coins, observing ruins, even turning over ancient bricks lying in the streets, Flavio did what his title promised. Humanists throughout Italy sketched old bridges and buildings, copied inscriptions, gathered coins. Their activities bring to mind ancient Roman antiquarians like Varro. Humanists were reviving an ancient program that Arnaldo Momigliano called "Varronian": recovering a civilization "by systematic collection of all the relics of the past." "Relics" included origins of place-names, historical events, and so forth, as well as physical remains. Antiquarians typically arrayed their finds—tangible or otherwise—in a mosaic of a place over time rather than in a linear narrative as a historian might.[6]

Above all, Italian humanists praised ancient elegance of expression; and classical rhetoric made a comeback. During the Middle Ages, squeezed between elementary schooling in grammar and the really serious higher education in dialectic, rhetoric had shrunk to a shadow of its ancient self. Humanist attitudes fed a resurgence. "The Christian religion does not rest on proof," declared the humanist Lorenzo Valla (1407–57), "but on persuasion, which is superior to proof." So much for Scholastic *scientia*. A crucial moment came in 1416. Attending the Council of Constance as a papal bureaucrat, Poggio Bracciolini, a tireless manuscript hunter, found at the nearby monastery of St. Gall a complete manuscript of Quintilian's *Institutes*, much of it lost since antiquity. Quintilian made rhetoric the master key to a complete educational curriculum. He also endorsed the hegemony of grammar and philology in the realm of scholarship. Recovery of Greek rhetoric from the faltering Byzantine Empire further stoked fervor for classical rhetorical education in fifteenth-century Italy. What effect the new rhetoric had in real schoolrooms is uncertain, but it gilded the prose coming out of Italian chancelleries where many humanists worked.[7]

This rhetorical revival did not cause humanists to abandon dialectic but to reimagine it. Petrarch sneered at technical Scholastic dialectical exercises yet accepted that students needed to learn logic. Lorenzo Valla proposed to rebuild dialectic as training in how to argue in ordinary words, as opposed to the formalized, arcane Scholastic version. This new dialectic could then play its *proper* role—as handmaid of rhetoric. In Valla's reformed *trivium*, rhetoric rules; dialectic makes rhetoric more effective; and grammar (meaning grounding in ancient languages and literatures) provides the raw material.[8]

The revival got interrupted, and a revised dialectic again pushed classical rhetoric into storage. The Dutch humanist Rudolfus Agricola (who had read Valla on the subject) carried Italian humanist rhetoric across the Alps in the later fifteenth century. But he merged it with dialectic—and gave dialectic the whip hand. Agricola's was a new humanist dialectic, engaged with Latin literature, not the despised Aristotelian logic of the Scholastics. His *De inventione dialectica* (1479) exerted wide influence. His equally anti-Aristotelian disciple Petrus Ramus (Pierre de la Ramée, 1515–72) may have exerted even wider. Ramus subordinated rhetoric to another new-model dialectic, less subtle than Agricola's, more schematic, better suited to schoolroom use. Ramus's program appealed especially to fellow Calvinists in England; in New England it shaped schooling into the eighteenth century. Practical rhetoric (teaching boys to write and speak well) remained important; and among grown-ups esteem for Ciceronian eloquence waned rather than vanished. So techniques of classical rhetoric survived in the classroom—and also in writings by people as famous as Kepler and Galileo. Yet not until around 1700 did classical rhetoric again become *à la mode*.[9]

Meanwhile, Italian humanists got lessons in historical change as, striving to emulate classical style, they learned more about ancient vocabulary and syntax. In 1355 Petrarch, then employed by Emperor Charles IV, used expertise in classical Latin (and Roman history) to prove fake an 'ancient Roman' document undercutting imperial authority. Because he worked so hard to copy classical eloquence, Petrarch saw the gap dividing 'barbarous' medieval Latin from the real, dead thing. And humanists soon learned that ancient literary Latin supplied a moving target, not one timeless style. Cicero provided one model, Tacitus another. By the early fifteenth century, humanists were studying how Latin usage changed over time in ancient Rome.* Lorenzo Valla showed an even keener historical sense than Petrarch. Purportedly, Emperor Constantine, after moving his capital east, granted authority over the western empire to the pope: the so-called Donation of Constantine. In 1439–40 King Alfonso of Aragon was feuding with Pope Eugenius. Alfonso's secretary was Valla. He applied to the 'donation' historical and linguistic analysis like Petrarch's, mixed with antiquarian expertise. With precision and acid tongue, he proved the document a medieval fabrication. Many had smelled a rat in the donation; but Valla's philology first nailed the rodent (a feat, apparently, with no practical result). Glen Bowersock called Valla's "analysis of language and style" the "beginning of serious philological criticism." Valla did not stop with Constantine. An influential Neoplatonic philosopher (today called Pseudo-Dionysius) was traditionally thought to be Dionysius the Areopagite, St. Paul's Athenian interlocutor. Tradition met Valla. He showed that a legal council, not philosophical academy, sat on the Areopagus, making Paul's Dionysius closer to jurist than philosopher. Valla went on: Neoplatonism hardly existed in Paul's day; a first-century date created historical absurdities in 'Dionysius's' writings; no one before Pope Gregory the Great (590–604) mentioned the book. Real historical criticism was at work.[10]

---

* Studies of Latin spilled over into vernaculars, increasingly vehicles for literature. Classical grammar supplied the model for vernacular grammars, such as the *Grammatica della lingua toscana* (ca. 1440) of Leon Battista Alberti.

Valla shows the possible, not the ordinary. Humanist emendation perhaps damaged more manuscripts than it improved. And for every genius like Valla, there was an Annius of Viterbo. A Dominican friar, Annius, in the spirit of Valla, laid out rules for critical evaluation of old sources. He practiced what he preached, in a sense. In 1498 appeared his *Commentaria super opera diversorum auctorum de antiquitatibus loquentium* (*Commentaries on Works of Various Authors Who Discuss Antiquities*). This tome melded excerpts from a raft of ancient authors with discussion of them by Annius. Expert philologists saw that Annius composed not only the commentaries but most of the 'ancient' writings. More typical humanists gobbled up the forgeries. Annius was far from the only counterfeiter.[11]

Still, by Valla's day, Renaissance erudition had staked out its territory. Humanist scholars salvaged forgotten manuscripts, chiefly from monastic libraries. (Some long-lost ancient texts were recovered; other manuscripts helped to correct or expand works already circulating.) Employing the ancient technical apparatus of critical marks, they emended these manuscripts—more often by conjecture than collation. They prepared editions. They wrote commentaries and similar works of criticism. They reformed Latin vocabulary, style, and grammar following the 'best' classical models. Parallel to this textual and rhetorical philology, they pursued antiquarian research into material relics such as buildings and coins.[12]

Angelo Ambrogini (1454–94), nicknamed Poliziano, showed the potential of Italian Renaissance philology. He had a couple of mangled manuscripts of Epictetus's *Enchiridion*; using quotations from the *Enchiridon* in a sixth-century commentary on Aristotle, Poliziano plugged holes and emended the text. In commenting on Ovid, he correctly traced the Latin word *nablĭum* (a sort of harp) through Greek ναῦλον (*naûlon*) back to Hebrew *nevel*—observing in the process the systematic consonant shift from Hebrew *v* to Latin *b*, a precocious insight foreshadowing nineteenth-century linguistics. Poliziano even inferred on philological grounds (off base this time) that Egypt influenced ancient Hebrew worship. And, unlike most contemporaries, he collated manuscripts as basis for emendation, turning to cautious conjecture only when manuscripts failed. With sometimes dazzling ingenuity and care, the best philologist of his generation was again doing textual and linguistic scholarship like the most skilled of his ancient forebears.[13]

But Renaissance philologists did such work from a historical point of view unavailable to their ancient models. Ancient philologists—emending old texts or recording civic myths—had seen their own times as continuous with the pasts they studied (Golden Ages and the like excepted). Even when lamenting his degenerate age, Varro knew it as part of the unbroken centuries of Roman history. Renaissance scholars differed. A long-dead ancient Rome, humanists believed, spoke through the words surviving from it. Philology enabled moderns to recover the historical reality behind these words. The literature, even the Latin, of classical antiquity had faded; now they were being retrieved. This gulf between the humanists' 'now' and their antique idols gradually added to philology a historical dimension. In emending Livy, Valla pioneered a genuinely historical approach to texts, where earlier humanists had seen only issues of form and style. To spot and correct errors that had crept into manuscripts, Valla showed, the philologist needed to imagine the gamut of problems faced by long-ago scribes. Philologists awoke to the possibility of anachronism. The most skilled of them insisted on interpretation alert to the historical contexts within which documents had been written. In fifteenth-century Italy, philology became a pursuit undertaken from a knowingly historical angle of vision.[14]

Yet 'historical angle of vision' is a hazy term, and its shifting meanings need continuous monitoring. As the centuries passed, changes occurred in what 'history' and 'historical context' meant for philologists. Humanists of Renaissance Italy looked back at a classical past that they knew was not their own, present world. But neither did they feel it an alien planet. Indeed, by the mid-fifteenth century, when humanism had fully leafed out, Aquinas may have seemed stranger to them than Cicero. Italian humanists came to believe it possible to breathe life not only into Cicero's Latin but also into his world-view—and to revive it in Christian form. (Choosing Ciceronian Latin as their model language ironically deprived them of a vocabulary for discussing things Christian.) The Christianity they created reached back beyond medieval writers to the Church Fathers; for the Fathers, too, had wrestled to reconcile Christianity and pagan writings. For Italian humanists, the ancient past spoke directly to present puzzles.[15]

But humanists also viewed antiquity as remote in time, divided from themselves by a barbarous age. Medieval chroniclers—like medieval painters who dressed Aeneas in the same clothes they wore—put Charlemagne and Frederick II on a list of emperors that started with Julius Caesar. Literate medieval people believed themselves to belong to the same world as ancient Romans. Humanists felt differently. Petrarch had not seen his own time as continuous with ancient Rome but as a distinct, degenerate era, beginning when pagan Rome ended.[16]

This new sense of history led two humanists to invent a chronology still used. Between about 1415 and 1442 Leonardo Bruni wrote a history of Florence from Roman times to his own. Bruni agreed with Petrarch that the Roman era had ended long ago; but he believed that a new epoch had then opened in the late 1200s. About 1440, in his history of Europe since the collapse of the western Roman Empire,* Flavio Biondo offered a similar schema. However, Biondo thought that the new, happier age began with the revival of letters in his own day. Thus Bruni and Biondo, probably independently, di-

---

* Biondo seems to have invented 'the decline and fall of the Roman Empire,' made famous a few centuries later by Edward Gibbon. Biondo took the sack of Rome by Visigoths in 410 CE as the starting point of his history, the same event that spurred Augustine to write *The City of God*.

vided European history into ancient, middle, and modern—a blueprint with us ever since. The term *medium aevum* came into use around 1600. In 1605 the antiquarian William Camden Englished it as "the Middle Age."[17]

To recapture antiquity needed therefore the tools of a historian, but humanists *did* think antiquity recuperable. They did not see it as—to use a later concept—a *culture* different in kind, unblendable with their own. They had historical perspective but not the sort that saw the past as a foreign country (as nineteenth-century historicism did).[18] They lacked the idea of distinct 'cultures.' Still, in making historical change basic to their art, the later Italian humanist scholars set themselves off decisively from philologists of Alexandria and Rome. For all their debt to antiquity, Italian humanists did open new roads for philology.

Yet the scholars who traveled them after 1500 came mostly from north of the Alps. The political balance within and among the various Italian states and statelets had always wobbled. Competing claims of pope and emperor for overall suzerainty had long unsettled the situation further. Ambitious local rulers sometimes drew in foreign forces to bolster their own agenda. In 1494 Charles VIII of France—egged on by Ludovico Sforza of Milan, wanting an ally against Venice—invaded Italy. This adventure began decades of war. Soldiers from several countries took turns devastating the peninsula. In 1527 Spanish troops and German mercenaries of Emperor Charles V Habsburg sacked Rome itself, imprisoning the pope in his own fortress. Besides rape and rapine, the *Landsknechte* "in the Campo dei Fiori and in every intersection, burnt an infinite multitude of books"; or so reported one of the pope's physicians, the humanist historian Paolo Giovio. In those bleak days Giovio found more comfort in Cicero's *Tusculan Disputations* than in Holy Writ. Refugees from the Italian wars included philology. Erudition never deserted Italy, but instability there moved humanism's center to Northern Europe.[19]

Before its flame guttered, the original, rhetorically oriented, Italian humanism changed the face of learning. It recovered much of the written record of Greek and Roman antiquity. (Petrarch and Poggio alone found about half the writings of Cicero now extant.[20]) It brought back to life the philological methods, linguistic inquiries, and antiquarian interests of ancient scholars. Valla even began to apply their techniques to the Bible as well as to 'pagan' texts. Italian humanists nurtured a deeper sense of the historicity of philological scholarship. And, when humanism died as a broad-gauged ideal of the life of the mind and of the citizen, humanist philology survived—mainly across the Alps.

Philologia Trilingua, the Bible, and History

Northern humanism differed from its Italian parent. Italian humanists devoted themselves chiefly to Latin and to ancient pagan authors. Northerners made more use of languages other than Latin—especially Greek and Hebrew—and used them in biblical as well as classical philology. 'Chiefly' matters: northern humanists did not break from the past but expanded what Italians began.

Consider Greek. Ability to read it never vanished in the Latin Middle Ages, but it became rare.* Italian humanists shifted the momentum. Petrarch took a stab at learning Greek until his tutor left. In the late 1300s, knowledge of Greek began to increase in Italy. In the mid-1400s, as the Ottomans closed in on Constantinople, refugees sped its spread. Even before, the Byzantine diplomat Manuel Chrysoloras taught Greek intermittently in Italy for a number of years from 1397. His pupils included Leonardo Bruni, the historian of Florence. Around 1500—when the number of Greek teachers got large enough to notice—the language began to meet some resistance. To Latin Christians, it could seem tainted with Greek Orthodox heresy; to some Scholastics who resented rhetoric and philology, it was tainted with humanism, too. Yet Scholastics also benefited from Greek: Aristotle, after all, was their great master.[21]

Scholastic and humanist stood at odds not in valuing ancient Greek writings but in how to approach them: the one philosophical, the other philological; the one dialectical, the other rhetorical; the one logical, the other historical. Both used Greek, but in dissimilar ways, on a differing range of texts. Bruni made controversial translations of Aristotle; but Aristotle the master of rhetoric and ethical guide intrigued him, not Aristotle the logician, physicist, and metaphysician. Bruni criticized Scholastic translators of Aristotle as so overly literal as to puzzle readers: the translator should grasp the broad meaning of a passage and mold it into elegant Latin prose for an educated general readership, not transliterate for a coterie of academic philosophers. Not Greek itself, but the typical philologist's disinterest in metaphysics, his interest in rhetoric, and his broader way of looking at the ancient world set philologist apart from Scholastic.[22]

Besides Aristotle and other pagan books, Greek opened to philological study the most high-risk text, the New Testament. Valla undertook—for practically the first time in the Latin west since antiquity—to examine Greek manuscripts of it. (No one knows which ones.) He worked up a string of notes, using the Alexandrian method of collating texts. But he compared Greek texts with the normative Latin Vulgate; for he planned to emend not the Greek Bible but the Vulgate itself. Circulated warily in his lifetime, his observations paved the way for later scholars, notably Erasmus of Rotterdam (ca. 1469–1536).[23]

By Erasmus's day a learned humanist would blush if he had no Greek, and Hebrew was spreading among Christian philologists. At first Hebrew mattered mainly for proselytizing Jews (urged already by the Council of Vienne in 1311).

---

* Readers will recall from chapter 1 that Greek had persisted since antiquity as a spoken language in out-of-the-way parts of southern Italy.

But, as noted in chapter 1, a handful of medieval Christian biblical scholars asked rabbis for help; by the fourteenth century a few even learned Hebrew themselves. A scattering of Italian humanists dabbled in the language. Motivated by philology and piety, Lorenzo Valla sought the *hebraicam veritatem* (Hebrew truth) of the Psalms. Pico della Mirandola studied Hebrew under Jewish teachers in order to read the mystical writings known as Kabbalah. (How far he got is unclear.) In 1416 Poggio Bracciolini found a converted Jew to introduce him to Hebrew. Poggio thought Hebrew "of no use in increasing our wisdom" but that "it adds something to our study of the Humanities"—specifically "Jerome's method of translation."[24] Both dismissive attitude and philological motive persisted, as Christian scholars reluctantly began to admit the value of rabbinic erudition in interpreting the Old Testament.

Until perhaps the late sixteenth century, Christian study of Hebrew was a minefield. Anti-Judaism made Hebrew odious to many Christians. (The street ran both ways; other Jews sometimes hassled those who helped Christian philologists, and Christian derision of Judaism got answered in kind. Christians flung a lot more mud.) Still, in 1524 Robert Wakefield, the first Hebrew lecturer in Cambridge, declared in his inaugural oration that he "judged worthy only that person who approached complex mysteries of sacred scripture . . . equipped with diverse languages"—Hebrew the essential one. The far more learned Hebraist who helped to make a Wakefield possible was the German Johannes Reuchlin. He published in 1506 a Hebrew grammar-cum-dictionary to help Christians learn the language.* His grammar squeezed Hebrew into the straitjacket of humanist Latin, and Reuchlin read Jewish writings through Christian glasses. Yet other Christians turned on him when he opposed a 1510 edict to destroy Jewish books throughout the Holy Roman Empire. Vitriol and cries of 'heretic' bombarded him until his death in 1522. Erasmus dragged his feet before finally endorsing Hebrew studies, and then he sweetened his backing with anti-Jewish bile. The great philologist Isaac Casaubon (1559–1614), who pored over rabbinic literature and treated it much as he handled Greek texts, stood out among Christian Hebraists in showing some tolerance, even amity toward actual Jews. Anti-Judaism was not the sole stumbling-block to Hebrew learning. In 1525 the French theologian Pierre Cousturier (Petrus Sutor)—with a sneer at the "little rhetorician" Erasmus—called it "completely insane" to learn *either* Greek or Hebrew for biblical study. The church had declared the Latin Vulgate version sufficient.[25]

Still, both languages spread; and their popularity among the learned spawned the 'trilingual college,' mixing in its curriculum Greek and Hebrew with the traditional Latin. The first *collegium trilinguae* appeared in 1498 within a new Spanish university at Alcalá de Henares, just east of Madrid. In

* From Reuchlin's and other Hebrew grammar books, Christian scholars also got the concepts of root, prefix, and suffix, previously unknown to Latin grammarians but soon applied to vernacular grammars.

1518 the Collegium Trilingue [*sic*], inspired by Erasmus, arose in Leuven in present-day Belgium (separate from the unfriendly Scholastic university there). In imitation, in 1530, François I established the Collège Royal in Paris (ancestor of the Collège de France). Under the aegis of Erasmus's humanist friend John Fisher, bishop of Rochester, St. John's College in Cambridge (founded 1511) morphed into a collegium trilinguae—followed by the slightly younger Corpus Christi College in Oxford. (In 1511 Erasmus, urged by Fisher, had become first to teach Greek in Cambridge, briefly.) In the 1540s Henry VIII founded regius professorships of Greek and Hebrew at both universities. In the next century a new Catholic congregation, the Oratorian priests in France, required seminarians to learn Latin, Greek, and Hebrew. In the 1630s a collegium trilinguae opened on Europe's far frontier: Harvard College in the young Massachusetts Bay Colony.[26]

From the later 1500s serious scholars commonly had Hebrew and dealings with learned Jews. Well-educated Calvinist Protestants might pick up the language in routine schooling, as Isaac Casaubon did. By the 1600s, Sephardic Jews in Amsterdam were writing books aimed at Christian readers, evidence of regular contact across a hostile border. A few Calvinist philologists, mostly Dutch, reciprocated by admitting in public that rabbinic books illuminated the Old Testament. By 1600 most Protestant exegetes also agreed on the trustworthiness of the rabbis' Masoretic Text of the Hebrew Bible. Their consensus made it tougher to howl about rabbinic corruption of the biblical text, as Christians had done for centuries. But, as a rule, neither this consensus, widespread use of Hebrew, nor links with erudite rabbis softened Christian animosity to Jews and Judaism.[27]

Hebrew and Greek together enabled a massive, precedent-setting, and delicate work of biblical philology: the Complutensian Polyglot Bible. (Complutum is the Latin name of Alcalá de Henares, home of the Spanish university where the Polyglot was made.) This sensitive enterprise went on under—and probably needed—the auspices of a powerful cardinal, Francisco Jiménez de Cisneros. Many converted Jews lived in Spain, their Hebrew at least baptized. The Polyglot's editors applied methods by then standard: seeking the oldest manuscripts available, collating many copies to fix the likeliest readings among variants. But it was *not* standard to pair the Vulgate with Greek and Hebrew versions of the Bible. The resulting Latin-Hebrew-Greek leviathan (the Pentateuch also in Aramaic) revived Origen's system of printing the text, in its different languages, in parallel columns. The method left prudently untouched choices of variants among the versions—and thus the authority of the Vulgate. The Complutensian Polyglot was published, in 1522, in a medium scarcely seventy-five years old: printing with movable type. *Printed* several years before the papacy allowed it to be *published*, the Polyglot contained the first printed Greek New Testament and thus opened a new era of scholarly biblical texts, copied by machine.[28]

Even before 1500, presses printed fourteen European languages, but print- 2
ing affected philology little. Procedures of emending and commenting on
manuscripts did not change because the final product appeared in print. Printing did tend to stabilize texts and reduce scribal error (though not as much as
one might think); but print also stabilized mistakes. Printer-publishers, philologists at their side, worked fast to get an edition into print as soon as possible; they commonly collated only one or two manuscripts rather than several;
they relied heavily on conjectural emendation: all practices guaranteed to generate errata. Printing did make texts more widely and cheaply available. In
particular, Hebrew texts became more accessible to Christian scholars. (But
then Catholic authorities came down on Jewish printers after the Roman Inquisition condemned the Talmud in 1553.) Changes other than printing mattered far more for philologists.[29]

One was growing knowledge and technique, as Erasmus's career shows. Indeed, one might characterize Erasmus (besides as a man with a disposition for
the boxing ring) as synthesizer of philological craft built up since Petrarch. As
peripatetic as Petrarch, Erasmus oscillated mainly among the Low Countries,
England, and Basel, with briefer stays elsewhere. *Errans-mus*, 'roving rat,' his
foes called him. In 1504 he discovered (in Parc Abbey near Leuven) and in
1505 published (in Paris) Lorenzo Valla's notes on the New Testament. Drawing again on earlier scholars, he promoted a new Greek pronunciation, believed closer to that of antiquity. His edition of the Greek New Testament
(1516) ultimately proved an albatross around the necks of later philologists:
Erasmus worked too haphazardly; yet his New Testament—owing to its priority and its editor's fame—long stood in the way of more accurate versions. But
his edition did fix two key principles: that the same philological rules apply to
the Bible as to other ancient texts and that a text in its original language over-
rules any translation. The latter might seem obvious. Not so. Erasmus's Greek
manuscripts of the first epistle of John lacked a verse in the Latin Vulgate up-
holding the doctrine of the Trinity; so he discarded it. But editors of the Complutensian Polyglot kept this 'Johannine comma' (as it is now called)—translating it from Latin and inserting it into their Greek text! The Latin Bible
sanctioned by the church trumped the Greek original.[30]

Erasmus's scholarship showed historical consciousness stronger even than
Valla's. Erasmus thought historical contexts vital for fathoming the origin and
transmission of any text, and thus for emending it. By imagining himself as a
long-ago copyist, he articulated a dogma of textual philology: the principle of
the 'harder reading.' Consider an uncertain scribe about to copy a confusing
line. The copyist might inadvertently slip in a clearer phrase for one hard to
get. Faced with two variants, the philologist should—counterintuitively—prefer the clumsier. It less likely reflected a copyist's error. In writing a biography
of St. Jerome, Erasmus discarded traditional hagiography and studied Jerome's
life as history—stripped of holy legends—in order to understand his writings.

Conversely, he scrutinized the works to understand the life. Text and context entangled in the same web of history. Erasmus wrote that he wanted to know "not only what is said but also by whom, to whom, with what words, at what time, on what occasion, what precedes and what follows." Students of the Bible, he insisted, needed to learn ancient history and geography as well as languages, but above all to ask what the biblical writer was thinking.[31]

Erasmus never questioned Valla's supposition of mental and moral continuity with the past. Antiquity seemed to both men a *distant* but not truly *different* world. According to Erasmus, philology could retrieve how a biblical author thought. The world where Paul and Luke walked and talked differed in many details from his own, but not in kind. The ancient past—classical as well as Christian—seemed at once unlike the present yet familiar.[32]

The past grew less familiar in writings by one of Erasmus's friends in Basel, Beatus Rhenanus. Beatus proved himself an accomplished textual philologist, notably in his 1526 *Annotationes* to Pliny the Elder's natural history. He insisted on great caution in emendation; on scrutiny of a whole manuscript for clues to the reading of any passage in it; on checking related texts and other writings of the same period for additional hints; on close attention to handwriting (what scholars now call paleography)—"the very letters in the old manuscripts"—to ensure that the philologist had gotten the word right (which some copyist perhaps misread). Unusually explicit about methods, his work became a model for reconstructing texts. History pervaded his writing: a history more alert to cultural difference (as we would say) than perhaps any before. In 1519 Beatus edited Tacitus's *Germania* (about German tribes encountered by the Romans). It hit Beatus that the people in Tacitus's pages behaved and thought nothing like modern Germans. (That ancient Germans were certified Barbarians, not St. Paul or Cicero, made it easier to realize how much they differed from modern folks.) Using skills honed in editions and commentaries, Beatus set out to make sense of masses of confused information about ancient and medieval Germans, scattered through motley sources. He assembled these data in *Res Germanicae* (*German History*, 1531). Beatus's compendium—a kind of anthology of primary material—supplied the first foundation for writing early medieval German history.[33]

PHILOLOGY REELING FROM REFORMATION

Historical sensitivity could get a philologist into trouble amid the upheavals of the Reformation era. It would be risky to suggest, say, that Moses had not actually composed the first five books of the Old Testament.[34] As Catholic and Protestant rulers struggled to impose their varied orthodoxies in the wake of the Reformation, heretics burned at the stake. Philologists rarely roasted; but they came under pressure to eschew any hint of heterodoxy and actively to defend orthodoxy—as defined locally. For obvious reasons, biblical philology

Q: humanism is the essence of philology?

Philology in the hands of humanists?

was at the center of the storm, but the Reformation changed the climate for erudition as a whole.*

On the Catholic side, foes of philology defamed it as abetting Protestantism. Some Scholastics had long griped—well before Martin Luther made trouble—that philologists undermined religion. By laying critical hands on the Vulgate, they sapped the authority of the church that declared it authoritative. It did not help philologists that Luther's ninety-five theses (1517) came the year after Erasmus's Greek New Testament—nor that Luther relied on Erasmus's text in his German translation of the New Testament. In reality, Scholasticism and philology were not matter and antimatter, annihilating each other on contact. Erasmus's English friends Thomas More and John Fisher appreciated both. Yet in the wake of Luther's revolt tensions reached boiling point. Scholastic critics of humanism intimated that the slippery slope of philology led to Protestantism. Erasmus turned around and accused them of fabricating the indictment to discredit humanism. Catholic leaders sometimes did react as if biblical philology were the wolf in the sheepfold. The Council of Trent reaffirmed the 'authenticity' of the Vulgate: "no one is to dare, or presume to reject it under any pretext whatsoever." The church forbade Catholics to read Erasmus's works. Yet philology never did divide along a Protestant-Catholic line. Erasmus stayed true to the Roman religion at some cost. So did Johannes Reuchlin, despite years of abuse from Catholic authorities and friendship with leading Lutherans (Philip Melanchthon was his beloved grandnephew). Erasmus's trilingual ally John Fisher died for the old faith.[35]

In fact, Protestants and Catholics both looked skeptically on biblical philology. The nondoctrinal, historical approach to the Bible practiced by scholars like Valla and Erasmus fell among the first casualties of the Reformation. Whether in university or pulpit, Protestant biblical interpreters sacrificed historical and linguistic precision to dogma as quickly as Erasmus's most grotesque caricature of a Scholastic. By the later 1500s even learned Protestants typically read the Bible as an arsenal of polemical theology, not as ancient books needing historical context to understand correctly. Catholics put perhaps even more distance between themselves and the perils of philology. Good Catholic scholars studied the Bible; but they worked on narrower lines, under closer scrutiny. Philologists who privileged history over creed were few.[36]

There were some. Calvin's disciple Theodore Beza prepared notes to the New Testament helpful to later scholars. Both Joseph Scaliger (1540–1609) and Isaac Casaubon treated early Christian writings as voices from the ancient world, not as premature Calvinists or Catholics. They insisted, innovatively, on placing the New Testament in ancient Jewish context. Scaliger massively

here, "philology" (humanist philology) is meant to stand for all philology.

---

* The other revolution of this era arose from European entanglement with the world beyond Europe and the Mediterranean region. The consequences for erudition were colossal, but also more gradual and diffuse than the Reformation's. I shall take them up as they affect my narrative.

augmented that context by uncovering the lost diversity of ancient Judaism. Astonished readers learned from Scaliger that Jews once lived who not only spoke Greek but read their scriptures in that language. Such historically minded biblical critics formed an endangered minority as long as the fires of the Reformation raged.[37]

However present-minded their reading of scripture, early Protestants unwittingly laid groundwork for historical biblical philology to come. In the texts used in medieval universities, marginal comments by Church Fathers and Doctors swathed every book of the Bible. Protestants stripped them. Luther, not yet Lutheran, had just such a 'clean' text printed for his lectures on the Psalms in 1513. Removing the blanket of commentary freed the Bible from Catholic tradition, left it open to individual exegesis. The principle of *sola scriptura*—scripture alone, liberated from the say-so of the church—became central to Protestantism. But, with no restraint on how individuals could interpret the Bible, chaos threatened. To ward it off, mainstream Protestant leaders preferred the least equivocal sense of the words—that is, the literal or 'historical' meaning. (Do not confuse this 'literal sense' with 'biblical literalism' that English speakers talk about today. The latter assumes a theory of verbal inerrancy only spelled out in the nineteenth century.) Efforts to settle the literal meaning had sooner or later to revive historical biblical studies; with no church to tell you, how else could you figure out what ancient writers meant in the words they penned?[38]

Protestant literalism turned the Bible into something closer to a historical document. Without the present-tense immediacy of medieval symbolic interpretations, the Bible became more like a record of distant places and times. True, in its pages the Holy Spirit still spoke to pious Protestant readers in the here and now.* But the pages themselves told of events long ago, not of allegorical meanings alive today. The Gospels became the annals of Jesus's life and the register of his teachings. So penetrating a philologist as Isaac Casaubon, like everyone else, took it for granted that historical sections of the Bible could not really conflict in their account of events. A sometime Harvard lecturer, Charles Morton, in 1694 read a patently metaphorical passage in Jeremiah literally, as evidence for his theory that birds migrate to the moon. The first chapter of Genesis became the chronicle of creation. Quite typically, the astronomer Johannes Kepler (1571–1630) referred to "historiae Mosaicae de creatione"—"the Mosaic history of creation." Kepler's contemporary, the Anglican priest-poet John Donne (1572–1631), insisted that "we defend and maintain this Book of *Moses* to be Historical, and therefore literally to be interpreted"; otherwise "we are utterly disprovided of a history of the World's

---

* The popularity of 'typological' interpretation among Protestants also moderated the historicizing effect. Thus Puritans in the Massachusetts Bay Colony could interpret the Exodus from Egypt as a 'type' foreshadowing their exodus across the Atlantic to escape their own pharaoh, Charles I.

Creation." Calling Moses "principal Secretary to the Holy Ghost," Donne declared the secretary's account of creation "infallible"—although exactly how long ago God did his work "is matter of reason, and therefore various and perplex'd." By Donne's day, Protestants began to ask questions that would not have troubled an allegorically minded medieval exegete unconcerned about biblical 'history.' Where exactly sat the Garden of Eden? How scientifically precise was Moses in recording creation?[39]

Aside from its effect on biblical studies, 'confessionalization' of learning replaced key humanist ideals with new ones. These met a need for dogmatic exactitude created by the quarrels within Western Christianity. Protestant schools gave up aspirations to broad learning (an ambition, as already noted, that perhaps never got far in grubby reality); they opted for a narrower focus on doctrine and classical languages: raw material to make good Protestant servants of the state. The new Jesuit schools did offer a broader rhetorical training of high quality, but with a whopping dose of Catholic doctrine. On both sides, religious policing took priority in the curriculum. Personally scholars suffered from the same confessional stresses. Within a few years of Luther's theses, neutrality became a dead option. Learned friendships dissolved in acrimony. Scholars fled to safer cities, gave up sensitive topics, or put down their pens altogether. In Paris both Catholics and hard-line fellow Huguenots bedeviled Isaac Casaubon. He decamped to the then milder climate of England in 1610.[40]

Interconfessional quarrels sharpened the ever-developing sense of history. Catholics and rival Protestant groups hurled competing claims about origin and development of doctrines, church offices, and religious practices. The need to back up assertions breathed new life into the old genre of ecclesiastical history. The shade of Eusebius must have smiled upon the thick, heavily documented volumes. Polemical such histories were—thoroughly. But they also honed standards of historical evidence, as one tome after another came under fire. Protestants, banging home the message that Rome had strayed far from true Christianity, stressed the yawning gap between Jesus's world and present papist institutions—while also commonly insisting that their own teachings and customs returned to the church Jesus had founded. Catholics, clobbering Protestants for ruinous innovation, insisted on the continuity between that primitive church and the Church of Rome. The wrangling never got settled, but it did force scholars to mull over differing features of historical epochs. A more nuanced awareness of Jesus's context convinced some church historians to try to fill in its background of Jewish rituals and beliefs. The new Christian Hebraic scholarship made the effort more feasible.[41]

A trajectory arcs from Petrarch to Valla to Erasmus to Beatus Rhenanus to these ecclesiastical historians. Scholars with different religious and philosophical commitments, applying philological method in different ways, contributed to growing mindfulness of cultural variance between historical periods.

Without invoking determinism, a later observer nonetheless sees the result of philology's comparative method, as it continually set the present against the past and varied pasts against each other.

Yet politico-religious motives, not any internal dynamic of erudition, spurred investigation of the past. In this sense, history in the age of the Reformation grew decidedly ahistorical. To cite one case, English Protestants battled with English Catholics in exile to control the distant origins of English Christianity. What had really happened in sixth-century Kent was secondary. Such learned wars of religion had institutional fallout. The great Bodleian Library in Oxford opened in 1602 as a battery of *Protestant* learning—to "beate the Papists," as its first keeper put it, "with the forcible weapon of Antiquitie." This warrior sought to blow out of the water Catholic scholarship on the early church by showing that "the Papists" had tampered with manuscript evidence. (Alas for him, they had not.) The papists of the Bibliothèque du roi in Paris, meanwhile, amassed their own manuscript arsenal to bombard the rebel Protestants. The Reformation made erudition a weapon of war.[42]

Philology in the Wake of Reformation

Yet the Reformation did not kill "humanism;" rather, humanism's own limitations, *along with* changes in the world around it, pushed it in new directions. The common humanist aversion to philosophy, for instance, made it too one-sided to work for long as a broad worldview, especially after the Reformation threw theological disputes into high relief. Then, when religio-political violence tore Europe apart, humanists abandoned the perilous civic arena to take refuge in the scholar's study and university lecture hall. Compare the humanist Thomas More (1478–1535) with another great legal humanist four decades younger, Jacques Cujas (1520–90). More served Henry VIII as lord chancellor of England. Cujas shrank from public involvement. He no longer studied Roman law to apply it to contemporary problems, as earlier scholars had; instead he interrogated ancient texts to discover their meanings in their own time. The violence of the Reformation swirled about both More and Cujas. The politically engaged More died on the scaffold. The politically withdrawn Cujas died in his bed. What the Reformation did in northern Europe, political turmoil had already done in Italy. Early Florentine humanists studied Roman republicanism to better their own republic. But in the late fifteenth century, with Florence under the thumb of Lorenzo de' Medici, Poliziano withdrew into pure scholarship; like Cujas, he tried to understand the past on its own terms, gave up on finding lessons for the present.[43]

Scholars between the Reformation and the late seventeenth century are still rightly called humanists because of their languages and methods, but they looked on their work differently than did their earlier namesakes. More and more, erudition ran as a self-contained business. Scholars saw in each other

@ humanism or philology ?

members of the same company, tied together with thick webs of correspondence. They formed the international Republic of Letters—a term that entered
common use during the tumult of the early Reformation. In 1875 Mark Pattison, biographer of Casaubon, remarked about the sixteenth century, "There
came now into existence, what has ever since been known as 'learning' in the
special sense of the term." He was onto something. Such learning remained
the animating ideal of the Republic of Letters until *philosophes* bumped *érudits* off their pedestals around 1700. By the time Erasmus died in 1536, the old
rhetorical humanism was already beating a retreat into the fortress of the
grammar schools. There Latin and Greek remained the touchstone of elite
education into the twentieth century. But even there teaching of classical languages became, as a rule, ahistorical gerund grinding, barely aware of the ancient civilizations that spoke those languages.[44]

Ironically, this narrowing of the meaning of humanism diversified humanist scholarship. When church authorities dampened historical scrutiny of the
Bible for a century after the Reformation, philological energy and ingenuity
turned in new directions. And, with many classical texts already in print by
the 1520s, erudition did not simply shift back toward text-oriented classical
philology.[45]

Classical studies hardly vanished. Massive collections of emendations, variant readings, and observations on ancient history and life rolled off the presses.
In 1557 Francesco Robortello published the first systematic handbook of classical textual philology; and in 1572 appeared the hefty, still authoritative Greek
dictionary of Robert and Henri Estienne. Unedited texts remained to print
(notably those of Sextus Empiricus in the 1560s, with widespread philosophical consequences in the revival of ancient skepticism). Classical texts already
in print needed betterment. And, more intimately familiar with classical languages, writings, and history, philologists made better-informed conjectures
about how to restore corrupt passages.[46]

Still, where philologists before the Reformation converged on classical and
then biblical *texts*, their later successors diverged into manifold fields. A German humanist physician, writing in 1578, included within the purview of philology the study of—among other things—linguistic matters, aphorisms,
proverbs, fables, histories, chronology, significant people, rivers, mountains,
landscape, cities, morals, the cultures of peoples and races, religious rituals; in
short, everything to be found in "good authors." He was no oddball. A quarter
century later, a manifesto called *De Polymathia* (*On Polymathy*) appeared in
Hamburg. It identified polymathy as historically oriented 'grammar' in the
spacious ancient Alexandrian sense, citing Eratosthenes as exemplar. The author envisioned the insatiable polymath traipsing "per omnes disciplinarum
campos"—through all fields of disciplines—filling up a bottomless bucket
with sundry facts and material objects. The philologist thus claimed all knowledge created by human thought and action, generously leaving to other inquirers the natural world, or most of it.[47]

This intellectual imperialism diluted the humanist's special relationship with classical antiquity and altered its focus. Antiquity still mattered a lot; but polyhistors—as these universally learned scholars came to be called—found much else to occupy their hours. Philological polymathy even bridged for a time the age-old gap between philosophy and philology. Since 'grammar' now commanded *all* realms of the human mind, it took charge of philosophy as well. Early modern philologists grew specially fond of preaching the ancient Stoics. Scholars also homed in on neglected, specialized areas of ancient knowledge, such as geographical, botanical, or critical writings. The learned jurist Guillaume Budé produced in 1529 a fat lexicon-cum-commentary of Greek legal terms. Two decades later, Conrad Gesner published an even more elephantine *Bibliotheca Universalis*. It provided biographies of all ancient writers of Greek, Latin, or Hebrew—together with an encyclopedia of all knowledge, more or less, though heavy on the classical past.[48]

In the encyclopedic spirit of Gesner but more concisely, it will be helpful to visit a few domains of philology and related erudition, as these grew from the sixteenth century through the seventeenth; for the proliferation of philological curiosity appears in hindsight a big step toward the modern humanities.

CLASSICAL ANTIQUARIANISM, CHRONOLOGY, AND THE EXPANSION OF ANTIQUITY

Since antiquity, artifacts had interacted with philology. The back-and-forth created a thicker, more nuanced sense of history. By the late sixteenth century, antiquarians were using more critical, better-informed methods to analyze ancient coins, buildings, tombs, and other relics; by the seventeenth, pictures of objects mentioned by ancient authors illustrated editions of their works. The study of inscriptions—much later named epigraphy—in particular grew more systematic. Epigraphers—to use that anachronistic term—borrowed approaches from textual philologists (such as studies of the historical evolution of Latin) to understand and date inscriptions. Catalogs and indexes made more usable the printed volumes of inscriptions that multiplied with every decade, while textual philologists checked their accuracy.[49]

In 1546 diggers in the Roman Forum uncovered monumental inscriptions listing dates of kings, consuls, and military victors, from the legendary founding of Rome in 753 BCE up to the end of the republic. Moved to the Capitoline Hill, the inscriptions became known as the Fasti Capitolini. (*Fastus*—plural, *fasti*—in this context means a calendar, listing such items as festivals or magistrates then in office.) A monk called Onofrio Panvinio prepared a scholarly edition of the find, *Fasti et triumphi Romani* (1557). Panvinio also put together a sort of companion to the Fasti, *Reipublicae Romanae commentariorum libri tres* (*Three Books of Commentaries on the Roman Republic*).[50]

This latter work showed how closely philology and antiquarianism cooperated. For instance, Panvinio wanted to sort out the confusingly diverse Roman priesthoods. He dragged in evidence from as many quarters as possible: coins, texts, long inscriptions from monuments, short ones from tombstones. Then he had to make sense of it. William Stenhouse described his predicament:

> How could Panvinio be sure of a particular arcane word in a text, for example, if the manuscript of the ancient author from which it came was known to have been carelessly copied? Could his correspondents offer any parallels, or any general pieces of advice? How was a particular abbreviation in the letters around a coin's edge to be interpreted, and did the figure on the coin represent a priest? How many inscriptions were known at Rome which featured a particular sacrificial officer, and how were the variations in the way the name was spelled to be interpreted?

To recover the ancient past, the written record could not be kept apart from coins, architecture, inscriptions; nor vice versa. Panvinio himself amassed some three thousand inscriptions and nursed a plan—unfulfilled—to publish all known inscriptions. The philologist and the antiquarian were often the same person.[51]

The Fasti Capitolini helped to make the ancient subject of chronology a hot modern one. The quest for correct historical dates traveled far beyond Rome. Comprehending ancient calendars and supplying absolute dates for early events—a renewed version of Eusebius's research—defined what Anthony Grafton called "one of the great encyclopaedic disciplines of late humanism, technical chronology." Chronology veered alarmingly close to the Bible but also puzzled over the history of recently conquered Americans. Its greatest practitioner, Joseph Scaliger, was also one of the finest classical textual philologists of his age; philology in his hands became key to unlocking chronology. Scaliger also pursued the history of languages, fretted over how to group them, and tried to put the ancient study of etymology on a scientific basis. The extent of Scaliger's polymathy amazes, but diversity of learned interests was normal.[52]

Chronological research like his supplied a springboard into study of ancient Egypt and Israel and farther afield. Topically these 'oriental' studies were the most innovative thing early modern philologists did. Scaliger played a big part. His chronology conjured an alluring vision: in Peter Miller's words, "a new history of Europe that integrated the ancient Egyptian, Israelite, and Phoenician worlds of the eastern Mediterranean with the Greek and Roman civilizations of the western." Other philologists, too, turned skills forged to study Greece and Rome onto ancient cultures of Asia and even beyond. Such soundings could subvert orthodoxy as severely as biblical philology. Isaac La Peyrère invoked ancient chronologies from the Near East and New World, antedating the biblical timescale, to argue in *Prae-Adamitae* (1655) that human beings existed long before Adam, the Bible's first man. The Jesuit missionary Martino Martini in 1658 tried to reconcile Chinese and biblical chronologies; he ended up implying that Chinese people antedated Noah, father of the whole human race after the universal Flood. In 1665 the English chronologer John Marsham showed Egyptian civilization to be older than either Greece or Israel.[53]

ORIENTALISM AND RELIGIONS

Other philologists ventured eastward. Even before 1600 a few transcended trilingual biblical philology to master Arabic, Aramaic, and Syriac;* they composed dictionaries and grammars as well for Ethiopic, Armenian, Turkish, and Persian. The erudite adventurer André du Ryer published French translations of the Qur'an (1647) and of selections (1634) from the thirteenth-century Persian classic *Gulistān* (*Rose Garden*). By his day, major universities throughout western and central Europe employed professors of Arabic and other 'oriental' languages. For a while, Oxford and Cambridge required of students a dash of Arabic. Little Harvard taught Aramaic and Syriac to all its sons. Meanwhile Leiden and Oxford Universities collected manuscripts in Middle Eastern languages. Oxford acquired even Chinese ones. So did the Bibliothèque du roi in Paris, and in 1687 it sponsored publication of Latin translations from Confucius. The *Journal des sçavans* [*savants*] gave this book more attention than another published the same year, Isaac Newton's *Principia*.[54]

Whence came the fad for 'oriental' languages in such decidedly unoriental places as Holland and England? (And it was partly a craze, fading in the late seventeenth century.) From the later 1500s, European commercial, diplomatic, and missionary activity expanded in the Ottoman Empire. These venturers learned languages and supplied raw material for oriental scholarship. This background helps to explain the popularity of Arabic, a language of secondary importance for Bible studies but primary for the Levant. European merchants in the East Indies stretched the range in the seventeenth century. Other overseas involvements would feed philology in later times.[55]

These oriental studies converged with antiquarianism, biblical philology, and chronology to expand inquiries into non-Christian religions. Where earlier Christian Hebraists worried about the Bible, Johannes Buxtorf's *Synagoga judaica* (1603) tried to decipher modern Jewish practice—to enrich anti-Jewish polemics. Buxtorf probably incited Leone Modena's *I riti degli Ebrei* (*The Rites of the Hebrews*, 1637): a Jew explaining Judaism to Christians. In 1617, John Selden wrote about Near Eastern mythology, including a Phoenician creation story. Italian scholars studied ancient Egyptian sun worship. The

* Syriac is a Semitic language, related to the Aramaic spoken by Jesus, and a medium for early Christian texts. Some medieval Christians had learned Arabic in Muslim Spain.

Dutch philologist Gerardus Vossius in 1642 wrote about many rites, ancient and exotic, from the cultic meaning of beans in pagan Rome to polytheism in Calcutta. Not all sun-worshipping idolaters (idolaters they remained, for Europeans gazed at them with Christian eyes) lived long ago. Fascination with strange *ancient* religions reflected *modern* efforts to fathom ceremonies seen by merchants, missionaries, or conquerors in Asia and South America. The Portuguese who in 1498 first saw Hindu gods painted on temple walls thought they were looking at Christian saints in a Christian church—though the extra arms must have puzzled them. Exotic observations, or reports of them, pushed some scholars beyond the binary between true religion (inward faith in Christian beliefs) and false (pagan idolaters, Muslim impostors, superseded Jews). Instead of calling Chinese rituals idolatry, Jesuit missionaries declared them a form of civil religion. Another Jesuit, in Peru, did think that Inca rites were idolatry inspired by the devil but no different in essence from Greek and Roman paganism—all evidencing a universal human instinct to worship. Ethnographic curiosity and philological research ran together. Scholars groped toward a concept of 'religion' as a category that might cover very different practices, of disparate peoples, in varied times and places.[56]

HISTORY, ANTIQUARIANISM, AND NATIONAL PASTS

Alongside study of faraway places, antiquarian research into European national and civic pasts thrived in the Republic of Letters. Antiquarianism in this spirit was nothing new, having been patriotically prosecuted by Lovato and Petrarch. As early as the twelfth century, Geoffrey of Monmouth traced "the history of the kings of Britain" (*Historia regum Britanniae*) and the island's name gloriously back to one Brutus, great-grandson of Aeneas—and Geoffrey had lifted Brutus from Nennius's *Historia Brittonum*, three centuries earlier. (Geoffrey added the deft detail that Britain was unpeopled when Brutus and his Trojans landed, "except for a few giants.") German scholars in the fifteenth century used etymology to recover supposed lost laurels of their cities. Sixteenth-century Spanish antiquarians treated local Roman inscriptions as evidence for Spain's early history rather than as a provincial piece of Roman history. From imagined Goths sprang the distinctive excellencies of the English.[57]

Such inquiries—and fantasies—gained new energy with the troubled mid-sixteenth century. Rulers in the contested world of the early modern nation-state strove to legitimate their regimes. Uncovering roots deep in native soil served the purpose. By applying philological tools to old political and legal documents, historians could manufacture plausible defenses of shaky institutions. In France, such erudition prospered especially during the religio-political wars of the later sixteenth century. (French readers then learned that France did not originate, as long believed, with yet more Trojan refugees—evidently once scurrying all over western Europe—but with a Germanic people called Franks.) French historians often acquired their philological skills through legal education, odd as that may sound. Legal scholars sought principles to bring order to the turmoil of their day, and civil law was inherited Roman law. So jurists applied philology, such as expert knowledge of ancient Latin vocabulary, to remains of Roman legal texts. They tried to figure out what each word meant to the ancient authors—in contrast to Scholastic jurists, who had rationalized such texts to fit current needs. Jacques Cujas, mentioned earlier, was preeminent among these philologically minded jurists. In their search, many of them saw—even more clearly than Bruni and Biondo—how different their times were from the ancient Rome that created the law Europe still tried to use. Disciples of Cujas went on to apply his approach to the medieval history of France, melding philology and historical narrative. Cujasians not only made scholarly readers more mindful of historical difference. They also sharpened methods that later historians would pick up.[58]

Such erudition was anything but disinterested. Nation-states evoked patriotic fervor: "after what I owe to God," wrote one student of Cujas, the historian Jacques-Auguste de Thou, in 1604, "nothing should be more dear and sacred to me than the love and respect owed to my *patrie*." A mix of nationalism and religious quarrels animated seventeenth-century English medievalist research. Christian antiquity fascinated scholars in the Church of England throughout the century, but the contents and meaning of ancient Christianity bounced around with every theological twitch.[59]

De Thou's English friend William Camden pulsed to his own nationalistic rhythms. He wrote an adulatory history of the reign of Queen Elizabeth, an account of the Gunpowder Plot, an inventory of the epitaphs in Westminster Abbey, and, above all, *Britannia* (first edition, 1586), a multivolume survey of Great Britain. It embraced scenery, Roman coins, folklore, monuments, law courts, customs, the sea, ancient and recent history, the kitchen sink.* It is worth a pause—a long pause—to get a flavor of the varied curiosity of the early modern antiquarian. Here is Camden introducing his account of the origin of the name Britain:

> [I]f you run over all particulars severally both new and old; you shall find, that every nation was of others called by divers names, from those that they themselves used. Thus they that in their native tongue had Israelites to their name, according to the Greeks were called Hebrews and Jewes, and by the Aegyptians *Huesi*, as witnesseth Manetho, because they had Heardmen for their governours. So the Greeks named them Syrians who, as Josephus writeth, called themselves Aramæans. They that named themselves Chusians, were by the Grecians of their blacke faces called Æthiopians. Those which after their own speech were named

---

* *Britannia* exemplified an early modern discipline called chorography, a topical survey of a region covering everything from soil types to antiquities.

than younger ones: so the size and dispersal of a language family suggested its age. But how to determine filiation of languages remained very uncertain.[64]

Second, the Adamic language debate invigorated inquiries into language itself as a general phenomenon. This thinking took two forms. One was an old quest for a universal language: an artificial tongue with which people could communicate across natural linguistic barriers. This pursuit carried with it (to some extent required) a second, parallel labor: to identify traits shared by all human languages. These lines of work—whether aimed at meta-analysis of human tongues or at invention of a universal language—hearkened back to the *grammatica speculativa* of the medieval Scholastics: turning grammar into rules that must underlie all languages.[65]

A perfect universal language would mirror without distortion the order of nature itself. (Recall the ancient thinkers who believed that words expressed the nature of the things they named.) Such a man-made tongue, easy to learn because of its logical structure, would allow people to communicate regardless of vernaculars and with exactness impossible in natural languages. It might replace Latin as the idiom of science. The idea traveled widely in the seventeenth century. René Descartes, lover of clear and distinct ideas, toyed with it. But in England the project of inventing a universal language really caught on. There, Francis Bacon had railed at the ambiguities of natural language and the barren, merely semantic disagreements it engendered. He called for a new kind of grammar to clarify how words related to things. Bacon's disciples in the new Royal Society (chartered 1662) stressed the need to report scientific research in lucid, simple language.[66]

One of these disciples—a founder of the Royal Society—was Bishop John Wilkins. He produced the best-known, most finished artificial language of the century. After working for a quarter century, Wilkins published in 1668 *An Essay toward a Real Character and a Philosophical Language*, supposedly founded on basic terms common to all natural languages and "legible by any Nation in their own Tongue." In 270 folio pages of tables, Wilkins laid out a classification starting with forty genera, branching into 251 "characteristic differences" and then into 2,030 species. Wilkins's new language did not, in fact, replace Latin as the language of learning. Rather, foreign savants begged the Royal Society to have his *Essay* translated into Latin so they could read it. But it did prepare ground for future nonnatural languages (such as American Sign Language) and, more significantly, for semantic theories. Wilkins would have boggled at electronic computers but not at the languages invented to program them.[67]

Related efforts to devise a universal grammar also thrived. Descended directly from *grammatica speculativa*, universal grammar promised analysis of natural language that would explain all tongues. In 1587, the Salamanca professor Francisco Sánchez de las Brozas published *Minerva sive de causis linguae Latinae* (*Minerva, or, On the Properties of the Latin Language*). Any language, Sánchez pointed out, could be translated into any other. Therefore, he argued, all languages must share an underlying structure, reflecting the elemental categories of thought. These categories would have formed the grammar of the original language ancestral to all existing ones. Yet extant languages have different structures. Therefore, all of them must include implicit rules for sentence formation that mediate between deep patterns (the elemental categories common to all languages) and the surface structure peculiar to a given language. Such rules comprise the grammar of any actual language like Latin. Sánchez influenced the next century's most famous searchers for universal grammar. This group gathered around the abbey of Port-Royal—a half-hour stroll from the philological monks at Saint-Germain-des-Prés. The generative thinkers in the Port-Royal coterie were Blaise Pascal and the younger Antoine Arnauld. In *Grammaire générale et raisonnée* (1660; often known simply as the Port-Royal Grammar), the Port-Royal grammarians equated grammar and mental processes. With unprecedented thoroughness they analyzed the structures of language on foundational rational principles, rather than on usage alone. Port-Royal deemed linguistic forms to be logical, not merely conventional. Work like this evolved into modern theoretical linguistics in the nineteenth century.[68]

The nineteenth century had not arrived, and rigorous linguistic research was shadowed by half-cracked speculations like those of the Jesuit polymath Athanasius Kircher (1602–80). Take Alexander Pope's dictum, "a little learning is a dangerous thing"; imagine it walking on two legs and you have Kircher in his wilder moments. A modern student of Kircher called him "the last man who knew everything." Among his feats of linguistic omniscience, he purported to decode Egyptian hieroglyphs (not actually done until the nineteenth century)—and to prove that Chinese characters derived from them. After all, he thought Confucius might have been Moses. Kircher's erudition so impressed contemporaries that most found his flights of fancy plausible.[69]

THE RETURN OF BIBLICAL PHILOLOGY

The persisting religious hostilities that cramped biblical philology eventually roused the Dutch humanist Hugo Grotius to turn to it. Grotius had studied, brilliantly, under Scaliger in Leiden before getting a law degree from Orléans. Even in the fairly tolerant Netherlands, religious politics got Grotius thrown into jail for life in 1618. In 1621 he escaped, aptly hidden in a trunk supposed full of books, and went into exile in Paris. There he wrote his most celebrated work, *De iure belli ac pacis* (*On the Law of War and Peace*, 1625), a founding text of international law. Grotius believed that philological research into the Bible would also help to bring peace and reunite Christian Europe. Philology could reduce doctrinal quarrels by emending corrupted texts that fueled theological fights. It could even bring to a reasonable minimum the articles of faith that Christians professed. Grotius may sound like Pollyanna Philologica, but his teacher Scaliger famously pronounced that "theological disputes all stem from ignorance of grammar." In this utopian spirit—and in the late-humanist philological tradition—Grotius wrote two volumes of commentaries on the New Testament (1641–50) and a third on the Old Testament (1644). His tolerance extended to the Talmud, which added "not a little to our understanding of the thought of the books which belong to the Old Testament." Grotius had absorbed at Leiden, perhaps from the historical scholarship of the learned French lawyers who taught Scaliger, a deeper sense of the distance between past and present than previous biblical philologists. Valla and Erasmus in essence used a historical sensibility to resolve textual problems. They knew that an exegete needed historical knowledge to interpret old texts, since usages specific to a time and place shaped the meanings of words and sentences. Grotius was a more fundamentally historical critic who grasped that the thought world of the biblical authors was not his own. (He needed, but lacked, our idea of 'culture.') His commentaries hinted at biblical ways of thinking alien to moderns, drawing analogies between practices of ancient Hebrews and ancient pagans.[70]

In England, Grotius's historical sensibility was shared by his contemporary John Selden, another polymath. Selden wrote on law and history as well as the world of the Old Testament. (He and Grotius sparred over the law of the sea, defending their respective national interests.) An adroit philologist, Selden used Arabic as well as Hebrew to explore the religious history of the ancient Near East. De diis Syriis (On Syrian Gods, 1617) prefigured the study of mythology and the comparative method of later scholars of religion. Despite profuse political entanglements, he continued until his death in 1654 to publish on institutions and customs of the ancient Hebrews, ranging from marriage and divorce to their calendar. In his writings the Old Testament became an object more of history than of theology.[71]

Another, slightly younger contemporary, Thomas Hobbes, honed a radical edge on the historical approach of Grotius and Selden. In Leviathan (1651) Hobbes—steeped in humanist studies as well as metaphysical materialism—reminded readers of the absurdity of the tradition that Moses wrote the entire Pentateuch. Could, for instance, Moses have described his own burial? Readers since antiquity had puzzled over such conundrums, offering various solutions, most often with later writers adding material to Moses's books. Questioning whether Moses penned every word in the Pentateuch was a yawner. La Peyrère, far more scandalously, had flatly denied that Moses wrote the books attributed to him. Hobbes took the next step. Relying on a passage in the apocryphal Second Book of Esdras, he claimed to identify the real composer. This was, he argued, Ezra the Scribe (alias Esdras, fl. 450 BCE), a priest of the period following the Babylonian exile. Some conventional biblical scholars accepted that an editor stitched together Moses's journals into a coherent narrative—a job for which Ezra made the most obvious candidate. But Hobbes hinted that Ezra, not Moses, actually wrote the Pentateuch. He declared clearly that the books contained only limited material by Moses; that they were written long after his time; and that other authors likewise wrote other Old Testament books long after the events they supposedly described. He treated the Bible as a human, historical document—to be understood as such, first of all, prior to any concession to divine inspiration.[72]

Baruch (or Benedictus) de Spinoza barreled through the door opened by La Peyrère, Grotius, Selden, and Hobbes. His *Tractatus theologico-politicus* (1670) aimed to undercut ecclesiastical authority in civil affairs. A good way to do this was to weaken its ultimate ground in a divinely inspired Bible. Spinoza combined metaphysical naturalism with Hebrew learning to turn the Bible into a product of human history, like any other ancient text. He elaborated Hobbes's argument that pinpointed Ezra, not Moses, as source of the Pentateuch. Indeed, Spinoza concluded that "one and the same chronicler," probably Ezra, wrote most of the Bible's 'historical' books. But he went further. Miracles never happen—an axiom that had nothing to do with philology but framed his argument about how to use it. And the biblical writers, Spinoza said, supplied no supernatural truths but only sought to foster piety. To interpret the Bible rightly—particularly the miracles and other supposedly imaginary bits—required, he argued, a philosopher's mind and daunting erudition: expertise in ancient Hebrew, comprehensive grasp of the historical circumstances in which the texts were written, a nuanced understanding of the worldviews of their writers. Even so equipped, Spinoza said, we may never have enough historical knowledge to comprehend large parts of the Bible. The implicit message was that the prating of priests, ministers, and rabbis amounted to empty babble. The explicit message was that the Bible sprang from a world alien to modern minds and obscured by the mists of time. In this new picture, only strenuous feats of philology could relocate the Bible in its proper historical setting and—slowly, arduously—yield some real insight.[73]

A French priest, Richard Simon, began to fill Spinoza's prescription. But where anticlericalism and naturalism shaped Spinoza's conclusions, philology probably guided Simon's. In 1678 appeared his *Histoire critique du Vieux Testament* (*Critical History of the Old Testament*). In it Simon examined methodically such matters as the history of the Hebrew text and the authorship of the Pentateuch (coming down roughly where Hobbes and Spinoza had). Simon showed how far, even for a sincere Christian, the cutting edge of criticism had moved from the verbal analysis of Erasmus. (Catholic philologists had less reason to fear textual instability in the Bible, since their church claimed authority to interpret it.) He illustrated a new—still rare—proclivity to plunge the text into history, into peculiarities of the alien time and place whence it came. To keep the Old Testament reliable as history, Simon posited that in each period secretaries recorded events for deposit in a public archive started by Moses. (A Flemish philologist vaguely foreshadowed this theory in 1574.) This hypothesis that multiple documents underlay the text would inspire innovative approaches to the Bible in the eighteenth century. Otherwise, Simon did not much innovate. Rather, he assembled systematically a mass of conclusions heretofore sprinkled over thousands of scattered pages.[74]

That was his offense. He laid out at length alterations in the Old Testament text, chronological faults, transpositions, variants, borrowings from lost documents, dubious authorship—all the defects of the inspired word of God. He insisted on analyzing the sacred book with the panoply of historical and critical methods that philologists applied to classical texts: let the results fall where they may. And he wrote not in Latin, hidden to all but scholars, but in lucid French. The police tried to burn all 1,300 copies. Simon's religious order expelled him. Simon tried to vindicate his orthodoxy: to no avail. A copy that escaped the bonfire made its way across the English Channel. A faulty Amsterdam printing soon circulated, then an English version ("ill translated," said John Evelyn). In 1685 Simon agreed to the book's republication in the more lenient Netherlands. In 1689 he brought out a *Histoire critique du texte du Nouveau Testament*, in 1690 a *Histoire critique des versions du Nouveau Testament*, in 1693 a *Histoire critique des commentaires du Nouveau Testament*, and finally in 1702 an annotated translation of the New Testament. Church authorities condemned it, too. Simon also compared rabbinic traditions and Jewish rituals with Christian theology and ceremonies, arguing that early Christians modeled their liturgies on synagogue rites. He immersed in history not only the biblical text but even the evolution of Christian belief and worship.[75]

A young firebrand of the Republic of Letters, Jean Le Clerc, crossed swords with Simon. Le Clerc had no objection to Simon's historical approach to the Bible; he simply thought the older man's scholarship shallow. In 1685 Le Clerc posed the questions *he* thought crucial to answer: did the time-honored authors of the ancient Hebrew books actually write them? if not, when could they have been written and when and how compiled? Le Clerc had his own evolving answers. Moses, for instance, wrote part of the Pentateuch, melded with other writings by later editors. A century earlier, it would have been practically impossible to phrase such queries. Modern historical criticism of the Bible had arrived.[76]

PHILOLOGY AND HISTORY AT CENTURY'S END

Le Clerc had broad notions of the task of 'criticism' and of historical writing in general. Finding out who had composed a text, tracing its transmission and the errors that crept in, only began the task:

> We still must discover, if possible, with what aim the author wrote, what occasioned him to take up his pen, and to which opinions, or to which events, this Work can refer, above all when it is not a matter of a book that contains general reflections or eternal truths, which are the same in all centuries and among all peoples of the world.

Le Clerc published in 1697 the first modern general theory of philology, *Ars critica* (*The Art of Criticism*). It summed up rules evolved to govern textual philology during the preceding century, an era of growing technical refinement. *Ars critica* made methodological axioms of textual philology explicit and displayed the deeper sense of historical distance between ancient texts and modern readers that philologists had developed. The book insisted that historically grounded philological criticism of a text, not speculative reason or authoritative tradition, offered the right road to biblical or any other interpretation. Le Clerc sharply distinguished between rhetoric—where history traditionally dwelled—and the *proper* practice of history. Historians must eschew bombastic, made-up declamations. Their job is watchful criticism of sources and realistic evaluation of possibilities, laid out in prose just as restrained. *Ars critica* influenced the English-speaking world into the nineteenth century, even as its Latin began to reek of an archaic scholarly world. In 1830 Cambridge University Press finally published a partial English translation.[77]

The Dutch scholar Jacob Perizonius showed how to apply principles like Le Clerc's—and showed to what extent European philology had grown 'historicized.' In *Animadversiones historicae* (*Historical Observations*, 1685) and later works, Perizonius fussed over the early history of Rome. He identified mistakes and confusions in ancient historians. Yet he argued that philological criticism could extract kernels of fact even from fables like that of Rome's founder Romulus. The historian should apply three criteria: reliability of the source; inherent possibility of the event; and contradiction by other sources (or its lack). In the case of the Romulus tale, Perizonius defended the trustworthiness of sources available to ancient Roman historians; dismissed yarns like the she-wolf suckling Romulus as absurd; and noted that Roman writers agreed on Romulus as founder. Ergo, a man named Romulus did found Rome, and afterward legend glorified him with claptrap. Perizonius also tried to ferret out lost sources hidden in surviving ones. He adopted a theory—suggested by a sentence in Cicero—that traditional songs (lost by Cicero's day) had preserved memories of historical events for early Roman historians to draw on. Perizonius's source criticism shows how historically conscious some philologists had become. And it shows the limits of that consciousness: Perizonius presumed that Romans would have found Romulus—bastard, fratricide, rapist—too disgraceful to invent. Ancient Romans still shared the values of modern Dutchmen.[78]

Unlike *Ars critica* and *Animadversiones historicae*, Simon wrote his *Histoires critiques* in French; and this was another step in a new direction. Spinoza's radical friend Lodewijk Meyer groused about the dominance of Latin in academic writing: it shut out ordinary people from intellectual life. That did not stop Meyer from writing Latin. But Simon broke the mold, and he was not alone. In the decades before 1700 a shift toward vernaculars began in the Republic of Letters. Latin remained the default language of the learned, but more and more followed Simon's example. International periodicals founded to inform the erudite—first Denis de Sallo's *Journal des sçavans* [*savants*] (1665), then Pierre Bayle's *Nouvelles de la république des lettres* (1684) and Le Clerc's *Bibliothèque universelle et historique* (1686)—commonly appeared in French. The Royal Society published its *Philosophical Transactions* in English from the first issue in 1665. In 1718 Christoph August Heumann issued in Hanover a survey of learning (an early form of intellectual history) entitled *Conspectus reipublicae litterariae* (*Conspectus of the Republic of Letters*). Sixteen years later Nikolaus Hieronimus Gundling produced at Frankfurt-am-Main a similar thing. (It was a popular genre among the professoriate.) But Gundling's appeared in German, *Vollständige Historie der Gelahrheit* [*sic*] (*Complete History of Learning*). And when Johann Erhard Kappen published at Leipzig in 1754 a new, more systematic history of the Republic of Letters, it, too, came out in his native tongue, not the traditional scholars' Latin. The slow emergence of vernacular intellectual cultures would affect philology. As time went by, English-speaking scholars, spending more and more time encased in their own language, would veer from usages of German or French peers.[79]

It is time now to focus on those English-speaking scholars. What did they inherit from earlier erudition? The hasty survey of European philology and allied braches of learning in this chapter has left out worlds more than it included. Where, for just one instance, is the study of mythology, which entered a new phase in the late seventeenth century?[80] But even this quick overview gives a sense of how philology evolved. Italian humanists recovered the legacy of ancient philology, grown mossy in the Middle Ages. This included rhetoric, textual criticism, and grammar, as well as related activities like antiquarian inquiries and chronology. Italian humanists often just copied methods of their Roman predecessors. But the most skilled of them learned to analyze and emend texts with new sophistication and even with a feeling for historical change missing in antiquity. They restored classical rhetoric before it got adapted to new forms of dialectic by their heirs north of the Alps. Those inheritors, dexterous in Greek and Hebrew, applied humanist methods to the Bible as well as to classical manuscripts. Buffeted by the Reformation, they settled down into something like 'professional scholarship' and greatly extended the range of their studies. Scholars reclaimed much of the material patrimony of Rome and taught themselves how to organize these remains, whether inscriptions, buildings, or coins. They pursued antiquarian research also into national pasts. They revived the ancient study of chronology and extended 'antiquity' beyond Rome and Greece, learning Arabic and other 'oriental' languages. They looked into religions beyond the familiar trio of Christian, Jew, and Muslim. They built on medieval grammar to deepen understanding of the phenomena of language, broaching the idea of language families and beginning awkwardly to assemble a few of them. Finally, daringly, even shockingly, some returned to scripture with a new historical approach.

In all these learned pursuits, history usually played some role—whether the history of languages, of nations, or of the biblical text—while comparison provided a common method—whether comparing tongues, customs, or manuscripts. Over time, the interplay of history and comparison amplified and nuanced a novel notion: that peoples in faraway epochs or places differed in basic ways from modern Europeans. Here is Charles Fleury, writing in 1681 about the mores of the ancient Israelites:

> One has to ignore history completely not to see the great change that distance in time and space brings to customs. We live in the same country where Gauls and then Romans lived. But how far are we in life-style from either? . . . And in our own century, what relation do our customs have to those of Turks, Indians, or Chinese? So if we join the two types of distance, we should not be astonished that men who lived in Palestine three thousand years ago had different customs than ours.[81]

It bears repeating (because so unlike our own system of knowledge) that the whole of this learning—rhetoric, textual philology, grammar, antiquarianism—formed a single world of erudition. Petrarch the rhetorician was Petrarch the antiquarian and Petrarch the textual philologist. Scaliger the chronologer was Scaliger the classical philologist and Scaliger the historian of Hellenistic Judaism.

In the later seventeenth century, philology, like the Roman god Janus, wore two faces. One peered back at scholars of earlier generations: its weathered visage mirroring their abilities as well as their limitations. The other—its features half formed—gazed toward the future. In that age to come, practices of early modern philology would evolve into ways of dealing with languages and understanding their pasts hardly imaginable before 1700. What did English-speaking philologists in this transitional era do with what was handed down to them?

...."shift in study of language from something philosophical and metaphysical to something empirical and historical ..." Seth Lerer

3

"A Voracious and Undistinguishing Appetite"

British Philology to the
Mid-Eighteenth Century

Philological Society 1842

Now the gaze narrows, focusing more closely on those philological traditions that eventually spawned the humanities as known today in Britain, Ireland, and North America. Learned Britons mostly populate this first chapter devoted to the English-speaking world. Irish and American scholars will grow more visible after 1750.

Geographically on Europe's edge, Britain's scholars long lived there intellectually. They never lost touch. The great English humanist Thomas More (1478–1535), like his Scottish counterpart George Buchanan (1506–82), belonged to Europe-wide networks of the learned. A scattering of erudite men with similar links dotted early modern British history: from Humphrey, Duke of Gloucester, in the fifteenth century to Cambridge's Gabriel Harvey at the start of the seventeenth. A meager tradition of active philological *production* in England went back at least to Thomas Linacre (ca. 1460–1524), who studied Latin and Greek in Florence, collaborated with the Venetian humanist printer Aldus Manutius, and translated the ancient Roman physician Galen. Yet, compared to continental scholars, the British only toyed with philology before the seventeenth century.[1]

Then, within decades, England became a hub of erudition (though not yet Scotland). The Thirty Years' War (1618–48) ravaged German-speaking Europe. French persecution of Protestants, intensifying from the 1610s, plagued Huguenot philologists. Much of European learning fled from Germany and France to the Low Countries—and to the island facing the Netherlands across the North Sea. Ties between the English and the Dutch tightened. Their mercantile rivalry led to war more than once, but proximity and long-standing trading links also drew the two Protestant countries together. When politics made England too hot for John Locke, he took refuge in the Netherlands. When a surviving copy of Simon's *Histoire critique du Vieux Testament* ended up to England, a transcription went to Amsterdam for printing. A North Sea–hopping Dutch philologist, Franciscus Junius, helped to open up the study of Anglo-Saxon in Oxford in the 1670s; his manuscript dictionary, housed in the Bodleian Library, and the Anglo-Saxon type cut for him served the small but active circle of Oxford philologists after he was gone.* Junius's nephew Isaac Vossius came to England in 1670, bringing a library that made other scholars salivate (and aided their research); there he produced a steady flow of chronological, biblical, and classical scholarship.[2]

Philology of all sorts blossomed in England; this multiplicity matters because distinct modern humanities disciplines would eventually arise on these different foundations. Imitating continental masters like Joseph Scaliger, English philologists pored over obscure Byzantine Greek manuscripts to catch glimpses of vanished classical writings quoted therein. Abraham Wheelocke, who taught both Arabic and Anglo-Saxon at Cambridge, published in 1659 the first printed Anglo-Saxon grammar. Oxford in his generation housed its own Anglo-Saxon philologists, including the Bishop John Fell who lives on in doggerel. ("I do not love thee, Dr. Fell / The reason why I cannot tell / But this I know and know full well / I do not love thee, Dr. Fell.") Oxford's Arabist, Rev. Edward Pococke, protégé of John Selden, set the model for the modern scholar by downing endless cups of coffee. (He picked up the novel addiction in Middle Eastern sojourns, when he studied with learned Arabs.) His *Specimen historiae Arabum* (1650)—first book printed in Oxford with Arabic type—translated into Latin part of Abu'l-Faraj's thirteenth-century *Compendious History of Dynasties*, with a learned commentary that dwarfed the text. This book inaugurated the study of Arabic as something more than adjunct to commerce or biblical studies. Pococke's complete edition of Abu'l-Faraj (1663) endured into the twentieth century. Working with Pococke, among others, Brian Walton produced the London Polyglot Bible of 1657, in nine languages, with erudite critical paraphernalia. A Cambridge scholar, John Spencer, in 1685 published the colossal *De legibus Hebraeorum ritualibus et earum rationibus* (*On the Ritual Laws of the Hebrews and the Reasons for Them*). In it he tried to show that Hebrew ritual derived from Egypt, extending Selden's comparative approach to ancient Israelite religion. Spencer ignited a Europe-wide polemic. By the late seventeenth century, English philologists worked as competently and as variously as anyone on the Continent.[3]

---

* In the later nineteenth century scholars came to prefer 'Old English' to label the language spoken in Anglo-Saxon England. Earlier it was called Anglo-Saxon (or variants thereof). I follow the custom of the time.

The Examples of Richard Bentley

One philologist sums up much of old and new in British erudition. Richard Bentley (1662–1742) can serve as tour guide to the varieties of philological research in Britain, before more prolonged looks at a few key fields of study.

He caught the learned world's attention in 1691. John Mill, head of St. Edmund Hall, Oxford, was overseeing an edition of a sixth-century CE Greek chronicle by one John Malalas of Antioch. The chronicle was of minor worth but an English denizen: the Bodleian Library owned the only manuscript. Mill knew Bentley, a precociously learned Cambridge graduate then settled in Oxford. Mill showed him the proof sheets—on condition that he submit comments for publication as an appendix. Enough came to Bentley's mind to fill a Latin text that runs to almost 125 pages in a modern printing. Bentley's *Epistola ad Cl. V. Joannem Millium* (*Letter to the Illustrious Man John Mill*) was far the best part of the edition.[4]

Bentley's imaginative leaps raised eyebrows, but his erudition awed. By emending and commenting on over sixty Greek and Latin authors quoted by Malalas, Bentley created a rich, if helter-skelter, study of vanished Greek drama. Almost in passing, he recovered a lost rule of poetic meter, correcting Grotius and Scaliger. He ranged over antiquity, in many cases drawing on manuscripts he had ferreted out in Oxford libraries. The extent of the young man's reading in both Greek and Latin—of all periods, printed and manuscript—was arresting. Bentley must have had nearly photographic recall to hold it all ready for use, tossing off the *Epistola ad Millium* on the spur of the moment. (He once claimed to have no great memory, the least plausible assertion in the history of learning.) He made some slips, jumped to some false conclusions, but shone in a virtuoso performance. "Had he but the gift of humility," his patron, Bishop Edward Stillingfleet, reportedly said, "he would be the most extraordinary man in Europe."[5]

Leading Dutch scholars appreciated the powers on display, even while some of Bentley's countrymen shuddered at the loosely fettered fancy of his conjectural emendations. At the behest of the Dutch philologist Joannes Graevius, Bentley collected, emended, and put in order over four hundred fragments of the Hellenistic poet Callimachus, culled from a hodgepodge of Greek texts. (Callimachus appeared in chapter 1 in connection with the Library of Alexandria.) This work, published at Utrecht in 1697, followed the example brilliantly set by Scaliger and Casaubon; and it etched the template for the many later classicists who reconstructed writings of ancient authors from scattered remnants.[6]

Yet to label Bentley a classicist grossly understates the range of his learning. He turned from writing the *Epistola ad Millium* to deliver in 1692 the first series of Boyle Lectures, endowed to confute "notorious Infidels, viz. *Atheists, Deists, Pagans, Jews and Mahometans.*" (Rev. Dr. Bentley later held the Regius Professorship of Divinity at Cambridge.) He used Newton's gravitational theory to prove God's existence. The Boyle Lectures had nothing to do with philology. The point is the extent of what Bentley could and did do—and a reminder of the polymathy of early modern erudition. Even his philological writings showed Bentley as a broadly 'literary' figure, not a closeted scholar.[7]

Bentley's most striking classical work derived, in fact, from trying to make a mark in the literary Quarrel of the Ancients and Moderns. The quarrel—one of the intermittent spats over whether writers and artists should imitate old models or find a new way—broke out in France in the 1670s. Was modern French a better literary vehicle than ancient Greek and Latin? Had modern writers outgrown the crudity and rambling wordiness of Homer? Did the telescope eclipse ancient science? In 1690 the *querelle* jumped the English Channel. Sir William Temple, a retired diplomat, published an "Essay upon Ancient and Modern Learning" intended to put the moderns in their place. Temple provoked a detailed reply in 1694 from Rev. William Wotton, "a most excellent preacher, but a drunken whoring soul" almost forty years younger than Temple and far more learned. For a second edition of his *Reflections upon Ancient and Modern Learning* in 1697, Wotton solicited contributions from scholarly friends, including Bentley—for philology counted as modern science even when treating ancient books.[8]

Bentley offered a 150-page *Dissertation upon the Epistles of Phalaris*, printed as an appendix to *Reflections*. Phalaris was a semilegendary tyrant of Syracuse in the sixth century BCE, with the winsome habit of roasting enemies in a hollow bronze bull. His 148 'surviving' letters had long entertained the classically educated. Scholars took them for a forgery or a prank. Poliziano thought their hilarious bombast pointed to the second-century CE satirist Lucian of Samosata. But hapless Temple imagined them genuine. In his "Essay" he praised "the Epistles of *Phalaris*" for having "more Race, more Spirit, more Force of Wit and Genius" than any other letters he knew, "antient or modern"—oldest books being, ipso facto, the best. Sir William brought down upon himself the erudition of Bentley. But now Bentley wrote in English and strove for elegance—in contrast to the ramshackle *Epistola ad Millium*, but in keeping with a literary performance for a genteel public. Temple managed no answer, but his partisans did. Their comeback provoked a second, free-standing *Dissertation* four times longer than the original.[9]

In either version, the *Dissertation* was a tour de force. Bentley showed that the letters could not fit their alleged place and time. Pseudo-Phalaris referred to cities not yet founded, cited texts not yet written, bungled the value of his own coins, but knew of literary genres not yet invented—and wrote all this, though himself a Dorian speaker, in Attic dialect—a kind of Attic, moreover, not heard until five centuries later. Bentley's erudition glittered. His numismatic expertise had no equal until the nineteenth century. Long digressions offered careful, empirical analyses dating the emergence of tragedy and comedy as genres—laying ground for scholarly literary history. Another excursion explained motives for literary forgery in the ancient world. A chapter on Attic dialect and its later imitators proved seminal in recuperating the history of the Greek language. The *Dissertation* was blue-ribbon scholarship, but Bentley tried to drag erudition out of the musty libraries of philologists into the elegant drawing rooms of Augustan literary debate.[10]

So, unsurprisingly, he turned to the popular Roman poet Horace, every schoolboy's old acquaintance. Bentley's edition of Horace (1712) won admiration and condemnation in equal measure, often from the same critic. The book pranced with a stupendously self-congratulatory preface. In it Bentley trumpeted the accuracy of his conjectural emendations, validated (he assured readers) by his peerless taste and insight. He then went on to make some *seven hundred* changes from the common readings, mostly on guesswork—richly informed with his truly unmatched erudition, feel for the language, and grasp of textual difficulties. "To us reason and circumstances carry greater weight than a hundred codices," he famously wrote in one note. (He did use manuscripts, quite shrewdly.) Few of his emendations survive today, but esteem for the qualities he brought to them does. Bentley conceived his Horace as a contribution to polite letters. Yet he smothered the poems in learned annotations.* Philology did not really qualify as light entertainment. In the *Dunciad* Alexander Pope dragged Bentley on stage as "The mighty Scholiast, whose unwearied pains / Made Horace dull."[11]

Bentley's philology ranged far beyond classical authors. He did complete an important edition of Terence—and started what would surely have been an ingenious edition of Homer. But he also worked on the New Testament (discussed later). And he notoriously applied his critical imagination to a modern text, *Paradise Lost* (1732).

Bentley edited Milton much as he had Horace. But—maybe to highlight his genius in conjectural emendation—he denied collating printed versions or consulting the one manuscript he certainly examined. Bentley declared all printings of *Paradise Lost* badly corrupt. Some errors, he alleged, infected the text when Milton's amanuensis misheard the blind poet's dictation; others when the printer goofed; still more when a "suppos'd Friend" interpolated lines when reading proof. The sightless Milton never knew. Bentley rode to his rescue. Wherever—in Bentley's view—lines went wrong metrically, violated consistency, or offended taste, he used the margins to delete or emend, to recover what Milton *must* have said. The author of the greatest English epic would never have uttered a pun. 'Milton' became, as Kristine Haugen put it, "the name attached to the sum of Bentley's criteria for poetry." Alexander Pope was hardly the only reader who found the performance ludicrous. Bentley's *Paradise Lost* induced winces, but it also exemplified a major innovation in

---

*Bentley gives a handy example of a Europe-wide shift in the dominant *form* of classical scholarship during his lifetime: from the commentary (as on the letters of Pseudo-Phalaris) to the edition. In editions erudition showed only in notes and perhaps preface, rather than in the text itself. Both forms of course were ancient.

philology. Other editors of his generation likewise applied methods pirated from classical studies to texts in English.[12]

One stroke of Bentley's philological genius stands out. The Greek alphabet once included a letter shaped like the English capital *F* and pronounced like the English *w*. Ancient grammarians knew of it from inscriptions in extinct dialects. They called the letter *digamma* (double gamma) because it looked like one *gamma* (Γ) atop another. The digamma gave the Romans (and us) the letter *F*. But it vanished from the Attic-Ionic dialect family in which Homer was first written down before the poems were recorded. (Homer, Bentley apparently believed, originally wrote his poems with the digamma; then later Greeks copied them after it had vanished.) Bentley tied the lost letter to puzzling gaps in Homer's meter. Restoring the letter would mend the meter: οἶνος (*oinos*), for instance, became ϝοῖνος (*woinos* = Latin *vinum*, 'wine'). Knowing from ancient texts some words that once began with the digamma, Bentley plugged these into Homer, replacing their later forms, and proved his hypothesis. Bentley's theory found its way into print in 1732. No known manuscript of Homer ever contained a digamma. Bentley's finely tuned ear—not just for scansion but for linguistic change over time—led to unimagined discovery.[13]

No one could hold as high an opinion of Bentley as he did of himself, but he was extraordinary. His meticulous, systematic historical discriminations—of anachronisms, of literary types, of the changing language—set a new standard for historical criticism of classical texts. Friedrich Wolf, the great Homerist of the late eighteenth century (a man who never met modesty), saw in Bentley his superior, "the greatest of all scholars." Bentley's reputation only grew during the nineteenth century. Near its end the poet-classicist A. E. Housman called him "the greatest scholar that England or perhaps Europe ever bred." Today that praise seems excessive. But even Bentley's failed New Testament project and his reckless Milton pointed toward innovation in biblical philology and in literary studies.[14]

What exactly was new in Bentley? His philological instruments were well worn by the time he inherited them. But Bentley wielded these tools with stricter attention to historical context and especially to variation over time. Thus he could explain changing literary fashions, track the emergence of new genres, and follow even the evolving dialectic forms of the Greek language. In doing such things, he showed new possibilities latent in philology and opened doors for later scholars. A modern authority not given to gush (E. J. Kenney) called Bentley "the innovating genius and founder of the science of historical criticism."[15]

Yet his classical philology remained 'historical' in a limited way. First, Bentley cared only about reconstructing texts. He studied antiquity to emend its writings, never to understand the ancient world itself. Language and literary form clutched his curiosity, while the chronological scholarship that fascinated Scaliger bored him. Second, nontextual relics of antiquity caught his eye—such as the Sicilian coins that confused 'Phalaris'—only if they aided textual criticism. (In this, he imitated his Cambridge teachers.) Third, though he appreciated change over time in literary forms and in language, he had little sense of change over time in human behaviors, customs, and ideas. In Bentley's view, Phalaris could not have written the letters ascribed to him because he spoke Dorian rather than Attic, *not* because people in the sixth century BCE just did not *think* in the same ways as whoever *did* write those letters centuries later. Bentley missed the most fundamental dimension of history for later scholars: how human societies, behaviors, and thinking develop as time passes. But what he did he did brilliantly. Most English classical philologists trailed in Bentley's wake. They did solid work but looked like cockboats chasing a ship of the line. But not every British philologist trailed his pennant.[16]

REIMAGINING ANTIQUITY

In the Quarrel of the Ancients and Moderns, the Moderns regarded Greeks and Romans as backward compared to modern Europeans. In French skirmishes of the *querelle*—known to educated British readers—Homer, most ancient of poets, came off as downright primitive. This did not automatically condemn. It could suggest primal force, rude strength, in language, imagery, and imagination. But 'primitive' in any case implied strangeness to modern eyes.[17]

A Scottish philologist, Thomas Blackwell, drew the implications. Blackwell exemplified the newly vigorous erudition north of the border, fostered by Scottish economic expansion after 1707 (for more about this, see chapter 4). Prosperity energized Scotland's ancient universities, with philology among the beneficiaries. Blackwell held the chair of Greek in Marischal College, Aberdeen. In *An Enquiry into the Life and Writings of Homer* (1735), he linked the form and content of the Homeric epics to their social and cultural environment. His psychological and sociological analysis took him far beyond Bentley's literary and linguistic approach. Blackwell thought it universally true "that *young Minds* are apt to receive such strong Impressions from the Circumstances of the Country where they are born and bred, that they contract a mutual kind of Likeness to those Circumstances." Thus, from the social and political usages of his early period in the evolution of Greek society, "*Homer* drew his *Imagery* and *Manners*, learned his *Language*, and took his *Subject*."[18]

The idea that a people's historical growth formed its culture and that its culture shaped its texts—the idea that Simon had struggled toward, that Bentley had shied from—this notion Blackwell warmly embraced. Specifically, he pioneered a schema in which all societies evolve through the same defined stages. (Think of hunter-gatherers settling down as farmers, who eventually ripen into city-dwelling merchants and artisans.) This so-called stadial (stage) theory became a core axiom of the Scottish Enlightenment. Blackwell attracted readers. The *Enquiry* went through five editions and earned a European reputation. Most notably, it helped to ignite a revolution in classical philology in Germany near the end of the century, as chapter 4 will tell. In one respect Blackwell did resemble Bentley. He conjured up his Homeric world entirely from texts. This would change.[19]

An even greater innovation in Homeric studies came from outside the library. Robert Wood was the son of an Irish Presbyterian minister. In a larger sense he was heir to Britons, like Pococke, who had since Elizabethan times traveled more and more often in Ottoman domains. During one Middle Eastern journey Wood spent two weeks in 1750 exploring the supposed vicinity of ancient Troy. These rambles stoked a long-smoldering ardor for Homer; and Wood set down to write about him. But in 1756 William Pitt appointed Wood under-secretary of state. This launched a lucrative political career and postponed Wood's Homer book for a decade. Privately printed at last in 1767 and again in 1769, *An Essay on the Original Genius and Writings of Homer* was finally published in 1775, four years after its author died.[20]

Wood's Homer upended conventional notions of the poetic colossus of ancient Greece. To begin with, the literary giant was illiterate. Writing, Wood deduced, came to Greece around 554 BCE. Homer lived long before—indeed, before any "cultivated" and "settled state of language," in "an early stage of Society" when "the business and pleasures of life were rude, simple, and confined." "Oral tradition" furnished "the only mode of recording events." "Verse and Music" served as "very necessary aids to Memory." The once urbane Homer, font of philosophy and arts, became in Wood's book a primitive bard, singing songs to amuse his smelly comrades. Others broached the scandalous idea of a Homer ignorant of letters (Jean-Jacques Rousseau for one), but Wood was first to do so with any rigor and to sketch a plausible historical context. The theory of oral epic was born.[21]

Wood's rude, unlettered Homer seized the imagination of Europe. Wood sent a copy of the 1769 printing to the philologist J. D. Michaelis at the University of Göttingen. (Michaelis, who visited England in 1741–42, had become a go-between for English and German scholars.) He loaned it to his Göttingen colleague C. G. Heyne, who applauded it in a 1770 review. A German translation appeared three years later, reviewed in Frankfurt by Johann Wolfgang von Goethe. By the next year, Wood had become well enough known among Germans for Goethe to allude to him in the wildly popular *Sorrows of Young Werther*. French, Italian, and Spanish translations followed formal publication of the *Original Genius of Homer* in 1775. Wood's thesis remained controversial but made influential converts—including one who mattered most for future Homeric studies, Friedrich Wolf.[22]

Together with Blackwell, Wood put Homer in a credible historical context. They recalibrated the study of early antiquity, gave that period a distinct cultural identity, and made clear how far its culture stood from modern ways of thinking and behaving.* Whether they were right in details hardly mattered to the conceptual transformation they initiated. Eventually this historicized philology would carry Richard Simon's project a giant step further and revolutionize biblical criticism.

BIBLICAL PHILOLOGY AND 'RELIGION'

Very few Britons in Simon's day were ready for this. Plunging the Bible into secular history veered too close to blasphemy. *Histoire critique du Vieux Testament* terrified so cosmopolitan an Anglican as John Evelyn. Yet Simon's book quickly penetrated England. John Locke likely had a copy by 1681, only three years after its aborted publication. Almost as rapidly Simon's most corrosive pages reappeared in abridged translations meant to undermine Christian belief. Why did English Protestants react so vehemently to biblical philology, and why did English infidels so easily assume that it chipped away at Christianity?[23]

Both questions had the same answer: the scary novelty of applying critical method to sacred words commonly believed unerring. (Jews at the time also simply assumed the reliability of the Hebrew Bible. For Catholics, church authority validated the Bible.) Learned English Protestants did study the Bible with an eye on the accuracy of the text: remember the London Polyglot. But comparing versions in different tongues, even compiling variants, did not tinker with the text itself. Actually *emending* sacred scripture like a classical text seemed too much like nit-picking the words of God. The standard form of biblical philology in English before 1700 remained the safe commentary, not the risky edition. English philologists applied scalpels to scripture with great delicacy, especially the more sensitive New Testament.[24]

John Mill—Bentley's older friend—worked long and hard on the Greek New Testament. For thirty years, Mill collated manuscripts from home and abroad; he scoured the Church Fathers for biblical quotations. But when he finally published, in 1707, he dared not tamper with the *textus receptus* (received, or standard, text). He instead reprinted the 1550 Estienne edition (essentially Erasmus's text) and piled up some 30,000 variants at the bottoms of the pages. A long introduction supplied a history of the transmission of the text from antiquity to the present. Though far from perfect, Mill's work put England for a while at the forefront of biblical philology.[25]

Around 1700 a few writers tried to use such evidence of textual corruption to undercut the Bible and thus Christianity. Two sincere Christians inadvertently started the fracas. In 1685 the pugnacious Amsterdam polymath Jean Le

---

*Some readers will wonder why I neglect parallel ideas of primitive society in Giambattista Vico's *Scienza Nuova* (*New Science*, 1725). The answer is that few paid attention to Vico—Blackwell one of the few—until Jules Michelet translated his book in 1827.

Clerc laid into Simon's *Critical History*, in revenge for Simon's ridiculing Le Clerc. The Republic of Letters could make bare-knuckle boxing look civilized. English Protestants would have applauded many of Le Clerc's hits, especially his jab at Simon's deference to the Catholic Church as authoritative interpreter of the Bible. But in the course of attacking popery, Le Clerc stumbled out of bounds. Simon had argued that parts of the Old Testament were not divinely inspired. Le Clerc applied this principle to the New Testament. Five years later this touchiest portion of Le Clerc's polemic appeared in English—author, translator, and publisher cloaked in wary anonymity—as *Five Letters concerning the Inspiration of the Holy Scriptures*. Holy hell broke loose among the clergy. The storm set the tone for a half century of clashes between post-Christian deists—who accepted a creator but rejected divine revelation—and more or less orthodox Anglicans.[26]

The so-called Deist Controversy mixed politics, theology, Newtonian science, logical confusion, high seriousness, japery, and biblical philology. The last matters here. Philology provided contestants a handy weapon more often than a serious pursuit. A young Irish writer, John Toland, ignited the fireworks with *Christianity Not Mysterious* (1696). Toland aimed to bring to bear on the Bible the methods of classical philology. His scholarly pretensions got hoots in Germany, where serious biblical philologists were clearing new ground. (His claim that early Christians divided into Jewish and Gentile factions did have a long afterlife there.) Toland maneuvered the little philology he did control to deny that God inspired the Old Testament; allusion to classical parallels only insinuated the unreliability of stories of Jesus in the New Testament. (Toland was not mad.) Other deists followed Toland in decrying the Bible as untrustworthy, morally unsavory, an imposture of priestcraft. Reverend writers rushed to defend the Holy Book (Bentley among them). Deists and parsons quarreled over the truth of 'facts' in the Bible, rarely asking what those statements might have meant in original context. Arguments on both sides were seldom more sophisticated than Hobbes's or Spinoza's, though much more long-winded.[27]

A few entries into the fray influenced scholars, notably Rev. William Warburton's *Divine Legation of Moses* (1738–41). Warburton meant to vindicate the supernatural origin of the Mosaic dispensation. His argumentative style specialized in paradox and convolution, and his contortions need not detain us. But, in the course of defending the Hebrews' intimacy with the deity, Warburton tossed off an astonishing farrago of particulars about the ancient world. He mused on everything from mystery cults to the origin of language. Almost incidentally—in trampling the theory of an ancient pagan wisdom superior to Moses's—Warburton showed that Egyptian hieroglyphs were not an esoteric code, as long believed, but a practical form of writing. He carried further John Spencer's research into the origin of Hebraic rituals in resistance to parallel Egyptian ones. Reading and misreading of Warburton swayed later writers, including Condillac. If Warburton's philological ramblings lacked order, they had power.[28]

So did the writings of another Anglican clergyman, Conyers Middleton. How close to deism he really stood remains foggy. He claimed to defend the integrity of scripture. Maybe. It *is* clear that Middleton had a sense of history. He applied it to ancient Rome more often than ancient Israel. Besides forays into the deist controversy in the early 1730s, he published a much-reprinted biography of Cicero and an argument that the Catholic Church derived its rites and offices from pagan Rome. In addressing the Bible, Middleton went beyond chuckling at the implausibility of the serpent in Eden or the Tower of Babel to explain rationally such apparently far-fetched stories. He tried to see these tales through the historical lens that he used to look at other ancient texts. Seemingly factual, but incredible, tales like these must have been meant allegorically. Middleton thought the Mosaic account of creation probably metaphorical. He also reckoned, like Spencer and Warburton, that the ancient Hebrews adopted some rites from the Egyptians—though in his case because primitive Israelites had to borrow from sophisticated Egyptians. Puzzling out what Moses got from his Egyptian background became almost a learned obsession in the seventeenth and eighteenth centuries.[29]

This particular fixation reflected a generally rising curiosity about religions exotic to Europeans. Encounters with peoples unfamiliar or unknown to Westerners earlier largely explain it. The Jesuit mission to China led to a Latin translation of Confucian writings in 1687. The Oxford orientalist Thomas Hyde in 1700 gave Europeans their first real view of Zoroastrianism. A Jesuit missionary in Canada, Joseph-François Lafitau, published in 1724 a tome on the religion of Native Americans. The elephant of such works was the seven-volume *Cérémonies et coutumes religieuses de tous les peuples du monde* (*Ceremonies and Religious Customs of All Peoples of the World*), compiled between 1723 and 1737 by Jean Frederic Bernard and illustrated by the engraver Bernard Picart. This pair not only told what they knew—less accurate the farther they got from Amsterdam—about Buddhists and Jews, Mayans and Muslims, Hindus and Protestants but also compared, looking for parallels, hinting at a universal substrate of all religions: a version of deist 'natural religion.'[30]

Comparison was the rule in this genre as in philology generally. Jesuits in China saw shadows of Christian doctrine in Confucian writings. (The same Jesuits turned the sage Kong Fuzi—Master Kong—into 'Confucius,' giving him a Latinized name as Western scholars had.) Lafitau compared Native Americans with barbarous tribes described by ancient writers like Herodotus to show that all peoples shared an innate religious impulse. Thomas Blackwell, the Aberdeen Homerist, paralleled the creation story in Genesis with a Phoenician myth—without asking whether the comparison reflected poorly on Yahweh's status as the sole, transcendent creator. Such similarities between biblical religion and other cults came up increasingly often. Writers like Blackwell, Warburton, and the deists were lifting the "veil of sanctity" (Leslie Stephen's phrase) that had shielded the Bible from the searching comparison applied to other ancient texts.* (In contrast, learned British colonists in North America showed vanishingly little interest in comparing religions, perhaps owing to contempt for native peoples who practiced the ones nearest to hand.) In making such analogies, these British writers showed a deepening if still largely inarticulate conviction that scholars better understand ancient *civilizations* by comparing them to each other, just as ancient *manuscripts* had long been treated.[31]

Deist ballyhooing of natural religion also gave wide currency to a novel idea: religion. The roots of natural religion went far down. Cicero claimed that human beings everywhere need to worship gods; Thomas Aquinas argued that unaided human reason teaches the existence, unity, and goodness of God. But to talk about the gods or God is one thing, to discuss an entity called religion quite another. The antithesis between 'true religion' (such as one's version of Christianity) and false belief (such as worshipping idols) is ancient. The concept of religion as a general category—a generic practice of which many species exist—seems no older than the seventeenth century, finally clarified in John Spencer's writings about the relation of Hebrew ritual to Egyptian ceremonies. Deist trumpeting of the sufficiency of 'natural religion,' along with the deist-inspired search for common truths underlying all faiths, first spread the notion of religion as a general class of inquiry.[32]

If deism scared Christians, it also loosened the shackles on biblical philology. Deists attacked the textual integrity of the Bible. In response, Protestant philologists needed to validate the text—to get the words right, and to show they were right. So the post-Reformation fear of fiddling with the New Testament text finally eased. Only two years after John Mill's Bible-cum-variants appeared in 1707—and on the foundation of his work—Rev. Edward Wells began issuing a new Greek Testament (completed in 1719); at many points he swerved shrewdly away from the *textus receptus*. The taboo on biblical emendation had faded away, but scriptural conservatism had not. Wells's contemporaries pretty much ignored his edition. In 1729 the Presbyterian minister Daniel Mace produced an even sounder one, its textual decisions far ahead of his time. His edition was not disregarded, like Wells's, but beaten black and blue in print.[33]

Yet none other than Richard Bentley defined the new editorial program. So good a classical philologist knew that, as more manuscripts were collated, more variant verses would appear. But he felt sure that expert analysis could recover the Greek New Testament as early Christians had known it. The aver-

---

* Transforming the Bible into an object of secular philological research did distance it from *holy scripture* as understood by ordinary Jews and Christians: the scholar's Bible was not and is not the divine revelation filled with spiritual meaning read in churches and synagogues. Since the philological rather than religious fallout of biblical studies is relevant here, this issue can be overlooked.

sion of Protestants to biblical philology got it backward, Bentley said. His masterfully emended edition would make the New Testament not "more *precarious*" but "more certain and authentic." Bentley never got close to finishing, but his methodological pronouncements much clarified the task. A pamphlet of 1720 spelled out axioms: (1) the original text of the New Testament books lay beyond recovery; (2) editors should aim instead to restore the earliest text feasible, which Bentley judged to be the Bible of the early fourth century; (3) this job required comparing "the most antient and venerable" manuscripts (those written before 500 CE), testing for accord among Greek and Latin versions, then checking readings against patristic citations and ancient Syriac, Coptic, Gothic, and Ethiopian translations. Bentley believed he could thereby reduce Mill's 30,000 variants to a couple hundred. Such an edition would give the Christian churches a "Magna Charta" to endure after "all the Antient MSS [manuscripts] here quoted may be lost and extinguish'd." Bentley believed the Bible divinely inspired, but he *treated* it as a historical document rather than as the living word of God. His precepts survived his abortive edition and set parameters for nineteenth-century philologists who did finally fix a new *textus receptus* to replace the one descended from Erasmus.[34]

Benjamin Kennicott capped the short-lived English ascendancy in textual criticism of the Bible. (For continuity, his story and Robert Lowth's will be told here, though they burst the nominal dates of this chapter.) As an Oxford student in the 1740s, Kennicott learned Hebrew and other biblical languages; he also absorbed some of the comparative methods of philology. In 1751 he began examining manuscripts of the Hebrew Bible. He decided to do for the Old Testament what Mill had done for the New Testament. In 1753 he explained his approach in *The State of the Printed Hebrew Text of the Old Testament Considered*:

> The rational and safe Method of proceeding in a Case of this important Nature is—to compare Scripture with itself—to explain a difficult Phrase or Passage by a clear one, that bears some Relation to it—to consider the natural Force of the Original Words, the Tendency of the Context, and the Design of the Writer—to compare the most ancient Editions of the Original with one another, and with the best Copies of the most celebrated Versions.

In short, like Mill and Bentley, Kennicott imported into biblical philology techniques long used on classical texts: "the only Method . . . universally apply'd by the Learned." Unlike Bentley, he chased the will-o'-the-wisp of recovering the original text. Kennicott sought to track down all existing Hebrew manuscripts (another fantasy). Copying and collating the almost seven hundred he did find required time, assistants, money. As his reputation spread, cash flowed in; subscriptions to the project exceeded £9,000.[35]

As was usual when Christian philologists dealt with their Old Testament, Kennicott created torturous relations with Jewish scholars and the Hebrew

Bible. On one hand, he needed erudite rabbis to help in tracking down manuscripts and in resolving linguistic and interpretive puzzles; and he made some use of scriptural quotations in the Talmud. On the other hand, like most Christians, he despised Judaism as inimical to "the Christian Cause." Kennicott was not rabid. But he tried to 'free' the Hebrew text from the interpretive control of the rabbis and hand it over to Protestant philologists. To this end he stripped the text of vowel points.* Their absence made many words less certain and allowed readings unsanctioned in rabbinic Judaism. Without Jews, Kennicott was helpless. With them, he was high-handed.[36]

In 1776 and 1780 appeared *Vetus Testamentum Hebraicum cum variis lectionibus* (*Hebrew Old Testament with Variant Readings*), printing the unpointed Hebrew and Samaritan versions in parallel columns. The volumes had weaknesses. The Göttingen philologist J. D. Michaelis jumped on Kennicott's decision to omit vowel points. Michaelis's student (and eventual successor) J. G. Eichhorn griped that Kennicott had only collected variants and not entertained that "great idea, *a critical edition of the Bible.*" At home, Kennicott took flak from both Jewish writers and suspicious Christians. His occasional preference for readings from the Samaritan Pentateuch rather than the received Masoretic Text chafed Protestant sensibilities. Nonetheless, scholars throughout Europe applauded him for greatly advancing knowledge of the Hebrew Old Testament. His *State of the Printed Hebrew Text* had already been republished in Leipzig, translated into Latin for a European audience. Now Germans also reprinted the appendix to *Vetus Testamentum Hebraicum* that discussed manuscripts of the Hebrew Bible. Except Bentley, perhaps no other British philologist of the eighteenth century won such repute. And after Kennicott's widely publicized labors an English writer could calmly admit that "a few errors" had crept into "our common translation of the Scriptures."[37]

Benjamin Kennicott's chief patron, Bishop Robert Lowth, took Old Testament philology in a more innovative direction. Lowth was raised to appreciate biblical innovation. His father, an Anglican cleric and respected biblical interpreter, defended Richard Simon and cited contemporary Persian and Arabian customs to illuminate the Old Testament. Highly regarded as a poet from his student days in Oxford, the younger Lowth was elected professor of poetry in the university in 1741. He held the position for a decade before leaving to climb the Anglican ladder, reaching eventually the see of London. Lowth knew Hebrew well (the tongue spoken by Adam and Eve, he unfashionably believed). Thus he delivered thirty-four lectures on an odd topic for a poetry professor: the parts of the Old Testament thought to be written in verse (for example, Psalms and Job). Lowth gave his lectures in Oxford's mother tongue, Latin. He published them in 1753 as *Praelectiones de sacra poesi Hebraeorum* (*Lectures*

---

* Written biblical Hebrew included only consonants, leaving readers to infer vowels. Rabbis in the early Middle Ages added small marks to indicate the vowels to be spoken when the text was read. These are vowel points.

on *Sacred Poetry of the Hebrews*). As it happened, J. D. Michaelis heard one of the lectures during a visit to Oxford. By the time Lowth published, Michaelis was professor in Göttingen ("justly celebrated for its eminent Professors," Lowth thought). Michaelis reprinted the work there, expanding some sections and adding his own notes—"about a third of the whole edition," Lowth wrote, "correcting what is wrong & supplying what [in Michaelis's view] is defective in my work." This edition assured the attention of German philologists. An English translation in 1787 brought Lowth a wider British and American audience.[38]

In *Sacred Poetry of the Hebrews*, Lowth offered a fresh understanding of the Old Testament by drawing on learned traditions rarely mined by earlier biblical philologists. Whereas Kennicott lifted methods from classical textual philology, Lowth borrowed from rhetoric: the idea of the sublime (an elevated rhetorical register transcending everyday life); the ancient instruction (seen in Isocrates) to compose in balanced clauses parallel in length, syntax, and structure; and the integral role of meter in Greek and Roman poetry. Every schoolboy studying Homer or Vergil learned how to 'scan': to recognize the varieties of poetic meter—the repetitive rhythm of each line. The neoclassical Augustan poets whom Lowth and his readers admired, such as Dryden and Pope, put classical poetry and its principles on a pedestal. In a very different vein, the new awareness of the foreignness of primitive cultures to modern ways of thought, awakened in the Quarrel of Ancients and Moderns, also affected Lowth. He conceived ancient Hebrews, like Homer, as remote from modern readers not just in time, but in circumstances, way of life, way of thinking.[39]

Marrying Israelite primitivity to neoclassical rhetoric bred startling results. Since antiquity, learned Christians had insisted that the 'poetic' parts of the Old Testament—surely a nobler literature than Horace or Homer—had metrical form like Greco-Roman poetry. Lowth looked for meter and, like others before him, could not pin it down. (It was not there.) He did not give up the conviction, but he declared knowledge of Hebrew meter irretrievably lost. More or less as a substitute for the missing meter, he announced that the distinctive essence of Hebrew verse lay in its figurative style and primitive fondness for repetition (parallelisms—a variant of the rhetorical dictum just mentioned). Lowth imposed poetry on the unwitting Hebrews, who knew no such genre; and he then analyzed it with current neoclassical categories of literary criticism, most extensively the sublime. He discussed varieties of imagery. He devoted successive lectures to poetic genres in the scriptures: lyric, elegiac, dramatic, and so forth. He scrutinized the individual styles of different prophets. Putting these ideas into textual practice, in 1778 Lowth published a translation of Isaiah, a book, according to Lowth, previously considered prose. Like Kennicott, he tried to toss out "the ill-founded opinion of the authority of the Jews, both as interpreters and conservators" of the Hebrew Bible. He also tossed out modern European ideas of what constituted poetry, showing how Isaiah's prophecies fitted the traits of ancient Hebrew 'poetry,' especially parallelism. With an introduction expounding Lowth's principles of Hebrew versification, the translation of Isaiah gave wider circulation to Lowth's ideas, then still locked up in Latin.[40]

Lowth never doubted that the writings he examined "are justly attributed to the inspiration of the Holy Spirit," but he also considered them "conformable to the principles of science" and "circumscribed" by the "rules of art." The philologist could and should analyze the writings "of Moses, of David and Isaiah" like those "of Homer, of Pindar, and of Horace." Lowth's explanation of Hebrew 'poetry' helped to spread the notion that 'oriental' style differed from European. Far more consequential, Lowth offered a new way of studying the Bible: by examining its literary forms. In the next century, biblical philologists would take up this idea, making waves that rippled widely. But their native language would usually be German, their philosophical axioms different. The center of biblical studies was shifting away from the English-speaking world even as Lowth published.[41]

CLASSICAL TOOLS, ENGLISH RAW MATERIAL

Just as British biblical philologists borrowed methods from classical studies, so did the first scholars to edit English literary texts. Bentley's *Paradise Lost* stood out solely for deranged editorial axioms, not for the project of editing an English author. By the early 1700s, readers had come to see well-known English authors of bygone eras as "Classic" like Cicero or Homer; so Lewis Theobald called Shakespeare in 1726. Like *manuscripts* of ancient classics, *printed texts* of modern ones crawled with variants: "the more the Editions of any Book multiply," Theobald explained, "the more the Errors multiply too." Shakespeare had grown "corrupt enough to pass for one of the oldest Stamp"—an English Homer. The evolution of the language likewise made old authors tough slogging for modern readers. "That which was written in *English* two hundred Years ago is now scarce intelligible," averred Anthony Blackwall in 1719. So editors rushed in to save the new canon of English classics from corruption and make it accessible. As early as 1688 Jacob Tonson produced a recognizable 'edition' of *Paradise Lost*—that is, one involving editorial labors like those expended on ancient texts. In 1721 a Chaucer edition used manuscript collation and conjectural emendation to restore a supposedly accurate text.[42]

Five years later, Theobald's *Shakespeare Restored* set out principles to guide in mending the "mangled Condition" of "our *British* HOMER." An editor should strive to recover the original autograph and to explain contexts for modern readers ignorant of them. To do so, the editor had to know thoroughly Shakespeare's grammar and usage, Elizabethan spelling, the practices of the stage in his day. Also required was intimate acquaintance with Shakespeare's plays such as Bentley had with Greek and Roman literature. Theobald's work prepared the ground for later editors and, more immediately, for his seven-volume edition of Shakespeare in 1733. In that work his collation of variants, cautious conjectural emendations, and explanatory commentary echoed practices of Greek and Latin philology. Theobald had edited Greek drama before turning to English. "*Shakespeare's* Case has in great Measure resembled That of a corrupt *Classick*," he wrote, "and, consequently, the Method of Cure was likewise to bear a Resemblance." Samuel Johnson, in his edition of Shakespeare, called himself a scholiast, the venerable name for a commentator on the classics. Not Bentley's absurd Milton but his "dull" Horace guided Theobald and other eighteenth-century editors of English 'classics.'[43]

Besides "Emendation of corrupt Passages" and "Explanation of obscure and difficult ones," Theobald added, an editor might also inquire "into the Beauties and Defects of Composition." Theobald did some of that, though mostly confining himself to "perfecting the two other Parts." More such aesthetic criticism, however, appeared in the next decades, assessing authorial style and effect—Samuel Johnson's famously. Critics borrowed categories from classical rhetoric (the 'sublime' got a lot of play). But they also drew on recent writings about 'taste,' notably the third Earl of Shaftesbury's *Characteristicks of Men, Manners, Opinions and Times* (1711). Why should aesthetic criticism have boomed when it did? Perhaps three causes conspired. First, a broader, bourgeois readership for 'polite' literature developed in the late seventeenth and early eighteenth centuries; and critics felt these new readers needed guidance, even herding like sheep. Second, canonization of monuments of English literature—Spenser, Shakespeare, Milton—presented readers with difficult texts whose obsolete aesthetic criteria wanted explication. Finally, a steady increase in new titles published, starting in the 1740s, and the rise of a new genre, the novel, left inexpert readers in need of counsel—or so critics felt. Johnson saw himself as just such a learned gatekeeper. Whatever the reasons, the fact remains.[44]

The earliest English writings attracted attention, too. Poking around in moldering English documents, some dating from Anglo-Saxon times, was no novelty as such. In the fourteenth century the abbey of Bury St. Edmunds cataloged its charters—in effect the deeds to its many properties—after townspeople resentful of its wealth sacked the abbey library. In the next century a try was made at an inventory of manuscripts in all English monastic libraries. The Reformation speeded Anglo-Saxon research. When Henry VIII dissolved the monasteries, vexed book lovers tried to salvage medieval manuscripts; meanwhile, royal agents seized any that served Henry's purposes (and used averse ones for toilet paper). A few Anglican apologists pored over records of the early English church to prove its primeval independence of Rome. (The Anglo-Saxon church actually doted on the pope, but wishful thinking long persisted.) One piece of antipapal propaganda, dating about 1566, contained the first printed Anglo-Saxon. Throughout the troubled seventeenth century, politico-religious purposes continued to inspire scrutiny of the remote English past, as parliamentarians and royalists, Laudians and Puritans, high churchmen and low threw historical evidence in each other's faces.[45]

Such motives spurred sustained research by a handful of scholars into "the Saxon tongue" (as it was then called), again using standard tools developed by classical philologists. Piously expecting to uncover Anglicanism *avant la lettre*, Abraham Wheelocke collated manuscripts to publish in 1643 the first editions of two chief sources for early English history: the Anglo-Saxon Chronicle (ca. 890) and the Anglo-Saxon version of Bede's history (731). Anyone who likewise hoped to assail popery or evil politicians with such weapons first needed to learn Anglo-Saxon. In 1659 two essential aids appeared in one book: the first printed (if puny) Anglo-Saxon grammar, by Wheelocke (dead six years earlier), and the first reasonably full dictionary of the language, by the Canterbury antiquarian William Somner. Several exuberant decades of Anglo-Saxon philology ensued. This small clan of scholars found its main home—in an era when English erudition typically resided in rectories and noble houses—in the two universities, especially Oxford. These philologists began to see that religious or political claims grew more plausible as scholarship grew more accurate. Besides, Anglo-Saxon manuscripts could fascinate in their own right.[46]

So rigor grew; and Anglo-Saxon scholars began to distance themselves from politics—as well as to take interest in related languages with no political import. In 1667, Franciscus Junius sought "a Commentator that should give anie light to Chaucers old language." Six months later his correspondent Thomas Marshall—who supplied Junius with just such a commentary—himself awaited "an Islandish [Icelandic] Lexicon" from "a frend at Hamburg." Thirty years on, Humfrey Wanley sent George Hickes a guess at the origins and pronunciation of an ancient Visigothic alphabet (a language remotely related to Anglo-Saxon). Wanley amazed the master of University College Oxford with his "Painful Searches, Judicious Examinations, and Correct Transcripts" of manuscripts and his "great Severitty of Studdy"—"17 Hours *per diem*." Wanley had no motive for such exertions but love of learning. He lived on the edge of penury for years to indulge his craving for manuscripts. At one point he stoically proposed to wed a well-off cousin to support his habit—"not very ugly," he told Hickes. Oddly, the cousin found his suit unpersuasive. So Wanley married his widowed landlady: one way to save rent.[47]

In the contest for hero of erudition, George Hickes left his correspondent Wanley in the dust. Hickes was a learned clergyman nurtured by the Oxford circle of Anglo-Saxon philologists. With their aid, he published in 1689 an improved Anglo-Saxon grammar. By then dean of Worcester Cathedral, Hickes was on the fast track to churchly preferment when the Glorious Revolution of 1688–89 ousted James II from his throne and Hickes from his hopes. Hickes believed the king's deposition a sin against divine appointment. No less stubborn than principled, he denied the legitimacy of the new regime, nailing defiance up in the cathedral. Outlawed from 1691 to 1699, he spent those years on the run, hiding out in friends' houses under aliases. While on the lam, Hickes plunged ever deeper into Anglo-Saxon studies—given books and manuscripts by partisans of the new regime and loyalists to the old. Born from religio-political divisions, Anglo-Saxon scholarship now reached across the deepest such rifts.[48]

From underground, Hickes marshaled philologists and antiquarians to compile the supreme work of Anglo-Saxon erudition to date. Its sonorous title left no doubt: *Linguarum veterum septentrionalium thesaurus grammatico-criticus et archaeologicus* (*Grammatical-Critical and Archaeological Treasury of Old Northern Languages*). Its two great folios came off the press in Oxford in 1703–5, after the crown lifted Hickes's outlawry in 1699. Hickes planned the book and provided much text. He shared duties with two other lead authors and many contributors. Hickes stressed the kinship of the Germanic languages, and his *Thesaurus* sped their comparative study. It included an expansion of his 1689 Anglo-Saxon grammar, plus 'Frankish' (Old High German) and Icelandic ones. A treatise on the study of Anglo-Saxon language and history broke ground substantively (by clarifying Anglo-Saxon governance and legal practices) and methodologically (by analyzing proper names to crack historical problems). Most decisively here, Hickes and Wanley did for England what Mabillon had done for France: laid down rules for analyzing ancient charters (the science of 'diplomatics'). Mabillon applauded. The book included many smaller contributions, such as an essay on Anglo-Saxon and Anglo-Danish coins by the antiquary Sir Andrew Fountaine. The second volume comprised a magisterial register of Anglo-Saxon manuscripts by Wanley. This catalog, with detailed descriptions of each item, vastly eased study of the Anglo-Saxon world. It was not superseded for 250 years. The *Thesaurus* laid the enduring basis of Anglo-Saxon philology. In its pages—as in the philological tradition generally—language study, antiquities, and history jumbled together.[49]

In the wake of the *Thesaurus*, other philologists focused on recovering and printing Anglo-Saxon texts. Such work required diligence and persistence rather than Bentleyesque brilliance. These qualities undergirded a 1709 edition and translation of Ælfric's tenth-century life of Pope Gregory the Great—critical apparatus in English, not Latin—prepared by Elizabeth Elstob, protégé of Hickes, crony of Wanley. Her older brother and fellow Saxonist, William Elstob, died in 1715 before publishing a planned edition of Anglo-Saxon laws; David Wilkins's 1721 collection *Leges Anglo-Saxonicae* redeemed the promise. The most impressive product of this textual erudition was John Smith's edition of Bede's *Historia ecclesiastica* (1722). The first true critical edition of Bede, it reproduced both Latin and Anglo-Saxon versions, rested on collation of the oldest manuscripts, noted variant readings, and included auxiliary materials throwing light on Bede's world (notably charters from the kingdom of Mercia, now lost). Smith used on Bede philological techniques honed over centuries by students of classical antiquity. And in his workmanlike way Smith squeezed more from these methods than the scintillating Bentley, for he used them not only to emend the text but to bring to life the age in which Bede wrote.[50]

Unlike editors of such newer 'classics' as Chaucer and Shakespeare, these Anglo-Saxon critics faded away after about 1725. Elizabeth Elstob did her best to popularize Anglo-Saxon (which she thought needed to grasp properly modern English). In 1715 she published a grammar "of the English-Saxon tongue" (as she called it)—and in English rather than Latin, for general readers. But debts that she and her brother ran up to finance their scholarship sank her campaign. After he died in 1715, she fled London to evade debtor's prison, living for years under an assumed name in Worcestershire. Her disappearance symbolized the state of Anglo-Saxon philology after the 1720s. But the foundation remained. Decades later, Thomas Jefferson used Elstob's grammar, alongside Hickes's, to teach himself Anglo-Saxon. In the 1820s, an elderly Jefferson included Anglo-Saxon in the curriculum he devised for his University of Virginia. A British university had created the first permanent position in Anglo-Saxon only a couple of decades earlier. These nineteenth-century philologists built on the erudition of the three decades either side of 1700.[51]

Philological scholarship on England *after* the Norman Conquest also flourished around 1700. Humfrey Wanley moved on from his catalog of Anglo-Saxon manuscripts to prepare a similarly detailed register of the huge manuscript collection of the politician Robert Harley, Earl of Oxford, now in the British Library. (Wanley worked as librarian to Harley and then to his son from 1708 until his own death in 1726.) Thomas Madox did foundational work on medieval charters. In his *History and Antiquities of the Exchequer* (1711) he composed the first detailed, archive-based account of medieval English governance. The list could go on at length. In 1717 Wanley helped to establish a Society of Antiquaries to encourage more research into the centuries before 1600.[52]

The society symbolized a golden age of British antiquarianism in the decades right around 1700—so thriving as to evoke satire. The antiquary had emerged as a type in the English world of learning in the sixteenth century: recall William Camden's 1586 *Britannia* and the investigations of his student Robert Cotton. In the later seventeenth and early eighteenth centuries, antiquarians multiplied. They treasured the sorts of written records that underlay Hickes's *Thesaurus* or that Wanley cataloged in Harley's library. But they also inherited the fascination shown by their Elizabethan ancestors with physical relics like funeral monuments and Roman coins, an appetite fed by local informants and a thriving trade in artifacts. In 1707 Dr. John Woodward sent Rev. John Strype drawings of "some Roman Urns & other Antiquities digged up near B[isho]psgate." Most antiquarians collected miscellaneously, like Sir Thomas Browne, whose house John Evelyn described in 1671 as "a paradise and cabinet of rarities . . . especially medals, books, plants and natural things." A few antiquarians specialized. Britain's Roman past appealed, given that many remnants survived; and John Horsley crisscrossed Britain to inspect Roman remains for his *Britannia Romana* (1732). John Aubrey did a little of everything; but his "Monumenta Britannica," still in manuscript when he died in 1697, zeroed in on what we now call prehistoric megaliths. William Stukeley (the first secretary of the Society of Antiquaries) obsessed over Stonehenge and the nearby henge monument at Avebury ('Abury' to him). Between 1719 and 1726 he visited the monuments time after time, sometimes for weeks. His careful drawings and measurements finally appeared in *Stonehenge* (1740) and *Abury* (1743). Stukeley studied barrow graves and ancient coins with the same care as henge monuments.[53]

Such 'archaeological' interests (to speak anachronistically) grew increasingly prominent among antiquaries as the seventeenth century turned into the eighteenth; and in detailed surveys like Stukeley's antiquarianism began to transmute into something resembling later archaeology. Underline 'began.' *Stonehenge* and *Abury* set Stukeley's empirical rigor in a fantasy world populated by 'Druids'—Phoenicians who brought the religion of Abraham to Britain. Stukeley also imagined chariot races around Stonehenge and identified some of the old coins he examined as prizes awarded to the winners. He snatched this last illusion out of thin air, but the Druids he concocted from a mishmash of early modern speculations linking biblical history with faint glimpses of Druids in classical sources. Modern archaeologists could admire Stukeley's measurements. His Druids might have excited Athanasius Kircher, but in the 1740s they inhabited a dying intellectual world.[54]

By then antiquarian scholarship itself was in decline. Stukeley's books reflected a curiosity about pre-Roman Britain booming in 1700, fading thereafter. In the 1730s learned interest in medieval philology, history, and antiquities also fell off, just as had Anglo-Saxon scholarship—in part, perhaps, because the religious and political disputes that once fueled them had also subsided. Antiquarianism never died, especially as a popular hobby; and it recovered scholarly health in the early nineteenth century. But in the latter half of the century other modes of study would colonize its territory.[55]

LANGUAGE ITSELF

Conjectures about the origin and nature of language by erudite Britons in the later seventeenth century roughly paralleled the thinking of such contemporary continental writers as the Port-Royal group. Near the end of the century John Locke shifted the center of gravity of linguistic speculation. The change came because Locke belonged to the tradition of Bacon and the circle of the Royal Society. He abhorred any notion that mere analysis of language opened the door to understanding nature. Natural knowledge could only be gained by empirical investigation, by 'experiment' in its broad seventeenth-century meaning. These principles determined his understanding of language.[56]

In his *Essay concerning Human Understanding* (1690), Locke outlined an experiential theory of knowledge—congenial to the Royal Society—and this theory depended on the conventional, arbitrary nature of language. Human language gave no immediate insight; rather, people created language out of their experience, as they did knowledge. All awareness of the world around us comes through the senses, said Locke. These sense perceptions produce ideas in the mind; and these ideas (not corresponding objects outside of our heads) are what we actually know. Human beings invent words to label ideas, so that they can communicate information to others. But the correspondence between word and idea is arbitrary, made up by people, not given in the idea or in nature. So far, so Alexandrian: tracing the history of words tells us something about human inventiveness, nothing about the nature of things.

But Locke expatiated. On one hand, language is inescapably social and in that sense objective: only if a word evokes the same idea in both speaker and listener can we communicate. On the other hand, language is inescapably personal and subjective: only *I* have the exact idea in *my* head that *I* indicate with a particular word. "Common use *regulates the meaning of Words* pretty well for common Conversation"; but it falters faced with the complex ideas of "philosophical [scientific] Discourses." What is more, we express abstract ideas by metaphorical extension of concrete words. So 'inspiration' derives from its literal meaning, breathing. The more abstract the idea, thus, the more uncertain is the word for it. How can I be sure that the idea in *my* head for which I use the word *cat* is identical to the idea in *your* head for which you use the same word? At least I can grab your shoulder, point to a small, furry animal, and say "cat—yes?" What about *gravitational force, corpuscles (atoms), love,* or *god*? "I could not avoid saying a great deale concerning words," Locke almost apologized, "because soe apt & usuall to be mistaken for things." Locke may have fallen into dubious linguistic psychologizing. But by stretching the millennia-long argument about natural versus conventional language to raise these new questions, he relativized words and, as Hans Aarsleff wrote, "laid the foundation of the modern study of language."[57]

Innovation did not immediately win him new friends. The assertion that language was human creation rather than divine gift distressed some pious souls. So did the implication that moral vocabulary had no "foundation in nature," as Rev. Jonathan Edwards worried in far-off Massachusetts half a century later. Edwards partly accepted Locke's conventionalist view of language. But he insisted that "Mankind in general seem to suppose some general standard" when using words like " 'good' and 'evil,' 'right' and 'wrong.' " Moreover, optimists who awaited the manufacture of a universal, precise, philosophical language (as Wilkins's *Real Character* had essayed) did not appreciate Locke torpedoing their boat. Among them was Leibniz, a fan of such projects. But Condillac admired Locke's *Essay*, and it partly inspired his own *Essai sur l'origine des connaissances humaines* (*Essay on the Origin of Human Knowledge,* 1746). Condillac, in turn, set off a Europe-wide debate on the origin of language. Meanwhile, in Britain and America over the course of the eighteenth century, Locke's conventionalist approach to language gradually seeped so deep into intellectual culture as to become almost second nature among the highly educated.[58]

Some Englishmen rebelled against second nature, none more flagrantly than James Harris. Born into a well-connected Salisbury family, Harris had a talent for friendship, a passion for music, a bent for scholarship, and moneyed leisure to indulge all three. He made himself into a learned student of classical writers, especially Aristotle. In 1751 he published *Hermes: or, A Philosophical Inquiry concerning Language and Universal Grammar*. *Hermes* stood in the tradition of *grammatica speculativa* and universal grammars such as the Port-Royal Grammar. But it differed from recent antecedents in unabashedly going back to Aristotle for much of its theory. Harris threw down the gauntlet before Locke. He made words expressing general ideas primary, those referring to specific things secondary. He defended innate ideas against Locke's claim that all knowledge comes through the senses. He said that God gave human beings the ability to form general ideas and thus language. He got a predictably chilly reception in England, a warmer one north of the border, and an enthusiastic one in France and Germany. In 1796 a French translation appeared by order of the French state. (A German translation had come out eight years earlier, under less-imposing auspices). Johann Gottfried Herder appreciated Harris's argument that peculiarities specific to a given language reflected the historical experience of the people speaking it. In applying Aristotle's categories of matter and form to phonetics and semantics, Harris anticipated Wilhelm von Humboldt's idea of *innere Sprachform* (see chapter 5). By going back to the ancients, *Hermes* pointed universal grammar toward linguistic thinking of the future.[59]

Locke and Harris seem at loggerheads, yet they coincided in moving language theory in a new direction. The old universal grammar—from *grammatica speculativa* to Port-Royal—sought a common structure underlying all languages. The old disputes about Adamic language focused attention on an Ur-time before human history. The old project of a universal language sought to heal the rupture of Babel by inventing a perfect language. None of these ways of theorizing about language had much to do with real human beings, caught in the toils of life. Neither Locke nor Harris utterly repudiated all these earlier ways of meditating on language; Harris even carried the flag of universal grammar. But both made language theory a way of probing not merely language but the human condition. For Locke, to study language meant to explore how people gather knowledge and to gauge its limits. For Harris, to study language meant to analyze—at least potentially—the uniqueness of a culture and its historical roots. (In passing, Locke also pointed out that customs of different countries produced words in one language with no counterpart in another.) The one man pointed mainly toward psychology and epistemology, the other chiefly toward history and anthropology. Both gave a new, broader meaning to questions about the origin and nature of language. They were not alone. Thomas Blackwell, too, had connected the state of a language with its speakers' historical development, as had Robert Wood. Indeed, throughout Europe, old imaginings of a primordial (or potential) language that mirrored the natural order were giving way to new understandings of language, as evolving from, and encoding, the slow development of human-kind or of particular peoples.[60]

FRAMEWORKS FOR PHILOLOGY

The many varieties of philology should not mask traits common to all human-istic learning. In important respects early modern erudition differed from the academic regime that gradually took shape after 1800. These disparities will eventually help to explain the distinctive traits of the modern humanities.

For one thing, most early modern erudition survived on institutional or aristocratic patronage. Personal wealth gave James Harris leisure for philol-ogy, but Locke lived as a dependent in a noble household before getting a government post and then retiring to a rich friend's country house. The Church of England was the greatest Maecenas, usually by accident. Many re-searchers earned their bread as clergymen, collating manuscripts or measur-ing ancient monuments when pastoral duties permitted. (Or, perhaps, when they did not.) The two English universities were Anglican institutions, with college fellows ordained or on the way to ordination; research was neither re-quired nor expected, but a fellowship could support it. Aristocratic patronage played a sizable part, too. Wanley worked as Lord Harley's librarian. The Lord Chief Justice paid for cutting the Anglo-Saxon type to print Elizabeth Elstob's grammar. Publishing by subscription began around 1700 to multiply many small patrons to raise money needed for a large philological project. Samuel Johnson financed his edition of Shakespeare by subscription. (His famously unpatronized dictionary was paid for by booksellers who hoped to profit by it—fruitlessly.) When Hickes's frighteningly costly *Thesaurus* appeared, it in-cluded a long list of subscribers, at its top twenty-six noblemen. One need not imagine all twenty-six peers paging intently through the *Thesaurus*. Patron-izing erudition redounded to the reputations of the powerful (which is not to deny genuine curiosity as well). In 1722 a physician and an Anglican rector got together to launch a periodical to publish medieval and classical scholarship. This *Bibliotheca literaria* survived for two years and ten issues, not a bad run for dry stuff, but also evidence that philology could hardly thrive on the open market. Absent modern research universities, scholars needed subsidy.[61]

Diffuse, uncertain, fluctuating pay worked against any neatly organized system of knowledge; finances thus reinforced the traditional habit of human-istic scholars to traipse from one subject to another. Biblical philology, for in-stance, rarely monopolized the attention of those who pursued it. Kennicott stood out in sticking pretty closely to his Hebrew last. Besides *Sacred Poetry of the Hebrews*, Lowth wrote a much-reprinted English grammar (1762). Bentley never pulled off his New Testament edition; but he edited classical writers and, unfortunately, Milton. John Mill worked at both Malalas and the New Testament. His older Oxford colleague Bishop Fell toiled learnedly, if not fruitfully, on Anglo-Saxon and Suetonius as well as the New Testament.

Such variety points up a decisive feature of the ordering of knowledge before the mid-nineteenth century. Academic disciplines, as we know them, came to life well after 1800. True, the word *discipline* (and its Greek and Latin ancestors) had long been linked to learning. At first the term referred to the instruction imparted by a master to *disciples*; by extension it came to mean a branch of knowledge. As one might expect, practitioners in different branches—law, theology, astronomy—evolved distinctive questions and methods. To this limited extent, early modern 'disciplines' looked like our own. But they differed in vital respects. First, they mostly lacked institutional walls, such as academic departments, to raise barriers between disciplines. Second, they typically covered a broader range of knowledge than modern disciplines: 'philosophy' encompassed physics as well as metaphysics; 'literature'—as surveyed in eighteenth-century German histories of learning—meant almost anything written down of a serious, thoughtful sort; 'natural history' embraced geology, biology, ethnography, and more. Third, disciplines did not challenge the unity of knowledge. Expertise in one area did not discourage a scholar from exercising it in another: a trait that further limited the height of methodological fences between disciplines. Neither the encyclopedic model of knowledge as a 'circle of learning,' which prevailed in the Renaissance, nor Aristotle's hierarchical model, which reasserted itself in the seventeenth century, allowed for a discipline marooned on its own island. So Bentley's emending Homer, editing Milton, and expounding on the New Testament raised no eyebrows. He was hardly alone—in his own day and for a long time to come—in hopping from one field of knowledge to another. Bentley's almost exact contemporary, Jean Le Clerc, translated Old and New Testaments, edited Hesiod and Servius, compiled a manual of physical science, wrote an influential treatise on methods of textual criticism, and composed a history of the Netherlands.[62]

Wide reach and lack of walls between fields of learning mattered. In this situation it seemed perfectly natural to take tools used to study classical or biblical texts—long-established areas of research—and apply them to materials of other sorts overlooked by philologists until lately. Remember this mode of innovation. It appeared in the invention of English literary studies and the creation of Anglo-Saxon philology, and it will reappear repeatedly.

Philology in Britain looked different around 1750 than it had in 1650. Bentley had brought to classical studies a deepened sensitivity to historical change in both context and language; Blackwell and Wood added a new alertness to what we would call cultural change—awareness of difference in kind between Homeric civilization and later eras. Biblical scholars approached the problem of textual corruption with a new frankness and new skill in emendation—and reimagined the literary form of parts of the Old Testament as they began to come to grip with the 'otherness' of ancient Hebrew ways of thought. Philologists took methods of Greek and Latin erudition and applied them to 'classic' English texts: far enough back in the past to have degraded textually and grown hard for moderns to read. A few antiquarians studied ancient British remains with almost unprecedented empirical precision. Antiquarians and philologists—and no line divided them—pioneered sustained, systematic, and even cooperative study of the long English past, its literature, its language, and its language's family. Theories about language itself broke out of the traditional explanatory frames of Bible stories and universal logics, growing more alert to how history shaped a language. If a common theme ran through these changes, it was a deepening and refining of the historical consciousness already developing in earlier philologists.

British philologists studied a lot more things in 1750 than 1650, but the novelty lay more in range of topics than in frameworks of method. Time-tested philological techniques were polished and extended into new fields of inquiry. Such work could lead to original outcomes, as in Bentley's studies of the evolution of Greek dialects or in Lowth's approach to the Old Testament via literary genres. It could even create a new field of study, as with Anglo-Saxon philology. But these novelties grew organically from old ways, not from inventing radically new ones. In applying tried-and-true philological methods to early medieval language, writings, and institutions, Hickes and the other Anglo-Saxonists opened a new scholarly field; but their originality lay in matter rather than means.

This accent on continuity, on the steady honing of techniques first forged in Alexandria, does not fall equally on every British philologist. In Lowth, in Locke, in Harris, and in Wood, philology, to different degrees, broke out of ancient fences. More innovation was to come.

4

"DEEP ERUDITION INGENIOUSLY APPLIED"

REVOLUTIONS OF THE LATER EIGHTEENTH CENTURY

It is no wonder that James Harris interested himself in idiosyncrasies of various languages. By his day there were a lot of new tongues to pay attention to, especially if you were British; for in the later eighteenth century the British Empire reached a high-water mark. British soldiers and administrators roamed North America and the Indian subcontinent, and the Royal Navy roved the watery world. In January 1771, HM Bark *Endeavour* was sailing homeward from its voyage of discovery in the South Pacific (where it had run across Australia). On board the young natural historian Joseph Banks puzzled over resemblances among Tahitian, Javanese and Malay vocabularies. And he wondered about their odd overlap with words he had just picked up in Batavia from a Madagascar-born slave.[1]

Such musings pointed toward one of several seismic shifts within philology to be discussed in this chapter—new ways of understanding languages, new methods of studying them, new approaches to history, new conceptions of the Bible and of classical antiquity, new modes of treating the literature and language of England itself. The age-old Christian framework of learning became, as one result, too narrow to contain all new erudition; non-Christian cultures and post-Christian methods became the topic not of a book here and there but of systematic exploration by generations of scholars. Sources of change were many and varied. But three stand out. One was fallout from Britain's development: its political integration, its colonizing, its imperial ventures. Another was cross-fertilization between sundry innovations within philology, none of which arose in isolation from all others. The third was a renaissance in Germany—a renaissance at first not closely watched by English-speaking philologists but which demands coverage here because its longer-term impact was transformative.

ORIENTALIST ERUDITION AND ITS RAMIFICATIONS

In 1767 Benjamin Kennicott took time off from Hebrew research to promote a professorship of Persian language in Oxford. His first sentence pointed out that knowledge of Persian had become "an object of national concern" owing to "the interests which this country has lately acquired in the political, as well as the commercial affairs" of India. (Persian supplied the language of diplomacy and commerce there.) Without facility in Persian, how could "the servants of the [East India] company" properly do their jobs as "magistrates and legislators" over their subject peoples?[2]

Less hard-boiled motives stirred Kennicott, too. "Every nation has," he added, "besides the mere difference of Language, an Idiom, and even a mode of Sentiment peculiar to itself." Study of language opened the road to understanding national character and to uncovering "the traces" of a people's "primitive manners and original forms of government." The human mind being everywhere essentially the same and yet differently cultivated in various regions of the globe, "every branch of knowledge" would benefit "from an acquaintance with the manners, customs, and practice of the most remote nations." From "the Asiaticks," though degenerated today, "we derive the first seeds of all the knowledge which we have carried to so much higher a degree of perfection." This lineage alone would "justify our search after the remains of that Wisdom" that "once reigned amongst them." Further, the comparative method familiar to Kennicott from biblical philology, if applied to ancient records of sundry nations, could clear up "many doubtful facts" that "length of time, and the want of collateral evidence, have contributed to render obscure." In his boldest claim for comparison, Kennicott argued that exploring parallel customs, analogous religious practices, and "even the similitude of words" among "distinct and remote people" might lead scholars back "to the first source from which the whole race of mankind derive their origin."[3]

The changes Kennicott rang on the promise of linguistic study were unoriginal: his tract repeated themes becoming common in his generation. If the unique historical development of each *people, nation,* or *race*—terms then interchangeable—shaped its language, then language became key to unlocking mysteries of cultural evolution and national character.

Yet when Kennicott issued his plea, the only nonbiblical Asian languages really accessible in Europe were three used in commerce, diplomacy, and Christian missions: Arabic, Turkish, and Persian. This would soon change.[4]

In 1755 a French student of Middle Eastern languages sailed to India. He bore the fragrant name of Abraham Hyacinthe Anquetil-Duperron and wandered from Pondicherry in the southeast to Surat in the northwest. In Surat he studied with Parsi (Zoroastrian) priests. By the time he returned to Europe in 1761, he had picked up a working knowledge of Sanskrit, modern Persian, and its ancient ancestors Avestan and Middle Persian—plus scores of manuscripts in all these tongues. In 1771 Anquetil-Duperron published three volumes of selections from Zoroastrian writings, under the title *Zend-Avesta, ouvrage de Zorastre* (*Zend-Avesta, Book of Zoroaster*). This translation introduced Europe to sacred Parsi texts. Anquetil-Duperron became the first European to decipher an ancient language of Asia no longer in use, to decode its alien alphabet—cracking open a window that would vastly widen Europe's view of the past. His sometimes shaky rendering also gave Europe its first look at an early Asian text neither biblical nor classical in its associations. Yet it had little immediate resonance.[5]

Twelve years later, on September 25, 1783, the British frigate *Crocodile* anchored at Calcutta, delivering one of those imperial "magistrates" whose training Kennicott fretted over. He would not have worried about this one. Sir William Jones commanded eleven foreign languages, ancient and modern.* He knew something of about fifteen others. He had won acclaim for a Persian grammar (1771) and for translations from Persian, Arabic, and Turkish. Lowth's lectures on Hebrew poetry inspired him to write a similar Latin commentary on Asian poetry; this book (1774) treated Chinese as well as Persian, Turkish, and Arabic verse. "Persian" Jones and "Oriental" Jones became his universal nicknames. But fame did not bring cash, especially fame in a field with almost no paying jobs. So even before his Persian grammar hit the bookstalls, Oriental Jones turned to a career in law.[6]

In that role Jones arrived in Calcutta in 1783, as a judge of the Bengal Supreme Court. Nor did he come to India with an eye on mainly philology but, like the other Britons there, with an eye on the main chance. He wanted to make as much money as possible, as quickly as possible, then retire to a life of repose back home. Only two motives set Jones apart: he wanted to make his fortune honestly and to use his later leisure for learning. Before leaving England, Jones mentioned to Edward Gibbon his hope that the judgeship would leave time to keep pegging away at orientalist studies, and on shipboard he drew up a longish list of potential inquiries.[7]

He sailed toward well-prepared ground. Bengal's governor-general, Warren Hastings, promoted scholarship as both tool of empire and contribution to knowledge—two projects not easily separated. (Hastings had proposed the Persian professorship urged by Kennicott.) Among the several young East India Company servants who responded to Hastings's encouragement, Charles Wilkins already knew Persian and Bengali and became the first Briton really to command Sanskrit, the language of the ancient sacred and learned texts of India. In 1785 the company published in London Wilkins's translation of the *Bhagavad Gita*. It circulated throughout Europe.[8]

---

*Greek, Latin, French, Italian, Spanish, Portuguese, German, Persian, Turkish, Arabic, and Hebrew. Jones was also a radical Whig, heavily involved in politics, as well as a pioneering legal scholar, aspects of his varied life necessarily passed over here.

Jones brought new focus and fame to scholarship on India. Not long after stepping ashore in Calcutta, Jones lobbied company employees who shared his philological bent to join in an association to foster Asian studies. Ill health—the nemesis of Europeans in India—forced Wilkins to Benares (and within a couple years back home). So he was absent on January 15, 1784, when the Asiatick Society of Bengal met in Calcutta to begin its inquiries "into the History, Civil and Natural, the Antiquities, Arts, Sciences, and Literature, of Asia." Twenty-nine European males attended. Jones timidly broached admitting "learned natives," unthinkable to most Britishers on the imperial periphery, however erudite. The Asiatick Society was the first organization in the world devoted to Asian studies. It continues today, under "learned native" leadership.[9]

The first obstacle to overcome was ignorance of Indian languages, which hobbled President Jones and most of the members. At first, Jones was reduced to presenting such secondhand materials as a speculative comparison of "the Gods of Greece, Italy, and India" and his rendering of an Italian translation of lines from an Indian legend. The August court recess of 1785 gave Jones—inspired by Wilkins—a chance to begin Sanskrit, near the ancient Hindu university in Nadia, under an Indian tutor, Rāmalocana. Jones continued lessons back in Calcutta when the new court term opened in the fall, rising at 4:00 a.m. to study.[10]

He was falling under the spell of ancient Indian culture, but its charms did not primarily prompt him to learn Sanskrit. Rather, mistrusting the competence of the Indian scholars (pandits) who advised British courts on Hindu law, he wished to make Indian laws available in English. (He later changed his mind about the pandits.) Once he had Sanskrit reasonably in hand, Jones began a digest of Hindu law governing contract and inheritance, completed after his death by Henry Colebrooke; Jones also supervised a parallel collection of Islamic law, for India's largest religious minority. But the ancient Brahman rules governing personal behavior, attributed to the sage Manu and recorded in the oldest major Hindu law code, the *Manava-Dharmasastra*, specially fascinated him. Jones finished translating this book, as *Institutes of Hindu Law: or, the Ordinances of Menu* (his spelling of Manu), only weeks before his death in 1794. This volume launched the word *Aryan* on its fraught European career. More to the immediate point, it gave European readers their first nuanced insight into some Hindu practices.[11]

Yet, if law mandated Sanskrit for Jones, literature and science also profited. Even before he had a solid grip on Sanskrit, Jones was writing poems retelling Hindu tales and extolling Hindu gods. After he did get a hold of the language, he learned from the pandit Rādhākānta Sarman about the great poet Kālidāsa (around 400 CE?) and about his greatest play, *Śakuntalā*. In the summer recess of 1787, with Rāmalocana's aid, Jones began to translate it into Latin. (He believed Latin's similarity to Sanskrit made it fitter for a literal version than English.) The Latin translation he then turned into English, publishing it anonymously in Calcutta in 1789 as *Sacontalá, or the Fatal Ring*.* The next year it appeared in London. The 'Indian Shakespeare' swept Europe. "Do you want heaven and earth comprehended in a single name?" asked Goethe in 1791, "I name you, Sakontala, and thus all is said." Schubert turned the play into an opera. Lamartine burbled that Kālidāsa combined the genius of Homer, Theocritus, and Tasso.[12]

Jones and his colleagues in the Asiatick Society recovered other artifacts of ancient Indian civilization for Europeans, including smaller-scale Sanskrit works—in effect, reprocessing Indian culture, in more or less inventive ways, as Europeans had long done with Greece and Rome. Jones himself, under the tutelage of Rādhākānta and other pandits (including his Sanskrit teacher Rāmalocana), began the mammoth effort of working out from Sanskrit documents a chronology of Indian history—in effect, trying to add another column to those old comparative, Scaligerian chronologies that started with Adam. (He utterly failed.) This project, in turn, led Jones to bully his friend Samuel Davis into investigating ancient Indian astronomical calculations. Jones himself dabbled in astronomy and became the first European scholar to study Indian music. All this information, along with reports on Asian culture and natural history, appeared in the Asiatick Society's irregularly published journal, *Asiatick Researches*. Although printed in Calcutta, hundreds of copies sailed to Europe. Reprints soon appeared in London. The Massachusetts Historical Society elected Jones a member; Harvard College begged him to send Indian manuscripts for its library. Abandoned by her lover in 1806, the Romantic poet Karoline von Günderode left a suicide note in Sanskrit. By 1812, the breathlessness over Sanskrit had spread so widely that E.T.A. Hoffmann could use it in satire.[13]

This sudden rage for ancient Indian culture had long-term consequences. *Asiatick Researches*, Wilkins's *Bhagavad Gita*, Jones's *Ordinances of Menu* and *Sacontalá*, and a few other publications from his Calcutta circle created, over the span of little more than a decade, a new field of philologically oriented European scholarship—now called Indology. The Calcutta scholars' achievement paralleled in form that of the Anglo-Saxonists around the beginning of the century—and had much stronger impact. Missionary reports had provided blurry glimpses of nonbiblical civilizations, notably in China; Anquetil-Duperron had opened a small window onto Zoroastrianism. But Indology offered the first wide-ranging, systematic studies by Europeans of an ancient literate culture outside the orbit of the three familiar 'religions of the book.' It set the stage for—not yet produced—a post-Christian frame of erudition. (For just this reason anti-Christian deists valued it, but Jones himself still thought

---

* *Fatal Ring* because the plot turns on a ring that allows King Dushyanta to recognize the heroine Śakuntalā. Kālidāsa's play is based on an episode in the *Mahābhārata*.

within biblical categories.) For the moment, the new field remained stunted by the fact that only in India could Europeans learn Sanskrit. This barrier fell at the beginning of the next century. In 1804, 1805, and 1808, three different Sanskrit grammars appeared in English. The last was by Jones's early guide in Sanskrit, Charles Wilkins, for students in a college started by the East India Company to prepare Britons for its service. Ironically, Wilkins's and Jones's fellow countrymen did little to advance the field these two had largely invented. A younger East India Company employee, the hyperactive Sanskrit scholar Henry T. Colebrooke, on retiring to Britain rallied other ex-Company hands to found, in 1823, the Royal Asiatic Society. But it and Colebrooke were soon eclipsed by continental Europeans, French and German, who came to dominate Indology. Until after 1800, though, Calcutta remained the center of European Indic studies.[14]

There Jones put flabby flesh on Kennicott's speculation that parallels among religions might lead scholars back to a common source of the human race. The first volume of *Asiatick Researches* included a revision of Jones's paper to the Asiatick Society on likenesses between Greek, Roman, and Hindu gods. These similarities extended, he now suggested, to gods of Egypt, China, Persia, Syria, and other lands, including old northern Europe and "some of the southern kingdoms, and even islands, of *America*." Such affinities, he argued, pointed to a common origin of all these religions in a single primitive people. He detailed parallel attributes of gods and made much of superficial verbal congruencies.

> I leave etymologists, who decide every thing, to decide whether the word MENU ['author' of the laws of Manu], or, in the nominative case, MENUS, has any connection with MINOS, the lawgiver, and supposed son of JOVE. The *Cretans*, according to DIODORUS of *Sicily*, used to feign, that most of the great men, who had been deified in return for the benefits which they had conferred on mankind, were born in their island; and hence a doubt may be raised, whether MINOS was really a *Cretan*. The *Indian* legislator was the first, not the seventh, MENU, or SATYAVRATA, whom I suppose to be the SATURN of *Italy*: part of SATURN's character, indeed, was that of a great lawgiver; . . .

This fantastic essay got much attention in Europe. It may also have set Jones to thinking along lines that led to a more consequential comparison.[15]

Comparative speculation was not new to Jones. He knew Adam Ferguson and had read and reread that conjectural historian's *Essay on the History of Civil Society* (1767), which claimed to unify the experiences of all peoples in a common pattern of social evolution. Jones's boss Warren Hastings had argued that collating "the cultures and languages of different nations will uncover analogies and similarities," which "in turn will lead us to the origin of humanity." ('Culture' was coming into use about this time to mean the whole of a people's arts, sciences, religion, mores, and so forth. The coinage suggested a new way of thinking needing a new word or, in this case, redefining an old one. Usage like Hastings's would evolve into the modern anthropological sense of 'culture'; but at this point stress fell on articulated ideas, and English speakers were more likely to say 'civilization.' German speakers imported *Kultur* around 1780 to meet the same need.) Jones himself, wearing his lawyer hat, had written a book comparing Roman, Greek, Hindu, Mosaic, Islamic, and Visigothic laws. He had puzzled, with a Polish correspondent, over why Persian and European languages had a lot of similar words. He gave a paper to the Asiatick Society proposing a link between Hebrew and Devanāgarī (modern Sanskrit) alphabets. When he sat down to master Sanskrit, he almost automatically compared this latest tongue to languages he already knew.[16]

After studying Sanskrit for six months, he made a striking observation; and what he observed changed fundamentally the study of language. On February 2, 1786, the Asiatick Society met to hear its president deliver his third "anniversary discourse." Jones devoted this lecture to a survey of Indian culture—inevitably a superficial one. In bouncing from philosophy to physiognomy, chess to chronology, Jones paused to comment on the ancient sacred language. Here is the paragraph in full:

> The *Sanscrit* language, whatever be its antiquity, is of a wonderful structure; more perfect than the *Greek*, more copious than the *Latin*,* and more exquisitely refined than either, yet bearing to both of them a stronger affinity, both in the roots of verbs and in the forms of grammar, than could possibly have been produced by accident; so strong indeed, that no philologer could examine them all three, without believing them to have sprung from some common source, which, perhaps, no longer exists: there is a similar reason, though not quite so forcible, for supposing that both the *Gothick* and the *Celtick*, though blended with a very different idiom, had the same origin with the *Sanscrit*; and the old *Persian* might be added to the same family, if this were the place for discussing any question concerning the antiquities of *Persia*.

This passage is arresting—and not only for ranking a language of a darker-skinned, colonized people above the revered classical languages of European palefaces. It offered a new view of the relationships among languages, implying a new program for studying them.[17]

Jones's contribution to philology needs specification. He himself took less interest in purely linguistic affinities than in genealogical relations among peoples that he believed these links showed. He wanted to place India on the biblical family tree, where all peoples descended from Noah's three sons, Shem, Ham, and Japhet. Jones neither began nor, unfortunately, ended projects of tracing race through language. (Equating movement of languages with

---

* *Copious* and *perfect* were conventional terms for rating languages, the former referring to vocabulary, the latter to grammatical structure.

migrations of human beings haunted philology for generations, climaxing tragically in the Nazis' 'Aryan race.') Nor was Jones first to notice similarities between Sanskrit and European languages; missionaries and merchants had observed them as early as the 1580s; one or two scholars even teetered on the edge of something like a family, including some of the languages Jones mentioned. Charles Wilkins's friend and mentor, Nathaniel Halhed, dabbled in Sanskrit and published a comparison with Greek; Jones's acquaintance and correspondent Lord Monboddo noted the same connection.[18]

Jones's distinction was to articulate clearly the hypothesis of a common lost ancestral language, to specify a broad range of supposed daughter languages, and to attract widespread attention to the idea. In 1779 he had speculated that an "almost primæval" language ancestral to Persian, Greek, Latin, and the Celtic tongues might explain apparent cognates in all these languages. Now, when he saw how Sanskrit resembled ancient languages of Europe and Persia, he postulated an unknown language ancestral to all. Jones was right. Every tongue he named evolved from a single language that "no longer exists," later named Proto-Indo-European. Of the daughters, Jones omitted most notably the Slavic languages, largely outside his ken and grouped by him with Central Asian tongues. He was also wrong, later, to add Egyptian and Ethiopian to the ancestry, probably influenced by his biblical theory of descent from Noah. Yet this extended family, whose genealogy was to be deduced by comparing languages, supplied what Thomas Trautmann called "the necessary elements for imagining the Indo-European language family and Indo-European speaking peoples." As we have seen, in the sixteenth century scholars already recognized connected groups of languages—and believed, without details, that all European tongues descended from Japhet. But the idea that languages formed families *as a result of branching descent from a common ancestor* gave a new basis for systematic research into languages. Thanks to Jones, the comparative, historical, and genealogical method central to textual philology had found a remarkable new use.[19]

This bombshell lay buried in one paragraph in a rambling lecture first printed on the far side of the world from Europe. (Jones did develop considerably the notion of language families in his "Eighth Anniversary Discourse" in 1791.) Had someone else uttered these words, they might have eluded notice outside Calcutta. But the speaker was Oriental Jones, known all over Europe: "the incomparable Jones," Goethe called him. Especially amid the craze ignited by his *Sacontalá*, nothing Jones said about Sanskrit would go unheard. But, as with the Indology he pioneered, the ears that perked up mostly grew on heads in Germany and France.[20]

Out of the marriage of European philology and Indian texts, then, came two new fields of knowledge: Indology and comparative philology (or comparative grammar). The first offered no new methods; earlier scholarship had forged the techniques there applied. Its novelty lay in opening to European eyes a civilization previously obscure. Indology became the first field in which a self-perpetuating cohort of European scholars—not the odd missionary, merchant, or chronologer—worked systematically to uncover the riches of a non-European civilization across a wide front.* In a narrow, academic projection, Indology foreshadowed area-studies programs in post-1945 universities. In a broad, cultural view, Indology immensely expanded European perspectives on the history and civilizations of the world.

Comparative philology or comparative grammar, in contrast, hardly transformed how Europeans saw the world; but its procedural originality deeply changed the study of language. Jones in effect invented a new *kind* of philology. The concept of language families formed by genealogical descent gave students of language a novel way to classify languages and track their development. This fresh approach retained philology's central dogma of historical comparison. But it radically changed what to compare and the kind of conclusions to be drawn from the comparison. Grammarians no longer analyzed only the histories of individual languages or closely related ones, seen in isolation; they now also began to contrast grammatical and lexical change over time in quite diverse languages believed to be related over vast spans of time and space. By doing so, philologists aspired to retrace the history of the languages and even to reconstruct tongues long vanished from the earth. Within a quarter century of Jones's discourse, Friedrich von Schlegel was using the term *comparative grammar* and sniffing around the regular consonant shifts between Latin and German. Less than a decade after Schlegel's book, Franz Bopp began rigorous comparison of Indo-European languages, starting with verb conjugations. Seventy-five years after Jones introduced the idea of a language family comprehending tongues from India to Ireland, August Schleicher partly reconstructed the mother of them all, Proto-Indo-European. Loose speculation about Adam's language became rigorous science.[21]

MAKING EUROPEAN SENSE OF AMERICAN LANGUAGES

'Rigorous science' only slowly came to describe research into other languages that European imperialism stumbled upon, but studies burgeoned. Missionaries needed to preach the Gospel to (they hoped) Christians-in-waiting; sailors needed to ask directions (if only to the nearest breadfruit); natural historians needed to sate their curiosity. Lists multiplied of newly heard words with their equivalents in a missionary's own language, as did less frequent stabs at grammar. When such stuff reached a critical mass—or when intellectual agenda shaped it—compilation could turn into something more coherent.

---

*I count as European here the Mediterranean littoral, for centuries part of the Roman Empire; the world of the Bible and early Christianity can hardly be left out of 'Europe.'

Research into languages of North American Indians offer an example of this process. The first English-speaking Americans to carry out learned, European-style philological research were the students of these tongues. (Spanish-speaking scholars in the Americas beat them by a couple of centuries.)

The first Europeans to hear native North Americans strove to understand them for practical ends: trade, diplomacy, war, missions. The last produced by far the most recorded linguistic data. Jacques Cartier's first voyage of Canadian exploration (1534) yielded a short Algonquian-French word list. When French missionaries moved into Canada in the 1610s, they quickly wrote down basic dictionaries of several Indian languages. By 1632 a rather large dictionary of Huron and a catechism in that language had made their way into print in the mother country. By the 1640s many word lists, dictionaries, grammars, and similar aids circulated in manuscript among far-flung missionaries. Decade after decade, they struggled to transliterate into Roman characters Ojibwe and Huron sounds never uttered by French tongues, concocting some ingenious solutions.[22]

However smart their grappling with native languages was, French missionaries' efforts remained mostly descriptive, particular, utilitarian. They did argue about Indian eloquence—or its absence—based on European rhetorical ideas. But to classify, to compare, to theorize about the languages themselves lay beyond their horizon and their purposes. The same was true of their seventeenth-century, mostly English-speaking counterparts to the south. These were, if anything, more flatfooted in approach, fewer in number, less accurate. A Swedish Lutheran missionary to the Lenapes in present-day Delaware in the 1640s mistook a traders' pidgin for the Indians' language. He composed a catechism in it.[23]

Sometimes those struggling to learn these unfamiliar tongues *did* puzzle over larger questions. The Jesuit Sébastien Rasles (1657?-1724) was not the only missionary to notice that Indian languages seemed "entirely different from the spirit and form of European languages." And, when taking ship for America, Europeans did not entirely leave behind debates about the language of Adam. A few bookish types asked from which earlier tongue the Indians' supposedly corrupted languages descended. Hebrew was the commonest answer. That Swedish Lutheran believed the Lenapes' pidgin debased Hebrew.[24]

The study of origins changed in the later eighteenth century. The Scottish Enlightenment brewed new theories of social and cultural development, and British North America had close ties to Scotland. As mentioned earlier, Thomas Blackwell's *Enquiry into the Life and Writings of Homer* had proposed in 1735 that human societies evolve through the same basic social orders—so-called stadial theory. Blackwell's fellow Scots Adam Ferguson, William Robertson, Adam Smith, and John Millar defined more clearly the steps of progressively complex social organization that all societies theoretically must pass through.* In Smith's version, hunter-gatherers evolved into nomadic herders, then herders into farmers, on their way to the highest phase, commerce—as seen in, well, Glasgow and Edinburgh. One might, these theorists averred, trace conjecturally the gradual advance of the human mind through such stages. Development of languages provided a key to such analysis. Indeed, throughout late-Enlightenment Europe, the origin of language became a hot topic, cast in just such broad terms. The decisive publications of Ferguson, Robertson, Smith, and Millar roughly coincided in time with the fight of the British mainland colonies south of Quebec for independence. Their books appeared, that is, when these Americans started to think of themselves as a distinct people. Significantly, Robertson worked out his version of stadial theory in a conjectural history of Native Americans.[25]

For white Americans in this time of ferment, the status of American Indians entwined with sensitive issues of nationality, manliness, and self-esteem. Thomas Jefferson sought to refute the Comte de Buffon's libel that animals, including human ones, degenerated in the New World: that the Indians, in particular, were cowardly, stupid, and undersexed. Like others, Jefferson believed that studies of Indian language could probe the origins and potentially the character of these original Americans.[26]

A key instrument for such comparison was the word list. A list giving equivalents in one language for words in another is a blindingly obvious device for anyone trying to learn a new language, like those French missionaries in Canada. The tool seems to have been formalized by Gottfried Wilhelm Leibniz shortly after 1700. Leibniz decided to collect and compare lists of basic words for common things, in all dialects of German, ancient and modern. He planned thus to track the migrations of Germanic peoples and evolution of their language. Then he got the idea of using the same instrument to trace the diffusion of European languages from the descendants of Japhet. With greater success William Jones used word lists to compare Sanskrit with other tongues. For Thomas Jefferson, word lists supplied a system for studying the interrelationships and evolution of Amerindian languages. His vocabulary collecting dovetailed with a late-Enlightenment flurry of surveys of languages. Best known is a comprehensive comparison of vocabularies that Peter Simon Pallas, a German naturalist, undertook in 1787 for Catherine the Great. Jefferson anticipated Pallas's idea in *Notes on the State of Virginia* (1781). It is no accident that projects like these engaged Russians and Americans. Both countries were expanding into vast hinterlands populated by speakers of many tongues and cultures. (Another German scholar exploring Siberia in Catherine's service coined the word *ethnography*.) Etymology, traditionally the study of the true

---

* Scots did not invent the idea of different peoples passing through similar cultural stages—it is present, for example, in writings about American Indians by the sixteenth-century Spanish Jesuit José de Acosta—but they developed it in unprecedented clarity, detail, and universality.

meanings of words, became in these undertakings the study of words changing over time.[27]

Like William Jones, Jefferson inquired into the origin of Indians' languages to learn where their speakers came from. Comparing word lists from different tribes would show linguistic relationships; these, in turn, were supposed eventually to reveal genealogy and migration. "A knowledge of their several languages would be," he wrote, "the most certain evidence of their derivation which could be produced." In June 1791 Jefferson squatted with another future president, James Madison, in a tiny Unquachog village on Long Island to make a word list. Only three "old women" remained, Jefferson reported, "who can speak its language." (The language, Quiripi, is long extinct.) The next year, as secretary of state, he ordered a form printed with some 280 English words next to blank spaces for Indian equivalents, to send to missionaries, soldiers, traders, Indian agents, explorers. (Convinced that no species can go extinct, Jefferson included the word *mammoth*. That space always turned up empty.) Jefferson kept changing his mind about the Indians' origin: maybe Asia; maybe autochthonous; maybe some even came from Wales like his own ancestors. The "infinite" number of "radically different" Indian tongues convinced him, at any rate, that the natives' presence on the continent was "of the most remote antiquity." "The time necessary for the generation of so many languages must be immense." His strategy of tracing linguistic affinities by comparing words in standardized lists long outlived Jefferson. The vocabularies he solicited landed at the American Philosophical Society in Philadelphia, raw material for later investigators. Such American work never went on in isolation. In 1786 George Washington, at Lafayette's request, got federal agents to supply word lists for the vocabulary Pallas was compiling for Empress Catherine.[28]

In 1797 the Philadelphia physician Benjamin Smith Barton compared word lists from a number of Indian tribes. He concluded that both North and South American languages "may, with confidence, be referred to one great stock, which I call the language of the Lenni-Lennàpe, or Delawares." (They of the pidgin that flummoxed the Swedish missionary.) Comparison with Asian languages then revealed that "the nations of America and those of Asia have a common origin"—a conclusion, Barton said, affirmed by the tribes' oral traditions and geographic distribution. A population transfer probably occurred when a land bridge connected North America to Asia. (William Robertson had said much the same twenty years earlier.) This last assertion might have come from a twentieth-century anthropologist; at other times, Barton sounds like Scottish conjectural historians. In fact, he stood betwixt and between: trying to find empirical ground—sparse ground, as knowledgeable contemporaries saw it—on which to build speculation about language typical of Enlightenment discourse. In this respect, a work like Barton's marked a shift in Americanist philology: toward a comparative study of languages *both* empirically grounded *and* theoretically reflective, like the revolution set in motion by

William Jones. More proficient scholars than Barton were needed to carry the effort forward.[29]

CLASSICAL RUINS AND 'ARCHAEOLOGY'

Like the study of languages, the search for physical vestiges of classical antiquity started to change after 1750. The mutation is harder to specify than in the case of comparative philology. The vigorous curiosity of traditional antiquarians remained unabated. But among more of them the appetite for artifacts grew more specialized, the study of finds more exact. No word then existed to unambiguously label detailed, precise study of ancient sites. Until after 1800, 'archaeology' meant any research into the past or even the past itself. But the word's meaning did narrow in the nineteenth century, for a reason. And the study that later monopolized 'archaeology'—to replace the too-capacious 'antiquarianism'—began to define itself in the late eighteenth century.[30]

Scholarly innovation came from an unexpected quarter, from "some Gentlemen who had travelled in Italy," as one of their number described them. These lovers of moldering ruins—and of well-liquored, ribald romps—wished to promote "*at home*, a Taste for those objects which had contributed so much to their entertainment *abroad*." They meant the ruins. To this end in 1732 the gentlemen founded the Society of Dilettanti.* Weakening of the Ottoman Empire and increased British presence in the Mediterranean—not least of the Royal Navy—now made accessible ruins beyond the traditional Italy of the grand tour. Richly furnished with peers as well as rakes (overlapping sets), the Dilettanti did not suffer fiscal cramping; and the society in the latter half of the century published magnificently illustrated archaeological folios. These made available for the first time accurate knowledge of the classical ruins of Athens and southwestern Asia Minor. Thus, to date classical archaeology in the English-speaking world from 1732 does not stretch credibility intolerably. But the question is complex.[31]

Robert Wood, author of *Original Genius and Writings of Homer*, took the first well-defined step toward new precision in studying classical ruins. Wood's longing to see ancient sites ranged far beyond Homer's supposed turf. He also had a knack for cultivating rich friends. Thus equipped, he journeyed in the eastern Mediterranean in the early 1740s, then again a decade later. Travelers before him had published sketches of ancient monuments or carted off pieces of them to adorn collections. But Wood's careful observations of Roman-era buildings, his exact measurements, and his fine draftsmanship resulted in two impressive folios, *Ruins of Palmyra* (1753) and *Ruins of Balbec*

---

* *Dilettante* did not have the connotation of superficiality and frivolity it now carries. Italians used it to mean simply an amateur of the arts. As yet unknown in English, the word underlined the Italian cachet of the Dilettanti. Kelly 2009, 11–12.

(1757). (Palmyra was an oasis city in Syria, on the caravan route to Mesopotamia. Baalbek—ancient Heliopolis—in present-day Lebanon was a religious center.) The Dilettanti elected Wood a member in 1763. His books impressed readers throughout Europe and quickly appeared in French. Wood's meticulously measured, integrated surveys of entire ancient sites in Palmyra and Baalbek set a model.[32]

Two fellow aficionados of decayed Mediterranean cities, James Stuart and Nicholas Revett, clarify both the advent of something *like* 'classical archaeology' and why it was not. In 1751 Stuart (newly elected Dilettante) and Revett traveled from temporary residence in Italy to Athens, then a nasty, perilous town for Englishmen. They went in the spirit of the Dilettanti—more particularly the spirit of Wood, whose design to study Palmyra and Baalbek helped to propel them. They planned to survey the major monuments of ancient Athens. Two and a half years of careful labor led, slowly, to four volumes of *Antiquities of Athens* (1762–1816, finished by other hands). Their strict measurements—reminiscent of William Stukeley (surveyor of Stonehenge) as well as of Wood—look now like a contribution to 'classical archaeology.' Their more slapdash French rival Julien-David Le Roy did think of his work as historical recovery when he studied Athenian 'ruins' (as the title of his competing book called them). Stuart and Revett called the same piles "antiquities," providing timelessly "the most perfect Models of what is excellent in Sculpture and Architecture." The Englishmen meant their book to inform architectural taste, not historical understanding. 'Athenian Stuart' became a well-known architect, until his career foundered on the Dilettanti's signature vice, booze. And the hugely influential *Antiquities of Athens* inspired not a wave of excavations but the Greek Revival in building.[33]

Before leaving Italy for Athens, Stuart and Revett had visited a site that mattered far more in the eventual renovation of antiquarianism into archaeology. Local residents on the Gulf of Naples had always realized that ancient ruins lay underground. Statues kept turning up in their wells. In the eighteenth century these artifacts attracted attention from the Spanish Bourbons who ruled the Kingdom of Naples. Under their aegis in 1738 an engineer in the Spanish artillery began to excavate Herculaneum, buried by the volcano Vesuvius in 79 CE. Work eventually extended to other victims of that eruption, Pompeii and Stabiae: like Herculaneum, complete Roman towns preserved by lava and ash. Royal efforts to shoo foreigners away from this private Bourbon treasure could not keep out every curious visitor—nor squelch illustrated publications based on clandestine sketches. Finally, beginning in 1757, nine authorized volumes of *Le Antichità di Ercolano Esposte* (*The Antiquities of Herculaneum Displayed*) depicted dramatic discoveries in engravings that amazed Europe. (Gossip about some *undepicted* finds amazed and troubled. Everyday objects shaped as phalluses—amulets, oil lamps, and wind chimes—routinely turned up. What did these say about renowned Roman virtue?) At first the burrowers into the ancient cities mined them higgledy-piggledy for art objects to embellish the

Naples palace of the Bourbons. The more exacting antiquarians of Britain and France complained that the Neapolitans ripped artifacts out of context, then destroyed the context in their haste to find more loot. In 1750 Karl Jakob Weber, a Swiss military engineer in Bourbon service, was appointed to supervise the excavation. He tried to introduce regularity. This proved an uphill struggle since chain gangs of captured Barbary pirates did the digging. But Weber kept careful journals and drew up exact building plans, including detailed lists of objects found and marks showing where found. After he died in 1764, his successor followed his methods—but not his wish to publish the discoveries. More even than Robert Wood, Weber could have passed for an archaeologist, if the discipline had been there for him to inhabit.[34]

THE RHETORICAL REVIVAL

Just as innovatory, oddly, was a reworking of old classical rhetoric, in which Scots took the lead. Closely allied with philology during antiquity and the Italian Renaissance, classical rhetoric had fallen into neglect thereafter, especially in Protestant lands and above all in Britain, in favor of Petrus Ramus's dialectic. French rhetoricians of the later seventeenth century turned back to ancient masters of rhetoric, applying classical canons to their own vernacular prose, poetry, and preaching.[35] This neoclassical rhetoric soon seeped into England; but it thrived especially, a little later, in Scotland, a country that flowered intellectually in the eighteenth century.

Both flowering and rhetoric stemmed in great part from one political event: in 1707 the Parliaments of England and Scotland voted to merge the two kingdoms into a new Kingdom of Great Britain. The Acts of Union, opening English financial centers and English overseas ventures to Scots, sparked economic growth in the Scottish Lowlands. Sleepy Glasgow leap-frogged into a booming port by capturing the Virginia tobacco trade; the East India Company kept its headquarters in London, but Scots lopsidedly staffed its ranks and ruled noncompany trade with India. A southward trickle of ambitious Scots had already begun in 1603 when James VI of Scotland ascended the English throne as James I; the dribble swelled into a flood after 1707. The Lowland Scots language, though closely related to English, baffled hearers south of the border.* And the Acts of Union made English official in Scotland. All these changes spawned demand among aspiring Scots to learn 'correct' (i.e., London) English, while new prosperity bolstered the universities where the demand might sate itself.[36]

---

* Lowland Scots descends from the version of Old English spoken in what became northern England, with Scandinavian influence from the Danish conquest of that area. During the later Middle Ages, the language gradually pushed Gaelic (the original Scottish language) out of the Lowlands, leaving Gaelic the tongue only of the highlands and islands.

So it came to pass that Scottish university teachers revised the classical rhetoric of Cicero and Quintilian—to the end of polishing English rather than Latin, in a project of cultural assimilation. Already in 1720 the University of St. Andrews pondered a 'chair of eloquence.' Medicine seemed more urgent to the faculty at the time, but three decades later St. Andrews added rhetoric to the duties of the professor of logic and metaphysics. By then, rhetoric had become as near to a fad as Scottish academia could work up. John Stevenson, professor of logic and metaphysics at Edinburgh from 1730–77, added rhetoric to his remit. Adam Smith gave public lectures on the subject in Edinburgh between 1748 and 1751; when in the latter year he moved to Glasgow, he continued to teach it. In 1760 Hugh Blair (having copped Smith's lecture notes) took up at Edinburgh a professorship specifically in rhetoric; two years later, his chair became a regius professorship (endowed by the Crown) of rhetoric and *belles lettres* ('literature,' we would now say, meaning writing with a consciously artistic aim). Other Scots—Lord Kames in his *Elements of Criticism* (1762); George Campbell in *The Philosophy of Rhetoric* (1776)—brought classical rhetoric up to date philosophically by welding it to the new psychology of their fellow Scot, David Hume; but this shift, crucial for theory of rhetoric, had little relevance to the issues at stake here. When in 1783 Blair finally printed his *Lectures on Rhetoric and Belles Lettres*, the publisher paid him the gargantuan sum of £1500 (something like two or three million dollars in today's earnings)—and rightly: the book was a winner.[37]

Rhetoric had returned in a big way—not only in Scotland but also among other English speakers on the margins of the metropole. Although Oxford and Cambridge felt no need to teach rhetoric, Scottish patterns shaped American higher education from the later eighteenth century into the middle of the nineteenth. Scottish-style rhetorical teaching and Scottish textbooks became standard in the United States, as they did in English academies for the children of Protestant Dissenters from the established Anglican Church. Tellingly, Trinity College Dublin—from its founding in 1592 an Oxbridge for Irish Protestants—deviated from its English models in the eighteenth century in paying serious attention to rhetoric, including the new Scottish variety. Most Trinity boys may have come from reasonably comfortable Anglican families, but like their counterparts in Edinburgh and Glasgow they stood outside the metropolitan elite peering in.[38]

The Scottish rhetorical tradition commonly yoked rhetoric to *belles lettres*, as in Blair's title, and to criticism, as in Kames's. What did these links signify? To answer, it helps to imagine oneself in the position of a young native speaker of Lowland Scots, with its distinctive vocabulary, idioms, and accent. (A verse by Robert Burns: "And there's a hand, my trusty fiere! / And gie's a hand o' thine! / And we'll tak a right guid-willie waught, / For auld lang syne."*) The

---

* *Fiere*: 'friend or partner.' *Guid-willie waught*: 'friendly (good-will-y) drink.' *Auld lang syne*: 'old times' sake' ('old long since').

Scottish boy was striving to fit himself for success in a world where making it required fluency in the English spoken by elite Londoners. First, the youngster needed to learn the rhetorical *principles* governing sophisticated use of the language of the metropolis. But knowing theory did not suffice. The next step needed was immersion in examples of refined use of the language, with a knowledgeable guide to show how to put principles into practice. Scottish rhetoricians were adapting the method by which grammar schools had taught Latin since at least the early sixteenth century: practicing grammatical rules by translating classical authors. The pioneer Stevenson read ancient rhetoricians to his students and illustrated their principles with examples from Addison, Pope, Dryden, and other modern authors.[39]

Consider Blair's more elaborated version of this approach. He began by discussing big, general categories: taste, sublimity, beauty; then launched into the (speculative) historical evolution of language and its structure; finally reached the structure of English, paying considerable attention to sentence construction. Then Blair explained at length figures of speech and their effect. This segued into a discussion of style and how to form a proper one. (By now the student was listening to the nineteenth lecture.) Blair then devoted four lectures to analyzing critically Joseph Addison's style—meaning, really, his syntax—in four successive issues of *The Spectator* (the *ne plus ultra* of 'taste' at the time). He did the same to a selection from Jonathan Swift in a fifth lecture. The remaining twenty-three lectures examined rhetorical genres: several types of public speaking; historical writing; philosophic prose; types of poetry; drama; and so forth—again with critical discussion of specific texts. Kames's *Elements of Criticism* leaned more toward theory but nonetheless larded the text with examples drawn from well-known writers.[40]

'Criticism'—a term derived from the name for a textual philologist (*criticus* in Latin)—here took on intensely utilitarian meaning. If the young teenagers listening to Blair's Edinburgh lectures learned to dissect Addison's style, they could grasp it well enough to craft for themselves a pastiche of it. Looking at *belles lettres* with the eye of a 'critic' bought a ticket to social advancement. It is no wonder that Blair's book became a widely used manual in cultural provinces of England on both sides of the Atlantic (including Protestant Dissenting academies in England). No wonder, too, that it made no headway at Oxford and Cambridge, whose mostly elite students already knew how to speak and write 'proper' English—that of their own class.[41]

Did Scottish rhetorical teaching inaugurate the academic subject called English literature? No—unless the *Antiquities of Athens* started classical archaeology. True, rhetoricians like Blair taught students to look 'critically' at 'literature.' But they did so with the ancient rhetorical aim of polishing the boys' style, making them more effective writers and speakers. Not until well into the next century would students begin to pore over English and American poetry, plays, and novels 'for their own sake.' As late as 1869 the radical Scottish intellectual Alexander Bain, then professor of logic at Aberdeen, gave as the only legitimate reason for teaching English literature "to extract from it everything that is of value for improving the diction of the pupils." Scottish rhetoricians and their American imitators did regard literature as a helpful, if decidedly ancillary, thing to study. In that limited sense, they 'introduced literature' to the curriculum.[42]

Outside educational institutions, however, scholarship on imaginative literature flourished. More or less scholarly editions of 'English classics' like Milton and Chaucer multiplied in the second half of the century. William Warburton, besides his writing as combatant in the deist wars, published in 1747 an eight-volume Shakespeare. Hugh Blair also edited Shakespeare (1753) and oversaw a collection of British poetry in forty-four volumes (1772). Few people today recall Warburton's or Blair's Shakespeare. But Samuel Johnson's (1765) is renowned; it took a more complex, balanced approach to resolving problems of textual philology than any earlier edition of the Bard. Johnson's *Lives of the Most Eminent English Poets; with Critical Observations on Their Works* (1779–81)—though conceived merely as prefaces to a London edition of fifty-two poets meant to undercut a competing Scottish project—adopted a sweeping and acute approach to literary history and criticism also not seen before. Editing proliferated after 1750. Some was done sloppily for a quick pound. The best of it elevated editing to a new scholarly level. Edward Capell's 1768 Shakespeare modeled unprecedented meticulousness. Johnson's *Lives of the Poets* represented a newly prominent genre of books *about* poetry or drama. Several authors wrote histories of the English theater. Bishop Thomas Percy's *Essay on the Origin of the English Stage* (1765) even tried to trace the evolution of modern drama from more primitive forms of public performance. (Percy remains best known for collecting folk ballads.) The poet Thomas Warton produced a three-volume *History of English Poetry, from the Close of the Eleventh to the Commencement of the Eighteenth Century* (1774–81). Densely written, more compilation than narrative, given to meanders, readers found it hard going. But it won admiration in its day and foreshadowed a literary history that smelled of the scholar's midnight oil.[43]

Putting Hugh Blair's rhetoric alongside Edward Capell's Shakespeare and Thomas Warton's literary history, one sees a newly prominent object of philological scrutiny: English literature. Its study did not comprise a coherent 'field,' as biblical or Anglo-Saxon scholarship did. Teachers of rhetoric used literature to drum into students principles of tasteful composition. Editors of Shakespeare used tried-and-true methods of textual philology to produce reliable, readable plays. Historians of the stage or of poetry recovered for readers a literary tradition. These scholars were not in the same business, even if they used similar raw materials. By the late eighteenth century, many more or less learned writers in the English-speaking world seriously studied vernacular literary texts. It cannot plausibly be said that they studied the same 'field,' still less that a new branch of philology had emerged.

A Revolution in History

In contrast, Edward Gibbon's *Decline and Fall of the Roman Empire* (1776–88), by adapting philology to new uses, precociously defined what would become—after a century of confusion—the modern discipline of history.[44] By 'historian' we mean nowadays someone who writes nonfiction about the past, based on factual evidence. The term in Gibbon's time had much wider range. Then, *history* could refer to a novel or to sheer speculation about bygone ages. Lacking any other label, for now the word will carry here its narrower present definition, because precisely such nonfictional writing about the past is in question.

Understanding Gibbon's innovation requires first recalling an eighteenth-century conflict over how to write about the past: 'philosophic history' versus what might be called 'philological antiquarianism' (for lack of a better label). Philological antiquarianism dwelled in the persons of Scaliger and Casaubon, Camden and Mabillon, Bentley and Hickes. Such scholars wrote painstaking, systematic treatises reconstructing particular topics rather than sweeping, connected narratives; they might freeze-frame a moment in the past rather than explain change over time; they collected and emended old charters, chronicles, and the like, in the spirit of the Maurists. Philological antiquarianism was early modern erudition surviving into the age of Enlightenment. Philosophic history was a suave, sophisticated granddaughter of the universal histories of the early modern period. It traced large patterns of human progress (often caring little about the accuracy of specific details) and spelled out their causes. It approached its subject from a cosmopolitan, tolerant stance. It wished to tell its tales with literary elegance. In all this, it aimed to offer compelling lessons to the present. In this view, proper history amounted to 'philosophy teaching by example.' Philosophic history was a facet of Enlightenment. Typical, if especially celebrated, exemplars included Voltaire's *Essai sur les moeurs et l'esprit des nations* (*Essay on the Customs and Spirit of Nations*, 1756), which started with ancient Chinese and Chaldeans and brought the reader up to the glories of the age of Louis XIV, and Adam Ferguson's *Essay on the History of Civil Society* (1767), which more ambitiously traced the evolution of "the species itself from rudeness to civilization," as its author put it. Much of the genre fell under what Dugald Stewart later named conjectural history (social or cultural evolution plausibly imagined rather than materially evidenced). It aspired less to erudition about the past than to making the past speak to present concerns—for different styles of history aimed at different goals. Some philosophic history, such as Voltaire's *Essai sur les moeurs*, hid genuine erudition—lest learning dull its polished pages, weigh down its fast-flitting wit.[45]

Not every philosophic historian bypassed erudition or concealed it. In his own day, David Hume enjoyed a much bigger reputation as historian than philosopher. His six-volume *History of England* (1754–62) made him rich. While not deeply researched by antiquarian norms, the work rested on substantial reading in sometimes arcane sources; and Hume cited these in reference notes as well as in episodic discussions of special subjects interlarded in the narrative. The three volumes of William Robertson's 1769 *History of the Reign of Charles V* (the sixteenth-century emperor) sat on an even solider documentary basis. Robertson partly exposed its learned foundations in abundant, terse footnotes citing sources, interspersed with less frequent, longer notes considering matters supplementary to the main narrative. He included a lengthy appendix giving "Proofs and Illustrations" keyed to specific pages of a yet longer preliminary essay on "the Progress of Society in Europe" from the fall of Rome to the start of his story proper. This appendix, like Hume's digressions, resembled the clunky dissertations characteristic of antiquarian learning and of ecclesiastical history. Neither writer seamlessly integrated erudition and narrative.* Yet on these two Scotsmen dawned the idea that an entertaining and edifying narrative needed documentary support to earn plausibility.[46]

In general, however, philosophic historians scorned the 'pedantic' labors of deeply learned philological scholars like Mabillon and Bentley—or at best thought their toils irrelevant to writing history. Engineers of erudition like these two focused not on instructive narrative but on recovering or restoring relics of a lost past. They made bricks with which to rebuild that past rather than erecting the whole reenvisioned structure itself. That archetype of Enlightenment, Jean D'Alembert, in his *Discours préliminaire à l'Encyclopédie* (*Preliminary Discourse to the Encyclopedia*, 1751), sneered—as Gibbon later recalled—that the "sole merit" of these "*Erudits*" lay in "the exercise of memory"—an inferior power now "superseded by the nobler faculties of the imagination and the judgement."[47]

At this Gibbon balked. He admired the broad views, the literary skill of philosophic historians. Like them, he aspired to write wide-ranging history ripe with meaning for the present. He endorsed the widening of historical vision to take in private life as well as politics. For models of narrative, he turned to the remotest source of philosophic history, classical historians, notably Tacitus. But Gibbon stood apart from the general run of philosophic historians in his esteem for hard-core philological scholarship, as well as for the thorough documentation long typical of ecclesiastical history. "Even as a child," Joseph Levine reported, "he had been fascinated by textual and chronological problems, and as a young man he dared to quarrel with the experts about dating and emending texts." His first publication, *Essai sur l'étude de la littérature* (1762), defended antiquarian erudition against Enlightened scoffers such as

---

* Robertson did stand out in writing the history of a modern country not his own—a detachment from national identity that would become commoner among historians in the next century. Both Hume and Robertson displayed, too, the sentimentalism of eighteenth-century literary culture. But this sensibility was a matter of genre rather than method, and method concerns us here.

Diderot. Gibbon took Bentley as a hero, not a butt of ridicule. What French philosophes scorned as fact grubbing, Gibbon admired as deep scholarship. He studied the Maurist scholars Mabillon and Montfaucon and the innovative numismatics of their German contemporary Ezechiel Spanheim. Gibbon believed that only the manifold techniques of philological antiquarianism, applied with hard labor of learning, could rediscover the lifeways and thoughtways of the faraway past: the philosophically minded narrator should explain the transition from one state of society to the next, but he could do so only if he understood in depth the conditions on either side of the changeover. A Voltaire who disdained philology was apt to write fiction when he meant to write history. And for Gibbon truth was sine qua non. History depended utterly on correctly attested facts. One might think of him as inheriting and putting to new use Mabillon's and Le Clerc's insistence on strict scrutiny of evidence.[48]

And so the *Decline and Fall* brought to stylish adulthood this new kind of history, excelling even Robertson. Gibbon paraded in the philosophic historian's shirt—worn over the antiquarian's undershirt. *Decline and Fall* emulated the chronologically sequential, stylistically refined narrative of the philosophic historians, alert to historical change and its causes. But Gibbon built that narrative on sequentially and causally incurious, but painstaking and culturally inclusive philological antiquarianism. He himself was no philologist. (A mostly admiring Göttingen reviewer called his source criticism superficial.) Rather than delve into manuscripts, he used materials collected by others, notably the great Italian antiquarian-historian-philologist Ludovico Antonio Muratori (1672–1750). To understand events, he depended on deeper scholars more than on the printed ancient sources that he read assiduously. But Gibbon combined the moral vision and narrative force of philosophical history with philology's insistence on critically certified documentary evidence, à la Mabillon—even though the certification came to Gibbon secondhand, from reliable scholars. He also melded the formerly distinct traditions of secular political history and document-heavy ecclesiastical history. His reference notes did not merely offer clipped citations of books but *discussed* sources—and digressed, often amusingly, into much else. John Burrow described Gibbon's footnotes as "a commentary [note the philological genre] in which he gives rein to a relaxed, garrulous intimacy which acts in counterpoint with the tautly controlled formality of the text." In the first volume in 1776 Gibbon tucked away the notes at the back of the book. An admiring David Hume advised him to move them to the bottom of each page, so readers could follow the basis of the argument as it moved along; and Gibbon did. In him, as Arnaldo Momigliano put it, "Philosophic history ceased to be approximate and arbitrary and was subjected to the traditional rules of historical criticism" evolved by philological antiquarians. A lot of philosophic historians judged philological criticism a fossil. Thanks largely to Gibbon, it entered the genome of later history writing.[49]

Without becoming an antiquarian himself, Gibbon made antiquarian methods of scholarship a new substratum of historical narrative, a new test of its validity. His Scottish predecessor William Robertson lauded him as inaugurating a new kind of history. Robertson immediately adopted Gibbon's footnote technique for his *History of America* (1777) as well as giving therein, at Gibbon's suggestion, a full account of his Spanish sources. With *The Decline and Fall of the Roman Empire*, the modern era opened of scholarly history writing based on thick documentation. Birth must not be confused with maturity. Other scholars, more laborious than Gibbon, would nurture the infant, fend off threats to it. But, admired or not, Gibbon loomed over historians writing in English during the next several decades as they struggled to define the proper practice of their vocation.[50]

A REVOLUTION IN BIBLICAL PHILOLOGY

During Gibbon's lifetime, a similar revolution shook biblical philology, though it took place mostly out of eyeshot of English-speaking scholars. Already before 1700, daring students of the Old Testament, like Richard Simon and Jean Le Clerc, had challenged the traditionally accepted authorship of its books. But ideas about *how* its authors—whoever they were—put the Bible together remained spotty and vague. Simon had conjectured that Israelite secretaries deposited records of events in public archives first set up by Moses. Then in 1753 appeared a work turning speculation into hypothesis by sustained analysis of the text: *Conjectures sur les mémoires originauz [sic] dont il paroit que Moyse s'est servi pour composer le livre de la Génèse* (*Conjectures on the Original Sources That Moses Apparently Used to Compose the Book of Genesis*). The book was published anonymously, allegedly in Brussels, where the French government's writ did not run. The cautious author was Jean Astruc, professor of medicine at Paris, reputed for a seminal treatise on sexually transmitted diseases. He noted that Genesis sometimes calls God Elohim and sometimes Yahweh. Astruc arranged in two columns all the text that use the one name or the other. He believed that he had thus reassembled two different source documents—or the pieces of them—that Moses had stitched together to construct the history recorded in Genesis. Like most good philologists, Astruc did not minimize the problems his theory faced. Yet without oversimplifying he had hit on a key idea: different textual strands in the Old Testament might be separated out by their distinctive language.[51]

Astruc did not tend his young shoot; rather, it blossomed in Germany. The soil there had been prepared by British deists' attacks on biblical revelation. Germans translated some of their works, starting with Matthew Tindal's *Christianity as Old as the Creation* in 1741. The deists profoundly unsettled two scholars in particular: Johann Salomo Semler and Johann David Michaelis. The Göttingen professor Michaelis has popped up more than once—introducing into Germany Wood's *Original Genius and Writings of Homer*, criticizing Kennicott's Old Testament, revising Lowth's *Praelectiones de sacra poesi Hebraeorum*. Semler likewise held a professorship, at Halle, instancing the growing role of universities as centers of erudition in Germany. (In contrast, neither Wood, Kennicott, nor Lowth made university careers.) Reading British deists pushed Michaelis and Semler to look at the Bible with disillusioned eyes, privileging reason over revelation. Philology did not dictate this outcome; rather, the Enlightenment rationalism that the two shared with deists guided their use of philological methods. But the deist critique was destructive, not affirmative. It convinced Michaelis and Semler to take the Bible as a product of human history but gave little idea how.[52]

In their unsettlement they appear to have turned specifically to Richard Simon and, under his inspiration, tried to craft a historical reconstruction of the Bible's meanings. Like Simon they retained Christian faith while reanalyzing its biblical basis. (Undermining its basis, detractors insisted—depending, again, on nonphilological premises such as theories of biblical inspiration.) In Michaelis's case, personal contact with English biblical scholars in the 1740s—then the most sophisticated in Europe—also mattered. Indeed, an English reviewer in 1769 summarized well the point from which Michaelis and Semler started:

> [I]n order to understand the Scriptures to any useful purpose, it is not barely sufficient to know the mere sense of the words and phrases of the original, but . . . it is likewise necessary to be acquainted with the circumstances of the world at the time of our Saviour's coming; to have a knowledge of the government, sanhedrim, sects, customs, traditions, and opinions of the Jews; a knowledge of ancient history, chronology, geography, and the general system of pagan mythology, which is not to be acquired by turning over a Lexicon; . . .

In principle, Erasmus would have said the same; but he knew far less of such matters as "sects, customs, traditions, and opinions of the Jews" or ancient chronology. By Kennicott's time, philologists approached the Bible not only with vastly richer historical contexts but also with an appreciation of the cultural gap estranging ancient Israel or Roman Judea from the European present. Michaelis and Semler viewed the Old Testament text as recording divine teaching (and other things) but also as reflecting the premodern worldviews of its writers. These two and subsequent German philologists immensely strengthened and radicalized treatment of the Bible as a historical document.[53]

The relation of Michaelis and Semler to Jewish scholarship was alternately dismissive and uncomprehending. On one hand, they could not ignore Jewish learning when trying to understand Hebrew scriptures. Semler, for example, published in 1771 a German translation of Eliyahu Levita's controversial essay in Hebrew philology, *Masoret ha-Masoret* (1538). On the other hand, they did their best to make rabbinic erudition immaterial in Old Testament studies. Semler translated Levita's book precisely because it argued that the vowel points in the received Masoretic Text were a post-Talmudic invention, unknown in antiquity. If so (and Levita was right), Christians gained flexibility to reinterpret the Hebrew text while (in Semler's eyes, not Levita's) rabbinic traditions lost authority. Semler dedicated his translation to the Jewish Enlightenment writer Moses Mendelssohn. Michaelis likewise sent Mendelssohn the first volume of his own work on Mosaic law, assuring him that nothing in it attacked Jews. Both Semler and Michaelis assumed that Enlightened Jews shared their contempt for the "unfathomable opinions spread by the common horde of Jewish scholars," as Semler referred to rabbinic writings. (Mendelssohn kept tactful silence. He and other Enlightened Jews took the "unfathomable opinions" of medieval rabbinic interpretation as starting point for biblical philology, not obstacle to it.) Moreover, because the Hebrews of Moses's day lived in so different a society and culture than rabbis of the early Christian era, Michaelis argued, Talmudic learning barely mattered for Old Testament philology. These "oral traditions of somewhat ignorant rabbis," as Michaelis called the two Talmuds, might inform us about Jewish law in the times of the ignorant rabbis, but not about Mosaic law. Predictably, Michaelis opposed giving Jews civil rights, as other Germans were starting to advocate; and he deployed the new concept of biological race, just then being articulated by his Göttingen colleague J. F. Blumenbach, to denigrate Jews. Timeworn anti-Judaism did not sate Michaelis. He was that modern devil, an anti-Semite.[54]

Even while sidelining Jewish textual scholarship, Michaelis and Semler themselves remained basically textual philologists who strove to understand the Old Testament by placing it in specific historical milieux of the ancient world. They tried to reconstruct Hebrew society and its institutions, using information gleaned from geography, philological analysis, classical and (even) rabbinic writers, Arabic and Syriac texts, studies of ancient Egypt, and modern travelers in the Middle East. The method in detail was not new. (William Lowth, Robert's father, had used modern Middle Eastern customs—like wearing nose jewels—to explicate Old Testament passages.) The thoroughness *was* new, in analyzing the Bible as *essentially* a historical document to be interpreted by secular means.[55]

Michaelis became celebrated for such efforts, odd and even offensive though some of them now seem. Recall the impression that Wood's *Original Genius of Homer* made on him. His ancient Hebrews likewise lived in the childhood of humanity and likewise saw the world through the veil of myth. Modern Arabs existed in a similar splendidly primitive state. Michaelis set the agenda for a famous Danish expedition in 1761–67 to Yemen, from which only Carsten Niebuhr returned alive. It may strike a reader as bizarre that present-day Arabs could cast light on ancient Hebrews. But Michaelis thought Arabic nomads an unchanging people, stuck at the same rude stage of social development as nomadic ancient Israelites. Even modern Arabic words for plants could help to identify vegetation known only by name in the Bible, given the very close relationship of Hebrew and Arabic and the very little that Arabic must have changed, by Michaelis's axioms, since Moses's day. By such means he sought to recover, as Rudolf Smend put it, the "relationships of life in the biblical world and time" in order to lay open the real meaning of the Bible—as he imagined it. Michaelis's idea of a distinct, preexilic, 'classical' Hebrew civilization owed much to contemporary efforts by classical philologists, such as his Göttingen colleague C. G. Heyne (see below), to grasp ancient Greek culture as a whole. Michaelis's "biblical world and time" lay light-years away from classical Greece or even from the coeval but more 'advanced' ancient Egypt. The six volumes of his *Mosaisches Recht* (*Mosaic Law*, 1770–75) made that clear. So did his Old Testament translation, conditioned not only by Kennicott-like standards of textual emendation but also by ethnological and archaeological data.[56]

When Michaelis applied similar historical-critical method to the New Testament, he invented a long-lived hypothesis: that the authors of the Gospels drew on earlier, written proto-Gospels, now lost. Ironically, in his 1787 introduction to the Old Testament, Michaelis fought Astruc's thesis of multiple, pre-Mosaic sources for Genesis, arguing that Moses wrote almost all of the Pentateuch—and Job, to boot. But in his 1788 *Einleitung in die göttlichen Schriften des Neuen Bundes* (*Introduction to the Holy Scriptures of the New Covenant*), Michaelis put forward an Astruc-like theory to explain the strong similarities among the Gospels of Matthew, Mark, and Luke. He contended that their writers had all drawn on "other apocryphal Gospels" long vanished. Increasingly, biblical philologists would analyze books of the Bible in terms of underlying but forgotten sources revealed in their internal structure—an approach dating from Astruc and Michaelis and eventually labeled 'documentary.'[57]

Semler's pupil Johann Jakob Griesbach took such source criticism—and a documentary approach—in a different direction. In 1774–75 Griesbach published an epochal edition of the Greek New Testament. Griesbach's textual philology mattered hugely for three reasons. First, his edition, though it started from the 'received text' (textus receptus) derived from Erasmus, did not hesitate to replace readings with Griesbach's own when he thought manuscript testimony warranted. Unlike the earlier editions of Edward Wells and Daniel Mace—in a more conservative place, a more cautious time—Griesbach's became widely admired. It slew the Erasmian textus receptus. Wells, Mace, and more powerfully Griesbach had tinkered with the old textus receptus. From now on, philologists aimed to build a new, more reliable one. Second, in research for his edition—conducted with great skill and rigor—Griesbach developed a new understanding of the history of the New Testament text. Building on work by his mentor Semler and Johann Albrecht Bengel, Griesbach concluded that all New Testament manuscripts came down from three ancient families of manuscripts, the third derived from the first two. Put differently, he reduced hundreds of manuscript witnesses to essentially two or three. The method immensely clarified—for all textual philologists, not just biblical ones—the problem of how to make sense of variant readings in a given textual tradition. Finally, Griesbach gave up age-old efforts to 'harmonize' the obvious variations among the four Gospels, such as their chronology of events. (Even Michaelis's *Einleitung* still tried to harmonize over a decade later.) Instead Griesbach recognized the fourth Gospel (John) as distinct, and he printed the other three in parallel columns as "A Synopsis of the Gospels of Matthew, Mark, and Luke." Ever since, these have been known as the 'synoptic Gospels.' This tool gave the critic a method for explicating the Gospels' sources, and biblical philologists have gnawed on the 'synoptic problem' ever since. Later scholars rejected Griesbach's theory of just how the Gospel writers used each other's material; but, as Werner Kümmel put it, his method "laid the foundation for a truly historical investigation of the literary interrelationships of the Gospels."[58]

In the next generation others carried further a historical approach to the Bible, notably Michaelis's student and successor at Göttingen, Johann Gottfried Eichhorn. (The surname means 'squirrel,' and in pictures he resembles one.) The absence of modern academic disciplines allowed cross-fertilization vital to the evolution of philology, and Eichhorn's writings give a prime example. Eichhorn wrote *Litterärgeschichte* (a precursor of today's intellectual history), Arabic studies, several volumes of general and political history, and, pivotally, biblical criticism. As to his teacher Michaelis, Eichhorn "regretted only," as Jonathan Sheehan said, that Michaelis "had not gone far enough in making the Hebrews strange," in failing to see that primitive customs must imply a similar spiritual state. Eichhorn refined Michaelis's idea, honed on Wood's Homer, that primitive Hebrews naturally filtered reality through myth. Eichhorn's Göttingen colleague C. G. Heyne conceived Greek myth as the poetic residue of primitive reactions to an often frightening world. Borrowing from Heyne (perhaps also from Lowth and Wood—more cross-fertilization), Eichhorn developed a parallel mythical explanation of parts of the Old Testament. Neither true nor false (the black-and-white categories deployed by deists), myth was a poetic mode of apprehending reality, typical of primitive cultures. This theory gave biblical scholars a new way of explaining, for instance, the origin stories in Genesis. To comprehend the Pentateuch, the philologist needed to enter into the primitive mind-set of its authors. In Moses's day the Hebrews, Moses included, remained in their childhood as a people, devoid of varied literature and real learning. The record of a slow, relapsing struggle to get from polytheism to monotheism, the Old Testament had no spiritual lessons to teach modern people. But it offered unique resources for probing the cultural evolution of the human race. Only scraps of Greek oracles survive; the Old Testament delivers complete Hebrew prophecies. Greek songs for divine worship are lost; the book of Psalms supplies age-old Hebrew temple songs. The oldest Hebrew historians antedate Herodotus and Thucydides by centuries.[59]

Eichhorn's *Einleitung in das alte Testament* (*Introduction to the Old Testament*, 1780) set a new benchmark for historicist biblical philology. Again, Heyne strongly influenced his approach, in this case by insisting on placing classical authors empathetically in their historical contexts. Unlike Michaelis, Eichhorn had no trouble accepting Astruc's notion of two sources of Genesis, even dissected it more finely. *Einleitung* dated Chronicles after the Babylonian Exile (sixth century BCE) on the ground that depictions of Satan and of angels showed Persian influence. But Eichhorn also argued that its author relied on materials earlier than the books of Samuel and Kings: by comparing the texts he detected traces of a common earlier source. He suggested that the book of Isaiah may have assimilated matter from diverse prophets. Other German biblical philologists among Eichhorn's contemporaries made similarly dramatic proposals. No other philologist of his day had Eichhorn's range nor his wide influence, but he did not stand out as a lonely radical like Spinoza or Simon.[60]

He stood, rather, as the leading figure of a new school of biblical philology erected on foundations laid by such foregoers as Semler and Michaelis. Eichhorn called it *höhere Kritik*—higher criticism. The name distinguished the new school from the ancient and supposedly 'lower' effort of textual criticism simply to establish the best possible text of the sacred books. Higher criticism aimed higher because it sought to decipher authorship, literary origins and form, date, composition, and ultimately meaning of the books of the Bible in original context. Although Eichhorn called higher criticism only humanism under a new name, it set in motion sweeping changes in biblical scholarship.[61]

A New Classical Antiquity

Study of those other ancient texts central to philology, the Greek and Roman classics, underwent in Germany a parallel, equally stunning transformation. This story begins with Johann Joachim Winckelmann. Winckelmann fell in love with ancient Greece as a youth and, in his thirties, moved from scholarly study of Greek literature to passionate engagement with Greek art, especially sculpture. The discoveries at Pompeii and Herculaneum also inspired him. His *Geschichte der Kunst des Altertums* (*History of the Art of Antiquity*, 1764) is commonly, if anachronistically, called the founding text of art history. More to the immediate point, Winckelmann's writings stirred in Germany zest for Greek antiquity as the aesthetic, even ethical apex for moderns to emulate. Ancient Rome, long the dominant study, soon took a back seat to Greece. And, Winckelmann insisted, Greek antiquity had to be grasped as an integral whole: each artifact understood in relation to the concepts and spirit that infused the artist and formed the artwork. The neo-Hellenism awakened by

Winckelmann so gripped the German imagination that its historian Eliza Butler labeled it "the tyranny of Greece over Germany."[62]

One of the despot's worshippers was Eichhorn's colleague at Göttingen, Christian Gottlob Heyne. Like Winckelmann, he saw in classical antiquity a whole, once breathing world to be revived, not a medley of artworks and manuscripts. Heyne's Grecomania, however, paid as much attention to texts as to torsos, while refusing to study either in isolation from the other. And whereas Winckelmann was a loner, who lived mostly in Italy, Heyne was a star at perhaps the most admired university in Germany. He not only breathed new life into German classical philology; he reinvented it. He gave scholarly definition to Winckelmann's romantic appreciation of Greek antiquity as a distinctive whole, with its own aesthetic and ethical norms. By doing so, Heyne effectively created a new field of academic research and teaching. He inspired a host of followers. Among them was the even more celebrated Friedrich August Wolf, who eventually wrote Winckelmann's biography.[63]

This broad new vision of antiquity led Wolf to articulate in its classic (so to speak) form 'the Homeric problem.' Wolf went to study at Göttingen in 1777. There he encountered both Heyne and Eichhorn. Characteristically, he fought with Heyne but learned from both. Heyne handed on the lessons of Winckelmann along with his own view of preclassical Greeks as primitives whose poetic slant on the world expressed itself in mythology. Heyne had gotten his theory about early Greeks in part from Wood's *Original Genius and Writings of Homer*, and Heyne may have introduced young Wolf to Wood's book. (Its German vogue would have made it hard for Wolf to ignore in any case.) "The inspired guesser," Wolf later called Wood. From Eichhorn's biblical philology Wolf inherited methods of reconstructing the history of an ancient text. Within Heyne's and Wood's conceptual framework, Wolf applied Eichhorn's biblical methods to Homer. (The porousness of the frontiers between various regions of philology once again mattered.) In 1795 Wolf published *Prolegomena ad Homerum* (*Prolegomena to Homer*). In it he meticulously traced, for the first time, the history of the Homeric text in antiquity. He showed the hopelessness of knowing anything of a text earlier than the one in the hands of the critics of Hellenistic Alexandria. (He much esteemed Bentley. Did Wolf have at the back of his mind Bentley's proof of the futility of recovering the original text of the New Testament—Bentley who had also doubted the unity of the Homeric poems?) Homer, Wolf argued, was not an actual person, not even the illiterate bard depicted by Wood. Rather, a series of rhapsodes had produced the poems eventually stitched together into the *Iliad* and *Odyssey* and attributed to 'Homer.' The book stirred a hornet's nest: damned as sacrilege, hailed as brilliantly original.[64]

But Wolf did far more than pose the Homeric problem for generations of classical philologists; he imposed Heyne's new approach to the study of antiquity—while typically trying to steal his teacher's laurels. Wolf melded the textual history of Homer with the historical development of ancient philology, and he set all in the larger context of Greek culture. Like Heyne but even more forcefully, Wolf insisted that philologists examine every piece of classical culture in connection with every other. He named this holistic scholarship of the ancient world *Altertumswissenschaft*—the science of antiquity. In the philological seminar he created and lorded over during his quarter century at the University of Halle (1783–1807), Wolf formed the philologists who would dominate the next generation of German learning. There were limits to Wolf's 'science of antiquity' that eventually undermined it. Unlike Heyne, Wolf privileged textual over material remains of antiquity; and art and archaeology would have their revenge. His Altertumswissenschaft encompassed only Greece and, almost grudgingly, Rome; but there was more to the ancient Mediterranean, and later scholars would insist on its inclusion. Nonetheless, the long European tradition of classical studies had been permanently transformed, as decisively as biblical philology.[65]

FIN DE SIÈCLE: END OF AN ERA, OMENS OF ANOTHER

But in the European tradition's English-speaking corner both revolutions were postponed, owing in part to a changing climate for international scholarly communication. (This was not the only reason, as will later become clear.) Latin remained a means of learned exchange, as since Roman antiquity. Throughout the nineteenth century scholars who shared no modern tongue could write to each other in at least basic Latin, since European and American schoolboys learned the language. But the drift toward publication of scholarship in vernaculars speeded in the later eighteenth century. Such works sometimes got translated into Latin, so that the learned in other countries could read them. Yet in 1803 an erudite American, Samuel Miller, observed that Latin had "ceased to be that familiar medium of conversation and of writing, among the learned, that it once was." "A singular revolution," he marveled, which "has rendered the intercourse between learned men more difficult, for want of a common medium." Although Wolf wrote his *Prolegomena ad Homerum* in Latin, his biography of Winckelmann and his programmatic lectures on Altertumswissenschaft appeared in German. Eichhorn's and Michaelis's introductions to the Old and New Testaments came out in German.[66]

English-speaking philologists often got only a vague idea of these revolutionary German works. The mother tongue of the eighteenth-century Republic of Letters was French; and few British, Irish, or American scholars understood German. The best English classical philologist of his generation, Richard Porson (1759–1808), is supposed (plausibly) to have declared, "Life is too short to learn German." Porson certainly did not appreciate German philology and proved deaf to his great contemporary Wolf. The wars of the French Revolution and Napoleon reinforced linguistic barriers. For much of the time between the mid-1790s and 1815, British and American travelers had a hard time reaching the European continent, and international scholarly contact became difficult. The earthquakes that transformed biblical and classical philology in Germany barely stirred the English-speaking world until well into the nineteenth century.[67]

Nonetheless, the faces of philology everywhere looked very different around 1800 than even in 1750. As German innovations in biblical criticism and classical studies trickled across the Rhine, explorations of classical sites such as Pompeii, astonishing to all Europe, hinted at other new approaches to antiquity—though for the moment more significant as art than as revelation of a different past. Investigations of Sanskrit by Jones and others had given birth to Indology, a scholarly field new to the West, and to the transforming methods of comparative philology. These were only the most spectacular children of European imperial expansion. Growing knowledge of languages across the world and increasingly rigorous study of them gave a new empirical basis for generalizing about the nature of language; some of these efforts, as in study of Amerindian languages, spilled over into new inquiries into the histories of their speakers. Even long familiar products of language gained new types of attention. A widespread, if diffuse, interest in the study of modern English literature paralleled a longer-standing, more focused study of Anglo-Saxon. And a merging of antiquarian scholarship and philosophic history in the hands especially of Edward Gibbon provided a new model of how to practice the ancient genre of history. Novelty was everywhere. Did this grab-bag display any unifying traits?

Diversity now teemed in so many different directions as to threaten dispersion. To move from William Jones and the discovery of the Indo-European family to F. A. Wolf and the invention of Altertumswissenschaft is to leap across the globe and, evidently, across intellectual worlds as well. What—in the world—did Jones's and Wolf's endeavors have in common? And what, to stretch further, did these share with the work of Benjamin Barton and Hugh Blair, Edward Gibbon and Johann Eichhorn?

One answer points to continuity, another to change. The first is that all these ventures augmented the historically oriented, contextualizing, at least implicitly comparative bias of philology. The historical sensibility fostered by philology and allied studies had grown deeper and richer than ever before. As a teenager Walter Scott studied at Edinburgh University when William Robertson was principal, hung around Adam Ferguson's literary salon. In the historical novels Scott started publishing in 1814, change over time determines what characters can think and say. In contrast, the novels of Daniel Defoe or Henry Fielding less than a century earlier, even when called 'history,' even when set in the past, show no sense that historical context shapes the people inhabiting them.[68] As in Scott, so in the writings of William Jones, Friedrich Wolf, or J. D. Michaelis, the perception of distance between cultures became greater than ever, and the urge to compare (at least tacitly) in order to understand became stronger than ever. Comparison, in the first place, had birthed the keener alertness to historical and cultural difference. In these respects, as the nineteenth century began, philology amplified rather than altered its heritage.

The second answer, foreshadowing shift of direction, is this: most of the philologically rooted initiatives in this chapter took a tradition of intellectual speculation—whether conjectures concerned Amerindian languages or authorship of the Pentateuch, philosophic history or Homer—and grafted onto it new empirical solidity and rigor, grounded in the historical-comparative methods of philology. This joining of—put very crudely—theory and evidence set in motion a process that eventually transformed several loose-jointed intellectual enterprises into something resembling new sciences. And this process carried philology during the nineteenth century into the heart of a revolution in academic knowledge.

PART II

On the Brink of the Modern Humanities, 1800 to the Mid-Nineteenth Century

By 1800 philology strained against its own skin. Philology—and activities within its extended family, such as antiquarianism, rhetoric, history writing—had grown more varied in expertise, had scattered over vast reaches of imperial space, had opened a host of new questions. To practice philological erudition as one, vast, intertwined endeavor became harder to do, even as scholars continued to conceive humanistic learning as a single activity at bottom.

Institutional evolution mirrored this tension. During the first half of the nineteenth century colleges and universities expanded in number in both the United Kingdom and, especially, the United States. In the larger ones, teaching became a little more finely subdivided. More specialized faculty positions appeared particularly in the natural sciences; but professorships philological in character also grew more specific. Harvard acquired its first chairs of modern European languages (1815) and history (1838). Trinity College Dublin got professorships in biblical Greek (1838), Irish (1840), and Arabic (1855). By no means every professor pursued research, but more explicitly defined academic jobs reflected a trend also in erudition.[1]

Rising population and resources fueled this slowly growing specialization. Between 1825 and 1850 Harvard University annually raked in some $40,000 in donations, over twenty times its eighteenth-century average; its total assets quintupled in the first half of the century. Ireland, long served only by Trinity College Dublin, got new colleges in Galway, Cork, and Belfast when Parliament voted a grant of £100,000 in 1845. Possibly, too, the larger environment had its subliminal effect on the learned world. In the United Kingdom and North America between 1800 and 1850, government bureaucracies grew a bit, became somewhat more specialized; division of labor was more obvious in the increasingly commercial and industrial economy. Scholars fitted the pattern. Still, neither specialization of erudition nor its funding amounted to much compared to the period after 1850—especially after the American Civil War, when new research-oriented universities in the United States fattened on the wealth of an industrializing nation.[2]

But specialization did creep in before then, a result of decisions by learned men who inhabited universities and other institutions of erudition. Associations to advance learning multiplied after 1800; and as the quantity of learned societies increased, their scopes of interest typically shrank. Such generalist organizations as the Royal Dublin Society (1731), the Bath and West of England Society (1776), or the American (i.e., greater Boston) Academy of Arts and Sciences (1780) came to seem too open-ended to people with more single-minded intellectual concerns. Individuals interested in history founded the American (i.e., Massachusetts) Antiquarian Society in 1812 and the Society of Antiquaries of Newcastle upon Tyne in 1813. Philologists working on Asian topics founded the Royal Asiatic Society in 1823 and the American Oriental Society in 1842.[3]

In this climate philology, stretched every-which-way, began very slowly to split under the strain. Classical scholars, though still linguistically equipped to emend the Greek New Testament, less often did so—and less often paid attention to the biblical philologists who did. Orientalists tended to fix more exclusively on a defined set of languages: Sanskrit and Persian, or Arabic and Hebrew, but not all. A Bentley oscillating between emending classical texts and editing the New Testament, a Jones moving from Persian to Turkish to Arabic to Chinese to Sanskrit, would by the mid-nineteenth century seem a little surprising.

No sudden revolution broke out. Lines of connection held. Classical *Altertumswissenschaft* inspired British historians. Grammarians of modern languages modeled their studies on ancient ones. Scholars studying modern literature used the methods of historians. A drift toward differentiation was definite, but only in retrospect does the tilt look decisive. Taking advantage of hindsight, the following chapters will each concentrate on a single broad area of philological study.

5

"THE SIMILARITY OF STRUCTURE WHICH PERVADES ALL LANGUAGES"

FROM PHILOLOGY TO LINGUISTICS, 1800–1850

The fascination with the phenomenon of language that gripped Enlightenment writers did not ebb after 1800. The most ambitious project yet, *Mithridates, oder allgemeine Sprachenkunde* (*Mithridates, or General Science of Language*) sampled myriad languages worldwide.* Johann Christoph Adelung put out a first volume in 1806, then died; by 1817 Johann Severin Vater had finished the job with three more. The idea of language families, boosted by William Jones, was by now pervasive, a new template for research. *Mithridates* used the "Our Father" as a lens through which to see affinities between tongues—an eyepiece like the Leibnizian word list, though sharper in focus. By glimpsing similarities of words and grammar, Vater sorted languages into families. Absent real grasp of how languages change over time, the groupings later proved mostly wrong. But at the time the work seemed to revolutionize comparative philology; for it brought into view strikingly distinct basic word forms of different linguistic groupings. Less hefty books more or less contemporary with *Mithridates* also tried to test family ties with actual facts. As Gibbon had wed philosophic history to philological research, so Vater and the others married Enlightenment speculation about language to data collecting.[1]

And they approached their research with a new sense of shared enterprise. When, a couple centuries earlier, the learned had stopped fussing about how Adam and Eve communicated, historical and comparative study of languages had faded into the episodic hobby of isolated scholars.[2] The Republic of Let-

---

* The title refers to Mithridates VI of Pontus who, according to Pliny the Elder, spoke all twenty-plus languages of the peoples he ruled.

ters usually did not behave that way. Philologists working on Greek and Roman texts had for centuries kept up with editions and commentaries by other writers on the same turf—with all of them self-consciously feeding on erudition of earlier generations of classical scholars. Biblical philologists, rhetoricians, chronologers, antiquarians did likewise. Griesbach's Greek New Testament took account of textual variants published by John Mill seventy years earlier; Mill worked in reference to Robert Estienne's edition a century and a half before him. Compare to them Thomas Jefferson or Peter Pallas around 1790. Both relied on a host of volunteers to amass vocabularies. But neither Jefferson, Pallas, nor the missionaries and soldiers who harvested words for them belonged to a self-aware community of linguistic scholars, building on and responding to the work of others within it, past and present. Ironically, the closest European thing to such a network in the eighteenth century came together in India in the late 1700s—the British students of Sanskrit encouraged by Warren Hastings, tutored by Indian pandits, and famously represented by William Jones. Yet, within two or three decades of his death in 1794, philologists who studied language itself had coalesced into an interactive guild—granted, not densely populated—with outposts stretching from Madras to St. Petersburg to Paris to Philadelphia.

Its members engaged in parallel but overlapping projects. During the first half of the nineteenth century, most scholars involved with the new comparative philology lived on the European continent. They belong to the story of modern humanistic scholarship in the English-speaking world because English-speaking scholars later followed their example. This chapter will look at four programs of linguistic research in turn. First, Indo-European philologists—starting where the Calcutta Sanskritists left off—developed the most elaborate body of learning and most robust academic establishment. Stressing languages' development over time, the Indo-European project moved in step with the historicizing impulse long animating philology. Second, one German comparativist, Wilhelm von Humboldt, created a general theory of language by looking through a Romantic lens at a different language family. Third, a handful of white Americans applied the new comparative approach to Native American speech. Though few, they set in motion a learned tradition aware of its lineage, integrated into European erudition, using empirical research to create and refine theoretical frameworks as European scholars did. Finally, however, most students of language in the English-speaking world before 1850 seemed, from a continental perspective, trapped in a time warp of Enlightenment conjectures. Even so, none of the people involved in these different projects worked unaware of the others. Vater and Humboldt corresponded with leading students of Amerindian tongues; they in turn followed avidly not only each other's work but also studies of other languages. Even the old-fashioned speculators knew something of continental philology while choosing to ignore it.[3]

Intensive collaboration—and rivalry—within and across national frontiers furthered methodological rigor and complexity. A bare half century after the first volume of *Mithridates*, the American philologist Benjamin Dwight dismissed the massive work as "a mere unarranged mass of curiosities, no higher in character than in mineralogy would be a collection of stones from different lands, divided into classes according to their mere resemblances of color or of shape."[4] This increasing sophistication and tighter focus fundamentally changed the landscape of language study.

COMPARATIVE HISTORICAL INDO-EUROPEAN PHILOLOGY

Sanskrit and the idea of an Indo-European family of languages passed from British hands to continental ones in the heated climate of German Romanticism. Johann Gottfried Herder pronounced the central linguistic dogma of Romanticism in 1772 in his *Abhandlung über den Ursprung der Sprache* (*Treatise on the Origin of Language*): "Man is, in his distinctive features, a creation of the group, of society; the development of a language is thus natural, essential, and necessary for him." He meant *literally* essential: Herder argued that language supplied the means of expression that allowed human beings to think—and a thoughtless primate was not "Man." Thought could not exist apart from language, nor vice versa, so thinking and talking must have evolved in tandem. But language could not possibly arise in isolated individuals with no one to chat with. "Man is," therefore, "a creation of the group." It followed that the language of each people—or race, or nation: terms still interchangeable—expressed in its vocabulary and structure that nation's distinctive sensibilities and ways of thinking. Language, that is, articulated a people's unique identity—or, as Herder believed, its spiritual essence. (One could agree with Herder on this last point but not believe language essential to thought.) Herder became thus the foremost advocate of a notion already circulating, for instance, in James Harris's *Hermes*: "how Nations, like single Men, have their *peculiar* Ideas; how these *peculiar* Ideas become THE GENIUS OF THEIR LANGUAGE, since the *Symbol* must of course correspond to its *Archetype*."[5]

Herder's argument reinforced, and was reinforced by, a venerable idea that languages corresponded to 'nations' in the special sense of peoples bound together by shared physical inheritance. (There is no less awkward way to say it. The concept of biological 'race' only lurked on the horizon. Realizing how promiscuously peoples had mixed in Europe, Herder himself believed in nations as cultural-linguistic, not genetic, entities.) Herder's older contemporary Samuel Johnson made the point in 1766: "The similitude and derivation of languages afford the most indubitable proof of the traduction [lineage] of nations, and the genealogy of mankind." Languages "often supply the only evidence of ancient migrations, and of the revolutions of ages which have left no written monuments behind them." This axiom grew from the biblical story of the repopulation of the earth after the Flood by Noah's sons, Japhet, Shem, and Ham. But the bond between language and nation proved sturdy enough to survive loss of faith in the Bible story, ignore obvious historical facts, and defy common sense. It was well known that the French language descended from Latin; no one assumed that *therefore* the French population descended from ancient Romans.* And if Bengalis in 1786 could learn English, presumably their remote ancestors could have learned a language of earlier invaders. Nonetheless, William Jones believed he could trace the genealogies of peoples through the affinities linking Sanskrit to Welsh and English, just as Thomas Jefferson hoped to trace American Indians' ultimate origin by following backward the tracks of their languages. This faith endured until the mid-nineteenth century—though never without its critics—when the concept of biological race undermined it. Herder's idea that a nation's language expressed its unique character meshed nicely with this belief that each nation kept its own evolving language more or less in perpetuity.[6]

Both ideas resonated with the distinctive German nationalism welling up around 1800. Napoleon humiliated German states and statelets. Wounded pride rebounded as swollen patriotism. Germans lacked a nation-state about which to thump their chests ("Rule, Britannia" but no "Rule, Germania"). For this reason, German national self-esteem obsessed on a unique *culture* supposedly uniquely conveyed in the German tongue. The collection of folktales by the Brothers Grimm remains the most widely known symptom of this syndrome. The elder Brother Grimm, Jacob, also studied the historical evolution of German legal institutions and, most influentially, of the German language. He had been initiated into the cult of Germanness at the University of Marburg during the winter of 1802–3 by a slightly older devotee, Friedrich Karl von Savigny—whose focus on Roman law did not inhibit his fervor for the German Middle Ages. What held true for the German nation and language was supposed to hold true, mutatis mutandis, for other peoples and their languages. This was Romantic linguistic nationalism.[7]

Into this hothouse were transplanted Sanskrit and the Indo-European idea, but moving them from Calcutta to Berlin took a while. British philologists in India continued to glean erudition from pandits. Such interaction led to the demonstration by F. W. Ellis in Madras in 1816 of a new family, the Dravidian languages (of which Tamil is perhaps best known to Westerners). As another fallout of East India Company scholarship, between 1805 and 1810 British philologists published four Sanskrit grammars in English, in England. These grammars and related aids made Sanskrit portable. Europeans no longer had to go to India to learn from pandits. The gain carried a loss: henceforth European Sanskrit philology was largely cut off from the wells of Indian learning that had irrigated it in its Bengal infancy. The Calcutta orientalists who survived India took their Sanskrit learning back to Britain with them. William

* *Some* correlation often exists between genes and language. Italian soldiers in the Roman army certainly left behind some DNA in what is now France. More French DNA, however, moved in with Germanic speakers who joined the genes of the aboriginal Celts and whose language yielded to early French.

Jones's mentor Charles Wilkins found work as the first librarian at East India Company headquarters in London. Another Asiatic Society repatriate was Alexander Hamilton (first cousin to the American founder of the same name). Perhaps the most learned of the Calcutta Sanskritists, Hamilton returned to Scotland in 1795. There he lived the life of a private scholar until in 1806 becoming professor of "the Sanscrit and other Hindoo languages" at a new college started in Hertfordshire by the East India Company to train the company's 'servants.'[8]

In between, he carried Sanskrit across the English Channel. In 1802, taking advantage of the Peace of Amiens, he traveled to Paris to examine Sanskrit manuscripts in the Bibliothèque nationale (née Bibliothèque du roi), the richest collection in Europe. Peace broke down, and Hamilton got stuck in Paris when hostilities resumed. There, a privileged prisoner of war, he cataloged the selfsame manuscripts. He also taught Sanskrit (and the notion of Indo-European comparative philology) to a handful of Parisians. The city sheltered a coterie of orientalist scholars (Anquetil-Duperron still lived), an audience receptive to this new import. Meanwhile, the imperial temperature in Britain grew icy for Indian learning, as the East India Company fell under the sway of a hard-edged anglicizing party today associated with James Mill, Thomas Macaulay, and racist contempt for Indians. These people wanted to hear nothing about the glories of Sanskrit literature or ancient Indian achievements in astronomy and mathematics. Sanskrit came to be studied in Britain as the hobby of a few retired colonial administrators or a minor tool of imperial governance. Not until 1832 did a British university get a professorship of Sanskrit—endowed at Oxford to help Christian missionaries. As a result of these shifting imperial currents, Paris became the new center of Indology almost by default. In 1814 the Collège de France established the first chair of Sanskrit at any European university. Until near midcentury, anyone wishing to dive into Sanskrit went to Paris.[9]

Hamilton's informal Sanskrit tutorship had another consequence, for the most eager of his pupils was the thirty-year-old Romantic scholar Friedrich Schlegel. Schlegel had shared the enthusiasm generated in Germany by the first translations of Indian literature near the end of the previous century. These works acquired European meaning from the idea that language expressed a people's spiritual essence; and India now tended to displace Egypt as the homeland of arcane ancient knowledge parallel to Mosaic revelation, an erudite fantasy as old as the Italian Renaissance. For Schlegel and other German Romantics, the 'discovery' of Sanskrit uncovered a new fount of numinous wisdom. The projection of deep significance onto Sanskrit should not surprise, given the centrality of language in the German Romantic worldview. And Sanskrit was kin to German. Schlegel, in fact, wrongly believed Sanskrit the mother of all Indo-European tongues (flouting Jones's argument that all, including Sanskrit, descended from a language now lost). Ancient Indian wisdom must therefore have fed primordially into the makeup of the German people. The blood of Sanskrit flowed into the veins of German—more or less literally: Schlegel believed that the forebears of the Germans wandered over from India. (Ancient Egypt and Israel he thought also Indian colonies.)[10]

These ideas—and feelings—gushed forth in Schlegel's *Über die Sprache und die Weisheit der Indier* (*On the Language and the Wisdom of India*, 1808). The author himself called his book a work of "the true living science." It made a huge splash, inspiring what Raymond Schwab long ago labeled "the oriental Renaissance" in Europe. When Prussia created a new university at Bonn in 1818, Schlegel's older brother August took up a professorship there—duties undefined—and chose to introduce Sanskrit teaching to Germany. (He vowed to apply the methods of classical philology to Sanskrit texts, a shrewd move in the Greek-drenched German universities.) The English scholar-politician George Cornewall Lewis wanted to learn Sanskrit—until the large "number of letters" (thirty-six) in its Devanāgarī alphabet daunted him. One might even speak of a mania for Sanskrit. True, if the maniacs who actually learned the language had assembled from both shores of the Atlantic, they would not have filled a decent-size lecture hall. But so pervasive was the allure of Sanskrit as key to mystic wisdom that E.T.A. Hoffmann, tongue in cheek, could call music "the secret Sanskrit of Nature," knowing readers would get the joke. These broader cultural resonances extended as far as Concord, Massachusetts, and Ralph Waldo Emerson's poem "Brahma" (1857).[11]

For philology itself, three things mattered most about *The Language and Wisdom of India*. First, Schlegel ignited passion in some young Germans for the study of Sanskrit. Second, he made more precise the project of tracing the genealogical relations of the Indo-European languages (despite his massive error about Sanskrit as the Ur-tongue). Third, he displaced for a while the long-dominant method of searching out affinities among languages by supposed etymology or similarity of words (as in *Mithridates*). Instead, Schlegel argued that philologists could best trace linguistic kinship by comparing the structure of words (a study named morphology a few decades later), especially the inflection of nouns. Similar grammatical form indicated family relationship. He was not first to take this position; Sámuel Gyarmathi had thus proved the filiation of Hungarian and Finnish a decade before. William Jones himself hinted at the method in the "Anniversary Address" that opened Indo-European research. But Schlegel picked up on the tip, made it popular, and propagated the term *comparative grammar* to label the new technique. *Über die Sprache und die Weisheit der Indier* proved decisive for the future of language study. As Sebastiano Timpanaro put it, Schlegel brought comparative grammar "into the field of genealogical comparison and showed how powerful it could be in ascertaining the common origin of different languages."[12]

Among those inspired by Schlegel was a German student named Franz Bopp. In 1812, financed by the Bavarian government, he settled in Paris. There he joined the orientalist circle, plunged into the study of Sanskrit, and immersed himself in Sanskrit manuscripts in the Bibliothèque imperiale (the once and future Bibliothèque nationale). In Paris he got to know Hamilton; later, in London, Wilkins and Colebrooke. A direct line thus connected Bopp with Calcutta and, at one remove, with Indian scholarship. In 1816 he brought out *Über das Conjugationssystem der Sanskritsprache in Vergleichung mit jenem der griechischen, lateinischen, persischen und germanischen Sprache* (*On the Conjugation System of Sanskrit Compared to That of Greek, Latin, Persian, and German*).[13]

The book revolutionized Indo-European philology. Bopp developed rigorously the program suggested by Schlegel, while abandoning Schlegel's stress on inflection as the crucial morphological element when comparing Indo-European languages. Starting with verb conjugations (instead of noun declensions) in the five languages in his title, Bopp began the grinding task of reconstructing the comparative historical development of the grammatical structure of the Indo-European family. Maturing through a series of monographs, this labor culminated in his *Vergleichende Grammatik des Sanskrit, Send, Griechischen, Lateinischen, Litthauischen, Altslavischen, Gothischen, und Deutschen* (*Comparative Grammar of Sanskrit, Zend* [i.e., Avestan], *Greek, Latin, Lithuanian, Old Slavic, Gothic, and German*), published in six parts between 1833 and 1849. Bopp put on a scientific basis the learned but loose European zeal for Sanskrit. Romantic glow faded. In his hands, Indo-European comparative historical philology became the paradigm for historical study of language families.[14]

Other Germans turned the new science to nationalist ends, glorifying the 'Indo-Germanic' languages. This road eventually led to a horror no one in Bopp's day could imagine: the Aryanism of the Nazis. The cosmopolitan Bopp, nurtured in Paris, conscious heir of the Calcutta Sanskritists, would have nothing to do with linguistic chauvinism. He would not let the Germans stand for "all the peoples of our continent"; and in his writings the family remained 'Indo-European.'[15]

Yet the power of Bopp's scholarship helped to shift the center of orientalist philology from France to Germany. Indo-European philologists had to fight an uphill battle against the classical philologists entrenched in German academia. Sanskritists owed their first five professorships to the propagandizing of August Schlegel and to the political pull of one powerful man, Wilhelm von Humboldt. Only around 1850 did tensions dissipate. By that year, seven other German universities had chairs—variously titled—involving Sanskrit, besides Bopp's own at the pinnacle in Berlin.[16]

For philology, the Indological content of Bopp's work mattered less than his comparative method of studying structural relationships of languages. A comparative approach had always lain at the heart of philology. William Jones instinctively, if fleetingly, applied it to Sanskrit; and Friedrich Schlegel called attention to its promise in this new domain. Now Bopp carried it through strictly, with nothing of Schlegel's Romantic fire. Indeed, in general, as comparative philology matured in the academic world, its practitioners severed ties to the Romanticism that midwifed it, formulating their scholarly questions with methodological precision and emotional ice.[17] And, even in his early days, Bopp was only the most wide-ranging of the philologists pioneering comparative historical grammar as a systematic study.

Another was a Dane, Rasmus Rask. Almost simultaneously with Bopp, Rask traced the morphological relationships connecting the historical development of Nordic languages with their Germanic and Slavonic cousins and with Lithuanian, Latin, and Greek. Rask finished the manuscript of his *Undersøgelse om det gamle nordiske eller islandske sprogs oprindelse* (*Essay on the Origin of the Ancient Scandinavian or Icelandic Tongue*) two years before Bopp's *Conjugationssystem*; but it waited for publication until 1818. In his book, Rask resurrected etymology from the grave that Schlegel had dug for it. But Rask also renovated it. He put lexical (word) comparison on the same systematic basis as comparative grammar: "If there is found between two languages agreement in the forms of indispensable words to such an extent that rules of letter changes can be discovered for passing from one to the other, then there is a basic relationship between these languages." For instance, Latin *pater*, Spanish *padre*, German *Vater*, English *father*, and Swedish *fader* show that these five tongues are cousins. Rask had articulated the key idea of systematic sound shifts, derived ultimately from study of ancient Indian grammarians. Etymology grew into comparative phonology (study of the sound systems of languages).[18]

A year later, in 1819, Jacob Grimm published the first volume of his *Deutsche Grammatik* (*Germanic Grammar*). As Bopp compared the (more or less static) grammars of different tongues to trace the relationships among several Indo-European languages, so Grimm used evolution in grammatical structures to reconstruct the historical relationship of the Germanic languages, from Gothic in antiquity down to the modern tongues of Germany, Scandinavia, and England. In the process he invented technical lingo still standard, such as *strong* and *weak* to label verbs, *Umlaut* and *Ablaut* to characterize vowel changes. Then he read Rask. In 1822 appeared a new edition of the first volume of *Deutsche Grammatik*, giving pride of place to phonology over grammar. Grimm schematized and extended Rask's regular patterns of consonant changes between languages into what became known as Grimm's Law. (Grimm never said 'law,' simply 'sound shift.') As Bopp had on his *Conjugationssytem*, Grimm labored on *Deutsche Grammatik* for many more years, tracing the grammatical evolution of the Germanic tongues from remote past to the present. As Bopp had systematized comparative philology, so Grimm provided the model for historical linguistics.[19]

The basic rules of the new linguistic game were laid down between 1816 and 1822 in Bopp's *Conjugationssystem*, Rask's *Undersøgelse*, and the second edition of Grimm's *Grammatik*. All three men advanced not only the comparative but also the historical bias of philology. Bopp aimed ultimately to reconstruct the extinct language from which Indo-European tongues stemmed. Rask saw his work as a means to recover the lost history of nations before the invention of writing. Grimm's many-sided explorations of German legal history, folktales, mythology, and language all sprang from his Romantic desire to recover, in the spirit of Herder, an essential Germanness in his people's past. All three tended to see the history of language as a declension from a purer past. But these rather traditional *attitudes*—not out of place in sixteenth-century quarrels about the language of Adam—now inhabited a transformed science: empirically much more meticulous, methodologically vastly more rigorous. The Calcutta Sanskritists had opened the way for a revolution beyond the wildest imaginings of Alexander Hamilton.[20]

Yet the revolution went little noticed in the English-speaking world before the 1840s. Granted, the few scholars who did pay attention mostly admired the new comparative philology. Anglo-Saxon had long been studied in connection with other Germanic languages; so, predictably, the handful of Anglo-Saxon philologists showed greatest interest in Rask and Grimm, who concentrated on these tongues. The Anglo-Saxonists were not quite alone in respect for comparative philology; and the number of sympathizers, at least in Britain, slowly grew. James Prichard in 1813 used a shaky comparative philology to vindicate the unity of the human race; indeed, as late as 1851 the new philology seemed chiefly to appeal to Americans for its utility in defending Adam and Eve. In 1833 George Cornewall Lewis applied comparative method to refute the theory of François-Juste-Marie Raynouard that all Romance languages descended from Old Provençal, the language of the troubadours. Comparing word forms in the major western European Romance languages, Lewis showed these to be compatible with individual descent of the languages from Latin, but incompatible with common descent from Old Provençal. Lewis's essay echoed the spirit of continental comparative philology but not its rigorous method. In 1839 John William Donaldson tried, in *The New Cratylus*, to improve the teaching of Greek by applying Indo-European philology to understanding its structure. Five years later, he made the same effort for Latin. Though better versed in comparative philology than Lewis, Donaldson appealed no more to learned readers broadly. (Both Lewis and Donaldson belonged to a narrower circle around the unconventional new London University, sympathetic to German erudition, unlike Oxbridge. Indeed, when the university opened in 1828, it hired a pupil of Bopp as professor of oriental languages.) In 1842 the Philological Society was organized in London, some members known for valuing German scholarship. But "the most striking fact" about the society's first two decades, said Hans Aarsleff, "is the virtual absence of non-English, Germanic philology."[21]

The striking fact cannot be laid to ignorance. Continental work got enough coverage, in both British and American periodicals, that English-speaking readers were hardly left in the dark. In 1820 Alexander Hamilton reviewed Bopp's *Conjugationssystem* for the *Edinburgh Review*, and Rask himself reviewed Grimm's *Deutsche Grammatik* (snarkily) in the *Foreign Review* in 1830.

In 1838 Rev. William Balfour Winning gave something approaching a general survey of Indo-European comparative philology in not much over a hundred pages, with a quotation from Bopp on the title page and large chunks translated from German scholarship. Rev. Joseph Bosworth's Anglo-Saxon grammar (1841) even included "an outline of Professor Rask and Grimm's systems" [sic]. John Pickering's 1843 address to the first annual meeting of the American Oriental Society praised Franz Bopp—granted, as "the first Sanskrit scholar of the age," only alluding to his comparative grammar in quoting a French savant. Nonetheless, the commonest English and American reactions to comparative philology before midcentury ranged from ignorant to dismissive to snappish. Bopp's seminal *Comparative Grammar* was not translated until 1845–53.[22]

HUMBOLDT AND LINGUISTIC RELATIVITY

Meanwhile, Wilhelm von Humboldt took these same methods of Indo-European comparative philology and applied them to other languages of the world—with a pivotal twist.* His linguistic studies covered a daunting range, from youthful fieldwork among Basques to studies in midlife of American Indian languages, then on to a theoretical investigation of how languages produce speech (which he thought more fundamental than grammar)—and much more. All this looked toward the same object, as he explained to B. G. Niebuhr in 1820: "to establish on a better basis the comparative study of languages which heretofore has been highly superficial, unphilosophical, and wrongheaded." He compared his goal to Linnaean taxonomy of plants. Space permits consideration here of only one book later influential in the United Kingdom and North America.[23]

Perhaps the greatest single monument of the Romantic conflation of language and nation was Humboldt's *Über die Verschiedenheit des menschlichen Sprachbaues und ihren Einfluss auf die geistige Entwicklung des Menschengeschlechts* (*On the Structural Difference of Human Languages and Its Influence on the Intellectual Development of the Human Race*, 1836). Humboldt wrote this work to introduce a massive study of Kawi within the context of other Malayo-Polynesian tongues. (Kawi or Kavi is an archaic literary language of the Malay Archipelago, combining Old Javanese with Sanskrit loan words.) Humboldt died in 1835 before finishing his 'Kawi-Werk.' Within a few years of his death, a former assistant edited most of it in three volumes. A landmark in modern research, it began comparative study of the huge Malayo-Polynesian subfamily of the Austronesian languages (a family whose existence Humboldt

---

* Even more than William Jones, Humboldt was a man of many parts. His reform of the Prussian educational system supplied a model for countries as far afield as the United States and Japan, and he was a key Prussian diplomat in the era of the Napoleonic Wars.

first demonstrated), spanning almost half the globe. The theoretical introduction was published separately, a kind of memorial, redacted to stand on its own as a compendium of Humboldt's ideas about language. This prelude represented Humboldt's ideas to most English-speaking philologists—especially as more of them learned German.[24]

Humboldt started from an axiom that had implications far beyond philology: the structure of every language reflects the mental characteristics of the nation that generated it. Languages are thus inherently subjective or relative when compared to other languages (a fairly common eighteenth-century idea). Language is also sociable by nature; it arises, after all, from the need of people to communicate with each other. *Within* any given language, sociability subdues subjectivity and creates stability; speakers, in effect, agree on what words mean and how sentences work. But a warlike race, say, will develop different linguistic structures than a peaceful farming people. Less blandly and more specifically, in Humboldt's view the Indo-European languages were structurally better suited to intellectual activity than those of the Semitic family. This enabled ancient Greeks and Romans—and more recently Germans—to advance science and engineering, while the poor Arabs (and tacitly, Hebrews) could only ape their feats.* Humboldt was no raving anti-Semite. He pushed legislation to admit Jews to the same civil status as Christians, though apparently so that assimilation might dilute their unfortunate Jewishness. Yet, as in the hands of a genuine anti-Semite like Michaelis, philology continued to exalt European nations and to denigrate both faraway Arabs and, of more immediate import, Jews close at hand.[25]

For the technical study of language, Humboldt's work had happier results. With details drawn from tongues as diverse as Mongolian and Lenape, Chinese and Sanskrit, looking at everything from agglutination to accentuation, Humboldt explored what he called "*innere Sprachform.*" This phrase might fairly, though not literally, be translated as "the deep structure of language." Humboldt believed that language really existed only in speech—the grammar of written language being derivative and secondary. Therefore, students of language needed to go beneath the external forms of grammar to analyze how a language generates speech. What mattered most was the creative activity of the speaker, conceived dually as language-producing individual and as language-producing nation; for every language was constantly in motion. Humboldt fully shared the Enlightenment conviction that the study of language revealed the history of nations: that comparing evolution of languages gave the surest evidence of the progress of civilization among different peoples. But because he collated so many historically unrelated tongues in *Über die Verschiedenheit des menschlichen Sprachbaues*, history had to drop out. Instead, he devoted himself to analyzing typology rather than reconstructing

---

* This was not the West versus the rest. The peoples of Persia and northern India spoke Indo-European languages.

structural development over time.* Humboldt's ahistorical approach jarred with the historicist treatment of languages favored by German philologists in his generation—who, anyway, cared little about languages *other* than Indo-European ones. So he influenced mainly philologists elsewhere, notably students of American languages like Du Ponceau, Pickering, and their successors. Nonetheless, he put empirical flesh on the bare bones of Herder's dictum that language voices each people's distinctive identity.[26]

In doing so, Humboldt reworked the axiom of textual philology that meaning gets teased out in the interaction of a text and its social and cultural context. He did so by putting a language in place of a text. He showed in concrete detail how the *innere Sprachform* of a language manifests the inner life and worldview of a people and how that *Sprachform* in turn shapes the spirit it conveys.[27] He invented a new version of the philologist's 'hermeneutic circle': text explaining context, context explaining text. *Verschiedenheit des menschlichen Sprachbaues* also gave the most commanding exposition of Herder's theorem that thought and language are inseparable, that each conditions the other, and that every nation has a specific spirit expressed in its language. Humboldt created a plausible linguistic basis for cultural diversity.

THE STUDY OF AMERICAN LANGUAGES

As Humboldt knew, Amerindian language studies in his day got their warmest welcome at the American Philosophical Society (APS) "for promoting useful knowledge" in Philadelphia. The society housed the Indian word lists amassed by Thomas Jefferson. Benjamin Smith Barton, another member, had used them for his 1797 book trying to decipher where Native Americans came from. Afterwards these materials lay fallow. In 1815—copying the New York and Massachusetts Historical Societies—the APS secretary, Peter Du Ponceau, formed a Historical and Literary Committee. It aimed to collect old documents and "interesting Historical & Statistical facts." The committee was little more than a front for Du Ponceau. As its corresponding secretary, he ran the show. Du Ponceau had a cosmopolitan life story. French by birth and upbringing, he came to America as a seventeen-year-old boy to fight in the revolution, stayed, and won distinction as a Philadelphia lawyer. Even in youth, he showed fearsome talent for languages and enjoyed linguistic puzzles. Several weeks after the Historical and Literary Committee got going, he met John Heckewelder, a Moravian missionary to the Lenape (or Delaware) Indians. Heckewelder of course knew Lenape; he lent Du Ponceau a manuscript German-Lenape dictionary from the Moravians' library in Bethlehem, Pennsylvania,

---

*Typological linguistics focuses on structural similarities between languages, apart from their histories. It can discern relationships between languages when data is lacking to establish a genetic kinship. Building words by clumping together morphemes—called agglutination (a word coined by Humboldt)—is the sort of defining feature that typology would look for.

helped him translate it, fed his growing appetite for details about the Lenape tongue. This philological partnership rekindled Du Ponceau's ardor for linguistic studies and turned it toward Indian languages. His research, ballooning to multiple tongues, kept him writing letters into the night and talking with Indians and others who spoke their languages.[28]

In 1818 mutual interest in linguistic questions brought Du Ponceau in touch with John Pickering, a Massachusetts lawyer.* The two rarely met in person. As Du Ponceau once lamented, "I wish I had you here for an hour only; armed with my books, I would throw volumes at your head, and we would swim together in a sea of philology." Their twenty-five-year correspondence rarely mixed metaphors so violently, but it eventually filled two thick volumes. Soon they were working together on Amerindian languages. Pickering had persuaded the Massachusetts Historical Society to reprint a few old missionary sources, with scholarly apparatus and introductions. He and Du Ponceau shared the "German labor," as Pickering called it, of seeing the first of these into print: Rev. John Eliot's 1666 grammar of the Massachusetts language. With less input from Du Ponceau, Pickering edited an early eighteenth-century manuscript word list compiled by the missionary Josiah Cotton, as well as Rev. Jonathan Edwards's 1788 *Observations on the Language of the Muhhekaneew* [Mahican or Mohican] *Indians*. (Edwards recognized as related several members of the subfamily now called the Eastern Algonkian group. He also pointed out analogies to Hebrew, which makes him look a good deal less modern.) The ample introductions and notes to these reprints integrated 'missionary linguistics' into American and European scholarship.[29]

As the editing of these primary sources may suggest, data came first for Pickering and Du Ponceau. The latter put his sarcastic finger on an "unfortunate" problem in Adam Smith's "very ingenious" conjectural essay on the origin of language: "it does not accord with facts, as far as our observations can trace them." Pickering explained the principle more soberly, "If we wish to study human speech as a science, just as we do other sciences," then we have to assemble "all the facts or phenomena." Only then can we "generalize and class those facts for the purpose of advancing human knowledge." Science thus demanded study of as many languages as possible—notably the "neglected dialects of our own continent." (Dialect and language still meant the same thing to Pickering.) Gathering linguistic facts meant not just scribbling words on a word list, as Jefferson had supposed. A missionary's idiosyncratic phonetic renderings of words in one Algonkian language rarely matched a trader's equally individual code for writing down another, making it impossible to compare the two word lists closely. This problem bedeviled students of nonwritten languages. To supply "the means of easily comparing the dialects with one another," Pickering devised in 1820 a uniform spelling system for

* Pickering's father, Timothy, served as Indian commissioner in George Washington's administration, interesting himself in Indian languages.

recording in Roman letters any language. Pickering believed his technique would work for "the barbarous and unwritten languages of the globe in general." ('Barbarous' was a technical term for a stage of social development, not a word of abuse.) European philologists seemed to agree. Sequoyah's syllabary for Cherokee eventually defeated Pickering's system as far as Amerindian tongues. But some missionaries in far corners of the world did adopt Pickering's spelling, and as a result it survives in written Hawaiian. So far, Pickering and Du Ponceau look like more careful, more ingenious clones of Jefferson or Benjamin Barton.[30]

Yet, unlike Jefferson or Barton, Du Ponceau and Pickering used their data to advance comparative analysis of languages. Jefferson and Barton wanted to deduce where Native Americans came from. That did not distract Du Ponceau and Pickering. Instead they tried to systematize study of Indian tongues, fit it into the broader frame of comparative philology, and generalize from it. (To this end Pickering learned German, a "well of science," as his German-speaking friend reminded him.) In 1819 Du Ponceau offered a hypothesis (a word he cautiously stressed) of a pattern evident in all New World languages, unlike any in the Old World. On this basis he suggested a single American family, distinct from all others.* Indian tongues "abound with highly compounded words." This feature led Du Ponceau to label them "polysynthetic" (a word that stuck). In polysynthetic tongues "the greatest number of ideas are comprised in the least number of words." Indian speech compressed utterances in two ways: sometimes by "interweaving together the most significant sounds or syllables of each simple word" to form a compound; sometimes by compacting subjects, objects, adjectives, conjunctions—any part of speech—with verbs. In 1835 Du Ponceau won the Prix Volney of the French Académie des Inscriptions et Belles-Lettres for a treatise on comparative grammar of Algonkian languages. The essay provided a model of linguistic typology and Americanist comparative grammar—and quietly refuted Humboldt's claim that American languages lacked full formal organization. Pickering, too, put forward original ideas, notably the distinction between 'inclusive' and 'exclusive' plurals. (The former—such as *we*—include both speaker and addressee; the latter exclude the person spoken to. Humboldt used this innovation in analyzing Malayo-Polynesian languages.) In 1831 Pickering sketched in twenty pages of the *Encyclopaedia Americana* a systematic program of Amerindian language research. It was translated into German three years later.[31]

The Enlightenment theory that "the science of languages" could reveal "the history of the progress and of the developments of the human mind" remained very much alive for both men—the quoted words were Du Ponceau's—but in practice the historical dimension dropped out of the study of Native American

---

*Linguists today reject the hypothesis of a single American language family but accept the feature Du Ponceau called polysynthetic. Sometimes one Native American word can express a meaning for which Indo-European languages need a sentence.

tongues, as it had in Humboldt's *Verschiedenheit des menschlichen Sprach-baues*. Du Ponceau and Pickering fully believed Amerindian languages to be genetically related. But they *had* to limit themselves to structure—typology and comparative grammar—because no one had a clue how these tongues evolved. In contrast to the Indo-European language family, genealogical analysis was impossible. Americanist philology became (to use terms of art) completely *synchronic*, losing the *diachronic* element of development over time so long integral to philological method. Du Ponceau and Pickering's philology seemed to them truncated, especially as compared to Indo-European philology; the loss of historical perspective put an unhappy limit on what they could say. But they hardly believed all was lost. Studying differing forms of language cast light on what Du Ponceau called in 1838 "the most hidden mysteries of the human understanding": the ways in which ideas present themselves and get linked together in minds operating under the rules of a given language. Some peoples express their ideas analytically, others (like Native Americans) synthetically. Nations *think* in their own distinctive ways—as James Harris and Johann Herder had insisted—because they *speak* in their own distinctive ways—as Wilhelm von Humboldt also claimed.[32]

As United States army expeditions fanned out west across the continent, and federal Indian agents followed in their wake, data about more and more languages drifted back east. In 1826 the War Department made such data accumulation an official initiative—using Pickering's spelling system. The Swiss-born Albert Gallatin, prominent in Du Ponceau's Philadelphia circle, took advantage of the flood of new information. American Indians had long fascinated Gallatin, once Jefferson's secretary of the treasury. After retiring as American minister to France in 1823, Gallatin—urged on by the renowned explorer Alexander von Humboldt, Wilhelm's younger brother—avidly pursued his old boss's hobby. In 1836 the American Antiquarian Society published Gallatin's "synopsis" of North American Indian tribes: over four hundred pages of small print. The bulk of them dealt with languages—the usual comparative vocabularies and specimens of grammatical forms. From this material the seventy-five-year-old Gallatin produced what Allan Taylor called the "first really thorough and rigorous classification" of North American Indian languages, a rock-solid foundation for future work. By meticulous, painstaking comparison, Gallatin transformed word lists into a systematic ordering of tribal language families. And, as will appear later, his "Synopsis" also assembled facts about Indian cultures and pushed the study of Indian languages toward ethnology.[33]

For Du Ponceau and Pickering, in contrast, such studies fitted into a larger world of language study, mostly divorced from culture. Du Ponceau published on subjects ranging from English phonology to Berber dialects to Chinese writing. Pickering wrote on classical lexicography, contemporary Americanisms, and an obscure Malayo-Polynesian tongue now called Tobian. In 1842 Pickering became the first president of the American Oriental Society. (By then, enough American scholars focused on languages and cultures of Asia—from ancient Israel to modern Japan—to sustain an organization devoted to orientalist scholarship. The AOS was the first learned society in the United States devoted to a specialized field of study, its *Journal* the first specialized scholarly periodical. These facts suggest how close to the center of intellectual life philology and its offshoots then stood. Indeed, the next such society and journal were the American Philological Association and its *Transactions*.) These two American lawyer-philologists joined European scholars in wedding Enlightenment-style conjectures about language ('theory') to the antiquarian/missionary tradition of amassing information on particular tongues ('data'). The two thus helped to birth the first scientific study of language: an articulation of general categories and rules, derived from or tested by empirical research, to apply in comparative analysis of any and all languages. The Prussian Academy of Sciences named Pickering a Corresponding Member; several European learned societies elected Du Ponceau to membership, including the Institut de France. Language study had become something like an integrated "science" (a word Pickering used), and a few learned American fully engaged in it.[34]

ANGLOPHONE SPECULATION ABOUT LANGUAGE

Their numbers, however, were small; nor did continental philology find a lot of fans in the United Kingdom before midcentury. A few English-speaking scholars trumpeted the achievements of comparative philology. Most clung to an older, eighteenth-century style of 'philosophic' speculation about language—typified in Adam Smith's essay on the origin of language that Du Ponceau disparaged. One of those books that began to bridge the English Channel around 1840, Donaldson's *New Cratylus*, likewise aimed "to oppose the extravagant nominalism and false philology" of John Horne Tooke's *Diversions of Purley*, "and others of a similar stamp."[35]

Diversions of Purley provides a handy entry into the sort of linguistic theorizing that exasperated Du Ponceau and Donaldson. Horne Tooke was an English political radical and sometime parson. He published *ΕΠΕΑ ΠΤΕΡΟΕΝΤΑ, or, The Diversions of Purley* in two parts, in 1786 (revised 1798) and 1805.* *Diversions of Purley* belonged very much to the Enlightenment mode of speculation about the nature of language as a means of inquiry into the human mind. "I very early found it impossible," Horne Tooke characteristically wrote, "to make many steps in the search after *truth* and the nature of *human understanding*, of *good* and *evil*, of *right* and *wrong*, without well

---

*Ἔπεα πτερόεντα/*epea pteroenta* means 'winged words': a Homeric formula familiar to every well-schooled male in Horne Tooke's day. Purley was the country estate of Horne Tooke's wealthy friend William Tooke, whose surname the former John Horne adopted, wrongly anticipating a legacy.

considering the nature of language, which appeared to me to be inseparably connected with them." Typical of the genre, fantastic etymologies based on surface resemblances between words crammed the book's thousand-plus pages. Horne Tooke's particular hobbyhorse was to reduce all thought to language. The mind receives impressions from the senses (as Locke said), but (contra Locke) it does nothing with them: "What are called its operations, are merely the operations of Language." A noun is the name or sign of a Lockean idea, while a verb is simply "the communication itself" of the idea/noun. Thought is an illusion. What we call 'thought' takes place outside the mind, in the ordering and reordering of words in human communication. Grasping this truth will abolish all general reasoning: philosophy, law, theology, political theories, morality. This is the "extravagant nominalism" that Donaldson denounced.[36]

But Horne Tooke's theory matters here less than the *kind* of thing he was up to. Philologists on the Continent had by and large abandoned the speculative language theory beloved of Enlightenment writers such as Adam Smith, Condorcet, and Herder, in favor of the focused, systematic, empirical investigations of a Bopp or a Rask. Meanwhile, debates about language in the United Kingdom continued for a while their freewheeling eighteenth-century ways. The Cambridge University polymath William Whewell argued with the Edinburgh freethinker Robert Chambers about the origin of language as late as 1845. Ten years earlier, the future cardinal Nicholas Wiseman—an orientalist then teaching in Rome and more up to date than philologists back home—bemoaned British ignorance of German comparative philology and the penchant instead to invent "fanciful etymologies derided to scorn by continental linguists." Wiseman had his eye most immediately on a Scottish minister, Alexander Murray—who "blends the rarest erudition with the most ridiculous theories." Murray's *History of the European Languages* (1823) lurched wildly between an Indo-Europeanist account (probably got from reading William Jones), on one hand, and conjectural etymologies and speculation on the origin of language, on the other. Several years later, such etymologizing became a fad among "the distinguished men" of Cambridge, according to John Wordsworth, a Trinity fellow. British disciples of the new comparative philology were much more the exception than the rule until around 1840.[37]

The appearance then of books like Donaldson's—and the translation of Bopp's *Comparative Grammar* that started in 1845—began Britain's gradual convergence with continental philology. From the late 1830s, London University students learned about the history of the English language, roughly in the style of Grimm. The founding of the Philological Society of London in 1842— with the Germanophile Bishop Connop Thirlwall in the chair—marks a symbolic watershed dividing old speculative philology from the new empirical sort. As Donaldson sneered, "we oppose to chimerical conjectures the results of a science founded on facts." Even then, British scholars by no means aped German comparative philology. Much British philology, especially textual editing and etymology, built on native traditions of scholarship. And not until after 1850 did the new empirical erudition bear much fruit: in Friedrich Max Müller's edition of the *Ṛg Veda* (1849–74); in Horace Hayman Wilson's translation of the same (1850–88); in Hensleigh Wedgwood's *Dictionary of English Etymology* (1857); and above all in the Philological Society's *New English Dictionary on Historical Principles*, begun at the end of the 1850s, using methods forged by German lexicographers, and completed three quarters of a century later. (The *New English Dictionary* is now called the *Oxford English Dictionary*.) Speculation did not vanish. Müller and Wedgwood, for instance, quarreled over the origin of language. But it retreated to the margins of British philology.[38]

In America the conjectural Enlightenment style ruled yet longer. In fact, the lexicographer Noah Webster—a fan of Horne Tooke—might even be classified as pre-Enlightenment. The etymologies in his *American Dictionary of the English Language* (1828) assumed that all languages descended from 'Chaldee' (biblical Aramaic), a notion more at home in the seventeenth century than the eighteenth. Webster's etymologies haunted the dictionary until 1864, when—its originator safely dead for two decades—the publisher put a trained German in charge of that part of the job. Most American discussions of language into the second half of the nineteenth century went on in a speculative mode like Horne Tooke's. Even intellectually robust American magazines paid relatively little attention before 1870 to comparative philology. When Americans did get interested, they tended to assimilate *wissenschaftliche* German scholarship to their own conjectural theories.[39]

One might even speak of a distinctive American species of speculative philology, alive well past 1850. The type was not defined by any consistent theory of language but instead by reliance on conjecture rather than research, by entanglement in theological polemics, and by recurrence to philosophical problems.

The Transcendentalist controversy that rent Massachusetts Unitarianism in the 1830s supplies an example. The fracas pitted Rev. Ralph Waldo Emerson against his divinity school teacher Andrews Norton. It blew up in large part over how language developed and what religious knowledge it thus could communicate. The Lockean conventionalist Norton insisted that words get their meanings from implicit general agreement—and so every English speaker understands pretty accurately what Jesus or St. Paul says in the English Bible. The Transcendentalist Emerson felt sure that words arise from intuitions of the real nature of the things they name—and so every individual is on a personal quest to mine spiritual realities underlying fallible words. As another Transcendentalist, Elizabeth Peabody, rephrased Emerson's theory of language in 1849, "there is some natural and inevitable reason why every word should be what it is." If a teacher used the right words to explain Newtonian physics, she went on, it "would be breathed into the mind and assimilated, as the body breathes in and assimilates air and food." Students could "skip the labored demonstrations without loss." But, as Norton would have asked, how do you know for sure the right words? Harvard did not adopt her curriculum. Neither did champions of Protestant orthodoxy swallow a linguistic theory that, as Norton feared, left the Bible and creeds subject to a near infinity of individual meanings.[40]

Writing about language in this conjectural mode, growing old-fashioned even in Britain, flourished in the United States until at least the 1860s. Indeed, Enlightenment-style surmise that speech evolved from gestures survives embedded in the mostly empirical writings of Du Ponceau. The Yale philologist Josiah Willard Gibbs argued in 1839 for a sonorous genesis of words. Different "articulate sounds have a natural adaptedness to express specific ideas." "*Bl* and *fl* denote *blowing, blooming,* and *flowing,*" while the "nasals *m* and *n* are employed to express *negation*, being the natural sounds to express refusal." A former student of Gibbs, the New England minister Horace Bushnell, published in 1849 a "Preliminary Dissertation on the Nature of Language, as Related to Thought and Spirit." In Bushnell's scheme, some words point directly to obvious "physical objects and appearances" (*horse, chair*). If abstract rather than concrete—you cannot point to 'god' or 'economics'—words derive from metaphors based on material entities. Etymologically, for instance, 'spirit' originated by analogy to the physical image of breathing—whereby 'inspire' can refer to both a spiritual impulse and the physiological act of taking in air. Because of this "analogic property" of abstract words, Bushnell went on, theologians and philosophers can only glimpse truths through a veil of words, not state them exactly. "Religion," he wrote, "has a natural and profound alliance with poetry."[41]

This kind of imaginative—and mostly imaginary—philology flourished. Alexander Bryan Johnson, a banker in Utica, New York, wrote *A Treatise on Language* that went through three revisions (1828, 1836, and 1854). Johnson categorized words by their referents: sensible (referring to sense perceptions), emotional (to inner feelings), or verbal (to other words). The 1854 edition added intellectual referents (to innate tendencies of mind). This analysis led him to a nominalism that might have pleased Horne Tooke. In 1836 a second philological banker, Rowland Gibson Hazard, wrote about the link between language and "the present condition and future prospects" of the human race, followed twenty years later by another volume speculating on language. William Cardell published in 1825 an *Essay on Language, as Connected with the Faculties of the Mind*—as Scottish Enlightenment in spirit as the title suggests. Charles Kraitsir, an immigrant protégé of Elizabeth Peabody, believed the proper "object of philology" was to recover the "natural language" that "lies at the basis of all languages." The key to unlock this lost treasure chest "is a knowledge of the elementary sounds, which are also expressed to the eye in the writing of different nations." Poor Bopp, Kraitsir thought, had lost himself in "considerations upon the vowel." (As the allusion suggests, Kraitsir knew contemporary European philology. He just chose not to practice it.) Thomas

Trautmann has uncovered the tracks of Adam Smith's *Dissertation on the Origin of Languages* in the early thinking about kinship of the anthropologist Lewis Henry Morgan. The linguistic theories of Americans floundered all over the map, but their method of probing language through philosophic conjecture united them.[42]

The handful of their fellow citizens who followed the newer, research-oriented philology of Europe cried out in despair of their countrymen. "Alas! one little upper chamber, how small! would hold the few elect spirits that have seen this new fire blazing on German altars, and snatched one spark from it to kindle the same glowing flame in their own hearts." So lamented one of these elect pyromaniacs, Benjamin Dwight, as late as 1859. Dwight also alluded to his remote cousin William Dwight Whitney, then professor of Sanskrit and comparative philology at Yale:

> Not only are very few works relating to general philology produced on our soil, but the number even of those imported from abroad is exceedingly scanty. We have in all the colleges of our country, only one professor of Sanskrit; and he, though a philologist of widely acknowledged eminence, finds but few pupils to avail themselves of his instructions.

Whitney in turn was the sole Sanskritist inducted by his Yale predecessor, Edward E. Salisbury. Salisbury himself had studied Arabic with Silvestre de Sacy and Garcin de Tassy in Paris, Sanskrit with Eugène Burnouf in Paris, Christian Lassen in Bonn, and Franz Bopp in Berlin—the leading men in Europe. A recognized scholar there, Salisbury stood utterly alone in American academe until the 1850s. Independently wealthy, he taught without pay at Yale. In twelve years as professor of Sanskrit, he had two students: the classicist James Hadley and Whitney. The story tells how marginal the new philology was to discourse on language in the United States.[43]

This had to be a matter of choice. As a dutiful reader of German philology and biblical criticism, someone like Harvard's Andrews Norton could hardly have remained unaware of changes in linguistic scholarship. Yet he refused to accept the narrowing of the field to topics amenable to empirical research. Other Americans proved equally stubborn. Norton's opposite number at Princeton, Charles Hodge, also knew of recent comparative philology but failed to bite. Henry Tappan, reforming head of the University of Michigan from 1852 to 1863, adored German universities. Yet his personal library held none of the new German-style philology while including *Diversions of Purley* and Nathaniel Fish Moore's *Short Introduction to Universal Grammar* (1844), just as old-fashioned. In his teaching Tappan set forth views of language hopelessly behind the times in Berlin or Copenhagen. The formidably learned Mary Lowell Putnam read and spoke Polish, Swedish, and Magyar (not to mention French, German, and Italian) and had more than a nodding acquaintance with several other tongues. She knew well the relations of language families as revealed by comparative philology; but she had no wish to speak this last argot. (Putnam was elder sister and early mentor of the equally learned poet James Russell Lowell—who lacked his sibling's facility for languages.) Americans continued to cultivate the broad-gauged Enlightenment approach to language even as it withered in the Germanic heartland of philology.[44]

Their resistance braked advances in empirical knowledge of human language, but it kept language study in touch with other realms of intellectual life, from which specialized European philology more or less cut itself off. Speculation about language probably played a role, for instance, in the shift toward modernism within American Protestant theology, as a quasi-symbolic view of the language of creeds developed. J. B. Stallo, a Cincinnati lawyer and ex-science professor, launched in *Concepts and Theories of Modern Physics* (1881) one of the first challenges to the conceptual foundations of classical physics. Stallo applied "laws governing the evolution of thought and speech" to analyze the axioms behind physical theories—"laws" that seem very like speculations by American language theorists, though he left his sources opaque. Stallo, in turn, influenced the celebrated Genevan linguist Ferdinand de Saussure. American language theories may also have lurked behind Chauncey Wright's famous 1873 essay on the "Evolution of Self-Consciousness"—one of the foundation stones of philosophic pragmatism—and its conception of linguistic signs. Such cross-fertilizations thwart a triumphalist narrative of the rise of comparative philology. Its victory involved losses as well as gains, as does every shift in modalities of scholarship. To put the point differently, American conjectures held together humanistic learning and philosophy—so often separated, if not hostile, in the long history of philology.[45]

Moreover, at a time when historical method dominated European study of language, the ahistorical American approach kept alive a synchronic alternative to diachronic comparative philology. The philologists studying Native American languages left history out because they lacked evidence for tracking change over time. The conjectural philologists did so because they wanted to. Both presented a model of how to analyze language without reference to its history. Granted, much of American thinking about language hardly merited the name of scholarship. But some of it, such as Alexander Bryan Johnson's writing, was analytically keen. If such synchronic theorizing ever paid serious attention to empirical data, it could generate plausible "general laws or general tendencies of language" that took into account "the known and recorded facts of human language." So said William Dwight Whitney, impatient with his fellow Americans' loose ruminations about language.[46]

The situation, as we have seen, was broadly the same on both sides of the English-speaking Atlantic. A few philologists in the United States before Whitney paid attention to German scholarship, took a comparative approach, worked with empirical rigor admired by continental European philologists: Pickering, Du Ponceau, Gallatin. But in the first half of the century, these students of American Indian languages remained a small European island in the midst of a sea of American speculation. They had no peers in the United Kingdom, save for a handful of Anglo-Saxon scholars. The few Britons who kept up with German comparative philology never enacted it in a research program. That would change.

Already, the work of the comparative, empirical philologists marked a decisive shift in organization of language study. Earlier, scholars mostly concerned with other matters made occasional (and occasionally brilliant) forays into linguistic questions—as American bankers and preachers still did. Bopp, Rask, and Grimm opened a period of systematic, *specialized* linguistic philology in German and Nordic universities and research institutions. (Even Jacob Grimm conducted his mythological, folkloric, and legal inquiries in parallel rather than in interaction with his *Deutsche Grammatik*; there seems to have been no conceptual melding.) Humboldt, after retiring from his political career in 1819, showed a like single-mindedness—focus even narrowing with age—and similar engagement with other scholars of language. So did Pickering, as far as the need to make a living permitted. (Du Ponceau remained the old-style sundry savant.) These philologists no longer spread their energies across wide fields of knowledge. And specific problems were now shared within a self-aware community and handed down from one generation of scholars to the next. "Only in our century," bragged Grimm in 1851, had language studies matured into "a true science." It looked more and more like a specialized modern 'discipline.'[47]

Its practitioners cast about for a name to set them apart from other philologists. In 1840 William Whewell suggested 'linguistic' as a label for "the science of languages"—following, he said, "the best German writers." Whewell had a knack for neologism: a few years earlier he had coined 'scientist.' This time Pickering beat him to the punch, in 1839, with the form that eventually stuck: *linguistics*, with an *s*. For quite a while, though, 'the science of language' (singular) was probably the commoner title. Pickering did not complain. He thought his work qualified as science.[48]

6

"GENUINELY NATIONAL POETRY AND PROSE"

LITERARY PHILOLOGY AND LITERARY
STUDIES, 1800–1860

John Pickering may have thought his new 'linguistics' a science, but no one yet believed that of the study of literature. Critical discussion and editing of vernacular literary texts began before 1700, but only after 1800 did such literary scholarship even get acknowledged as a distinct area of philological endeavor. This chapter will follow that process—not yet complete in 1860—to track how older modes of philological erudition evolved into a field teetering on the verge of a 'discipline' if not a 'science.'

Eighteenth-century writers applied to modern literature philological methods developed to deal with classical and biblical texts. Richard Bentley emended *Paradise Lost* in the same way (overly imaginative) he emended Horace. Other studies of modern literature then derived less obviously from classical and biblical philology but still showed their roots: Thomas Warton's *History of English Poetry* and Samuel Johnson's *Lives of the English Poets* both adapted the form of the classical or biblical commentary to postclassical literature.

These variations of philology did not amount to a coherent field perceived at the time as the study of 'literature.'* From the mid-eighteenth century, Scottish universities, American colleges, and English Dissenting academies did teach literature—*belles lettres*. But they taught it to train students to write rather than for intrinsic merit. Such teaching adapted the age-old study of rhetoric rather than studied literature in the modern sense. Students did not

---

* Literary scholars brawl about defining their object of study. I cannot referee. For their ancestors in the nineteenth and early twentieth centuries, 'literature' meant—very approximately— works with artistic, imaginative, or creative qualities that set them apart from everyday writing (newspaper reports, pop songs, memos to the boss, the words you are now reading).

peruse *Paradise Lost* for its own value; rather, it helped them to learn grammar. If you could parse Milton's lines, you could parse anything. Despite the editing of plays and poetry in the eighteenth century, despite the histories of poetry and of drama then composed, despite the use of Milton and Addison to teach grammar and rhetoric, 'literature' did not emerge as a distinct scholarly endeavor until after 1800. In 1720 you could call Richard Bentley a 'classical philologist' or a 'biblical philologist'; and the labels pointed to well-established, clearly understood domains of scholarship (though not modern academic disciplines). You could not locate Samuel Johnson writing the *Lives of the Poets* in any defined field of erudition.

Enter Literature

This changed after 1800, but not immediately. What happened at Harvard College is instructive, insofar as the advent of a teaching field suggests that contemporaries saw there a province of scholarship. In 1785 the Hancock Professor of Hebrew began to teach English grammar and composition (demand for Hebrew having dried up). Through this back door Harvard got a Scottish-style professor of rhetoric—without the name. In 1804 the Boylston Professorship of Rhetoric and Oratory regularized the situation, with John Quincy Adams the first incumbent. Upon resigning in 1810, the future president published his lectures. The book shows that Adams followed in Blair's footsteps, teaching students to write and speak effectively, not to cherish Shakespeare and Dryden. The college did not yet teach 'literature' in the sense of poetry, drama, fiction, and artistically crafted nonfiction, studied for its own sake. Literature of that sort invaded Harvard in 1819, when George Ticknor became the first Smith Professor of French and Spanish. Abiel Smith, donor of the chair and a practical man, meant for his professor to do what the chair's name implied—teach French and Spanish. Ticknor wanted instead to lecture on literature. The college president caved in, hiring a low-level instructor to drill students in the languages. For the next fifteen years, Ticknor gave annually a course of lectures on Spanish "literary history and criticism" and another such on French. His successor, Henry Wadsworth Longfellow, continued to lecture on literature, leaving language teaching mostly to others. And, like Ticknor, Longfellow began his tenure of the Smith chair by taking leave to study in Europe. Both men conceived themselves as literary researchers, not simply teachers. Ticknor's erudition eventually issued in his *History of Spanish Literature* (1849), Longfellow's in his translation of Dante's *Divine Comedy* (1865–67).[1]

Ticknor possibly counts as the first professor of postclassical literature in the English-speaking world, but others soon arrived.* In 1828 the new London

---

* I say "possibly" because little or nothing is known about what foreign-language instructors in colleges and universities taught before 1819.

University named Rev. Thomas Dale as the first professor of English in the United Kingdom. The choice seems odd given Dale's devout Anglicanism and London University's devout secularism. Like Scottish professors of rhetoric, Dale taught composition; unlike them, he also surveyed English literature, in lectures running from Anglo-Saxon times through the eighteenth century. King's College (the Anglican riposte to London University*) named its own professor of English literature and history in 1835—Rev. Thomas Dale. William Spalding, Edinburgh's professor of rhetoric in the early 1840s, possibly included literature in his lectures as more than aid to rhetoric. Literature as a university study popped up around this time on the continent as well. In 1830 Claude Fauriel turned down a chair in French literature in Geneva to accept a new one of foreign literature in Paris, the first in France. Shortly thereafter, the University of Basel created a chair in French literature and rhetoric for Alexandre Vinet. Literature professorships appeared erratically. The United Kingdom may have had none *outside* London until 1849, when George Craik became professor of English literature and history at the new Queen's College Belfast. Canada got its first in 1853 when the University of Toronto named the Scot Daniel Wilson Professor of History and Literature. (History and literature were commonly yoked when the subjects first appeared.) Literature had surfaced as something like a recognized learned field, typically divided along national or linguistic lines. Another indicator: in 1808 the Royal Institution sponsored a lecture series on literature (delivered by Coleridge), the first major such event in England.[2]

Yet the modern idea of a discipline, with its reasonably clear if artificial borders, lay in the future. Even after professors began to profess it, literature took a long time to congeal as a field apart. One of F. A. Wolf's students, Karl Morgenstern, held the now mind-boggling title at the University of Dorpat of *Professor der Beredsamkeit und altclassischen Philologie, der Ästhetik und der Geschichte der Literatur und Kunst* (Professor of Eloquence and Classical Philology, of Aesthetics, and of the History of Literature and Art). What sounds today like confusion of tongues may at the time have composed a larger harmony. Consider a man who appears later in this chapter, John Mitchell 'Anglo-Saxon' Kemble—elder brother of the renowned actress Fanny Kemble. Fanny's brother published a study of an Anglo-Saxon dialect in the spirit of comparative Germanic philology. He edited Anglo-Saxon charters. He used such records to probe problems in pre-Norman institutional and legal history. He edited Anglo-Saxon poetry. He excavated barrows and the like. He never thought of himself as moving to and fro between comparative grammar, history, literature, and digging in the ground. He simply pursued his fascination with the Anglo-Saxon world.[3]

---

* In a compromise, in 1836 a royal charter created a new degree-granting University of London, of which King's College and London University, renamed University College, became constituents.

Even when perceived as a discrete field, literature covered diverse terrain, owing to varied inheritances from philology. Indeed, for many decades after Ticknor's appointment, informed observers considered literary scholarship a branch of philology. This comes as no surprise when one recalls that in 1867 William Dwight Whitney defined *philologist* as any "student of human thought or knowledge as deposited in literary records." ("Literary" here just meant written.) It helps to remember that in antiquity 'criticus' (though rare in classical Latin) was virtually a synonym for philologist. When its child 'criticism' appeared in English in the seventeenth century, the new word meant both textual criticism and (as John Dryden put it, hiding behind Aristotle) "a Standard of judging [a written work] well. The chiefest part of which is, to observe those Excellencies which should delight a reasonable Reader." The study of vernacular literature in the eighteenth century had included both of these elements: *textual criticism* in editions of poets and playwrights; *evaluative criticism* among rhetoricians drumming into students the "Excellencies" of Augustan prose. The inchoate studies that became 'literature' in the next century also included *literary history*, à la Warton and Johnson.[4]

Understanding how the new field of 'literature' grew after 1800 requires tracking all three types of philology—quests for the perfected text, for its fullest meaning, and for the historical evolution of its genre. In these pursuits, English and American philologists chased mostly after English-language works, just as German scholars usually studied texts in German, and erudite Italians worked on writings in Italian and its ancestors. Accordingly this chapter looks mostly at English literature. While skills of *textual philologists* of modern literature grew only incrementally more sophisticated, *evaluative criticism* and *literary history* changed profoundly. The era of *Altertumswissenschaft* and 'higher criticism' of the Bible had dawned. The literary historian still traced a chronological sequence of poets or dramatists. But he or she now tried to place them in richer contexts and to use them to illumine their age or vice versa. The critic not only assessed the 'excellencies' of a text according to some accepted standard; he or she also sought the *meaning* of a text. Explaining its sense still involved clarifying words by historical context, but also entailed seeking 'meaning' in some deeper sense.

EDITING TEXTS

Developments in textual editing pose no puzzles; for while volume grew, principles changed little. Whether Bentley's edition of *Paradise Lost* in 1732 or Elstob's edition of Ælfric's life of Gregory the Great in 1709, textual editors constructed editions of English writers by applying methods worked out over centuries by classical and biblical critics. Bentley did the job expertly and wildly; Elstob did it unfussily and lucidly. Nineteenth-century editors behaved much as Bentley and Elstob. They probably rarely thought of their classical or biblical ancestors, since English textual philology was by 1800 naturalized. The greatest beneficiary and victim of such editing was William Shakespeare, thanks to the iconic status he achieved in the previous century.[5]

Shakespeare instances the *kind* of author likeliest to receive editorial attention: an older writer, whose works contained variant and uncertain readings, whose archaic language sometimes needed explanation. Nationalism played a role, too: English poets and playwrights provided some of the stuff of English identity. Technical issues challenged editors. The texts of Shakespeare's plays were (and are) notoriously unstable. The First Folio misleadingly seemed to set in stone lines that varied from performance to performance, from copy to copy. Lesser but like problems dogged texts of other pre-1700 writers—Milton, Dryden, Donne, Skelton, Chaucer, and Spenser. They all appeared in new versions between 1800 and 1860. Their editors emulated, consciously or unconsciously, the well-worn craft of classical and biblical philologists, though by and large with less sophistication. It says something about the increasing self-awareness of literary scholars that the intended audience of Shakespeare editions underwent a sea change. Eighteenth-century editors typically aimed at theater-goers. Starting with the Irishman Edmond Malone's 1790 edition—and even more obviously in the massive notes to a twenty-one-volume revision of Malone finished in 1821 by the younger James Boswell—editors had in mind readers of scholarly bent and stamina. The first variorum Shakespeares appeared in 1803 and 1813.* Mary (Novello) Cowden Clarke compiled a *Complete Concordance to Shakespeare* in 1845.[6]

At the expert end of the editing spectrum stood Alexander Dyce (1798–1869). A few classicists today remember Dyce as editor of Bentley's works (an act of piety repaying his debt to Bentley's editorial model). Otherwise the black hole of history has sucked him in. But Dyce shows the growing professionalism of textual editing in this period. "Huge, shambling, awkward, ungainly," in Hazlitt's portrayal, Dyce as editor was the opposite. He edited classical texts as a hobby. He paid the rent with erudite editions of early modern writers, especially playwrights of Shakespeare's era. His output included the works of George Peele, John Webster, Robert Greene, Christopher Marlowe, James Shirley, Thomas Middleton, John Skelton, Francis Beaumont, John Fletcher, and Shakespeare himself—as well as William Kemp(e)'s account of morris dancing from London to Norwich in 1600, *Kemps Nine Daies Wonder*. Capable contemporaries judged his Shakespeare text the best yet made. Dyce also edited eighteenth-century authors, including the poets William Collins, Mark Akenside, and Alexander Pope, and the Scottish philosopher James Beattie. In 1825 he put out an anthology of women writers, *Specimens of British Poetesses*. Despite titanic productivity, he kept a reputation for acumen and learning. A few years after his death a commentator remarked, "His wide

---

* A variorum edition, such as the Boswell-Malone, contains either notes by different scholars, or variant readings of the text, or both.

reading in Elizabethan literature enabled him to explain much that was formerly obscure in Shakespeare; while his sound judgment was a sure check to anything like extravagance in emendation"—the ancient virtues of the comparative method, the meticulous philologist. Biographies attached to his editions added to literary history. His five-hundred-page Shakespeare glossary clarified the texts while advancing the history of the language. His leadership in groups formed to underwrite editions of premodern English texts—the Camden Society, the Percy Society, the Shakespeare Society—testified to Dyce's scholarly stature.[7]

Until midcentury, circumstances almost barred American philologists from this branch of erudition. A young Harvard philologist, Francis Child, explained why in letters to the English antiquarian James Halliwell in 1849. North America had no manuscripts, vanishingly few early printed texts, ill-stocked libraries. Of the "many private collections of rare volumes in the Northern states," none hold "much to assist the student of English literary antiquities." Publicly accessible libraries, like Harvard's, "have very limited means, and are therefore under the necessity of laying out their money on books of general usefulness." Child wanted to edit the plays of John Marston (ca. 1576–1634) but saw "the obvious impracticality of doing such a thing properly out of England." "Of his plays, except in reprints, I suppose not one is to be found in America. To acquire the necessary materials by purchase is of course out of the question, since some rarities are not to be bought, and one would not easily be satisfied without examining all the various editions." Harvard's library, Child pointed out, though "the largest in America" (not, he knew, big by European standards*), "is extremely deficient in the department of English Literature, wanting many of the commonest books." Two decades later another Harvard literary scholar, James Russell Lowell, still griped about this.[8]

When the SS *Great Western* began scheduled transatlantic steamship service in 1838, it started to lift these obstacles to American research in English literature. Inauguration of Cunard Line service in 1840 made frequent, scheduled crossings a reality. The earliest steamships took about two weeks to cover the New York–Liverpool route. Within a few years that fell to ten days; by the late 1870s, a week. Prices fell, too. Summer research trips to Europe became feasible. As important, mail moved much faster.[9]

Francis Child took advantage of this transportation revolution—and he became the first American scholar of English literature highly regarded across the Atlantic. In 1848, two years out of college, he had published a collection of four sixteenth-century English plays, with introduction and notes. Recognizing his promise, Harvard gave him leave to study in Germany for a year. He learned much in a short time, at Berlin and Göttingen. Jacob Grimm's comparative work on Germanic languages supplied a key Child later used to solve English philological puzzles by examining Danish and German parallels. He

---

* Child told Halliwell in 1849 that Harvard held "60000 or 70000" volumes in toto.

returned to Harvard in 1851. Thereafter, except for rare trips to Britain, he conducted research through a thick network of correspondents. In this way he did fundamental work on Chaucer's grammar and meter (1863), authoritative for twenty years, and, most famously, edited a five-volume *English and Scottish Popular Ballads* (1883–98), still a standard. First, however, Child oversaw for the Boston publisher Little, Brown the first reliable American texts of British poets. Child himself edited a five-volume Spenser (1855), solid enough that forty years later one expert (partial to Child) thought it still the edition of first resort.[10]

Another volume in this series supplies a good example of how midcentury editors went about their work. In 1855 James Russell Lowell edited the poems of John Donne for Child's series. Lowell, though best remembered for his own poetry, was deeply learned in languages and literatures (entirely self-taught). Indeed, in 1856 he became Child's colleague at Harvard, succeeding Longfellow as Smith Professor. The lapses of an autodidact with small editorial experience marred his edition of Donne here and there. And Lowell painfully felt the handicap he worked under without access to materials in England: no manuscripts, many fewer early editions. Constrained by time as well as materials, fueled by common sense more than expertise, Lowell nevertheless doggedly followed long-standard canons of textual editing. Seven collections of Donne's poetry had been printed in the seventeenth century. The textual tradition in Lowell's day mainly went back to the last of these, in 1669, although the poet's most recent editor (1839), Henry Alford, had used the first edition of 1633. Alford however omitted the grunt work of collating different texts. Lowell, in about four months and with fewer editions to examine (possibly only one from before 1700), did a more thorough job. He shrewdly triangulated among editions available to him and made occasional inspired inferences from them and from internal evidence in the poems. His notes, according to the Donne expert Dayton Haskin, "printed more textual variants than any reader of Donne's poetry had ever seen before" (over eighty). Lowell also "began to show that the earliest editions sometimes contain readings" better than in modern editions. While basically hewing to the textual tradition stemming from 1669, he emended it more than any previous scholar.[11]

Lowell's work displayed a novel strength of nineteenth-century textual work: the ability to produce accurate editions—exact even in specifying unresolvable uncertainties in the text—by imaginative study of a growing number of *earlier* versions of the same author. None of these early Victorian editors stood on the shoulders of giants. But by piling up the works of run-of-the-mill precursors, the better editors did see farther than previous ones. Granted, a few were cockeyed. The best-remembered Shakespeare from midcentury is a six-volume edition in 1858 by the respected philologist John Payne Collier. It used emendations in seventeenth-century handwriting that Collier discovered in a copy of the Second Folio (1632). In fact, he had forged the 'corrections,' in a plausible script. You cannot help but admire both expertise and chutzpah. (Collier was a genuinely talented and productive scholar as well as compulsive forger.) Less ingeniously, Child supplied a better text of Spenser through increasingly sophisticated mastery of textual history and language. Child's was the usual story—no dramatic discovery, just plodding progress.[12]

In Anglo-Saxon texts, honest-to-goodness novelty did sometimes surface. In most technical respects, Anglo-Saxon editing did not differ from editing Shakespeare. However, these manuscripts did raise trickier linguistic and cultural questions; on these, recent research in comparative grammar by philologists like Grimm could cast light. More sensationally, recoveries of texts 'lost' for centuries grabbed the attention of the reading public. Emending Spenser altered a well-known text slightly; Anglo-Saxon philologists revealed works hardly known before. Finally, Anglo-Saxon editing fed, and fed on, an identity politics more intense than, say, the cult of Shakespeare as the English Bard.

Once again nationalism fueled philology; and, once again, language, race, and fanciful identities ran together. In King Alfred's day lay the time-shrouded origins of English culture, society, polity. In 1840 'Anglo-Saxon' Kemble told Jacob Grimm, "We Englishmen, tho' we do not read Anglo[-Saxon] much, are beginning to feel very proud of our Teutonic element." The last three words were key. In the nineteenth century a stronger stress fell on Germanic ancestors as foundation of Englishness. Nor were imagined Angles and Saxons the only Teutonic folk in English genealogy. (Few historians today would bet on Angles and Saxons ever having existed as distinct peoples swarming into England.) Vikings—irresistibly bold, blond, and berserk—had conquered northern and eastern England in the ninth century. They settled in large numbers in this so-called Danelaw (i.e., where laws of the Danes ruled); and they contributed to England's vocabulary as well as its gene pool. The Anglo-Saxon Chronicle despised the pagan Vikings. Victorians loved them. (Vikings also founded Dublin but without elevating English opinion of the Irish.) Well-educated English people added Norsemen to their national lineage, adopted eddas as an honorary Anglo-Saxon literary genre.[13]

Many 'old-stock' white Americans, too, started to see 'Anglo-Saxon' as a badge of identity (Vikings not so often). Anglo-Saxon fervor rose in the 1840s, in the face of two antitypes: hungry Celtic immigrants pouring in from Ireland and Mexican soldiers fighting in the Mexican-American War. Meanwhile, in the United States, as in England, study of Anglo-Saxon language was spreading, although its heyday came after 1870 (as did the heyday of racial Anglo-Saxonism). Formal instruction began, at Jefferson's urging, at the University of Virginia. In 1825 the new university recruited a German-born Londoner, Georg Blaetterman, to teach the language. By the 1840s—with Anglo-Saxonism rising—a handful of other schools mimicked Virginia. A native Virginian, Louis F. Klipstein, after a few years in Presbyterian ministry, went off around 1840 to study in Giessen. He returned to publish an Anglo-Saxon grammar, an anthology, and a couple of texts. Badly edited, freeloading on English publications, they showed more enthusiasm than skill.[14]

Across the Atlantic both were in evidence. Anglo-Saxon erudition had gone to sleep after its burst of energy in the decades either side of 1700—the age of Hickes, Wanley, the Elstobs. Every now and then, it woke up briefly. In 1772 Rev. Edward Lye published a dictionary of Anglo-Saxon and Gothic. In 1819 Anna Gurney translated the Anglo-Saxon Chronicle into modern English. But a chair of Anglo-Saxon founded at Oxford in 1755 sat empty for forty-five years, then fell to a man largely ignorant of the language. The alarm clock finally rang in 1826 when Benjamin Thorpe traveled to Copenhagen to sit at the feet of Rasmus Rask, the comparative philologist. In 1830 Thorpe translated into modern English Rask's Anglo-Saxon grammar. He returned home the same year, to a long career of editing Anglo-Saxon texts. (Thorpe's younger contemporary Frederic Madden did the same for what we now call Middle English texts, such as *Sir Gawain and the Green Knight*.) In 1838, Rev. Joseph Bosworth published his *Dictionary of the Anglo-Saxon Language* (the first to give definitions in English, not Latin). By then Henry Wadsworth Longfellow declared that more had been done "within the last fifteen years, to excite an interest in the Anglo-Saxon language and literature" than in the previous three hundred. He did not mention that the interest excited few people enough to learn the language.[15]

Comparative philology did make its study more rigorous and accurate, as John Mitchell Kemble showed. A bemused William Whewell reported in 1834 that Kemble "founds himself altogether on James Grimm." (Bosworth's dictionary would have benefited from founding itself on Grimm.) Kemble's mother came from Austria, and he grew up hearing German. This gave him a leg up on almost all British contemporaries. While still nominally a Cambridge student, he spent much of 1829 in Germany, studying philology with Andreas Schmeller in Munich and developing a taste for Anglo-Saxon. He learned then of Grimm's work in comparative grammar. In 1832 Kemble settled back in Cambridge to study medieval law and Anglo-Saxon manuscripts. He drilled himself in Grimm's *Deutsche Grammatik*; he visited Germany again. Before turning thirty, Kemble published comparative Germanic philology in the spirit of Grimm and in the city of Munich, *Über die Stammtafel der Westsachsen* (*On the Lineage of the West Saxons*, 1836). (Late West Saxon, the literary language of England in the hundred and fifty years before the Norman Conquest, is also the Old English dialect in which most writings survive.) Kemble had made himself the linguistically best-grounded Anglo-Saxon scholar in Britain. In 1832 he began a twenty-year correspondence with Grimm; they met face to face in Göttingen two years later. In 1833 Kemble made the first stab at a scholarly edition—not all that scholarly—of three of the four major Anglo-Saxon poems then known. He dedicated it to Grimm.[16]

One of the three was *Beowulf*. In 1700 Humfrey Wanley had found the sole manuscript of *Beowulf* in Robert Cotton's library. Wanley briefly described it in his catalog, making it known to an erudite few. The saga then sat lonely in the library—getting badly singed in a fire in 1731—until 1786. In that year

Grímur Jónsson Thorkelin, an Icelandic philologist in Danish service, looked it over, arranged for a transcript, and at last published it in 1815, with a Latin translation. He thought *Beowulf* a Danish saga written in Anglo-Saxon. Ten years earlier, Sharon Turner had called attention to *Beowulf* in his *History of the Anglo-Saxons*, claiming it for England, mangling its plot, translating a few gobs. J. J. Conybeare, onetime professor of Anglo-Saxon at Oxford, translated longer selections with commentary in 1826. Five years later, Longfellow commended the poem to readers of the *North American Review*. Word was getting around. Meanwhile, the Danish philologist N.F.S. Grundtvig published in 1820 a proper learned edition, with Danish translation. He rounded up a list of subscribers headed by the king of England and archbishop of Canterbury. A foreigner laying hands on what had by now become an Ur-text of Englishness outraged the patriotism of the Society of Antiquaries. Kemble stepped in. First came his 1833 stopgap edition—prefaced with a defense of the Anglo-Saxon identity of Beowulf himself, no less robust for being wrong. In 1836 Kemble finished his aforementioned treatise on West Saxon, the dialect of the *Beowulf* manuscript (though probably not of the poem originally). Grimmian philology rescued him from blunders of his earlier version. In 1837 he published *Beowulf* in full philologic array, with notes, glossary, and modern English translation (dedicated again, even more aptly, to "James Grimm"). Thus the king of the Geats stepped onto the stage of English literature. Mere editors of Shakespeare could do naught but envy the glory of it all.[17]

Little glory attached yet to editing of ancient Irish texts; but it, too, became a learned pursuit in the first half of the century, if a lonely one. Old Irish texts posed greater problems than Anglo-Saxon ones. Irish editors lacked the erudite aids—dictionaries, grammars, printed editions of comparable texts—that Anglo-Saxon scholars had refined since the seventeenth century. Comparative Celtic philology scarcely existed, while comparative Germanic studies thrived. If seeing Anglo-Saxon texts into print was tough, barriers to publishing Irish texts, far lower in status, stretched to the sky. Nonetheless, a few learned, stubborn men began to try. In 1831 John O'Donovan—who described himself as "so infatuated with such studies as to be unable to take delight in any other pursuit"—tackled "Leabhar Í Eadhra" ("The Book of O'Hara"). This sixteenth-century manuscript contained bardic poems mostly about the chiefs of O'Hara (Ó hEadhra in Irish), compiled at the behest of the Elizabethan head of the clan. One Mícheál Óg Ó Longáin had already transcribed it in 1826; and the "highly judicious, learned" Dr. Heard had made (O'Donovan reported) "a literal translation of some poems in the MS." O'Donovan now proposed to translate the whole thing, "with notes to elucidate idiomatic peculiarities, peculiar Irish phrases, old names of *places*, *men*, *Rivers* &c, with the derivation of such, and to postfix an Index referring to every subject and curious passage in the whole Book." In short, he wanted to do for "The Book of O'Hara" something like what Kemble was about to do for *Beowulf*. How far O'Donovan got beyond a twenty-four-page, handwritten description of the manuscript and its difficulties—if any distance at all—is unclear from extant records. Not until 1951 did a learned Irish Jesuit actually publish *The Book of O'Hara* under the aegis of the Dublin Institute for Advanced Studies.[18]

Neither O'Donovan's nor Kemble's work—nor that of any other editor of ancient languages of the United Kingdom—added a truly new implement to the tool box of textual criticism. Even the use of comparative philology to cast light on obscure words simply extended the analysis of grammar and vocabulary familiar to philologists since antiquity. Puzzling out the likeliest form of a text by close attention to its words, by comparison to related texts, by drawing on contexts such as legal institutions or religious practices—these procedures had long been stock-in-trade of textual philology.

The New Literary Critic

Evaluative criticism (henceforth in this section simply 'criticism') was more innovative. Like textual editing, such criticism continued old philological habits: close attention to the words of a text; elucidation of their meanings by comparison with other texts. Unlike textual philology, criticism underwent a revolution in the half century after 1800.

Eighteenth-century Scottish rhetoricians held no monopoly on evaluating writing against some standard principles. This was timeworn rhetorical practice, although particular principles fell in and out of fashion. Samuel Johnson assessed literature by moral probity, faithfulness to life, expression of abstract and universally applicable truths, and adherence to neoclassical canons of diction, prosody, and rational coherence. This kind of criticism survived into the next century. For a decade or more after 1800, American critics insisted on 'purity' of poetic diction—meaning abstract rather than concrete, elevated rather than everyday language. (Wordsworth flunked.) Reviewers of novels in American magazines as late as the 1850s judged them by (in Nina Baym's words) "the artistic execution of formal features, the picture of life provided by the novel, and the interest achieved by the work"—especially the last. The critic should, according to New York's *Knickerbocker Magazine* in 1840, "apply the standard of the immutable laws of nature to the productions of art."[19]

By then, however, such pronouncements sounded to sophisticated ears like bombast—for three reasons: the simple fact of growing erudition, the circulation of certain German ideas, and the transfer of biblical interpretation to secular texts.

First, learned critics applied to "the productions of art" something harder to come by and less rigid than "immutable laws of nature": they applied wide reading and tempered judgment. Such erudite criticism rose to prominence gradually, hit or miss. The literary output of a small but growing number of eighteenth-century writers included criticism. Samuel Johnson was most eminent; but others, such as Bishop Richard Hurd and Elizabeth Montagu and her so-called Bluestocking Circle, belong on the list. By 1800, critical commentary on earlier writers had become a familiar genre. Some writers made a living from magazine articles of this sort and introductions to reprints of poets or playwrights. Mary Wollstonecraft did so before *A Vindication of the Rights of Woman* made her famous. The thick quarterly reviews that dominated highbrow journalism for much of the century—starting with the *Edinburgh Review* in 1802—made such writing a centerpiece of intellectual life in the United Kingdom and North America. Some regular reviewers did it to make money (Edgar Allan Poe), others to make points (another Southerner, Hugh Swinton Legaré—pronounced 'Legree'). Something resembling professionalism spread during this period, even among writers who did not work for money.[20]

But was this quasi-professional criticism truly erudite, a plausible offspring of learned philology? One needs first to ask what counted as 'learning' in literary critics. The answer is pretty much what counted as erudition for any philologist: knowledge of languages; awareness of theoretical or methodological canons; wide familiarity with context (chiefly, in this case, other literature with which to compare the work under the microscope); skill sharpened through on-the-job training. Measured by these criteria, reviewers ran the gamut. The English poet and essayist Anna Letitia Barbauld and the South Carolina lawyer Hugh Swinton Legaré—both highly educated (informally, in Barbauld's case); both avid readers all their lives—qualified as learned by any standard. No one would have said so about Elizabeth Inchbald. A mediocre English actor who became a successful playwright and novelist, Inchbald made the mistake of contracting to write critical introductions for a series of British plays (1808). She quickly found her brain too thinly stocked for the job but could not get the publisher to let her go. In general, writers for the quarterlies worked at a high average of erudition, while reviewers for less exalted magazines were often unfitted for critical reactions more nuanced than panting or outrage. ('Often' is a key qualification.) Extremes of competence reflected the state of the art. Study of modern literature was crawling out of its chrysalis as a field of learning. Whereas theological seminaries or college fellowships set informal minimums for biblical and classical philologists ('minimum' often the exact word), no such controls regulated literary scholarship, however 'professional' it sometimes looks in retrospect. Yet *some* critics did wield real erudition specific to the emerging field of literature.[21]

The second reason why evaluative criticism changed in the early 1800s came from German-speaking Europe. In the later eighteenth century, two currents of thought revolutionized how erudite Germans approached literature. The first, discussed earlier, was the way of thinking—like Herder's—that saw language and thought as inseparable. It viewed each people's language (and therefore literature) as expressing its culture's distinctive inner character. And it believed that all cultures develop their potentialities through evolution over time. These axioms encouraged critics to understand authors by situating them in the historically specific cultures that produced them—an old philological principle given now a philosophical foundation and a stronger stress on differences dividing civilizations.

The second current stemmed from the philosophy of Immanuel Kant and his disciples, developers, revisers, interpreters, and misinterpreters. Most notable in the English-speaking world was Samuel Taylor Coleridge. In lectures on literature in the 1810s and in *Biographia literaria* (1817), Coleridge stole from post-Kantian German idealist writers, pillaging August Schlegel with special thoroughness. Coleridge propounded an aesthetics and a theory of poetry centered on the mental states of writer and reader and the organic oneness of the poem or play; to wit, "images and feelings . . . brought together without effort and without discord." For present purposes, details of Coleridge's critical theory do not matter. What signifies, rather, is a turn away from analyzing a literary work in terms of formal qualities (as did Scottish rhetorical critics) toward analyzing it in terms of how the work relates to psychological states of imagined readers. This introduced a new kind of 'meaning' into literary works.[22]

These two new German ways of grappling with literature—in shorthand, cultural-historical and psychological—combined to shape British and American literary studies. Coleridge was only one mediator of German ideas to English-speaking audiences. Germaine de Staël's *De l'Allemagne* (*On Germany*) first circulated in an 1813 English translation (Napoleon's censors having pulped the French printing). *On Germany* introduced many British and American readers to the new waves of German thought. In 1818 John Gibson Lockhart translated Friedrich Schlegel's *Vorlesungen über die Geschichte der alten und neuen Literatur* as *Lectures on the History of Literature, Ancient and Modern*. Perhaps most widely read were the 1808 Vienna lectures of Schlegel's brother August, *Vorlesungen über dramatische Kunst und Litteratur* (*Lectures on Dramatic Art and Literature*), translated in 1815 by John Black. All these works circulated in America almost as soon as they appeared in the United Kingdom. William Prescott recorded Friedrich Schlegel's "reflections on the poetry of the Middle Ages" in his notebook in 1823 and knew of his brother as well.[23]

These German ideas influenced Britons and Americans because they resonated with native-born notions, especially Scottish Enlightenment ones. Thomas Reid's "intuitions of the mind" chimed in roughly the same register as Kantian epistemology. The psychological explorations of writers like Reid, James Beattie, and Dugald Stewart sometimes ran on similar lines to the concepts of Schelling and August Schlegel. Above all, Herder's literary insight— that the literature of a people expresses distinctive, evolving cultural traits— flowed smoothly alongside Scottish theories of the evolution of the mind through progressive stages, not to mention James Harris's *Hermes*. And these Scottish ways of thinking did not lurk on the fringes of Anglophone culture. They had a commanding intellectual presence—in Scotland, obviously; in Scotland's cultural province, northern Ireland; in England, where they did face more competition; and in the United States, where in higher education the

Scottish Enlightenment cloned itself. Even Hugh Blair's ubiquitous *Lectures on Rhetoric and Belles Lettres* explained how language mirrors the "sensibility" of a people and their developmental level in terms that might serve as prolegomenon to Herder.[24]

So a Germanized conceptual vocabulary became general among critics in Britain and the United States—at least among those who brought erudition to the practice. New York reviewers in the forty-five years before the Civil War, according to John Paul Pritchard, seem mostly to have judged literature by "the moral qualities or effects of the work, its appeal to popular taste, and its emotional appeal." Superficial judgments may have been generic in slapdash magazine reviewing, as opposed to the highbrow quarterlies. But Rev. George Allen, professor of languages at Delaware College, familiar with Herder and Coleridge, articulated in 1838 a sophisticated theory of "reproductive criticism" in which the critic's job was to replicate the creative process of the author. Another disciple of Coleridge, the Boston Unitarian minister William Ellery Channing, offered a variant in 1828. A work "of fiction or of imaginative art" brings us "delight" because in it "our own nature is set before us in more than human beauty and power." "Poetry has," he said, "a natural alliance with our best affections." The passions depicted in poetry "excite a deep though shuddering sympathy" in the reader. And a reader properly understands a poem only by its resonance with the state of the reader's mind. One more American Coleridgean, Edwin Whipple, introduced the word *interpretation*—previously a term of art among biblical critics—to distinguish a proper, Coleridgean procedure from the criticism of those who wished to judge rather than to understand a work.[25]

Whipple's borrowing from biblical philology points to the third fruitful source of this new critical mentality. In interpreting the Bible, Protestants stressed its literal sense. But, particularly in preaching, the 'spiritual' senses—allegory, typology, and so forth—continued to thrive in the English-speaking world. Stephen Prickett has pointed out how these patterns resurfaced in the structure of novels. So Jane Austen (a pastor's daughter) secularized "old-fashioned biblical typology" to create double meanings in the scene in *Mansfield Park* (1814) where a locked garden gate stops Rushworth, Crawford, and Maria Bertram. Likewise, in *Adam Bede* (1859), George Eliot (translator of the German biblical critic David Strauss) used typology and allegory to contrast the self-absorbed Hetty with the pious Dinah as the two prepare for bed in their chambers.* Austen and Eliot underline a general point. Authors writing prose fiction reworked—and no one suggests Austen was the first—long-familiar methods of biblical reading to create secular literary symbolism. The adaptation was not necessarily self-conscious. Bible reading saturated Anglophone Protestant culture.[26]

---

* These scenes appear in chapter 10 of *Mansfield Park* and chapter 15 of *Adam Bede*, respectively.

Here was a two-way street. For literary critics—again, almost instinctively—analyzed authors using modes of interpretation engrained by centuries of biblical exegesis. In 1863 Matthew Arnold, denying that "arithmetical demonstrations" could tell us anything worth knowing about the Bible, drew a sharp line between scientific truth and religious truth. Yes, science and reason (he had his eye on German 'higher criticism') could show how the Bible was assembled, could destroy the historical credibility of the Pentateuch. But science could not draw out the positive meanings of Scripture, could not edify; for "the Bible-language is not scientific, but the language of common speech or of poetry and eloquence, approximate language thrown out at certain great objects of consciousness which it does not pretend to define fully." In genre, that is, the Bible was literature; and it came alive within the conscience and consciousness of the reader. Literary language called for literary criticism, to awaken the reader to the Bible's spiritual power. If literary critics could discuss the Bible in an edifying way, so, too, secular literature. For English-speaking critics after him, Arnold's discussion of literary interpretation of scripture became a model for literary interpretation in general.[27]

Given how the Bible perfused Anglophone culture, German-inspired psychological criticism resonated with the multilayered meanings readers found in scripture. As allegorical or typological reading of the Bible gave readers lessons for their own conscience or understanding, so analogously did Coleridge's focus on the mental state of readers suggest similar personal lessons from secular literature. Disciples of Coleridge swung back and forth between applying his ideas to biblical and to secular interpretation. In 1837 George Allen explicitly coupled the two realms. "Profound study of works of creative art" was linked with "religious cultivation" in "the constitution of the mind itself." A slide from biblical criticism to literary interpretation makes sense given what Protestants believed about scripture. God meant His revelation to be understood by all readers; the Bible needs no authoritative interpreter (like the Catholic church). The biblical philologist Moses Stuart therefore insisted in 1832 that *principles* of biblical interpretation—as distinct from linguistic and historical expertise—must be the same as applied to all books. True, only the sanctified can fully grasp verses relating to spiritual life. But, Stuart went on, this differs little from secular reading. "Who, for example, can read and fully understand Milton and Homer, without the spirit and soul of poetry within him which will enable him to enter into their views and feelings? Who can read intelligently even a book of mathematics, without sympathizing with the writer?" *Sympathy* would become a catchword of literary criticism; and, as the century wore on, critics increasingly would preach canonical works of literature as secular scripture.[28]

In sum, learned critics laid down a new methodological dogma. Few rejected formal criticism as *part* of their job. After all, the older criticism had much to say. It was neither arid, rigid, nor obsessed with grammar and syntax. Eighteenth-century critics celebrated the sublime. Hugh Blair taught that poetry grew from "rude effusions" of bards in the primeval "age of hunters and of shepherds," like Robert Wood's Homer; so the poet (unlike "The Historian, the Orator, the Philosopher") spoke "to the Imagination, and the Passions." Learned nineteenth-century critics built on earlier ideas of the imaginative power of poetry. Yet categories like sublime or primitive lay outside a text— 'objective' gauges with which to measure a literary artifact. The newer criticism, in contrast, wanted to study a work from inside; to understand it in terms of psychological effects, authorial intentions, philosophic implications; to treat it as a singularity—not just to apply off-the-shelf criteria but also to pry open the work in its uniqueness. Here emerged a new idea of erudite criticism to fit a new field of erudition.[29]

One sees it in Hugh Legaré, the most learned critic in the American South before 1860. Writing about Byron in the 1830s, Legaré rang changes on traditional categories such as pathos and the sublime, commented on diction and figures of speech, like Hugh Blair lecturing on *The Spectator*. Yet Legaré also brought to bear on Byron's poetry the poet's personality traits, psychological makeup, individual situation. For Legaré, a poem must be grasped in terms of its own specific interiority: a lesson possibly learned from August Schlegel, whose lectures Legaré read carefully. The philologist's method of comparing texts remained essential to Legaré's criticism. But the range of qualities of a work of art available for comparison crucially expanded.[30]

At the same time, as Legaré shows, this 'inward turning' did not repudiate earlier practices. Literary scholars seemed more likely to meld the new criticism with older approaches than to replace one with the other. George Craik, the first professor of English literature and history at Queen's College Belfast, lectured on "great" English writers in an apparently modern critical mode but also published *The English of Shakespeare, Illustrated by a Philological Commentary on Julius Caesar* (1856).[31]

LITERARY HISTORY

Literary history made up the third subdivision that eventually merged into the new study of 'literature.' If evaluative criticism intensified the philologist's spotlight on the text itself, in literary history context triumphed over text.

The genre had antecedents. 'History of literature' existed in eighteenth-century Germany (*Litterärgeschichte*), and German philologists churned it out in quantity. But literature here meant roughly what we call today 'the literature' of academic fields, not 'artistic' literature (what August Schlegel labeled "*schöne* [beautiful] *Literatur*"). Think of the *American Journal of Sociology*, not the Great American Novel. Besides biblical philology, Johann Gottfried Eichhorn wrote Litterärgeschichte. He defined it in 1812 as "the narrative of the origin and chief developments of all parts of learning," tracing the causes. By causes, he had in mind the sociocultural contexts that philologists had long valued to help them understand texts. "The history of arts and learning," Eichhorn insisted, "can never be expounded apart from the history of social conditions. For culture and literature are twin sisters.... Culture, as first-born daughter, prepares for the birth of literature, her younger sister; from then on, they live and work together inseparably and die with one another." Histories of imaginative writing did appear in Britain before 1800, in the form of narratives of English theater and English poetry. Thomas Warton's *History of English Poetry* was mentioned earlier. But no one then thought of this sort of literary history as a self-conscious, erudite pursuit.[32]

Litterärgeschichte and British-style histories of literature converged right after 1800. Individual works had appeared in various countries on poets or dramatists, like Warton's book. The first general narrative came from the pen of Friedrich Bouterwek, yet another Göttingen professor: *Geschichte der neuern Poesie und Beredsamkeit* (*History of Modern Poetry and Eloquence*, twelve volumes, 1801–19). By poetry Bouterwek meant any work of imagination, regardless of form. In adapting the Göttingen tradition of Litterärgeschichte to studying "schöne Literatur," Bouterwek kept the stress on explaining sociocultural causes of developments. His book provided a chronological narrative from the later Middle Ages, highlighting authors who influenced subsequent development of a national literature. His third volume, on Spanish literature, though spotty in coverage, proved the biggest hit and was translated into French and English as well as Spanish. Jean Charles Léonard de Sismondi cribbed from it for the Spanish portions of his four-volume *De la littérature du midi de l'Europe* (*On the Literature of Southern Europe*, 1813). Sismondi is justly better known as an economist; but his "beautiful, & comprehensive picture" appealed even to readers like William Prescott who recognized its errors. Prescott also knew Friedrich Schlegel's lectures on literary history. "The English," lamented Prescott in 1823, "are behind every cultivated language in Europe, in similar works of general literary criticism." He must have been thinking of a book he was reading alongside Sismondi, the *History of Fiction* (1814) by John Colin Dunlop (actually a Scot, not English)—"a laborious, dry but a comprehensive and faithful register of fictitious prose composition from its [Greek] origin to the present day." "A fine field this, therefore, for a scholar," Prescott mused.[33]

In the end Prescott pursued civil rather than literary history, and few British and American scholars in the first half of the century did join Germans and French in writing the historical species of the emerging genus of 'literature.' None of this handful attempted a general history of English or American literature comparable to Sismondi's history of southern European literature. John Payne Collier's three-volume history of early modern English drama (1831) supplied a mass of data rather than a coherent narrative. In 1830 Thomas Carlyle started a history of German literature but never got further than Luther or close to publication; the couple of articles that Carlyle printed from the project suggest it would have been derivative. Henry Hallam's four-volume

Introduction to the Literature of Europe in the Fifteenth, Sixteenth and Seventeenth Centuries (1837–39) aped the Göttingen Litterärgeschichte of the previous century, mixing Grotius and Galileo with Shakespeare and Scaliger—surveying all of intellectual life rather than literature in the narrower modern sense.[34]

The newer literary histories, such as Bouterwek's and Sismondi's, reeked of German historicism: specifically a historicism formed by Herder's idea of national character unfolding over time. Here philology melted into philosophy. The philologist's need to establish precise contexts for understanding texts had spawned the notion that each human culture at each period was historically unique. One sees this axiom at play in Lowth's *Sacred Poetry of the Hebrews*, in Wood's *Homer*, and in Eichhorn's higher criticism. (Eichhorn and Bouterwek collaborated in Göttingen—where August Schlegel had attended Eichhorn's lectures.) It followed logically—and, from the workaday philologist's point of view, practically—that any given cultural moment must evolve into its unique successor. Herder, and German Romantics following him, had turned these philological principles into philosophic axioms. Karl Otfried Müller applied the method in his 1840 history of ancient Greek literature:

> Our object is to consider Grecian literature as a main constituent of the character of the Grecian people, and to show how those illustrious compositions, which we still justly admire as the *classical* writings of the Greeks, naturally sprang from the taste and genius of the Greek races, and the constitution of civil and domestic society as established among them.

To cast light on the pre-Homeric period from which no poetry survived, the historian turned to "those creations of the human intellect" that "naturally precede poetical composition": "*language* and *religion*." Likewise, the new literary histories of more recent epochs aimed, as Hugh Legaré understood, to trace "the history of modern literature up to its sources, with a view to show its connection with national history and manners." The parallels to Altertumswissenschaft and to comparative philology are clear. Legaré realized that "a new order of researches, and almost a new theory of criticism have been proposed to scholars."[35]

This philosophized philology interested more American than British scholars. (Altertumswissenschaft itself engaged more American classicists, too, as the next chapter shows.) When embarking on his career teaching European literature, Longfellow made heavy if idiosyncratic use of Sismondi in sorting out his ideas. Likewise, Legaré's fellow Southerner, Richard Henry Wilde, preparing a book on Dante, assumed that, to understand the poet, the historian must understand "the age in which he lived, and the learning, arts, manners and government of his country."[36]

The only English-language scholar before 1860 to write a major literary history along these lines was likewise American: Legaré's friend George Ticknor.

From 1815 to 1817, in the Göttingen heyday of Eichhorn and Bouterwek, Ticknor studied there. "Literary history" then afforded his "amusement." He grew close to Eichhorn, who by this time had moved into a Herderian, organic approach to writing history. When F. A. Wolf visited Göttingen, Ticknor discussed Altertumswissenschaft with him at length. The young Bostonian not only read the literary histories of the brothers Schlegel but talked with them both. In Paris he studied transitional forms of Latin as it evolved into early southern Romance languages. In short, with no intent to do so, he equipped himself to write literary history in the new mode: as a narrative of the unfolding of national character. In November 1817 he accepted the new Smith chair of French and Spanish at Harvard. In 1818, to prepare himself for the job, he traveled throughout Spain, settling in Madrid for several months. There he came to know men of letters, deepened his knowledge of the Spanish language in its historical evolution, and began to collect an impressive library of Spanish literature. In 1835, frustrated by his failed campaign to drag Harvard up to German standards, he resigned his professorship. He returned to Europe for three more years, renewing old acquaintances, making new ones, adding still more books to his now fabulous library of 14,000 volumes.[37]

This library, and his Harvard lectures, provided the resources for Ticknor's three-volume *History of Spanish Literature*, published in 1849. It was the solidest work of humanistic learning yet to appear in the United States. (As works of art, the histories by Ticknor's friend William Prescott far surpassed it; as contributions to scholarship, the gap yawned as wide in the other direction.) Ticknor transplanted into English-speaking soil the Bouterwek-like literary history he had met as a young man in Germany. His first volume treated literature from the advent of written Castilian in the twelfth century through the polemics of the New World in the early sixteenth. The second volume focused on the 'golden age' of Spanish literature: Cervantes, Lope de Vega, Calderon. The third, most diffuse took the story up to Ticknor's own youth and the expulsion of Napoleon from Spain. At every stage, Ticknor surrounded his accounts of literary works with the explanatory context of Spanish history and culture. In effect, he updated in this new medium the old contextualizing practice of textual philologists—and emulated the newer *Altertumswissenschaftlich* axioms that permeated Göttingen erudition during his studies. Ticknor aimed not only to show how Spanish literature expressed the supposed character traits of the Spanish people: loyalty, chivalry, superstition, violence. He also lauded, in contrast to a Spain under the heel of tyrants and the Inquisition, the virtues of ordered republican liberty in the United States. These stereotypes make a reader today wince, and the whole idea of national character is long discredited.[38]

But the scholarly qualities of Ticknor's work commanded admiration. There was good reason why the *History of Spanish Literature* was quickly translated into French, German—and Spanish. Spanish readers in particular snapped it up, despite having to swallow hard at some of Ticknor's prejudices.

His research was far more accurate and thorough than Bouterwek's or Sismondi's. For more than fifty years, the *History of Spanish Literature* had no serious competition. And, regardless of one's opinion of the story he told, Ticknor did have a narrative line.[39]

Indeed, Ticknor's *History* marked a turning point in philology in the English-speaking world. It combined deep erudition with a coherent narrative that placed literature in historical and cultural context. In following the axiom that a text can be well understood only in cultural-historical context, Ticknor merely applied philology to the study of imaginative literature. But in subsuming such contexts within a chronological, causal narrative, he turned Anglophone philology into something new. His true originality consisted mostly in writing English, for his German masters taught him all he knew, methodologically speaking. Still, Ticknor was the first scholar to produce a fully realized work of literary history in English. No literary historian today would tell the story of any literature as Ticknor told of Spain's. But every literary historian after Ticknor who aspired to recognition as a scholar *would* feel obliged to conduct serious research and to discuss texts in historical or cultural context.

By midcentury, then, the components of the emergent field of 'literature' were in place in the United Kingdom and United States: textual editing, evaluative criticism, and literary history. Born out of philology, they had grown into something recognizably modern. Whether they hung together, whether one could now plausibly call literature a single field, still less a 'discipline,' is another question. In the 1850s few universities taught literature; and especially—but not only—in medieval studies lines remained blurred between literary research, general history, and the linguistic inquiries of comparative philology. To raise these questions points toward the solidifying of the modern discipline of literary studies in the decades to come. It also inspires curiosity about what was happening to other studies of the cultural legacy of European civilization, the subject of the next chapter.

7

"An Epoch in Historical Science"

THE CIVILIZED PAST, 1800–1850

Eighteenth-century philologists and social theorists distinguished differing *types* of human societies or cultures: a trend even more evident in the nineteenth century. (The word *culture*, in something approaching its modern anthropological usage, circulated after 1750, though not fully naturalized for a century.) More and more, various species of sociocultural order came to be seen as phases in a progressive historical evolution, from lower to higher. Robert Wood's primitive Homeric era of myth and poetry led to a rational classical Greece, while Adam Smith envisioned a more complex, steplike progress from a hunter-gatherer status through pastoral barbarism and then settled agriculture to commercial society. Most nineteenth-century social theorists assumed cultural evolution of this general sort, leaving modern tribal peoples stuck in an 'earlier' epoch. One line of demarcation gleamed sharp and bright: that between 'civilization' and all ruder stages leading up to it. Exactly what civilization meant remained hopelessly nebulous, though often the invention of writing had something to do with its origin.

Historians try to penetrate the world of the people they investigate, not impose today's axioms. This chapter will therefore lump together diverse studies of the 'civilized' past—even though the hazy concept of civilization rarely played an explanatory role in them. Scholars examined here include classical philologists plus two more or less learned groups with roots in philology and antiquarianism—newfangled archaeologists, opening a fresh field, and long-familiar historians, sorting out new practices that would eventually define the modern humanistic discipline of history. Classicists, archaeologists, and historians sometimes interacted, sometimes ignored each other. But they dealt with common problems and responded to some common influences. A later chapter will survey scholars who studied 'primitive' peoples, staking out the discipline of anthropology.

PART I: ALTERTUMSWISSENSCHAFT AND CLASSICAL STUDIES

Classical erudition's educational role camouflaged its status as a discrete field of knowledge. In 1800—and long before—Latin and Greek ruled the one Irish, the two English, and the many American universities and colleges. (The several Scottish ones went their own way; but even the prestige of mathematics at Cambridge did not spare students endless Latin and Greek.) Classical texts supplied the core of undergraduate education, occupied the largest fraction of students' academic hours. Other studies growing from philology, rhetoric, or antiquarianism—history and modern literature, linguistics and anthropology, even classical archaeology—did not enter higher education in the English-speaking world until well into the nineteenth century. They stood out as conspicuously new. Their practitioners could more easily come to see themselves as members of a group devoted to research in a particular field and—in the long run—as practitioners of a 'discipline' apart from other disciplines. Classical philologists, however, could seem just teachers—some of whom worked to improve Greek and Latin texts like those their students read. To regard their research as a defining pursuit of one specific clan of scholars among others—eventually to see 'classics' as one 'discipline' among many peers—did not come easily. Confronting *Altertumswissenschaft* began a long, thorny process of a new self-recognition.

The invention of Altertumswissenschaft, the science of antiquity, by German scholars like Heyne and Wolf transfigured classical philology. The study of texts became the study of civilizations. Use of historical and cultural context to illuminate ancient texts evolved into use of ancient texts to light up the history and culture of Greece and Rome. As the nineteenth century wore on, the idealistic spirit animating the Hellenism of the Age of Goethe choked on the dust of philological minutiae.[1] Still, ardor distilled in Altertumswissenschaft put classical erudition on to a new track. For varying, complicated reasons, British and American classical philologists only timidly set foot on it during the first half of the century. Their reactions form the gist of part 1 of this chapter.

German Classical Erudition

Altertumswissenschaft opened not merely a wider but a post-Christian view of classical antiquity. Early Christian writers such as Augustine had 'baptized' Greek and Roman pagan writers for Christian use. For well over a millennium thereafter, the church and its educational institutions—most European schools and universities—controlled the meanings of classical texts. Congruences with Christianity got stressed. Lapses from Christian ethics or belief got suppressed. The pagan gods became literary and artistic conceits, while Vergil prophesied the birth of Christ.[2] But eighteenth-century writers skeptical of Christianity began to smash the shackles binding classical antiquity to Christianity. Gibbon made the religion a villain in his story of Rome's decline. In the Germany of Gibbon's day—the Age of Goethe—the cult of ancient Greece displaced traditional piety for those, like Goethe himself and Winckelmann, who no longer found Christianity compelling or even plausible. Pagan statues and temples provided, for this small but potent minority, an aesthetic surrogate for dogmatic religion. Although most German philologists remained Protestant or Catholic, worship of Greece had a lasting effect.

Altertumswissenschaft licensed scholars to find difference in the pagan past. Classical antiquity no longer walked side by side with Christianity. Socrates and Cicero regained their pagan integrity, even under the gaze of pious Lutheran professors. Altertumswissenschaft brought a new sense of the otherness of the ancient world, missing even in a scholar so immersed in classical writings as Bentley.[3] German philologists viewed remote antiquity as a world vastly different from their own—although, not entirely consistently, they also venerated ancient Greece as fount of timeless canons of beauty and value.

The old work of editing and emendation of classical manuscripts still went on, for trustworthy texts provided much of the raw material for Altertumswissenschaft; but classical studies broadened far beyond textual criticism. The new way had its enemies. A long-simmering quarrel pitted the great textual philologist Gottfried Hermann and his disciples, who advocated verbal criticism of a sort familiar in England, against August Boeckh and his followers, who argued for comprehensive Altertumswissenschaft. Barthold Georg Niebuhr of the University of Berlin blew the new trumpet, with a Romantic undertone, in a letter to Count Adam Moltke in 1812:

> Oh how would philology be cherished, if people knew the magical delight of living and moving amidst the most beautiful scenes of the past! The mere reading is the smallest part of it; the great thing is to feel familiar with Greece and Rome during their most widely different periods![4]

This letter came to Moltke just after he received the second volume of Niebuhr's pathbreaking study of early Rome, *Römische Geschichte* (*Roman History*).* Inspired in part by Wolf's inquiry into ancient Homeric philology, Niebuhr dug through the misty legends in Livy's history, the main ancient source for Rome's early centuries, to a substratum of institutions and social structure. He uncovered the legal dimension of plebian-patrician agrarian conflict and, as Arnaldo Momigliano put it, "virtually created the modern study of Roman history." Niebuhr did so by adapting imaginatively the traditional approach of the philologist. He compared antiquity to

---

* *Römische Geschichte* originally appeared in two volumes in 1811–12, based on 1810–11 lectures at the University of Berlin. After years as a Prussian diplomat, Niebuhr returned to scholarship and in a second edition (1827–32) revised his earlier volumes and added a third, bringing the story to the end of the First Punic War in 241 BCE.

an immeasurable city of ruins, of which there is not even a ground-plan extant; in which each one must find his way for himself, and learn to understand the whole from the parts,—the parts from a careful comparison and study, and a due consideration of their relation to the whole.

In this passage, one hears the philologist straining to elucidate a difficult text by tacking back and forth between the text itself and its context: the hermeneutic circle—transplanted from textual philology by Niebuhr, under the influence of Altertumswissenschaft, into history writing. Comparative contexts stretched far and wide. Agrarian problems in modern Europe and India implicitly framed those in ancient Rome. Niebuhr reported that Aztec chronology helped him to grasp "the cyclical system of the old Italian mode of reckoning the years."[5]

Niebuhr was hardly the only revolutionary. August Boeckh, a student of Wolf's, trawled Greek texts and inscriptions. From his colossal catch, he reconstructed lost worlds of Greek music and poetic meter, of ancient chronology and natural science, and, in *Die Staatshaushaltung der Athener* (*The Public Finances of Athens*, 1817), of the economic basis of the Athenian state. Boeckh stood to subsequent historians of Athens somewhat as Niebuhr did to his successors in Roman history. His book laid open for the first time the fiscal operations of any ancient state, a topic neglected by text-oriented philologists before Altertumswissenschaft. Boeckh thus began the process of understanding the social and economic foundations of Greek history and culture—a past he was less apt to idealize than earlier Hellenists, as Romantic glow faded. His use of inscriptions in research for the book led him to launch the Corpus Inscriptionum Graecarum, founding Greek epigraphy as an organized scholarly undertaking. Karl Otfried Müller—inspired originally by Niebuhr—followed in Boeckh's footsteps. Müller produced in 1820 and 1824 the first modern accounts of ancient Greek peoples founded in thorough command of all types of sources, *Orchomenos und die Minyer* (*Orchomenos and the Minyae*) and *Die Dorier* (*The Dorians*).* Cases multiplied: the start of modern scholarship on mythology in the differing theories of Müller and the philologist George Friedrich Creuzer; Müller's pioneering handbook of ancient art; his history— the first—of Greek literature, broadly conceived.[6]

Müller had studied with Boeckh; and he carried out his master's principle that philology comprised "the historical construction of the collective life of a people in its practical and spiritual tendencies, therefore of its entire culture and all its products." (The political disunity of German-speaking Europe stimulated this displacement of the vital bond of a people onto culture, as Boeckh

---

*Orchomenos was a city in Boeotia, the Minyae a legendary people associated with it. The Dorians were one of four supposed major ethnic groups into which ancient Greeks divided themselves. These books were meant as the first in a series on Greek peoples and cities cut short by Müller's early death.

implicitly conceded.) Boeckh elaborated his maxim systematically in a course of lectures he delivered regularly between 1809 and 1865, surveying for students the whole domain of classical philology—theory of interpretation, theory of criticism, general character of Greek and Roman antiquity, public life, private life, religion, art, mythology, philosophy, mathematics, empirical study of nature and of society, literature, and language.[7]

British Classical Philologists Turn Their Backs

Nothing so sweeping was imagined in the United Kingdom. There, well after 1850, most classical scholars in universities focused closely on textual emendation and linguistic questions. Some of this work proved solid and useful, such as Charles Blomfield's editions of Aeschylus (1810–24) or William Veitch's thorough *Greek Verbs, Irregular and Defective* (1848). But it lacked the scope and holistic grasp of antiquity that came with the German breakthrough into Altertumswissenschaft.[8]

Some British scholars did try to bring Germany home, but few belonged to the Oxbridge classical establishment. Oxford and Cambridge—including former college fellows who moved on to Anglican rectories—turned out the bulk of classical scholarship in the United Kingdom; and these almost 'professional' classicists saw their job as improving texts through emendation and editions. Other universities in the United Kingdom played minor roles in classical philology before 1850. The new University of London and the ancient Scottish universities—St. Andrews, Glasgow, Aberdeen, Edinburgh—downplayed Greek and Latin compared to Oxford and Cambridge. In this period few learned publications came out of either Trinity College Dublin or tiny Durham University (founded in 1832). Some British academics did value German learning, notably philologists around the secular University College London. George Long and Thomas Key stand out—both earlier taught at Thomas Jefferson's equally modern-minded University of Virginia. But Key focused on comparative philology, while Long soon left the university to spread his energies across educational reform causes. He published most of his classical scholarship after 1850.[9]

Until then, erudite interest in Altertumswissenschaft came largely from scholars outside universities. Before midcentury, most British historians of ancient Greece and Rome, most British commentators on Homer or Vergil were bankers, clergymen, politicians—'amateur,' if deeply learned, independent scholars. So were most British translators of German books on classical antiquity. Such 'amateurs' did much to put the study of ancient history on its modern scholarly footings, and they devoured German erudition. But British disciples of Altertumswissenschaft failed during the first half of the century to shift the mainstream of publications in classical philology away from a traditional focus on textual criticism.

Oxbridge scholars did not totally ignore Altertumswissenschaft. In fact, for a few years a Germanophile cell roiled Trinity College Cambridge, shrine of echt-English classical philology. In 1828–31, two Trinity fellows, Julius Hare and Connop Thirlwall, translated Niebuhr's Roman history, with the author's heartfelt backing. Altertumswissenschaft had absorbed both men for some time. (In the background lay their general passion for German literature and learning, which raised hackles in Cambridge. Further in the background lay Hare's partial schooling in Germany and partial upbringing by William Jones's widow, his aunt.) Their Niebuhr translation found use in universities, even a few schools; and it impressed some English historians and biblical critics—but not classical philologists, to judge from their publications. In 1831 Hare and Thirlwall sought to broaden philological erudition with a thrice-yearly journal, the *Philological Museum* (echoing the title of one founded by Niebuhr four years earlier.) The *Museum* focused on "the literature, the philosophy, the history, the manners, the institutions, the mythology, and the religion of Greece and Rome" in the spirit of Altertumswissenschaft, although now and then wandering off into matters like English spelling reform (Hare's hobby). Five of the thirty-five articles in the first volume simply translated German publications. The two editors meant to inspire English philologists to emulate Germans: "If Niebuhr and Müller and Boeckh do not excite some of their [English] readers to think and look about them, they might as well have been allowed to remain in the obscurity of their native language."[10]

Hare and Thirlwall were oddities in an uncongenial Cambridge—both had left by 1834—but not alone in England. In the same year as the first volume of their Niebuhr, a precociously learned Oxford undergraduate, George Cornewall Lewis, translated Boeckh's *Staatshaushaltung der Athener* as *The Public Economy of Athens*—with a long preface chiding the author for his feeble grasp of modern political economy. Two years later, now studying law in London, Lewis and another young lawyer, Henry Tufnell, translated Müller's *Die Dorier*, adapted to British insularity. Rather than calling Greek gods by Greek names, *The History and Antiquities of the Doric Race* followed "the English custom" of "using the names of the corresponding deities of the Romans." Passages discussing *Knabenliebe*—boy love; bluntly, pederasty—vanished. Even with *Knabenliebe* out of the picture, Oxbridge classical scholars kept on emending and editing, disinclined to emulate Boeckh or Müller.[11]

Outside the circle of classical philologists narrowly defined, however, Altertumswissenschaft enjoyed some respect, even acclaim. In 1831 the *New Monthly Magazine* praised both the "profound and varied scholarship" of K. O. Müller ("well known to every classical student of German literature") and the "attainments of the lamented Niebuhr" ("too well known in this country to require any laboured eulogy from us"). Three years later the *Quarterly Review* declared flatly that in Greek and Latin learning "the Germans have taken the lead, not only of us, but of all the rest of Europe."[12]

Why did most English classical philologists resist Altertumswissenschaft, when other learned writers embraced it? Four very different problems seem to have hampered transmission to Oxbridge: linguistic barriers, religious concerns, the structure of education at Oxford and Cambridge, and long-held scholarly commitments.

The language problem was real but not decisive. Few among the learned knew German in the early 1800s—more, it seems, in Scotland than England or Ireland. Even laying hands on German books could require expeditions worthy of an Arctic explorer. Prior to Hare and Thirlwall, only Edward Blomfield among Cambridge classical scholars read German; his early death in 1816 reduced the number to zero. When Edward Pusey set out to learn German in the early 1820s, allegedly only two other people in Oxford knew the language. Looking back from the 1850s, Arthur Stanley identified Julius Hare and Connop Thirlwall as "probably the only Englishmen thoroughly well versed in the literature of Germany" in the 1820s. "Thoroughly" was a much needed qualifier. George Cornewall Lewis, after all, translated both Boeckh and Müller. Classical *textual* scholarship throughout Europe still routinely took the form of Latin notes to editions of Greek or Latin texts, easily accessible to scholarly English speakers. But Wolf's *Prolegomena ad Homerum* was among the last major works of broader German classical erudition published in Latin. Translations could bridge the linguistic gap, if it were the only obstacle. Around 1830 Henry Hart Milman was potting German erudition for readers of the *Quarterly Review*. In 1822 Thomas Arnold in the *Quarterly Review* estimated that fewer than a half dozen Britons had read Niebuhr's *Römische Geschichte*. After Hare and Thirlwall's translation, Niebuhr's readership spread—not exactly like wildfire (no one ever mistook *Römische Geschichte* for a gripping read) but pretty widely among British *historians*. Even in translation Niebuhr did not lure classical philologists, a group growing distinct from biblical and other critics. (The existence of journals nominally devoted to classical philology show a drift to such specialization; their habit of wandering off into other topics show the limits of the trend.) Not the language barrier, then, so much as disinterest cooled classicists to Altertumswissenschaft.[13]

For some of them, coolness perhaps was a reaction to the whiff of paganism arising from German neo-Hellenism, seedbed of Altertumswissenschaft. Reminding readers of the pagan integrity of antiquity made Altertumswissenschaft obnoxious to some pious Protestants. Niebuhr—as will later appear—even threatened the Old Testament. Most British (and American) college teachers before 1860 were ministers of the Gospel. They would have noticed that Altertumswissenschaft appealed to the tiny minority of post-Christian writers, such as Thomas Macaulay, whose *Lays of Ancient Rome* were inspired by Niebuhr, and George Grote, atheist historian of Greece. The 'godless' University College London—which Grote and George Cornewall Lewis backed—notoriously welcomed German philology. Still, the liberal Anglican Connop

Thirlwall ended as a bishop, his fellow Niebuhrian Thomas Arnold as Regius Professor of Modern History at Oxford. Religious implications of Altertumswissenschaft probably disturbed only more conservative Christians.

The structure of Oxford and Cambridge before 1850 would anyway have hamstrung classical scholarship along the lines of Boeckh's or Müller's. In German universities, lifelong professorial careers devoted to ancient Greece or Rome fostered the deep learning underlying Altertumswissenschaft. In Oxbridge—where the comparatively few professors were marginal to instruction—the college tutors taught all subjects, generalists not specialists. Most tutors were celibate Anglican clergy, the normal prerequisite for a college fellowship; after several years, they typically moved to parishes, lured by opportunity for marriage and ecclesial promotion. Few devoted entire lives to erudition. Altertumswissenschaft edged into Oxbridge's teaching long before its scholarship. (By the late 1830s exams expected students to know something of Boeckh and Niebuhr secondhand.) Even then, tutors habitually treated ancient writers pretty much as contemporaries who dispensed useful advice to young men of the ruling classes, not as denizens of a foreign past. Such Oxford and Cambridge tutors supplied the great majority of publishing classical scholars, and some were deeply engaged with classical texts. But their working conditions deterred the kind of research that would encourage them to go beyond emending those texts—had they been inclined to do so. Oxford and Cambridge would have to change before Oxbridge philology broadened beyond what Germans called 'word philology.'[14]

Finally, engrained scholarly method undercut Altertumswissenschaft. Bentley was an innovator in using historical context to clarify ancient writings and a genius at textual emendation (when not gone wild). Those who followed him appreciated mostly the latter half of his legacy. Consensus calls Richard Porson Bentley's greatest inheritor. Porson was an alcoholic and a slob on a Herculean scale; his rooms smelled so bad that visitors threw open windows. William Hazlitt saw him in the London Institution's library "dressed in an old rusty black coat with cobwebs hanging to the skirts of it . . . looking for all the world like a drunken carpenter." Drunken he may have been. He was also charismatic, arrogant, brilliant. No less an authority than Ulrich von Wilamowitz-Moellendorff credited Porson as the man who "established the metrical rules of tragic dialogue and did the same for its language." Wilamowitz lamented that Porson died in 1808 with only a translation of the Lexicon of Photius, the Byzantine scholar, completed; "otherwise his life's work consists of admittedly splendid emendations to a rather small number of Greek authors." In fact, those "splendid emendations" included important editions of four plays by Euripides. Still, sharing in Bentley's genius for textual criticism, Porson used his erudition and phenomenal memory with the riddle-solving mentality of a code cracker or crossword puzzle addict. He simply had no interest in understanding texts in historical context.[15]

Oxbridge scholars routinely adopted his approach, toughened with an alloy of amour propre. The English, along with the Dutch, were through most of the eighteenth century Europe's undisputed masters of classical (and biblical) erudition. Anglo-Dutch primacy rested on exactly the kind of textual scholarship that won Porson fame. It is hardly surprising, given human nature, that English classical philologists would stick to the methods that had set them atop the philological world, turning up their noses at German upstarts. Through the first half of the nineteenth century Porson remained the admired model.

Early in the century he had important disciples in three other fellows of Trinity College Cambridge: Charles James Blomfield, James H. Monk, and Porson's close friend Peter Paul Dobree. They piously brought their master's remains into print. Of the three, Dobree was shrewdest and broadest-ranging. However, during his abbreviated lifetime (he died in 1825, at forty-three) he published nothing. Like Porson's reputation, Dobree's rests mainly on his notes—in his case, marginalia—printed after his death: more textual emendations. Perhaps Porson's strongest successor was an Oxford rival of the Cambridge trio, Peter Elmsley, who was amiable, rich, widely learned, and simply wide—memorably obese. Elmsley entertained far-reaching historical interests, but his published scholarship stuck in the Porsonian mold. After the collapse of Napoleon's army reopened the continent in 1813, Elmsley trekked through France and Italy, industriously collating manuscripts—and just as studiously ignoring the new erudition across the Rhine and over the Alps, immaterial to his textual research.[16]

Indifference to Altertumswissenschaft at times strains credibility. Taking advantage, like Elmsley, of revived continental travel, a talented young classical scholar from Cambridge, Charles Blomfield's younger brother Edward, toured German universities in 1813. Edward knew German. Yet he contrived not to notice Altertumswissenschaft, even after chatting with Wolf in Berlin. On returning, he published in a Cambridge philological journal a summary of recent German classical philology, with a view to bringing British scholars up to date. The article amounted to a listing of editions of classical texts in progress. Blomfield failed even to note the publication the previous year of Niebuhr's history of Rome. Elmsley had indirect contact with Niebuhr in aid of manuscript collation yet apparently took no notice of the man's own writing.[17]

The journal in which Blomfield's account appeared, the *Museum Criticum; or, Cambridge Classical Researches*, took a view of its terrain broad enough to encompass articles on the Rosetta Stone. But evidently neither of the editors—Blomfield's elder brother Charles and his Trinity colleague J. H. Monk—could read German. Predictably, English classicists did attend to Boeckh's text-oriented rival Hermann (who communicated with them in Latin). The few allusions in the *Museum Criticum* to German philology mostly concerned editions of Latin or Greek texts, where scholarly apparatus appeared in Latin. The

Cambridge group had started the *Museum Criticum* to set a higher scholarly standard than the *Classical Journal*, a quarterly published in London between 1810 and 1829 by the erratically learned printer A. J. Valpy, an Oxford graduate. Higher did not mean broader: the journal stuck resolutely to an exclusively verbal or linguistic approach to criticism.[18]

Like the *Museum Criticum*, the *Classical Journal*'s contents tilted heavily toward old-style classical studies (including original poems in Greek and Latin, such as every Oxbridge student composed). Defying its name—and, as a money-making business, needing to attract readers—it also published articles on biblical criticism, Zend and Pahlavi manuscripts, the origin of language and writing, Chinese coins, travels in Arabia, and more. The philological articles, classical or biblical, waved the Union Jack of traditional English verbal criticism (feebly, the Cambridge Porsonians thought). The journal did publish a two-part biography of C. G. Heyne in 1819 and, by the late 1820s, included a handful of German books in its lists of foreign works noticed (as distinct from reviewed); but most foreign-language books mentioned were in French or Latin, as if the Republic of Letters still thrived. Valpy appeared as blind as any Cambridge scholar to the German revolution in the study of antiquity. In celebrating the heroes of the "new era" in "Classical Literature," Valpy named "HEMSTERHUIS, RUHNKEN, VALKENAER, VILLOISON, BRUNCK, DAWES, MARKLAND, TOUP, TYRWHITT, and PORSON." Classical philology apparently had no meaningful life beyond the enlightened terrain of Britain and the Netherlands. And the "new era" remained the one that began with the "labors of BENTLEY."[19]

Prolegomena ad Homerum and *Römische Geschichte* started nothing that mattered much in Oxford or Cambridge. The philologists of Göttingen and Berlin—and University College London—were realizing that ancient Greeks and Romans did not encounter the world in the same ways as modern Europeans. Oxbridge philologists still thought of the ancients as like long-dead English gentlemen with odd taste in clothing.

But English classical philology had not merely gotten stuck in a narrow rut; even as it creaked along in its groove, the road headed downhill. A. E. Housman quipped in 1903 that

> our own great age of scholarship, begun in 1691 by Bentley's *Epistola ad Millium*, was ended [in 1824–25] by the successive strokes of doom which consigned Dobree and Elmsley to the grave and Blomfield to the bishopric of Chester. England disappeared from the fellowship of nations for the next forty years.

(England's ancient *historians*, in contrast, would lead the fellowship of nations.) Attentive eyes at the time saw the collapse. Julius Hare lamented in 1831 that "the mite which England has contributed during the five years from 1825 to 1830 toward the increase of our knowledge concerning classical antiquity, is in truth little more than a mite." Perhaps no erudition that cut itself off from the generative currents of its time could stay healthy. Housman was savage on this point: English classicists, "having turned their backs on Europe and science and the past, sat down to banquet on mutual approbation, to produce the Classical Museum and the Bibliotheca Classica, and to perish without a name."* In fact, publishing by English classical philologists did greatly slacken after the 1820s.[20]

Instead they threw themselves into teaching—an act Porson never committed even while Greek professor at Cambridge. And teaching now became principally the labor-intensive business of helping students to translate classical texts and write Greek and Latin compositions. Student papers left little time for "making any real advances in philology," as J. W. Donaldson moaned in 1839, even were tutors inclined to scholarship. Few were, in any serious way. Professors, with lighter workloads, did not publish a lot more classical scholarship. The period between the 1820s and 1870s were great years of university reform in England: renovation of instruction and of organization of higher education. Academic energies came to be diverted to the practice and politics of modernization—when teaching left energy. Mark Pattison, glum rector of Lincoln College Oxford, *did* carry out research during the latter phase of his career, in the peculiarly Germanic field of the history of scholarship. He remarked that Oxford had plenty of talented young MAs "but that each was rapidly set to turning some wheel in the vast machinery of cram." Thus, just when Altertumswissenschaft transformed the meaning of classical philology, Oxbridge opted for teaching over research. Hare and Thirlwall's *Philological Museum* fell victim early. Most copies went unsold. Not enough articles came in to fill the pages. After two years, the printer gave up: scholarship provided a sinkhole for his money. "We tried to enliven the taste of the English public for philology in the highest sense of the word," Hare wrote to his friend Christian von Bunsen, "but the effort was premature." Classical philology in the United Kingdom entered a long lull.[21]

Hare did not despair. "Classical studies" remained the core of education; "and not a few persons leave these universities every year, richly furnisht [Hare's reformed spelling, cherisht till he perisht] with the knowledge and qualifications requisite to prepare them for becoming accomplisht scholars." A German observer, visiting English universities in 1850, marveled, "Genuine culture of the classics and reverence for classical antiquity is more common in England than among us, though we may be able to produce a longer list of famous names in philological scholarship." Composing pseudo-Sapphic lyrics and ersatz Horatian odes evidently persuaded Oxbridge students of the charms of classical antiquity, certainly honed competence in its languages.[22]

This sort of classically infused, educated public (many not university graduates) kept Altertumswissenschaft alive in the United Kingdom. Following the

* Housman was unjust to the *Classical Museum* (see below); he was expert at both savagery and injustice. The Bibliotheca Classica was a series of texts for school use.

translations already mentioned of Niebuhr, Boeckh, and K. O. Müller around 1830, other landmarks of Altertumswissenschaft made their way into English from the later 1830s onward. In 1836 Sarah Austin translated Heinrich Hase's *Die griechische Altertumskunde* as *The Public and Private Life of the Ancient Greeks*. Two years later F. A. Paley published Georg Friedrich Schömann's seminal work on Athenian politics (translated, exceptionally, from Latin) as *A Dissertation on the Assemblies of the Athenians*. In 1844 the Scotsman John Leitch translated another of Müller's major works as *Introduction to a Scientific System of Mythology*, yet another in 1847 as *Ancient Art and Its Remains*. Müller, remarkably, wrote his final work for an English audience, under the aegis of George Cornewall Lewis and the Utilitarian circle to which he (and Sarah Austin) belonged. This last book, unfinished at Müller's early death in 1840, was a history of Greek literature, published in London in that same year. As Müller was writing, Lewis presumed, in the spirit of Altertumswissenschaft, that his author would deal with "manners" and the arts along with literature, in order to "give an idea of the *character* of the people, of their literature, art, manners, institutions, & origin." The book (a handy manual for students) went through multiple editions in its truncated state before J. W. Donaldson completed it in 1858. German books about ancient Greece found enough readers in the United Kingdom—some even in Oxford and Cambridge—to keep getting printed. They just did not shake the loyalty of Oxbridge classical scholars to Porsonian erudition.[23]

Yet in 1844 appeared a premonition of organized, learned opposition to purely textual philology: *The Classical Museum: A Journal of Philology, and of Ancient History and Literature*. Leonhard Schmitz, a student of Niebuhr's settled in Britain, edited it. Schmitz recruited correspondents from several German universities. His journal reviewed German books along with British. It reported on German learned institutions. It featured articles by British writers who took interest in Altertumswissenschaft—George Cornewall Lewis, George Grote, George Long, A. P. Stanley, J. S. Blackie, and Henry Malden. It paid attention to art and archaeology and to ancient history, topography, and culture, as well as to textual philology. It mixed in a little comparative philology, articles on lesser-known Asian and African languages, some scholarship on church history and the Bible. It drew several subscribers from Oxford and Cambridge colleges—including a couple of younger men who later in the century would promote German-style scholarship there. But after a few years the balance of its contents begin to shift toward traditional textual and linguistic topics, and after the 1850 volume the *Classical Museum* folded.[24]

Classical Studies in North America

North America could not even boast of the United Kingdom's solid if stolid attainments. Interest in classical antiquity helped to define the educated classes on the western shore of the Atlantic just as on its other side. In the republican

United States classicism held deep meanings even for women, who as a rule had no Latin and less Greek. But the United States lacked an infrastructure of erudition to support textual philology, still less Altertumswissenschaft. Private libraries enabled Jefferson or Madison to join the Republic of Letters; such collections did not come close to meeting technical demands of philological scholarship. In 1816 George Ticknor compared Harvard's library with Göttingen's. Harvard held fewer than 20,000 volumes, perhaps then the largest library in America, but was closed most of the time; Göttingen held more than 200,000, "liberally administered." "We have not yet learnt that the Library is not only the first convenience of a University, but that it is the very first necessity,—that it is the life and the spirit." Canada had even poorer provision. 'Classical scholar' in North America meant a bright lad who did well at Greek and Latin. Teaching of Latin and Greek in even the best American colleges resembled an elementary version of Oxford and Cambridge, minus the English stress on verse composition. As late as 1818 a highly regarded Harvard professor sneered at "those learned labourers, who have spent their lives, in settling disputed readings, or explaining doubtful passages, in a Greek or Roman classick."[25]

Contempt aside, poverty of all sorts of academic resources prevented serious philological scholarship. The United States and Canada prior to 1850 had no library fitted to support research, no university competent to train classical scholars, no professor free to teach Latin or Greek at an advanced level—and no stock of classical manuscripts on which to exercise philological skills. In 1815 Harvard sent Edward Everett and George Bancroft to study in Göttingen. When they hopefully returned, the college's single-track, elementary instruction could make no use of their new learning. German biblical criticism, despite some vehement religious objections, took root earlier in America than Altertumswissenschaft—for the United States did have a few seminaries and divinity schools within which erudite men had time for scholarship. From Göttingen in 1818 Ticknor howled, "What a mortifying distance there is between a European and American scholar . . . we do not even know the process by which a man is to be made one. . . . Two or three generations at least must pass away before we make the discovery and succeed in the experiment."[26]

Nonetheless, American college teachers of Greek and Latin warmed to German classical scholarship more readily than did their British cousins. The United States had no native tradition of philology to defend (no Porson could conceivably have existed in America before 1850). And, although Latin and Greek provided the core of education in American colleges, those colleges (influenced by Scotland) did offer a fairly wide range of other subjects. Professors of classics could a little more easily see their work as a distinct field, parallel to other fields, than could tutors in Oxford and Cambridge. They could slightly more readily empathize with German professors and *their* ideals.

Hints of a more abundant—and more Germanic—future appeared fleetingly. As early as 1803 a book by the young Presbyterian minister Samuel

Miller, *A Brief Retrospect of the Eighteenth Century*, dangled scholars like Heyne and Wolf before American eyes. True, their names amounted to little more than marks on Miller's pages, and he scarcely understood the state of erudition in eighteenth-century Germany. In 1831 George Bancroft, not yet a famous historian, gushed over Boeckh, in Lewis's translation, in the *North American Review*. *The Public Economy of Athens* also got a long, admiring explication the next year by Hugh Legaré in the *Southern Review*. For a while in the 1820s, the College of New Jersey (the future Princeton University) housed a Nassau Hall Philological Society, centered on the thousand-volume personal library of Robert Bridges Patton, a Göttingen PhD. Patton even put his Princeton seniors to work on an edition of Aeschylus's *Seven against Thebes*, a project redolent of the philological seminar Patton knew in Göttingen. Both Patton and the philological society proved transient. College fiscal woes forced him to jump ship in 1829 to run a prep school, taking his library with him. In 1832 he published a Greek-English dictionary—a revision of a British version of a German work. That was as high an order of classical scholarship as America provided for.[27]

A few other Americans likewise began to value classical philology as a learned pursuit, to admit their national deficiencies, and to set about overcoming them. From 1815 on, a trickle of young men sailed off to study in Germany—knowing full well, as one of them said, that "very few of what the Germans call scholars are needed in America." Americans (leaving aside German immigrant communities) struggled under the same linguistic handicap as British readers. When George Bancroft prepared for Göttingen in 1818, he recalled, he found only one person around Boston who could teach him German: Sidney Willard, the Hebrew professor at Harvard—who had no clue how to pronounce it. (Bancroft's memory overstated how arid the desert was, but not by much.) In the early years these academic pilgrims went especially to Göttingen, which welcomed foreigners and had strong ties to the United Kingdom.* George Ticknor, among the first, dejectedly confessed that his fellow countrymen did "not yet know what a Greek scholar is." Yet more and more young Americans of scholarly bent shipped out to Germany, a few to study classical philology.[28]

And, in general, nineteenth-century Americans esteemed German culture more than did the English. A growing number of Americans learned German, to sample its literature and learning. The versatile Charlestonian Hugh Legaré, when chargé d'affaires in Brussels in the early 1830s, picked up German with an eye specifically to classical scholarship. Acquiring the language became easier as more and more colleges began teaching it. Another Charlestonian, Basil Gildersleeve, learned it as a Princeton student in the later 1840s and took it to Berlin shortly thereafter.[29]

* From 1714 to 1837, the Hanoverian dynasty ruled both the United Kingdom and Hannover, the state in which Göttingen lay. George II founded the university.

By the 1820s the best informed American professors accepted the superiority of German over English philology; rejected the context-free grammar grinding that ruled American teaching of Latin and Greek; and tried to import into their classrooms a trace of Altertumswissenschaft. Harvard's Greek professor, Cornelius Conway Felton, stressed a holistic approach to Greek culture: "the Art and Literature of the ancients shed light upon each other to a degree unknown in modern times," for they were "different developements [sic] of the same idea of the beautiful." He groused that Americans teach classical texts "with little knowledge of ancient history, and none of mythology"—without "transporting ourselves back to the time" when their authors lived. He knew that Greek plays were religious events rather than mere entertainment; and he insisted that understanding "the Greek drama fully" required learning "the spirit of the people and the light in which they regarded it," along with "the architectural construction of the theatre, and the scenic details." To elucidate any ancient work, students must reflect on "the connexion of the passage in question with the context," considering as well "the style of ancient thought." (Felton's close friend and older colleague Andrews Norton, also German-influenced, gave identical advice a decade earlier to Harvard Divinity School students studying the Bible. Felton may have felt the force of Norton's as well as German example.) "Style of ancient thought" points to the efforts of scholars like Eichhorn and Wolf to use the Bible and Homer to conjure up the spirit of Hebrew and Greek civilizations and then use this 'spirit,' recursively, to understand texts. Eulogizing Felton in 1862, Theodore Dwight Woolsey of Yale observed that the late professor "was not so much drawn" to "linguistics and general philology and to the verbal side of Greek learning" as he was "to all the manifestations of the Greek mind and life"—that is, something like Altertumswissenschaft.[30]

In 1843 Felton collaborated with two biblical philologists, B. B. Edwards and Barnas Sears, in a work meant to bring Americans up to date in classical philology. (Only Sears had studied in Germany, from 1833 to 1835.) Their *Classical Studies* ranged broadly across the later eighteenth and nineteenth centuries, from Oxford to Leiden to Berlin. But it highlighted German classicists, starting with Heyne and Winckelmann, the fathers of Altertumswissenschaft, before moving on to Wolf, Boeckh, Creuzer, Müller, and others. The American authors paid due credit to German textual philologists, most effusively Hermann. But they lamented that English philology, once "the admiration of the learned of all countries," had "through Porson and his followers" grown "so limited to the mere language and metre of the Greek tragedians" as to sink into near irrelevance. Today, they declared, August Boeckh's renown outshines that of all other German classical philologists. "In mere language," Hermann surpasses him. "But in a knowledge of what the Greeks and Romans were practically—in the power of reproducing Grecian and Roman life, in all its thousand forms—no one can pretend to be his equal." Only his student Müller came anywhere near. The "excellence of Boeckh and his followers" lay in bringing together "the better portions of the methods of Wolf and of Niebuhr."[31]

Starting in the 1830s teachers like Felton and Woolsey brought a little of Germany into American colleges. They began to edit Greek plays for classroom use, based on German recensions. These little books did not amount to research as it was known in German universities. Looking back from the next century, the Chicago classicist Paul Shorey observed that New England in the age of Emerson

> had accumulated enough in books, education, and social tradition to support a literature and the kind of culture that he [Emerson] calls scholarship. Technical, professional, productive scholarship it could not support. The minimum condition of that was the libraries, the university apparatus, the body of workers trained in the old-world tradition that we have acquired only in the last thirty or forty years.

Indeed, in Felton's day, as Caroline Winterer noted, scholarship and teaching blurred in the minds of American professors:

> Their chief avenues for scholarly output were college textbooks, articles in literary and popular journals, and lectures directed at the learned public. In these venues they did not display the results of their own new research; rather, they distilled the fruits of German and English scholarship for a broadly educated American readership.

Secondhand, admittedly, such work showed American academics perking up their ears at Altertumswissenschaft and laying a foundation on which original investigations might some day arise.[32]

Felton tried something more ambitious. Karl Beck—a new colleague in Latin (who doubled as Harvard's physical education teacher)—abetted him. Beck had fled Germany to escape political persecution. He knew the new historical philology not only from German university studies but also as stepson of the biblical scholar Wilhelm de Wette. In 1831 Felton and Beck—frustrated by drilling restless teenagers—set up what they called a philological seminary. They admitted only college graduates seeking serious training in classical philology, either for personal enrichment or to prepare to teach Greek and Latin. Beck would have known seminars from his own education. Where he and Felton got the idea to admit only postgraduate students makes a puzzle—possibly from theological seminaries such as Harvard's Divinity School. In any case, their philological seminary foreshadowed the distinctive American contribution to the structure of the modern university: the graduate school. The shadow fell fleetingly: the seminary lasted two years. But it implied longing for a classical philology more substantial than Aristophanes for adolescents.[33]

The next generation would satisfy the yearning. Having learned German at Princeton, in 1850 Basil Lanneau Gildersleeve put it to work at the University of Berlin. He arrived a self-described "Teutonomaniac"—"Goethe's aphorisms were my daily food"—but not intending a career in classical philology. At matriculation he encountered the decidedly unromantic August Boeckh. Boeckh, Gildersleeve recalled, "made a passionate classicist out of an amateurish student of literature." However, studies in Berlin left Gildersleeve discouraged. After a semester, he decamped for the American-infested University of Göttingen, where he became friendly with George Martin Lane and Francis J. Child, who would make their marks at Harvard—Lane in Latin, Child in English. After two Göttingen semesters, Gildersleeve moved to Bonn. The particular pattern of migration had its effect. As it happened, Boeckh's lecture topics during the semester Gildersleeve heard him were Demosthenes and Greek literature. Gildersleeve got comprehensive lectures on 'encyclopedia of philology,' not from Boeckh, but from the eminent Latinist Friedrich Wilhelm Ritschl in Bonn. Ritschl, while not endorsing Gottfried Hermann's purely textual philology, harbored suspicions of Boeckh's all-inclusive Altertumswissenschaft. Had Gildersleeve spent his German years primarily in Berlin, he may have emerged depressed but broader-gauged. After returning to Göttingen to defend a dissertation on Porphyry (a topic suggested by the great Jacob Bernays in Bonn), Gildersleeve sailed home in July 1853 to begin a major career in American classical studies, first at the University of Virginia, then at the new Johns Hopkins University—a story that belongs to a later chapter.[34]

And if his scholarship did not range as broadly as expected from a student ordained classicist by Boeckh, the historical depth and cultural breadth of Altertumswissenschaft did affect Gildersleeve's writing and teaching. He not only admired German philology but held in contempt the narrowness of English classical scholarship. "It is astonishing with what vehement obstinacy, so to speak, England prides herself upon the mere negative merit of keeping her quantity void of offence."* He recommended, "as a motto for their future productions, the words of Sir Andrew Aguecheek—'I am a great eater of beef, and, I believe, that does harm to my wit.'" The torch had long passed from sinking England to rising Germany. "The Germans are now dominant in the science of classical philology, and we must harmonize with them or make a senseless discord."[35]

As far as seriously grappling with the German revolution in classical philology before Gildersleeve's generation, classicists in North America stood largely helpless, their counterparts in the United Kingdom mostly oblivious. Both situations would change profoundly later in the century. For now, Altertumswissenschaft, especially the shock of Niebuhr, echoed mainly outside classical philology as practiced in the English-speaking North Atlantic up to 1850.

---

* In this usage, "quantity" refers to the grouping of long and short syllables basic to Greek and Latin verse.

PART II: ARCHAEOLOGY

During the nineteenth century, antiquarian fondness for digging up Roman remains and ancient English graves evolved into a distinct field called archaeology. In 1871 E. B. Tylor defined it as the specialized study of "old structures and buried relics of the remote past."[36] Deleting "remote" as inessential, we have in Tylor's phrase the heart of the discipline as it still exists. But only erratically over the first half of the century did archaeology begin to emerge as a discrete, well-bounded field of study. Even the word got used irregularly and inconstantly, evidence of a subject not yet sharply outlined.

A key difference already separated protoarchaeology in the English-speaking world from German work. Gildersleeve named among his "chief masters" in Bonn Friedrich Gottlieb Welcker. By then doyen of German classical archaeologists, Welcker all his career tried to integrate material culture and philology in a holistic science of classical antiquity. He pioneered in using plaster casts of ancient sculpture to show evolving artistic styles, but he also edited Greek literature and wrote a trailblazing treatise on Greek religion. Welcker fitted smoothly into German classical studies—as evidenced by his many students in the next generation of classical scholars. In the British classical establishment, he would have stuck out as weirdly as an abstract bronze among his plaster deities. In the United Kingdom the written word ruled. The few serious American classical philologists were more curious about ancient marble; but, pending speedier transatlantic voyages, they usually sat home. Despite these obstacles, several Britons, even one American helped before 1850 to shape the archaeology of the 'civilized past.' But these 'archaeologists,' unlike Germans, inhabited a parallel universe to academic classical erudition, rather than blending into it. Still, since most Anglophone pioneers were alert to—even involved with—archaeologists working in continental Europe, a glance there is needed.[37]

Continental Counterparts

Since antiquity, gathering material pieces of the past had gone along with philology; but such collecting did not equal archaeology as Tylor meant the word. Newfangled archaeology inherited much from old-fashioned antiquarianism, but shed much. Antiquarians trawled a wider sea than modern archaeologists. The haul that antiquaries picked over and classified included written records, information about old customs and institutions, and all sorts of other lore. A particular antiquarian might obsess over physical artifacts, just as archaic words might preoccupy another. Jacques Spon of Lyon hugely favored tangible relics—so much so that he has been called the first (in 1685) to use *archaeology* in its modern sense as the study only of material remains. But this is wrong. His traditionally broad antiquarian's definition of "ARCHAEOGRAPHIA" (his actual term) included manuscript records. For, whatever individual preferences, the antiquarian enterprise as a whole attempted—and had since Varro, if not before—to reconstruct past worlds from all stuff available. Indeed, reflecting this omnivorous scavenging, the word *archaeology* itself (and variants in other European languages) originally meant simply a distant past or its retrieval. As late as 1807 F. A. Wolf used *Archäologie* to refer to study both of legal and political institutions and of Greco-Roman art.[38]

The last, in fact, provided the nucleus around which archaeology in our sense gelled. Renaissance excavators of ancient Roman sites had hunted for statuary and other artworks; eighteenth-century diggers at Herculaneum and Pompeii did the same. Collectors right through the first half of the nineteenth century appreciated Greek and Roman antiquities much more for aesthetic qualities than for insight into ancient cultures. Cycladic figurines from the third millennium BCE sometimes got mixed in with classical marbles shipped to northern Europe from Greece. They were derided as crude and barbaric—irrelevant to a scholar of the civilized past—rather than valued as voices of a people otherwise silenced by time. In 1827 excavators uncovered painted tombs at Corneto (now Tarquinia), some sixty miles north of Rome. The murals showed remarkable details of daily life in the little-known Etruscan culture, but what they revealed about classical Greek painting caught eyes at the time. In the mid-nineteenth century casts of classical sculpture still formed the core of Friedrich Welcker's 'archaeological' museum, and the lectures Gildersleeve heard him deliver as professor of archaeology concerned Greek *art*. As late as 1881 Boston architects underwrote American excavations at Assos in northwestern Anatolia in hope of clarifying for modern use principles of ancient Greek architecture.[39]

What made 'archaeology' out of artworks? It was changing *treatment* of excavations and objects they yielded—systematizing, historicizing, interaction with philology. The beauty of a 'find' very slowly became secondary to 'disciplinary' archaeologists, though far from irrelevant.

Excavation itself became after 1800 a more precise, careful business. The military engineer Karl Weber had begun tightening up in the eighteenth century: imposing order on helter-skelter mining for Roman art at Herculaneum and Pompeii, drawing up accurate plans of buildings, marking on charts where artifacts were found. His successors refined his example. In the first decades after 1800, removal of rubble and mapping of walls revealed Pompeii as a city, not unconnected buildings, statues, frescoes. The hunt for art, subjected to system, thus unexpectedly yielded insight into Roman life. By mid-century best practices included precise recording of where artifacts lay within a site, faithful drawings of structures excavated, accurate charting of areas dug up. This paradigm guided the Egyptian expedition of the Prussian archaeologist Richard Lepsius in 1842–45. Granted, around 1850, more excavators still flouted the ideal than followed it, and no dig of a Greek site yet lived up to Lepsius's standard. But more and more exact technique was a precondition for archaeology's emergence as a new, at least semi-independent field.[40]

In this same period students of classical art were placing its remnants in history. Again, first steps belonged to the previous century. In 1764 Winckelmann—modeling his work on J. C. Scaliger's periodization of Greek literature two centuries before—divided classical Greek sculpture into four phases. His initial dating of works depended on literary sources and inscriptions. Then, having sorted the objects into groups, he worked out a four-stage succession of artistic *styles*; this made rough dating of newfound statues theoretically possible without written evidence. Winckelmann's system teetered on very scant data. His early nineteenth-century heirs kept historical evolution central in study of classical art but beefed up evidence. In the museum developed by Welcker in Bonn from 1819, he organized coins, pottery—and, above all, the first university collection of casts of Greek sculpture—to display historical development of ancient art. From time to time, Welcker and other museum directors rearranged their casts to reflect changing theories of how Greek art evolved. In 1833, using K. O. Müller's handbook of ancient art, Eduard Gerhard began to order historically the classical collections in the new royal museum in Berlin, the most prominent in Germany (now the Altes Museum). Gerhard had credentials. A student of Wolf and Boeckh, he had published in 1831 a long report on some three thousand Greek vases found in Etruscan tombs at Vulci, not far from Corneto and its wall paintings. The vases showed, for the first time, classical Greek painting developing in unbroken sequence. But Gerhard valued these spectacular finds chiefly as visual evidence to better parse Greek mythology. In his philologically trained hands, art served Altertumswissenschaft: archaeology shed light on Greek worldviews as well as artistic technique.[41]

In cases like this, philological Altertumswissenschaft helped to form archaeology into a cultural study. None other than K. O. Müller, after all, had written the first handbook of ancient art. Succeeding German scholars like Welcker and Gerhard pushed archaeology gradually away from the 'timeless' artworks that supplied its main motive in the early 1800s; they moved it closer to a science of the past allied (as antiquarianism had often been) with the historical, interpretative concerns of philology. Making archaeology a branch of Altertumswissenschaft subordinated it to the study of texts but also broadened its purposes beyond digging up beautiful objects. German archaeologists in the nineteenth century tended to treat archaeology as philology—objects as texts, so to speak. After all, students of Boeckh ruled the field until nearly 1900. Richard Lepsius believed himself to be 'reading' Egyptian monuments according to philological methods. Eduard Gerhard called archaeology "the philology of monuments." Otto Jahn—expert on classical pottery, disciple of Boeckh—in 1849 insisted that scholars apply to the "language of artworks" the heedfulness with which philologists had for centuries read texts. In reconstructing a fragmentary inscription, archaeologists thought as if it were a damaged manuscript. Given distance between surviving pieces, and considering time, place, and subject, what words or letters could most plausibly fill the gap? Philology thus tied archaeological finds more firmly to historical contexts, made them more revelatory of a particular culture. It also ruled out timeless patterns linking objects that some antiquarians might once have visualized. German philologists not only transferred their methods to the 'reading' of archaeological data but also consistently preferred written records to those wordlessly registered in stone and bronze. Nonetheless, just such Germans took the lead in forging independent institutions for archaeology.[42]

A little reflection makes it less odd that text-minded scholars led in institutionalizing archaeology. Antiquarianism had entangled itself with textual philology to an extent that made it hard to drew clear lines between the two. Antiquaries collected coins and statues, studied topography, and restored ancient Rome (at least on paper). But they also marshaled written sources and applied philological methods to interpret them. New-style archaeology specialized in material objects to the exclusion of manuscripts. The same scholar might study Greek monuments and Greek manuscripts, even integrate the two types of sources to illuminate the ancient world more completely. Welcker did. But well before midcentury everyone understood that 'archaeology' covered the stuff in his museum, not written sources on his desk.

Thus learned Germans began to organize archaeologists into specialized societies. This started in Rome, mecca of archaeology after Napoleon's defeat in 1815. Among Germans there was Eduard Gerhard, who moved to Rome in the early 1820s. He linked up with fellow countrymen as well as leading Italian antiquarians who shared his passion for archaeology. Fretting over how slowly information about finds spread—despite their growing number—in 1829 he drew his antiquarian acquaintances together into a multinational Instituto di Corrispondenza Archeologica (Institute for Archaeological Correspondence). Its first president was a French diplomat, its patron the crown prince of Prussia (whom Gerhard had guided through the archaeological sights of Rome the year before), its general secretary the learned Prussian ambassador Christian Bunsen. English and Italian antiquaries headed their own sections. As subsecretary, Gerhard sat at the center of the web, receiving news of discoveries from all over Italy and beyond, then reporting it in the institute's publications. Not least was his own study of those thousands of Greek vases from Vulci. The institute, Stephen Dyson wrote, "played a key role in the creation of a more scholarly brand of classical archaeology." In 1835 Crown Prince Friedrich Wilhelm paid to build a headquarters on the Capitoline Hill. In succeeding years Prussian subsidies erratically but steadily increased, eventually including stipends for young German archaeologists. In 1871 the now-named Institut für Archäologische Korrespondenz in Rome became a Prussian state institution, and in 1873 an imperial one, the Kaiserlich-Deutschen Archäologischen Institut, overseen from Berlin.[43]

Meanwhile, archaeologists outside of Rome also put the field on a more formal, more scholarly basis. Events moved quickly in the early 1840s, as if archaeologists suddenly recognized themselves as a new species. In 1842 Francesco Avellino, head of excavation at Pompeii, began the *Bullettino archeo-logico napoletano*. In 1843 Gerhard—having left Rome in 1833 for the new royal museum in Berlin—started another journal, *Archäologische Zeitung*. The *Archaeological Journal* appeared in London the same year. In 1844 Charles Lenormant, lecturer on ancient Greece at the Sorbonne, founded the *Revue archéologique* in Paris. In its inaugural issue he differentiated 'scientific' archaeologists from ancient historians and from antiquarians: historians knew little about monuments; antiquarians had not mastered critical methods; archaeologists knew both. It was a first stab.[44]

Most European archaeological activity centered on ancient Greece and Rome, not all. Invading Egypt in 1798, Napoleon took along savants to survey the country physically and archaeologically. This learned battalion published its findings in some twenty gorgeous volumes between 1809 and 1829—essentially creating modern Egyptology. One soldier came upon the Rosetta Stone, carved with essentially the same inscription in hieroglyphic, Demotic (late ancient Egyptian), and Greek script. Nabbed by victorious British troops in 1801, the stone ended up in the British Museum. But it allowed scholars at last to read ancient Egyptian hieroglyphs after Jean-François Champollion translated it in 1822. All this bustle left some French *érudits* with unslakable thirsts for Egyptian archaeology. Lenormant, in fact, after joining the Sorbonne in 1849, taught only that subject. France also nurtured many local, more or less learned societies of antiquarian bent. Beginning in 1833 the Congrès archéologique met annually in different towns to connect these groups with the larger world of French erudition. The Congrès devoted much attention to medieval archaeology; journals of local societies also ushered in scrutiny of Roman Gaul. Similar groups flourished in Germany, especially in the Rhineland. They, too, by the 1840s were discovering artifacts from all periods of the Germanic past and displaying them in local museums. In Rome, opening a new front in his war against secular liberalism, Pope Pius IX sponsored excavation of early Christian remains—an antiquarian pursuit languishing since the Renaissance. The first great success came in 1849 with rediscovery of the catacomb of Saint Callistus on Via Appia. This dig brought to prominence Giovanni Battista de Rossi. He went on to shape a new subfield, Christian archaeology.[45]

Anglophone Classical Archaeology

Antiquarianism was giving birth to archaeology; and, as it did, Anglophone scholars and adventurers—almost all British—supplied some of the midwives. British classical archaeologists in the making were shaped not by university training like Welcker and Gerhard but by the achievements of eighteenth-century antiquarian explorers of ancient Greece like Robert Wood, James Stuart and Nicholas Revett, and other Dilettanti.

In the spirit of the Dilettanti, well into the 1800s British students of antiq-uity traveled to the Mediterranean mainly to describe topography and build-ings—and to cart off stones. (Classical relics from the eighteenth-century grand tour already crammed country houses.) The most ambitious mover of marble was Thomas Bruce, Earl of Elgin. From 1801 to 1803 Elgin 'rescued' the Parthenon frieze and other gems of Athenian art from potential defacement and deterioration. He genuinely feared for the monuments, and Ottoman au-thorities licensed his removals. But some English-speaking Hellenophiles saw him as latter-day Vandal. Cried Byron: "Frown not on England; England owns him not: / Athena, no! thy plunderer was a Scot." Frowning was far from uni-versal, plunder common. Edward Clarke was in Athens in 1801. He censured Elgin—but he himself at Eleusis bribed officials to snatch a decayed caryatid (upsetting local peasants who supplicated it as a fertility goddess). Clarke had earlier visited the region of ancient Troy. There, from inscriptions and coins on site, he recognized a hill called Hisarlik as the ancient city of Ilium Novum (New Troy)—though no one then realized that old Troy lay beneath. Identifi-cation of Hisarlik as Ilium Novum (or Recens) first appeared in print in *The Topography of Troy* (1804) by William Gell. Gell, among the most painstaking of these antiquarian observers, also published surveys of antiquities in Attica and Ionia, an overview of the Pompeii excavations, and a precise *Topography of Rome and Its Vicinity* (1834). Gell's even more meticulous contemporary William Martin Leake, an army man with engineer's eye, traveled through Greece intermittently from 1802 to 1810 on duties military and diplomatic. During his journeys he recorded ancient remains throughout the land. After retiring from service he published books on ancient Greek topography essen-tial to later archaeologists. *The Topography of Athens* (revised 1841) remained standard until the twentieth century.[46]

Well-educated Americans visited the Mediterranean with similar interests but little scholarly effect. The American elite grew up in the same classically infused culture as British counterparts. Stuart and Revett's *Antiquities of Ath-ens* circulated in the colonies and young republic; Thomas Jefferson owned *Le antichità di Ercolano*. After 1800, casts of ancient sculpture began to adorn public collections as well as a few private parlors. Few Americans had jour-neyed as far south as Italy during the colonial period, and continental travel remained difficult until the end of the Napoleonic Wars in 1815. In 1802 the young South Carolinian Joel Poinsett did get to Sicily to admire Greek ruins; four years later, twenty-year-old Nicholas Biddle even traveled extensively through Greece. After 1815, Americans with sufficient means began visiting Italy in growing numbers (usually a once-in-a-lifetime experience, given the slowness of transatlantic travel in the age of sail). The more scholarly or adven-turous among these pilgrims not only examined seriously excavations in Rome but trekked to Pompeii and even onward to Greek temples at Paestum. Visits to Greece itself remained unusual before midcentury—although in 1818

Edward Everett went there, fresh from hearing Welcker lecture on archaeology in Göttingen. These Americans wrote only in letters and diaries about the remains they saw—with one exception. John Izard Middleton, a South Carolinian educated at Cambridge, lived most of his life in France and Italy. In 1808 and 1809 he studied and drew the so-called Cyclopean walls in Latium southeast of Rome. (He mistakenly linked them to similar Mycenaean masonry in Greece.) In 1812 he published in London color plates of his careful drawings, with explanatory comment, in a volume called *Grecian Remains in Italy, a Description of Cyclopian Walls and of Roman Antiquities*. It sank without a trace.[47]

What did all this amount to? For the Americans, little except a broad, if shallow, acquaintance among the privileged classes with classical sculpture and temples. The first American classical archaeologists would exploit this interested public in the late nineteenth century. A lot of British travelers drifted through the region with the same nebulous veneration as Americans—like Richard Monckton Milnes, making a "pilgrimage" to Delphi in 1842 before wandering on to Jerusalem and Cairo. But writers like Gell and Leake expanded knowledge of ancient civilizations. They contrast with the eighteenth-century expeditions sponsored by the Dilettanti. These resulted less in deepened understanding of ancient Greek culture, more in new fashions of modern building: the Greek Revival. Architects in the making still prowled temples in Leake's day. One, C. R. Cockerell, as we shall see momentarily, even made important finds while studying Greek architecture. Cockerell befriended Leake (and drew pictures for his *Topography of Athens*), but Leake and Gell sought something other than architectural inspiration. Their surveys of ancient topography and monuments offered relatively little to an architect. But they greatly helped later scholars trying to put material relics of classical antiquity into geographic and cultural context to understand ancient Greeks and Romans better. The *literary* custodians of this same antiquity—the Oxbridge classical establishment—did virtually no research into physical remains; and this apathy highlighted by contrast the archaeological sensibility of writers like Leake and some other British travelers. Christopher Wordsworth (nephew of the poet and first to decipher graffiti at Pompeii) did study at Trinity College Cambridge—during Hare and Thirlwall's brief ascendancy. As E. D. Clarke had done for New Troy three decades before, in 1832 Wordsworth located the lost city of Dodona, where once spoke the oracle of Zeus. Thirty years later excavations confirmed his speculations.[48]

Actual digging by British 'classical archaeologists'—a label premature in 1832—proceeded haphazardly, well below Pompeii standards. Cockerell, exploring Aegina with pals in 1811, hired locals to do shallow, hit-or-miss digging around the Temple of Aphaia. They turned up sculpture of unknown style, in transition from archaic to classical. Cockerell and friends also figured out that the temple had been painted in bright hues; when he published, he challenged the long-settled consensus that Greeks did art in marmoreal white. The next year, by chance, he uncovered a sculptured frieze while clambering over the ruined temple of Bassae in the Peloponnese. And in observing temples closely, Cockerell noticed entasis in classical columns—first to do so. (Entasis is a slight swelling of a column as it rises. It made columns *appear* straight to an observer at ground level as they went up.) Cockerell had luck as well as a good eye. More typical were two English student-architects searching in 1823 for artworks at Selinunte, a Greek colony in southwest Sicily. Officials kicked them out for trying to sneak metopes back home. But in 1838 the intrepid (and usefully rich) Charles Fellows led a small band up-country from the southwestern Anatolian coast to the ancient Lycian capital of Xanthus in Asia Minor—a place unknown to western Europeans and illumined by no written record. Fellows carefully explored the site and other ruined Lycian cities nearby. His published account ignited such enthusiasm that the British Museum got the government to back three return expeditions. On the last a hundred Royal Navy sailors marched up to Xanthus, along with carpenters, stonecutters, and the now indispensable cast makers. On these trips—sanctioned by a *firman* (permit) from the Ottoman sultan—Fellows's men stripped the place. They worked with all the skill expected from untrained sailors, smashing the so-called Horse Tomb into pieces. The navy carried the crated swag back to London. In his way, Fellows had pulled off an archaeological triumph; but his feat looked more like looting than methodical excavation.[49]

Still, soundings as different as Leake's and Fellows's awoke interest and expanded erudition back home. Classical scholars in English universities still obsessed on texts, and almost everyone valued ancient artifacts mainly as art. Inevitably, then, the British Museum in London became the central warehouse of expertise in classical archaeology. (Britain had no parallel to specialized museums of classical art that Germans built in this period, like Welcker's in Bonn or the Glyptothek in Munich.) By 1800 the British Museum already owned much classical material—coins, Greek vases, Roman statuary: legacies of the antiquarian sensibility of the eighteenth-century grand tour. It now acquired more and more pieces of note. Cockerell persuaded the government to buy in 1814 the frieze he found at Bassae. Two years later Parliament finally agreed to purchase the Elgin Marbles. The so-called Harpy Tomb, Nereid Monument, and other booty from Xanthus came to the museum in the 1840s.[50]

The person there who ultimately mattered most for classical archaeology was a young man named Charles Newton. An 1837 BA of Christ Church Oxford—where he befriended John Ruskin—Newton had an artistic eye, antiquarian tastes, and solid grounding in Oxford-style, wholly textual classical philology. Philip Bliss, an antiquary who then served as university registrar, took Newton under his wing. In 1840 Bliss found his protégé a job as junior assistant in the British Museum's Department of Antiquities—"a very nice place for a young man fond of the kind of thing," according to Bliss's contact at the museum. The phrase says all that needs saying about the professionalism of museum curatorship at the time. 'Antiquities' at the British Museum

included everything from Greek to medieval to Asian artifacts. Classical artworks had pride of place. Newton did not delight in the job, but he learned a
lot. His interests at this point had not yet zeroed in on Greek and Roman antiquity. But by 1847 he had developed strong views on how to study classical
antiquity. These owed much to Altertumswissenschaft.[51]

A breathless letter to his mentor Bliss, written in that year, shows the holistic cast of mind within which British classical archaeology would develop after
1850, with Newton among its leaders. He chided the old-fashioned Bliss for
Oxford's resistance to change in its dealing with the ancient world:

> That for example the classics should be taught & studied without the il-
> lustration of ancient art, that the Greek & Latin languages should not be
> considered in relation to the great family of languages to which they
> belong, & the comparative anatomy of cognate tongues more dwelt
> upon, that ancient history should be so feebly & imperfectly delineated
> in college lectures, that there should be no English Handbooks of an-
> cient history bridging over great chasms when the history is not told
> continuously but picked up by inference out of fragments, & by labour
> too difficult for students to accomplish for themselves, that there should
> be no maps of ancient countries embodying all that recent travellers &
> the hydrographers of the navy have added to our knowledge,* that in a
> word the great University of Oxford, the officina [workshop] and labora-
> tory of learning for many centuries should have no tools to dig with ex-
> cept what she imports from Germany, these things are crying & mon-
> strous defaults, I do not say, abuses, because Oxford tutors are not aware
> how little they are doing to extend the knowledge of that they profess to
> teach.[52]

"Tools to dig with" would soon turn literal and would not be imported from
Germany—though not forged in Oxford or Cambridge either.

English-Speaking Protoarchaeologists Elsewhere

The classical world held pride of place for educated Anglophones, but not always the most advanced erudition. Middle Eastern archaeology, for one, developed more speedily than its classical counterpart in the decades up to 1850.
Perhaps the heavy legacy of classical textual philology did not weigh it down,
or perhaps material remains had to fill in for largely absent literary sources.
Ancient Egypt had long fascinated European philologists, not least owing to
its salience in the Old Testament. Both scripture and Greek sources spoke also
of Persians, Babylonians, other ancient peoples of the region. The massive bar-

* An early project of the Society for the Diffusion of Useful Knowledge, a Utilitarian organization in the orbit of University College London, was to produce such maps.

rier to investigating any of these civilizations was inability to read their writings—if writings were known. This made digging things up appealing.

Egypt still loomed larger than other ancient Middle Eastern empires; and
in the three decades after 1820 Britons, like continental scholars, came to develop techniques recognizable as scholarly Egyptian archaeology. (Americans
at best collected artifacts when touring Egypt.) The essential breakthrough
came in cracking the code of hieroglyphic writing. Decipherment of the triple-
language text on the Rosetta Stone—in which the English natural philosopher
Thomas Young played a crucial part—at last became available when Champollion published a complete translation in 1822. This key unlocked the door, and
students of ancient Egypt over the next few decades learned to read hieroglyphs with growing fluency.[53]

Literacy transformed explorers and adventurers into scholars. Henry Salt,
British consul in Egypt from 1816 to his death in 1827, spent much of his last
few years copying inscriptions, decoding them, expanding the vocabulary of
hieroglyphic names and letters. From 1828 to 1839 an expedition put together
by Robert Hay, a wealthy Scot, surveyed methodically ancient monuments of
the Nile Valley, from Giza and Memphis into Nubia. Joseph Bonomi, one of
the team's artists, delicately reproduced inscriptions and wall paintings. For
twelve years starting in 1821, John Gardner Wilkinson studied inscriptions and
murals in tombs and temples, mostly around Thebes. (William Gell had
turned him toward Egypt.) The result in 1837 was *Manners and Customs of the
Ancient Egyptians*, a richly illustrated description of daily life, the first drawn
from Egyptian rather than classical sources. Readers devoured it; Queen Victoria knighted its author. Shortly before Wilkinson published, the retired soldier Richard Vyse opened and explored many Giza pyramids. His gunpowder
damaged most of them. But he atoned by funding a painstaking, nonexplosive
survey of pyramids in Upper Egypt by the English civil engineer John Shae
Perring from 1837 to 1839. Perring's drawings, site plans, and maps, published
in *The Pyramids of Gizeh* (1839), seriously expanded knowledge of ancient
Egypt.[54]

Archaeology elsewhere in the Middle East required shovels. Unlike Egypt's
stone-built pyramids and temples, the mud-brick monuments of Assyria and
Babylonia had long ago melted into mounds. Over the centuries, a rare European traveler now and then had sat foot on fallen Persepolis or what he
thought was Nineveh; in 1786 a French abbé even dug into Babylon. But Englishmen did most to create Middle Eastern archaeology. The antiquarian-
minded Claudius Rich served as East India Company 'resident' in Baghdad—
a sort of consul—between 1808 and 1821, the year he died. Besides amassing
manuscripts and coins, he identified the site of Nineveh and explored Babylon. His *Narrative of a Residence in Koordistan*—not published until 1836—
first described the region's archaeological remains. His collections, purchased
by the British Museum, brought the first cuneiform tablets to Europe.[55]

In 1839 twenty-two-year-old Austen Henry Layard set out to travel overland to Ceylon (today Sri Lanka). He never got there. He wandered Ottoman lands and Persia, learned Arabic and Persian, lived as a tribesman for a while. In early 1842 he grew interested in mounds across the river from Mosul. The new French consul in the city, Paul-Émile Botta, had begun to dig there. Eventually Layard persuaded Stratford Canning, British ambassador in Constantinople, to fund excavations. Layard's stint of tribal living paid off in good relations with local workers. Most important, he hired and soon became friends with an unusual native of Mosul. Hormuzd Rassam was born a Chaldean Christian; an English missionary's wife converted him to Anglicanism and taught him English. Starting in October 1845 Layard's crew dug at Nimrud—which he believed to be Nineveh. He uncovered three palaces and remarkable artifacts, including the startling winged lions and bulls with human heads that now seem the Assyrian trademark. His finds induced the British Museum to shell out. In 1847 he dug at the mound of Kuyunjik, the real Nineveh. There he discovered Sennacherib's palace, the biggest Assyrian building. He returned to celebrity in Britain. He took Rassam home with him and enrolled him at Oxford. But in 1849 Rassam went back to Mesopotamia as second in command to Layard. More excavation at Kuyunjik in 1849–51 produced more Assyrian splendors. In 1852—persuaded by Layard—the British Museum sent Rassam back for more digging. At Kuyunjik (working by night to evade French rivals) his men uncovered the palace of the seventh-century BCE king Ashurbanipal. Besides more glorious artwork, the site yielded thousands of clay cuneiform tablets. This 'library' of Ashurbanipal would open ancient Assyrian culture to modern eyes. Yet Assyrian archaeology was still more an adventurer's than a professor's pursuit.[56]

Biblical archaeology *was* a professor's pursuit—and an American professor's to boot. Edward Robinson, a Connecticut minister's son, in 1823 became Hebrew instructor at Andover Seminary in Massachusetts. Middle Eastern archaeology intrigued him; by 1822 he knew Rich's reports from Babylon. In 1826 Robinson left for Germany to make himself into a serious biblical philologist. From the orientalist and biblical philologist Wilhelm Gesenius of Halle, his chief mentor, Robinson learned to examine sources critically and not to let his own beliefs color the evidence. (Neither did Robinson let evidence unsettle his beliefs.) At Halle and Berlin he also acquired some skills of an orientalist, notably Arabic. In Berlin, lectures on geography by the explorer Alexander von Humboldt and the renowned geographer Carl Ritter intrigued him. In 1830 Robinson returned to the United States. There he made a reputation in biblical philology—a part of his career discussed later. But even before he left Germany, orientalism, geography, and the Bible swirled together in his mind. He began to contemplate a book on sacred geography. Opportunity knocked in 1832. A former student of Robinson's at Andover, Eli Smith, came to visit. Now a missionary in the Middle East, Smith was fluent in Arabic, familiar with the Levant, well connected with local Muslims as well as missionaries. Illness and scholarship delayed Robinson's adventure for several years. But on March 12, 1838, he and Eli Smith left Cairo, with a pack train of camels and a crew of Arabs, headed for the Holy Land.[57]

Biblical philologists had long believed linguistic and cultural contexts essential to understanding scripture; Robinson meant to provide physical context, what he called "the historical topography." Supplying it required careful attention and much research—Robinson seems to have read every previous trekker through Palestine—all sifted by the skeptical mulling of evidence taught by Gesenius. (The journey also needed stamina and courage. Palestine had no roads, only trails haunted by bandits.) Robinson showed his basic method in Suez when trying to pinpoint where the Israelites crossed the Red Sea. The book of Exodus put the number of adult males at 600,000, plus women and children—and many, many moseying sheep. Robinson frankly admitted the improbable logistics of getting this mob through the Red Sea in the few hours the Bible gave. Yet he never questioned Exodus's statistics, and he accommodated these fantastic data as well as the lay of the land allowed. When he got to Palestine, Robinson continued to look facts in the face and to weigh evidence carefully pro and con, without doubting for a moment that 'facts' in the Bible were exactly that. He blundered in Jerusalem. But in locating biblical sites outside of the city—Beersheba, Shiloh, Bethel, Jericho, and many others—his technique worked pretty well, especially when he could triangulate with other ancient sources and linguistic clues from place-names. (Smith's fluency in Arabic proved a godsend.) In less than four months, under harsh, often perilous conditions, Robinson and Smith crisscrossed the biblical lands. Though unable to excavate, they identified scores of biblical places. Their inferences held up under scrutiny of later archaeologists better than one might guess. Over the next two years, working in Germany, Robinson prepared the three-volume *Biblical Researches in Palestine, Mount Sinai and Arabia Petraea* (1841).* Together with its superb maps, his text laid the basis for later archaeology in the Holy Land. Halle gave him an honorary degree, and the Royal Geographical Society of London bestowed a gold medal.[58]

British modernity presented a challenge to archaeologists almost opposite to Middle Eastern underdevelopment: massive railroad building and industrial expansion threatened to wipe out medieval structures. What we now call historic preservation seems largely to have motivated the founding in 1843 of the British Archaeological Association (BAA). (One might reasonably guess that the same visible changes in physical environment also inspired the romantic medievalism that made modern people worry about ancient piles.) The new group meant not to displace the Society of Antiquaries but to complement it with a more specialized focus on material relics of the British past,

---

* Pace the title, the book contains ethnology, description of flora and fauna, and postbiblical history; it remains a valuable source for nineteenth-century Palestine. In transliterating Arabic place-names into Roman characters, Robinson used the system John Pickering had developed for American Indian languages!

including the *Archaeological Journal* established by the BAA in 1844. As in classical archaeology, no sharp lines separated archaeology from art and architecture: a Gothic revival paralleled the Greek revival. Nor did British 'archaeologists' yet clearly distinguish themselves from antiquarians. Many founding members of the BAA belonged not only to local antiquarian groups but also to societies created to print medieval and early modern texts—and fully a third of the early members were clergy, long the main engine of antiquarian research. But, in agitating for more attention to 'national antiquities' at the British Museum and other repositories, these 'archaeologists' gave a special dignity to physical remains. Only two years after its birth, the BAA split. In what seems from afar a petty quarrel, some of its founders hived off as the Archaeological Institute of Great Britain and Ireland—taking the journal with them. Charles Newton, still more interested in British antiquities than in Greek archaeology, jumped ship, serving briefly as secretary of the new Institute. Just what British archaeology meant in these early years is foggy. Meanwhile, Americans, lacking a medieval or Roman past, contented themselves with historical societies focused on a more recent past and its paper remains.[59]

Archaeology at Midcentury

From such endeavors a new discipline called archaeology emerged, but this future was not quite obvious in 1850. The word *archaeology* in its newer sense (meaning the study of material remains rather than the past, generically) came into English before 1850, as the names of the BAA and the Archaeological Institute showed. Charles Newton talked without self-consciousness of "historical archaeology." But Edward Robinson used the term only indirectly, citing German works on *biblische Archäologie*. As late as 1849 Henry Layard still wrote of 'antiquities' rather than archaeology. These inconstant usages suggest flux. Whether uttering the word or not, the new archaeologists inherited much from older antiquarianism. But they set their work apart from antiquarianism by exclusive focus on the physical past, whether Robinson's and Leake's "topography" or Layard's and Fellows's artifacts.[60]

Yet textual and linguistic philology profoundly shaped the new archaeology. Leake's *Topography of Athens* closely followed Pausanias's second-century CE 'tour guide' to Greece. Herodotus and Homer gave Charles Fellows his framework for understanding ancient Lycia; and he touted the "great value" of inscriptions he copied "as supplying a key to the hitherto unknown Lycian language" and illuminating "questions of remote history." Decipherment of hieroglyphs by Champollion and other philologists made possible Wilkinson's *Manners and Customs of the Ancient Egyptians* in particular and Egyptology in general. Robinson was not only trained as a biblical philologist; he also explicated the "historical topography" of the Holy Land by relying utterly on the Bible, other ancient written sources, and linguistic clues in modern Arabic place-names. Bible stories also sparked British interest in Babylon and Assyria, and Layard decorated the title page of his *Nineveh and Its Remains* (1849) with verses from Ezekiel.* The medieval texts churned out by the specialized printing clubs that so many BAA members patronized affected their thinking about medieval buildings. And while Charles Newton believed it ludicrous that "the classics should be taught & studied without the illustration of ancient art," he never dreamed that ancient art should be studied without the illustration of the classics.[61]

Study of material relics of all sorts of pasts—Greek, Roman, Egyptian, Mesopotamian, biblical, British and Irish—started in the half century before 1850 to break away from broader-gauged traditions of old-style antiquarians. But it had not yet become archaeology in the modern disciplinary sense: specialized, expert study of material stuff left behind by human beings. And, for now, it continued to receive much nourishment through the umbilical cord that connected it to philology.

PART III: HISTORY

Philology likewise fed the child that would mature, after many decades, into the modern discipline of history. In February 1776 history writing had taken a new direction. With publication of volume 1 of the *Decline and Fall of the Roman Empire*, Edward Gibbon became, as chapter 4 showed, the 'philosophic' historian who firmly set the paradigm of erecting historical narrative on historical philology. The fastidious antiquarian learning of the Academy of Inscriptions in Paris, hooted at by moderns like Voltaire, appealed to Gibbon, who actually read Mabillon and Montfaucon. The *Decline and Fall* counted as philosophic history insofar as it included the sequential narrative that the philosophic historians had honed, attentive to causation and crammed with implicit lessons for the present. But Gibbon based his narrative on control of pertinent sources—the kind of documentary evidence that philologists traditionally commanded—discussed in about eight thousand footnotes. No philologist himself, Gibbon made the achievements of philological erudition the substratum of historical narrative.[62]

This philological turning had, over the course of the nineteenth century, gradual but profound effects on writing history. For a philologist, old texts merited an inherited respect for their individual and collective integrity that they never enjoyed in the erratic, instrumental use of documents by a Voltaire. Gibbon arrayed his sources to support his broad narrative of the "triumph of barbarism and religion." But, like a philologist, he respected the integrity of texts underlying this narrative. He felt it necessary to take account of the range

---

* The verses, bland in themselves, come from an allegory that has a personified female Jerusalem playing the harlot with Assyrians and Babylonians. Layard, who had a cynical streak, probably knew exactly what he was doing.

of available sources, pay attention to conflicts among them, clarify ambiguities, dispel confusions: hence those thousands of footnotes. This union of history and philology gave birth to a belief that history becomes reliable—as distinct from merely entertaining—only when it rests on balanced research into
a comprehensive scope of sources. 'Sources' usually meant documents more or
less contemporary with the events described. (Ancient historians often had to
rely on echoes of earlier authors preserved in writings of later ones.) This new
conviction did not sweep through the English-speaking learned world like a
summer thunderstorm. During the first half of the nineteenth century,
document-based history struggled to vindicate its claim to hegemony amid
luxuriant varieties of inquiry and amusement that traditionally went under
the label of history.

Documents

On both sides of the Anglophone Atlantic, this new historical outlook fostered
institutions to furnish the documentary sources needed. In 1790–91 a group of
Bostonians organized the Massachusetts Historical Society with the aim of
"preservation of books, pamphlets, manuscripts, and records" in order to "rescue the true history of this country from the ravages of time and the effects of
ignorance and neglect." Tellingly, what these New Englanders first called an
Antiquarian Society quickly took the name of Historical Society. The Connecticut Historical Society followed in 1799, the New-York Historical Society
in 1804, and the American Antiquarian Society in 1812 "to assist the researches
of the future historians of our country" by collecting historical documents. By
1860 well over a hundred such organizations existed in the United States. Private citizens did not act alone. Between 1803 and 1807, senator William Plumer
of New Hampshire singlehandedly collected all congressional journals since
1774, together with four or five hundred volumes of related documents. In 1810
Congress authorized a fireproof structure to house such federal archives (although neglecting to provide bureaucrats to care for them until 1859). Starting
in the 1820s state governments designated agencies to preserve their records.
A few states even hired transcribers to copy material in European repositories
relevant to their colonial histories.[63]

The United Kingdom moved in the same preservationist direction, also by
fits and starts. From time to time since the seventeenth century, individual
scholars had printed collections of historical documents, including notable
efforts like the pre-1066 ecclesiastical records in Henry Spelman's *Concilia*
(1639). In 1800 the House of Commons named a committee "to inquire into
the State of the Public Records of this Kingdom." Their state turned out to be
crumbling, resulting in the creation of a Record Commission later that year to
carry out reforms advised by the committee. This Record Commission and its
successor survived until 1837. Several rat skeletons found amid the Exchequer
records, together with a long-dead cat suggest both problems faced by the

commissioners and one old solution. The two Record Commissions excelled at wasting money and losing records, but they did publish volume upon volume of sources for early English history. In 1838 Parliament established a permanent Public Record Office. In that same year, three members of the Society of Antiquaries founded the Camden Society in London to partly fill a gap left when the second Record Commission expired: to print historical manuscripts and reprint rare books of historical importance. The Camden Society turned out to be first of several such private organizations. The Record Commission had started a Monumenta Historica Britannica to print medieval records, in imitation of the Monumenta Germaniae Historica begun in 1826; but it fizzled after belated publication of a single massive volume in 1848. In 1857 the United Kingdom finally got its monumenta historica when the Rolls Series—officially the Chronicles and Memorials of Great Britain and Ireland during the Middle Ages—began under government auspices.[64]

Yet writers of what went under the name of history remained equivocal about such records. In the decades around 1800, Voltaire and Gibbon did not between them exhaust the varieties of historical practice. Authors could craft a self-consciously historical past in several genres—not to mention antiquarian collecting and the sketching of ruins. A novel could still be called 'history' without affectation. Walter Scott's historical novels formed many readers' view of the Middle Ages. Mason Weems composed a best-selling biography of George Washington with parts manufactured out of whole cloth. The erudite American clergyman Samuel Miller, writing around 1802, set next to histories like Robertson's and Gibbon's a made-up correspondence among an invented "set of [ancient] Greek gentlemen." Miller used as his general label for novels and romances "Fictitious History."[65]

Like Miller, everyone knew that fact differed from fiction; but history could be either. Readers saw the stark difference between Weems's fanciful account of Washington and Mercy Otis Warren's effort to portray his doings factually in her *History of the Rise, Progress and Termination of the American Revolution* (1805). But no one cried foul when Weems called his work a history. A cleft—not so yawning but pretty wide—also divided a history like Warren's from one like Thomas Carlyle's *French Revolution* (1834–37). Warren's *History* relied on her own experience rounded out by contemporary writings, self-consciously tried to stir the reader's imagination, and aimed, as Lester Cohen put it, "to form minds, fix principles, and cultivate virtue." Carlyle's *French Revolution* was meant as a revelatory work of art and picked up documentary detail here and there to get to its prophetic ends. Both books stood apart from a history like Gibbon's, grounded in mastery of sources. Warren claimed authority on the basis of personal knowledge, Carlyle on the basis of something like moral insight, Gibbon on the basis of comprehensive attention to the documentary record. This last type of history, ancestral to the later humanistic discipline of history, eventually pushed the kinds of history written by Warren and Carlyle—not to mention Weems—to the margin of academic history. Narratives grounded in extensive research in documentary sources, especially archival sources, became history in the disciplinary meaning of the word.[66]

But only in retrospect was the merger of philology and philosophic history to create modern historiography complete by the early 1800s. What counted as good historical research and writing took decades to work out. It is no accident that thinking about history became intense and innovative at the end of the eighteenth century and start of the nineteenth. The French Revolution and Napoleonic conquests then scrambled the European continent's past. Europe's oldest university shut its doors. Political and legal institutions stretching back to when the mind of man runneth not vanished overnight. The thousand-year-old Holy Roman Empire vaporized. No wonder people pondered the processes of historical change. In particular, these dramatic institutional metamorphoses focused eyes "on the growth of [a state's] form of government and constitution,—on everything which serves to throw light on the relation of the whole people to the life of the State," to quote a historian of the time. Talk of freeing serfs in Denmark and Prussia and of redistributing land in France probably got Niebuhr interested in early Rome, when seemingly similar issues rent Roman politics.[67]

Indeed, battles to define proper methods of history often raged on the terrain of ancient history. In the early nineteenth century, Greece and Rome governed schooling of elite boys and remained storehouses of political exempla for them when, grown up, they ran the show. As late as 1895 an English biographer could reproduce a long letter in Latin, confident that his upper-crust readers wanted no translation. A twenty-year-old American on the grand tour in 1816 wrote to his parents that opening "a Greek or Latin book" gave him "much the same sensation" as "look[ing] on the face of a dead friend, and the tears not infrequently steal into my eyes." When women aspired to a voice in public matters, they wore metaphorical stolae even if illiterate in classical languages. In 1846 the polymathic Southern author George Frederick Holmes could take as given that "Of all histories, that of Rome is unquestionably the most important."[68]

But Greeks mattered a lot, too; and Gibbon's history of Rome provoked two of ancient Greece: the Scot John Gillies's *History of Ancient Greece, its Colonies and Conquests* (1786), written to instill Whig principles, and the Englishman William Mitford's *History of Greece* (1784–1810), which drew Tory lessons from ancient Hellenes. Both Gillies and Mitford were revulsed by Athens and democracy; the idealization of Athens came later in the nineteenth century with the drift of contemporary politics toward democracy. No less a master than Arnaldo Momigliano identified Gillies and Mitford as the inventors of Greek history (neglecting, perhaps, earlier claimants to the title). As acolytes of erudition, both followed in Gibbon's train; both trudged far behind the high priest. But even Gibbon fell short of German expectations. German critics admired *Decline and Fall* as a literary masterpiece; but Ludwig Spittler, professor of history at Göttingen, lamented Gibbon's scholarship. Such judgments signified, because well into the nineteenth century ancient history set methodological standards for all history. As Niebuhr quipped, "All ancient history eventuates in Roman history, all modern history starts from it."[69]

Scholarly judgments like Spittler's lie at the heart of our inquiry.* It means nothing for present purposes that Gillies was a Whig, Mitford a Tory—nor that William Prescott was a Romantic historian of Spain, Henry Thomas Buckle a Positivist one of England. Nor is it of any moment (again, for present purposes) that most historians in this chapter focused on politics and law, neglecting social, cultural, and economic history. The topics that engage historians shift from generation to generation. What matters here is not what divided historians over the last couple of centuries but on what practices they came to agree. The question is how history eventually defined itself as a humanistic discipline in the English-speaking world: what basic canons of procedure made a work of history good or bad, acceptable or unacceptable, *as history*.

Disagreement on that topic, usually implicit, swirled in the decades after Gibbon published his final volume in 1788. The only consensus even among scholarly historians was that histories must *somehow* use sources coeval with the events. But how? For the Scottish historian and numismatist John Pinkerton, who knew Gibbon, "history is a science, and must, like other sciences, have rules peculiar to it: of which the most essential is, that, when conformable to ancient authorities, it is to be regarded as true; and, when not, as false." But Pinkerton's rules did not ask historians to probe the *accuracy* of what their ancient authorities said. Sharon Turner's pioneering *History of the Anglo-Saxons* (1799–1805) also approached documents uncritically. Henry Hallam's *View of the State of Europe during the Middle Ages* (1818) raised the bar for medieval political history, but Hallam sometimes fell back on secondary sources and believed the dating of original records of minor moment.[70]

John Lingard took vigorous issue with that sort of slackness. An ecumenically minded Catholic priest, Lingard had studied for a decade at the English College in Douai. There, in northern France, he encountered at least indirectly the powerful philological tradition associated with the Benedictine Maurists (most famously Mabillon and Montfaucon) and the Jesuit Bollandists, all expert in interrogating ancient manuscripts. Lingard not only came away convinced of the crucial importance of original sources, but he also understood better than any previous English-speaking historian how to put documents through a critical sieve. Gibbon judged reliability of sources by such common-sense tests as internal consistency or the author's reputation for honesty; he did not know to ask about the origin of the sources themselves or to triangulate among different documents to infer what might be accurate in each of them. In contrast, Lingard grasped the need to handle sources with the con-

---

* For this reason, Walter Scott gets ignored in these pages. His novels powerfully influenced history writing, but in style and subject matter rather than method.

structive hermeneutic suspicion cultivated by centuries of sophisticated philology. He appreciated, as no other English-speaking historian of his time fully
did, that *authenticity* did not equate to *credibility*. A sixteenth-century letter
might be genuine, but where did its author learn the facts retailed in it? Did he
or she have motive to mislead? Might the document be forged? Do date and
provenance match other evidence of the author's whereabouts? Do extant accounts of the same events jibe? Questions that skilled historians later routinely
asked about sources were imported from philology into English historical
practice by Lingard.[71]

He both anticipated later historical practices and echoed earlier models.
His first book, *The History and Antiquities of the Anglo-Saxon Church* (1806),
applied philological rigor to surviving evidences of early English Christianity.
He demolished the cherished Anglican fantasy that the Anglo-Saxon church
had kept Rome at arm's length. (Mere fact did not easily slay so handy a theory.) His most widely read work, *A History of England, from the First Invasion
by the Romans to the Revolution in 1688* (eight volumes, 1810–30), was the
most deeply researched and reliable general history of England yet composed.
Inevitably, as a hardworking pastor rather than leisured professor, Lingard relied heavily on the growing volume of primary sources available in print and
on a network of erudite correspondents who ferreted out manuscripts for
him. But he was also, as Peter Phillips pointed out,

> the first English historian to make serious use of rare printed material
> and manuscript sources in the Vatican and other Italian libraries, as well
> as French dispatches, and material from the state papers of Ferdinand
> and Isabella and Philip II of Spain preserved in an almost inaccessible
> state in the Spanish castle of Simancas.

As a result, Lingard wrote the most cosmopolitan history of England to date,
rich in European context. Still, in the French origin of his method, Lingard
echoed the same eighteenth-century antiquarian traditions that had influenced Gibbon—but did so just when scholarly rigor moved its main residence
across the Rhine.[72]

Most American historians in this period hovered somewhere between a
Lingard and a Carlyle. Recognizing documents as essential, they remained in
other ways closer to the philosophic history of Hume or Voltaire. William
Hickling Prescott wrote best-selling histories of early modern Spain and its
American conquests. But he regarded himself as a man of letters, not a scholar.
A rich Bostonian (and friend of George Ticknor, the historian of Spanish literature), Prescott amassed a huge collection of Spanish historical material, including numberless copies of original records. His biographer rightly calls him
a pioneer among American scholars in "multiarchival research" and "biobibli-
ographical essays." He scrupulously footnoted his sources. Given the paucity
of recent histories of his topics, Prescott had to draw much of his information
from old chronicles. But he did not build his narratives by painstaking analysis

of his source base. Rather, he seems to have put together a timeline of key events and then mined his trove of documents for dramatic details to rivet readers. He had, he admitted, "neither the knowledge or talent" to "make my history profound"; he aspired instead to "make it *entertaining*." "I must not be too fastidious," he warned himself early in his research, "nor too anxious to amass every authority that can bear upon the subject." A decade later, he had grown no more meticulous: "The Mexican Antiquities are an appalling subject. I shall step gingerly over them." At the same time, and in contrast to Carlyle, he took sources seriously and used them critically. (Carlyle sneered at a fellow historian of Cromwell "learned in parish-registers and genealogies," who did "much research of old leases, marriage-contracts, deeds of sale and suchlike.") Yet, methodologically, Prescott apprenticed himself to the Abbé Mably, an eighteenth-century philosophe who stressed drama in the writing of history, rather than to the more severe Germans, who accented erudition.[73]

Mably proved a great favorite of Prescott's generation of historians in the United States: they tended to care less about scholarship, more about rhetoric, than British counterparts. American reviewers swooned over George Bancroft's ten-volume *History of the United States* (1834–74); but a younger, stricter scholar wrote in 1858 that Bancroft "ought to be flayed alive" for omitting footnotes. Notes hardly mattered: Bancroft already had conclusions ready at hand before he did research. His scholarly slovenliness supplies particularly good evidence of American ambivalence about erudite history, because he knew firsthand the new standards of scholarly practice: he held a Göttingen doctorate and had translated his teacher Arnold Heeren's survey of ancient Greece. Prescott's and Bancroft's younger contemporaries John Lothrop Motley and Francis Parkman resembled Prescott more closely than Bancroft in their serious attitude toward documentation and their fidelity to original sources. But they, too, wrote as men of letters more than as men of learning.[74]

A transatlantic fracas in 1852 revealed the gap between British and American standards of documentary rigor. Between 1834 and 1837 Rev. Jared Sparks edited twelve volumes of George Washington's writings. Unwilling to let the Father of His Country utter bad English, Sparks cleaned up Washington's grammar, spelling, vulgarities. In the United States readers still expected this piety toward the great dead, and Sparks made no secret of it. In 1838 Harvard rewarded his labors by naming him its first professor of history (probably the first in North America). Fourteen years later an English historian, Viscount Mahon, writing about the American Revolution, laid into Sparks for corrupting the documentary foundation of history writing. A pamphlet war ensued. Americans leaped to Sparks's defense, outraged that anyone should accuse him of guile. After all, George Bancroft sewed together quotations from different sources to construct one seamless speech. It was how he portrayed 'authentically' what had really happened.[75]

The dispute was not trivial. For Prescott or Bancroft, documents served to enliven a narrative that, in essentials, preexisted research in original sources.

For Mahon, history *derived from* interpretation of documents, construed in political, economic, or cultural context as philologists had long done. Tampering with primary sources poisoned the well from which (in Mahon's view) every truly scholarly historian drank. Yet it would be wrong to convict Sparks or Bancroft of dishonesty. They adhered to older canons of historical practice than those becoming standard among the learned in the United Kingdom. In this respect American historians reversed the behavior of American classicists. Leading American classicists emulated German models when Oxbridge classicists shunned them. Erudite British historians patterned themselves after learned Germans while most American historians still yearned to be eighteenth-century Frenchmen.*

Niebuhr's Example

Yet by 1830 or so, even a Mably manqué knew that Germans had forged a stricter historical erudition, reshaping it to fit norms of Altertumswissenschaft. Niebuhr became for educated Americans as well as Britons the model of hardcore historical scholarship—after Thirlwall and Hare translated him. (Several years later Leopold von Ranke won esteem as great in the English-speaking world. Unlike Niebuhr, Ranke fueled rather than ignited methodological change. So he gets neglected here.) Niebuhr had a fanciful theory that long-vanished folk ballads about early Rome echoed in later Roman historians; few learned British and American readers bought it. Rather they admired his hard-headed, meticulous deconstruction of the reliability of traditional sources for early Roman history, especially Livy.[76]

Contemporaries, like later observers, attributed Niebuhr's triumph to bringing philological method to bear on historical problems—and victory it was. Even before the Thirlwall-Hare translation, the *Edinburgh Review* placed his Roman history among the most remarkable books of the age. Although his corrosive skepticism rattled some conservative cages, Niebuhr massively influenced most major British historians writing after 1830. Thomas Arnold, famed headmaster of Rugby School, actually learned German in order to read Niebuhr—and (as he later told Julius Hare) "devour[ed] with the most intense admiration" *Römische Geschichte*. Once Thomas Macaulay could read it in English, he decided that Niebuhr's history "created an epoch in the history of European intelligence." George Grote, not a man worshipful by temperament, declared it "impossible" to utter Niebuhr's name "without veneration and gratitude." Even in Oxford, suspicious of most things German, Niebuhrean approaches to history carried prestige. Henry Liddell—of Liddell and Scott Greek dictionary fame but also author of a two-volume history of Rome—

---

* A notable exception to this generalization was the New Englander Richard Hildreth—not coincidentally a Utilitarian, like George Cornewall Lewis and other Germanophiles around University College London—whose *History of the United States of America* (1849–52) adhered to German standards. Note, however, its relatively late publication date.

wrote about "The Revolution of Niebuhr" with "reverence," recalling how Oxford students in the 1830s "applied his lamp to illuminate the pages of Livy."[77]

If American historians did not rush to copy Niebuhr, it was not for ignoring him. At least three American editions of the English version of *Römische Geschichte* appeared by 1860. His reputation preceded his translation: Prescott in 1825 mulled over writing the history of ancient Rome; but competing with "the great & learned Niebuhr" scared him off, and he opted for Spain. The *Princeton Review* averred in 1852 that modern historical scholarship "well nigh reached perfection in Niebuhr's History of Rome"—and in later eminent historians "animated by his example." In between Prescott and the *Princeton Review*, John Calhoun "greatly admired" Niebuhr; Edgar Allan Poe saw in him "a very powerful influence on the spirit of his age"; and in 1850 the author of a smarmy romance assumed her readers knew of him, much as later novelists tossed around the name Darwin. Magazines routinely called him "the great Niebuhr," "the illustrious Niebuhr." One suspects some name-dropping, but American readers did get a tolerable idea of Niebuhr's achievement. Writers explained to them how he applied to ancient history "the principles of philological criticism, which Wolf had pushed to their utmost in his Homeric studies"; how he collated ancient texts with each other; how he used "fragments of the older historians, preserved in the Scholia." American assessments of Niebuhr lacked clear understanding of the critical techniques for evaluating sources that he derived from philology—maybe because few Americans yet knew well the European tradition of classical and biblical philology. Still, when a writer admired "the boldness, tempered by consummate skill and steadiness of hand, with which he [Niebuhr] deals with his vague and fragmentary materials," a reader grasped loosely what this meant. A reflective reader might have gone on to wonder why her own country's historians rarely pursued "the true method of historical inquiry" created by the "learning, the sagacity, and the critical acumen of Niebuhr."[78]

British historians more often did pursue. Niebuhr's most literal follower was Thomas Arnold. He even used the Hare-Thirlwall version as a textbook at Rugby School, probably flummoxing the boys. Arnold knew that Niebuhr was not reader-friendly. English-speaking admirers on both shores of the Atlantic called his prose arid, his organization dismaying. Arnold tried in his own *History of Rome* (1838–43) to adapt for a larger readership the "thoughts and notions which I have learnt from him." Deliberately unoriginal, Arnold's work did not wear well. But it mattered in its day for making Niebuhrean history accessible to many readers scared to plumb the depths of Niebuhr's own book.[79]

Greek History in England

Niebuhr's translator Connop Thirlwall fashioned a more impressive work of ancient history than Arnold's rehash. For rashly proposing that Cambridge award degrees to non-Anglican Protestants, Thirlwall got fired from Trinity. From 1835 to 1840 he labored in a rural Yorkshire parish. In these unpromising circumstances he showed astonishing powers of scholarly concentration. Spending up to sixteen hours a day in his study, he mastered the many recent German studies of discrete aspects of Greek history: everything from Karl Otfried Müller on early mythology to Johann Gustav Droysen on Alexander the Great. Steeped in Altertumswissenschaft and ancient sources, Thirlwall wrote an eight-volume history of Greece (1835–44) along Niebuhrean lines. Not merely the most solid history of Greece in English, it was the first truly erudite general history in any tongue. In 1852 the first two volumes were translated for French schools. Even before Thirlwall finished, his friend Leonhard Schmitz began a German version, for German philologists without good English. Thirlwall must have savored the irony.[80]

He learned of a deeper irony belatedly: his onetime schoolmate at Charterhouse, George Grote, was preparing his own history of Greece. Pulled out of school early by his father, Grote went directly into the family bank in Threadneedle Street. Exile from education did not quell a scholarly bent, and young George devoted free hours to classical and other studies. A Lutheran minister taught him German. He began to write a little, not yet for publication. In 1819 he met James Mill and Mill's master, Jeremy Bentham. Soon Grote converted to Bentham's reformist utilitarianism, and Bentham's circle completed his truncated education. He married; rather than cut back on reading, he woke up earlier. In 1822 Grote decided to write a history of ancient Greece. No one now knows why, though the subject had long attracted him. Writing took many years, interrupted by banking and politics. (Grote sat in Parliament from 1832 to 1841.) In 1843, empowered by a fat legacy, he retired from banking to devote full time to erudition. The first two volumes of his *History of Greece, from the Earliest Period to the Close of the Generation Contemporary with Alexander the Great* came out in 1846, two years after Thirlwall finished his. Grote's twelfth, final volume appeared a decade later.[81]

To understand Grote's *History*, the reader needs to distinguish two different influences on his writing. In one respect, his most powerful model seems to have been James Mill's Benthamite *History of British India* (1817–18). From this venomously anti-Indian work, Grote learned (somehow) to respect evidence deeply and (less surprisingly) to judge the people he wrote about. His *History of Greece* did not hesitate to adjudicate, its chief target being William Mitford's antidemocratic *History of Greece*. Democracy was Grote's hero, rationality his religion. His Benthamite liberalism guided the history: "an awkward measuring-stick," as Wilamowitz commented, "and foreign to the Greeks themselves, but still a standard." In fact, Grote's Athens strikingly resembles his own Britain, with reformers pitted against conservatives and Pericles as prime minister. This present-minded political agenda distinguishes Grote's history from Thirlwall's equally scholarly, better-written, but drabber work.[82]

Yet, like Thirlwall, Grote admired Niebuhr's methods and knew the German historians of Greece. In this respect he stands in Niebuhr's tradition, not James Mill's. Mill approached India's history equipped with strong prejudices against its inhabitants, a clear idea of the judgments he would preach, and absolute ignorance of Indian languages. George Grote shared only Mill's Benthamite axioms, not his scholarly ones. Indeed, in treating early Greek history, Grote out-Niebuhred Niebuhr in source criticism. A survey of ancient and modern literature convinced Grote that extant sources permitted no real historical knowledge before the first Olympiad (ca. 776 BCE). (This judgment was reasonable in Grote's day, before archaeology supplied evidence for earlier times.) So Grote divided his history, in effect, into a prehistoric account of legend and myth and a much longer, chronological history of real events. His linguistic sensitivity matched any German's, even K. O. Müller's. In *Die Dorier*, Müller described a 732 Olympic winner, Oxythemis "Κορωναῖος," as from Koroneia in Boeotia. (Κορωναῖος—Koronaios—is a geographic epithet.) Grote showed (using Boeckh's massive assemblage of Greek inscriptions) that Κορωναῖος was the adjective for Korone on the Messenian gulf, not for Boeotian Koroneia (which was Κορωνεύς or Koroneus)—and he then articulated the principle "that a town ending in–η [e] or–αι [ai] following a consonant had its ethnical derivative in–αιος [aios]," whereas one ending in–εια [eia] had its in–ευς [eus]. In Grote's *History* fastidious philology ultimately served his grand philosophic narrative, and these politics put him at odds with Niebuhr and most of Niebuhr's English disciples. But writers who politically might stalk each other with daggers drawn could agree on how history worked as scholarship.[83]

History in English around 1850

Because Grote and Niebuhr's model of how to write history soon became simply 'history' in the scholarly sense, it has no specific label. One could call it 'Niebuhrean,' but the word does scant justice to the range of philologically informed history writing. Ancient history was far from the only site where historical narrative melded with a philologist's scrupulous source criticism. Nor did only Niebuhr exemplify the new gospel, as the independent case of Lingard shows. Better than 'Niebuhrean history' is 'philologic history'—in distinction from the Enlightenment-style philosophic history being gradually discredited.

Some British historians of the first half of the nineteenth century—James Mill reviled by posterity, Thomas Carlyle celebrated by the same fallible tribunal—still wrote history with a philosophe's insouciance about where evidence led. So did an American like Bancroft. Carlyle, biographer of Oliver Cromwell, privately regarded each newly discovered Cromwell letter, swaddled in scholarly commentary, as "an ancient rusty nail embedded in half a ton of dust"—

interesting only to "the owls." At least in the United Kingdom, Carlyle and his ilk looked increasingly old-fashioned.[84]

By midcentury most erudite writers accepted philologic history as the only reliable type. Niebuhr himself became its victim in George Cornewall Lewis's *Inquiry into the Credibility of the Early Roman History* (1855). Lewis applied to Roman origins a skepticism as austere as his friend Grote's. Lewis rounded on Niebuhr's ballad theory: no poetic meter echoed in Livy's prosaic prose (a fair point). After a thousand learned pages, Lewis decided that Roman history before 280 BCE lay beyond recovery. (In 280 Pyrrhus of Epirus invaded Italy; reliable accounts of his campaign survive, along with the phrase *Pyrrhic victory*.) Historians should stick to the period after 280, when the "great outlines" become as clear as in modern history. Only "an occult faculty of historical divination" allowed Niebuhr to reconstruct Rome's earlier history, and Lewis did not believe in oracles. (He did not foresee that numismatics, epigraphy, and archaeology could supplement divination.) John Mitchell Kemble, in his groundbreaking *The Saxons in England* (1849), applied a scrutiny learned from German philologists to the earliest records of English history. (He owed debts to Jacob Grimm as well as Niebuhr.) Kemble's two volumes even mimicked the clumsy form of Niebuhr's history: individual dissertations treated, in no discernable order, various knotty problems in Anglo-Saxon history, such as serfs' lives and the duties of an official called *geréfa* or *geróefa*. Clumsiness never became a British ideal, but philological rigor did. Grote's *History of Greece*, however controversial its politics, displayed the new norm for how an up-to-date British *scholar* wrote history.[85]

This union of philosophic history and philological antiquarianism, developing from Gibbon to Lingard to Grote, created 'history' pretty much as conceived today. Even in America, the *Princeton Review* in 1852 distinguished "the poetical-historical narrative" early in a people's existence (citing Herodotus and Froissart) from "the historical-philosophical disquisition—the nearest approaches to which among the ancients, we find in Thucydides and Tacitus; and which among the moderns has well nigh reached perfection in Niebuhr's History of Rome."[86] History of this 'perfected' sort was distinctive. It issued from an erudite *community*. Even a popular synthesizer drew ultimately on the research of scholars; these scholars themselves depended on work by other scholars. Philologic history, like the older philosophic history, studied not only change over time but also its causes. But now the historian learned about such changes (and inferred their causes) as philologists did—by consulting documents or quasi-documents (inscriptions, pictures, maps) from the period under study. Yet, unlike the antiquarian, the historian did not focus on documents themselves, as artifacts, but used them to tell a story structured by change over time. Philological skills (diplomatics, paleography, emendation) became only 'ancillary sciences' of philologic history. The historian might devote himself to solving a particular problem (say, how fourteenth-century East Anglian farmers rotated crops) without regard to change over time or to storytelling. But all historical research in the end *contributed* to a chronological narrative of historical development—never fully settled—available to all historians.

Gibbon would have recognized this description of 'history,' just as do most academic historians in the English-speaking world today. Where philologic history left Thomas Carlyle, James Mill, William Prescott, Walter Scott, Mercy Warren, and their many readers is another question. Only after 1850 would a new humanistic 'discipline' fully emerge, limited to philologic history. Academic historians then would seek, with no little success, to impose their self-conception on the whole genre of history, once far more capacious.

In 1850 the meaning of 'history' remained in flux, as did 'archaeology' and studies of classical texts. The new practices emerging from philology and its allied studies mostly developed, for now, outside of universities—as was true of linguistics and literary research as well. That would change, in several decades to come. Within universities, history, classics, and so forth would become 'disciplines'—transforming the landscape of humanistic erudition.

8

"Grammatical and Exegetical Tact"

Biblical Philology and Its Others, 1800–1860

Biblical philology in the English-speaking world began to change during the first half of the nineteenth century. Understandings of the Bible affected, and were affected by, theological developments. But in this chapter the spotlight falls only on the erudite philology of Bible study, insofar as one can untangle philology and theology. In 1800, biblical scholarship (or 'criticism,' the old synonym for philology derived from 'criticus') partook fully in the holistic world of textual philology. It shared ideas and personnel especially with the other great study of ancient Mediterranean texts, Greek and Roman philology. By 1860, biblical philology was evolving into a distinct field whose practitioners spoke mostly to each other. And because students of the Bible more often worked under direct ecclesiastical control, flouting received beliefs carried risk. Heretics no longer feared fire, but they were fired. The place of biblical scholarship within the structure of knowledge shifted.

So did its axioms. In 1800, English-speaking Christian biblical critics almost all considered the Bible a unitary source of timeless truth: a single, inspired "Sacred Volume" unique among ancient texts.[1] Philologists sought only to correct cautiously textual errors that had crept in over centuries of transcription and translation: the kind of emendation undertaken by John Mill a hundred years earlier. By 1860 some Anglophone philologists had come to regard the Bible as a miscellany of ancient texts. The critic could grasp the character and meanings of each book, they thought, only in light of its own peculiar history.

As a result, study of the Bible became more explicitly historical, and comparisons with other ancient texts came to seem more apt. This last impulse would in the long run encourage a new, philologically grounded, historically oriented discipline often called comparative religion.

German Innovation

The unitary Bible's woes began in German-speaking Europe. As already seen, *Altertumswissenschaft* developed in interaction with biblical philology: Eichhorn applied to the Bible Heyne's ideas about myth; Wolf used on Homer Eichhorn's methods of reconstructing the biblical text. Like the pioneers of Altertumswissenschaft, Semler, Michaelis, and Eichhorn strove to explain the Old Testament by assembling information on the ancient Hebrews and their neighbors and then using this historical context to illumine the biblical text. And, also like Altertumswissenschaft, this new biblical philology began to conceive ancient peoples as thinking in very different ways than modern scholars trying to understand them. The characters who filled the pages of the Bible, especially the Old Testament, saw their world through the mythological lens of an extinct 'oriental' mind. They seemed as far removed from present mentalities as Homer's heroes chatting with Athena and Hera.

Eichhorn had coined the term *höhere Kritik*—higher criticism—to name this attempt to understand the Bible's authorship, literary forms, and meanings in light of deep history. He thus distinguished higher criticism from the less ambitious 'lower criticism' that tried simply to get the words of the text right using such tools as grammatical analysis. (The border was blurred. By examining vocabulary and style alone, Wilhelm Gesenius showed in 1815 that Chronicles was composed comparatively late and that Deuteronomy had a different author than the rest of the Pentateuch.[2]) Following Astruc, Eichhorn went so far as to disassemble books of the Old Testament and to hypothesize earlier, multiple sources from which ancient editors stitched them together. Moses became not so much author of the Pentateuch as compiler. Eichhorn interpreted some biblical stories as mythical in character and believed all to be refracted through their authors' primitive, 'oriental' cast of mind. But none of these eighteenth-century philologists questioned the basic historical accuracy of the Bible narrative. Like earlier readers, they assumed the Old Testament to relate the history of ancient Hebrews pretty much as events had unfolded: the doings of Abraham and Isaac, Moses and Joshua, David and Solomon really happened. A philologist might need to decipher the mythology encoding this history; but the facts were there, much as the *Iliad* draped with gods and goddesses a real Trojan War.

Wilhelm de Wette attacked this assumption and put the Old Testament narrative itself in question. In his *Beiträge zur Einleitung in das Alte Testament* (*Contributions to the Introduction to the Old Testament*, 1807), De Wette denied that the apparently historical books of the Old Testament told of real events. Far from a historical Moses having put together the Pentateuch, Moses himself may have been mythical. But De Wette understood myth differently than did Eichhorn. For the younger philologist, myth was, to quote Tal Howard, "simply a spontaneous religious and poetic expression whose relation to possible historical events was not only elusive but, more important, irrelevant to the religious content of the Old Testament." Composed hundreds of years after the 'events' it described, the Pentateuch was a work of poetic imagination, an Israelite national epic. Its author or editor never intended to relate historical facts. Together with the 'later' historical books, it served to validate the religious orthodoxy of the monarchical period by reading this orthodoxy back into an immemorial time of origins. In the background of this demotion of the Hebrew scriptures lurked the anti-Semitism that infected many German scholars, most virulently Michaelis. From a more strictly philological point of view, De Wette suddenly flipped the Bible from a source of historical truth into a text itself a product of history. Its truth claims themselves required historical assessment.[3]

Historical criticism of the Bible had set its modern compass, though its course ran neither straight nor smooth. De Wette made little immediate impress on contemporary scholarship, and his ideas had foes as well as followers among German biblical philologists. German universities housed plenty of traditional biblical scholars suspicious of historical criticism.[4]

But challenges to the historical truth of the Bible had come to stay. Soon enough, at the University of Tübingen, Ferdinand Christian Baur analyzed the New Testament in terms parallel to De Wette's dissection of the Old Testament. Far from reporting straightforwardly the life and teachings of Jesus, the authors of the Gospels and Epistles composed them as weapons in struggles among Jesus's early followers to define his legacy. These scriptures resembled wartime propaganda more than factual narrative. De Wette had suggested that "the mythic principle" could apply to New Testament as well as Old. Baur's student David Friedrich Strauss took the hint. In the two volumes of *Das Leben Jesu, kritisch bearbeitet* (*The Life of Jesus, Critically Examined*, 1835–36), Strauss pronounced the Gospel stories of Jesus a mythic expression of early Christian faith. Any historic realities lying behind the narratives were lost in the mists of time. Anyone could have forecast the ensuing storm. Baur repudiated his student. But even fairly moderate German scholars now placed themselves outside Bible stories looking in, trying to discern what each book meant in historical context.[5]

British and American Reactions

Shocks radiating out from the German epicenter of innovation reached Anglophone biblical philologists erratically. As with Altertumswissenschaft, language gave one reason for delay. Relatively few Britons or Americans could read German in De Wette's day, even fewer fluently. As to German biblical criticism, Unitarians dabbled in it from the 1790s on, and it deeply influenced Coleridge. But all four of the leading American biblical philologists between 1800 and 1860—Moses Stuart of Andover Seminary; Andrews Norton of Harvard Divinity School; Charles Hodge of Princeton Theological Seminary; and Edward Robinson of Andover and later Union Theological Seminary—learned to read German only *after* appointment to teaching positions in biblical studies.[6]

Linguistic isolation gradually faded. As early as 1819 Norton, having just acquired German, declared knowledge of it essential for scholarship. This recognition put him ahead of the learning curve for Anglophone biblical critics. But ability to read German spread in philological circles in the 1830s and 1840s. By 1850 or so, on both sides of the Atlantic, serious English-speaking philologists recognized German as a necessity, in Sanskrit or Greek studies as well as biblical ones. Still, the initial linguistic barrier slowed the reception of German biblical philology.[7]

American biblical philologists suffered also—like American classicists—from a dearth of scholarly infrastructure. As Moses Stuart quipped in 1838, "We have so few men who can afford to bury themselves for a long time in the closets of libraries, and so few libraries that have closets well stocked with books."[8]

A deeper reason why German biblical scholarship made few quick converts lay precisely in its innovativeness. Anglophone Protestants clustered nearer the conservative end of the Protestant theological-critical spectrum. If they feared truly pagan Greeks, still more they wanted their Bible as sanctified by the ages. Even midcentury theological liberals like F. D. Maurice and Thomas Arnold believed the Old Testament to provide a basically accurate history of ancient Israel. In the 1830s Andrews Norton rejected as spurious the first two chapters of Matthew's Gospel. This conclusion would have fazed no German philologist, but it sent reeling Norton's fellow Unitarians, America's most avant-garde denomination intellectually. De Wette shocked; Strauss could hardly be imagined. When in 1825 Connop Thirlwall translated Friedrich Schleiermacher's study of Luke, an appalled *British Critic* undertook the inescapable "task of demolition"; the reviewer presumed his readers unfamiliar with Schleiermacher's writings but "terrified by the name." John Conybeare used his 1824 Bampton Lectures at Oxford to denounce German divinity. "The candour and earnestness displayed by the author," Connop Thirlwall dryly observed, "increase our regret that his studies had not led him to feel the necessity of acquiring the German language." In Oxford, he sighed, mere "knowledge of German" seemed to bring a cleric under "suspicion of heterodoxy." Arthur Stanley said of the decades before midcentury that "the panic of Germany amounted almost to monomania in many excellent persons." Thirlwall himself, more than fifteen years after the flap over Schleiermacher, accused English theological magazines of still deliberately leaving readers "in the dark as to everything that is said and done in German theology," to safeguard their tender faith. And shouldn't they have? Charles Hodge in 1822 pronounced it "unquestionably a fact" that much German scholarship wallowed in "false doctrines, and the most irreverent treatment of the Sacred Scriptures."[9]

But Hodge recognized Germans, equally without question, as the nation "most distinguished for its progress in Biblical Literature." Quite a few German critics—"of as great erudition as any others"—offered no offense to Hodge's conservative version of Christian belief. As to the many "offensive" ones, well, the pious philologist needed "to separate the poison from the food." As soon as feasible after joining the Princeton Theological Seminary faculty in 1822, Hodge sailed to Germany to study. As he arrived in Halle in 1827, a slightly younger Oxford contemporary, Edward Pusey, was wrapping up his own German education in Bonn. (Pusey assured his friend John Henry Newman that he "would introduce no German theology" into his Oriel College teaching.) Moses Stuart never got closer to Germany than Boston harbor, but he early saw German biblical criticism as essential. Whatever their reservations, many American and British biblical scholars had begun to see the need to absorb German innovations—if only to learn technical skills needed to defend orthodoxy from some of their German teachers.[10]

For the next half century, Anglophone attitudes toward German biblical criticism careened between admiration and alarm. As a rule, the most competent British and American scholars devoured German philological expertise but choked on any serious revision of inherited biblical orthodoxy. In Eichhorn's terms, they loved German textual ('lower') criticism and loathed higher criticism. Pusey had a better informed, more nuanced opinion of German philology than most English contemporaries. Even he condemned Michaelis's fairly moderate writings as stuffed with "perverted applications of mere civil, often of modern, principles, unfounded theories and low views." In 1826, after briefly lauding the "critical and philological knowledge" of the eminent Hebraist Wilhelm Gesenius, Moses Stuart launched into twenty pages decrying the man's denial that Moses wrote the Pentateuch.[11]

Stuart's pupil Edward Robinson radiated the sort of German attainments that Anglophone biblical critics welcomed. Robinson appeared in the last chapter as founder of biblical archaeology, but he also made a large mark on biblical philology in America and Britain. None other than Gesenius shaped his studies in Germany in the 1820s, and Gesenius's grammatical interests 'took' in his student. While still in Halle, Robinson began translating Philipp Buttmann's Greek grammar—a version long used in American colleges. Immediately on his return home, Stuart enlisted him as editor of a new journal, the *Biblical Repository*. In it Robinson not only published American scholarship but also provided a conduit for German erudition. Robinson's own articles sidestepped theology, devoting themselves to 'objective' philological issues. He believed the orthodox teachings of his Congregationalist church, but he never felt the alarm at German philology so common in it—probably because Robinson, like his teacher Stuart, understood true philology as grammatical and verbal in nature. In 1836 Robinson published a translation and revision of Gesenius's Hebrew dictionary. Edition after revised edition, this book supplied a standard foundation for Hebrew studies in the English-speaking world—and in its latest, much altered reincarnation (Brown-Driver-Briggs) still does today. In that same remarkable year Robinson published a New Testament Greek lexicon of his own devising, likewise in common use for decades. These works, other reference manuals he prepared in the 1830s, and the *Repository* laid a solid basis for biblical learning in the United States. Robinson imported the meat of his erudition from Germany but left higher criticism on the farther shores of the Atlantic.[12]

A partial English parallel to Robinson was Rev. Henry Alford. Unlike Robinson, Alford began as, and largely remained, a miscellaneous man of letters. He published poetry, lectured at Cambridge on Christian evidences, edited John Donne, translated the *Odyssey*. But for twenty years from 1841 his obsession became editing the Greek New Testament. Having studied at Trinity College Cambridge in the heyday of Hare and Thirlwall, Alford appreciated German philology. (Niebuhr he called "one of the greatest men in this ignorant and obstinate world.") He started from the readings of Philipp Buttmann and Karl Lachmann. But he moved on to recent collations of the oldest manuscripts themselves—the Codex Alexandrinus in the British Museum, the newly recovered portion of the Codex Sinaiticus, the newly available Codex Vaticanus. In 1847 he took three months off to travel to Bonn to improve his German. By the time his fourth and final volume appeared in 1861, he had given English-speaking scholars a rich new resource: the Greek text surrounded by marginal notes illustrating idioms and constructions, ballasted with English footnotes on exegesis and philology. Alford's edition for the first time fully integrated modern German textual philology into English-language biblical erudition. Yet he retained the typical Anglo-Saxon suspicion of German rationalism and drew his philological lines carefully. His biographer noted the "strictly critical character" of Alford's scholarship. "Abbreviations, punctuations, elisions of orthography, systematic ellipses, the merest turns of the pen in this or that manuscript" got his careful attention. Higher criticism got the cold shoulder.[13]

HISTORY CREEPS IN

Despite a grudging, defensive reception, the "perverted" methods of higher criticism oozed into the United Kingdom and United States. Churchly fingers in the dike kept seepage sluggish for a long while. Consider the Scot Alexander Geddes, who abetted Germans and suffered for it. Geddes was a traditionally broad-gauged philologist who translated Horace and published on Scottish-language poetry. He was also a Catholic priest. In 1800 he trained his philological spotlight on the Bible. Stimulated by Lowth, Kennicott, and German scholars, Geddes tried, like Eichhorn, to distinguish mythical from historical elements in the Old Testament. The creation narrative in Genesis he took to be "a most beautiful *mythos*, or philosophical fiction, contrived with great wisdom, dressed up in the garb of real history, adapted, as I have said, to the shallow intellects of a rude[,] barbarous nation." Geddes declared the location of the Garden of Eden "a question of no importance" despite all the ink Michaelis had spilled over it. Every nation has a myth of a golden age, he thought, and Eden represented the golden age "of Hebrew mythology." Whoever composed this mythology, it was not Moses; for Geddes denied that Moses wrote the Pentateuch. Geddes had not absorbed as fully as Eichhorn the notion that modes of thought in an ancient culture might differ radically from modern ways of thinking. The ancient Hebrews had "shallow intellects," not a mythologizing mind. And, like a rationalistic deist, Geddes treated biblical miracles as actual events for which some natural explanation existed rather than as a way of understanding the world characteristic of ancient Hebrew culture. Bad enough. His bishop forbade Geddes to exercise his priestly office and, on his demise in 1802, refused a funeral Mass. The Catholic hierarchy condemned his translation of the Bible. But Geddes knew German scholarship, and German scholars knew his.[14]

Such intercourse became rarer during the wars of the French Revolution and Napoleon near the end of Geddes's life; but a Cambridge man, Herbert Marsh, lived in Germany off and on from 1786 through the 1790s and met German scholars. Growing interested in biblical studies, he decided to translate Eichhorn's *Einleitung in das alte Testament*. A friend warned him that Cambridge University Press deemed Eichhorn too hot to handle. Marsh instead translated (1793–1801) Michaelis's less radical introduction to the New Testament. By treading more carefully than Geddes, Marsh ended as an Anglican bishop. He defended Mosaic authorship of the Pentateuch and the historical reliability of the Gospels. But his Cambridge lectures as professor of divinity made explicit his admiration for Eichhorn, and some of the new German critical ideas slipped through fine cracks in his orthodoxy. The notes he added to his translation of Michaelis brought English readers up to date on German criticism. His own *Dissertation on the Origin and Composition of the Three First Canonical Gospels* (1801) amplified Eichhorn's idea of a common, lost source for the synoptic Gospels. Conservatives muttered of heresy. The American Unitarian Joseph Buckminster—who helped to persuade Harvard in 1808 to reprint Johann Jakob Griesbach's edition of the New Testament—sent students to study with Marsh.[15]

The pattern exemplified by Geddes and Marsh persisted in Britain and America through most of the century. Speak too brashly about scripture and get slapped down. Tiptoe around traditional pieties and get a hearing for innovative biblical philology, even if a skeptical one.

Institutional context mattered. Within the Roman Catholic hierarchical system, Geddes's bishop could punish his heterodoxy directly. Marsh sheltered under the University of Cambridge, where the Church of England's jurisdiction was indirect and mediated. Anglican bishops did sometimes try to root out advanced ideas about the Bible. One of Marsh's successors as bishop of Llandaff, Alfred Ollivant, in 1857 officially warned his diocesan clergy to steer clear of German criticism. The rare radical forays into biblical study in this period were made by individuals who had lost ties to any church: Marian Evans's translation of Strauss's *Leben Jesu* (1846);* Francis Newman's *History of the Hebrew Monarchy from the Administration of Samuel to the Babylonish Captivity* (1847); Theodore Parker's 1843 'translation'—expansion, interpretation, simplification—of De Wette's introduction to the Old Testament. Scholars in institutions under direct church control could suffer real harm. In England this primarily meant colleges run by Protestants outside the Anglican establishment. In 1857 the distinguished philologist Samuel Davidson lost his job at Lancashire College for publishing German-influenced commentary on the Old Testament (by German standards conservative). He did not help his cause by keeping a collection of German portraits at home, including Schleiermacher's.[16]

The churches kept watch over biblical philology most routinely in the United States. A movement began early in the century to segregate ministerial training within special-purpose seminaries or university-based divinity schools. Beginning with the founding of Andover Seminary (1808), Princeton Theological Seminary (1812), and Harvard Divinity School (ca. 1816), such ecclesial confines housed a growing proportion of American biblical philologists. In fact, the first four important American biblical scholars—Stuart, Robinson, Hodge, Norton—taught at these first three theological schools, under more or less direct Congregationalist, Presbyterian, and Unitarian control, respectively. Episcopalians and Baptists were not far behind. By the 1830s, when New School Presbyterians pulled apart from the more conservative Old School faction, their leaders in 1836 almost instinctively set up Union Theological Seminary in New York City—where Robinson moved—to compete with the Old-School-dominated Princeton Seminary. This church-oriented system long helped to ensure cautious approaches to the Bible in the United States. No major blowup over higher criticism roiled an American seminary until 1879. In that year, Crawford Howell Toy resigned from Southern Baptist Theological Seminary because of heterodox views of the Old Testament. Certainly no American *inside* a seminary believed Germany "the only land where theology was ... studied as a science, and developed with scientific freedom"—as the lonely radical Theodore Parker did. Parker's version of De Wette fell predictably flat. "It has never," he wrote thirteen years after its publication, "had a friendly word said for it in any American journal"—never even "received any reasonable notice."[17]

A side effect of seminaries was very slowly to isolate biblical philology within institutions devoted to training clergy. Biblical scholarship thus drifted faster and farther from other areas of philology in the United States than in the United Kingdom. This segregation not only hastened the development of biblical criticism into a distinct 'discipline.' It also meant that innovations in

---

* Marian Evans is better known by her later pen name George Eliot.

biblical philology less often influenced secular scholarship, and vice versa. The first generation of American academic biblical critics indulged wide-ranging intellectual interests. Even Moses Stuart, most biblically focused among them, published occasionally on affairs of state; Andrews Norton and Charles Hodge roamed all over the intellectual map. Lines remained porous for a while. Well after 1850, the Yale classicist James Hadley served on the American Committee for the Revision of the English Bible; he also presided over the American Oriental Society, which prior to 1880 included biblical scholars.[18] But such connections grew fewer in the second half of the century, especially in its closing two decades, as the professional seminary ambience began to constrain biblical philologists' sense of intellectual identity.

All the while, a historical approach to the Bible seeped drop by drop from Germany into the English-speaking world. In 1829, to place "within the reach of students some treatises, which are not now readily accessible," a few New York City clergymen published an anthology including long, translated excerpts from Gesenius, Michaelis, and Eichhorn—bowdlerized to omit or correct "inadequate views of revelation." In introducing his 1825 translation of Schleiermacher, Connop Thirlwall surveyed the course of German biblical philology in the quarter century since Marsh had summed it up in the notes to his translation of Michaelis. Hugh James Rose used his own knowledge of German to launch a diatribe against German theology and philology in 1825. Most of their practitioners, he warned, had abandoned "the old and sound grammatical interpretation" of scripture for "false and misapplied philology." In course of condemnation Rose let slip much specific learned wickedness. The English could learn of German historical philology from its enemies as well as its friends.[19]

Charles Hodge and Moses Stuart fed Americans such information. In 1825 Hodge started the *Biblical Repertory and Princeton Review*; about the same time Stuart unloosed a decades-long flow of articles on biblical subjects. Both men respected technical German philology; both detested higher criticism's questioning of the Bible's integrity and authorship. Stuart early found his critical epitome in J. A. Ernesti's 'lower critical' *Institutio interpretis Novi Testamenti* (1761), "among the *first* respectable efforts to reduce the principles of interpretation to a science." Ernesti summed up for biblical scholars long-set practices of classical philologists. Stuart abridged, translated, and rearranged the book for American students as *Elements of Interpretation* (1814). For Stuart, manuscript variations did not endanger the Bible's unchanging truth, independent of historical context. But *language* did change; and Stuart gave careful attention, closely informed by German philology, to understanding the words of a text in historical context when commenting. Sometimes grammatical interpretation—"the *usus loquendi* [current usage in speaking] and context"—sufficed. Sometimes "the meaning of words, phrases, and sentences" needed to be "illustrated and confirmed by historical arguments." Stuart went so far as to accept Eichhorn's higher critical theory that Moses used two dis-

tinct sources in compiling Genesis. Hodge was less historical. He did not ignore philology, but Reformed theology determined how he read the essentially timeless words of the Bible. Still, articles issuing under Hodge's editorship
and from Stuart's pen told American readers of major results of German historical criticism. Americans illiterate in German had to wait to read Strauss's
Leben Jesu until Evans translated it in 1846. But they read *about* it in Hodge's
review within two years of German publication. True, Hodge spent more
words on Strauss's conservative opponents than on Strauss; but "that Strauss
denies the *historical* truth of the gospel altogether, and explains it as a mere
philosophical or religious *mythus*" makes the main idea clear.[20]

Very few Anglophone biblical philologists—Stuart among them—appear
to have consulted Jewish colleagues, a change from earlier centuries. (Collaboration behind the scenes is hard to determine.) Reasons besides Christian
coldness help to explain lack of contact. In America before the Civil War the
Jewish population was relatively tiny, the learned Jewish population absolutely
tiny. The United Kingdom had more Jews, but few pursued biblical philology
in this period. Those who did shied away from topics favored by Christian
philologists, such as biblical history. The most visible achievement of Jewish
biblical learning anywhere in the English-speaking world was the American
Isaac Leeser's English translation of the Hebrew Bible—gently derided by a
modern Jewish biblical scholar as a "Judaized King James." (Leeser preceded it
with an 1848 Masoretic Hebrew version that he published with an Episcopalian minister, Joseph Jacquett.) Completed in 1853—and admired by Charles
Hodge—the Leeser translation remained in wide use until replaced by a better
one in 1917. Yet to call Leeser a 'biblical philologist' by nineteenth-century
standards is a stretch. He was a general-purpose publicist of all things Jewish,
who borrowed his solid Hebrew scholarship from Europe.[21]

Isaac Nordheimer was the rare Jewish biblical philologist in academe. Born
in Bavaria, he got an excellent Talmudic education and then a Munich PhD in
philology, focused on Semitic languages. He migrated to the United States in
1835, barely twenty-six years old. For a Jew, absent Jewish institutions of higher
learning, a formal position like Stuart's teaching the Bible lay beyond imagining. Nordheimer taught Hebrew and other 'oriental' languages, first at the University of the City of New York from 1836, then at Union Theological Seminary
when it opened in 1838.* His great work was a highly regarded *Critical Grammar of the Hebrew Language* (1838), drawing on both his rabbinic learning and
his German philology. He also published, among other things, a few articles in
the *Biblical Repository*. These included an introduction to the book of Ecclesi-
astes and an exchange with Stuart over the interpretation of two passages in the
Hebrew Bible taken by Christians as messianic prophecies. Nordheimer would
doubtless have published much more had tuberculosis not killed him at thirty-
three—"snatched away in the commencement of what promised to be a distin-

---

* Union Theological Seminary next appointed a Jew to its faculty in the 1960s.

guished career of learning and usefulness," as Edward Robinson lamented. Stuart also greatly admired him. But Jewish biblical erudition was as scarce among Christian scholars as German philology was plentiful.[22]

When a few Anglophone biblical philologists began cautiously to try out German higher (or historical) criticism, they took inspiration from German classical as well as biblical philologists. The two fields of study, after all, had not yet hived off into different 'disciplines,' deaf to each other. And in the schooling of boys and young men, revered ancient texts such as Homer and Livy occupied a canonical status parallel to the Bible's, if far less exalted. Wolf's deconstruction of Homer, then, not only borrowed from Eichhorn's approach to the Old Testament; it also might encourage readers oblivious to Eichhorn to wonder if the Old Testament had likewise been cobbled together from folk stories. Pusey claimed exactly as much: "scepticism as to Homer ushered in the scepticism on the Old Testament." Niebuhr depicted Livy's history of primitive Rome as a fiction crafted from popular ballads. He seems to have rocked the Bible harder than Wolf did—maybe because Niebuhr explicitly compared fabulous Roman tales of origins to Old Testament stories, or just because he had more Anglophone readers. His frank disbelief in biblical chronology and the creation story sharpened the hermeneutic of suspicion. Niebuhr even hinted that ancient Hebrews lent authority to the Mosaic Law by claiming Yahweh as its author, just as Etruscans and Romans shored up "the laws of the state" by ascribing them to their gods.[23]

In 1861, tongue in cheek, the Oxford bishop Samuel Wilberforce asked "whether the human mind, which with Niebuhr has tasted blood in the slaughter of Livy, can be prevailed upon to abstain from falling next upon the Bible." In flat fact, one of the biblical 'skeptics' he was then in the process of lambasting, Benjamin Jowett, traced his doubts about the factuality of Old Testament narratives precisely to college lectures based on Niebuhr. (Niebuhr's picture later adorned Jowett's study.) Jowett was not alone; during his stay in Paris in the mid-1840s, Max Müller argued with "young Renan" over how much of "the Old and the New Testament would stand the critical tests enunciated by Niebuhr." Frederick Denison Maurice found "the Niebuhrian investigations" bringing him "face to face with the characteristics of the Hebrew history." Already in 1835 Thomas Arnold urged scholars to do for Judea "what Wolf and Niebuhr had done for Greece and Rome."[24]

Two Moderately Shocking Historicists

One writer impressed by Niebuhr's "slaughter of Livy" did not wait for Arnold's urging. In 1829 Henry Hart Milman published a three-volume *History of the Jews*. Milman combined a successful career in the Church of England with a calling as man of letters. Besides histories of Christianity in different eras, he wrote poetry and plays, translated Euripides and a portion of the

Mahābhārata (with the Sanskritist H. H. Wilson), composed a life of Horace, and edited Gibbon. Milman knew wide ranges of philological erudition but expertly commanded none; he was no new-model, specialized scholar. And his *History of the Jews* paid correspondingly little attention to heavy-duty German Old Testament philology. He wrote the three volumes in a little over a year, amid pastoral duties, far from any well-stocked library. But he did read German and appreciated the stress on progressive historical development in German theology, while Niebuhr's *Römische Geschichte* had impressed him with its theory of popular ballads as sources for early Roman history. Milman shared the widespread notion that primitive peoples naturally related events in poetry. He had absorbed the teaching of eighteenth-century writers like Robert Wood: humankind in its childhood perceived the world through imagination rather than logic. In that faraway time people expressed experience by elaborating myth, not recording fact. In such a "heroic or mythic age," as Milman called it,"history, law and religion are alike poetry."[25]

This idea Milman applied to the ancient Hebrews, especially in his first volume. Like a Scottish stadial theorist, he made "the ancestors of the Jews, and the Jews themselves, pass through every stage of comparative civilization." The Old Testament showed the evolution of the Hebrews from primitive mythmaking to the threshold of rationality. "God, who in his later revelation, appeals to the reason and the heart, addressed a more carnal and superstitious people chiefly through their imagination and their senses." Milman depicted Abraham as "the Sheik or Emir" of "a nomadic tribe." The sexual aggression, bloodthirstiness, and crude mores on display in the Pentateuch in fact proved the Books of Moses to be authentically early records, not a later composition as some supposed. Milman's *History* provoked outrage. He discreetly kept his name off the title page of the first edition. ("The clergy," he had written some years earlier, "must not unnecessarily seek unpopularity.") Everybody knew anyway. Readers assumed he was spreading the toxin of German historical criticism.[26]

And, indeed, Milman's younger ally Arthur Stanley wrote decades later that *The History of the Jews* was "the first decisive inroad of German theology into England; the first palpable indication that the Bible 'could be studied like another book.'" The poison was much diluted, and it worked with slow, homeopathic effect. Milman still believed that God providentially guided the history of Israel. He still thought even the earliest Hebrews monotheists. He still presumed that the Old Testament told a real history, though cloaked in the mist of the primitive mind. And he basically retold that story, garnished, as John Rogerson put it, with "references to classical authors, to the accounts of travelers to the East, and to [older] biblical scholars such as Richard Simon, John Spencer, and J. D. Michaelis." But *in the Anglophone context* Milman innovated. His novelty and his impact—and both were real—lay in his treatment of the Old Testament history as a history parallel to that of other ancient peoples, his insistence that the Bible be scrutinized like other ancient books, and his placement of the Hebrews within the larger world of ancient Semitic peoples. For most readers in Britain and America, these lessons would have come as a shock. But because they appeared in a book written for a general audience by a clergyman, because they did not challenge the veracity of the Bible, and because they were cloaked in reverence, they sometimes sank in. Oxford, Milman's alma mater, roused itself in fury at his *History*. Thirty-three years later it invited him back to deliver an annual lecture—on "Hebrew Prophecy."[27]

Equally conservative at heart, yet equally corrosive of a timeless view of the Bible, was Andrews Norton's *Evidences of the Genuineness of the Gospels*, published in three volumes in Boston between 1837 and 1844. This was the most substantial work of biblical philology yet completed by any American. At the time English-speaking readers thought it a huge achievement. Milman himself judged it superior to any other work on the "great question" of "the antiquity and genuineness of the New Testament." The Harvard professor Francis Bowen, widely read and no fool, thought it "an almost unrivalled monument of patience and industry, of ripe scholarship, thorough research, eminent ability, and conscientious devotion to the cause of truth": "one of the great works in theological science of the present century." Such encomia indicate how far most Britons and Americans still were from appreciating German biblical philology. The enthusiasm for *Genuineness of the Gospels* probably owed much to Norton's *purpose*—to prove that the Gospels "remain essentially the same as when they were originally written; and that they have been ascribed to their true authors." In common with the even more conservative Stuart and Hodge, Norton stood appalled at the theory, widespread in Germany, adopted by Herbert Marsh, that the synoptic Gospels relied in part on a now-lost earlier account of Jesus's life and teachings.[28]

Yet the Unitarian Norton understood the *divine revelation* in the Bible very differently than did most American and British Protestants, including Stuart, Robinson, and Hodge. In the most common view God had guided the authors so that they wrote what God intended them to record, at least insofar as their words bore on religious truth. (Commentators differed whether God inspired the exact words, as well as whether biblical accounts of natural events and secular history were inspired.) The Bible text itself was, in this sense, God's word. Norton, like other Unitarians, differed. Yes, the Bible recorded teachings by divinely inspired individuals. But its authors wrote down this inspired doctrine as would any other human writer. God did speak through Jesus. But the disciples who recorded Jesus's words had no supernatural guidance. Nor did divine care protect subsequent manuscripts from essential error as they were copied over and over. The Gospels thus needed evaluation for accuracy just as other ancient historical texts.

This Norton proceeded to do through standard philological practices. Among other things, he showed the agreement of the many manuscripts of the Gospels, both extant and as quoted by ancient authors. He argued from their internal consistency. He adduced the peculiar Hebraistic inflection of the

Greek *koiné* in which the Gospels were written. He explored the comments of early Christian writers. And he concluded,

> The Gospels, as I have said, remain *essentially* the same as they were originally written. In common with all other ancient writings, they have been exposed to the accidents to which works preserved by transcription are liable. In the very numerous authorities for determining their text, we find a great number of differences, or various readings. But, by comparing those authorities together, we are able, in general, to ascertain satisfactorily the original text of the last three Gospels, and of the Greek translation of St. Matthew.*

Norton freely conceded that some passages in the extant biblical text were "spurious." In particular, he advanced "strong reasons for thinking, that the first two chapters of our present copies of the Greek Gospel of Matthew made no part of the original Hebrew." He singled out other verses in each of the Gospels he judged dubious. He even suggested that the original authors themselves may have got wrong some of Jesus's words.[29]

This hardly sounded like David Strauss; but Norton did make the biblical text itself (as distinct from revelations recorded in it) a product of history. The Bible threw up the same problems, required the same methods of interpretation, as any other historical document. After all, ordinary human beings wrote the Bible, recording on papyrus what they had seen and heard. So Norton often found himself agreeing with German critics and 'advanced' British writers like Milman about the culture-bound character of scripture. The modern critic had to penetrate the "oriental style" of the New Testament writers. (So far Stuart agreed.) These men of another culture in the distant past typically "embodie[d] intellectual & moral ideas" in metaphor. Such "expressions . . . will certainly be mistaken" by any reader who "puts that sense upon the words in which we would ourselves employ them." Norton thought the Pentateuch largely mythical and legendary, the story of Jonah and the great fish "fabulous." (Overall, Norton took a low view of the Jewish scriptures. Yes, God had revealed Himself to the Hebrews. But the Old Testament mixed truth with so much ludicrous religious practice, made-up tales, outright immorality that no rational Christian could mistake the books themselves for divine revelation. And Norton was not an anti-Semite.)[30]

Norton shied away from the conclusions of radical German critics; but, like them in method, he immersed the Bible deeply in the historical context of its production. Everyone accepted the philological axiom that the words of an ancient text could only be rightly understood in historical context. As Hodge stressed, any serious biblical interpreter needed to know "the manners and

---

*Norton presumed, as did other scholars at the time, that the author of Matthew (whom Norton believed to be the apostle himself) originally wrote in Hebrew, then was translated into Greek.

customs, the laws, character, and circumstances of the persons to whom the sacred writings were addressed, their civil history, with that of neighbouring nations, together with whatever light, geography, chronology, natural history, and philosophy, can cast on the Sacred Volume." But Norton opened the door to history far wider than Hodge. Hodge feared that historicizing the Bible would undermine its authority as timeless truth. He believed not only that Moses wrote the description of Creation in Genesis but also that he recounted the events precisely. Where did the inspired author pick up his facts? Hodge found plausible a hypothesis that Moses as a boy in Egypt heard the story of Creation from the patriarch Jacob, who learned the details from Noah's son Shem, who had gotten them from Methuselah, who had it all directly from Adam. It works if you believe the Old Testament's chronology to be literally true. Norton did not.[31]

There is no reason to think that Norton ever read F. A. Wolf, but he applied to the Bible the same philological maxim that Wolf applied to Homer: place a text within the holistic ancient milieu—we would say 'culture'—from which it had emerged. Odd though it may sound, Norton adopted a more strictly historical, or at least more empirical, attitude toward scripture than the most advanced German critics. For them, idealist, progressivist philosophy (generally Hegelian by the time Norton published) undergirded the upward ascent of history. Norton, in contrast, adhered to Scottish Common Sense Realism. For him, history did not rise on the wings of the World Spirit. History involved only ascertainable, solid fact. True, the Common Sense philosophy itself shaped Norton's conception of 'science,' of what counted as data, and of how he should handle these. But he and other American biblical critics hit the target in griping about how often philosophy drove German philology to its conclusions.

THE CRISIS OF 1860

With the creeping in of historically minded biblical philology in Britain and America, pressure gradually built up, as in a magma chamber, under the traditional Bible. The volcano erupted in 1860. By then, writers from Marsh to Norton had habituated well-informed readers to the axiom that they needed detailed historical context to understand the Bible fully. The few direct intrusions of advanced German biblical philology into English print—chiefly Parker's version of De Wette and Evans's translation of Strauss—perhaps extended limits of acceptable discussion. A few decades earlier, trashing two chapters of Matthew's Gospel would have set off the fire alarm. But De Wette and Strauss terrified people, making a philologist like Norton seem reasonable, despite an occasional lapse into heterodoxy. In 1853 a Cambridge prizeessay competition set as its historicizing topic, "The gospels could not have originated in any or all those forms of religious opinion which prevailed among the Jews at the time of our Saviour's incarnation"—a question stemming from Strauss's *Leben Jesu*. In 1857 Oxford's Mark Pattison praised in print German "Historico-Critical" philology, in the scary person of Tübingen's F. C. Baur. By bringing history to bear on the Bible, Pattison wrote, Baur and his cohorts "have relieved Scripture criticism from the incapacity under which it laboured, from the opprobrium of dishonesty which had attached to it." This slow erosion of the Bible's uniquely sacrosanct position among ancient writings—once the only ancient text exempted from history—opened the way for *Essays and Reviews*.[32]

In March 1860 this volume appeared: seven essays by six liberal Anglican clergymen (including Pattison) and one layman. The essays shared no overall theme but converged in criticizing some traditional orthodoxies and demanding greater latitude of thought within the Church of England. All but one writer had a link to Oxford; most taught the rising generation. The lead article in the *Westminster Review* for October 1860 notoriously declared, "A book has appeared which may serve to mark an epoch in the history of opinion." Numerous other reviews at least made clear that the book marked an epoch in the history of outrage. (In his review, the Göttingen Hebraist Heinrich Ewald made clear that *Essays and Reviews* opened no new era in scholarship—indeed, that Oxford had not yet learned what scholarship was.) "Cries of horror, grief and pain rang from the press and the pulpit," wrote Basil Willey; "the Bishops protested; the Court of Arches [forum for Anglican heresy trials] and the Judicial Committee of the Privy Council came into action." Within a year the book went into its sixth edition, having by then sold over five thousand copies, a smashing success. American publishers pirated it within months of English publication. The furor may have grown all the more furious because *Essays and Reviews* followed close on the heels of another shock to Anglo-Protestant orthodoxy, Darwin's *Origin of Species*, on sale four months earlier. Looking back from the 1890s, William Lecky thought *Essays and Reviews* began a major shift in mores, "the great enlargement of the range of permissible opinions on religious subjects." But liberalization of drawing-room chat does not concern us here.[33]

What the book certainly set in motion was public discord between the historical-critical approach to the Bible and the older philology that revered the Bible as the unitary, timeless word of God. *Essays and Reviews* did not deal solely with biblical studies. German influence riddled the Broad Church circles from which *Essays and Reviews* emerged, and German-inflected theology as much as German-style philology sat in the eye of the storm that swirled around the book. 'Liberal' did not mean only advanced critical views. But historical-critical philology did concern all the authors; most of the essays touched on the Bible; three focused on it; and on this subject Germanic assumptions glared from the pages.[34]

Of the biblical essays, most explosive was the last, "On the Interpretation of Scripture" by Benjamin Jowett. Jowett in 1860 was a forty-two-year-old Balliol

College tutor who had already dismayed the orthodox with a commentary on some of Paul's Epistles. A legendarily effective teacher, he lagged considerably behind that mark as a scholar. More interested in theology than biblical criticism, Jowett had a shaky hold on German biblical philology. But he wielded sharp skills as a controversialist, and he looked on *Essays and Reviews* as a chance to show that ecclesiastical retaliation would no longer cow theological liberals. He wanted to fire a shot across the bow of "this abominable system of terrorism, which prevents the statement of the plainest facts, and makes true theology or theological education impossible." Jowett did believe that the Bible imparted a divine revelation—a gradual one, accommodated to progressively fuller capacities of its audiences in their different periods. But he denied that divine inspiration made the Bible a unified whole, in which one book could explain the meanings of another. He hailed modern German biblical philology as "great steps onward." He insisted on the use of historical evidence, particularly as to the circumstances in which various books were written. He nailed to the masthead his banner "*Interpret the Scripture like any other book*" (i.e., as classical scholars did, without theological presuppositions). And he steered straight into gales of orthodox wrath. Nothing Jowett wrote was novel, and the book changed no one's mind. But, as John Rogerson said, *Essays and Reviews* signaled the "readiness of liberals to come out into the open."[35]

Thus began decades of conflict that might be called the Bible Wars. (In the United States hostilities did not open until the 1870s and really heated up in the 1880s.) Confused tendencies within the ranks of Old Testament philologists in particular became two opposing camps.[36] The warriors fought not so much over philological techniques, but over what philology ultimately implied about the Bible's relation to its own history and historical contexts. The nature of scripture and its authority seemed at stake.

For German-influenced biblical philologists, as for classicists and other textual philologists, to try to understand a text without immersing it deeply in its historical contexts now seemed simply amateurish. If *Essays and Reviews* in 1860 did not mark a watershed, it did signal a tipping point.

And in its wake a different question arose. Had biblical philology, after long obsession with its own unique trials, turned in on itself? Would biblical scholars after 1860 have anything to say to philologists working with different texts?

THE COMPARATIVE SETTING OF BIBLICAL PHILOLOGY

In the remote background of turmoil in biblical studies sat growing awareness of non-European religions with their own truth claims.* In "On the Interpre-

---

* I use the term *non-European religions*, for lack of a better one, to label collectively religions other than Christianity and Judaism. These two faiths held a virtual monopoly over religion in Europe in the period covered by this book, although certainly not confined to Europe; so I call the *other* religions—not Christian, not Jewish—non-European religions.

tation of Scripture" Jowett wrote, "Even the Vedas and the Zendavesta, though beset by obscurities of language probably greater than are found in any portion of the Bible, are interpreted, at least by European scholars, according to fixed rules, and beginning to be clearly understood."[37] No one can now recover how such parallels between the Bible and the 'scriptures' of India or Persia affected Christian or Jewish biblical critics. Presumably such effects—if any— often worked subliminally. But as biblical philologists began to look at their own scriptures through the eyes of history or mythology, they could scarcely avoid knowing of the history and mythology of other, faraway faiths with their own revered writings.

European curiosity about religious practices and beliefs of alien peoples hardly waited for the nineteenth century to begin. Such nosiness started long before Europe: Herodotus tiptoed gingerly around Persian and Egyptian divinities (gods are best not toyed with), but he managed to say quite a bit. In the seventeenth century, John Selden and John Spencer undertook learned inquiries into ancient Semitic religions; Jesuits translated Confucian writings; Thomas Hyde introduced Europe to Zoroastrianism. Early in the eighteenth century, Picart and Bernard published their seven volumes of *Ceremonies and Religious Customs of All Peoples of the World*. Toward the end of that century, Sir William Jones in Calcutta compared the gods of India with those of Greece and Rome. His employer, the East India Company, published in London Charles Wilkins's translation of the *Bhagavad Gita*. And deists made hay by comparing Christianity to 'heathen' faiths.

Knowledge of these alternate faiths deepened and spread more widely in the nineteenth century. Wilhelm de Wette not only revolutionized Old Testament criticism but also delivered lectures comparing religions, which he published in 1827 as *Die Religion, ihr Wesen und ihre Erscheinungsformen und ihren Einfluss auf das Leben* (*Religion: Its Nature, the Forms in Which It Appears, and Its Influence on Life*). His lectures covered 'primitive' religions; those of the ancient Mediterranean (stretching to Persia); and Judaism and Christianity. De Wette ranged widely, as John Rogerson noted, over "traditions, rites, laws, architecture, art, poems and hymns"; for he wanted "to place biblical studies in the widest possible context of the study of religions, philosophy and culture." Both Hegel and Schopenhauer made the history of religion do heavy lifting in their philosophizing. But such stuff was far from a German monopoly. Vans Kennedy, an East India Company man well versed in Sanskrit, puzzled over the relation of India's gods to those of ancient Greece and Rome (like Jones half a century before). His conclusions appeared in 1831 as *Researches into the Nature and Affinity of Ancient and Hindu Mythology*. (He had earlier published on Islam.) An odder Englishman, Godfrey Higgins, with ample money and leisure, devoted himself from 1813 to studying the history of religions. He wrote learnedly from what seems a rather musty quasi-deist perspective, though he called himself Christian. He published a study of the Sabbath, a book vindicating Mohammed from Christian slurs, and another on

Celtic Druids. His death in 1833 cut short an ambitious comparative history of religions aiming to reveal the ancient ancestor of all (two volumes appeared posthumously). This *Anacalypsis* sometimes brings Vico to mind, sometimes Madame Blavatsky.[38]

White denizens of what became the United States, through their colonial years, had given little attention to religions other than their own; but interest perked up after independence from Britain. A bookish New Englander, Hannah Adams, badly needed money. She earned some by writing what came to be titled, in its fourth and final edition in 1817, *A Dictionary of All Religions and Religious Denominations, Jewish, Heathen, Mahometan, and Christian, Ancient and Modern*. This started in 1784 as an alphabetical compendium of Christianity, with an appendix—an obvious afterthought—hastily surveying non-Christian religions. As the book grew, it morphed into an increasingly balanced and accurate account of all religions Adams could learn about (still weighted heavily toward Christianity). It also grew popular enough to bring in regular income for Adams—and for an English publisher to pirate the third edition in 1815.[39]

Such surveys became fashionable, rarely showing Adams's effort at even-handedness. Several flaunted Protestant self-esteem. The English Baptist missionary William Ward produced in 1811 a four-volume *Account of the Writings, Religion, and Manners, of the Hindoos*. A reader discovers repeatedly that the Hindoos' religion amounted to "idolatry" and "superstition." Rev. Charles Goodrich, an American, cribbed his *Pictorial and Descriptive View of All Religions* (1842) from an English abridgment of Picart and Bernard. But he improved their aged book by adding proofs of the ongoing conquest of "idolatry" in "every portion of the globe" by the "crucified Redeemer." Goodrich's work was often reprinted. James Moffat, a professor of the Bible in the Presbyterians' Cincinnati Theological Seminary, delivered in 1852 a lecture called "Biblical Criticism as an Object of Popular Interest." It made clear the hierarchy of truth:

> The various shades of philanthropy may be traced from nation to nation, by the corresponding degrees of Christian knowledge. From the midnight blackness of Hindooism, through Mohammedanism, and Romanism, and formal Protestantism, to the humble, intelligent and faithful follower of the Word of God [i.e., the Presbyterian], you may distinctly grade the ascending scale of humanity.

Moffat's color-coding put 'Hindooism' at a safe distance from the Bible.[40]

Not all Christian discussions of Asian religions assumed such a gap. In the 1820s and 1830s, English-speaking Unitarians saw in the Hindu reformer Rammohan Roy a fellow Unitarian in all but name. The most radical Unitarians—the American Transcendentalists—in the 1840s printed excerpts from Sanskrit, Confucian, Buddhist, and Zoroastrian texts, explicitly as parallels to the Bible. In 1855 the Unitarian minister Thomas Wentworth Higginson declared, "Every year brings new knowledge of the religions of the world, and every step in knowledge brings out the sympathy between them. They all show similar aims, symbols, forms, weaknesses, and aspirations." Higginson's words supplied almost a prospectus for a comparative history of religions. Another Unitarian, Lydia Maria Child, wrote it—three volumes, nearly simultaneous with Higginson's proclamation. Child's husband, a Harvard-educated lawyer, proved a fiscal disaster; Mrs. Child turned to writing to keep body and soul together. Like Hannah Adams's dictionary, Child's *Progress of Religious Ideas, through Successive Ages* was a much-needed potboiler. But it showed her deep-felt concern for religious toleration and substantial reading. She abjured the Christian habit of explaining away "apparent contradictions and absurdities, in Jewish or Christian writings" while snickering at irrationality in other religions. She tried to abstract herself from her own Christianity and to place all faiths "precisely on a level" with it—to treat "all religions with reverence." Such generosity was unusual but not unheard of. In *The Religions of the World and Their Relations to Christianity* (1847), the Broad Church Anglican Frederick Denison Maurice sought to dispel Christian prejudices and depict non-European religions honestly. Rev. Charles Hardwick thought him soft on the heathens. Ten years later Hardwick wrote a long refutation of Maurice's thesis of significant parallels between Christianity and other ancient faiths. The rebuttal might have gone on even longer had a hiking accident in the Pyrenees not abruptly ended its author.[41]

Few popularizers of non-European religions strove to be serious scholars—as, say, Vans Kennedy and Godfrey Higgins did. But all helped to bring greater attention to religions from outside the European cultural sphere, including the attention of scholars. In the latter half of the century philologists would take these materials and shape them into a new learned discipline, devoted to the comparative study of religions.

Meanwhile the effect on biblical philology was hard to measure. There was Jowett's passing—and laconic—allusion to "the Vedas and the Zendavesta." Theodore Parker—solitary American disciple of De Wette—read widely and thoughtfully about Asian religions. He saw Hinduism as an improvement over Presbyterianism but concluded that a purified Christianity would beat all comers. A key step in purification, he believed, would be inquiry into the relationship between Christianity and other widespread faiths of the world. What this project meant for the Bible is foggy, though certainly Parker saw it through the same mythographic, historicist lens as he saw the *Bhagavad Gita*. Time would tell if Anglophone biblical philologists might bring what Ralph Waldo Emerson called "ethnical scriptures" to bear on what was once God's unique Word.[42]

History now mattered in new ways and in new depth. Perhaps, for a Parker, the history of world religions clarified the Bible's meanings. Certainly, for a Jowett, historical criticism was needed fully to uncover them. In a changing academic climate after midcentury, all these inquiries—and the other studies descended from philology—would be transformed.

PART III

⤙ ⎯ ⤚

THE MODERN HUMANITIES IN THE MODERN UNIVERSITY, MID-NINETEENTH TO TWENTIETH CENTURY

In roughly the first half of the nineteenth century, philology began a prolonged process of fragmentation and re-formation. Tasks long seen as facets of a single enterprise hived off as semiautonomous areas of scholarship. Since the Renaissance, textual philologists had preoccupied themselves mostly with ancient texts, secular and sacred, written in one of the historic 'trilinguae': Greek, Latin, or Hebrew. Now emenders of classical texts less often pored over biblical ones, while more and more biblical philologists carried on their craft within theological institutions, writing in the first instance for a clerical audience. No hard-and-fast line yet separated classical and biblical philology around 1850. After all, ancient Greek remained ancient Greek, whether Attic or Hellenistic. It raised no eyebrows when the Yale classicist James Hadley served in the 1870s on an American committee to revise the English Bible.[1] But hindsight sees two distinct fields taking shape.

Porous but genuine frontiers became normal. Some philologists had moved on from trilinguae to 'new' ancient languages brought under European scholarly gaze by imperial expansion. Study of these tongues, in practice if not yet principle, likewise tended to fall into discrete philological spheres. A Sanskritist might deal also with Old Persian texts; he was unlikely seriously to touch Greek or Latin ones, even though he knew those languages pretty well, like every highly educated male. Still, the many classicists in the decades after 1850 who thought it proper training to learn a bit of Sanskrit showed division far from absolute, as did overlap between Sanskrit textual philology and research into comparative Indo-European grammar and phonology. Yet if lines were not bright, they existed. Anglo-Saxon comparative grammar stood apart from Sanskrit studies; Sanskrit studies seemed different from classical studies. An eighteenth-century polymath like Oriental Jones looked increasingly the stuff of legend—or dilettantism.

In some areas of research, aspects of philology melded with other, related types of scholarship to produce new learned fields. An early instance was Edward Gibbon's *Decline and Fall of the Roman Empire* (1776–89). It merged the narrative style of philosophic history with the research methods of philological antiquarianism to produce perhaps the first clear-cut example of the scholarly history prevailing today. The influence of Barthold Georg Niebuhr's philologically grounded *Römische Geschichte* (1811–32) decisively confirmed this new genre for influential English-speaking historians in the first half of the nineteenth century—though 'history' still teetered between entertainment and scholarship in the works of learned popular historians such as William Prescott or Francis Parkman. Likewise, the study of texts in archaic forms of modern languages (notably Anglo-Saxon), the editing of 'classic' vernacular authors like Shakespeare and Donne, and the relatively recent practice of 'criticism' evaluating modern poets and playwrights flowed together to form a precariously erudite field of 'literature,' recognized by at least some scholars and universities. A few philologists investigating American Indian or Austronesian languages cross-bred traditional speculations about language with methodical data gathering to produce a 'science of language' that one of them named linguistics.

Such movements, usually amorphous and unself-conscious during the first half of the century, became more systematic, more intentional after about 1850. There came into existence, for the first time in the English-speaking world, academic disciplines in the modern sense.

This key shift blurs in retrospect because we lack clear language for discussing it. The word *discipline* (coming from the *disciple* of a teacher) had been used in academic contexts for centuries. It could mean 'instruction' (apparently its original meaning in English), but it could also mean a branch of knowledge. Chaucer used the word in this latter sense in the *Canterbury Tales*. This linguistic fact obscures the novelty of the new kind of disciplinary specialization that appeared in the nineteenth century. Early modern textual philologists agreed broadly on the kinds of problems to address and on methods to resolve them. They also developed characteristic instruments for keeping track of information (such as commonplace books) and for spreading knowledge (such as commentaries and editions). In this sense textual philology formed a discipline. So did, for instance, chronology and chorography. But early modern disciplines were far from exclusive; the same people might pursue classical studies and chorography, biblical learning and chronology. Late Victorian and twentieth-century disciplines also had their mutually understood problems and methods, their distinctive technologies for organizing data and sharing knowledge (like index cards and discipline-specific journals). Yet modern disciplines grew much more strictly subdivided. By the 1920s notably few scholars worked in both history and linguistics or studied both anthropology and literature.[2]

Two institutional developments set this shrinking focus into context. Neither was sui generis. Both were, rather, two faces of a much wider cultural change—a professionalizing ethos that reshaped attitudes in the upper echelons of the workforce in both the United Kingdom and North America.[3]

The first of these two developments was the creation of organizations ('learned societies,' 'professional associations') focused on subvariants of philology and its offshoots. Such groups fostered a new level of self-consciousness about, say, 'literature'; they helped practitioners of this field see themselves as distinct from 'classicists' or 'historians.' Again, there was nothing unique here. In the same period, physicians, engineers, natural scientists, and others formed similar groups, while government employment began to evolve away from patronage toward a professional civil service.

The second development was a revolution in higher education. Since the Renaissance—with periodic updating—English, Irish, and North American universities, colleges, and academies had taught a curriculum centered on classical languages, though never confined to them. (Scottish universities taught more diverse subjects to younger boys. Cambridge stood out in giving mathematics more prestige than Greek and Latin.) For complex reasons largely irrelevant to this book, this old, classical curriculum broke down in the later nineteenth century. The breakdown went on more rapidly in America, and in newer English and Irish institutions, than at Oxford and Cambridge. During this time of muddle, most of the emerging fields of research mentioned above seeped into university teaching. Soon a substantial body of teachers professed 'history,' 'literature,' eventually even 'anthropology' and 'art history.' In the increasingly research-oriented environment of turn-of-the-century universities, these teachers also pursued erudite investigations in their fields. The formation of these scholarly corps had an effect like that of the new learned societies. By teaching students under these new labels, and by spawning learned journals specific to them, they marked off each field of philological or postphilological study as an independent realm, like male marmots flagging with urine the boundaries of their territories. When this happened, classical scholars, too, found themselves in just another academic field, instead of the default option of college teaching. Since university professors usually took the lead in founding and running the learned societies, one can reasonably suspect the newly research-minded universities as the main locus of change.

And once certain scholars had wandered off into their own separate garden, they tended to speak directly mostly to each other, ignoring other grandchildren of philology on the other side of the wall. The walls grew higher, specialization more exclusive. Research universities not only encouraged the emergence of this sort of specialization but such specialization also reinforced itself, in a feedback loop fostering more and more self-isolation. Academic disciplines in their modern sense now first saw the light of day. Their birth was unprecedented and momentous for erudition, as the links tying together the different realms of human knowledge snapped. The process transformed all academic knowledge, from the natural sciences to the human ones.[4]

In this setting, the fragmentation of philology sped up in the United Kingdom and United States. Biblical philologists now tended to divide more clearly into (Greek) New Testament and (Hebrew) Old Testament specialists. Oriental philologists who pursued Arabic, Chinese, or Sanskrit increasingly focused on one or the other language and its close relatives. Students of Amerindian languages and cultures less often paid attention to classical or Polynesian tongues as well, as John Pickering had once done. Historians and literary scholars—who were often the same person when the two subjects first appeared in university teaching—hived off into separate learned societies.

Thus, after midcentury, bits and pieces precipitated out of the complex solution called philology, then crystallized into new 'disciplines.' Biblical philology, classical philology, and orientalist philology all contributed to a new field called history of religion or comparative religion. Occasionally such new studies melded with nonphilological methods or topics, becoming intellectual hybrids. The relatively late-blooming discipline of anthropology makes a good example, concerning itself with both human bodies and human cultures. As each new discipline came to self-consciousness, it evolved its own distinctive, defining institutions—learned societies, journals, university departments. Its ties to its old intellectual neighbors frayed. By and by it forgot that it had once formed a part of something much larger.

In the waning decades of the century, the rubric 'humanities' came to label most of the new disciplines spawned by philology. (Anthropology, theoretical linguistics, and biblical criticism were not usually called humanities; and one central humanistic discipline, philosophy, did not have roots in philology.) Like 'discipline,' the plural 'humanities' was a new term descended from an old one. From the late Middle Ages, the singular word *humanity* served to distinguish classical studies from natural sciences on one side and sacred studies (*divinity*) on the other side. Francis Bacon used humanity in this way in *The Advancement of Learning* (1605). The term's modern career is not well charted. But by the eighteenth century *humanity* in its academic sense seems to have fallen out of widespread use, except in Scottish universities (where it meant the study of Latin). Its revival as a plural in the course of the following century apparently arose from the need for a label for the multiple new 'liberal studies' or 'culture studies' entering university curricula. As late as 1911, an observer familiar with higher education in both the United Kingdom and the United States signaled the novelty of the humanities by calling them "the so-called 'humanistic' subjects." Yet by 1900 the humanities seemed central to liberal education throughout the English-speaking world, and the disciplines comprising them took their place among the fields of academic research represented in any full-fledged university.[5]

Almost all of them—and a couple of disciplines not usually grouped with the humanities—have a common origin in the splintering of philology after 1800. These family ties prevented the philologically grounded humanities from ever completing their disciplinary divorce. Their common foundation left always open a basis for interaction. Time and again, one humanities discipline, at some critical point in its evolution, drew on another for ideas and inspiration. The numerous calls for 'interdisciplinarity' since the mid-twentieth century are not forward-looking but—if unknowingly—backward-looking. The rest of this book will tell this story of departure, division, and return.

Thus were born—out of philology, with the university as midwife—the disciplines of the humanities in their modern forms. It remains now to trace the final stages of the long journey from ancient Greece to modern Britain, Ireland, and North America.

9

‿◦‿——◦‿

"This Newly Opened Mine
of Scientific Inquiry"

Between History and Nature:
Linguistics after 1850

L inguistics became a university discipline—lightly populated—in North America and the United Kingdom in the decades after 1850 (though by no means confined to universities). Whether it remained a humanistic study presents a more complex question. The topics of linguistics were legion—Amerindian languages; Indo-European comparative philology; historical grammar of various individual tongues, Indo-European and other; studies of Pacific, Asian, and African languages and language families—with methods ranging from typology to phonology to lexicography to morphology to etymology.

To bring so sprawling a field into focus, this chapter looks at linguistics mainly through the eyes of its two most prominent practitioners in the English-speaking world at the time. They provide good lenses because they shared a starting point in Vedic scholarship; they dealt with lots of philologists elsewhere; they pursued diverse research themselves; and they detested each other. Academic blood feuds may be small-minded, but they can reveal fault lines dividing a discipline. Close-up scrutiny also gives a finer-grained view of the complex texture of linguistics as it matured. The two stars are the Yale philologist William Dwight Whitney (1827–94) and his Oxford counterpart Friedrich Max Müller (1823–1900). To start, a little biography.

Müller

Max Müller (always called Max) was born in the duchy of Anhalt-Dessau, one of the miniature states dotting German-speaking Europe before 1871. His father Wilhelm (a popular Romantic poet) was the duke's librarian, his mother Adelheid daughter of the prime minister. The father died before Max turned four. He left Max to grow up as a poor boy with unusually well-placed friends. They insured that he got a good education at the famous Nicolai School in Leipzig, and he then went on to the university there. Somewhere along the way, he read Friedrich Schlegel's *Über die Sprache und die Weisheit der Indier.* At the University of Leipzig, Müller fell in love with Sanskrit. After taking his degree in 1843, he went to Berlin to hear the lectures of Franz Bopp and the idealist philosopher Friedrich Schelling. Bopp disappointed him, but Müller caught mysticism from Schelling—a mild but chronic fever with decisive results for Müller's later writings on comparative religion, as chapter 13 will show. It even inflected his Sanskrit scholarship. From Berlin, Müller migrated to Paris, then still the European capital of Sanskrit. There he honed his fluency under the eminence Eugène Burnouf. Encouraged by Burnouf, he decided to edit the *Ṛg Veda,* the oldest of the Hindu scriptures,* together with Sāyana's magisterial fourteenth-century commentary on it.[1]

Seeking manuscripts of the *Ṛg Veda* and Sāyana, in 1846 Müller sailed to England and into an unexpectedly permanent berth. In London the formidably learned and well-connected Prussian ambassador, Christian von Bunsen, shared the young man's scholarly vision. He took Müller under his wing. Bunsen and Horace Hayman Wilson, Boden Professor of Sanskrit at Oxford, convinced the East India Company to subsidize Müller's edition. Müller settled in Oxford to collate manuscripts. He figured the edition would take five years. The first volume duly appeared in 1849; the sixth and last twenty-five years later. Müller stayed in Oxford, beavering away at the *Ṛg Veda,* making English friends, lecturing on linguistic and literary topics as deputy for the decrepit Taylorian Professor of Modern European Languages. In 1854 he became Taylorian Professor himself. In 1858 All Souls College elected him fellow, and the next year he married an Englishwoman. In 1868 he became Oxford's first professor of comparative philology. Müller's fluent, even theatrical books and public lectures made him eventually an international academic celebrity—a man, rumor had it, who called Wilhelm II "the nicest emperor I know" and had the Ottoman sultan over for lunch.[2]

But Müller hit one big bump on the way up. In 1860 the Boden Professorship of Sanskrit fell vacant, and he stood for election. No one doubted he was Britain's best Sanskritist. Many did doubt his religious orthodoxy. He notoriously hobnobbed with friends like Benjamin Jowett, known for admiring 'advanced' German biblical criticism. Müller avowed his own Christian faith with a straight face; but people suspected—rightly—that he had drifted pretty far from the Lutheranism of his youth (a drifting perhaps set in motion by

---

* Scholars date the *Ṛg Veda,* a collection of hymns, in its present form between 1500 and 1200 BCE, though many of its hymns are older—some possibly echoing the third or even fourth millennium.

Schelling's Berlin lectures). The religious business gained extra weight because Joseph Boden had endowed the chair for missionary ends. Traditionalist Oxonians also resented Müller as icon of the new Teutonic scholarship rustling the ivy on the medieval walls of their beloved colleges. Yet so orthodox an Anglican as Edward Pusey campaigned for Müller, stressing his erudition and averring that he had "already done more for the Gospel in India than any other Sanskrit scholar, by opening to our missionaries their [Indians'] sacred books." (Müller's opponent for the chair, Monier Williams, rightly pointed out that 'scriptures' for modern Indians were the classical Sanskrit texts in which *he* specialized, notably the Mahābhārata—not Müller's ancient Vedas.) Had only college fellows voted, Müller would have won. But election lay in the hands of Convocation, dominated by rural clergymen with Oxford MAs. They flocked to town to elect a second-rank philologist but first-rate English Christian, Monier Williams.[3]

The defeat left Müller bitter, sucked energy from his Sanskrit scholarship, and set him chasing other hares. Sanskrit had never excluded related work. The language's historic connection with the larger Indo-European project meant that European Sanskritists commonly dabbled in comparative philology. As early as 1849, Müller won the Institut de France's Volney Prize for an essay explaining how comparative Indo-European philology could cast light on the lives of "our Arian [*sic*] forefathers" who spoke the vanished ancestral language.* (Collect all words with "the same form & the same meaning" in the "principal" Indo-European tongues; "the objects which they represent must have been known to the Arians before they separated." You could cull possibly misleading loan words because they would not show the sound shifts of, for instance, Grimm's Law.) As his Volney Prize essay hinted he might, Müller published in 1856 the *Essay on Comparative Mythology*, grounded in comparison of languages; and, shortly before the Boden chair election, he accepted an invitation to lecture at the Royal Institution in London specifically on comparative philology. These talks, and a follow-up series two years later, began an extraordinary broadening of Müller's scholarly work. (A 'shallowing' as well: Müller was a good Sanskritist, but his skills faded as he moved further away.) Müller devoted the first volume of his collected essays, *Chips from a German Workshop* (1867), to what he called 'the science of religion.' (Chapter 13 will discuss his subsequent books on comparative religion.) A seismic shift had shaken his scholarship. Sanskrit still mattered, but the center of gravity swung far from ancient India.[4]

When Müller stepped beyond philological studies of Sanskrit texts, he took with him the belief that such texts figured in the larger history of the evolution of human consciousness. As he wrote, "The growth of language is continuous,

---

* Words like *race*, *nations*, and *blood* were used loosely in Müller's day (and by Müller himself). He consistently taught that ethnicity arose from shared language, not biology, and opposed the 'racial science' of Aryanism that developed during his lifetime.

and by continuing our researches backward from the most modern to the most ancient strata, the very elements and roots of human speech have been reached, and with them the elements and roots of human thought." And "humanity begins," he said, "when language begins." It will soon appear how expansive Müller's linguistics was, but first we need a quick overview of Whitney's career.[5]

WHITNEY

William Dwight Whitney was the son of a merchant and banker in Northampton, Massachusetts. Of seven Whitney children, five held academic or scientific jobs. That tells something about his upbringing. William looked up to his brother Josiah, seven years older. After Yale, Josiah studied geology in Berlin. He heard Bopp and Grimm lecture—and half longed to turn to philology. He did not, returning home to become a famous field geologist (honored in the name of California's Mount Whitney, the highest mountain in the contiguous United States). But tales of Berlin philology stirred William, who excelled in natural science, too, at Williams College in western Massachusetts. There the Congregationalist Christianity in which he had been reared faded. He soon lost his faith altogether. Imbued with his brother's positivistic natural science, he did not, like Müller, swap his Christianity for a diaphanous theism but settled into tactful, quiet agnosticism and a lifelong aversion to metaphysics. After graduating Williams in 1845, at age eighteen, William said he yearned to "go to Berlin and study Philology." Finances instead dictated working for three years in his father's bank. European languages, old and modern, and eventually Sanskrit, the holy grail, filled his evenings. The family pastor, who studied Sanskrit with him, put him in touch with Yale's Edward Salisbury, sole professor of the language in America. Whitney spent 1849–50 at Yale, studying Sanskrit with Salisbury, Anglo-Saxon with Josiah Gibbs, and advanced Greek with Theodore Woolsey. In September 1850 he sailed for Europe. In Berlin, Bopp disgruntled him as he had Müller. Albrecht Weber appealed—a Sanskrit professor just two years older than Whitney. So Whitney became an orientalist rather than comparative philologist. He learned Arabic, Persian, and, under Richard Lepsius, Egyptian and Coptic. Weber, a Vedic specialist, sent Whitney to Rudolph von Roth at Tübingen, top of the field. Impressed, Roth enlisted him as coeditor of the *Atharva Veda*, second-oldest of the four Vedas, dating from perhaps just before 1000 BCE.* On Whitney's long way home in the spring and summer of 1853, he collated and copied every manuscript in Europe—in Paris, London, and Oxford.[6]

Whitney returned a professional orientalist, but where to profess? Salisbury—who after a fruitless decade decided that teaching was not his forte—

---

* The *Atharva Veda* treats mostly pragmatic concerns such as medicine and warfare.

surprised his protégé by resigning his position at Yale in Whitney's favor. Whitney became "Professor of the Sanskrit and its relations to the kindred languages, and of Sanskrit literature"—as roundabout a way of saying 'Sanskrit and comparative philology' as ever devised. His post was in Yale's new Department of Philosophy and the Arts, founded in 1847 to supply postgraduate study. (Not until 1861 was a degree awarded, the first American PhD.) The study on offer lay mostly in philology—classical or Indo-European. In form and aim, the department teetered uneasily between the philosophy faculty of a German university and the not-yet-invented graduate school of an American one. Like Max Müller at Oxford in the same period, Whitney also had to teach modern languages to undergraduates. He enjoyed it as little as Müller did.[7]

Like Müller, he soon established himself as a leader in Indology. In 1855–56 his and Roth's definitive edition of the *Atharva Veda* appeared. Many other Sanskrit publications followed. Already in 1861 Breslau recognized his stature with an honorary degree; the Berlin Academy awarded his 1871 edition and translation of an ancient grammar its triennial Bopp Prize for the most noteworthy Sanskrit publication. This line of work culminated in his own Sanskrit grammar (1879), still authoritative, never out of print—"epoch-making," said Karl Brugman, a leading Indo-Europeanist in the generation following Whitney. In the 1860s Whitney started to diversify beyond Sanskrit. He published grammars and dictionaries of modern languages. By far greatest of these was the masterful *Century Dictionary* of English in ten volumes, which he edited between 1889 and 1891, shortly before heart disease killed him at sixty-seven. Elected to the American Oriental Society even before his German studies, he became its librarian in 1855 and editor of its journal two years later, before election as president in 1884. By then he had also served as founding president of the American Philological Association in 1869. In that year Yale staved off a try by Harvard to kidnap Whitney for its faculty. In 1867, like Müller a few years earlier, Whitney turned a public lecture series into a general survey of linguistics for popular consumption, *Language and the Study of Language*. A similar work, *The Life and Growth of Language*, followed in 1875. Whitney's sober restraint and cautious empiricism contrasted with Müller's flamboyant showmanship and sometimes ungrounded speculations. They were fated to clash.[8]

THE VEDAS

Müller and Whitney's temperamental discord showed even in their Vedic scholarship. The four Vedas were the hottest topic in Indology when they entered the field. Both men made their initial reputations with learned, often arcane redactions of Vedas. Whitney was the better technical Sanskritist, seen in what Michael Silverstein called "beautiful studies of accent" and in his use of statistical methods to elucidate the grammatical development of Sanskrit. But the two experts had contradictory notions of why their work mattered.[9]

Müller believed he was bringing to light the 'childhood' of the peoples who speak Indo-European languages. As his mentor Bunsen put it, language provided the "greatest prehistoric fact," opening the window on any civilization. Müller conceded the Ṛg Veda to be full of "childish, silly, even to our minds monstrous conceptions"; but it also contained "sparks of profound truth." The "childish" Vedic way of thinking—earliest recoverable evidence of the human mind—developed through "youth" into the mental "manhood" of modern Europeans, specifically their religious thinking. Müller was like a Scottish conjectural historian who had passed beyond ungrounded speculation to what he thought text-based reality. The reconstructed Proto-Indo-European word for a god

> stands still, as the most ancient monument of the human race—aere perennius: breathing to us the pure air of the dawn of humanity, carrying with it all the thoughts & sighs, the doubts & fears of our by-gone brethren, & still rising up to heaven with the same sound from the Cathedrals of Rome & the temples of Benares—as if embracing by its simple spell millions & millions of hearts in their longing desire to give utterance to what is unutterable, to express what is inexpressible.

No wonder Müller leaped from the Ṛg Veda to mythology. In his preface to volume 3 (1856)—and in his essay on comparative mythology, published that same year—he insisted that studying the Ṛg Veda gave insight into mythology. By 'mythology' he meant an inevitable early stage of human thinking in which metaphorical uses of words overwhelm their actual references. (Robert Wood's notion of a primitive era of poetic thinking still echoed.) Deva—'shining,' one attribute of a god—came to mean 'god.' Indo-European speakers stopped thinking in this primeval way before separating into distinct groups with their own daughter languages like Sanskrit. So Vedas postdated the age of mythology. But they lay closer to it than any other text. Like a "patient" geologist, reconstructing ancient earth from "recent formations," the careful philologist could tease mythology out of the Ṛg Veda.[10]

Whitney admired Müller's skills as a Sanskritist, but dismissed his Romantic vision of a mythological age lying behind the Vedas as mere conjecture, unworthy of science. He would have agreed in spades with Müller that the Vedas were full of "childish, silly" verses but would have laughed at the "sparks of profound truth" Müller also saw there. Whitney found the "unlimited praises" lavished on the philosophic and poetic merits of the Ṛg Veda's so-called cosmogonic hymn "well-nigh nauseating." Why, then, study Vedas? Two reasons: for better understanding of the Sanskrit language and for historical information embedded in them. The cosmogonic hymn did have "the highest historical interest" as the earliest speculation on the origin of the world in India and "probably anywhere among Indo-European races"—"grossly anthropomorphic" though it was. Whitney stood ready to pour cold empiricism on Müller's Romantic imagination. The time to decant came in the 1860s, when Müller branched out from Sanskrit into general linguistic theory.[11]

Interlude: August Schleicher

By then, the linguistic landscape had evolved. In the nineteenth century linguistics (or 'the science of language,' preferred by Müller and Whitney) was overwhelmingly identified with comparative historical philology, embodied with most prestige in Indo-European linguistics. But this philology never stayed still. Among many agents of change after 1850, the main one was perhaps August Schleicher, professor at the University of Jena. At least he makes a good representative figure. A series of publications beginning in the late 1840s culminated in Schleicher's *Compendium der vergleichenden Grammatik der indogermanischen Sprachen* (*Compendium of the Comparative Grammar of the Indo-Germanic* [Indo-European] *Languages*, 1861). In these works, especially the last, Schleicher summed up, clarified, and elevated to a new stage the Indo-European project sparked by William Jones in 1786 and turned into a serious research program by Franz Bopp in 1816. Schleicher was no incandescent genius, but he had what Whitney justly called "immense industry and erudition" and a masterful hand at synthesis. A mound of research by many linguists on Indo-European in large and on individual family members in detail came coherently together in his *Compendium*.[12]

In 1853 Schleicher formalized the key idea that languages develop by branching descent from a parent language. The principle was present in Bopp's method but not articulated. Schleicher was an avid, well-informed gardener and plant breeder. As he knew, some natural historians used an *arbre généalogique* (genealogical tree) to display botanical relationships (as in the Linnaean system of classification). Schleicher borrowed it. He used this *Stammbaum* (family tree) to show how the Indo-European family evolved as each branch grew from its parent limb—all stemming ultimately from the trunk that he called Indo-Germanic (Proto-Indo-European). As soon as Schleicher made Bopp's semitacit axiom clear, it came under attack as implausible. Did languages really split off and lose all contact with each other? Did Indians never speak with neighboring Iranians? Did French people never talk with Italians? As different dialects of a language evolved into distinct tongues, would they not continue to affect each other? Specific alternatives to Schleicher's Stammbaum do not matter here, only that he triggered brisk debate. The underlying issue mattered to every linguist concerned with historical development of languages, not just Indo-Europeanists.[13]

As his tree suggests, Schleicher viewed language as a natural organism; and this belief led him to define linguistics as a natural science, sharply distinct from philology. To think of the 'birth, life, and death' of languages in organic terms was hardly new. Bopp himself wrote in 1827 that "languages are to be looked upon as organic natural bodies, which form according to definite laws; carrying within themselves an inner life-principle, they develop and bye and bye perish. . . ." But "are to be looked upon as" is not quite the same as saying, as Schleicher did, "Languages *are* natural organisms." (It was Schleicher who imported 'morphology' from biology to label study of the structure of words.) Independent of the will of their speakers, languages grow, evolve, and die according to fixed laws, like a cabbage or a rabbit.* Therefore, linguistics is a natural science, "part of the natural history of human beings," applying methods like those of other natural sciences. Therefore, it is not philology. Philology, he told readers, treats texts handed down from earlier times, interprets these texts, tries thereby to comprehend the culture that produced them. Linguistics, in contrast, investigates a law-bound natural process outside of human control, not a human culture. Such claims made other linguists sit up. Both Müller and Whitney would weigh in.[14]

Schleicher's contention that fixed laws governed the slow march of language change, just as they ruled the rest of natural history, had another key implication. Fixed laws do not allow for variation. They can generate very complex outcomes, as different laws interact in different natural conditions. Schleicher the gardener knew that not every bean plant of a given type grew to the same height, produced the same number of pods, yielded beans of exactly the same color. But each underlying, law-determined subprocess must always go on with unvarying regularity. Grimm did not use the word *law* to describe the regular sound shifts he described, for the pattern had exceptions. Fixed law allowed none. In Schleicher's world, as a language family evolved, sound shifts must always occur in the same sequence, for a natural law governed them. In geology, this principle of slow but steady, law-governed transformation was called uniformitarianism. Erosion by wind and water, and other such natural operations, the same today as millions years ago, shape and reshape the face of the earth. The great champion of geological uniformitarianism in Schleicher's era was the Scot Charles Lyell. Schleicher invoked him as a model. Schleicher brought uniformitarianism to linguistics.[15]

But Schleicher's main claim to fame after 1861 lay apart from his scientism or even his Stammbaum; it was instead his partial reconstruction of the Indo-European protolanguage, not a single word of which had existed for thousands of years.† In his *Compendium* he laid out in detail the phonology (including sound laws) and morphology of several ancient written Indo-European

---

* Not long after *Origin of Species* appeared, Schleicher published a short book arguing that natural selection applied to languages as well as to biological organisms. Readers of *Origin of Species* will recall that Darwin invoked comparative philology as a parallel to lend plausibility to his theory. The relations between philology and biological evolution remained thick through the rest of the century. There is no space here to go into this story, but see Alter 1999.

† Readers curious about the culture and whereabouts of the people who spoke Proto-Indo-European may consult the accessible account in Anthony 2007.

languages (including Sanskrit, Avestan, Greek, Latin, Old Irish) *and* of the *unwritten* mother of them all. In an appendix he even provided paradigms of declensions and conjugations for all the languages treated, starting with the "Indogermanische Ursprache" (Indo-Germanic primeval tongue: Proto-Indo-European). He re-created the "primeval tongue" by working backward from attested forms in daughter languages. Schleicher doggedly compared known forms in different Indo-European tongues, in various stages of development. He thus inferred words, sounds, and grammatical forms that likely existed in the mother language. He even composed a little fable in it, "Avis akvasas ka" (The Sheep and the Horses). Only Schleicher's uniformitarian axiom of unvarying linguistic laws allowed him to make such bold leaps. Some linguists contested in principle his achievement in bringing Proto-Indo-European back from the dead, others in detail. But it lent prestige to his claim for linguistics as natural science.[16]

MÜLLER'S SCIENCE OF LANGUAGE

Against this background, Max Müller entered the fray over the status of linguistic laws. Smarting from his defeat for the Boden chair, Müller appeared at the Royal Institution in London in April and May 1861 to deliver lectures on 'the science of language.' They drew an immense crowd from London's intelligentsia—John Stuart Mill, Arthur Stanley, the Duke of Argyll, many more—and, when published a couple months later, a large readership. Reviewers cheered. The published *Lectures* won for Müller a second Prix Volney. The book went through three editions in the first year. Letters poured in from Germany as well as England. The Royal Institution asked for a second series, delivered in 1863, published in 1864. Both volumes of *Lectures on the Science of Language* quickly appeared in French, German, Russian, Italian, Swedish, and Dutch. Müller sporadically published articles on linguistics—sometimes embroiled himself in controversy—into the final decade of his life.[17]

What, broadly, did he have to say? At the heart of his linguistic theory lay his conviction of the unity of language and thought: no words without thought, no thought without words. This principle was so integral to German Romantic language theory that it is futile to guess where Müller got it—Herder? Humboldt? Schlegel? Schelling? All, and others? It followed, in Müller's eyes, that language sharply and utterly divided human beings from 'lower' animals: the "Rubicon" that "no brute will dare to cross." Heaven had given human beings the capacity for abstraction—which no beast had, however clever—and language "is the outward sign and realisation of that inward faculty." Darwin's *Origin of Species* had appeared less than two years before Müller stood before the crowd at the Royal Institution. In 1871 Darwin speculated in his *Descent of Man* that language possibly arose from imitating natural sounds (a notion Müller had already derided in 1861 as the "bow-wow" theory)—and that brutes might have crossed the Rubicon. Müller went on the offensive. The dispute got nasty, with Darwin's son George serving as surrogate for his non-combatant father. (Müller appears not to have grasped well Darwin's theory of evolution, which furthered misunderstanding.) Whitney—already on Müller's enemies list for deriding some of his linguistic theories—weighed in on Darwin's side, with the result that ill-feeling turned into bad blood that lasted as long as both of them lived. Indeed, longer: Mrs. Max Müller continued to assail Whitney after he and her husband had both died.[18]

If the bow-wow theory was wrong, how did Müller think language originated? In answering this question, another of his distinctive linguistic ideas is essential. Müller asserted that the elementary particles of language were "roots" (also called "radicals")—monosyllabic words that "cannot be reduced to a simpler or more original form." They came in two varieties, "predicative" and "demonstrative" (i.e., verbal and substantive). The truly primitive predicative roots, each expressing a broad category of action, consisted of either a single vowel or a vowel and a consonant. From modifications of a small number of such primary roots—plus "a small class of independent radicals," with meanings such as 'this' or 'there', 'he' or 'she'—language was built up. "Language is a thrifty housewife," said Müller. From a scanty supply of roots "she might form a dictionary sufficient to supply the wants, however extravagant, of her husband—the human mind." These roots were at once primary—irreducible—and yet very wide in meaning—abstract. Müller believed that this theory of origin from a few utterances of highly general import dissolved the paradox of Romantic language theory: how language and thinking could grow up together, neither preceding the other. Very simple utterances were yet so abstract as to exercise the cognitive capacities of the human mind. And since these primary roots were abstractions, they could not have arisen in mere animal sense impressions. No brute could cross that Rubicon.[19]

Müller's explanation also laid a theoretical foundation for the long-cherished notion that the development of the human mind could be traced through the history of language. "Childern [sic]," he wrote, "do not recollect before they begin to speak, nor have nations any historical recollections before their own language has been formed." So the early history of language—and of the human mind—belongs to a seemingly vanished past—yet not really lost. Sciences such as geology teach us "that by a careful investigation of given historical facts and by generalising these facts as far as we safely can, it is possible to go back to periods previous to the beginning of history."[20]

Müller thought of language organically, as growing and dying, much as Schleicher did—and with a similar uniformitarian principle. The "very keystone of Comparative Grammar" is "that language follows none but her own laws, & that consequently," there "can be nothing irregular in language." Language is a "part of nature" and, as such, "is regulated by its own invariable laws, which, even when we are not able fully to understand them, must yet be admitted to exist." Unsurprisingly, then, Müller began his lectures on the science of language by insisting that it belongs to the physical sciences. And, like Schleicher, he distinguished philology from comparative philology. Drawing on a well-known distinction made by William Whewell between physical and historical sciences, Müller assigned philology—he meant textual philology—to the historical sciences, which dealt with the results of what Müller called "human art." Comparative philology belonged to the physical sciences, concerned with the works of God. Philology began explicitly to splinter. But was not comparative philology patently historical? Müller believed "a confusion of terms" clouded the issue. "There is a difference between historical development and natural growth." Every "production of man" has "a history" properly speaking, whereas "language or any other production of nature, admits only of growth. The laws of growth are invariable & can be deduced by repeated observations. The laws of history are not invariable and it is impossible to deduce them by observation ever so minute." Müller added to the confusion he deprecated by constantly using "historical" to describe the methods of comparative philology. But historical change *in languages*, Müller consistently claimed, "is not in the power of man either to produce or prevent."[21]

It was, however, in the power of man to investigate. And "no other branch of nature" was "so intimately connected with the history of man, as speech." It matters for the comparative philologist whether the language he is studying belonged to a literate or illiterate people, a dominant or subordinate nation. It matters which other languages it interacted with. But the historical nature of Müller's science of language went much deeper than the need to know the contexts within which languages developed. Classifying languages by their historical relationship to each other was far "safer" than the synchronic, purely structural method of Humboldt. More profoundly, languages shape human history and culture. The "artificial structure of the agglutinative languages," such as Turkish, supposedly prevented Turks from writing "great works of art in literature." In Turkish "all expressive elements are carefully glued one to the other." The "human mind" can hardly "adapt itself so much to this complicated machinery" as to use it with enough fluency to produce an *Iliad* or a *Hamlet*. In contrast, the "more highly developed" Sanskrit, Greek, Latin, or German "seems almost to think for man & to carry him on to the loftiest thoughts & speculations." The clumsier languages of those unlucky souls who did not speak an Indo-European tongue "act as an impediment to the free action of thought." This accounted for "Chinese character & nationality"—enough said, to an Oxford audience. In Müller's schema, man does not shape language, but "language to a great extent models the reasoning & imaginative faculties of man." And in a kind of linguistic archaeology the comparative philologist could dig down through the strata of a language's (or language family's) development to excavate fossil words that would reveal *how* language had once shaped "the reasoning & imaginative faculties of man." "Comparative Philology is the means, the Science of Language is the end." And its "higher purpose" is "to discover the secrets of thought in the labyrinth of language, after it has been lighted up by the torch of Comparative Philology."[22]

Three things, in sum, stand out about Max Müller's linguistics. First is its virtual identity with comparative philology in range and method, though not in ultimate aim. Second is its thoroughly diachronic character, its irreducibly historical approach (even if sometimes Müller wanted to say "growth" instead of "history"). Third is its main use and ultimate aim—as a spade to excavate the history of the human mind. And for Müller, the most fascinating facet of human thought was its religious dimension: no wonder that after 1870 he devoted most of his considerable energy to the *comparative* study of religions.

WHITNEY'S SCIENCE OF LANGUAGE

Whitney's linguistic studies, in contrast, had a more complex (and ultimately more fruitful) relation to comparative philology and to history, none at all to religion. Unlike Müller, who began lecturing on comparative philology in 1851, Whitney until the end of the 1850s confined his scholarship to sober, stubbornly empirical Indological research. He scorned the sort of speculative leaps and Romantic fervor that kept bubbling up in Müller.

A learned Indological dispute first drew him into print on linguistic theory and soured him on Max Müller. The elderly French physicist Jean-Baptiste Biot had long interested himself in the history of ancient astronomy—Egypt, China, India. In 1860, in a lengthy review of a translation of a Hindu astronomical text first published in the *Journal of the American Oriental Society*, Biot set off a ruckus over the lunar zodiac. (He died in the thick of it.) Had Chinese or Indian astronomers invented it? The astronomical issues do not matter here. The debate really came down to textual interpretation: how to understand celestial allusions in the Vedas. Whitney's old teacher Albrecht Weber disagreed with Biot. Max Müller stepped in with a theory melding Biot's and Weber's positions. His interpretation rested on his peculiar notion—reflecting post-Kantian idealism rather than empirical research—that a word's abstract meaning appeared earlier than its concrete one. Müller also, in Whitney's opinion, dished out "abominably mean treatment" to his friend Weber. In 1863 Whitney replied to all parties in a ninety-four-page article in his *Journal of the American Oriental Society*. He characteristically professed skepticism: the evidence did not clearly support any resolution of the problem. Then he turned to Max Müller. He did not quite denounce Müller for deciding "important historical questions" on the basis of pro-Aryan prejudice instead of factual investigation, but he came as close as minimal politeness allowed. Politesse did not stop him from calling Müller's idealist etymological theory "strange and hardly credible." Whitney—the agnostic empiricist—must also have had in mind the theist Müller's idealist, speculative performance in his

Lectures on the Science of Language two years earlier. In 1858 and 1859 Whitney had already delivered a couple of talks on general linguistics. The clash with Müller foreshadowed heavier involvement.[23]

In March of 1864 Whitney got a chance to respond directly to Müller's science of language. The Smithsonian Institution invited him to deliver in Washington a series of lectures on "The Principles of Linguistic Science." The next winter he expanded these in a lecture series in Boston. Revised, the Boston lectures appeared in 1867 as *Language and the Study of Language*.[24]

As post-Kantian idealism lay in the background of Müller's thinking, so Whitney had his own, distinctly un-Romantic philosophical perspective, with a linguistic outcome directly counter to his foe's. Whitney came to intellectual maturity in an America where Enlightenment-style speculative language theory, philosophically and theologically inflected, still dominated. He borrowed from Scottish Common Sense philosophers—especially Thomas Reid and Dugald Stewart—the conviction that language is *arbitrary* and *conventional*. Words have no 'natural significancy,' to be excavated from their long-ago origins, as both Müller and Whitney's late colleague Josiah Gibbs believed. Rather, the fact that an American says "chicken" and a Frenchwoman "poulet" to refer to the same fowl is purely arbitrary: "gibbelblatt" and "cronk" would work just as well. That *all* Americans say "chicken" and *all* French speakers say "poulet" is a matter of convention, not of deep hidden meaning. So far, nothing original. But Whitney extended the notion of convention—and took a slap at Müller—with a principle that Stephen Alter, Whitney's biographer, nicely labeled "semantic presentism." All words get their meanings from past usages, Whitney gladly conceded; and comparative philologists must unpack word histories to understand how languages developed. Yet knowing a word's history in no way affects how a person uses it. We simply use words with the same conventional meanings as everyone we talk with—or read—uses them *today*. To fathom a language *as it is used now*, no one needed to follow Max Müller into the labyrinth of Sanskrit roots. That diachronic approach distracted from accurate analysis of actual linguistic usage. For the latter purpose, a synchronic method sufficed. For a Sanskritist like Whitney, throwing down this gauntlet was unexpected.[25]

With this striking aperçu in *Language and the Study of Language* Whitney did *not* take a giant step away from comparative philology, but he did distance himself from both Müller and Schleicher on its nature. Whitney devoted the core of the book to Indo-European and other language families, and he insisted on history as the proper method for studying language. His discussions of phonetic change and dialects were thoroughly diachronic. He lumped together all such language study as 'linguistic science,' a variant of Müller's 'science of language.' He even distinguished, like Müller, between philology—which investigates "thought and knowledge as deposited in literary records"—and linguistic science—which "deals with language as the instrument of thought, its means of expression, not its record." But then he drew a sharp line. Language is "an organism" only in "trope and metaphor." In blunt fact it exists solely "in the minds and mouths of those who use it." Language "is in their power, subject to their will"; it has no "life and growth independent of its speakers." True, individuals cannot alter a language by their own will, but that is not because fixed natural laws govern language. It is because all speakers of a language comprise "a democracy." One person may coin a word, but "general suffrage" must ratify it. And just as each individual of a biological species varies somewhat from "the specific type," so does individual speech vary from the average of the language. As in Darwin's natural selection, such divergences can spark evolution. But language is not actually an organism; it is an institution—"the work of those whose wants it subserves." Like other complex institutions, it will change over time without "conscious intent." So, pace Muller and Schleicher, linguistics is not a physical science but "a historical or moral science." "It is a branch of the history of the human race and of human institutions," not of the 'natural history of man,' as Schleicher had it. Americans in 1867 still used *science* as Germans today use *Wissenschaft*—though Whitney warned of physical scientists trying to capture the word. For the moment, Whitney's formulation gave linguistics all the prestige it needed.[26]

His voluminous writings ranged far from the general linguistics of *Language and the Study of Language*, and they give a fuller idea than Müller's publications of the scope of linguistics as it became a university-based discipline in the English-speaking world. There was a second general treatise, *The Life and Growth of Language* (1875). Whitney's Sanskrit and Indological studies continued, adding much to the bulk of the *Journal of the American Oriental Society* during his long editorship. His monumental Sanskrit grammar departed from traditional dependence on the abstract ancient Indian grammarians, most notably Pāṇini; the ever empirical Whitney instead built up a descriptive grammar from actual usage in Sanskrit literature. (He was motivated by relative neglect of syntax in Hindu grammar and by its lack of correlation with standard categories in Western grammatical analysis.[27]) He published on phonology, on dialect formation, on the origin of language, on the relation of comparative philology to ethnology, on mixture of languages, and more. He compiled a German grammar and a German-English dictionary. He wrote on English usage and English grammar—more descriptive, less prescriptive in both areas than predecessors. (He nonetheless looks like a prig to his intellectual grandchildren today.) He edited the *Century Dictionary* (1889–91), the best grounded, most thorough, most scholarly American dictionary of English up to that time. In 1892, two years before he died, he fired a last salvo across the Atlantic: *Max Müller and the Science of Language: A Criticism*. The subtitle was redundant.

But his "semantic presentism" best places Whitney in his evolving discipline. He always insisted that the 'linguistic scientist' could only explain language diachronically, by its history. An almost Darwinian kind of feedback drives change over time in language, as the community of speakers unconsciously selects which mutations will survive. Yet, viewed synchronically, in the present, language is to all appearances arbitrary; it simply is what it is, and it works perfectly well without knowledge of its history. His mode of historical explanation was uniformitarian, like Schleicher's; but Schleicher did not explain Whitney. The latter's youthful ardor for natural history and participation in his brother Josiah's early geological fieldwork gave him in effect a training in that science. His view of language mirrored contemporary uniformitarian geology. To understand *why* the earth is as it is, you needed to uncover the slow workings of geological change over time. But the earth is as it is, and you do not need to know its geological history to farm it, mine it, sail its seas, or climb Mount Whitney.[28]

Without his clearly intending it, the diachronic and synchronic in Whitney's linguistics became linked—at least in others' eyes. Whitney developed an original theory of dialect formation, based on how phonetic changes spread from their place of origin. But in its own phonetic history, every language stood alone. The linguist "cannot tell why sounds are found in the alphabet of one tongue which are unutterable by the speakers of another." More broadly, Whitney's writings on general linguistics, most notably *Language and the Study of Language*, put forward theoretical statements more compact, more generic, and more sophisticated than in predecessors like Bopp and Müller. Müller in effect regarded comparative philology and 'the science of language' as two sides of the same coin. Whitney thought of 'linguistic science' as a theoretical field, drawing on comparative philology but distinct from it. Thus he distilled 'timeless' generalizations from the many decades of research by historically oriented scholars like himself. As Ferdinand de Saussure put it in 1894, Whitney's works, starting with *Language and the Study of Language*, "deduce from the results of comparative grammar a higher and general view of language." As a result, linguistic elements produced by history became readily available components in research that ignored their history.[29]

This is more or less what happened to linguistics in the twentieth century, as it gradually turned away from comparative historical work toward investigating linguistic structure synchronically. Certainly historical research continued, especially on Indo-European languages, and it continues today; but it no longer provided the discipline's center of gravity. The figure who usually stands out in this revolution is Saussure. His posthumously published *Cours de linguistique générale* (*Course in General Linguistics*, 1916) treated language as a formal system of arbitrary elements. It proved enormously influential, giving birth to what came to be known as structural linguistics—and to 'structuralism' in other fields, including anthropology and literature. A young Saussure met Whitney in Berlin in 1879. More to the point, he met Whitney's ideas, especially in *The Life and Growth of Language*. Whitney's extremely 'structuralist' teaching in parts of that book set Saussure off on his own original course. And his course moved linguistics far from Whitney's understanding of the discipline. The Americans prominent in the shift to a synchronic structuralist or 'descriptive' linguistics—Franz Boas (German-born), Leonard Bloomfield, and Edward Sapir—might admire Whitney, might adopt bits and pieces of his thinking (especially the sociological idea of language as an institution). But they rejected his fundamentally historical science.[30]

WHITHER THE DISCIPLINE

Focusing closely on two men has given a fine-grained view of key issues in linguistics as it developed into a university-based discipline. Max Müller's genuinely humanistic vision of 'the science of language'—effectively defined, if you will, as the larger human meaning of comparative historical philology—did not lead to an enriched philology. It led instead out of the discipline of linguistics and into a new discipline of comparative religion, examined in chapter 13. William Dwight Whitney's linguistics was more 'professional,' more technically proficient, more theoretically sophisticated, and more inward-looking. It was also, ironically, more in tune with contemporary German work than the German-raised Müller's old-fashioned Romantic version of the field. Perhaps even more ironically, it helped to inspire and make possible abandonment of the historical method that both Müller and Whitney thought essential.

Zeroing in on Müller and Whitney might leave the impression that these two adequately 'represented' the discipline of linguistics; they did not. A hasty glance at some other researchers between 1850 and 1900 gives a fairer picture of work in a diverse discipline—though only a list of names and topics. It starts with Americans. The Swedish-born, German-educated Maximilian Schele De Vere (1820–98) and the deep-rooted New Englander Benjamin Dwight (1816–89)—a relative of Whitney—both produced surveys of comparative philology in the 1850s; neither can be said to have contributed much to it. In 1872 Schele De Vere published a study of Americanisms (as John Pickering had done in his first venture into philology in 1816.) George Perkins Marsh (1801–82)—politician, diplomat, pioneering conservationist and ecologist—was also a philologist. In 1838 he compiled and translated Rask's writings into *A Compendious Grammar of the Old Northern or Icelandic Language*; his *Lectures on the English Language* (1859) provided a more original history of English in the spirit of comparative philology. Daniel Brinton (1837–99) and Franz Boas (1858–1942) continued the tradition of Amerindian linguistics, though Boas became better known as anthropologist than linguist. (Through Brinton passed down Humboldt's legacy, and Boas's student Edward Sapir seized on Humboldt's idea that languages shape their speakers' worldviews. Sapir's student Benjamin Lee Whorf in turn influentially argued that linguistic differences produce differences in cognition, the theory of 'linguistic relativity.' But this goes deep into the twentieth century.) Maurice Bloomfield (1855–1928) studied Sanskrit with Whitney before becoming professor at Johns Hopkins

University; although he published in comparative linguistics, he was Whitney's true successor in Vedic scholarship. Of these linguists, all but Dwight, Marsh, and Whorf became professors; Whorf was on that track when cancer cut him down young.[31]

The United Kingdom housed a similarly varied batch of linguists. Charles Darwin's favorite cousin, Hensleigh Wedgwood (1803–91), helped to found the Philological Society in 1842; his *Dictionary of English Etymology* (1857) featured superb research hampered by feeble grasp of comparative philology. Fitzedward Hall (1825–1901), an American expatriate (Harvard 1846), taught Sanskrit in India before settling in as professor at King's College London. He edited a number of Sanskrit texts (and wrote on Indian philosophy), then turned in later years to severe crankiness and English philology. This latter area—specifically English etymology—was the métier of Richard Trench (1807–86) and James Murray (1837–1915). The former, an Anglican cleric (ultimately Archbishop of Dublin), became best known for an odd and immensely popular amalgam of moral exhortation and etymological research titled *On the Study of Words* (1851; reprinted many times on both sides of the Atlantic). Trench subsequently published more conventional works advancing etymological scholarship and, as an influential member of the Philological Society, pushed hard for a new English dictionary "on historical principles." Murray—after leaving school at fourteen a sometime bank clerk, an off-and-on schoolmaster, and all the while knee-deep in extracurricular philological and literary research—became the editor of this new dictionary, now called the *Oxford English Dictionary*. A. H. Sayce (1845–1933) pioneered study of Assyrian in England. He then turned to comparative philology, with large contributions in semantics. Then he flitted off to Hebrew linguistics and early history of Israel, before ending his career as a Middle Eastern archaeologist. Henry Sweet (1845–1912) concentrated his powers in several works in phonology (though dabbling in grammar, the history of English, and general linguistics). His *Handbook of Phonetics* (1877) proved foundational to twentieth-century development of that field. Examples could be multiplied, but this gives a fair sample of linguists in the United Kingdom. A little less apt to inhabit a university than the Americans, they found a center of gravity in the Philological Society.[32]

It is clear that a discipline focused on multisided study of language and languages thrived in the later nineteenth-century English-speaking world; it is not so clear how this discipline stood in relation to the philologically grounded humanistic erudition from which it emerged. Max Müller insisted that 'the science of language' belonged among the natural sciences, not the humanities. Whitney may have been right to suspect that Müller and others who shared his opinion wanted to piggyback on the rising prestige of natural science. But search for unvarying 'laws' governing linguistic change stood far from the contextualizing, interpretative method of philology. When linguistics shifted from a historical study to a predominantly synchronic approach, it moved even further from the philological tradition. Structuralist linguistics—treating language as a formal system rather than comparing actual languages—dropped even the comparative method central to philology since antiquity. The arcane, highly technical jargon that such linguists began to write in the twentieth century (and still do)—nearly impenetrable to outsiders—hardly reminds one of humanistic scholarship. At the same time, comparative, historical Indo-European linguistics did not vanish; nor did similar research on other language families. And the etymological, historical lexicography that produced the *Oxford English Dictionary* looks familiar to anyone acquainted with the history of philology. For that matter, so does Sayce's career, including its ending in archaeology—a latter-day reincarnation of antiquarianism.

Perhaps the most accurate assessment is that, when the discipline of linguistics took its modern form around 1900, it stood betwixt and between. Parts of it identifiably linked to the humanistic philological tradition. Other parts left that tradition far behind.

10

"PAINSTAKING RESEARCH QUITE EQUAL TO MATHEMATICAL PHYSICS"

LITERATURE, 1860–1920

The discipline of 'literature' did not quite exist in the English-speaking world in 1860.[1] The practices that would comprise it—literary history, textual editing, evaluative criticism—had by then gained recognition as at least episodically scholarly endeavors. But a single, discrete field of literature absorbing all these subfields had not. After 1860, within the matrix of the modern university, the pieces gelled into the discipline we know today.

As already observed, studies of literary works developed as erudite discourses during the nineteenth century from the confluence of two ancient, historically related fields of knowledge: philology and rhetoric. Neither had earlier treated the subject 'literature' in the modern sense, although many texts that rhetoricians and philologists *did* study eventually joined the canon of the new discipline. Within the English-speaking world, literary studies of works written in English predominated at first. As a rule (though not always), Anglophone scholars of other modern literatures followed this lead, as Romance languages and German, then Slavic languages and other tongues found homes in new or newly reformed universities. Because of this sequence of events, this chapter will concern mostly study of literature in English.

The diversity of its philological and rhetorical sources showed in the new discipline. Philological ingredients came from both textual philology and comparative grammar. Textual philology bestowed the elements of scholarly editing and literary history, as well as of a historically sensitive criticism on very roughly the model of *Altertumswissenschaft*. Comparative grammar produced a parallel study of the English language and its historical evolution— topics as much a part of the new field in its formative years as Shakespeare and Browning. Rhetoric contributed to literary study much of its critical vocabulary as well as the germ of the idea of 'criticism' in the modern literary sense (as distinct from its original meaning, learned emendation of texts).

Like other humanities, literature declared and fortified its disciplinary status by generating a panoply of professional institutions specific to the discipline. And, as in most humanities, professionalization moved faster in the United States than in the United Kingdom. 'From amateur to professional,' if not exact, points in the right direction. More precisely, during the first half of the century, various literary studies existed as dispersed enthusiasms that did not cohere as a single field, were only erratically erudite, and rarely figured in university curricula. After midcentury—even though types of literary study remained as diverse as ever—these manifold practices congealed into a single, reliably learned discipline. Research-oriented universities certified this outcome by setting up English chairs, departments, faculties, or the equivalent.

LITERATURE IN HIGHER EDUCATION

The clearest symptom of emergent 'disciplinarity' was the spread of literature in colleges and universities. The subject came to be seen as sufficiently 'academic' and 'scholarly' to merit a place in curricula. The appointments of George Ticknor at Harvard in 1819 and Thomas Dale at University College London in 1828, mentioned earlier, provided the earliest instances of literature taught as literature, rather than as aid to composition. But such cases remained rare until after midcentury. Then numbers swelled. In 1855 Francis March began teaching English literature at Lafayette College in Pennsylvania. In 1858 Andrew Dickson White and James Russell Lowell lectured on it at the University of Michigan and Harvard University, respectively.[2]

English literature then spread through American colleges like a contagious fever. By 1866 so out-of-the-way a place as Baylor University in the village of Independence, Texas, began teaching it—in conjunction with rhetoric and Old English. By 1870 over sixty colleges had literature courses, commonly lectures to seniors. In that year even the bastion of Greco-Latin conservatism, Yale, started offering English literature, though at first quarantining it in the déclassé Sheffield Scientific School. By the 1880s literature was everywhere in America. Any new institution—no matter how remote, no matter how feeble—offered it instinctively. Even at the Illinois Industrial University, where the lamp of liberal learning flickered feebly indeed, grammar gave way to literature in the early 1880s. By 1900, English literature had displaced Latin and Greek at the heart of the humanities even in Yale College.[3]

The same thing happened in the United Kingdom. Teaching in the University of London at first veered erratically from literature to rhetoric, depending on the professor. But Henry Morley, who began teaching English at King's College in 1857, then switched to University College in 1865, gave a lasting shove toward literature. In 1861 the Inglis Commission made English literature (though not professors of it) compulsory in Scottish universities. At Edinburgh, William Aytoun, Hugh Blair's latest successor as professor of rhetoric, was by 1864 devoting a large chunk of his lectures to a "complete review of British literature." The English section of the MA examination in that year comprised two questions in rhetoric, two in language, and eight in literature. David Masson, who followed Aytoun at Edinburgh in 1865, further downgraded rhetorical teaching and instituted a parallel course devoted entirely to the history of English literature (defined as literature *in* English, with lavish attention to Scottish writers). The provincial 'redbrick' universities that developed in England from the mid-1870s incorporated courses in English literature early in their histories.[4]

Predictably, English crept in more sluggishly in Oxford and Cambridge, where it vied against the entrenched prestige of Greek and Latin. In 1873 Oxford included English literature in requirements for a pass (i.e., not an honors) degree. Twenty more years went by before the university conceded an honors degree in English. Even then detractors thought the subject too soft: "a miserably inadequate training, however well taught"—according to the professor of modern literature (!) at University College Liverpool. In 1904 Oxford got its first professor devoted to English literature, none other than the selfsame Liverpool man, Walter Raleigh. He really set the English School in motion. In 1911 the Board of English Studies shrewdly commissioned a lecture series on echoes of Greek and Roman classics in English literature, delivered mostly by classicists, sprinkling on English some secondhand dignity. Cambridge hemmed, hawed, and grudgingly set up in 1878 a board to supervise, as the faculty senate put it, "the study of modern and medieval *languages* in the University." A degree in modern languages—including English—became possible in 1886, with some attention to literature along with the purely linguistic studies. Is it any wonder that early methods of English teaching there exactly paralleled classical philology of the older verbal sort, save for a larger dose of phonology? Students almost universally ignored the option. Finally, in 1917, with the winds of war shaking old habits, Cambridge established an English tripos, and literature came into its own in the university.[5]

ENGLISH LANGUAGE, ENGLISH LITERATURE

So something called English literature existed as an academic discipline, eventually even at Cambridge; but what was it? As perhaps expected of a discipline descended from philology and rhetoric, pioneers of English literature rarely separated study of literature from study of language. Take William Spalding, professor of rhetoric first at Edinburgh, then at St. Andrews. He had serious pretensions to scholarship. In 1833 he had published a monograph arguing for Shakespeare's joint authorship (with John Fletcher) of *The Two Noble Kinsmen*. Over forty years later F. J. Furnivall, competent to judge, thought it still "one of the ablest (if not the ablest) and most stimulating pieces of Shakspere criticism I ever read."* The book mattered enough to be reissued in 1876 by the New Shakspere Society. Spalding took the two-pronged approach to his problem inherited from classical and biblical philologists. He first examined historical evidence surrounding the text for clues to its authorship, then—"the decisive test"—analyzed the language of the text itself to uncover distinctive traits of Shakespeare's style.[6]

This conviction that language mattered crucially to literary studies animated Spalding's *History of English Literature* (1853). This book did not aspire to scholarship, only to support elementary teaching; and the text probably incubated in Spalding's lectures to the teenagers at Edinburgh and St. Andrews. But it illustrates his idea of literature as an academic field, and the manual's many editions shows his thinking not eccentric. (In the University of Alabama's only stab at teaching English literature before the Civil War, the text assigned was Spalding's.) "Systematic study of English Literature" explained "some of the leading facts in the Intellectual History of our Nation." Thus 'literature' included Occam's philosophy as well as Chaucer's poetry, John Knox's history of the Scottish Reformation along with Shakespeare's plays, Jonathan Edwards's theology and Gibbon's history, Macaulay's essays plus Walter Scott's novels—though Spalding said a lot more about poets than philosophers, dramatists than divines. The book had three parts: a brisk survey of Old English and medieval writings; a longer narrative of English literature since 1500 (accompanied with "Illustrative Extracts" from major writers); and, sandwiched between, "a brief Summary of the Early History of the English Language" that "fills about one-seventh of the volume." Spalding conceded that this last section "must have, through the nature of the matter, a less popular and amusing aspect than the other Parts." But, he insisted, the "story which this part tells, should be familiar to every one who would understand, thoroughly, the History of English Literature."[7]

From philology, scholars like Spalding inherited a tight link connecting a language and its literature, and this premise shaped English in its formative decades as a discipline. When the "scientific" journal *Modern Language Notes* started at Johns Hopkins University in 1886, it "translated into the study of modern languages" the "aspirations of classical philology," according to Richard Macksey. (August Boeckh presided as its tutelary spirit.) These "aspirations" showed in diversity of what counted as 'literary' topics at Johns Hopkins. The Teutonic Seminary in 1890 featured a paper on the Alemannic dialect, relating it to the region's rugged geography, as well as one on echoes in later German literature of the Battle of the Teutoburg Forest (where, in 9 CE, Germanic tribes wiped out a Roman army). The English Seminary indulged even greater promiscuity. Subjects ranged from recent poetry through investigations of the history of the language (diphthong shifts, for instance). Perhaps

---

* "Shakspere" was a common Victorian spelling.

Old English and medieval literature won pride of place, but no topic or method dominated. Morgan Callaway Jr. got his PhD in English at Johns Hopkins in 1889. He went on to a long, successful career at the University of Texas. (The distinguished Harvard literary scholar Hyder Rollins was his student.) Callaway published mostly on Old English syntax, taught mostly Shakespeare. Even in analyzing literature, he applied a philological method, seeking "analogues" for a passage under study in other writings known to the author. Such comparisons aimed both to fix a historical genealogy for the work in question and to clarify its meaning. Endorsing Callaway to head Texas's English department in 1900, Yale's Albert Cook admitted some might want a man with a "larger scope" to run a literature department. They would be wrong: "this view, it seems to me, could only arise from a misconception of the term 'Philology'— such a view as would prevent men like Professor Gildersleeve [the Johns Hopkins classicist] from being considered professors of literature."[8]

Like Callaway, English professors on both sides of the Atlantic made students study the history of the language as essential to experiencing literature written in it. "The chief use of the study of English before Chaucer," wrote Lafayette College's Francis March, is "better understanding and mastery of English in Chaucer, and since Chaucer." Benjamin Meek's English course at the University of Alabama in 1872 covered almost nothing *but* the language and the history that shaped it. He was extreme. David Masson at Edinburgh devoted four lectures to the evolution of the language before surveying literature in modern (post-Anglo-Saxon) English. By 1877 thirty-one American colleges taught Old English; by 1888 forty-four also offered courses in subjects like "English philology" and "history of the English Language." At Princeton, freshmen read Thomas R. Lounsbury's *History of the English Language*, and sophomores studied Francis March's *Origin and History of the English Language*. Henry Morley began his university teaching career with an evening course at King's College London in 1857 on "The Origin and Structure of the English Language, illustrated by our literature from the earliest times to the invention of printing." He ended his professorial life presiding at University College over three-part examination requirements in English for a pass degree: "History, structure, and development of the English language," "Anglo-Saxon Grammar and Translation," and a set of special subjects including authors like Shakespeare and Spenser but also Benjamin Thorpe's edition of the Anglo-Saxon Chronicle. In 1891 the Cambridge examinations in "Mod[ern]. & Med[ieva]¹. Languages" covered six subjects: "(1) Shakespeare; (2) 16th & 17th century writers; (3) Chaucer; (4) Middle English selections; (5) Anglo-Saxon verse; (6) Anglo-Saxon prose & Icelandic."[9]

This philological approach to literature through language did not impose a regime of grim grammatical nit-picking. Morley was an effervescent lecturer who drew crowds and wrote a series of books popularizing English literature. Yale's Thomas Lounsbury, a former teacher of Greek and Latin, penned the aforesaid *History of the English Language* (1879), *English Spelling and Spelling*

Reform (1909), and a history of the *text* of Shakespeare (1906). The list at first glance almost caricatures dry-as-dust philology. But his history of English was remarkably readable; and he also produced (among other works) *Shakespeare as a Dramatic Artist* (1901), *Shakespeare and Voltaire* (1902), biographies of James Fenimore Cooper (1882) and Alfred, Lord Tennyson (posthumously published 1915), a narrative of Robert Browning's early literary career (1911), and *The Yale Book of American Verse* (1912). A competent coeval called Lounsbury's deeply learned, three-volume study of Chaucer (1891) "the most important contribution yet made by an American scholar to the great unwritten history of English literature." Lounsbury may have been the first college teacher of English in the United States*—in 1870—to make students read literary works rather than merely *about* them.[10]

In that same year, he published in the *New Englander* magazine a plea for teaching English not via manuals or "elegant extracts" but through reading complete works by the "greatest authors." Forty years earlier C. C. Felton at Harvard had made the same appeal regarding Greek and Roman texts—where Lounsbury started teaching. The ideal literature teacher, Lounsbury explained, would put the student's mind "into such sympathy with the author he is reading, that he will appreciate him fully and therefore enjoy him,—appreciate him in his spirit, his style, his manner of presenting his thoughts, in everything, indeed, even to his weaknesses, which displays the essential characteristics of the man." Such "close and constant intimacy with the words and ideas of a great writer" would, Lounsbury believed, develop the immature student's own character. For the next twenty years, professors dropped into New Haven to observe Lounsbury's classes firsthand. His ambitions may sound fustily Victorian to jaundiced twenty-first-century ears, but they cannot be described as narrow linguistic study. Yet Lounsbury's philological conception of the discipline of literature mandated that freshmen first spend a year learning about the evolution of the English language, in preparation for beginning to appreciate, as sophomores, literary works written in it.[11]

And, like any philologist, Lounsbury insisted on putting works in historical context to elicit their meanings. Since "all books in English literature are more or less full of references and allusions to the political and military history of the times in which they made their appearance," students should look up and explain "all such references and allusions." Literary history itself, of the sort found in the manuals that Lounsbury demoted to ancillary status, supplied part of the needed context. Indeed, literature, he believed, could not be taught apart from history; and students must read literary works "in a chronological order." "A separate portion of the life of a nation is not wrenched out by itself and considered apart from what follows and what precedes, but is connected naturally with a past that has already been made the subject of investigation,

---

* We know far too little about early teaching of college English to say certainly who first did what when.

and with a future for the investigation of which it paves the way." Lounsbury warned against obsessing over "grammatical and philological details": "We study the language for the sake of the literature, not the literature for the sake of the language." Linguistic history and cultural contextualization became tools to reveal how literature expressed "the life of a nation."[12]

This last aim was widely shared. A very different type of literature teacher, Cornell's Hiram Corson, believed that the great "Masters of Song" (writers, not tenors) offered a wellspring of timeless spiritual regeneration for their readers. Yet even he found "the secret of their vitality and power" in each author's "imbibing and reflecting" the "spirit of his age and the state of society around him."[13] To fathom an author, one must understand his time and place; by understanding an author, in turn, one comprehends better his time and place. K. O. Müller agreed.

There echoes in this credo the Altertumswissenschaft that inspired the Johns Hopkins philologists who fifteen years after Lounsbury's manifesto started *Modern Language Notes*. "At its best," commented Richard Macksey on the journal's hundredth anniversary, "this first vision of language and critical method could aspire to a total view of civilization and a command of its major languages in their historical dimension. It was dedicated to a scrupulosity of attention, an honesty in assessing detail, an alert historical awareness, and a sense of obligation to a community of scholars." Lounsbury himself fretted less about grammar-grubbing sucking the life out of literary study than about "that widely-spread habit, born of newspaper and novel reading, of running over the words of a book" without paying close heed. The wide-ranging literary scholarship of a Lounsbury had hidden roots in Altertumswissenschaft.[14]

HISTORY AND LITERATURE

Thus it becomes clearer how these early literature professors saw language study—notably of Old English—as integral to the historically informed criticism that they yoked with it.* Hiram Corson insisted that a student could not appreciate Elizabethan literature ("the goodliest heritage of every educated Englishman and Anglo-American") without bringing to it "a respectable knowledge of the previous language and literature" from Alfred the Great onward. His textbook of early English accordingly began with the Old English Gospel of John and ended with selections from Chaucer and Gower. The history both of England and of its language informed historical analysis of literature. As James Morgan Hart, professor of modern languages and literature at the University of Cincinnati, put it in 1884, "the study of English literature

---

* Institutions, too, at first saw literature and history as naturally allied. The Universities of Michigan and Toronto, Queen's College Belfast, and King's College London all started by hiring a single professor to teach both history and literature.

means the study of the great movement of English life and feeling." Atypically, Hart did not want undergraduates to learn Old English, but only because he thought the Anglo-Saxon worldview too remote from later historical evolution of English thinking. (He did believe that college *teachers* of English literature must know Old English.)[15]

His idea, the textual philologist's idea, saturated literary studies: literature reflected its times; history in turn clarified literature. William Aytoun's 1864 Edinburgh lectures depicted British literature against British history. Moses Coit Tyler often gets called father of the academic study of American literature. His four volumes on the literature of colonial and revolutionary America are equally often said to have begotten American intellectual history. Tyler moved to Cornell in 1881 as, aptly, professor of "American History and Literature." There he helped to found the American Historical Association. Edward Dowden of Trinity College Dublin began his much lauded book on Shakespeare (1875) by analyzing the "Elizabethan atmosphere" shaping the Bard—even linking Shakespeare to his contemporaries Francis Bacon and Richard Hooker in their aversion to "ideality" and their "devotion" to "the vital, concrete, and ever-altering facts of human society." David Masson, teaching at Edinburgh about the same time, likewise believed literary works fathomable only if plunged into historical context. The opening fifteen percent of his lectures delivered nothing *but* history, mostly political and cultural; many of the following also dished up history and biography. Perhaps this came as no surprise from a man who wrote a six-volume biography of Milton "in Connexion with the History of His Own Time" (1858–60) and who ended his career as Historiographer Royal of Scotland. But twenty-five years later Stockton Axson at Princeton, no historiographer, lectured on Victorian poetry as "interpretative of the thought of the 19th cent[ury]." Axson's colleague George Harper taught Elizabethan drama against a thick background of history. Harvard's Barrett Wendell believed literature to be "of all the fine arts the most ineradicably national," growing from a shared history rooted in shared language (a principle analogous to Max Müller's axiom that ethnicity grows from a common tongue). Accordingly Wendell's *Literary History of America* (1900) started with history, not literature, and throughout drenched literature in political and social history.[16]

W. P. Ker, lecturing at University College London around the same time, judged relevant historical context differently. Ker focused on literature per se. He pretty much ignored political, social, and economic developments. At the same time, he interpreted literature historically in so far as he explained literary works in relation to earlier and later *writing*:

One is compelled to pay attention to the way in wh[ich]. one author or school of authors is related to another, to consider the revolutionary & reactionary changes of taste, the conflict of ideas, the decay & regeneration of literary power in successive periods of history. One is compelled to do this because one is compelled to make the history of literature intelligible . . . one is naturally led from the study of any great book to require all sorts of knowledge about other books, about the place of the one book in relation to the rest of the universe of letters.

He often invoked as context a *kind* of writing peculiar to a place and time. "There is a certain type of conceit that is mediæval, the comparatively simple sort. The sort taken from natural history, the comparison of the phoenix, the butterfly [he meant moth] seeking the flame—you get these conceits used over & over again by the Troubadours, & the Ital[ian]. poets." Ker remained 'philological' in two ways. First, he explained a piece of literature by relating it to its context. Although for him context consisted almost entirely of other pieces of literature, at times he took writings as showing some basic trait of the 'mind' of an age. Second, he moved back and forth from text to context, expecting each to cast light on the other. One must be, he said, "both telescopic and microscopic."[17]

Equally philological in tack, but with a different take on historical context, was Herbert Grierson. He followed Masson in the Edinburgh chair, and it is revealing to compare Masson's lectures in the early 1880s with Grierson's some forty years later. Grierson's students also got a big helping of general historical context, but usually intellectual and cultural history immediately germane to literature, rather than the mishmash of political and cultural narrative that Masson ladled out. Literary study remained deeply historical, but the history that counted as relevant had become more sharply defined. Moreover, Grierson had a clearer sense of gradual, causal development over time than Masson, for whom shifts came abruptly.[18] The philological method of literary study had not changed fundamentally but had grown more sophisticated. All of Grierson's academic writing—literary history, editions, criticism—relied on exceptional historical erudition. But he stood out only in depth of learning. In general, a high proportion of nineteenth- and early twentieth-century scholarship in English literature took the form of biographies, literary history, and historically grounded editions.

Literary Editing

Of all varieties of literary scholarship, editing most directly inherited methods from classical and biblical philology. After all, resources needed to emend Chaucer or Shakespeare were in principle those needed to emend Manilius or Terence—close familiarity with the language, wide knowledge of contemporaneous authors. In 1860 Charles Norton was reading proof for his friend Richard Grant White's edition of Shakespeare. Therein White asserted that use of 'shall' to express obligation and 'will' to express futurity dated from around 1550. Norton pointed out just such usage in Chaucer and Gower nearly two centuries earlier.[19] Textual philologists had called on this kind of skill set since antiquity. The process of adapting it to English texts, begun around 1700, continued unbroken into the later nineteenth century. Nothing basic changed after 1860. Editing and emendation of English works simply became more skilled, more rigorous, more thoroughly researched—on average.

No one accused Frederick James Furnivall of averageness, and his career highlights the ups and downs of editorial scholarship. As eccentric as he was energetic, a Christian socialist turned agnostic, Furnivall gained a reputation for hot pink neckties, sculling on the Thames with shopgirls, and hours toiling over manuscripts in the British Museum. He made a signal contribution to learning when, as honorary secretary of the Philological Society, he initiated what became the *Oxford English Dictionary*. But he also ruled editing of early English texts. He founded several societies devoted to publishing such editions: the Early English Text Society in 1864, the Chaucer Society and the Ballad Society in 1868, the New Shakspere Society in 1873, and the Wyclif Society in 1882. (He then shattered some of them with his love of quarrels, the bitterer the better.) These groups churned out edition after edition—some 250 from the Early English Text Society alone before Furnivall's death. The Cornell professor Corson in 1896 declared "the whole learned world" more in debt to Furnivall "than to any other living man." In 1884 Berlin honored him with a doctorate. Oxford followed suit, and Trinity Hall Cambridge—his own college—made him an honorary fellow.[20]

Furnivall advanced a 'scientific' approach to Shakespearean philology in keeping with the temper of his age. By 'scientific' Furnivall meant more than the German-style scholarship he urged on the Shakspere Society. Working with Rev. F. G. Fleay, Furnivall proposed to settle the chronology of Shakespeare's plays by systematically analyzing language and meter in each work. (The Irish scholar Edward Dowden, a far subtler mind, appreciated the potential of this method, though quickly repented with regard to Fleay.) The metrical test mattered most, Fleay explained, "because in it, and in it only, can quantitative results be obtained." Fleay also warned that "any critic who attempts to use these tests" needed "a thorough training in the Natural Sciences, especially in Mineralogy, classificatory Botany, and above all, in Chemical Analysis." This last admonition left readers struggling to keep a straight face, and even Furnivall soon realized that Fleay had crossed the border into dottiness. Still, their effort to date plays and assign authorship by quantitative assay foreshadowed computer-based textual analysis by scholars today.[21]

Yet erudition often fell victim to Furnivall's eagerness. He rushed as many early English manuscripts into print as he could, and he cut scholarly corners to do so. When "every MS. is in type," *then* would come "the higher task of re-editing all the best texts, with the knowledge gained from a survey of the whole field of early literature." He worked hard but rarely persistently. His own editing was often slapdash, and at times he handed over manuscripts to rank amateurs in his societies. His friend Alois Brandl, the University of Berlin's specialist in English philology, wondered whether Furnivall could even conjugate an Old English verb. (He probably could—but not necessarily many.) Furnivall cheerfully confessed his scholarly lapses. Yet he could grow fierce when he believed philology flouted:

> When I see imposters like . . . Swinburne, [and] Fleay, who know as much early English as my dog, & who fancy they can settle Chaucer difficulties as they blow their noses, then I ridicule or kick them. But earnest students I treat with respect, & am only too glad to learn from them.[22]

Furnivall might well have tried to teach his dog Old English. He was odd and ardent enough.

And, despite lapses, he made capital contributions to editorial scholarship. The greatest stemmed from one of his learned friendships, with Harvard's Francis Child. Cut off from Chaucer manuscripts by the Atlantic, Child pleaded with his pen pal to print a few of the most complete. Furnivall borrowed from biblical philology the idea of printing the best manuscripts of the *Canterbury Tales* in parallel columns (a scheme dating back to Origen, revived in the early modern 'polyglot' Bibles). Better textual scholars, notably the Cambridge Chaucerian Henry Bradshaw, loaned skills Furnivall lacked. To muster money, he created the Chaucer Society. So equipped, he published between 1868 and 1877 *A Six-text Print of Chaucer's Canterbury Tales in Parallel Columns*—and for once he did the job pretty accurately. Furnivall went on to do the same for Chaucer's *Troilus and Criseyde* and (less accurately) his so-called minor poems. The *Six-text Print* became the foundation for modern critical editions—the first (1894–97) by Furnivall's younger coworker Walter Skeat. Nor should one discount the scores of manuscripts printed by the Early English Text Society, sloppily edited as most were. Furnivall's steam-engine brought into the public domain much, if not most, of the corpus of Old English and (as we now say) Middle English texts. These supplied material for later editors, who corrected hasty errors by him and his fellow zealots—as Furnivall had predicted.[23]

Furnivall stood between two worlds. He aspired to 'scientific' scholarship but lacked the philological equipment to produce it. He evinced flashes of genuine methodological originality but not the expertise to bring them fruitfully down to earth. He helped to show that English studies merited a place in universities yet rejected academic rigor himself. When he founded the Early English Text Society in 1864, his amateur zeal linked him to typical editors of previous generations. When he died in 1910, he lumbered like a disputatious dinosaur among professional, often university-based scholars.

The editorial evolution that bypassed Furnivall resulted in progressively more sophisticated handling of major authors. Editions of English writers approached more and more closely, in accuracy and method, those of classical or biblical texts. John Donne makes a convenient example, continuing a case begun in chapter 6. There, one saw how, with shrewd collation of the few texts available to him, James Russell Lowell produced in 1855 an edition of Donne's poems superior to any previous—and first to print variants. The next editor, Alexander Grosart, claimed to have painstakingly compared several manuscripts and all previous editions for his two-volume set (1872–73). In fact, he leaned heavily on one manuscript and worked carelessly. But rising expectations compelled Grosart to brag as he did, and his stress on the manuscript tradition did make a key advance. Lowell, late in life, set out to improve his earlier work. He died first, in 1891. His daughter Mabel Burnett and his friend Charles Norton (philological skills honed by his work on Dante) finished the job in 1895. The next year, in England, E. K. Chambers issued his own version—unaware that the other was under way. Both Chambers and Lowell-Burnett-Norton raised to a new level of accuracy Donne editions based on the print tradition. An 1896 article by Norton, "The Text of Donne's Poems," pointed the way toward still more expert editing.[24]

That came in Herbert Grierson's edition of 1912. Grierson remained convinced of the superiority of early printed editions for reconstructing Donne's poems. But he also made extensive use of manuscripts, applying rigorous techniques commonly ascribed to the German classical and biblical philologist Karl Lachmann. (The so-called Lachmannian—or stemmatic—method arranges manuscripts in families by identifying shared errors; this reduces the number of 'witnesses' and supposedly makes it easier to discern which textual tradition lies closer in time to the original.) In elucidating the poems, Grierson deployed his own deep knowledge of their scholastic context. Both Grierson and Norton learned from Edward Moore's *Contributions to the Textual Criticism of the "Divina Commedia"* (1889), a book on the cutting edge methodologically. Grierson's work had its defects, but it remained a standard until the great variorum edition of our own day. His edition evidenced the highly skilled, professional qualities that editors of English literary texts had achieved by the early twentieth century. Grierson was also the first Donne editor to make his career in universities.[25]

FOLKLORE AS LITERATURE

In contrast to Donne's editors, Harvard's Francis J. Child applied traditional methods of textual philology to untraditional oral materials. He showed the continuing fluidity of philology, even as it fragmented into distinct humanistic disciplines. (Child appeared in chapter 6 as editor of Elizabethan playwrights and a Chaucer scholar.) However, biblical scholarship had likely first introduced him to philology. So a broad sense of the remit of textual philology became second nature. Studies in Germany further expanded it. These brought him under the spell of Jacob Grimm, from whom he probably got the idea of comparing similar tales in different tongues. His chief scholarly interest shifted in the later 1850s from literary texts to oral traditions, from editing Spenser to editing British ballads (sung narratives). Many erudite students of ballads flourished in the English-speaking world; Child proved far and away the most thorough.[26]

He began in 1857 with an eight-volume collection of ballads garnered from printed sources—a strategy he soon regarded as deficient. (Donne's editors more slowly realized their need for manuscripts.) Child took cues especially from his contemporary Svend Grundtvig, Danish collector of folk ballads, and from a man who affected Grundtvig, William Motherwell, early nineteenth-century gatherer of Scottish folksong. Child set out to print every extant English and Scottish oral ballad. Mostly this meant finding manuscripts where some long-dead antiquarian had written down traditional songs heard from singers. Child approached his massive task with increasing methodological expertise gleaned from comparable work by European philologists (especially Grundtvig). He also mustered an indispensable army of ballad seekers. A typical case: In 1872 Child's old chum Charles Norton was living in London, where his friends included Thomas Carlyle. Norton enlisted Carlyle's Scottish connections to procure names of schoolteachers north of the border. To some thirteen hundred of these Norton sent Child's printed plea for ballads. Child dragooned other Americans visiting Britain, but his chief coworkers were British. By far most important were the omnipresent Furnivall in London and William McMath, a law clerk, in Edinburgh. Child did not care to trace origins or pinpoint geographic sources, as did Grundtvig. Rather, he wanted to compile every variant. He compared ballads not only with other British ones but also with similar types in other European languages. (A helpful rabbi translated from Polish and Hungarian.) Child well knew that many songs had perished irretrievably, but by the time he begin to print in 1882 he believed he had assembled the great majority of surviving ballads. Most dated from the seventeenth and eighteenth centuries, though his collection reached back as far as 1400.[27]

By combining well-known methods of literary editing with those of comparative northern European philology, Child created a fascinating hybrid. The first volume of *The English and Scottish Popular Ballads* appeared in 1882, the last in 1898 (edited by his student George Lyman Kittredge, following Child's death two years earlier). Experts at the time recognized "Child's Ballads"—as folklorists and folksingers still call it—as the banner achievement of American literary research to date. The collection mattered to literary scholarship because it added to the canon oral poems like "Lord Randall," "The Unquiet Grave," and "Mary Hamilton," material haphazardly and partially known before his work. An obvious parallel points to Kemble's edition of *Beowulf* earlier in the century. But "Child's Ballads" also helped to establish the new—or newly recognized—field of folklore,* which, not quite a discipline of its own, floated between literature and another new discipline, anthropology.[28]

In these ways, Child, with other scholars of his generation, helped to define the boundaries and practices of 'English literature.' Taking his work as a whole, Child stood at a point where three different subdisciplines of English studies diverged: (1) historical linguistics, specifically the history of the English language (his monographs on the language of Chaucer and later of Gower); (2) folklore or oral literature (the ballads); and (3) English literature 'proper' (his editions of Spenser and other English Renaissance writers).

LITERARY CRITICISM AS SCIENCE AND ART

Increasingly prominent in literary scholarship was criticism in its newer, narrower sense: evaluative analysis of specific works of poetry, prose, or drama. Like Child's and Grierson's editing and the crowded genre of literary history and biography, this sort of criticism owed something—not as directly—to timeworn textual philology. In evaluative criticism resurfaced both the careful linguistic scrutiny typical of textual philologists and their inclination to illuminate texts by placing them in historical context.

In some critics sharply focused, concentrated attention to words and phrases joined with historical consciousness. "Criticism has now become a province of history," commented W. P. Ker in 1889, as he prepared to move from a provincial professorship to the Quain Chair of English Language and Literature at University College London:

> The growth of history in the 19th century is hardly less remarkable than the growth of physical science itself. . . . The author of the Origin of Species represents much more than mere natural history, & his general view of the world is anticipated or shared by many historians, many poets & romancers. By their methods of observation, by their regard for the minutest particulars bearing on their study, by their sense of the vastness of the world, & the power of time to work changes, history & criticism share the same intellectual character with studies in widely different subject matters.

In contrast to the "*à priori* & *dogmatic*" criticism of "the 17th and 18th centuries," criticism "now follows the prevailing fashion—if it is scientific, it resembles natural history rather than the exact sciences; it uses historical & comparative methods, when it uses any methods at all."[29]

---

*William J. Thoms coined "Folk-Lore" in the *Athenaeum* in 1846. The word quickly caught on, suggesting a newly felt need to give its own label to one scholarly practice that precipitated from antiquarianism.

Yet, as chapter 6 showed, evaluative criticism developed chiefly from melding philology's historic ally rhetoric with its historic rival philosophy. The practice of closely analyzing individual works grew up within rhetoric, as did kinds of stylistic analysis applied to them. To illuminate deeper meanings in such writings, critics turned to categories borrowed from biblical criticism and philosophy. And the newly 'professional' literary critics of the later nineteenth century pretty much carried forward the basic critical method that emerged in the decades before 1860: some combination of judging a work's formal qualities by universal standards while seeking idiosyncratic deeper meanings through interpretation.

But these later critics did so in a new spirit, within a new environment. As literature became a university subject, criticism—still flourishing in newspapers and magazines—moved into new English departments or schools along with philology, literary history, and textual editing. At the same time, research mattered more and more within universities. 'English' often awoke suspicion as a 'soft' subject, with criticism its spongiest side. 'Research' had pretty clear meaning for historians of language (Child's rigorous analysis of Middle English pronunciation) or for literary historians (Masson's massively researched volumes on Milton) or for textual editors (Grierson's painstaking work on Donne). How did a literary critic pursue research? Did criticism amount to more than hyperventilating about the genius of Shakespeare or the beauties of Keats's odes?

A new breed of literary critics devoted themselves to proving their rigor, a toughness always implicitly tested against the erudition of classical philologists, the high priests of humanistic learning in British and American universities. The English critic John Churton Collins longed for a professorship but got one only three years before he died in 1908. All this time, from his redoubt in the quarterlies and newspapers, he flayed flabby criticism. As an editor friend put it, Collins regarded "the great mass of modern criticism" as "shamelessly inadequate, ignorant, injudicious." In a notorious spat with the prolific Edmond Gosse in 1886, Collins raked him over the coals for gross blunders of fact, routine carelessness about historical context, even ignorance of texts he pretended to know. In his own writings and in fierce attacks on other critics, Collins modeled what learned criticism demanded: erudition in several languages, fastidious accuracy in details, command of multiple comparative contexts. He agitated for bringing this sort of criticism into Oxford and Cambridge.[30]

Some university-based literary critics even insisted that criticism was—or could and should become—a science. They did not propose to ape astronomy or biology. Until the end of the nineteenth century, 'science' still meant something like rigorous, systematic knowledge. "Ultimately, science means no more than organized thought," said one English critic. Mark Harvey Liddell, after postgraduate training at Princeton, Oxford, and Berlin, taught English from 1897 until 1932 at the Universities of Texas and Louisville, at Butler College, finally at Purdue University. Whether writing criticism or editing Shakespeare, he thought of himself as working "in a scientific spirit" and "by scientific methods." One of Liddell's projects, "Prolegomena to a science of Prosody [*sic*]," meant to show the critic of poetry how to approach it 'scientifically.' In 1895 Charles Mills Gayley of the University of California agreed that "trustworthy principles of literary criticism depend upon the substantiation of aesthetic theory by scientific inquiry."[31]

This theorem was neither brand new nor solely American. In 1885 Richard Green Moulton, an extension lecturer at Cambridge, published *Shakespeare as a Dramatic Artist*. It aimed "to claim for Criticism a position amongst the Inductive Sciences, and to sketch in outline a plan for the Dramatic side of such a Critical Science." Moulton contrasted this new, empirical science with "judicial criticism" that judged a work as better or worse by general standards. Critical science instead explored literary works "to get a closer acquaintance with their phenomena" and to identify emerging literary types. Critical science's "foundation axiom" sounded a little like physics: "*Interpretation in literature is of the nature of a scientific hypothesis, the truth of which is tested by the degree of completeness with which it explains the details of the literary work as they actually stand.*" Liddell's and Moulton's reactions put them on one end of the spectrum of literary critics. On the other, Matthew Arnold *contrasted* study of poetry with science: the two being complementary precisely because one did what the other did not. Few critics regarded themselves as scientists, but many did stress their rigor—if only in self-defense within increasingly research-oriented universities. A historian of American literary criticism, Robert Falk, summed up the change: "Criticism became more of a business and less of an art. Technical matters displaced philosophy. In place of Emerson's 'metre-making argument' one finds [Sidney] Lanier's involved and specialized *Science of English Verse*."[32]

Yet lecture halls filled with undergraduates also pushed English professors in the opposite direction, with some effect on what counted as literary criticism. Few twenty-year-olds pined to mix scientific rigor with their *Hamlet*. Moreover, a reigning ideal of 'liberal culture' in Anglophone collegiate education in this period made literature into a tool for civilizing elite young barbarians. This job called more for inspiration than perspiration.

The nature of the inspiration was deeply affected by the secularization of academic knowledge. The traditional Protestant framework of knowledge crumbled between 1850 and 1900 in both North America and the United Kingdom. Intellectually alert men and women no longer easily assumed that all knowledge cohered because it concerned a single divine creation—still less that all knowledge pointed to God.* Also, in the northeastern United States especially, a growing number of Catholics and Jews entered once Protestant colleges in the years around 1900, making explicit Protestantism awkward in

---

* Catholic colleges did not reach this crisis until well into the twentieth century.

the lecture hall. Yet many professors, along with a lot of students and even more parents, worried over what would replace the Christian formation that colleges could no longer readily offer. For reasons not clear—perhaps absence of an established church—Americans felt the problem more strongly.[33]

In this situation, the humanities, willy-nilly, filled the hole left when explicit Christianity largely evaporated from university teaching. Literature courses, in particular, offered not a definable religion, certainly not theology—but a vague 'spirituality' that served to bridge the gap left by the exit of Christianity, to reassure uneasy students and parents. (Explicitly religious extracurricular groups also thrived.) Moreover, the promise that literature could build 'character' (as Lounsbury averred) took on a little of the burden of moral formation once shouldered by Protestantism. Poetry's "power of forming, sustaining, and delighting us"—especially its aid in raising a person's character to ever higher levels—formed the basis of Matthew Arnold's claim in 1880 that "most of what now passes with us for religion and philosophy will be replaced by poetry."[34]

Literary criticism thus emitted a lot of fuzzy 'spirituality' around 1900, especially in the classroom, especially in the United States. The spirituality had to be woolly. Its consumers ranged from evangelical Christians to agnostics or near agnostics like Arnold himself. This context may help to explain the late-Victorian fascination with authors heavy with allegory or metaphor, like Dante, Spenser, and Donne. At Harvard at the end of the 1870s, William Roscoe Thayer studied Dante with both James Russell Lowell and Charles Eliot Norton. Thayer judged Norton ("the minute and indefatigable searcher of texts") clearly superior to Lowell as *philologist*. But Norton the *evaluative critic* also showed "a spiritual insight which made his interpretation of the deep and holy passages of the 'Divine Comedy' almost a religious exercise." That Dante was a Catholic, Thayer a Protestant, and Norton an unbeliever hardly figured. Looking back, Thayer could not say whether Norton impressed him more with "the spiritual significance or the supreme beauty of the poem"—no surprise, since Norton "never divorced the spiritual from the beautiful." Either way, "to read Dante with Mr. Norton was almost an act of worship."[35]

There was no "almost" about Hiram Corson of Cornell. Norton's erudition, as Thayer said, "despised inaccuracy or misstatement." Corson scorned such learned pickiness in the lecture hall: "inspiring power must come from an author's or a teacher's *being*, and not from his brain." Accordingly, in editing texts for classroom use, Corson minimized the significance of textual variants, where other professors in their quest for scholarly rigor highlighted them. To "discover the secret" of a poem's "aesthetic power" lay "within the reach of any one of ordinary emotional appreciation and analytic skill." Corson defined imaginative literature as "an expression in letters of the life of the spirit of man co-operating with the intellect." Hence the critic's job qua professor was to bring "the spirituality which constitutes the real life of poetry" to "the consciousness and appreciation of students." A great fan of elocution, Corson deemed declaiming literature from the podium the best way to achieve this goal. Undergraduates did not need to think so much as to hear and feel. It worked for some of them. While listening to Corson, one student felt himself transported into a mystical ecstasy—the turning point of his life, he later recorded, converting him to a profound and permanent love of poetry. Other students read the newspaper, even tossed an occasional shoe.[36]

If some of Corson's colleagues thought him daft, he nonetheless rode a main current of criticism in his day. William Morton Payne, for many years an editor of the influential literary journal the *Dial*, claimed in 1895 that literature sent "a personal message to the individual, which enshrines it, along with music and religion, in the most sacred recesses of the soul." A "spiritual glow," a "kindling of the soul," came "with the hearing of some ineffable strain, or the reading of some lightning-tipped verse." Harvard's Barrett Wendell defined literature as simply "the lasting expression in words of the meaning of life."[37]

As far apart as Barrett Wendell and the 'scientific' Richard Moulton appear, do not exaggerate the distance between them. Tensions cropped up, especially over control of curriculum. But Hiram Corson began as an instructor of Old English and continued to teach it after moving to Cornell. In the 1890s he wrote a technical book on prosody with a strong literary-historical element. George Lyman Kittredge—"the quintessential philological scholar" according to Gerald Graff—could tell an audience in 1914 that Chaucer's *Book of the Duchess* has "a haunting charm about it that eludes analysis, but subdues our mood to a gentle and vaguely troubled pensiveness."[38]

Neither 'scientific' nor 'spiritual' criticism had staying power in their specific late Victorian forms, but both shaped literary criticism for many years to come. Scientific criticism was the sharpest edge of a new-forged, learned, scholarly mode of literary criticism as it moved into research-oriented universities. Its animus long endured in the requirement that academic critics command multiple languages (including earlier forms of English), detailed knowledge of a wide range of literatures, persnickety accuracy, and scalpel-like skill in parsing fine distinctions in texts. Spiritual criticism took to an extreme earlier nineteenth-century critics' search for nonobvious or latent meanings in literary texts. Out of this older, broader quest precipitated spiritual criticism, in reaction to the secularization of academic knowledge. If spiritual criticism proved temporary, it cemented as an enduring goal of critical inquiry penetration beneath the literary surface. The ghost of spiritual criticism haunted later academic literary criticism's "systematic preoccupation with 'hidden meaning,'" for which (as Gerald Graff and Michael Warner suggest) "academization" bears the responsibility.[39] And both spiritual and scientific criticism fitted (as well as sometimes competed) with linguistic and historical literary scholarship. Clear distinctions rarely divided different sorts of literary scholars. The same person assumed different roles, and few took strong positions against the legitimacy of other modes of literary scholarship. But many now did stand firm against 'loose,' 'careless'—that is, nonscholarly—treatment of literature.

PHILOLOGY BECOMES A GHOST

By around 1900 all these varied practices—linguistic scholarship, editing, literary history, evaluative criticism—hung together as a single scholarly enterprise, housed in the same professorship or academic unit. By then North America had the Modern Language Association (1883)—serving both Canada and the United States—while the United Kingdom soon got the English Association (1906). Learned journals marked the new discipline's emergence, as in other disciplines. Having "contributed a valuable article to the Modern Literature Quarterly" won a young academic job seeker a check mark in the eminent Edward Dowden's ledger in 1899. By this time Dowden got routinely consulted when jobs opened up at colleges and universities throughout the United Kingdom—indeed the empire. In his own angling for a professorship at Oxford fifteen years earlier, disciplinarity appeared in more embryonic form. He offered letters of recommendation, evidence of recognized stature in the field, proof of being valued by his own institution, an active scholarly program—all very modern. But the notion that a college should appoint its own lingered on, as did the power of endorsement by influential outsiders to the discipline (in this case famous poets rather than actual literary scholars). The new discipline of literature bore the clear marks of its ancestry in philology: concern with analysis of language, close attention to texts, historical contextualization—with the master philological technique, comparison, displayed in editing, linguistic studies, literary history, and criticism alike. But 'literature' now stood on its own two feet, a distinct discipline.[40]

Ironically, given their multisided philological inheritance, scholars of English began to narrow their understanding of 'philology' around the turn of the century. Philology came to mean mere "study of words" or "linguistic science" in *opposition* to study of the forms of literary works, to literary history, and to exploration of the "spiritual and aesthetic" meanings of poetry and fiction. As early as 1888 Furnivall thought that a learned paper on *Beowulf* by an Oxford scholar needed "a bit or two about the language" in order to "give a flavour of Philology." This cramped construal of philology was largely a red herring—sometimes reflected rank ignorance of its varied character.[41]

But it led, in two or three decades after 1910, to widespread repudiation by literary scholars of a straw man called philology (best described as linguistically oriented erudition with a bias toward Middle and Old English). In the early years of English faculties, linguistic and historical scholars—more nearly 'scientific,' more clearly 'rigorous'—held the upper hand. After the First World War literary history remained prominent, but the pendulum began to swing away from linguistic erudition toward criticism. The critics took revenge on those who once lorded it over them. By the 1920s the Old English expert Morgan Callaway had gained enough eminence to collect honorary degrees. A younger English professor, Jay Hubbell, wrote him off in 1924 "as a dryasdust philologist."[42] A close reading of such sneers suggests not denigration of philology, but redefinition of it. Critical, historical, and textual practices that classicists and biblical scholars—and indeed continental European scholars of modern literature—still knew as philology acquired different names in Anglophone faculties of literature. Even while Old English scholars got pushed to the margins of the discipline, the basic methods of literary study—including a newly prominent social history of literature—remained those that had evolved out of philology and its sister, rhetoric.

Here lay a double irony. Having identified themselves as antiphilology, scholars of modern literature cut themselves off from the cross-disciplinary breadth of philological erudition. They not only confined themselves to literature. Even within literary studies, more and more specialized scholars sought to bite off only as much as they could very thoroughly chew. George Saintsbury, a learned literary journalist before succeeding David Masson at Edinburgh, fretted about the effect on literary criticism. Caught "between reviewers of all work who don't know, & specialists who won't see, the chance of books is not rosy." As early as 1878, when T. H. Ward planned a new, four-volume anthology of English poets, he enlisted different experts to edit individual poets. The "various sections and stages" of English poetry "have become the objects of so special a study" that no one scholar could handle it all—or even a large chunk—competently. Ward exaggerated but did not lie. In contrast to the new specialism, Charles Eliot Norton not only edited Donne but also published serious research on Dante, medieval architecture, art history, and classical archaeology. He died in 1908, among the last of his kind.[43]

11

"NO TENDENCY TOWARD DILETTANTISM"

THE CIVILIZED PAST AFTER 1850

If anything, the line between civilized peoples and their primitive opposites grew brighter after 1850. In 1908 an Oxford anthropologist awarded the "lower kind" of "human culture" to his discipline, turning over "the higher life of society" to "the Humanities."[1] The distinction certainly grew more invidious: more racialized, more racist. Tribal peoples in Africa or aborigines in Australia—supposedly unchanging folk with oddly timeless pasts, no real history—barely belonged to the same human race as Egyptian pharaohs, Roman soldiers, medieval English villagers, Renaissance artists, American and French revolutionaries.* Yet, as the nineteenth century ended, the primitive reared its unexpected head in such long-time bastions of civilization as ancient Greece and Israel. For most of the learned, these intrusions barely dimmed the vivid border dividing civilization from those without it; but a fox had been let loose in the henhouse.

By 1900, scholars who devoted themselves to the civilized past, including the few who cracked its veneer, did so mostly within universities and colleges, under rising pressure of disciplinarity. Leaving aside the literary historians of chapter 10, three major disciplines pursued research into past civilization by 1900: classicists (including now archaeologists); historians; and art historians. (Smaller groups focused on ancient civilizations beyond Greece and Rome, such as Egyptologists, are overlooked here for reasons of space.) Like scholars of literature or language, classicists, historians, and art historians each worked in growing segregation from the learned in other fields. Classicists dealt routinely with classicists, not so often with New Testament critics or medieval

---

* Denying civilization to some nonwhite peoples, such as those of India and China, strained credibility. They could be rendered inferior in other ways: as degenerated from ancient civilization, or as infected with racial defects limiting their capacity for true civilization, or both.

historians. In this new world of ever more distinct 'disciplines', erudite men—now women, too, in small numbers—forgot the philological ancestry that made them cousins. Still, the adventurous among them crashed through these newfangled barriers.

PART I: 'CLASSICS' BECOMES A DISCIPLINE

The advent of a novel discipline in the English-speaking world named classical studies, or simply classics, says worlds about the peculiarities of the modern humanities. The first philologists, in ancient Alexandria, emended and edited authors we call classical; their Renaissance successors began their revival of learning with classical Greek and Latin texts. If classical textual philology stretched back before Caesar, why call classics new in the late nineteenth century?

There are four answers. First, classics then became a modern discipline: a university-based field of study, inward-looking, gauging individual achievement by quality of research. Its practitioners published increasingly for each other. By 1920 they rarely dabbled in studies other than classics (and, if so, saw themselves as dabblers). And they differentiated serious scholarship for specialists from popularizing for general readers. Second, classicists set up new institutions specific to their discipline. These included professional societies and journals. Third, a consensus slowly took hold that classical scholars must go beyond texts to recover the Greek and Roman worlds. Thus archaeology, epigraphy, art history, architecture, ancient history, and numismatics melted into 'classics', not as optional adjuncts or even ancillary subdisciplines (like paleography for historians), but as integral to the new discipline. Classics became the study of ancient Greece and Rome, not of ancient Greek and Roman texts, however weighty these remained. (Later, 'ancient Mediterranean world' often seemed fitter than 'ancient Greece and Rome'.) Seen in the longest perspective, this broadened 'classics' sprang from the marriage of antiquarianism and philology, much as Gibbon had wed philology to history. A nearer-sighted vision sees German *Altertumswissenschaft* conquering the English-speaking world.

Fourth and finally, the slowly gathering effect of all these developments made Greece and Rome less familiar, sometimes alien—in a few erudite depictions even alarmingly savage. For centuries, classical texts had furnished readers not only Greek and Roman ideas but values for contemporary life. That latter use grew tricky. More and more, classicists highlighted differences separating ancient from modern. Most dramatically, anthropology began to illuminate earlier cultures from which 'classical' Greece and Rome emerged. A few daring scholars gave the Greeks and Romans barbaric rites, alien customs, ways of thinking apter for cannibals in New Guinea's highlands than for proper Victorians. Civilized people? The primitive but peaceful Homer once proposed by Robert Wood now might lend a hand in human sacrifice. *This* ancient world could not plausibly provide the chief formation of elite young men. And, in fact, the weirding of Greece and Rome followed upon the weakening of the educational monopoly of Latin and Greek. When weakening became collapse, classics took its new place as merely one among several humanistic disciplines.

Broadening of classical philology into 'classics' moved faster in the United States than in the United Kingdom. Well into the second half of the nineteenth century, most British classical scholars continued to hymn the timeless charms of the classical text and to resist incursions of nontextual studies. As late as 1903 Thomas Page—who in 1910 became the first editor of the canonical Loeb Classical Library—railed against classical archaeology: "the real, the imperishable substance of a great writer has scant connection with mouldering stones or decaying ruins."[2] By 1903 Page's diatribe made him seem almost "mouldering" himself, but in Britain he would not have looked so a quarter of a century before.

A Discipline Takes Shape in the United States

He would have in America, however. There early gestures toward ampler classical studies by college teachers like Harvard's Cornelius Felton picked up scholarly impetus in midcentury. The Yale philologist James Hadley's enduring *Greek Grammar* (1860), traditional in form, showed a professionalism new for American classicists. In the same year appeared a book by a twenty-nine-year-old Harvard professor who had studied in Berlin before returning home with a Göttingen doctorate. William Watson Goodwin's *Syntax of the Moods and Tenses of the Greek Verb* made the first major original contribution by an American to classical studies—reprinted as recently as 2009. Then, in 1869, in an important essay fast translated into German, Hadley explained how Greek and Latin accents—seemingly different systems—followed similar laws of musical modulation. Both Hadley and Goodwin deployed comparative philology and German modes of analysis. In other ways, too, American classicists had a broader outlook than Oxbridge peers. No later than 1872—probably earlier—the University of Michigan taught ancient art as part of undergraduate instruction in classics.[3]

Two changes in the educational environment fostered broader-gauged classical teaching and research. First, curricula shifted. American colleges had long required wider studies than Oxford or Cambridge, while keeping classical languages at the center. At Harvard, with one of the most diverse programs, classics in 1856–57 still took 40 percent of student hours before senior year. The number of subjects on offer—sometimes no longer required—kept growing everywhere. The buildup eventually pushed Latin and Greek off their thrones. As a rule, the more eminent the university, the sooner the monarchs toppled. In 1867–68 Harvard ceased to require Greek and Latin except for freshmen; in 1884–85 freshmen, too, were set free. (Goodwin gagged at the idea of a student graduating "with the highest honors without ever having read a line of the Iliad.") This revolution left teachers of Latin and Greek looking and feeling more like professors of geology or history—that is, specialists responsible for a body of field-specific knowledge, rather than general-purpose educators dragging all students through standard texts. Second, highly regarded universities started to expect faculty research. It became a factor in hiring and salary. Institutions further down the ladder of prestige sooner or later aped those higher up. Professors in all fields reacted predictably. Many teachers of Greek and Latin (conceiving themselves now as scholarly specialists) morphed into professors of classics alert to research in their field. More and more of them understood classics *as* a 'field,' not general education.[4]

For such Americans, initiation into broad-gauged, historically sensitive classical studies as practiced in German universities became a common rite of passage. Young Ernest Sihler of Fort Wayne, Indiana—fresh from a Lutheran seminary in St. Louis—fetched up in Berlin in 1872. There he studied textual philology with Moritz Haupt and Emil Hübner but also Roman literature with Hübner, Greek history with J. G. Droysen, Greek literature with Adolph Kirchhoff, Roman history with the illustrious Theodor Mommsen, Greek philosophy with the Aristotle scholar Hermann Bonitz, and more. Under the eye of the archaeologist Ernst Curtius, Sihler acquainted himself with ancient sculpture in the Altes Museum. From Haupt he learned a lesson untaught in the English Cambridge: understanding Aristophanes required not only analysis of his language but also immersion in the history of his time. Mommsen began his lectures, Sihler recorded, by warning against treating antiquity as Oxford did: "We must not fancy that the political sentiments of the Romans were in the slightest degree tinged with those humanistic ideas with which the moderns, with their idealization of classic antiquity, are accustomed to endow them."[5]

Sihler went on to further study in Leipzig; to the first PhD in classics awarded by the new Johns Hopkins University; to a respectable career at New York University; and to personifying the new, disciplinary classicist. On his way home from Germany, Sihler stopped in England but sought out no classicists. Why bother? His first research back in Indiana was a monograph on the relation of Attic Old Comedy to the history of the period.* An abridgment became his first scholarly paper, read to the 1876 meeting of the American Philological Association. A year later Sihler was analyzing "the critiques of Dionysius Halicarnassensis [ca. 60–7 BCE] bearing on Attic orators and oratory of the IV century B.C." with other members of the weekly "Greek Seminarium" at Johns Hopkins University.[6]

The "seminarium" was a German institution reimagined in Baltimore by its director, the German-trained Basil Gildersleeve. Sihler's seminar presentation

---

* Attic Old Comedy is the comedy of the fifth and early fourth centuries BCE, surviving in Aristophanes and fragments of other writers.

showed how German experience—both his own and mediated through Gildersleeve—pushed an American classicist of the mid-1870s beyond mere verbal criticism. Gildersleeve did comment on grammar, syntax, and etymology: future Greek professors needed to perfect their Greek. But Sihler's research in the seminar, though text-based, was not merely linguistic. He explored the *substance* of rhetorical technique—how fourth-century orators differed in style and aesthetics—by contrasting passages in different authors. (Gildersleeve stressed "the importance and fruitfulness of crossreading," the age-old comparative method of philologists.) Without going into detail (or so seminar minutes suggest), Sihler traced rhetorical differences among orators to their differing historical situations. One of Gildersleeve's students claimed to "have acquired no small degree of general culture" in the seminar. Students more often acquired specialized papers to deliver to the American Philological Association (APA).[7]

The APA gave the new discipline a home. Classical philologists had helped to found the association in 1869 but hardly monopolized its earliest years. At first the group paid more attention to comparative philology, electing William Dwight Whitney as its first president. Although amateurs sprinkled its ranks, the great majority of members—and the leadership—were research-oriented and university-based. The APA explicitly modeled itself on German precedent, and the classical scholars involved shared its founding aim of "the advancement of knowledge." Among its first acts was a yearbook, its *Transactions*, to publish members' research. From the start the organization intended to divide into specialized subsections, sign of incipient disciplinary fault lines. Before *Transactions* reached its tenth year, articles on classical subjects drowned all others. As soon as the new battleship of research, Johns Hopkins, lowered its gangplanks, the APA boarded for its annual meeting, Gildersleeve at the helm. Two other Greek philologists molded in Germany—Thomas Seymour of Yale and William Watson Goodwin of Harvard—played leading roles in the organization. The Modern Language Association, founded in 1883 (another artifact of disciplinary specialization), sucked away members interested in modern tongues. Latin and Greek scholars thereafter dominated the APA.[8]

The association both sprang from and nurtured the new discipline of classics. It promoted a range of classical studies that would have unnerved Thomas Page. It cooperated closely with the Archaeological Institute of America from its founding in 1879. (From 1905 the two coordinated annual meetings, although their journals did not overlap in coverage.) Early on, professional disciplinary ambitions shaped the APA. The annual meetings became the place for young scholars to make a mark and (as one early member put it) achieve their "much desired migration" to a university higher in the pecking order. A brilliant paper at the 1871 annual meeting in New Haven catapulted young Frederic Allen from Knoxville, Tennessee, to Harvard. Migration required rising into "the first class of men who have made considerable reputation" (to quote the president of the University of Virginia in 1912)—though an ambitious classicist also needed the imprimatur of an eminence like Gildersleeve. By its fiftieth anniversary in 1919, the APA in practice—though not yet officially—defined itself as the disciplinary organization only for American scholars of the ancient Greek and Roman worlds, a niche it still occupies.[9]

Journals like the APA's *Transactions* announced the new genus, the professionalized academic discipline; and they spread modestly. The most influential American classicist of his generation, Gildersleeve, began in 1880 the *American Journal of Philology*. The *AJP* was a thoroughly research-oriented enterprise, underwritten by its editor's research-obsessed university, aimed solely at professional readers. After consulting "the leading scholars," Gildersleeve solicited subscriptions from professors "representing most of the institutions of note in thirty States of the Union [out of thirty-eight]." Recently APA president, Gildersleeve intended the quarterly as the main outlet for scholarship by APA members. (The cramped *Transactions* appeared only once a year.) Accordingly, the *AJP* at first enveloped "the whole cycle of philological study" from "Comparative Grammar" to "the Teutonic languages." Gildersleeve did seek balance, but coverage inexorably slipped toward Greek and Latin. After a decade or two, articles on medieval German dialects or Amerindian languages stood out as odd guests amid a welter of studies of Greek chthonic gods, the subjunctive in Cicero, papyrus fragments of Homer—although not until the 1930s did the *AJP* abandon pretense. The truth is that 'philology' was no 'discipline' but a set of related scholarly practices. It provided no academic center of gravity. Classics *was* a discipline, or at least a discipline aborning; and its acolytes wrote for each other. Gildersleeve considered himself lucky to find time to "read a book outside my special line of work." More periodicals appeared as the discipline gelled: *Cornell Studies in Classical Philology* (a monograph series) in 1887, *Harvard Studies in Classical Philology* in 1890, *Classical Journal* in 1905, and *Classical Philology* in 1906.[10]

Their contents show how American professors understood 'classics.' Philology in the narrower sense dominated in these early decades, when mere language teaching still ruled the workdays of almost all classicists. But readers could also learn about Roman private life, the role of women in Athenian murder trials, travel in the ancient Mediterranean, and the staging of Greek drama, as well as more traditional philological subjects like manuscripts of Aristophanes or the imperfect indicative in early Latin. Even textual studies stretched beyond Oxbridge tradition. American classicists sought the roots of Greek mythology in "*Primitive worship*—assoc[iated] with nat[ura][l] objects" like mountains, trees, and stones"—even in "Hindoo" precedents, like "Indra ag[ain]st serpent."[11] And journals kept readers abreast of 'the profession,' reporting conferences, memorializing deceased colleagues.

Provision of graduate training was another prerequisite for a native-born discipline. The earliest leaders of American professional classics—Gildersleeve, Goodwin, Harvard's Latinist George Lane—wrote dissertations in Germany in the 1850s. (Only World War I finally stopped pilgrimages to Germany.) Through the 1870s American universities awarded few PhDs. But in the 1880s Johns Hopkins, Harvard, Yale, and Columbia began to churn out classical dissertations in meaningful numbers, supplemented in the 1890s by Princeton and the Universities of Michigan, Chicago, and Wisconsin. In 1893 the regents of the University of California fired their Greek professor; failure to publish unfitted him to train graduate students. In 1919 Chicago's Paul Shorey recalled early dissertations as "naturally largely linguistic." But, Shorey went on, "the American doctor's dissertation now covers a wide range of varied and interesting topics from the cults of Lesbos to the scolia on hypokrisis." One Princeton graduate student showed "that the traditional account of the way in which Gyges gained the throne of Lydia is derived from a folk-tale of the Hittites."* Shorey believed that doctoral work improved in the 1890s; and he judged the average American dissertation by the 1910s "distinctly superior" to its German equivalent. Shorey's barefaced nationalism now raises eyebrows, but American graduate training had become fully competent by 1900.[12]

So had research by the graduate students' teachers. Shorey's patriotic fantasy that Gildersleeve rivaled Wilamowitz invites chuckles, and Germans looked down their noses at American classicists in the early twentieth century. But already in 1881 a Cambridge scholar mentioned Gildersleeve, Goodwin, and Harvard's John White—"the leading 'classics' in America"—in the same breath with the top men of the United Kingdom. Prominent American classicists were on easy personal terms with British counterparts. Both Oxford and Cambridge gave Gildersleeve honorary degrees. He produced valuable editions of Justin Martyr and Pindar, vital studies of Greek syntax. (A South Carolina professor oddly called Gildersleeve's "Problems in Greek Syntax" in the *AJP* "the most inspiring & spiritual piece of work I have ever seen.") His comments on current scholarship in the *AJP*'s "Brief Mention" section guided a generation of English-speaking classicists. Less Olympian Americans did work internationally respected—Goodwin's *Syntax of the Greek Verb* and his commented edition of Demosthenes's oration on the crown; White's writings on Greek metrics and his study of marginal commentary in manuscripts of Aristophanes's *Birds*; Edward Morris's *Principles and Methods in Latin Syntax*; the exhaustive vocabulary of the Latin playwright Plautus compiled by Gildersleeve's student Gonzalez Lodge; and much more. As this list suggests, linguistic and textual philology at first dominated research. This did not make Americans clones of Richard Porson. Harvard's Greek philologist Frederic Allen focused so closely on texts that he laughed at himself as a pedant. But his colleague James Greenough said of Allen, "For him classical learning was a real science, a great branch of anthropology, giving insight, when rightly studied, into the mental operations and intellectual and moral growth of ancient

---

*Presumably this refers to a story in Herodotus. The Lydian king Candaules showed off to Gyges the beauty of his naked wife. Furious, the queen told Gyges to kill her husband and seize the throne or else die himself. Other ancient accounts explain how Gyges became king, but this is the most famous.

peoples. To him literature and monuments were records of life, and they were to be interpreted by it, and in turn were themselves to interpret it." Text interpreting context, context interpreting text, bespeaks traditional philology. But the context is "life."[13]

In any case, after 1900 a broader range of research topics became common. Two examples must suffice. In 1914 Bryn Mawr's Tenney Frank published *Roman Imperialism*, a transformative book. Six years later *Greek Theater of the Fifth Century before Christ* by the University of California's James T. Allen began his years of research illuminating the production of ancient drama. A few of these early works remain useful, even continue in print. Most show—especially compared to writings before 1850—keener awareness of the historical distance separating ancient Greek and Roman cultures from the American present. One reason is audience: other specialists, not eighteen-year-olds wanting convincing that classical antiquity mattered to modern life. As classics developed, some of the eighteen-year-olds wised up. Two University of California undergraduates griped to the regents in 1893 that their Greek professor taught them only to read and translate, neglecting larger cultural contexts of texts he assigned.[14]

Perhaps these undergraduates dimly saw that American classical scholars had created from college teaching of Greek and Latin a new discipline—new both in scope of inquiry and in being a modern discipline.

Archaeology and Classical Studies

One large piece of it was classical archaeology. In the late nineteenth century this study grew more distinct from, say, Egyptian or medieval archaeology precisely because it merged into 'classics.'* The disinterest of most Oxbridge classical scholars in anything but texts, plus passivity on the part of most Irish and Scottish classicists, kept Greco-Roman archaeology out of universities in the United Kingdom until fairly late in the century. A location five thousand miles from Athens disabled Americans almost as long. Nonetheless, the continental Europeans who dominated digging of the classical past had English-speaking competitors.

Of these, most influential was Charles Newton (seen already in chapter 7). Focusing on him best shows how classical archaeology evolved from pre-1850 antecedents, for Newton has a strong claim to be the first modern classical archaeologist in the English-speaking world. In 1861 Richard Jebb called him the "recognized head of classical archaeology" in the United Kingdom. And by then classical archaeology in the English-speaking world had become what it remains: specialized study of material relics of ancient Greeks and Romans,

---

*For reasons of space, this book omits the post-1850 development of Egyptian, Mesopotamian, and medieval European archaeology, especially as they did not differ *basically* from classical archaeology in method or relation to philology. Assyriology and Egyptology do get fleeting notice in connection with biblical criticism in chapter 13.

found most often by systematic excavation. Still, into the twentieth century English-speaking archaeologists valued such artifacts more for artistic interest than for light cast on daily life. (Germans began shifting emphasis a little earlier.) In fact, 'archaeology of art' became a common synonym for classical archaeology, and archaeology considerably overlapped with art history in its first decades as a discipline.[15]

In June 1850 Newton, addressing the Archaeological Institute of Great Britain and Ireland, signaled a transition. He still included in 'archaeology' linguistic evolution, oral traditions, and "Manners and Customs," along with "Monumental" evidence. (The last comprised both inscriptions and "Monuments of art and of handicraft.") But he strongly stressed "Monumental" or material archaeology. His experience in the next decade would make the emphasis exclusive.[16]

Newton understood archaeology as an extension of textual philology, as did most nineteenth-century Mediterranean archaeologists. The archaeologist strives "to collect, to classify, and to interpret all the evidence of man's history not already incorporated in Printed Literature"—just as "the researches of the Palaeographer of classical antiquity" extend from writing on parchment to inscriptions in granite. Newton shared the faith of the documentary historians discussed in chapter 7. He compared Greek and Roman coins (and "sepulchral brasses of the Middle Ages") to archival records. (After "a Muratori," he said, comes "a Gibbon.") Paleographers must become "deeply versed in history and philology"—not merely handwriting—to interpret old documents properly. So, too, archaeologists must know "the meaning or motive" pervading an artistic style, not just its "external characteristics." Only such erudition equips them "to read and interpret" the style. The archaeologist "is the Scholiast and the Lexicographer of Art," and ancient literature and ancient art interpret each other. As in the hermeneutic circle of textual philology, archaeological artifact and cultural context mutually illuminate: "the type of the Roman coin completes the historical record of its legend; the legend explains the type." As Muratori made the documentary record available for Gibbon, so archaeologists "read and interpret the indirect record" of ancient architecture "as evidence for the Historian." "Wherever man has left the stamp of mind on brute-matter"—"a ship, a garment, a piece of glass"—there archaeologists belong. Their motto*: "HOMO SUM, HUMANI NIHIL A ME ALIENUM PUTO."[17]

Newton developed these ideas into a mature classical archaeology by digging up a tomb. As assistant in the Department of Antiquities at the British Museum in 1846, he had studied twelve slabs of an ancient frieze recently pried from the walls of a Crusader fort in Bodrum (ancient Halicarnassus) on the southwest coast of Anatolia. Halicarnassus contained the Mausoleum, the fourth-century BCE tomb of the Persian satrap Mausolus, one of the Seven

---

* "I am a human being; I deem nothing human foreign to me": a tag from the second-century BCE Roman playwright Terence, familiar to every elite Victorian male.

Wonders of the Ancient World. The Mausoleum's exact site had evaporated from memory, but the newly acquired reliefs must have come from it—looted by the Crusaders to build their stronghold. In 1848, in Leonhard Schmitz's *Classical Museum*, Newton published an article about the sculptures; in it he speculated that the Mausoleum's remains lay buried in the center of modern Bodrum. In 1852 he quit the museum to become British vice consul on the Aegean island of Lesbos, not far from Bodrum—"in reality," Jebb noted, "an archaeological mission." Over the next six years Newton explored ancient Greek sites in Bodrum's vicinity, shipping trophies back to the British Museum.[18]

His triumph came in Bodrum itself. In 1855 he visited, examining remaining segments of frieze in the castle walls. He lobbied Britain's minister in Constantinople (Stratford Canning, financier of Layard's dig at Nimrud) and the foreign secretary for support. Newton got a couple thousand pounds, plus the loan of HM Steam Sloop *Gorgon* and several royal engineers. After an engineer pinpointed a likely site, Newton's Turkish crew began digging on New Year's Day 1857. His museum experience helped Newton find the Mausoleum's ruins. Textual philologists emended manuscripts by cross-referencing an uncertain passage with, in effect, a database of texts stored in memory. Newton applied the same subconscious comparative procedure to fragments of sculpture dug up by his workmen, separating later chaff from the fourth-century grains that led him to the prize. Newton had photographers to record the site exactly—one of the first archaeologists to use them. And he had Royal Engineers. Military engineers did a lot for archaeology (beginning with Karl Weber at Herculaneum). They had sapper's skills for difficult digging, mapping proficiency for precise plotting, construction know-how for moving heavy marbles safely with makeshift cranes and pulleys. By early April, Newton's crew had excavated most of the foundations of the Mausoleum, revealing its shape. In August the British Museum dispatched an English architect "for the purpose," Newton reported, "of delineating and describing the site and remains of the Mausoleum." By December the job was almost over. In Bodrum Newton worried what "science would demand," a revealing anxiety. Even more valuable than the artworks carried home by the Royal Navy was the expertise amassed, the example set. In 1861 the British Museum made Newton keeper of a new Department of Greek and Roman Antiquities. The next year he detailed the excavations in a learned, mildly technical volume. It served future archaeologists as a how-to guide.[19]

Newton had invented modern classical archaeology for the English-speaking world. Around 1700, antiquarians like William Stukeley honed techniques of digging and surveying; adventurers in the circle of the Dilettanti brought site surveys to a new standard of exactness; Henry Layard took both skill sets to Mesopotamia in his quest for Assyrian 'antiquities.' Newton cross-bred this technically astute antiquarianism with military engineering, then tutored the offspring in classical philology. Even Germans learned from him.

A half century later the archaeologist Adolf Michaelis summed up Newton's achievement. Prior to Bodrum, knowledge of buried Greek and Roman art and architecture came "almost exclusively" by "accidental discoveries." During the 1840s Richard Lepsius and Henry Layard excavated "more systematically" in Egypt and Mesopotamia, "extending our horizon beyond the classical countries." Newton first applied "this more systematic method on Greek territory." He not only "greatly widened the range of our knowledge, especially of the art of the fourth century," but also laid a solid basis for further advances— "more rigidly organized" expeditions in the 1860s and eventually "a more definite technique of excavation" that "preserved and reconstructed." The pioneers in these methods came chiefly from Michaelis's Germany, especially in the big Olympus excavations between 1875 and 1881. Newton in 1877 acknowledged German preeminence in "every branch of archaeological and philological study."[20]

He used his own eminence and his post at the British Museum to promote classical archaeology in the United Kingdom. He plied Parliament with pleas for grants and came away, over his career, with well in excess of £100,000— money he used both to buy on the antiquities market and to fund British excavations. At his retirement in 1885 no other collection of Greek sculpture, not even in Germany, rivaled the British Museum's. He pushed for teaching classical archaeology at Oxford and Cambridge and himself filled, in 1880, a new chair in it at University College London. His stature—and access to cash— made him arbiter among the growing number of British classical archaeologists in the field.[21]

John Turtle Wood provides a case in point. Wood's classical education in the 1840s left him peculiarly obsessed with the Temple of Artemis at Ephesus—another of the Seven Wonders of the Ancient World. After studying architecture, he practiced in London from the early 1850s (refining engineer-like skills). But Ephesus would not go away. In 1858 he got a job with a British firm building the first railway in the Ottoman Empire. The line ran from Smyrna (today's Izmir) to Aydin—opportunely passing through Ayasoluk (now Selçuk), an easy walk from the ruins of Ephesus. In 1863 Wood took his savings, quit the Oriental Railway Company, and began to dig. Once again, classical textual studies pointed the way for archaeology. Once again, excavation in Ephesus's waterlogged sands demanded engineering aptitude. Wood got— from the British Museum, thanks to Newton—grants to support his work, in return for any ancient art he found. Five more years of drudgery, danger, disease, and detective work followed. In December 1869 Wood found the Temple of Artemis, under twenty feet of soaked sand. (Immediately Newton had the museum buy the site.) It took another five years fully to excavate the pitifully shattered remains. The museum got only fragments, but these included large architectural elements blanketed with reliefs, along with decorated columns illuminating the evolution of Greek design. Dragging these massive pieces up from deep in the swamp taxed Wood so much that he never traced the overall layout of the temple. Works of art still trumped what "science would demand." In 1874 Wood went home, his dream fulfilled, minor fame achieved. In 1877 he published *Discoveries at Ephesus*.[22] Newton sponsored other British digs—in Rhodes, Cyprus, Sicily, eastern Libya, and multiple sites in Anatolia.

One, by Alfred Biliotti and Auguste Salzmann at Ialysos on Rhodes, helped to nudge Greek archaeology in a new direction. In 1868 the two started to dig artifacts from some ancient tombs. By sheer luck, an Egyptian scarab among their finds roughly dated them. In 1877 Newton and a young colleague, Percy Gardner, traveled to Greece on behalf of the museum, to examine Heinrich Schliemann's recent discoveries from Mycenae. Comparing Schliemann's material with that from Ialysos, Newton realized that Biliotti and Salzmann's graves were Mycenaean—and began to crack the mystery of Mycenaean civilization. He cast some of the earliest light on the Greek bronze age. His efforts to enlighten classicists at Oxford and Cambridge had less effect.[23]

If Newton created modern Anglophone classical archaeology, Americans first built institutions to house it. Classicists in the United States had long had more sympathy for the broad-gauged understanding of their field pioneered in Germany. University-based classical scholars helped to organize the Archaeological Institute of America (AIA) in 1879. Significantly, not only classicists took part. University leaders in the United States—some trained in Germany—chafed at their country's failure to keep up in archaeology even with the English, much less the Germans. The AIA sprang from these frustrations. Whereas the British dug Hellenic sites before they had organizations for the purpose, Americans started an institute to get themselves digging. Like the American Philological Association, the AIA did not begin with an exclusively classical focus (though a school in Athens was intended from the outset); but classicists quickly claimed most of its turf. Yet, where the APA showed clear marks of 'classics' becoming a discipline, the AIA seemed torn between old and new modes of erudition. Its main instigator and president until 1890, Professor Charles Eliot Norton, held no advanced degree, never studied in a German university, never supervised a dissertation, and published more scholarship on Dante, medieval architecture, and English poetry than on archaeology. He regarded the many nonprofessional members of the AIA as a strength, and he recruited young men untrained in archaeology for the Institute's first excavations, in Asia Minor.[24]

Still, if ambivalently, the AIA tilted toward disciplinarity. Norton saw need for supervisory experts even while worrying that disciplinary narrowness might strangle broad learning. In 1881 the AIA set up for graduate students the American School of Classical Studies in Athens. (France and Germany already had similar institutions.) A different American professor headed it each year. Norton failed to recruit as permanent director the archaeologist Charles Waldstein of Cambridge University—American-born, German-trained. Next to Norton himself, his Harvard colleague John Williams White was the key early organizer of classical archaeology in the United States. White worked in the linguistic-textual philological tradition, chiefly on Aristophanes. Yet in 1897 he became the first professional classicist to head the AIA. Such breadth of interests within the discipline was normal. Classical archaeologists with substantial careers in United States universities prior to 1920 invariably combined archaeology with philology. ('Pure' archaeologists ended up as museum curators or academic nomads.) The AIA also committed itself—and still does—to forging bonds between university-based scholars and a larger educated public. Yet its leaders increasingly understood this mission as translating disciplinary research for a passive popular audience—not as working hand in glove with part-time, avocational scholars, as did the American Oriental Society before the Civil War.[25]

Teetering between new-model discipline and old-style general culture muddled the AIA's *American Journal of Archaeology* from its first issue in 1885. Its editor, Professor Arthur Frothingham of Princeton, wanted a German-style *Zeitschrift*, fattened with monographic reports of research, to keep scholars up to date. Officially, however, the quarterly aimed to "make all the important work done in the field of Archaeology" accessible "in a convenient but scholarly form, to *all* who wish to inform themselves of the progress made in this branch of study." Confusingly, the journal also explicitly conceived itself as a venue for specialized research by classical archaeologists. It is hard to imagine general readers riveted by, say, an article in the first volume discussing an obscure inscription in Boeotian characters on a bronze statue-base dated circa 500 BCE. Such technical reports filled more and more of subsequent volumes. But only in the twentieth century did the journal definitively declare itself a specialized publication for classical and Mediterranean archaeologists, supplemented in 1912 by a new magazine for general readers.[26]

The American School of Classical Studies at Athens (ASCSA) had at first a personality split along the same lines. Classical learning long meant broad education and culture, and some early students treated the ASCSA as a classical finishing school—"for general cultivation in Greek studies" rather than "for special research in a particular department," as the first annual director put it. But many did come for "special research." The first class (1882–83) included future Greek professors at Cornell, Western Reserve, Columbia, and Chicago. Chicago's Paul Shorey became an eminence. Two of the others, Harold Fowler of Western Reserve and James Wheeler of Columbia, cowrote in 1909 the first English-language college textbook of Greek archaeology, for many years a standard; Fowler edited the *American Journal of Archaeology* from 1907 to 1916. Of the first thirty students, four were women; in 1899–1900, exceptionally, eight of fifteen were. This female presence mirrored not only women's entrance into the academic profession generally. It reflected, in particular, an embrace of classics by elite northeastern women's colleges founded in the decades after the Civil War (though the first woman at the ASCSA, Annie Peck in 1885, graduated from the University of Michigan). With classical studies the badge of elite male education, to offer a degree equal to a man's meant Greek. Bryn Mawr made itself a major center for classical research. In 1886 Wellesley became the first women's college to join the smallish group of institutions sponsoring the ASCSA. But ASCSA directors still believed women too delicate to root in dirt. So Harriet Boyd (Smith College 1892) took her fellowship money in 1900 and financed her own dig on Crete. It resulted in the first paper delivered by a woman to an AIA annual meeting and, in 1908, the first monograph on a Minoan site. (Boyd, later Harriet Boyd Hawes, went on to teach at Smith and Wellesley.) If not all early male students were discipline-minded, some females were.[27]

American Greek and Roman specialists embraced archaeology on the principle that 'classics' investigated all aspects of Greek and Roman civilizations—an axiom ultimately rooted in Altertumswissenschaft. (Not surprisingly, given tradition, well into the twentieth century British and American archaeologists still regarded textual evidence as more reliable.[28]) Some Americans—like Felton—had worked since the 1830s to widen the field in this way. By 1890 they had won. The humanistic discipline of classical studies, in a form recognizable today, had securely rooted itself in the United States. The story across the Atlantic was more complicated.

Classical Erudition in the United Kingdom

Broadly speaking, one can say that classical scholars in Britain and Ireland clung longer to purely textual philology. Many resisted archaeology, even epigraphy and numismatics. Quite a few acted as if they needed little historical context to make the meaning of texts clear and shrugged off theoretical or technical erudition. Most held out against separating classical studies from general culture. Broadly speaking, one can say all this; on the ground the situation grew confused.

Scotland stood out because its universities traditionally rejected Oxbridge models. A translation of Aeschylus in 1850 won John Stuart Blackie the Edinburgh Greek professorship in 1852. He held it until 1882, publishing a translation of the *Iliad*, with commentary, in 1866 before getting distracted by other hobbies. As a young man, he had studied in Göttingen with K. O. Müller and in Berlin with Boeckh; he developed an interest in archaeology as well as texts and adopted a historical approach to the study of antiquity. He sent his own students off for summer study of Greek in German universities. He sneered at the "absurdities" of the "Porsonian school." But Blackie had pursued theology in Germany more vigorously than classical philology. He trained as a lawyer, published a translation of part 1 of Goethe's *Faust*, taught Latin at Aberdeen before moving to Greek at Edinburgh. Neither persistent researcher nor proficient teacher, he yet became the best-known Scottish classicist of his generation. Blackie lectured with bubbling fervor and took an unconventionally broad view of classical studies—beyond even whose faraway fences he routinely wandered. His many works included a life of Burns; *The Wisdom of*

Goethe; *Christianity and the Ideal of Humanity*; and political tracts flavored by Scottish nationalism. He spent years plumping for a Celtic chair at Edinburgh. Whatever Blackie was, he was no close textual scholar in the Oxbridge line. Indeed, one of his "rambling" philological papers left his successor in the Greek chair, Samuel Butcher, hopeless of "following the movements of a genius so erratic." "An accomplished and amiable man, blessed with a fortunate want of sensitiveness" (Caroline Jebb's view), Blackie was more sage than savant.[29]

More thorough scholars were pushing the boundaries of 'classics' beyond explicating ancient texts. Rev. Charles MacDouall began his university career as professor of Hebrew at Edinburgh in 1847—then immediately got expelled for deserting the Church of Scotland. In 1849 the new Queen's College in Belfast hired him as its first Latin professor. A year later, when the chair of Greek opened, he hopped to it. MacDouall discharged his duties conscientiously; but his real interest lay in neither Hebrew, Latin, nor Greek, but in all of them and more. He certainly stood far from a 'discipline' of classics—or any modern discipline. 'Comparative philologist' may best describe him, but any single label falsely pins him down. The range of his personal library stuns: grammars and texts in Chinese, Turkish, Burmese, Telegu, Tamil, Persian, Armenian, Avestan, Mongolian, Japanese, Tibetan, and many other tongues, including early forms of several European languages. Always and everywhere he preached the philologist's gospel that "the peculiarities of any one language,—like the characteristic features of any one country,—are best illustrated by collation with others." But he *was* professor of Greek for twenty-eight years; his library and his manuscript remains contain much in that line. As a classicist he admired Niebuhr and his methods. He regarded ancient Greeks as remote from modern values, not as Victorians in chitons. He generally admired them, though lamenting their polytheism. He did see them as connected to moderns through ongoing influence of Greek culture and common human nature. But in writings and classroom lectures he was apt to compare Greeks with their linguistic relatives in ancient India, rather than to treat them as like 'us.' He put Greek culture in the context of an extended ancient world, not his own modern one.[30]

Trinity College Dublin, founded in 1592 as an Oxbridge on the Liffey, on the whole sniffed at intellectual innovation—but then there was Rev. John Pentland Mahaffy, its professor of ancient history. Born in Switzerland, partly raised in Germany, Mahaffy was not the typical Trinity don. As early as the 1870s he maintained contacts at German universities, worked on a social history of ancient Greece, and anticipated a history of Greek literature in the spirit of Otfried Müller. In 1871 he published a study of Assyrian, Egyptian, and Persian materials as prolegomena to Greek and Roman history. Not every classicist thought highly of Mahaffy's syntheses. But he did technical work, valued by German experts, emending papyrus fragments of Greek authors. Among the sources for his several books figured not only such Egyptian papyri but also German collections of fragments and inscriptions, Sir John Lub-bock's writings about primitive peoples, and Henry Rowe Schoolcraft's books on American Indians. Oxford and Cambridge did not talk like this.[31]

Yet they remained the center of gravity of classical erudition in the United Kingdom, and what happened there mattered more than anything in Scotland or Ireland. The two universities approached the ancients differently. At Cambridge, the tradition of Porson endured until the 1870s. Scholars (and the students they taught) kept their eyes fixed on the language of the text in front of them; even issues of literary style counted as illicit wandering from grammar. D'Arcy Thompson, Greek professor at Queen's College Galway from 1864 to 1902, tongue barely in cheek, described the Cambridge classicist: "All information, historical, antiquarian, geographical, or philosophic, as connected with the classics, he regarded with contempt: any dunderhead, he considered, might cram that at his leisure: but it pained him to the quick if a senior pupil violated the Porsonian pause,* or trifled with the subjunctive." At Oxford, in contrast, classical studies centered on philosophy. Aristotle had ruled the roost since the Middle Ages, but Plato knocked him off after 1850. Plato's best known Oxford friend was Benjamin Jowett, from 1855 Regius Professor of Greek, later powerful master of Balliol College. Jowett's translation of the *Dialogues* stood as the monument of Oxford classical scholarship. A. E. Housman's jibe at Jowett's looseness in translation reflected the temperamental conflict between Cambridge and Oxford. He called Jowett's Plato "the best translation of a Greek philosopher which has ever been executed by a person who understood neither philosophy nor Greek."[32]

Classical scholars in the two universities, however, typically agreed on two matters. Both encountered the ancients almost exclusively in writing; both swept their awkward antiquity under the carpet. Both treated Plato—words or thoughts, respectively—as if timeless, as immediately present to the reader of 1870 as to his contemporaries. (What ever-living Plato tried to say did change over the years.) Neither university had much use for material remains of antiquity, because neither had much wish to take antiquity on its own terms rather than the nineteenth century's. Texts were all. Housman dated the revival of English classical erudition from publication in 1864 of Hugh Munro's edition of Lucretius. Wilamowitz thought it began with Housman's own first paper in 1882, another purely textual performance. Between 1854 and 1859 Cambridge University Press published the *Journal of Classical and Sacred Philology*, with contributors from both universities. Three youthful Cambridge philologists edited it; two later became celebrated biblical scholars, the third a learned Latinist. The journal appreciated German learning—so long as it was verbal criticism. The editors got nearest to classical archaeology in recording briefly the discovery of some new inscriptions and a couple of statues.[33]

---

* The Porsonian pause is a caesura occurring in a particular metrical situation in Greek tragedy; Porson set forth the rule in his preface to Euripides's *Hecuba*.

Only late in the century did this situation change fundamentally, under external pressures. They took two forms.

First, competitors to the two ancient universities multiplied. From the late 1820s, the new University College London dumped the classics-drenched curriculum of Oxford and Cambridge and embraced German-style philology, English literature, and other 'modern' fields. (Tiny University of Durham, founded in 1832, aped Oxbridge.) In 1845 Parliament authorized nondenominational colleges in Belfast, Cork, and Galway, to give Irish Catholics substitutes for Anglican Trinity. Civic leaders in English cities outside London hankered for a 'useful' higher education for their city's boys (and soon girls). In 1851 Owens College was founded in Manchester. Between 1874 and 1882 other university-level colleges opened in Leeds, Birmingham, Bristol, and Liverpool. Together with a later one in Sheffield (1897), these institutions gained degree-granting authority between 1900 and 1909—the so-called redbrick or civic universities. (Until then, students got degrees through the University of London or a now defunct Victoria University, set up in 1880.) In the 1870s and 1880s three similar colleges were founded in Wales, then in 1893 the University of Wales to award degrees to their graduates. In all of these schools 'modern' subjects such as English literature, history, modern languages, and natural science dominated. Latin and Greek, if at first taught at all, took a decidedly subordinate position. Though lacking the prestige of Oxford and Cambridge, the new colleges offered an alternative education that appealed to many—and suggested a model for updating the ancient universities.[34]

A majority in Parliament saw need for updating even before Owens College opened, and government exerted the second, direct form of external pressure. Starting in 1850 with Royal Commissions to investigate Oxford and Cambridge, and continuing for some thirty years, parliamentary interventions pushed the ancient universities toward curricular modernization, funding of research, abolition of religious tests, and a faculty structure more nourishing of permanent academic careers. Feeling some duress, both universities created in the 1850s new paths to honors degrees. As with the expanding subjects in American colleges, but more dramatically, these new courses gradually turned classics into one field among many rather than simply essential liberal education—and eventually turned classicists from general-purpose teachers into specialists. Parliamentary nudging toward more research suggested what such specialists might do.[35]

These circumstances created an opening for inside agitators wanting a more 'scientific,' research-friendly, German-style classical scholarship. At Oxford a prime perturber of the peace was Mark Pattison, Rector of Lincoln College from 1861 to 1884. Thomas Arnold's teenage daughter Mary remembered Pattison and his friend Ingram Bywater,* in Pattison's library around 1870,

---

* Mary Arnold would later be known as the novelist Mrs. Humphry Ward, famous for *Robert Elsmere* (1888).

talking warmly of Ranke and Curtius, sneering at Oxford's pretense of erudition, and fuming (as Mary recalled) at Balliol College, "which aimed at turning out public officials, as compared with the researching ideals of the German universities, which seemed to the Rector the only ideals worth calling academic."[36]

Pattison saw research, especially research alert to history, as a form of high culture, not distinct from it. In 1869 he helped to launch *The Academy*, the first magazine devoted to book reviews by academic specialists—but covering books in all fields of knowledge. In the 1850s Pattison had become seriously interested in German scholarship. One of the first fruits of this curiosity—perhaps even the impetus for it—was an encounter with Jacob Bernays. Among the most brilliant German classical philologists of his generation, Bernays was a Jew, thus effectively barred from a university chair. (Ministers of education, holding power of appointment, enforced anti-Semitism even while some of the greatest German classical scholars admired and befriended Bernays.) He spent the first half of his teaching career at a Jewish theological seminary, the second at his alma mater, Bonn, as librarian and 'extraordinary professor' (roughly equivalent to untenured assistant professor in the United States today). In 1855 Bernays published a biography of J. J. Scaliger—whom Pattison was then investigating for a projected series of lives of French Renaissance scholars, never completed. The coincidence brought the two men together. They became friends. Pattison spent a good deal of time in Germany in the late 1850s and grew into a shrewd and by no means uncritical observer of German academic life. He admired the rigor of German erudition, above all Bernays's, but wanted to smooth its rough edges with the suavity of the English man of letters. As a prose stylist, Pattison ranked high; as a scholar, he had serious weaknesses. (His autobiography may be his greatest work.) But Pattison knew himself to be knee-high next to Bernays and channeled his best students to Bonn for advanced work. Bernays become a conduit for inflow of German scholarly ideals into Oxford classical erudition.[37]

The most consequential beneficiaries of his tutelage were Henry Nettleship and Ingram Bywater. Nettleship eventually became Corpus Christi Professor of Latin in Oxford, Bywater Regius Professor of Greek. Pattison sent Nettleship to Bernays in 1865, Bywater three years later. (Bernays, not yet teaching in Bonn in 1865, affected Nettleship less than did Moritz Haupt in Berlin.) Both returned to Oxford to advocate and exemplify rigorous, Germanic classical research. Both sent their own promising students to Bernays. Nettleship contributed important work in Vergilian studies and in Latin lexicography— and edited Pattison's essays after his mentor's death. He also seems to have taught the first German-style classical seminar in Oxford. Nettleship stressed (in Christopher Stray's words) "the opposition between gentlemanly compositional classics and the learning of the academic scholar." Bywater, who traveled frequently to Germany, became, like Pattison, a friend of Bernays. Bernays advised on Bywater's 1877 edition of fragments of the pre-Socratic philosopher Heraclitus that made his scholarly reputation. Bywater continued to seek Bernays's advice, and Bernays encouraged his interest in Aristotle. This resulted ultimately in Bywater's magnum opus, a 1909 edition of the *Poetics*. Bernays's last known letter before his death in 1881 was to Bywater. Unusually for a British or Irish scholar, Bywater published in German journals. Almost equally odd, he shared Pattison's and Bernays's fascination with the history of scholarship. Peerless in his generation as editor of Greek texts, Bywater received high honors in Germany as well as the United Kingdom. As a longtime Delegate of Oxford University Press, Bywater acted as a gatekeeper for classical scholarship published in English, enforcing his German-stained standards.[38]

Yet Bywater and Nettleship applied German research norms to traditional textual philology; even Germanophile Oxford classicists hesitated to move beyond the text. A turning point came in 1887 when Percy Gardner became first incumbent of a new Lincoln and Merton Professorship of Classical Archaeology. But the turning creaked slowly. Gardner (primarily a numismatist), bred up at the British Museum under the shadow of Charles Newton, admired German methods of excavation. Oxford, by and large, admired nothing so far outside the text as archaeology. It took Gardner years of struggle to sneak the camel's nose under the tent of Literae Humaniores ('Greats,' the historical-philosophical Oxford classical course), and its nose never got further inside than a 'special subject' in Greek sculpture in Honour Moderations in the 1890s. Archaeology did not come into its own at Oxford until appointment in 1907 of Francis John Haverfield—an archaeologist specialized in Roman Britain—as Camden Professor of Ancient History. As late as 1900 Oxford students studied ancient history chiefly by reading ancient texts.[39]

At Cambridge the classicists—who, after all, had long endured the greater prestige of mathematics—moved slightly faster toward change. Suspicion that Plato and Cicero differed from Victorians in more than native language crept over even diehard Porsonians. Might one gaze on the ancients through the lens of history? A telling moment came in 1879 when reform of the Cambridge classical tripos allowed students to add a new part 2, testing work in philosophy, archaeology, history, comparative philology, or art—if they wished. Few did, a fact that says as much about their teachers as them. Not until 1918 was part 2 required.[40]

The career of Richard Jebb exemplified the slow shift toward more holistic 'classics.' Coming from a prominent Anglo-Irish family, Jebb stood slightly askew English life. He went through the Cambridge classics mill at Trinity, taking his degree in 1862. He excelled at composing Latin and Greek verses but found the requirement "utterly barren." (Later he appreciated this linguistic drilling as foundation for broader-gauged scholarship.) Elected fellow of Trinity in 1863, Jebb enjoyed Cambridge life, but his approach to classical studies fitted poorly. "What time he can spare from the adornment of his person," said the master, "he devotes to the neglect of his duties." He learned German, went to Germany to improve it, monitored German scholarship. (Predictably, he got on well with Ingram Bywater at Oxford.) With the new Sanskrit professor Edward Cowell, he founded the Cambridge Philological Society in 1868, a small-scale analogue to the contemporaneous American Philological Association, with a parallel *Journal of Philology*. Jebb and Cowell's journal floated between the learned generalism of Hare and Thirlwall's *Philological Museum* and the disciplinary periodicals in the United States. In 1875 Jebb accepted the Greek chair at Glasgow—but lived half the year in Cambridge.[41]

Glasgow began a new phase for Jebb. In 1878 he visited Greece to look into archaeological outfits set up by France and Germany. He seemed puzzled by the contrast between English classicists, who ignored material relics, and English biblical critics and historians, who valued facts archaeology furnished. Returning from Greece, Jebb aided Charles Newton, the publisher George Macmillan, and the Greek chargé d'affaires John Gennadius in creating a Society for the Promotion of Hellenic Studies (1879); under its aegis, a *Journal of Hellenic Studies* (1880) pushed British classical studies beyond texts by highlighting history and archaeology. The classical establishment mostly stayed aloof: under a fifth of the founding members came from universities. But in 1883 even Cambridge got a classical archaeologist—though it had to hire a German-trained American, Charles Waldstein.* Jebb's own scholarship remained textual and interpretively conservative—like that of John Williams White, America's energetic advocate of archaeology. The Irishman's monument is a seven-volume edition of Sophocles's plays. A century later his commentaries "remain the yardstick by which all subsequent ones are measured," according to Roger Dawe. Jebb's caution in conjectural emendation stood out in an era of fond imaginings. Yet this fastidious philologist—who in 1896 helped F. G. Kenyon piece together papyrus fragments that restored to the world the odes of Bacchylides (fl. 475 BCE)—led in promoting archaeology. With Newton's backing, he midwifed the British School at Athens in 1886 as a base for excavations and for training classical archaeologists, like the American School founded five years earlier. So when Cambridge, appreciating his textual scholarship, called Jebb to its Greek professorship in 1889, it signaled at least tolerance of a broadened 'classics.'[42]

Soon Cambridge stepped almost unimaginably far from verbal philology. In the early 1880s a young classical philologist of Trinity College, James G. Frazer, was at work translating the 'guidebook' to Greece written by Pausanias in the second century CE. Pausanias described architecture and landscape but also pried into local lore. Offbeat rituals and myths particularly fascinated him. Like Jebb, Frazer grew up on the Celtic fringe, but in Glasgow, where he attended university before matriculating at Trinity, finishing high in the clas-

* Since 1851 Cambridge had a professor of archaeology, endowed by an enthusiast for classical art, John Disney. But no Disney Professor actually specialized in archaeology until 1880, when Percy Gardner arrived from the British Museum.

sical tripos, and getting elected fellow. He came from the Free Church of Scotland, a bookish lot, overpopulated with independent thinkers given to theological dogfights. Frazer dropped Christianity but not the maverick Free Church intellectual style.[43]

In late 1883 a slightly older Free Churcher, William Robertson Smith, showed up in Cambridge. Smith will appear in the last chapter as a biblical philologist and founder of the comparative study of religion. For now, it matters that his studies had led him into totemism and other ethnological topics—and that he edited the *Encyclopædia Britannica*. When Smith arrived, he joined Trinity and moved into rooms in the neo-Gothic pile of Whewell's Court, a kind of annex to the main buildings of the college across Trinity Street. Some weeks later, in the combination room after dinner, Smith settled down to chat with the thirty-year-old Frazer. Homesickness perhaps drew Smith to his fellow Scot. Whatever the attraction, it hardly matched the magnetic effect he had on the younger man: "I never afterwards," Frazer recalled, "attempted to dispute the mastership which he thenceforward exercised over me by his extraordinary union of genius and learning." A walking tour of Scotland that September cemented the bond. Frazer was never Smith's best friend, but Smith had become Frazer's.[44]

Frazer was primed to fall for Smith. A few years earlier, he had read and been much taken with E. B. Tylor's *Primitive Culture*. Tylor drew Frazer to anthropology, and this enthrallment resonated with Smith's ethnological interests. As Frazer said, "my interest in the subject might have remained purely passive and inert if it had not been for the influence of . . . Smith." Yet Tylor and Smith touched a nerve ready to tingle. Any philologist who chose to translate Pausanias—a big job—must have had a powerful ethnographic curiosity to begin with, and likely one tilted toward myth and cult.[45]

The encounter with Smith turned Frazer's abundant energies in a new direction. Smith recognized his new friend's considerable talents. He assigned Frazer to write on "Taboo" and "Totemism" for the *Encyclopædia Britannica*: subjects close to Smith's heart, especially the latter. As Smith privately admitted, he stood over his colleague's shoulder as he wrote about totemism, "guiding Frazer carefully on his treatment." This apprenticeship launched Frazer on the study of primitive religion. In 1887 appeared his first book, *Totemism*. As his biographer Robert Ackerman says, this small volume "was the most considerable monograph on the subject" published to date, "bringing together data from all over the world": "it immediately became the standard authority in the then sparsely populated field." Pausanias went on the shelf (finally to emerge from the press in 1898, in six volumes). For the rest of his long life, Frazer oscillated between classical philology and armchair anthropology. With the latter, he tried to track the evolution of the human mind—as other Scots had done in the eighteenth century. There resulted in 1890, in two volumes, *The Golden Bough: A Study in Comparative Religion*. Frazer dedicated the book to Smith, "in gratitude and admiration." He even asked his publisher to design his book after Smith's *Religion of the Semites*. *The Golden Bough* learnedly speculated on the origin and nature of mythology and religion. Information piled up for revised editions. Frazer promised his publisher to "try to study brevity." If sincere, he was an appallingly bad student. The third edition, finished in 1915, reached twelve volumes. In 1922, he took pity on readers and boiled it all down into a single volume.[46]

Conceptually, *The Golden Bough* of 1890 showed little originality. Frazer started from Smith's fascination with rituals where a god itself became sacrificial victim. The key organizing principles came from Tylor and Smith. Frazer adopted Tylor's notion of 'survivals'—"processes, customs, opinions, and so forth, which have been carried on by force of habit into a new state of society different from that in which they had their original home, and they thus remain as proofs and examples of an older condition of culture." From Smith he got the theory that, in primitive religion, practice precedes doctrine—that is, a ritual comes first, then devotees devise an explanation for it, typically in the form of a myth. Frazer pioneered only in subject matter: in applying these notions to classical antiquity. (To say that he elaborated on ancient sources is an understatement.) Frazer elucidated the origins of 'civilized' Greco-Roman religion by deploying comparative data from 'primitive' religions. He used much material about agricultural rituals collected in the 1860s by the German folklorist Wilhelm Mannhardt.[47]

Frazer studied rituals to recover primeval religious ideas otherwise lost—his real fixation. Precedence of ritual to myth mattered to him only for validating this technique. In the second edition (1900), with Smith dead, Frazer moved away from totemism, dropped the ritual theory. He pivoted his revised study instead on a "sharp distinction between magic and religion" (as he told his publisher), a difference blurred in 1890. The subtitle changed to *A Study in Magic and Religion*. Frazer now argued that primitive worshippers understood sacrifice as *magic* with which their priest-king made gods do as he wished. Later, truly *religious* sacrifices, in contrast, appeased an offended deity or prayed for its aid. The "true subject" of *The Golden Bough*, as Robert Ackerman observed, was "nothing less than humanity's long upward struggle towards an understanding of itself and the world." "A necessary stage in mental evolution," religion was now "superseded by a world-view based on rationality: positive science." Frazer did not invent the magic/religion polarity; but his elaboration of it introduced an original theme, influential for a while, into comparative study of religion. But the academic world was changing. By the time the third edition appeared, the anthropologists with whom Frazer identified were fleeing his comparative method, grand speculation, and armchair travels for the particularities of fieldwork. Notwithstanding, *The Golden Bough* may be the most widely read (or skimmed) work of anthropology ever written in English. To follow its fortunes would travel far afield from classics.[48]

But—and this matters now—*The Golden Bough* remained tightly linked to classical studies. Even though Australian aborigines may have engrossed

Frazer more than ancient Greeks and Romans, Pausanias kept popping up in *The Golden Bough*. Its title came from an event in the *Aeneid*—"the legend of the Golden Bough," Frazer explained, "as that legend is given by Servius in his commentary on Virgil." And Frazer's book began by exploring a ritual combat linked to a cult of Diana at a temple in Nemi, southeast of Rome, site of a recent archaeological dig. Greeks and Romans dot the book. Unlike a study that *only* discussed the outré doings of people in New Guinea or Polynesia, *The Golden Bough* might fascinate classical scholars.[49]

It did. *The Golden Bough* inspired a few younger classicists at Cambridge: Jane Harrison, F. M. Cornford, and Arthur Cook—plus one at Oxford, Gilbert Murray. They responded to Frazer to different degrees, under different influences. What they shared was the axiom that Frazer took from William Robertson Smith: ritual begot mythology. Before backing off in later editions, Frazer passed Smith's precept on to Harrison and the others. Thus, this constellation of scholars came to be called the Cambridge Ritualists. Harrison held the group together, to the extent it held together at all. Frazer himself never belonged, a distant icon. Distance had a reason: the Ritualists fully (if temporarily) accepted Smith's maxim, just when Frazer was backpedaling. The most influential expression of Ritualism was Harrison's 1903 work *Prolegomena to the Study of Greek Religion*. (Wolf's *Prolegomena ad Homerum* echoed.) Harrison limned turbulent, exotic rituals beneath the long-supposed serenity of the Olympian gods. The first chapter announced the key contrast between Olympian and chthonic ritual—between rituals of "service" to the mild gods of Olympus and rituals "of 'riddance' or 'aversion' addressed to an order of beings wholly alien," terrifying gods of the underworld. The book went on to show how the cult of Dionysus and the Orphic mysteries even undermined the Olympians. Smith's leverage showed in Harrison's interpretation of totem, taboo, and exogamy as instruments of social cohesion, as well as in her attention to rituals of initiation. Her friend Gilbert Murray's *Four Stages of Greek Religion* and her own *Themis*, both published in 1912, furthered their case that religion centers on the nonrational. What "we tend to worship," wrote Murray, are "things not of reason, but both below and above it, causes of emotion which we cannot express." Rituals—such as the Orphic rites that attracted and appalled Harrison—spring from and let worshippers vent primal feelings inspired by such sub- or suprarational apperceptions of an unnerving world lurking beyond the everyday.[50]

Specifics of Harrison's argument and her famous distinction between Olympian and Chthonic ritual need no detailed discussion, for her impact on 'classics' came chiefly through the more general picture of Greek religion she painted. In it, the familiar Olympian deities originated as transformed animal spirits of the underworld. (Probably this claim ultimately traces back to Smith's writings about totemism.) Real, barbarous, bloody rituals lay behind the symbolic violence in later cults of Dionysius and Orpheus. Whether the sacrificers of children could already read and write made a nice question—not clearly answered—because in other respects they belonged on the 'primitive' side of the watershed parting civilization from what came before. Harrison got the nickname "Bloody Jane," but the sex and bloodshed she postulated repulsed her.[51] At every step, Harrison privileged emotion and the unconscious over rationality and conscious thought. Scholars found her often unconvincing. Still a sense lingered of ancient Greeks closer to primitive folk than modern people. Harrison's approach also struck at the hegemony of the text: for her, *thoughts* and *beliefs* documented in the canonical literature of ancient Greece took second place to *actions* and *rituals* recorded on a clay seal found in Knossos, on gold plates dug from ancient tombs, on the painted vases that Harrison studied early in her career.

Put succinctly, the Cambridge Ritualists leached from the Greek past its familiarity, its direct relevance to the present, its traditional entailment in the cultural life of the here and now. And they made essential to classical studies the nontextual evidence that German philologists had long welcomed, that Americans had greeted hospitably, but that most Oxbridge philologists had scorned until recently. As both of these achievements sank into the workaday research of other classicists, the changing content of higher education would matter. When classical texts no longer dominated the classroom, they no longer seemed so obviously central to the disciplinary inquiries of the classical scholars who taught there.

By no means all classicists appreciated the Ritualists. Harrison's books made Wilamowitz shudder; and most classicists, like him, continued to focus on canonical texts. Even a not unfriendly writer in the *Classical Review* in 1913—who called Harrison "the Scholar Gipsy of Hellenic studies" for ranging through "dark and devious coverts of savage anthropology"—ticked off error after implausibility before concluding that her method resembled wishful thinking more than "science." Training of classicists in the United Kingdom and Ireland typically remained staunchly "verbal and stylistic," as David Grene, a 1936 MA of Trinity College Dublin, testified.[52]

Still, classical research broadened. The work of the Ritualists led eventually to such seminal books as E. R. Dodds's *The Greeks and the Irrational* (1951) and permanently changed the face of ancient Greek civilization. By the early twentieth century, then, even some leading Oxbridge classicists opened up to nonliterary evidence and stressed the historical distance separating themselves from their subjects very much as American classicists did—in fact, in the case of the Ritualists, going a lot further than Americans.

Two telling differences from American experience stand out. First, although German example proved decisive in both countries, it sometimes came from different quarters. German classical philologists influenced Nettleship and Bywater—like Gildersleeve and Goodwin. German philologists lay behind Frazer and the Ritualists, too, but not German *classical* philologists. German Old Testament scholarship pushed William Robertson Smith to assert the primacy of ritual over myth and doctrine: the principle he handed on to Frazer and thence to Harrison. Second—as this cross-fertilization between biblical and classical scholarship may hint—discipline formation moved at different speeds. In the United States specialization marched hand in hand with the historicizing and broadening of classical studies. In the United Kingdom serious discipline formation came later, *after* the crucial intellectual developments of the 1880s and 1890s. Both Oxford and Cambridge had philological societies by the 1870s, but neither specialized in classical philology. No national organization for classicists existed before the Classical Association in 1903. And this new association aimed more to defend the place of Latin and Greek in education than to promote research—the motive behind founding of the American Philological Association thirty-four years earlier. Creation of the Society for the Promotion of Roman Studies in 1910 added both a sister for the Society for the Promotion of Hellenic Studies and further confusion about the center of gravity of classical scholarship. Similar stories could be told about journals available for classicists to publish in. 'Classics' did not jell as a 'discipline' in Britain until perhaps the 1920s.[53]

But it did, and any reader of the Classical Association's *Classical Quarterly* will recognize the melding of American and British classical scholarship into a single disciplinary whole. So the oldest mode of philology became one discipline among the humanities. In becoming a discipline, 'classics' absorbed not only classical philology but also related inquiries long grouped together as 'antiquarianism'—archaeology, numismatics, epigraphy, the study of 'art objects' like statues and vases. For this reason, classicists studied evidence perhaps broader in scope than any other humanistic scholars—and needed training in more numerous technical practices. No other of the humanities exhibited so little of the narrowness associated with modern academic disciplines, because no other retained so much continuity with the multiple practices of early modern philology and its erudite neighbors like antiquarianism and chronology. Classicists today may talk routinely only to each other, but they talk about a remarkable range of things.

One can see the trajectory leading to 'classics' in still longer perspective. The philologist's original and still core job—from Hellenistic Alexandria to twenty-first-century Austin, Texas—was to (re)produce a text as faithful as possible in words and meaning to a putative, lost original. This original might be an imagined oral recitation of a Homeric bard or an imagined letter from St. Paul to a Christian community in Anatolia. To recover the lost words, the philologist scrutinized all available texts purporting to replicate the original, excised all additions, corrected all errors, filled plausibly all gaps. This task was the first meaning of 'criticism.' To carry out the job, the critic needed to know intimately the milieu whence came the lost original. Without such knowledge, no critic could recognize locutions current in that context, identify implausible words and phrases, make a well-informed guess how to fill lacunae. At first, the philologist got this expertise by comparing the text under inspection with (at least implicitly) other texts from roughly the same time and place.

Other learned persons (including many philologists) independently pursued interests in collecting artifacts of various sorts—statues, coins, seals, vases—from past places.

The revolution of the later eighteenth and early nineteenth centuries—carried through mostly by German-speaking philologists—brought together systematically philological knowledge derived from texts with antiquarian information derived from other artifacts. Data gleaned from a coin minted under the Emperor Diocletian or from a Hellenistic inscription in an Anatolian ruin could illuminate the meaning of texts as usefully as data gathered from manuscripts. But antiquarian material had always held its own allure apart from its utility for textual philologists. When Wolf and Boeckh and Müller melded manuscripts and material objects to create Altertumswissenschaft, their gaze also shifted from individual classical texts to the ancient world whence they came. The aim of even textual philology became, for them, to understand Greek and Roman antiquity in their completeness. This new undertaking American scholars admired from afar and finally succeeded in joining after 1860, while many British and Irish classical philologists resisted until near the end of the nineteenth century.

Once domesticated in the Anglophone world, holistic study of classical antiquity demanded that researchers stay abreast of such diverse subfields as archaeology, epigraphy, papyrology, art history—and textual philology. The pressure tended to separate classicists from philologists once their near neighbors, such as biblical critics and orientalists. As late as 1800 the same scholar might comment on Attic tragedy, Anglo-Saxon poetry, and the Old Testament. Not in 1900. Distance between fields grew greater, boundaries clearer, as stresses of professionalization and specialization in newly research-inclined universities detached the learned into disciplines. Philology fragmented into several of these, most of them collectively labeled humanities. Classics became one.

PART II: HISTORY

History was another. The British ambassador James Bryce, who knew the United States well, observed that in American colleges around 1910, "among the so-called 'humanistic' subjects," history drew "the largest number of students," many more than those "occupied with Greek and Latin." While fewer studied history at Oxford and Cambridge, the subject had existed as an honors course in both universities from the early 1870s—and, yoked with English literature and political science, at Trinity College Dublin from the 1850s. By 1880 or so history had firmly established itself as a distinct and distinctly academic member of "the so-called 'humanistic' subjects" in universities throughout the United Kingdom and United States.[54]

How did history develop from a literary vocation, practiced mostly outside colleges and universities, to a leading discipline of the new humanities? Classical philology evolved into 'classics' by expanding its range; historical writing became disciplinary 'history' by contracting its. British and American classical scholars—following German example—shifted focus from Greek and Roman texts to the civilizations that produced them; classicists then adopted a holistic approach to studying antiquity, again more or less in German style. These academics absorbed into classics almost any method or evidence that could cast light on ancient Greece and Rome: coins, statues, ruined buildings, inscriptions, and of course texts alongside things dug up. Historians did the reverse, erasing whole classes of evidence and experience.

Boundaries of what qualified as history remained wide and fluid before 1850. True, many histories written in English between the late eighteenth and mid-nineteenth century look much like history as we know it today: Gibbon, Grote, Prescott, less celebrated authors such as Lingard and Thirlwall. But 'history' included writings that no longer bear the name. Speculations about ancient societies that left no written records—say, Greeks at the time of the Trojan War—counted as history, even though a kind of philosophical-anthropological guesswork. Putting botany and politics under one roof seems odd now, but writers commonly linked natural with civil history. The third volume of Jeremy Belknap's *History of New Hampshire* (1792) included ten pages describing the state's birds, and two years later Samuel Williams published a *Natural and Civil History of Vermont*. Scottish universities retained chairs combining natural and civil history well into the nineteenth century. Birds and barons, Burke and unlettered Boeotians all bumped elbows in the roomy hall of history. The Ohio author Alexander Kinmont in 1838 included religious doctrine in "the Natural History of Man," strange as it looks now to fold Persian Magi and St. Paul into natural history.[55]

This terminological promiscuity came under stricter policing around the middle of the nineteenth century. History then began to assume clearly its modern disciplinary definition. The marriage of philosophy and philology had already produced, in Gibbon's hands, a fresh and admired model of erudite historical narrative. Niebuhr's history of Rome injected philology even more deeply into the genes of this new history in the English-speaking world. (In 1895 Herbert Baxter Adams knelt to Niebuhr as "the real founder" of the modern disciplinary history that Adams taught at Johns Hopkins.[56]) After 1850, 'philological' history became, at least for professors, simply history *pur sang*.

The Invention of Prehistory

A decisive break came right around 1860. As late as the 1850s, the accepted timeline of human history still derived largely from the Bible and specifically from the Pentateuch, the five 'books of Moses.' The seventeenth-century Irish chronologer James Ussher calculated that the Creation began on Saturday, October 22, 4004 BCE. Not every scholar accepted Archbishop Ussher's arithmetic, and both Egyptian records and Chinese traditions raised questions. By the later eighteenth century, moreover, serious natural historians agreed on a vastly older earth.[57] In Charles Lyell's widely persuasive *Principles of Geology* (1830–33) the earth preceded humankind by millions of years. But until the mid-nineteenth century a consensus prevailed that *human beings* had existed no more than a few thousand years longer than the earliest Egyptian hiero- glyphs. History based on written records covered most of humanity's time on earth.

This consensus collapsed right after 1860, when perspective suddenly shifted on long-accumulating evidences. Diggers in Danish peat bogs and old grave mounds had from time to time found well-preserved bodies and artifacts of ancient people; the director of the national museum in Copenhagen, Christian Thomsen, in 1819 first organized such material according to a tripartite divi- sion of Stone Age, Bronze Age, and Iron Age. And natural historians had, for some decades, explored sites where human remnants—weapons, tools, even skeletons—mingled with remains of animals known as extinct. But all this could be explained, or explained away, without compromising the Mosaic chronology. A human skeleton found with mammoth bones had been buried there by later people; bodies discovered with stone axes meant that Danes four or five thousand years ago lived as primitively as modern savages.[58]

Yet the scaffolding for understanding such finds was creaking. Growing knowledge of fossils in rock strata millions of years old strained the Genesis creation story (though did not refute it if 'six days' of creation were metaphori- cal). Karl Richard Lepsius's *Chronologie der Aegypter* (*Egyptian Chronology*, 1849) demolished the Old Testament time frame for the learned. So, when in 1858 a team of geologists excavated Brixham Cave in Devonshire, the Mosaic chronology had a slacker grip on their thinking. The dig, supervised by lead- ing scientists, was meticulously carried out. It found implements made by human hands intermingled with bones of extinct mammals in sealed strata inches below the modern cave floor. There could be no mistake. The impact was immediate. A year later the doyen of geologists, Charles Lyell, long resis- tant to deep human antiquity, announced his conversion to a new, long chro- nology of human existence. In 1863 he published *Geological Evidences of the Antiquity of Man*.[59]

The "revolution in ethnological time," as Thomas Trautmann called it, does not figure in standard accounts of the evolution of history as a discipline; but it helped to create history as we now know it. Document-based historians could only throw up their pens in despair upon learning that during most of humanity's time on earth no one could write. This illiterate near eternity thus became written out (one might say) of 'history.' In 1851 the archaeologist Dan- iel Wilson, knowing the recency of human life, expected seamlessly to inte- grate material relics of preliterate Scots into a history resting on documents: Scotland's "Prehistoric Annals" fitted unproblematically into its historic ones.

But, when describing ancient Danish finds in the *Antiquity of Man*, Lyell declared that they belonged to a distinct "pre-historical age." Two years later, the banker and natural historian John Lubbock published *Pre-Historic Times, as Illustrated by Ancient Remains, and the Manners and Customs of Modern Savages*. The label stuck. Scholars who explored the human past in the countless millennia before script became prehistorians, not historians. Historians proper did not necessarily elide prehistory, might even take an imagined Teutonic or Aryan prehistory as a starting point. But the distinction between history, based on written records, and prehistory, without documents, had come to stay—a distinction between 'civilized' and 'savage.' A journal of prehistoric archaeology began publishing in 1864, and in 1866 the International Congress of Anthropology and Prehistoric Archaeology held its first meeting. The methods of prehistorians became those of archaeology, paleontology, and physical anthropology, not history. *History* began at Sumer, with words on clay tablets.[60]

Lubbock's subtitle flags another excision of human experience that shaped history as a humanistic discipline. Notions of social evolution current in Lubbock's day had roots in eighteenth-century Scottish thinking about the 'progress of civilization.' They assumed that all peoples developed through similar stages of social organization—say, from primitive promiscuity through polygamy to Victorian monogamy; or from hunting-and-gathering through nomadic herding through settled farming to a mercantile economy. If this were true, then prehistoric human beings and modern tribal peoples both lived at an early stage of human development. Primitive was primitive, today or ten thousand years ago. As Lubbock said, both "ancient remains" *and* "the manners and customs of *modern* savages" could illustrate "pre-historic times." Living in the childhood of the race, modern savages could not write, could not produce the documents essential to historians—now clearly understood as students of the literate, ipso facto civilized, past.[61]

Anyone tempted to see here only racist disdain of light-skinned imperialists for darker-complected people they routinely kicked around would be wrong. Many nineteenth-century Britons (though not all) dripped with contempt for their colonial subjects in India. But Indians had history because they had written records—in fact, records of great antiquity. The other Indians, in North America, did not; even sympathetic white observers thought it impossible to recover these Indians' history before literate Europeans arrived. So British historians poured out histories of India, from James Mill's venomous one in 1817 through Mountstuart Elphinstone's more sympathetic one in 1841 to W. H. Moreland's dispassionate *India at the Death of Akbar* in 1920. Between 1867 and 1877, H. M. Elliott published eight volumes of badly translated Arabic and Persian texts in an effort to provide *The History of India, as Told by its Own Historians: The Muhammadan Period*. Meanwhile, the pre-European past of *American* Indians became the domain not of historians but of anthropologists. Anthropology (about which there will be more in chapter 12) emerged precisely as the discipline studying those whom Hegel called peoples without history.*[62]

Philology, Documents, and History

That disciplinary history had textual philology as a parent mattered hugely. The philologist's habits of carefully scrutinizing a text, of studying contemporaneous texts to find information to elucidate the first text; the philologist's concern to date texts exactly, to sort out genuine from spurious passages—all these practices translated fairly directly into the new historian's ideas of what counted as 'evidence' and how to use it properly. Evidence meant information gleaned from perusal of documents, preferably texts coeval with events under review. A historian often found such papers in archives, and this old word now became peculiarly associated with historical research. The Reformation philologist's motto "ad fontes" ('to the sources') evolved into the historian's cry 'to the archives.' Archival research became a distinguishing, if never universal, hallmark of historical practice and training of historians. Data amassed in this way had to be verified against other such pieces of evidence, in a historian's version of the hermeneutic circle through which philologists had long cross-checked manuscripts.[63]

Data thus confirmed counted as 'facts,' and insistence on facts separated 'history' from speculations about the past once *thought* to be history. Lord Kames's admired *Sketches of the History of Man* (1774) confessedly comprised "the substance of various speculations, which occasionally occupied the author, and enlivened his leisure hours." In how different a spirit Sir James Bryce wrote in 1911 that "it is better to be tedious and monotonous and dreary almost up to the verge of unreadability than that our facts should be wrong or that such of them as are right should be smothered under festoons of florid verbiage." "Whether we like it or not," declared Frederick York Powell, Regius Professor of Modern History at Oxford in 1898, "history has got to be scientifically studied, and it is not a question of style but of accuracy, of fulness of observation, and correctness of reasoning, that is before the student." A young Bryn Mawr historian and Johns Hopkins PhD, Charles M. Andrews, took pride in 1892 that no reader could accuse his first monograph "of being hastily put together or of being based on second hand authorities." Not long thereafter the University of Chicago's Andrew McLaughlin regarded historical method—he used the philological term "critique"—as firmly fixed, "as far as it outlines the task of the sleuth seeking to detect truth from falsehood in documentary statement."[64]

---

*Hegel also believed that no Hindu writings qualified as historical records in the proper sense, which reinforces the suspicion that great philosophers make bad historians. Certainly he and Ranke did not get along.

This absolute insistence on documentary foundations, acquired from philology, did more than elevate 'facts' to the sine qua non of real history; it also limited history to periods and societies that used writing. Writing did not necessarily mean ink on paper. It could be letters graven in stone, scratched into a clay tablet, struck on a coin. History after 1850 flaunted its text-oriented, philological roots by making documentary evidence essential to scholarly historical research and writing. "No documents, no history," as the French historians Charles-Victor Langlois and Charles Seignobos bluntly put it in their widely read *Introduction aux études historiques* (1897)—translated as *Introduction to Historical Studies* the next year, with preface by the Regius Professor of Modern History at Oxford. "Manuscripts have come into use almost without limit"—so Lord Acton in 1896—"crowds of scholars are on the watch for them, and the supply of documents exceeds the supply of histories." "The printing of archives has gone on parallel with the admission of enquirers," he went on, "and the Master of the Rolls alone has made public five hundred volumes of sources. Other countries are as profuse." This philological heritage created a boundary, defined history by separating it clearly, for the first time, from prehistory and anthropology. Such a border made no sense apart from its philological origin. Human beings remain human even when they do not write. So it is no wonder that elementary history textbooks often start with some account of human prehistory: *Homo erectus* and Cro-Magnons in world history books, pre-Columbian native peoples in American history books, Celts and Druids in an 1886 *History of the Scottish Nation*. And it was simply human that history from time to time has enjoyed a fling with anthropology ever since the two disciplines divorced. Infidelity to texts once in a while never threatened to break up the marriage.[65]

In wedding philology, history got more than a fixation on writing. It contracted a serious case of rigor. Classical philologists had grown used to obsessing over minutiae of language, handwriting, or date. The point, after all, was to get the text exactly right. With the possible exception of chronology, no other science devoted to human affairs sweated the details so exhaustively. In contrast, earlier *historians*—Clarendon, Voltaire, Kames, even Gibbon— had used textual sources but rarely parsed them closely. But, for historians cumbered with the shade of Niebuhr, their tutelary ghost demanded not only grounding every assertion in textual evidence but also verifying the authenticity of the text and hewing scrupulously to its words. Techniques evolved by classical philologists to date manuscripts and place them in context filtered into the workaday routine of historians. Granted, historical practice rarely grew as strict as that of classical or biblical philologists; but supposed severity in method became a mark of identity. Richard Garnett in 1900 would not even allow into a bibliography "writers who make no pretensions to original research." In 1872 Henry Adams, teaching medieval history at Harvard, offered a former student advice about writing in "the historico-literary line." "To do it requires patient study, long labor, and perseverance that knows no limit. The Germans have these qualities beyond all other races. Learn to appreciate and to use the German historical *method*, and your *style* can be elaborated at leisure."[66]

As history became a university-based discipline after 1850, philological rigor inherited from ancient textual studies showed in minimum norms of professional practice that distinguished scholarly from 'popular' history, 'scientific' from amateur history. Admiration for methods of historians in German universities stiffened the spines of their English-speaking cousins. The key to professional training in history, the young Johns Hopkins University instructor J. Franklin Jameson wrote in 1882, is to "get away from all secondhand work and get practice in the use of sources." And when in 1885 Jameson assailed at the American Historical Association's annual meeting the feebleness of existing histories of individual American states, the words that first tripped off his tongue were "deficient in research." "Insight," he told a University of Chicago audience in 1901, is no "substitute for the laborious sifting of authorities." He continued with a revealing assessment of a great historian of an older type. Thomas Carlyle, he sneered, in the end "care[d] more for eloquence than for accuracy," despite "all his vociferous groanings over the assumed toilsomeness of his research, all his excited posing as the lynx-eyed destroyer of shams." As a result, when people "wish to know exactly what happened in Cromwell's time or in the French Revolution they will turn to Professor Gardiner or Professor Aulard." Harvard's Henry Adams cast like aspersions on the pioneering historian of the American West H. H. Bancroft, a mere "compiler": "it will be a disgrace to let such a work out as the measure of our national scholarship." Jameson declared that, if he had not become a historian, he probably would have taken up philology as a career.[67]

Professional History as Academic Discipline

This tightening of research methods was also a must for legitimacy as a university subject, once universities began to take the research imperative seriously. And in turn acceptance as a university subject certified the academic respectability of the field—testified, that is, to rigor appropriate to real scholarship. This mattered; for, unlike classical studies, history did not normally belong to curricula in English and American colleges and universities before 1850. True, students traditionally struggled through a few ancient historians, but as classical literature rather than as history for its own sake. Oxford and Cambridge both got Regius Professors of modern (i.e., postclassical) history in 1724; but because modern history formed no part of any degree program, students had no incentive to listen to their lectures and rarely did. In Scottish universities, as already mentioned, history was confounded with natural history; and natural history seems usually to have trumped the civil kind.

But in the mid-nineteenth century, history began to vie for academic gravitas. In 1838 Harvard established the McLean Professorship of Ancient and

Modern History: a straw in the wind. The first incumbent, Jared Sparks, pioneered in editing American historical documents (even if deficiently, by later benchmarks like Jameson's). Queen's College Belfast taught history in conjunction with literature from its opening in 1849. Toronto followed suit in 1853, and Trinity College Dublin in 1856, with an honors course uniting history, literature, and political science. In 1853 Oxford introduced modern history combined with law as an examination option—but only for students who had successfully completed classical studies. In 1872 modern history became an honors degree on its own, and by 1900 students in history outnumbered those in classics. A similar pattern unfolded at Cambridge, on about the same schedule; and the university began an independent historical tripos in 1873. By this time, American colleges commonly taught modern history, extending even to the history of the United States itself, though not usually with a professor solely dedicated to history. On both sides of the ocean, the earliest professors of history seldom had much in the way of specialized background for teaching it. Still, the widespread implantation of history as an academic subject showed that history had more or less arrived as a 'science.'[68]

Indeed, history's ambition to scientific status led to confusion about its relation to the humanities. A few historians after 1850 fell so deeply in love with natural science that they hoped to find in history general laws governing human affairs, like laws of physics. The best known of these seekers was Henry Thomas Buckle. His unfinished *History of Civilization* rested on the axioms that scientific laws control all human activity and that Buckle could discover them. His early death kept readers from learning if he was right, but the two volumes he did publish (in 1857 and 1861) made a splash. More modestly, many historians imagined their field as somehow scientific in disposition, even if a social rather than natural science. Some of this talk simply echoed contemporary use of 'science' to refer to any rigorous, organized study. When Henry Adams in 1875 decried Hubert Howe Bancroft's history as lacking in "scientific analysis," he was not thinking of test tubes and Bunsen burners. Boasting of history's scientific nature could simply mean bragging about its academic credentials. Other historians, however, did attempt in some—usually vague—way to imitate natural science, including Adams's brother Brooks in his *Law of Civilization and Decay* (1895). The semantic confusion does not much matter. Whatever the ambitions of its practitioners, the roots of 'scientific' history sank deep into philology, like those of other disciplines that unquestionably belonged to the humanities. Like them, history held a secure place in the 'liberal culture' that, in the decades around 1900, students were supposed to absorb from the humanities.[69]

If 'science' is one red herring misleading us about history's formation as a discipline, another is the supposed fixation of nineteenth-century historians on national or imperial politics. The German masters of the trade, notably Ranke, half drunk on visions of German unification, put an idealized nation-state at the center of history. But political history did not freeze out other topics, certainly not among English-speaking historians. Early annual reports of the American Historical Association show a lot of social and economic history. Herbert Baxter Adams emblazoned the wall of his seminar room at Johns Hopkins with E. A. Freeman's dictum that history is past politics; he claimed to embody "the union of History & Politics" at Johns Hopkins; and he pushed the semiracialist thesis that American political institutions descended from ancient German tribal gatherings. (Adams, by nature an archive rat, had to sneak these undocumented immigrants across the border dividing prehistory from history.) Yet he also insisted that Freeman "used the word 'political' in a large Greek sense" embracing even "art and literature." Adams made graduate students study Herodotus and ancient Hebrew religion along with American constitutional history. Despite such elasticity, most publications emerging from his seminar did deal with political institutions, and much of the history written in British universities before World War I also worked this vein. True, Paul Vinogradoff's admired *Villainage in England* (1892) studied medieval peasantry and village communities. But more typical was William Stubbs, Regius Professor at Oxford for eighteen years before becoming a bishop in 1884; he exerted huge influence as a historian of medieval English constitutional development. His successor, E. A. Freeman, focused on political institutions between the Norman Conquest and the late thirteenth century. In sum: political (including constitutional) history supplied the bread and butter of historians in the United Kingdom and United States in the later nineteenth century, not their entire cuisine.[70]

In any case, it is wrong to take political-constitutional history—even if historians really *had* written nothing else—as the *foundation* of the modern historical discipline. To do so mistakes contents for container. And when content changed in the twentieth century, the documentary framework of the discipline did not. Our moral universe has altered. Adams's racialism troubles us. Less profoundly, fashions shift. Stubbs's constitutional history now makes most historians yawn (which says as much about them as him). Yet at bottom his *method* is still that of most historians today, well over a century after his demise—but was *not* Hume's method a century before him. Stubbs began his historical career by editing medieval manuscripts. He pioneered in importing into the English-speaking world criteria for source criticism honed by nineteenth-century German historians. His chief works were an anthology of original sources for the study of medieval constitutional history and a three-volume history of that subject, grounded in close study of just such documents. Frederick Jackson Turner at the University of Wisconsin wrote a different type of history. But he was just as anxious as Stubbs "to get the students working on the original authorities." His motto? "All history is comment on a text." (With few original sources ready to hand, he longed for "something like Stubbs's Select Charters" for American history.) Most historians in the English-speaking world still build up their narratives and analyses from written documents; they still spend hours of research poring over these documents in archives, formal, informal, or online; they still insist on citing documents in reference notes giving location of these sources (see the back of this book); they still bash each other for misinterpreting documents; they still argue over the correct meaning of words; they still compare documents with other ones. Even when using images, they tend to 'read' them for content like written sources. They still behave, in brief, like textual philologists, even if now bored by constitutional history.[71]

And in the 1880s and 1890s philological history became a modern humanistic discipline in the United States, with learned societies, journals, and PhD programs. Almost upon taking charge of his seminar in 1882, Herbert Adams began the Johns Hopkins Studies in Historical and Political Science to publish monographs, the first such series in the United States. As in classical studies, graduate students angled for fellowships, young professors for better jobs. The doctoral degree became a badge setting the research vanguard apart from proles who merely taught—although a lot of eminent historians lacked the degree, including Andrew C. McLaughlin of the University of Michigan and later the University of Chicago. (Marrying the daughter of Michigan's president jump-started his career, or so colleagues in Ann Arbor believed.) In 1884 Herbert Adams led in organizing an American Historical Association (AHA). With his usual shrewdness, he located its headquarters in Washington, D.C., knitted an official tie to Congress, and lured into the AHA well-heeled amateurs alongside the minority of professors sworn to the (aspirationally) tough standards of disciplinary history. Most early AHA members, notably presidents, had no link to universities beyond having attended one. But professors called the shots. Publishers soon used the annual meetings, held in the college lull between Christmas and New Year, to hash out details with academic authors. Documentary research ruled. The AHA set up a Historical Manuscripts Commission (borrowing name and example from a UK government office created in 1869), to improve archives and ease access to their contents. The AHA battled for setting up a National Archives. Only "papers based strictly on original research" merited publication in the AHA's annual report. In 1895, two AHA members started the *American Historical Review* (absorbed into the organization in 1915 but linked to it ab initio), to provide a venue for disciplinary scholarship in history.[72]

A 'learned journal' exclusively for history appeared in the United Kingdom in 1886, bringing together (in Lord Acton's sardonic but accurate words) "a Sacred Band of university workers." The *English Historical Review* mimicked continental models, expressly the *Historische Zeitschrift*. Herbert Adams's Studies in Historical and Political Science may also have lurked in the background. Certainly the new journal sought American subscribers. In its earliest years, the *EHR* struggled to find direction. It teetered between the model of the older, profit-making, general-interest quarterlies and the paradigm of a specialized academic journal for which no British template existed. Under the editorship of Mandell Creighton, Dixie Professor of Ecclesiastical History at

Cambridge, only book reviews at first lived up to the *Review*'s German foster parentage. Acton, soon to become Regius Professor of Modern History at Cambridge, stood at Creighton's elbow. Acton kicked off the first issue with a sweeping survey of German historical scholarship in the past seventy years or so, "to mark the growth," he explained, "of a specifically German view of history." Acton raised an Olympian eyebrow at the nationalism of German historians but applauded their scientific methods—originating in Niebuhr's philology. By the 1890s fairly strict and consistent scholarly standards set the journal's tone. Creighton, at least, believed that the *EHR* rather quickly raised the standard of editing historical sources in England.[73]

Despite these 'professional' attitudes, British historians, like peers in classics, professionalized more slowly than American counterparts. The hegemony of Oxford and Cambridge, and the dominance there of colleges (with their tutors) over the university (and its professors), may help to explain the lag. The Royal Historical Society (1868; "Royal" was added in 1872) strolled along as a mixed set of parsons, lawyers, and the odd peer interested in history; only after 1900 did it start developing into what it became by the mid-1920s: a disciplinary organization for university-based scholars. British historians took longer than Americans to shut themselves up behind disciplinary walls. Right up to the twentieth century serious historical scholarship appeared in general-interest magazines like the *Quarterly Review*. When in 1896 Lord Acton was designing the early monument of professional disciplinary history in Britain, the fourteen-volume *Cambridge Modern History*, concern arose that he enlisted "too many professors" as authors. One familiar symptom of disciplinary specialization is prose clunky enough to ward off ordinary readers. ("College professors," an American historian sighed in 1903, "often write so badly that their work is unacceptable to the reading public.") By that benchmark perhaps the generation of British historians coming of age in the 1970s first fully earned the disciplinary label, though by the gauge of *topics* appealing to general readers academic historians in the United Kingdom merited the tag decades earlier.[74]

Meanwhile other disciplinary institutions and periodicals appeared on both sides of the ocean. A historian of Tudor politics based at University College London, A. F. Pollard, spearheaded in 1906 the founding of the Historical Association. Again, like the Classical Association three years earlier—and unlike American learned societies in either field—the Historical Association united teachers of history in both secondary and higher education. A year later, Americans set up yet more clearly disciplinary group. Historians from Midwestern universities started the Mississippi Valley Historical Association, apparently to foster a more focused, tougher-minded brand of scholarship than the AHA. But Pollard was no disciplinary softie. In 1920 he established the Institute of Historical Research in the University of London, which became the center of a substantial graduate program and a key link in the nexus connecting historians in American universities with British counterparts. Already by the 1890s, when an American historian traveled to Britain for summer research, he tended to spend leisure hours with British historians.[75]

As the discipline grew more inward-focused, its institutions became yet more specialized. In 1924, George Sarton of Harvard and the Carnegie Institution started the History of Science Society, with the HSS absorbing the scholarly journal *Isis* that Sarton had launched earlier. In 1925, to improve research and scholarly training, American medieval historians helped to establish the Medieval Academy of America; the next year it began publishing *Speculum*. The Medieval Academy, unusually, crossed disciplinary lines—or, perhaps more accurately, it defined 'medieval studies' (of the Latin west) as a chronologically and geographically demarcated discipline, like classics. In 1926, British economic and social historians founded the Economic History Society, with its own journal, the *Economic History Review*. And so it went, to ever more specialized associations for ever more specialized subfields.[76]

Such institutions provided walls within which the discipline could nurture its philologically grounded practices. Societies also functioned as feedback loops to correct deviations from orthopraxis—through book reviews, editorial vetting of manuscripts, supervisory criticism of dissertations, and the like. As classicists did, historians turned in on themselves. Some, from time to time, translated professional research for audiences outside the guild. Mostly they wrote for each other—and modeled for each other shared professional standards and humanistic scholarly procedures. Now and then, they slept through each other's conference papers, a custom still extant.[77]

PART III: ART HISTORY

At first glance, art history has been around almost as long as any study in the family of philology and antiquarianism. In the first century CE, Pliny the Elder wrote about the evolution of Greek sculpture and painting. Giorgio Vasari published his first biographical anthology of painters, a model for other books, in 1550. Art historians today commonly claim Johann Joachim Winckelmann's *History of Ancient Art* (1764) as their modern progenitor. But to write about art occasionally is one thing; it is quite another to investigate its history systematically and cumulatively, paying steady attention to other scholars using recognized methods to do the same thing.

In fact, art history as an academic discipline appeared only in the nineteenth century and, in the English-speaking world, only in its second half. In the United Kingdom, art history did not fully come into its own until the twentieth century.

Any connection between philology and this new discipline seems almost counterintuitive. Art, after all, involves images and forms, not words and texts. The paradox begins to dissolve when one realizes that some roots of art history grew from early modern antiquarianism: its practices paralleled philology and engaged many philologists. Winckelmann, grandfather of art history in most genealogies, recycled antiquarian texts in his own writings.[78] It is also worth recalling that Winckelmann inspired not only art history but also the philological Altertumswissenschaft invented by Heyne and Wolf. Early on, then, philology and art history rubbed shoulders. Finally, much evidence for the history of art is textual, including foundations like Pliny's *Naturalis historia* (77 CE*) and Vasari's *Vite de' più eccellenti pittori, scultori, ed architettori* (*Lives of the Most Excellent Painters, Sculptors, and Architects*, 1550, 1568). Establishing and interpreting such texts required philology. Mixed-up dates and dubious anecdotes, for instance, riddle Vasari's book.

But teasing out philology in the family tree of art history gets tricky, because the discipline developed in the English-speaking world along two main lines. One began with classical archaeologists. Art historians of this stripe concentrated on Greek and Roman material and flourished especially in the United States. The other track began with adaptations of German art historians by British writers, mostly focused on painting after the Middle Ages. The story becomes still more complicated. Two different types of institutions with distinct missions shaped the new discipline, universities and museums. A plethora of untrained curators—often painters—taught themselves history of art while helping to run museums. Often they fitted poorly into either main tradition.

Confusion does not stop here; for writings about early practitioners are sparse, relative to studies of, say, historians in the same period. American art history, in particular, during its formative Victorian days would puzzle most art historians today, for whom respectable art history in the United States starts with Bernard Berenson. In fact, Berenson came relatively late and marked a decisive shift in previously well-established meanings and methods of the field. And, of all humanities, art history was most robustly reshaped by the wave of intellectual refugees from Nazism in the 1930s and 1940s. The émigrés brought ideas and methods that masked—even erased—native traditions. So, after the 1930s, art history acquired a largely German pedigree. Erwin Panofsky is a name to conjure with today. Charles Eliot Norton casts no spell. To discover how art history joined the humanities requires digging.

The German Invention of Art History

The roots of museum-based art history in the English-speaking world lead back, once again, to German universities. Philosophic history had united with philological erudition to produce the modern discipline of history. So, too, during the first half of the nineteenth century, the marriage of philology (broadly conceived) and philosophy gave birth to art history as a distinct field in Germany. ('Philology' here includes archaeologists who interpreted arti-

---

* Despite the title given it, books 34–36 concern sculpture, painting, and architecture.

facts according to contextualizing principles of philologists.) Art history's philosophic lineage needs only fleeting notice, for it scarcely mattered in the English-speaking world. The key element was the rise of aesthetics as an independent field of European philosophic speculation in the eighteenth century. The British invented modern aesthetics, in the writings of the third Earl of Shaftesbury and Francis Hutcheson. But the aesthetic theories of Kant, Schiller, and especially Hegel shaped some German writers who pioneered art history as a self-conscious field, notably Karl Schnaase (1798–1875).[79]

Most German art historians felt the tug of philology more strongly. This group included Johann Dominico Fiorillo, for whom Göttingen created the first professorship of art history in Europe in 1813. (He really was German: his Neapolitan parents settled in Hamburg, where he was born.) Despite starting as a painter, Fiorillo wrote the history of art in a mode inherited from philology. So did Karl Friedrich von Rumohr, perhaps the closest thing to a 'founder' of the discipline. His intellectual father was Barthold Niebuhr, and Rumohr's *Italienischen Forschungen* (*Italian Researches*, 1827) applied to Vasari the philologically based skepticism that Niebuhr brought to bear on Livy. Rumohr's protégé Gustav Waagen, the first professor of art history at Berlin (1844), also leaned to philology by education and inclination. None of this startles, considering the force of Altertumswissenschaft in German scholarship and the fact that both art history and Altertumswissenschaft traced back to Winckelmann. Like any good philologist, Winckelmann insisted that a 'text'—say, a Greek statue—could only be understood in terms of its context. Thus he thought that Mediterranean climate helped to explain Greek ideas of beauty.[80]

The basic principle, if not the specific example, became standard in nineteenth-century German art history. The first survey of postclassical art was Fiorillo's *Geschichte der zeichnenden Künste von ihrer Wiederauflebung bis auf den neuesten Zeiten* (*History of the Visual Arts from Their Revival to the Present*, 5 vols., 1798–1808). Fiorillo took account of the influence of political and cultural factors on trends in painting, and he tried to situate individual painters within their social world. Waagen—personally very influential in England—advised, in Mitchell Schwarzer's words, "that in order to understand an artist, art historians should discuss political history, the constitution, the character of a people, conditions of the church, customs, literature, and the nature of the land." Waagen's seminal study of the Van Eyck brothers (1822) limned the history of the Low Countries and then surveyed Netherlandish painting during the half millennium preceding the Van Eycks—54 pages in all—before actually discussing the brothers and their work in another 187 pages. Even Waagen's overview of German and Netherlandish painting, meant to guide English tourists to specific works, took care to sketch at least a very broad historical context.[81]

This notion—that the history of art should nest within a large-scale historical narrative—became stock in trade of the field: Karl Rumohr, Franz Kugler, Karl Schnaase, Jacob Burckhardt. Regardless of philosophic underpinnings—

Schnaase embraced Hegel; Kugler spurned him—all the Germans who became models for British or American writers believed it essential that art history place artists and works of art in the broad sweep of history. Inevitably, the narrative concentrated on art and artists; but this art history fitted within a broader story of religious, cultural, even political history. Many art historians thus behaved like philologists: supplying context to make a 'text' intelligible, or using a 'text' to illumine the world from which it came (as in Altertumswissenschaft). Franz Kugler structured his widely used *Handbuch der Kunstgeschichte* (*Handbook of Art History*, 1842) in this philological way. As Burckhardt wrote—in the Victorian art historian Elizabeth Eastlake's translation—art history "should assist in the development of the history of civilisation," and works of art "should take their places as witnesses of the century to which they belong." So, when art history developed in the United Kingdom and United States later in the century, philology left a much bigger mark than philosophy.[82]

Amateurs on the Way to Expertise

Two midcentury writers illuminated the situation of art history in the English-speaking world. One was the New Yorker William Dunlap, a man of considerable energies and varied, if mediocre, talents. He worked as portrait painter, playwright, merchant, theatrical producer, biographer, schoolbook author, more or less at the same time. In 1834 he wrote the *History of the Rise and Progress of the Arts of Design in the United States*—a biographical *vade mecum* to its subject and the first stab at charting the evolution of a distinctive American artistic heritage. Aside from two or three magazine articles, Dunlap seems to have done nothing else in the art-historical line. The other figure was Anna Jameson. Daughter of a Dublin miniaturist painter who moved his family to London, Anna lived there most of her life. Married in 1821, Mrs. Jameson waved goodbye when her disappointing husband sailed off to a colonial post in 1829. She had published a melodramatic novel in 1826. Now she supported herself, and probably her parents and sisters, by writing. Her oeuvre included travel books, potboilers about female monarchs and poets' love lives, and a study of women in Shakespeare's plays that Gerard Manley Hopkins thought ranked her with Schlegel and Coleridge. In 1834 Jameson began a magazine series about quattrocento painters, later collected in a book. Henceforth art became her main literary line, and she proved very good at it—widely read in America as well as her own country. In 1840 she wrote an appreciative introduction to a translation of Waagen's book on Rubens, in 1842 a guide to public art galleries in London, and in 1844 a handbook to the city's private collections. Ambition expanded with literary success and knowledge of art history. In 1848 she produced a methodical, two-volume survey of Christian iconography in art, followed by three volumes expanding the same subject before her death in 1860.[83]

Jameson was a prolific art historian with knowledge and insight, well regarded by contemporaries and later readers, Dunlap a minor writer whose sole book on art matters only for registering facts otherwise forgotten. Yet the two share revealing commonalities. Both began as miscellaneous writers: Dunlap remained one; Jameson never stopped writing on subjects other than art. Both seem to have gravitated to art history because painting lay in their personal backgrounds, but also because of growing interest in the subject in their milieux. Both wrote not as scholars but as popularizers. Dunlap derived his information largely from hearsay; Jameson cannibalized hers from standard sources such as Vasari's *Lives of the Painters* and Franz Kugler's handbook.[84] Vastly different in quality and quantity of output, both writers reveal a new appetite for the history of art in America and Britain and nonprofessional authors trying to satisfy it.

It is not hard to find others of the type. Frederic Stephens, a failed painter, was art critic of the *Athenaeum* for four decades up to 1901. He wrote books on British artists of the day and historical overviews such as *Normandy: Its Gothic Architecture and History* (1865) and *Flemish and French Pictures* (1875)—frankly disclaiming "original researches." John Ruskin stood out from the crowd for the luminous prose, close observation, and impassioned argument of his *Modern Painters* (5 vols., 1843–60); but he differed in quality, not kind. Readers found a similar mélange of art history and aesthetic meditations in *The Art-Idea* (1864) by the American James Jackson Jarves, with an added dollop of Yankee uplift.[85]

More old-fashioned than Jarves—and more scholarly—was the Englishwoman Elizabeth Rigby. Like Anna Jameson an aspiring painter and sundry writer, she translated J. P. Passavant's *Kunstreise durch England und Belgien* (1833) as *Tour of a German Artist in England* (1836). After marrying Sir Charles Eastlake in 1849, she continued to translate German art history into English. Her versions included the second edition of Franz Kugler's history of Italian painting (1851; her new husband had translated the first) and Gustav Waagen's survey of pictures in British collections (1854). (She also completed the last two volumes of Anna Jameson's study of Christian art, unfinished at her death.) Later in life Lady Eastlake contributed to the *Quarterly Review* and *Edinburgh Review* her own studies of cinquecento painters. She kept up with continental scholarship, processing it into fare easily digestible by British readers. And, like her German mentors, she taught that historical context made the artist comprehensible, and vice versa: "The painter" is, "in a certain sense, the sure thermometer of the atmosphere he breathes." "We perceive" in Titian "the unmistakable reflex of a Republic [Venice] under which its subjects traded, wrote, and painted with a freedom then unknown elsewhere." Another legacy of philology appeared when she discussed the key skill needed in her husband's museum work. Connoisseurship—"a strictly modern science"—required not "the highest taste" but "the closest comparison." While amateurs like Eastlake might be very well informed, they did not belong to an acknowledged discipline of 'art history,' as the Germans they depended on now did.[86]

The Museum World

Eastlake's husband, Charles, continued the crab-like crawl that ended in an academic discipline of art history. In the husband's case, too, work as artist led to art history. Charles Eastlake began as a successful painter, chiefly of historical and biblical scenes. Painting piqued interest in the history of his craft, and in 1842 he translated Franz Kugler's history of Italian painting. Now reputed for both art and art history, Eastlake was named keeper of the National Gallery in 1843, its highest office but under the thumb of trustees. Frustrated by constraints, he resigned four years later. Painting now largely abandoned, he returned to art history. In 1847 he published *Materials for a History of Oil Painting* and the next year the first volume of an ongoing miscellany, *Contributions to the Literature of the Fine Arts*. This scholarship cemented his reputation, and in 1850 the Royal Academy elected Eastlake president. In 1855 he went back to the National Gallery in the new, more powerful post of director. In the ten years before he died, he enriched its collections, notably with earlier Italian masterworks. Together, he and his wife did much to move British taste toward such Italian 'primitives.'[87]

What matters most about Eastlake here is the institutional frame of his later career. Service at the National Gallery (and on a commission to oversee decoration of the new Houses of Parliament) pushed him toward a type of art history more scholarly and sophisticated, yet less historical and contextual, than his wife's version. These jobs amplified certain areas of expertise. His 1847 book, written to inform the commission's work, showed the effect. *Materials for a History of Oil Painting* rested on solid historical research in medieval and early modern manuscripts and early printed works. But *Materials* took a narrow view of the "history of oil painting"—as if a chronicle of the petroleum industry discussed only drill bits and pump jacks. Eastlake's book dwelled on technical expertise and physical materials used by Old Masters (Flemish artists in particular); for instance, purifying linseed oil. This nuts-and-bolts lore improved skills later required as director of the National Gallery. There Eastlake's remit included buying paintings for the collection. In this dealing, connoisseurship—scrutinizing technique and style to identify the painter of a work—was all-important, lest a shady seller palm off on Britain a fake Perugino. Poring over a painting for signs of an individual artist prioritized the object over its cultural context. Eastlake became a celebrated connoisseur, refining the norms of the craft. As director, he used historical context only in the limited (but innovative) practice of hanging paintings according to chronology and 'school.' Britons in Charles Eastlake's lifetime did not yet recognize a specialized field labeled art history, certainly not a 'discipline.' But institutional scaffolding for it was going up, and the framework helped to determine what later counted in the field.[88]

His kind of experience became more common as public art museums sprang up throughout Britain and America. The National Gallery dates from 1824,* but the golden age of public museums began during Eastlake's own museum career and glowed ever brighter as industrialization spawned vast wealth. The Victoria and Albert Museum (originally South Kensington Museum) opened in 1852 to showcase the arts of design. Glasgow's civic art collection dates from 1854. The National Gallery of Scotland opened in 1859, the National Gallery of Ireland in 1864, the National Museum of Wales in 1907. In the United States, within a single decade, five of the six largest cities as well as the capital acquired major art museums: New York's Metropolitan Museum opened in 1872, Washington, D.C.'s Corcoran Gallery of Art in 1874, Boston's Museum of Fine Arts in 1876, the Philadelphia Museum of Art in 1877, the Art Institute of Chicago in 1879, the Cincinnati Art Museum in 1881. By 1920, the United States supported at least 120 art museums.[89] A similar pattern appeared in England's provincial cities: Liverpool's city art gallery was founded in 1874, Manchester's in 1882, Birmingham's in 1885, Leeds's in 1888. The Tate opened in 1897 to highlight British art; the Syracuse Museum of Fine Arts (also 1897) decided in 1911 to focus on American art. What became the Montreal Museum of Fine Arts began in 1879, the National Gallery of Canada in 1880.

These museums required curatorial leadership and connoisseurship. This need made something resembling 'art history' a viable profession, if neither well defined, populous, nor purposefully trained. Even resemblance was often dubious. Sydney Cockerell transfigured the Fitzwilliam Museum. He had no formal art education, only much experience with manuscripts and engraving and many friends in the art world. Apparently he had nary an art-historical bone in his body, nor did he pine for one. With nothing else to recommend him, in 1908 he became director of the Fitzwilliam. Cockerell complained that his predecessor, M. R. James (now better known for his terrifying ghost stories), left the place "a pigstye." Cockerell cleaned it up, hung the pictures more elegantly and sparely, invented the "Friends of the Fitzwilliam" to raise money, hounded millionaires to procure more, coaxed from them their own art treasures, and created the modern Fitzwilliam. ("I turned it into a palace.") In his sledgehammer way Cockerell was a genius. But he was not, and had no way to become, an educated professional. Not until the 1930s did demand for qualified curators generate in the United Kingdom an institution to supply them.[90]

---

* The National Gallery was not the earliest art museum in England accessible to the public. The Ashmolean in Oxford opened its doors in 1683, before the concept of an art museum existed, and the Fitzwilliam in Cambridge in 1816.

Art History in the Universities

Meanwhile, colleges and universities incubated art history as a distinct learned pursuit. As mentioned, the University of Göttingen created the first chair in art history in Europe in 1813, Berlin the most prominent in 1844. France partly followed suit in 1863, with a professorship in the École des Beaux-Arts that blurred the line between art history and aesthetics. In 1868 a rich antiquarian, Felix Slade, bequeathed funds to establish professorships of art in the universities of Oxford, Cambridge, and London. Slade's will mandated that these professors "promot[e] the study of the Fine Arts" but did not specify how. The carrying out of Slade's legacy showed that art history, aesthetics, and the study of practical technique still jumbled together in many minds. London University made arrangements to train young artists (the famed Slade School). Oxford chose John Ruskin as its first Slade Professor. He decided to "establish both a practical and critical school of fine art for English gentlemen," to make his elite students competent draftsmen and effective patrons of the arts. Ruskin being Ruskin, he added moral prophecy to his job description. His Oxford successors until the twentieth century were all painters and such, and they largely ignored art history. Cambridge named Matthew Digby Wyatt, an architect and historian of applied arts. Wyatt gave his auditors a little history, a little theory, and a little practical advice. The man who followed Wyatt in the chair, Sidney Colvin, did attend to art history of a sort, the sort being object-oriented connoisseurship like Charles Eastlake's. In neither Oxford nor Cambridge did the lectures tie into a degree program or attract students. Only with the Watson Gordon Professorship of Fine Art at Edinburgh in 1880 did a university in the United Kingdom begin seriously to teach art history, still apart from any degree. And there, too, art history mingled with theory.[91]

At first, American colleges also puzzled over what teaching 'art' meant. Consider Yale: it got an art gallery in 1832 by happenstance because the American painter John Trumbull had lots of pictures on hand, while his nephew Benjamin Silliman was a prominent Yale professor. Colonel Trumbull gave lectures to the Yale boys in 1839, apparently how-to lessons that were never repeated. Thirty years later, Yale's museum spawned a School of the Fine Arts, offering "practical instruction for both sexes who are desirous of pursuing the Fine Arts as a profession." Yale hired the painter John Ferguson Weir as director, and he presided for forty-four years. The school gave ancillary instruction in art history, but not until 1940 did Yale organize a department of art history to teach undergraduates.[92]

Early American women's colleges pioneered in teaching art, mixing studio instruction with a moralism worthy of Ruskin had it not been so explicitly Christian. When Vassar opened in 1865, it had an art gallery integrated into its only—ample—building. Its "Professor of Drawing and Painting," a painter named Henry Van Ingen, lectured on art history to supplement practical teaching. Vassar separated art history from studio art in 1911 when Oliver

Tonks arrived to head the art department. Harvard's first PhD in classical archaeology (1903), firmly grounded in classical philology, Tonks taught disciplinary art history. He hired a painter to handle studio art. Wellesley College (1875) moved faster in the same direction. When it began, only six or seven colleges taught art in any way. From the outset, Wellesley trained young women to draw, paint, and sculpt. In 1878 it established a distinct School of Art—with a single ancillary art history course. Art history soon expanded to three courses (ancient, classical, modern); and in 1886 a separate department opened, parallel to the School of Art. In 1897 the college hired Alice Van Vechten Brown, trained as a painter before becoming head of a museum-affiliated art school in Connecticut. Brown turned the tables and made drawing and sculpting subserve art history: teaching technique aimed to make students better understand the historical development of art. Wellesley's liberal arts curriculum soon swallowed the School of Art. By 1900 students could major in art history: the only college with this option.[93]

Such new professorships both demanded and encouraged deepening expertise, but of what kind?* What did 'art history' mean in its formative years in American colleges and universities, methodologically speaking?[94]

A promising place to look for an answer is the only college or university that from the start clearly distinguished artistic training from art history. The school was Harvard, and the man accountable was Charles Eliot Norton, already discussed as chief organizer of American classical archaeology and as editor of John Donne. Norton held the first professorship of art history in the United States. His close friendship with John Ruskin rested in part on their similar ideas about art. But Norton knew German art history, too, better than probably any other American of his generation. In 1871 he weighed in on an adjudication by German art historians of the authenticity of two nearly identical 'Holbein' Madonnas in Dresden and Darmstadt. (Norton plumped for the Darmstadt version, correctly.) The next year he published research on the Siena Duomo in a Leipzig art-historical journal. When he came to teach art history at Harvard in 1874, Norton at first expected more advanced pupils to read German historians of art and archaeology: K. O. Müller, Franz Reber, Karl Schnaase, Jacob Burckhardt, and Adolf Michaelis. This turned out a ludicrous overestimate of Harvard undergraduates, and Norton soon junked the requirement.[95]

But firsthand awareness of German erudition may have made clearer that art training was one thing, art history quite another. At Norton's long-distance urging, Harvard had already in 1871 hired Charles Moore, a disciple of Ruskin, to teach drawing—in the vocationally oriented Lawrence Scientific School,

---

*The advent of the electric slide projector (lantern slides) in the late 1880s—replacing awkward, expensive, less easily visible large photographs—made teaching of art history more practicable and almost certainly aided its spread. Photographic slides changed the discipline only pedagogically but not in basic method. Therefore I ignore them, despite their centrality in art history.

not in Harvard College. When Norton himself joined the faculty, he unambiguously divided responsibilities between Moore's studio instruction and his own art history lectures. He thought acquaintance with artistic technique helpful in understanding artworks, and he arranged for Moore's teaching to move into the college. But Norton required of his own students no facility with a pencil beyond ability to take notes.[96]

Norton brought to art history a method decisive during its formation as a discipline in the United States. He cut his scholarly teeth on Dante in the later 1850s, with a commentary on and partial translation of the *Vita nuova*. Only ten years later did he begin art-historical research. He continued to translate Dante and to edit other poets for the rest of his life. As a young man, he brought to Dante the sensibility of a textual philologist, and not only because of the subject. Norton's father, Andrews, had been one of the first biblical philologists in the United States; he approached the New Testament as shaped by the Hebraic and Hellenistic cultures of its authors.[97] The son's closest friend during his late teens and twenties was Francis Child, just starting his philological career. By the time Charles Norton worked his way through Dante into art history, his philological cast of mind was fixed. He taught and wrote art history *as a philologist*, an interpreter of texts. He sought to place texts—literal or metaphorical—in historical context, to tack from text to context and back, casting a bit more light on each with every oscillation, in the tradition of philological hermeneutics established in the Renaissance. Where Andrews had taken the Gospels as texts, Charles's 'texts' were paintings and buildings as often as poems and charters. Andrews ultimately aimed always to clarify the text: the Gospels were primary for him. Charles more often strove to illuminate the context. In the spirit of Altertumswissenschaft, the civilization of ancient Greece or of medieval Italy mattered more than specific works of art.

But the method did not essentially differ. Norton intended his students to interpret the Parthenon as expressing Athenian culture, to find in the Athenians' temple, therefore, an aid to understanding the Athenians themselves, "the moral & physical elements of the Athenian nature." For Norton, the "same principles" underlay all of the 'arts of expression,' as he called literature, music, and the visual arts collectively. It made sense, then, that the interpretative methods of philology applied to understanding Greek architecture and Florentine painting just as to elucidating Dante's poetry. In Norton's eyes, the ultimate aim of art history was to widen students' imaginations and sympathies, but the methodological road to this moral goal began in the hermeneutic circle of philology.[98]

For at least three decades after Norton's appointment as professor of art history, the center of gravity of the field in America lay in classical art and archaeology. Vassar's museum principally boasted casts of classical and Renaissance sculpture; and in 1876 the college granted its first MA in fine arts— also first in the United States—for the thesis "The Progress of Art in Ancient Times." Bryn Mawr (opened 1885), most scholarly in ambition of the new women's colleges, at first taught art history from within the classics depart-ment. Its first full-time faculty member in art history was Norton's son Rich-ard, who had trained under the classical archaeologist Charles Waldstein in Athens and Cambridge and then burnished his archaeological credentials in Berlin. When Bryn Mawr finally created a separate art history department, its name was Classical Art and Archaeology. Princeton's department, founded in 1883, was also Art and Archaeology; and its teaching tilted heavily toward ancient and medieval art, as did its new art museum. (And, as at Harvard and Bryn Mawr, studio art ran a distant second to art history.) In 1895 the Univer-sity of Michigan's dynamic classicist Francis Kelsey still treated archaeology and "Greek and Roman art" as synonyms. This concentration on classical art reflected the historic hegemony of classical studies in higher education, but it may have magnified Norton's influence. Founding president of the Archaeo-logical Institute, no American had a higher profile in classical archaeology. Moreover, the textbooks most often used in courses on ancient and medieval art were the two volumes of Franz von Reber's survey, translated under Nor-ton's direction by his student J. T. Clarke as *History of Ancient Art* and *History of Medieval Art*.[99]

Whatever the reason, other American leaders in the new field echoed Nor-ton's philological, historical approach to art history. Princeton makes a good example. This bastion of Presbyterian orthodoxy viewed liberal Harvard with grave suspicion; and the agnostic Norton got a lukewarm reception when he lectured there in 1882—though less chilly than he expected. Teaching at Princeton also proceeded on philosophic principles of Scottish Common Sense realism that Norton had abandoned decades earlier. Yet Norton might have ghostwritten the founding manifesto of Princeton's Department of Art and Archaeology. William Cowper Prime and George McClellan actually composed it.* They insisted that the department focus on "Historic Art," not "principles of aesthetics"; for "works of art are the only trustworthy record of—not alone the history—but of the tastes, the mental character, and the manners and customs of various peoples in various ages." They added,

> In effect, the works of art of any people are another form of their litera-ture. They are thoughts, purposes, wants, necessities, habits, customs, tastes, recorded not in phonetic or hieroglyphic characters, but in plain objects, which can be understood by every ordinary intellect. And this is equally true, whether the works of art be the simplest objects of com-mon utility, or statues, architecture, and paintings, which record the cul-tivated and educated tastes of peoples, and show what were their stan-dards of beauty.

---

* This was indeed the Union Army general who ran against Abraham Lincoln in the 1864 presidential election. He later moved to New Jersey, made a ton of money, and served a term as governor.

Prime and McClellan went on, as if channeling Norton, to stress the value of art history "in making the student acquainted with his race" (Norton would have said "civilization," not "race") and "opening, constantly, new and clear views of sacred, as well as profane, literature." Such instruction required a "museum of art objects"—not just painting and sculpture, but "all works of art which are in any degree valuable as records of human tastes, desires, and habits of life."[100]

The person who cast this vision in stone, chiseling it to his own idiosyncratic specifications, was Allan Marquand. The son of a rich New York banker—a founder of the Metropolitan Museum of Art—Marquand got a philosophy PhD at Johns Hopkins in 1880. In 1881 he returned to Princeton, his alma mater, to teach logic and Latin. After a year Princeton president James McCosh drafted him to teach art instead. As befitted a logician, Marquand thought 'the scientific method' applicable to all knowledge. Subject rather than method defined art history. Marquand valued "the most careful studies of specific examples" more than Norton did: "iconographic elements" could provide "a sure guide as to whether a certain composition is to be classed as Hellenistic in general or more specifically as Syrian, Palestinian, Coptic, proto-Byzantine, or Provençal." (The German archaeologist Robert Koldewey praised this "strictly systematic treatment.") Yet Marquand advanced sweeping generalizations: "The fundamental quality of all Italian [Renaissance] art is draughtsmanship or design"—in "architecture, sculpture & painting"—whereas "the Greek genius was essentially plastic," the French "fundamentally architectural." And he took the same historical, developmental approach to art as Norton. But he differed from Norton in caring less about art as expressing a culture, more about evolution of art per se, fixing his eye on the objects. He believed "the historical or scientific method"—a telling equivalence!—as "productive" in art history as in "other sciences." By putting "architectural, sculptural or other forms" in "groups or families, their characteristics noted and their sequence traced," art historians could gain insights into "the origin & evolution of artistic species very similar to those which have figured so prominently in biological science in recent years." Such achievements depended on "*comparative methods* of research." Looking to Darwinism rather than philology, privileging objects over their cultural contexts, made Marquand an outlier. Yet he, too, imagined a historical, developmental, comparative art history.[101]

Methodological consensus in the founding generation of American art historians reflected the models they had to imitate. However suspect in the eyes of Princeton Presbyterians, Norton loomed as the great native example of art historian. And when looking across the Atlantic, American art historians, like classicists and biblical philologists, gazed raptly at Germany (admiring the erudition, wary of the philosophy). As noted, the major German texts known to Americans borrowed method from philology. Even if Marquand chattered about biology, his actual models came from philology. The first major German professor to dissent from this philological orthodoxy was the prickly Anton Springer (1825–91). He valued connoisseurship over cultural context.[102] Tellingly, Springer seems to have fallen flat among art historians in the United States during his lifetime. So a philologically formed—if not in Marquand's case philologically conceived—sense of the subject prevailed when art history became a discipline in the United States in the late nineteenth century.

Graduate study in art history showed it solidifying into a discipline capable of reproducing its corps of researchers. Individual courses for postgraduates popped up here and there before 1886. In that year Princeton started the first ongoing graduate program. Ten years later, at least thirteen universities and colleges in the United States listed courses in 'fine arts' open to graduate students—three others in classical archaeology, usually taught from an art-historical perspective. Princeton, oddly, did not award its first PhD until 1908, for a dissertation on Roman catacomb painting (early Christian art having become a Princeton specialty). By this time American schools had given eight or nine doctorates for art-historical dissertations clearly distinct from technical archaeology (such as work on cuneiform tablets). By 1920 some eight universities offered a doctorate in art history. Princeton was first to establish a museum primarily to support instruction in art history, in 1888. (Vassar's earlier collection aided teaching of studio art.) Harvard followed with the Fogg Museum in 1895.[103]

All these indicators show art history ripening as a discipline in the United States, but the specialty remained small. Departments at Harvard and Princeton led the field, and Chicago established one a decade after the university's founding. Yet Yale waited until the eve of World War II, Berkeley after the war. Art history doctorates awarded in the United States through 1920 totaled fewer than thirty. Museum executives and curators formed the American Association of Museums in 1906, a sign of professionalization, though probably of connoisseurs rather than historically minded art scholars. Not until 1912 did art historians in higher education organize a professional association roughly parallel to the American Philological Association or the American Historical Association, though less erudite in ambition: the College Art Association. They did so in conjunction with college-level teachers of studio art, and apparently the need for a learned journal did not occur to the founders. By 1912 fewer than a hundred colleges and universities—about a quarter of those granting bachelor's degrees—offered any art history courses. Only sixty-eight had a professor specialized in the subject. Comparisons with literature or history would have been ludicrous.[104]

To the extent that art history had a minimal presence in British universities before 1900, it displayed the same philological approach ruling American schools. The reason was simple: classical archaeology ruled the roost. Even Edinburgh's Watson Gordon Professor was a classicist. The Slade Professors at Oxford and Cambridge ranged more widely, but with few pupils and no tie to degree programs. The apparent exception that proved the rule was Charles Waldstein, Slade Professor at Cambridge from 1895. As lecturer in classical archaeology since 1883, his teaching bore marginally on the classical tripos. Lecturing more broadly as Slade Professor made him wholly irrelevant to student ambitions—until in the early twentieth century the classical and historical triposes allowed students to slip some art history into exams. Percy Gardner, from 1887 Oxford's first professor of classical archaeology, struggled to get fellow classicists to concede his salience. At least classics existed as a reputable field in which he might win recognition—and eventually did. Academically meaningful art history thus nearly equaled classical archaeology in universities until 1900. And from Charles Newton onward, British classical archaeology showed its philological parentage. Newton (from 1880 professor of classical archaeology at University College London) treated ancient relics as artworks. Like Charles Norton in America, he approached their history as a philologist. If Newton's philologic method sounds more like Altertumswissenschaft than today's art history, that is because it was. Richard Jebb explicitly compared Newton with Winckelmann. So art history shared a method spanning the Atlantic. But *postclassical* art history barely existed in British universities, and this absence limited the 'disciplinary' relevance of people like Newton to classics.[105]

On the margins of the university world, a learned archaeology conceived as art history stretched beyond the classical world. Independent or museum-based scholars probed the arts of Anglo-Saxon England and its Celtic neighbors. Margaret M'Nair Stokes provides a striking example. Daughter of a wealthy Dublin physician infatuated with Irish antiquities, brother of the Celtic philologist Whitley Stokes, Margaret grew up surrounded by antiquaries, archaeologists, manuscripts, and artifacts. She caught the fever early. Her self-acquired knowledge piled up until it spilled over in several respected works: among them a two-volume edition of Christian inscriptions in Irish, collected by her father's antiquarian friend George Petrie (1872–78); a profusely illustrated study, *Early Christian Architecture in Ireland* (1878); and an authoritative survey, *Early Christian Art in Ireland* (1887), in a series of art handbooks put out by the South Kensington (today Victoria and Albert) Museum. Its two volumes covered everything from illuminated manuscripts to church architecture. More monographs followed until she died in 1900, honorary fellow of the Royal Irish Academy, the Royal Society of Antiquaries of Ireland, and the Antiquarian Society of Scotland. Hers was a learned, philologically informed art history; but in it 'art' kept the sweeping range of an older antiquarianism.[106]

Farewell to Philology

In the United Kingdom art history did not exist as a true university subject before the 1930s. Aside from the feeble and flickering presence in higher education just mentioned, 'art historian' in the early twentieth century meant connoisseurs employed in museums or as art dealers. The first art-historical periodical in Britain (1903) was the *Burlington Magazine for Connoisseurs*, written mostly by such self-interested experts and designed to be a force in the art market. No degree program in art history then existed in any university in Britain or Ireland. As W. G. Constable paradoxically put it vis-à-vis the 1920s, art history "didn't exist but it was very seriously pursued by museum people." "Museum people" had to learn by doing jobs like cataloging; there was "no place to which anyone could go to have foundations laid." Constable got his own hands-on education first at the Wallace Collection and then as assistant director of the National Gallery. There he also began to lecture occasionally. An area of erudition does not need university endorsement to gain recognition as a distinct field of research: anthropology was fully acknowledged before entering the academy. Yet, when research-oriented universities increasingly set the agenda of learning, a field was apt to remain amorphous and uncertain of itself without academic embrace and provision for training—more so when most of its practitioners used their know-how to hawk artworks. Art history in Britain suffered a severe case of such arrested development. The celebrated 1911 *Encyclopædia Britannica* had no article on art history—only "Art Sales."[107]

Still, demand for expertise kept growing, fueled by museums and galleries. Even the great national museums—as well as first-class provincial ones like the Fitzwilliam and Ashmolean—cast about for educated young men with some background in the art world, like Sydney Cockerell or W. G. Constable. Lesser provincial collections could only hope to find tolerably self-educated curators, often settling for less. "Naturally no man or woman can be expected to be an expert on all art subjects," the artist-curator Sydney Herbert Paviere conceded in 1926, but at least curators "should have a good general knowledge of the history of art, both fine and applied." He wondered why the Museums Association did not step in and "consider some form of qualifications for curators." But where to acquire credentials? In 1930 a Royal Commission on National Museums and Galleries lamented that provincial museums too often had no choice but to hire "ill-prepared and unqualified persons."[108]

The next year Viscount Lee of Fareham, rich politician and art-lover, recruited Constable to develop the Courtauld Institute of Art as a unit of the University of London. (The Maecenas was Samuel Courtauld, a textile magnate.) To learn how to do it, Lee dispatched Constable to talk with art historians in the United States and Germany. As Constable recalled, "the early days of the Courtauld were largely shaped on the model of the Fogg Museum." He thought the Fogg paradigm better fitted to English university structures than German alternatives; it certainly fitted better his own museum experience. The first Courtauld teachers of necessity came from museums and art dealerships. Constable himself, with the same background, focused on analysis of individual paintings. He later wrote a fine book, *The Painter's Workshop* (1954), on physical details of the painter's craft—in the lineage of Eastlake's *Materials for a History of Oil Painting*. Otherwise, Constable cared little for historical context beyond getting chronology right. But he hoped that "from teaching research would emerge." Hope solidified in 1934 when the Courtauld gave shelter to the refugee Warburg Institute, fleeing Hitler. The Warburg's scholarly expertise immediately spilled into the Courtauld. The Warburg also brought a philological-historical mentality lacking among English art scholars—for instance, in using historical context to uncover past meanings of images, then using the meaning-laden images to explain the work of art. This influence eventually shifted the Institute away from Constable's vision of training curators in connoisseurship. (Constable himself resigned in 1936, over what he saw as the governing committee's preference for 'soft' undergraduate 'art-appreciation' versus training of graduate students.) Even the Warburg offered a more 'internalist' ideal of the discipline than the art-and-times model of Kugler, Waagen, Norton, Newton. It stood somewhere between connoisseurship and philological history, not too far from Marquand.[109]

For all the buzz around the Courtauld, little went on elsewhere in British or Irish higher education for a long time. When Slade Professor at Cambridge in 1935, Constable proposed a fund to bring in foreign lecturers, there being so few native experts.[110] The Association of Art Historians—the British professional society parallel to the College Art Association—did not organize until 1974. Postclassical art history in the United Kingdom grew into full being as an academic discipline much later than other humanities and not by the standard process of philological mutation. It emerged, rather, initially out of museums, later as a product of the postwar academic environment—more alert to the wider world.

Even in the United States art history soon lost the commodious philological disposition it had when emerging as a discipline. Such a broadly historical, contextual approach had always been tenuous in the United States. Marquand at Princeton started to rein it in. Many college teachers of the subject had begun as artists, not (like Norton) from a philological background. They lacked the wide-ranging erudition that enabled him to situate a work of art firmly in political, social, and cultural contexts, whether those meant classical Athens, medieval Paris, or Renaissance Florence. Most students, including graduate students, came to the field because they loved paintings or vases, not because they adored dusty archives and crumbling documents. They cared about the object, not the political system or religious institutions surrounding it. A majority of knowledgeable experts who made a living from art did so not in universities but in the rapidly expanding museums and private galleries. Their workaday lives resonated with the art market, and their most relevant learning lay in massive mental databases of individual works and artists. All of this militated against an art history whose salient contexts were social, economic, political, religious, and broadly intellectual. What mattered were narrower, more technical backgrounds in which works of art were compared with other works of art, rather than multiple broader facets of culture.

Such pressures re-forming American art history became all the more potent owing to the larger transatlantic situation. At the outset of the twentieth century, American collectors—including fortunate university art museums—thickly engaged with European art markets. Industrial wealth ensured that canvases flowed westward across the ocean in huge number. Knowledge needed to explain a picture in historical context mattered far less than the erudition needed to attribute it to the right artist securely (or at least persuasively) and to nail down its details. No collector or curator wanted to buy a portrait of Michelangelo if it actually depicted Baccio Bandinelli.* Moreover, the great weight of German authority, firmly on the side of historical-cultural contextualization in the days of Waagen and Schnaase, had now shifted decisively to favor object-oriented stress on the relation of art works to other art works. Norton's own student Bernard Berenson became a famous, if controversial, icon of the new connoisseurship. By the 1920s Norton's old department was pioneering at the Fogg Museum a novel, 'scientific' art history focused relentlessly on the individual object—the very model that Constable adopted for the Courtauld.[111]

In the 1930s the pendulum began to swing back. Just as Warburg scholars pushed the Courtauld Institute away from an ahistorical connoisseurship toward a more philological art history, so other learned refugees from the Nazis reshaped the discipline in the United States. German émigrés like Erwin Panofsky at the Institute for Advanced Study and Rudolf Wittkower at Columbia University brought the Warburg approach to America. (Wittkower made a twenty-year stopover in London before arriving to take command of Columbia's art history department in 1956.) Sometimes these erudite refugees had roots in philosophy as well as philology. And they always kept a tighter focus on the world of painters, sculptors, and architects than the more comprehensive historical contexts of Lady Eastlake or Charles Norton. But philology shaped the 'Warburgian' view of art history to an extent unknown in a connoisseur like Constable or Berenson. By around 1970, interest revived in yet broader historical contexts and meanings, in the scholarship of social historians of art like T. J. Clark—though an interest with very different roots from Norton's philology (in Clark's case, Marxism).[112]

But these developments do not alter the ironic, if not downright paradoxical, position of art history with respect to the other humanities that formed in the late nineteenth century. As with classics and history, philology decisively

---

* Bernard Berenson tried to sell Isabella Stewart Gardner "the only authentic portrait of Michelangelo." Norton pointed out that the subject was probably Baccio—although Norton likely erred in attributing the painting to Sebastiano di Piombo: it is now regarded as a self-portrait. See Turner 1999, 404.

shaped a new humanities discipline—at least in the United States, where art history actually took root in this period. Indeed, without this claim to deep erudition, art history might have struggled to legitimate itself as an academic discipline, as opposed to a commercial skill or cultural polish for young college women. But almost as soon as securely ensconced in American universities, art history tossed aside the tradition of learning that gave it birth.

Still, the afterglow of philology flickered even in connoisseurship. Consider habits of textual philology bequeathed by centuries of critics. The philologist pored intently over fine details of a work—comparing (sometimes subliminally) the text at hand with other relevant exemplars: the surer and wider the range of comparison, the more certain the emendation. These practices persisted among 'postphilological' art historians, applied by them to paintings, drawings, and sculptures rather than manuscripts. The twentieth-century English art historian Kenneth Clark made the tie explicit:

> To say whether a picture is, or is not, by Bellini or Botticelli involves a combination of memory, analysis and sensibility, which is an excellent discipline for both mind and eye. The nearest analogy is the textual criticism which was considered the ultimate end of classical scholarship from Bentley to Housman. No one complained that they were wasting their time when they emended, once again, the text of a third-rate author like Manilius. They were not even judged by the correctness of their emendations, but rather by some combination of memory, patience and elegance of mind which gave these minute revisions a quality of intellectual beauty. In connoisseurship memory of facts and documents is replaced by visual memory, not only of the Morellian criteria of ears and fingernails,* but of spatial and compositional elements, tone and colour; all of which must be related to what was happening in the rest of European art at the time (hence the necessity of dating) and even to mere fashion. It is an exacting discipline.[113]

Philology did not utterly vanish from art history.

Yet, as art historians set about organizing their new discipline in the first half of the twentieth century, they did turn their backs on the full-bodied philological method of Newton or Norton. Their favored approach neglected general history and rejected contextualization beyond the bounds of the art world. Exclusive focus on artworks became the norm for research, and 'art appreciation' became a synonym for 'art history' among undergraduates.[114]

Classics, history, art history: together with literary history they covered the civilized past. None, in the decades when they took shape as humanities, had a lot to say about savages who lurked beyond the chronological and geographic boundaries of Western civilization.

---

* Giovanni Morelli (1816–91) advocated a 'scientific' method of attribution by attention to small, distinctive characteristics of individual artists. Berenson was his most celebrated disciple.

12

"THE FIELD NATURALISTS OF HUMAN NATURE"

ANTHROPOLOGY CONGEALS INTO

A DISCIPLINE, 1840–1910

Just as a lot of nineteenth-century scholars tossed around the word *civiliza-tion* without knowing exactly what they were talking about, so they did *primitive*. The word meant, really, the opposite of civilized—whatever that de-noted. In contrast, a well-informed person could use *savage* and *barbaric* more precisely. These words labeled specific early phases of human society (hunter-gatherer, or nomadic-pastoral-agricultural in modern language). These terms of art derived from theories of the 'progress of civilization' through universal stages, circulated by Enlightenment Scots. Thus the Republican Party platform of 1856 indicted "those twin relics of barbarism—Polygamy, and Slavery." This terminology put both Utah Mormons and Southern planters in their obsolete place alongside the patriarchs of Genesis, one notch above savagery. In slack actuality, not many writers used *savage* and *barbarian* as carefully as the Re-publicans, although 'primitive' peoples had long caught the attention of 'civi-lized' Europeans in their own nomadic wanderings as Europeans visited or overran the lands of the primitives. Today 'primitive', 'civilized', 'savage', 'bar-barian' require scare quotes to signal that we find the distinctions foggy or of-fensive. Not so in the nineteenth century. In discussing scholars from that era, this book will adopt their language, if only to avoid littering pages with in-verted commas.[1]

The time revolution not only defined more sharply what counted as 'his-tory'; it also clarified ethnology.[2] In the early 1860s the 'long chronology' of human existence displaced the much shorter Mosaic chronology. Humanity—most well-educated people soon agreed—had walked the earth for perhaps a hundred thousand years, not a paltry six or ten thousand. Biblical literalists dissented. But a consensus among scholars drew a bright line between the few millennia of civilization and the vast depth of time before the invention of writing created it. The time revolution sealed the victory of philological, documentary history—the modern academic discipline of history—over other modes of history writing. As in a mirror, the modern academic discipline of anthropology also began to shape up.

In the 1860s—following the Brixham Cave finds—anthropology grew self-conscious as a modern field, if not yet a discipline. Its classic founding texts appeared between 1861 and 1871: Henry Maine's *Ancient Law* in 1861; Edward Tylor's *Researches into the Early History of Mankind* in 1865 and his *Primitive Culture* in 1871; Lewis Morgan's *Systems of Consanguinity and Affinity of the Human Family* in 1870. The "peoples without documents"—therefore without history—now belonged of right to anthropology. Uncivilized, primitive folk may have lived thousands of years ago, hunting animals now extinct with stone-tipped spears and arrows. They might live now, in Africa or Australia or Alaska, hunting today's animals with stone-tipped spears and arrows. They might even live in long-settled villages in New Mexico, farming corn, beans, squash, and chiles, looking and acting like their Hispanic neighbors.

If they sprang from a nonliterate culture, they were primitive, given over by historians to anthropologists. The literary scholar W. P. Ker observed in 1896 that *culture* had stretched its meaning: "It is the regular word among anthropologists & antiquarians for the civilisation of any form of society, even the most illiterate—you hear of the culture of the Stone Age, of the Bronze Age, & so on." And, as Oxford's R. R. Marett said with a pained smile in 1922, anthropologists had claimed "squatter's rights" over the "virtually unoccupied territory" of primitive culture. Today an anthropologist is as apt to do fieldwork in a suburban high school in Pennsylvania as in a tribal community in New Guinea. Even in 1890 or 1900 an anthropologist might scrutinize folklore in an Irish village or the crania of English schoolchildren. In theory anthropology studied all of humanity. (So Daniel Brinton insisted in 1893, and Marett agreed.) But in the formation of the discipline the archetypal object of the anthropologist's gaze (as both men grumpily admitted) was primitive man, whether fossilized or still roaming the earth. Either way, primitive man was, strictly speaking, prehistoric—lacking 'history' as understood after 1860.[3]

The philological foundations of documentary history are clear enough, but how could philology shape the study of people who never wrote anything? Anthropology presents perhaps the most tangled case of philological influence on a humanistic discipline. Different varieties of philology fed into anthropology, and anthropology itself precipitated out of very distinct studies. This composite makeup explains why today universities often group anthropology with social sciences rather than humanities, even though some of its founders thought it unmistakably a "science of the humanities."[4] Certain tesserae in the mosaic of anthropology bore the stamp of philology; others did not. To sort out these origins requires first a detour to an era before the discipline started to gel.

ANTHROPOLOGY BEFORE ANTHROPOLOGY

During the early decades of the nineteenth century, philology and antiquarianism together evolved a more 'scientific' approach to savages and barbarians. This area of learning became "the science of savages," in George Stocking's words, "in the sense that it was the only scholarly discourse that took them seriously as subject matter." The useful word *ethnography*, emerging from Russian explorations among primitives to the empire's east, provided one tag for this field in the making. *Ethnology* was a commoner one, usually implying comparison of different peoples. Sometimes one heard *anthropology*, but in this period that word customarily meant studying physical traits of peoples. Researchers gauged cranial capacity, for instance, by filling a skull with peppercorns and then counting them. But physical anthropology (better known today as biological anthropology) plays almost no part in this book. The omission violates nineteenth-century reality. Then the same inquirers who compared pottery shards or explored linguistic affinities might also measure skeletons. Their bone work gets neglected here because physical anthropology had thin connections to philology or antiquarianism, and no one called it a humanity when the category later emerged. In contrast cultural and social anthropology grew directly from philology and allied studies. Universities now typically confine all breeds of anthropologist in the same disciplinary cage, and anthropology seldom finds a place among the humanities. But its socio-cultural varieties—all descended from nineteenth-century ethnology and ethnography—belong there by historical origins and interpretative method.[5]

Formulation of a more self-conscious "science of savages" formalized centuries of experience. Reports on strange peoples by European travelers go back to Marco Polo and much earlier. Herodotus often gets tagged as the father of anthropology, though one might as well call Ptolemy the father of astrophysics for amassing observations of the heavens. Starting in the fifteenth century, imperialist ventures vastly multiplied data about tribal peoples. But a traveler in 1600 might comment on Andaman hunter-gatherers and on Hindus heir to millennia of civilization with similar curiosity: both were exotics who caught the eye. By 1800, investigators of primitive peoples started to see each other as engaged in a study distinct from inquiries into civilized peoples, living or dead.

Many of these sleuths were antiquarians engaged in inquiries that anthropology would later commandeer, including precursors of prehistoric archaeology; but methods and attitudes were shifting. Consider Sir Richard Colt Hoare's *Ancient History of Wiltshire* (1812–21).* Hoare and his coworker William Cunnington (who died in 1810) scrutinized the same ancient remains that intrigued another Wiltshire antiquary, William Stukeley, seventy years

---

* Hoare's book on prehistoric and Roman Wiltshire was preceded by years of antiquarian explorations in Italy and succeeded by a six-volume *History of Modern Wiltshire*.

earlier. Yet Hoare resolutely distanced himself from the druidic speculations of Stukeley's *Stonehenge*. "WE SPEAK FROM FACTS, NOT THEORY," he blared. (This was not entirely true: when Cunnington died, Hoare lost a restraining hand.) Where Stukeley had sketched and measured and fantasized, Cunnington—who mostly did the digging—shoveled, wrote down what he uncovered, and stuck to the physical record. He excavated chiefly Neolithic burial mounds called barrows—round barrows, long barrows, bell barrows. Other antiquaries "pretend to appropriate the different forms of barrows to different nations"—Phoenicians, Britons, Romans, "etc."; but he refused to speculate. He noted the location within barrows not only of human remains but also cultural artifacts such as pottery and "the horns of red deer." Skeletons, he observed, usually had "the limbs drawn up." He reburied them "in the exact spot where they originally lay." He noted the likeness of Egyptian artifacts in the British Museum to faience beads found in barrows—which later turned out to be Egyptian imports. Scarcity of iron convinced him of the barrows' great antiquity: he would not guess how old. Antiquaries had poked in barrows since the seventeenth century. Cunnington did it with new caution and care. He and Hoare even devised specific tools for delicate digging to replace the mason's trowels they first used. The excavations, written up by Hoare, supplied consistent data for clearer understanding of ancient tribes of England—or, as another antiquary put it in 1851, "treasuries of the facts on which an archaeological system must be built."[6] Linking "facts" to "system" hinted at a new erudite regime.

After Hoare and Cunnington, techniques for excavating ancient Britain changed little until after midcentury; but archaeologists did increasingly stress classifying and comparing what they found. Rev. John Marsden, the first Disney Professor of Archaeology at Cambridge, in his 1851 maiden lecture defined the archaeologist's job as "to collect, analyse and classify those relics of the past which form a very important portion of the materials of history." Marsden merely echoed real archaeologists, apparently never putting a spade in the ground himself. But Thomas Bateman did know whereof *he* wrote. The son of an antiquary who dug barrows, Bateman far outdid his father, shoveling across Yorkshire, Staffordshire, and Derbyshire. In one season he excavated no fewer than thirty-seven barrows. He underlined the key role of categorization and resemblance. The "List of Skulls" and "Remarks on the Pottery of the Mounds" appended to his final book, he bragged, "are likely to remain permanent standards of comparison in their respective classes." Bateman agreed with Hoare in deploring "theory, the bane of nearly all the older Antiquarian books." Bateman claimed instead to have provided enough "recorded facts" to "enable the student to elaborate his own theory with regard to the origin, affinities, belief, customs, personal appearance, and civilization" of the ancient peoples whose bodies populated the barrows. For twenty years Sir William Wilde published data from his excavations of Irish crannogs—ancient stockaded lake houses on man-made islands—starting with a 1840 report in the

Proceedings of the Royal Irish Academy. The founding of the British Archaeological Association (BAA) in 1843 brought such prehistoric archaeologists together with those of later periods. Bateman himself served as BAA secretary for Derbyshire.[7]

America lacked barrows and henge monuments; but it had massive manmade mounds in the Ohio and Mississippi valleys, as well as burial mounds elsewhere, attesting to ancient peoples.* Thomas Jefferson (who carefully recorded what he dug out of a tumulus in Virginia) called such mounds "Barrows," evoking English parallels. Many of the Ohio-Mississippi mounds stood out dramatically in the landscape, hard for a passer-by to miss. Army officers in the Ohio valley mapped a few in the late eighteenth century (soldiers once again kicking archaeology into motion). In 1787 Benjamin Smith Barton speculated that the mysterious "Mound Builders"—perhaps, he thought, progeny of Danes who landed in Labrador—had migrated southward and become the Toltecs of central Mexico. (Barton held living Indians in such low esteem that he could not conceive their ancestors building huge earthworks. His contempt was commonplace.) The next year, while the settlers of Marietta, Ohio, demolished mounds, Rev. Manasseh Cutler counted the rings of trees that had grown atop them, to make a stab at their age. In 1813 Hugh Henry Brackenridge, Scottish lawyer settled in western Pennsylvania, distinguished burial mounds from 'temple mounds,' a classification that lasted. He believed the burial mounds to be earlier (as archaeologists do today).[8]

Nothing like a general survey took place before 1820. In that year the American Antiquarian Society published in its periodical *Archaeologica Americana* 160 pages of reports from Caleb Atwater of Circleville, in south central Ohio. His town got its name from a circular earthwork on which it sat. The author—a "queer talker," one acquaintance said—had repeatedly failed to make a living in New York. Moving to Ohio in 1815, Atwater tried lawyering there with no better luck. Not much bothered by clients, he had time to roam. He persuaded Isaiah Thomas, president of the Antiquarian Society, to pay him to explore "these wonders of ancient days." Atwater, like Hoare, aimed "to collect and convey FACTS." He assembled, from his studies and from informants, descriptions of many mound complexes, usually with sketch maps and records of artifacts found in and around the mounds. His focus on "FACTS" often blurred. Atwater barely got started on his report before pausing to imagine some earthworks as forts built to protect mound builders from attack by "ancestors of our Indians." Guesses about "the ORIGIN and HISTORY" of the mound builders crowded his last seventy pages. His fertile fancy drew inspiration now from ancient Israel, now from ancient Rome, now from Scythians. Atwater shared the belief that the mound builders drifted southward to become the Toltecs

---

* Archaeologists today link the Ohio-Mississippi mound complexes—which stretch as far as Florida and east Texas—to the Adena-Hopewell and Mississippian cultures. These flourished respectively from around 800 BCE to 500 CE and from 500 CE to the advent of Europeans.

who erected pre-Aztec monuments in the valley of Mexico. But whence had they first come? They were, the evidence suggested, Hindus from the banks of the Ganges. (Atwater lifted this surmise from two denizens of Lexington, Kentucky: John Clifford, a merchant, and his friend Constantine Rafinesque, professor of natural history at the local college.) A reader of Atwater's reports can almost watch the cautious William Cunnington shape-shifting into William Stukeley of wild imaginings, an instability signaling transition in the antiquarian tradition.[9]

Transition to *what* became a little clearer a quarter century later. Two men from Chillicothe, Ohio—a town besieged by mounds—set out to improve on Atwater. One was a local physician, Edwin Davis, an Ohio native with long-standing antiquarian interests. The other, ten years younger, was Ephraim Squier, a twenty-three-year-old journalist who rode into Chillicothe in spring 1845 to edit a local weekly. Forthwith, the two began jointly to explore the local mounds, hiring crews to dig. Squier had more time for hands-on work, and Davis paid the bills, to the tune ultimately of $5,000. By the time they finished writing-up in May 1847, they had opened over two hundred mounds. Davis and Squier's survey of artifacts and contour maps of mounds outclassed in accuracy anything done previously. Squier and Davis took their manuscript to the new Smithsonian Institution in Washington, chartered the year before. *Ancient Monuments of the Mississippi Valley: Comprising the Results of Extensive Original Surveys and Explorations* appeared as the initial volume in the Smithsonian's Contributions to Knowledge series. It was not quite the book Squier wanted. The Smithsonian's first head, the physicist Joseph Henry, was dead set on molding the infant ethnology into a science based on induction from meticulously collected facts. He ruthlessly edited the manuscript to cut speculation not clearly grounded in fact. Out went, inter alia, Squier's cherished conjecture that the mound builders were racially distinct from present-day Indians and were ancestors of—who else?—the Toltecs. Squier got his own back. He had recently met young Charles Eliot Norton, who was writing a long review of the book for the *North American Review*. Squier tutored Norton in his Toltec theory. Norton made it central to his article—which probably had more readers than the sanitized *Ancient Monuments* itself. Squier went on to explore earthworks in western New York and Inca ruins in Peru—and to unchastened speculation about serpent symbolism in Amerindian cultures.[10]

Ancient Monuments in its published form, shorn of Squier's fancies, set a new standard of empirical rigor and theoretical restraint for American archaeology. Systematically categorizing and comparing the structural elements and artifacts they uncovered, Davis and Squier began to sort out mounds by type. This laid groundwork for trying to understand their meanings and functions. As another ethnologist put it at the time, "Out of confusion, system began to develop itself, and what seemed accidents, were found to be characteristics. What was regarded as anomalous, was recognized as a type and feature of a class, and apparent coincidences became proofs of design." System did not

everywhere develop itself. Even as Davis and Squier began carefully to excavate mounds in Ohio, a Philadelphia physician named Montroville Wilson
Dickeson was finishing his own digging in Mississippi and adjacent states.
A geological background led Dickeson to attend to stratigraphy, and he
showed unusual caution as to who the mound builders were. But he clam-
bered about the ancient mounds, shoveling with abandon, exaggerating what
he dug, guessing wildly about its meaning.[11]

Moving from *Ancient Wiltshire* to *Ancient Monuments*, a reader sees antiquarianism shifting—by fits and starts—toward more empirical restraint on
speculation, stronger stress on comparative method, greater analytic rigor.

A book of 1851 gives a snapshot of 'best practices' in prehistoric archaeology
in the English-speaking world at midcentury. Daniel Wilson, an Edinburgh
boy, dropped out of the university after a year. He eventually grew fascinated
with the Scottish past. In 1847, not much over thirty, he got elected an honorary secretary of the Society of Antiquaries of Scotland. The office put him in
touch with antiquarians across Scotland and opened privileged access to the
society's museum. The result was *The Archæology and Prehistoric Annals of
Scotland*, profusely illustrated. Wilson put it about that his book introduced
the term *prehistoric* into English—and convinced a lot of people. (*Pre-historic*,
with a hyphen, goes back at least three decades earlier.) Wilson adopted the
three-stage schema devised in Denmark by Christian Thomsen, grouping his
Scottish artifacts into stone, bronze, and iron ages. He drew an analogy between the geologist's use of fossils and the antiquary's of artifacts: both allowed
systematic dating and description of past eras. Comparison of pottery types,
he opined, might make chronology more precise. Applying a consistent
chronological system to ancient cultural remains added a new element to earlier tries at classifying by such diggers as Cunnington and Squier. (Wilson also
measured skulls and skeletons to prove that other peoples had preceded Celts.)
He believed scholars could infer prehistoric beliefs and customs from "weapons and implements," burial practices, "personal ornaments," pottery, and the
like. He wished archaeology to become a science. (The historian Henry Hallam thought Wilson had made it one). Wilson stressed "the close relations"
between "the researches of the ethnologist and the archaeologist, and the perfect unity of their aims." Wilson saw ethnology and prehistoric archaeology as
branches of a single science, comparative in technique, drawing data from all
cultures of the world. The comparative method of philology had transformed
into the program of Victorian anthropology.[12]

FROM AMERINDIAN LANGUAGES TO AMERINDIAN CULTURES

Philology led more writers to 'culture' than did the revamped antiquarianism
that inspired Squier's or Wilson's archaeology, for research on Amerindian
languages reverberated beyond linguistics. John Pickering and Peter Stephen

Du Ponceau larded their discussions of languages with detail about customs and beliefs of the peoples who spoke them. In 1818 the American Philosophical Society published a long "Account of the History, Manners, and Customs, of the Indian Nations, Who Once Inhabited Pennsylvania and the Neighbouring States" by Du Ponceau's informant John Heckewelder—soon translated into German and (by Du Ponceau) into French. Such unsystematic descriptions fell more or less within the venerable genre of travel writing. In fact, a decade later Lewis Cass, writing in the *North American Review*, dressed down Heckewelder for sentimental distortion, recommending the more "accurate and animated" ethnological reports by his protégé Henry Rowe Schoolcraft.[13]

Albert Gallatin, too, began to turn philology into something more ethnological. In 1836, as mentioned in chapter 5, appeared his closely printed four-hundred-page "synopsis" of North American Indian tribes. The date signified. Six years earlier, the Indian Removal Act lent new urgency to a long-standing fear that scholars raced against time to record Indian cultures before they vanished. In roughly 125 pages following a preface, Gallatin provided summaries of information about the languages of all known tribes (including some long gone), geographically organized. He included historical and demographic information—more or less of it, as available. For the more easterly, better known groups, Gallatin's tribal histories typically overwhelmed his relatively brief comments about languages. His account of tribes east of the Mississippi concluded with comparative descriptions of clan and family arrangements—foreshadowing the fascination with kinship systems that marked later anthropology. Some twenty-five pages of "General Observations" followed. Here Gallatin addressed the question of Indian origins (Asia) and the mystery of the mounds (ancestors of living Indians could have built them). He also sketched in a few pages a comparative overview of the subsistence basis of Indian cultures. Here Gallatin did with culture something akin to what Pickering and Du Ponceau did with language: grafted empirical data onto an analytic grid. His framework was the Scottish Enlightenment's conjectural history of human progress, and for Gallatin theory ruled data. He concocted a progressivist, socioevolutionary framework that could function as a tool for organizing comparative empirical investigations of human societies. This amounted to little more than a hint. Gallatin remained centrally concerned with language, and it is more accurate to hear him as a last echo of Enlightenment philology than as herald of Victorian innovation. Yet Gallatin's philological research did give the 'science of man' a push in a new, more systematic direction.[14]

Henry Schoolcraft shared Gallatin's faith in philology, but it took Schoolcraft on a fresh path into Native American cultures. A federal Indian agent in Michigan, Schoolcraft married Jane Johnston, daughter of an Irish trader and an elite Ojibwe woman. Tutored by Jane and her family, Schoolcraft studied Ojibwe language and oral lore. Clumsy at languages, he published not grammars or word lists but ethnological articles and, in 1839, two volumes of Indian stories called *Algic Researches.** (He coined "Algic'" to conjoin Alleghany and Atlantic, supposed origin of the tribes whose tales he told.) Schoolcraft wanted to get beyond "external customs and manners" and "physical traits and historical peculiarities," to "the philosophy of the Indian mind." Indians' "mythology" offered "insight into their mental constitution." While collecting legends, Schoolcraft got religion and joined the Presbyterian Church. Hanging around with Presbyterian migrants from the east initiated a steep drop in his opinion of "the Indian mind" and of mixed marriages like his own. This *volte-face* estranged his wife and gave his long introduction to *Algic Researches* a schizoid character. The mythologies of the tribes and the "genius" of their languages at first sounded splendid, especially when readers learned that myths conveyed "instruction, moral, mechanical, and religious, to the young." But, no, the myths were the "rude" efforts of a "barbarous people." Schoolcraft's relief became almost palpable when he left his confusion behind and turned to long accounts of linguistic structure and history, pausing only now and then to belittle the Indians' "rude rites," "habits of sloth," or "childlike attainments in music and poetry." Later, still in disparaging mood, Schoolcraft edited for the federal Bureau of Indian Affairs six helter-skelter volumes of *Historical and Statistical Information Respecting the History, Condition, and Prospects of the Indian Tribes of the United States* (1851–57). There he continued to insist that philology supplied the master key to unlock puzzles of the aboriginal world. In a sense he updated and vastly expanded Gallatin's "Synopsis."[15]

The immediate need for updating explains how Schoolcraft came to assemble his huge handbook. A tide of information about indigenous peoples—with contradictions muddling it—swamped policy makers. To worsen their plight, between 1845 and 1848 the United States annexed Texas, acquired the land now Oregon and Washington, and hijacked most of Mexico by force of arms. The country grew half again as large. The number of tribes under federal jurisdiction vastly multiplied almost in the wink of an eye. In 1847 Congress ordered the secretary of war "to collect and digest such statistics and materials as may illustrate the history, present condition, and future prospects of the Indian Tribes of the United States." The secretary recruited Schoolcraft for the job, and his *Historical and Statistical Information* resulted. Congress was prompted to act by a petition from a young group called the American Ethnological Society. Gallatin had taken the lead in founding it in 1842; Schoolcraft soon became a vice president. The lawyers, teachers, and ministers who attended its early meetings read papers to each other about a jumble of topics, most recognizable today as anthropology. But the society's chief feat was simply bringing into contact leading white students of American Indian life. The Ethnological Society only numbered about forty (though including intellectual luminaries like George Ticknor and William H. Prescott; but its exis-

---

* To it we owe Longfellow's *Song of Hiawatha* (1855), whose singsong rhythms were recited by millions of American schoolchildren for the next century (myself included).

tence—like the demand for Schoolcraft's compilation—suggested that the study of American indigenes teetered at a tipping point. The Victorian discipline of anthropology glimmered on the horizon—or just below it, for language study still mattered a lot to the Ethnological Society.[16]

ETHNOLOGY IN THE WIDER WORLD

More or less learned Americans began to study savages beyond their shores, too. For decades merchants and whalers had told tales of exotic peoples they chanced upon. Only in 1838 did the United States undertake deliberately to peer at such folk, as part of a broader scientific enterprise. On August 18 of that year—after scholars and scientists had cajoled Congress for a decade—the six vessels of the United States Exploring Expedition stood to sea from the navy yard in Norfolk, Virginia.[17]

The philologist on board was Horatio Hale, just graduated from Harvard but nominated by Yale's professor Josiah Gibbs. While still a sophomore, Hale had caught the eyes of his philological elders by publishing a vocabulary of an undescribed Algonkian language. True to form, when the USS *Peacock* reached the Cape Verde Islands, Hale made a Mandingo word list. In Rio de Janeiro he found newly arrived slaves from other African tribes and recorded more vocabularies. In Australia he traveled to the edge of European settlement to meet aborigines and collect their words. He paid attention to culture as well as to the technicalities of language, especially in the Pacific islands where the Exploring Expedition spent much time. When the "Ex. Ex." reached Oregon in autumn 1841, Hale left it to devote months to studying native languages there. Making his way cross-country to home in Philadelphia, Hale wrote up his observations from the voyage in a 666-page behemoth called *Ethnography and Philology* (1846). Congressional pigheadedness limited each of the expedition's scientific reports to a hundred copies, so few experts got to read Hale's work. Those who did were impressed. An English ethnologist called it "the greatest mass . . . of philological *data* ever accumulated by a single enquirer." But it was more than a mass of data. By comparing vocabularies and grammars, Hale became the first person to reconstruct the migrations of the far-flung Polynesians as they colonized island after island. Comparative philology thus recovered history, and Hale's account held up a century later. In *Ethnography and Philology*, he did not limit himself to language and what might be deduced from it. He recounted what he saw of social organization, religious ideas, means of subsistence, sexual practices, burial customs—without speculating or generalizing. His observations were not fieldwork as a later anthropologist would understand it, but they were ancestral to fieldwork.[18]

Hale sailed in the wake of a much longer history of British ethnographic reconnaissance. Captain Cook's ships traversed the Pacific in the 1770s mainly for geographic knowledge, but they also carried back much information about islanders encountered. And, just as a few East India Company servants wrote about languages and literatures of the peoples they ruled, so other bureaucrats of empire wrote about other subject peoples' customs and beliefs. Explorers and missionaries, too, described what savages ate, how they dressed, when they married. Missionaries usually reported more reliably, for they watched their hoped-for Christians for months and years, not in passing. Almost all these Britons—like Hale and other Americans—stared at the exotic other through glasses colored by ethnocentrism, religious prejudice, and certainty of their own superiority. This did not mean they could not see. It did mean that they missed some things and saw other things in distorted shades. Though far from perfect in quality, the data streamed back to the United Kingdom in massive and growing quantity.[19]

Sir George Grey was among the most energetic gatherers. A reform-minded liberal and fanatical imperialist, an avid collector of rare books and manuscripts, a sincere Christian and racist, he sympathized with subject peoples even as they suffered under his brutality in the interests of empire. In 1837, at age twenty-five, he headed an expedition to jump-start British settlement in northwest Australia; at twenty-eight he returned to the continent as governor of South Australia; at thirty-three he became governor of New Zealand. He went on to administer the Cape Colony in southern Africa and, eventually, to serve as elected prime minister of New Zealand. Throughout, he observed the indigenous peoples he ruthlessly ruled. His earliest Australian experience issued in two volumes (1841) about his explorations, including two hundred pages on Australian languages, laws, and mores. He learned local languages and, with remarkable persistence, untangled aboriginal social structure and kinship practices. Tumult in southern Africa kept him from close observation there, but he prodded officials and missionaries to amass ethnographic information. In New Zealand, collaborating with native experts, he collected Maori lore and translated it as *Polynesian Mythology and Ancient Traditional History of the New Zealand Race* (1855)—predictably taking all credit for himself.[20]

Given the horde of reports from Britain's worldwide empire about peoples encountered, it surprises that an ethnological society only came together in London in 1843, a year after Gallatin founded the American one. The birth of the Ethnological Society of London was delayed in part because an earlier Aborigines Protection Society (1837) had aimed to gather "authentic information concerning the character, habits and wants of the uncivilized tribes" as a step toward protecting them. The new Ethnological Society—more purely 'scientific' in purpose—intended to provide a "centre and depository for the collection and systematization of all observations made on human races." As with the American Ethnological Society, members felt themselves battling time to record facts about primitive peoples before civilization wiped them out—literally or by civilizing them. The society tottered for its first few years. But in 1848 it began publishing a journal. Two years previously, the British Association for the Advancement of Science (BAAA) created a subsection for ethnology. In

1847, meeting in Oxford, the BAAA heard some twenty-five papers on the subject. As in the United States, the science of savages was gaining recognition.[21]

Recognition *as what* is the question. Methodological and theoretical eclecticism raged. Gallatin—presciently, it would turn out—applied an evolutionary framework borrowed from Scottish Enlightenment stadial theory to organize nonlinguistic information about Native American tribes. He was lonely in the first half of the century in thinking in evolutionary terms. Schoolcraft collected oral tales to crack the secret of what he imagined as an unchanging 'Indian mind.' Many American and British ethnologists simply reported 'raw' data, as Hale had largely done. Others—perhaps most—used their findings to spar over polygenesis versus monogenesis. Had God created a single set of human ancestors or multiple separate races? The quarrel almost split the American Ethnological Society in the 1850s. James Prichard, the best-known English ethnologist of the earlier nineteenth century, usually concerned himself with skin color and skull shape; but even he enlisted comparative philology in his crusade to prove monogenesis. As the 1850s began, the transformations of antiquarianism and comparative philology had produced Ethnological Societies on both sides of the Atlantic, a small but burgeoning population of ethnologists, and a growing mound of data. But there was no 'discipline' to house it all and whip it into shape.[22]

Defining Anthropology

One developed after 1860 but amid confusion. Late nineteenth-century scholars throughout Europe had a hard time figuring out what to call this new discipline and agreeing on its contents. Germans tended to reserve *Anthropologie* for the study of human bodies (what in English became physical and eventually biological anthropology); social and cultural studies fell under the distinct science of *Ethnologie*—a term itself largely displaced by *Völkerkunde* before 1900. An Italian work of 1884, in contrast, called *antropologia* so "vast" a science that it tended "to absorb many branches of other specialized sciences." The French appear to have wavered between open-armed Italians and narrower Germans.[23]

British and American views matter most here. Anglophone anthropology certainly included prehistoric archaeology. Alice Fletcher made her anthropological reputation with fieldwork among living Native Americans. But in 1907, nearing the age of seventy, she talked the Archaeological Institute of America into setting up a School of American Archaeology in the Southwest; and she chaired its managing committee for its first five years. In her day Americanist archaeologists proved much more adept at characterizing vanished cultures—the terrain of cultural anthropology—than at putting them in chronological order. In 1898 the Cambridge anthropologist Alfred Haddon led the first British anthropological expedition, to the Torres Strait and New

Guinea. Haddon urged that 'anthropology' denote "the study of man in its widest aspect." He included within a single discipline of anthropology three major areas: physical anthropology, ethnography (both description of particular peoples and "comparative study of human groups"), and ethnology. This last subfield he severed "into several branches, the four more important of which are Sociology, Technology, Religion, and Linguistics." Haddon also linked archaeology and folklore with anthropology, more as methods than "branches," and waxed lyrical about insights to be had from comparative study of customs, religions, folktales, and so forth. He included as an appendix to his book a labyrinthine "classification and international nomenclature" of "the anthropologic sciences" that had influenced his thinking—a scheme "proposed by Dr. Brinton."[24]

This maniacal pigeonholer was Daniel Brinton of Philadelphia. Brinton became in 1886 the first professor of anthropology in the United States, at the University of Pennsylvania. (He may never have taught. Anthropology remained a museum science at Penn until 1910.) He first laid out his taxonomy of the discipline in a lecture to the Anthropological Society of Washington in April 1892, afterward altering it chiefly to increase the word count. In his version, anthropology split into four major "sciences": "*Somatology*: Physical and Experimental Anthropology"; "*Ethnology*: Historic and Analytic Anthropology"; "*Ethnography*: Geographic and Descriptive Anthropology"; and "*Archaeology*: Prehistoric and Reconstructive Anthropology." Ethnology (to take one example) further fissioned into "Definitions and methods" ("stages of culture, ethnic psychology, etc."), sociology, technology, religion, linguistics, and folklore. To give some flavor of the enterprise, here is how—in the longer-winded redaction reproduced by Haddon—the ethnological subcategory religion splintered: "Psychological origin and development; personal, family, tribal, and world religions; animism, fetichism, polytheism, monotheism, atheism; mythology and mythogeny; symbolism and religious art; sacred places and objects; rites, ceremonies, and mortuary customs; religious teachers, classes, and doctrines; theocracies; analyses of special religions; philosophy and natural history of religions." John Wesley Powell, one-armed explorer of the Grand Canyon and now head of the Smithsonian Institution's Bureau of American Ethnology, commented on Brinton's paper at the Washington Anthropological Society meeting. Powell sketched his own, alternative "scheme of classification and nomenclature"—but "tentatively," since he thought it "futile" to try to legislate such things. Powell and Brinton differed in how they sliced up anthropology, hardly at all in the substance of what they stuffed into it.[25]

As the concurrence of Haddon, Brinton, and Powell suggests, anthropology had stabilized as a discipline in the English-speaking world by the 1890s. An American writer surveying the field in 1906 pronounced anthropology "well out of its teens." This is not to say that theoretical positions were fixed for eternity: quite the reverse. Haddon and Powell both subscribed to a notion that human societies evolved through similar cultural stages, from brute savagery up to Victorian rectitude; they both believed the workings of this process best revealed by comparing different tribes, peoples, nations. Such views were typical in their day. (They were not universal: biblical literalism led the Canadian geologist-anthropologist John William Dawson to reject evolution and all its wiles. Brinton harbored more nuanced suspicions of full-bore ethnological evolutionism.) Then, within a couple of decades of Haddon's comments, an anthropological revolution in the United States, led by Franz Boas, guillotined evolutionism and sent the comparative method into exile. (Evolution died a more lingering death in the United Kingdom.) But—and this is the point—the discipline's *coverage* and most basic *method* did not change with its interpretative framework. The major topics that Haddon, Brinton, and Powell considered to belong to anthropology remained there. And 'fieldwork,' pioneered by Haddon's expedition and Powell's bureau, continued as the standard way of studying these topics.[26]

STRUCTURING A DISCIPLINE

Discipline formation took a few decades.* In 1851 a lawyer from upstate New York, Lewis Henry Morgan, published *The League of the Ho-de'no-sau-nee, or Iroquois*. Looking back from 1880, Powell called it "the first scientific account of an Indian tribe ever given to the world." Something was stirring, and it began to look like an academic discipline. In 1857 Daniel Wilson—author of *The Archæology and Prehistoric Annals of Scotland*, now settled in Canada—offered at the University of Toronto the course "Ancient and Modern Ethnology"; it was evidently the first anthropology course in any university. (In 1883 he got the title of professor of history and ethnology.) In 1866 Harvard opened the Peabody Museum of Archaeology and Ethnology. In 1871 the Ethnological Society of London and a newer Anthropological Society merged to form the Anthropological Institute of Great Britain and Ireland, groundwork for a professional association. The American Association for the Advancement of Science (AAAS) created an anthropology section in 1875; and none other than Lewis Henry Morgan, the ethnological lawyer, was elected president of the entire AAAS in 1879. In that year Powell established the Bureau of American Ethnology in the Smithsonian and sent Frank Hamilton Cushing to the Zuni Indians in New Mexico. Cushing's extended fieldwork—far beyond his boss's imagining or wish—made him, in Fred Eggan's reckoning, "probably the first professional ethnologist." Another certainly came along in 1884 when Oxford named Edward B. Tylor as reader in anthropology. Two years later Pennsylva-

---

* The stabilization of anthropology as an academic discipline did not at first inhibit the activities of 'amateurs,' whether missionaries and imperial administrators recording savages abroad or investigators at home poking around long barrows and Anasazi ruins.

nia appointed Brinton. In 1893 an International Congress of Anthropology met in Chicago in conjunction with the World's Columbian Exposition. The year before, Clark University awarded the first PhD in the discipline. By 1910 a well-posted road to becoming a professional anthropologist was paved for graduate students, including the enduring principle that it would be "wrong" to train as an anthropologist without fieldwork among some tribal people.[27]

A discipline needs a journal of record, and anthropology got one for each side of the ocean. After its organization in 1902 the American Anthropological Association took over *American Anthropologist*, published since 1888 by the Anthropological Society of Washington. *Man* was, from its first issue in 1901, "published under the direction of the Anthropological Institute of Great Britain and Ireland."

Man's origin shows how rapidly anthropology moved to specialized discipline. The magazine's chief promoter was John Linton Myres, a twenty-eight-year-old classical archaeologist, ancient historian, and anthropologist at Oxford. At first, Myres and his cohorts intended *Man* to replace the weekly *Academy*. Since 1869 *The Academy* had functioned as Britain's review of scholarship in all fields outside mathematics and natural science. But in 1896 an American businessman bought the magazine and made it a less academic, more 'literary' journal. Myres hatched *Man* to fill the void. The Egyptologist Flinders Petrie suggested the title *Man* "as the counterpart of the 'Nature' which exists already." Just as *Nature* surveyed the natural sciences, *Man* would take the human world as its domain—"all archaeology, anthropology, some history (down to French Revolution, say) and some psychology & folklore." No sooner than imagined, this grand vision starved to death in the new ecosystem of academic disciplines. "To avoid collision" with existing disciplinary journals, *Man* excised "practically all the 'history', and a large part of the 'archaeology'" (the classical part). When the first issue came out in 1901, psychology had also gone; and *Man* carried the subtitle *A Monthly Record of Anthropological Science*. It covered only subjects—like prehistoric archaeology, ethnology, folklore—by now well understood to pertain to the new discipline of anthropology.[28]

Topics represented in the first few issues of *Man* and the *American Anthropologist* suggest what the discipline comprised. Those in *Man* included Japanese Buddhist iconography; folk superstitions in Ireland; designs on Etruscan pot shards; "Kaffir" smoking pipes from southern Africa; grave goods from Tang dynasty China; California Indian basketwork and stone tools; "early religion" in light of southern African folklore; an unusual Australian boomerang; field notes (cultural and physical) on a tribal people of southern India; a prehistoric Egyptian cemetery; textual evidence for human sacrifice in late Roman paganism (sent, no surprise, by James Frazer); and carved doorposts from western Africa. The *American Anthropologist* predictably gave more space to Native Americans among otherwise similar diversity. It featured an obsidian arrowhead or spearhead found in Pleistocene deposits in Nevada;

human "beasts of burden" in "primitive commerce"; Navajo gambling songs; "linguistic and sociologic notes" about twenty tribes in Oregon; voting procedures in contemporary Britain and America; Franz Boas's field notes on a Coast Salish tribe of British Columbia; the myth of "Robin Redbreast" in early English poetry; the sociological theory of free trade and protectionism; Lakota and Ojibwe folklore; a Pueblo Indian dance in New Mexico; and, yes, "Cherokee Mound-Building."

THE PHILOLOGICAL LEGACY

What did philology have to do with this mishmash? Nothing, so far as free trade or secret ballots. But collection of curious objects—the boomerang, the grave goods, the obsidian implement—remind of philology's bosom companion, antiquarianism. For that matter, old-fashioned antiquaries took notes on folk dancing and traditional tales, too. Anthropologists carried old scholarly habits into new territory. At least some newfangled anthropologists understood themselves as continuing modes of inquiry familiar from older, European studies. "Perhaps," wrote the author of the report on the piñon dance at Jemez Pueblo, "these songs may yet be traced to some barbaric Ossian or Homer."[29]

Even the novel method at the emotional heart of social and cultural anthropology—fieldwork—echoed axioms about studying culture gestated in philology. James Frazer explained to a classicist colleague in 1888 that "the mental attitude of the savage to the external world is so unlike ours that it is only by perpetually soaking oneself in descriptions of savage life & thought that one can to some extent realise that attitude." Almost certainly without meaning to, this philologist-becoming-anthropologist restated the dictum that a scholar can fathom a text (itself, after all, a cultural practice) only "by perpetually soaking oneself" in the culture in which the text floats. Frazer sat at home among his books, pleading for money to send *other* anthropologists "to collect information about savages before it is too late." But take the ambition of perpetually soaking in ancient Greek culture that *Altertumswissenschaft* nurtured, load it on a boat to Samoa, and you have anthropological fieldwork.[30]

More generally, echoes of philology varied in resonance from one area of anthropology to another. *Physical anthropology*, the study of human bodies (and latterly also of 'ape-men' and apes), owed almost nothing to philology.[31] (The comparative method of physical anthropologists superficially resembled philological routine but derived from comparative anatomy.) In contrast, *linguistic anthropology* originated as comparative philology under a new name (at first focused on tribal languages), although it has broadened in recent decades. *Archaeology*, as already noted, grew out of philology's neighbor antiquarianism. Connections even linked archaeology with more strictly philological enterprises. Study of Amerindian languages preceded and to some extent inspired archaeological excavations of New World sites. Other non-European or preclassical Mediterranean digs occasionally demanded philological expertise—for instance, to decipher cuneiform, glyphs from Mayan ruins, and eventually the Linear B syllabary found at Knossos by Arthur Evans.

But philology left its deepest impress on the vast ethnological ranges of anthropology—*social and cultural anthropology*. One widely adapted tool exemplifies the stamp of philology. To compare systematically Native American vocabularies, Thomas Jefferson picked up the Leibnizian idea of listing parallel words in different languages. A half century later Lewis Henry Morgan adapted the word list to assemble vocabularies of kinship worldwide. A couple decades further on, James Frazer retailored Morgan's word list, possibly even hitting up a few of the same missionaries. Frazer used his questionnaire to amass cultural data, rather than words, for what became *The Golden Bough*. (A second version in 1907 included detailed instructions on how to cross-examine savages.) Philology decisively shaped Americanist anthropology. Albert Gallatin, writing the first general overview of Native Americans, moved directly from languages to ethnography. The immediate successor to Gallatin's survey—Henry Schoolcraft's six volumes of *Historical and Statistical Information*—grouped tribes by linguistic affinity rather than geography. When John Wesley Powell set up the Smithsonian's Bureau of American Ethnology he, too, made Indian languages its practical organizing principle. Daniel Brinton spent far more time on Amerindian languages than on any other anthropological topic. But these quick glances give too superficial a picture. It is better to plumb philology's presence by looking in somewhat more detail at three leading early anthropologists—necessarily passing over many others who mattered.[32]

Between about 1860 and 1900—the formative era of the discipline—ethnology flowed in two main channels. One was study of primitive religion as primal expression of beliefs and values ('culture'); the other, study of kinship as a system of social organization. Contributors to these two discourses did not always wear the badge 'anthropologist.' Chapter 11 glanced at two major influences on anthropology of primal religion from other realms of learning: William Robertson Smith (biblical philology) and James G. Frazer (classical philology). Historians of anthropology will never agree on who—however labeled—stands at the head of either stream. But, everyone agrees, three Anglophone anthropologists were seminal. One mattered chiefly for primal religion: Edward Burnett Tylor; the two others loomed large in making kinship a major anthropological inquiry: Henry Sumner Maine and Lewis Henry Morgan.

TYLOR, MAINE, AND MORGAN

All three shared two postulates taken for granted by most anthropologists in their day: belief in sociocultural evolution and commitment to comparative method in studying it. In the deep background of their evolutionism lurked the stadial theory of the Scottish Enlightenment: the understanding that all human societies developed through the same basic stages, at varying speeds. "How different," swore James Frazer, "are the motives and trains of thought that influence men in different stages of culture, moral and intellectual. No one who does not realise this difference ought to go in for anthropology. Or if he does he ought at least to stick to skulls and not try to know what goes on inside them." From the Scots, Tylor, Maine, and Morgan inherited the division of human social evolution into stages of savagery, barbarism, and civilization. None of them stuck to the details religiously, and Maine sometimes questioned the universality of evolutionary stages. But stadial theory allowed Victorian anthropologists to conflate contemporary primitives with early humans, even "appealing to existing European folk custom as evidence of prehistoric religion," as Frazer did. When around 1860 the 'long chronology' displaced the shorter biblical scale of human existence, the boundaries of prehistory stretched immensely further back; assimilation of present-day tribal peoples to early human beings then became, if anything, more salient. John Lubbock's influential 1865 book *Pre-Historic Times, as Illustrated by Ancient Remains, and the Manners and Customs of Modern Savages* illustrates the framework. Into it could fit all data about primitive people, from Cro-Magnon man to Torres Strait islanders living in 1898.[33]

The basic tool for sorting and analyzing such information was to compare in different societies apparently similar institutions, beliefs, customs—a method borrowed chiefly from comparative philology. The loan made sense: Anglophone social theorists all through the later nineteenth century deeply admired comparative philology. The American historian J. Franklin Jameson declared in 1906 that nothing "occurring in the physical sciences during the last fifty years has done so much to improve the quality of European thinking" as "advances" springing from "comparative religion and comparative jurisprudence, based on comparative philology." An older Oxford counterpart, Edward A. Freeman, asserted in 1872 "that the discovery of the Comparative method in philology, in mythology—let me add in politics and history and the whole range of human thought—marks a stage in the progress of the human mind at least as great and memorable as the revival of Greek and Latin learning" in the Renaissance: "hardly less than a second birth of the human mind." He declared in biblical cadence, "On us a new light has come." The guru of comparative philology and mythology whom Freeman here tacitly venerated was his colleague Max Müller. Freeman cited Müller along with Tylor and Maine as the pervasive influences on his *Comparative Politics* (1873). He described comparative philology as the first triumph of the comparative method, from which the others followed; and he imagined himself as treading "the same path" as Müller and Tylor.[34]

Be that as it may, the 'comparative method' as Victorian ethnologists practiced it could not have existed without the gift of the Indo-European family from comparative philology. The philologist who put it directly into their hands was most often Müller—a gift he sometimes regretted giving. He protested the ill-considered leap from linguistic relationship to biological kinship essential to at least Maine's use of the method. "Races," Müller reminded readers, "may change their languages, and history supplies us with several instances where one race adopted the language of another." Still, even Maine (not to mention Morgan) treated the lessons of comparative philology more judiciously than Tylor. Tylor took the basic idea of comparison and ran with it. He paralleled evidence from one culture to data from another without regard to whether the cultures shared any link whatsoever—the "promiscuous intercomparison of the customs of all mankind" that Müller decried. When drawing comparisons, Maine and Morgan paid much closer attention to historical connections—or contact—between the societies involved.[35]

Because mainstream anthropology soon enough sloughed off the comparative method, some anthropologists regard the practice as a historical curiosity with no lasting effect—wrongly. The comparative method in anthropology did go to its grave not long after 1900 (with Franz Boas preaching the funeral sermon). But it played a vital part in implanting anthropology as a discipline in the Anglophone world—as three individuals key in that process demonstrate.

Edward Burnett Tylor probably gets called 'father of anthropology' more often than any other author in English. That paternity is open to question. But Tylor did write the first introductory textbook in anthropology, in 1881; in 1884, when the British Association for the Advancement of Science added an anthropology section, Tylor served as president; and he held the first professorship of anthropology at Oxford (and apparently the first in the United Kingdom). His magnum opus, *Primitive Culture* (1871), famously began with the first definition of anthropology's most enduring concept: "Culture or Civilization, taken in its wide ethnographic sense, is that complex whole which includes knowledge, belief, art, morals, law, custom, and any other capabilities and habits acquired by man as a member of society." To be sure, believing in universal stadial evolution, Tylor did not treat 'culture' as anthropologists did after around 1910 or 1920; he could not imagine real cultural pluralism or cultural relativism. But in his famous sentence he did specify the subject of what would become 'cultural anthropology,' and his definition lasted well into the twentieth century.[36]

Tuberculosis made him an anthropologist. Tylor was working in his father's brass foundry—the family's Quaker faith ruled out university—when symptoms appeared. In 1855, following a route well-worn by consumptive, prosperous Victorians, he traveled to the sunnier regions of the Americas to recover. In Havana he met an older English Quaker, Henry Christy, a rich prehistoric archaeologist with ethnological interests.* Together, they traveled for four

---

* Christy was partner and funder of the French palaeontologist Edouard Lartet, who discovered Cro-Magnon man three years after Christy's death in 1865.

months in Mexico, Tylor learning to see through his mentor's ethnographic eyes. The result was Tylor's first book, *Anahuac, or, Mexico and the Mexicans, Ancient and Modern* (1861). It combined travelogue with inquiries into ancient Mexican cultures. In this latter interest Tylor had found the intellectual path he would follow the rest of his life.[37]

He plunged into research in archaeology, languages, ethnography. Despite his Mexican wanderings, Tylor afterward worked from the library rather than the field. Like Enlightenment Scots, Tylor hunted for the evolutionary development of human culture; and, like them, he associated the origin of culture with the origin of language. Unlike his Scottish predecessors, Tylor ferreted out details of the process rather than sketching it in broad, fictional strokes. Also unlike them, he had comparative philology to inspire him methodologically. *Researches into the Early History of Mankind and the Development of Civilization* (1865) comprised, in effect, a preliminary report of his findings. The book "brought together," as Adam Kuper put it, "the themes of linguistic, mythological and technical development to buttress a general argument about the intellectual progress of mankind."[38]

Max Müller's speculative riffs on comparative philology proved a key influence, both positively and negatively, when Tylor next turned to working out his theory of primal religion. On one hand, Tylor's understanding of the evolution of language owed much to Müller: a debt explicit in 1866 in a pair of articles in the *Fortnightly Review* and *Quarterly Review*. In them Tylor drew on, but heavily amended, Müller's theories to elaborate his own explanation of the origin of language. His theory of linguistic development in turn was key to his understanding of the cultural evolution—or intellectual progress—of humankind. On the other hand, Tylor reacted strongly against Müller's pet theory explaining mythology as a 'disease of language.' In another article in the *Fortnightly* in 1866, Tylor sharply dissented from Müller to put forward his own hypothesis that religion originated in anthropomorphic conceptions of "Sun, or Rain, or River" as "animated beings." "To write in a modern English book that a child is 'animated by a spirit of disobedience' is to use what a school-master would call a figure of speech; but there was a time when such words simply meant what they said, that there is a real concrete creature, a Spirit of Disobedience, who enters into the child and possesses it." This is Tylor's famous theory of primitive religion as animism. He supposed animism the "elementary religious phase" characteristic of early human history and modern tribal societies. The idea was central to his most celebrated book, *Primitive Culture*.[39]

And it mattered greatly in the early years of the discipline. Tylor did not invent animism by an act of creation *ex nihilo*. The notions of primal religion to which this new word pointed had long wandered about in the European imagination. Nothing Tylor wrote would really have startled Vico or Robert Wood, and Auguste Comte had offered a very similar theory under the label of fetishism. But in animism Tylor brought these older ideas together in a simple, lucid category, giving them new precision and sharper focus. By doing so, he gave anthropologists in his day a tool with which to organize research, a benchmark by which to distinguish primitive stages of human cultural evolution from succeeding ones, and a fruitful takeoff point for their own theorizing. He gave later anthropologists an easy target and a foil against which to devise alternate explanatory categories. The fact that animism finally sank from sight does not diminish its importance in the birth of anthropology as a discipline.[40]

It would be stupid simply to call Tylor's anthropology philological, but blind to ignore how philology furnished a matrix for its formation. Animism was not a philological category, but it formed in Tylor's reaction to Müller's stretching of comparative philology. And (turning to a still vaster Tylorian concept) 'culture' went far beyond language, but philology shaped Tylor's understanding of culture. And his bent for comparing cultures and customs he derived, sloppily, from comparative philology. (In 1889 he temporarily repented his methodological looseness and argued for injecting statistical rigor into the comparative method. This episode proved a momentary aberration for Tylor, with no discernable effect on other anthropologists.[41]) Philology plays an equally underground but even more clearly essential role when we turn from Tylor to Henry Sumner Maine.

The claim that philology mattered much to Maine at first seems off base. He was a lawyer, not a philologist. He served as Regius Professor of Civil Law (i.e., Roman law) at Cambridge from 1847 to 1854, then as reader in civil law at the Inns of Court from 1852. He practiced law for a time (unhappily) before going off in 1862 to serve as law member of the governor general's council in India. When he got back in 1869, he became Professor of Historical and Comparative Jurisprudence at Oxford. In 1877 he gave up that sinecure to become master of his old Cambridge college, Trinity Hall—the university's law college. He ended his career as Whewell Professor of International Law at Cambridge. His first and best-known book was *Ancient Law* (1861). It looks like law all the way down.[42]

Appearances deceive, and the first words of *Ancient Law* tell us how. Maine focused on a society's legal conceptions ("particular ways of thinking about obligations, rights, and authority that defined relations between members or units of a society," in Roslyn Jolly's words). He believed these key to unlocking the society's patterns of thought and symbolic action: its culture. Maine's "chief object" in the book was, he said,

to indicate some of the earliest ideas of mankind, as they are reflected in Ancient Law, and to point out the relation of those ideas to modern thought. Much of the inquiry attempted could not have been prosecuted with the slightest hope of a useful result if there had not existed a body of law, like that of the Romans, bearing in its earliest portions the traces of the most remote antiquity and supplying from its later rules the staple of the civil institutions by which modern society is even now controlled.

When composing *Ancient Law*, Maine lived in the last days of the short, biblical chronology; and he assumed that several thousand years took him back to the earliest days of humankind. Max Müller's Indo-European philology helped him by hinting at a buried cultural tradition linking Rome with an even more ancient India. Maine took little interest in Roman law for its own sake. It mattered to him, rather, because it provided precious evidence—otherwise practically unobtainable—of "some of the earliest ideas of mankind" and "traces of the most remote antiquity" of social institutions.[43]

Maine's book would have reminded alert readers of a prior probing of early Roman evidence: Niebuhr's Altertumswissenschaft-inspired history. Like Maine, Niebuhr tortured refractory ancient Latin sources to extract hints of institutions and practices lying behind them. Maine knew his Niebuhr. But Maine added to Niebuhr's kit a theory of social evolution connecting past to present and an explicitly comparative method.[44]

Maine had been thinking along these lines for a long time and never swerved far. Mountstuart Grant Duff, who attended Maine's lectures in the Middle Temple from 1853, said that *Ancient Law* contained their "expressed essence." John Burrow, whose chapter on Maine in *Evolution and Society* remains the most astute short gloss on his writings, observed that "most of his subsequent work may be regarded as an amplification of the theories of *Ancient Law*, enriched but not fundamentally altered by his Indian experience." Maine came back from India calling it "the great repository of verifiable phenomena of ancient usage and ancient juridical thought." Roman law now mattered to him more as linking "these ancient usages and this ancient juridical thought with the legal ideas of our own day."[45]

Maine's quarry in *Ancient Law* was "the primeval condition of the human race." To track down this "primeval condition," Maine emulated, in his own metaphor, a natural scientist who studies the physical universe by "beginning with the particles which are its simplest ingredients." Maine "commence[d] with the simplest social forms in a state as near as possible to their rudimentary condition." By tracing Roman law laboriously back to its archaic roots, and by comparing it to other ancient codes such as the Sanskrit Laws of Manu,* Maine believed he could recover the 'elementary particles' of social organization. More reliably than other sorts of evidence, ancient law rendered up authentic "fragments of ancient institutions." Humans' "mental, moral, and physical constitution" being basically stable, knowledge of early societies would yield invaluable clues to the process of social development eventuating in "the civil institutions by which modern society is even now controlled."[46]

---

* Maine would have used Sir William Jones's translation.

According to Maine, "evidence derived from comparative jurisprudence" pointed to kinship as the primal system of social organization. Specifically, ancient law (like the Bible) indicated that society originally revolved around patriarchal extended families in which the "eldest male parent" ruled "absolutely supreme." In this "empire of the parent" gestated "the immature germ of a state or commonwealth, and of an order of rights superior to the claims of family relation." The "*unit* of an ancient society was the Family, of a modern society the Individual." Social structure (at least in "the progressive societies") evolved from kinship to individualism—or, in Maine's more famous formulation, "from Status to Contract." Maine concentrated on this progression; kinship mattered to him merely as starting point, central only to ancient societies. But Victorian anthropology equated ancient and primitive: present-day tribal peoples were 'ancient' in cultural and social forms. Maine thus taught anthropologists to look to kinship to understand the social structure of the primitive societies they studied. That was a crucial step, though he provided little in the way of tactics for analyzing this new object of anthropological affections.[47]

What enabled the investigations that led to *Ancient Law*? The most immediate answer is expertise in Latin philology. Maine outshone all other classical students during his Cambridge years, sopping up virtually every Latin honor on offer—the Camden Medal; three Browne Medals; the Craven University Scholarship—graduating as senior classic, with the First Chancellor's (classical) Medal in hand. Without philological skills, Maine would have stood helpless before the ancient Roman evidence. With them, as in the later case of James Frazer, classical philology opened the door to anthropology. Maine "approached the study of society," John Burrow wrote, "as a classical scholar"—though not only as a classical scholar.[48]

Classical philology was not the only one at work in *Ancient Law*. Immediately before springing on readers the news that their forefathers could slay wives and children on a whim, Maine paused to defend the reliability of his conclusions. "It will at least be acknowledged," he blandly asserted, that the methods of comparative jurisprudence "are as little objectionable as those which have led to such surprising results in comparative philology." He must have had the Indo-European language family specifically in mind, because he used the shared genealogy of an Aryan culture sphere to underwrite his comparative linkages of ancient Indian and later European institutions. The evolution of languages studied by comparative philologists paralleled methodologically the evolution of social institutions "from Status to Contract" at the heart of *Ancient Law*. When Maine died, the *Times* of London noted an analogy between *Ancient Law* and *Origin of Species*, published two years before it: "the pregnant conception of evolution being the link that binds them together." But Darwinian evolution had no impact on Maine's writings, whereas he recurred often to comparative philology. No surprise: Maine came to intellectual maturity just when English readers and writers began paying serious attention to comparative philology.[49]

Comparative philologists assumed that present forms relate genetically to past ones from which they evolved. This axiom fitted tightly with Maine's design in *Ancient Law*. And the effort to reconstruct past ancestral forms—the goal of Indo-European research—was what Maine attempted in his book. These homologies support Burrow's argument that Maine's comparative, evolutionary anthropology owed much to comparative philology. And, for Maine as for comparative philologists, the cultural area within which a researcher could reliably compare institutions was that constituted by a single language family—a dictum of Max Müller's. In Maine's studies, 'family' became biological as well as linguistic: the Indo-European 'races.' As the like-thinking Oxford medievalist William Stubbs wrote, "it is quite lawful to work back, through obvious generalisations and comparisons with the early phenomena of society in other nations, to the primitive civilisation of the Aryan or the Indo-Germanic [synonyms for Indo-European] family." With Nazism coming between Maine and us, it is important to stress that, in the nineteenth century, belief in an Aryan racial family did not necessarily denigrate other 'races,' such as the Turanian or Semitic families—although in fact Maine often did seem to think only Aryans capable of *real* civilization.[50]

Maine did not drain comparative philology of all its lessons, and the greatest architect of kinship for anthropologists extracted more. This draftsman was Lewis Henry Morgan. He popped up earlier as author of an 1851 book on the Iroquois that John Wesley Powell called "the first scientific account of an Indian tribe." In later life Morgan got nicknamed Beaver, for *The American Beaver and His Works* (1868). "Beaver" Morgan may be best remembered for *Ancient Society* (1877), a grand synthesis in the socioevolutionary mode familiar to us from Tylor and Maine. (*Ancient Society*, written by a Presbyterian Republican who abhorred socialism, greatly impressed Karl Marx and Friedrich Engels. As a result Victorian evolutionary ethnology survived in the Soviet Union long after the Free World had given it up for dead.) Remarkably, Morgan did most of his research and writing amid an active, lucrative law practice in Rochester, New York. His most laborious and, for the formation of anthropology, most important work appeared in 1870 from the press of the Smithsonian Institution: *Systems of Consanguinity and Affinity of the Human Family*.[51]

Systems of Consanguinity carried analysis of kinship to a level of technical sophistication and intellectual rigor unimagined by Maine. Studying the Iroquois in the 1840s, Morgan discovered that they grouped family members into different categories than he knew: for instance, a girl would call her father's brothers also Father and her mother's sisters also Mother. Several years later, Morgan learned that Ojibwes did the same. Curiosity inspired broader inquiry. Eventually, Morgan enlisted in his information-gathering network the Smithsonian Institution, the State Department, and several Protestant missionary agencies. In the end he collected "the system of relationship of upwards of seventy Indian nations," plus, "by means of the foreign correspondence," equivalent systems "of the principal nations of Europe and Asia, of a portion of those of Africa, of Central and South America, and of the Islands of the Pacific." Morgan figured that he had assembled the kinship terminology of more than eighty percent of the human race. In 1870, after epic travail and unprecedented cost, the Smithsonian published Morgan's data, laid out in 139 schedules grouped into three units: (a) Semitic, Aryan, and Uralian families; (b) the Amerindian family (Morgan called it Ganowánian); and (c) Turanian and Malayan families.* These schedules alone covered almost two hundred pages, Morgan's commentary another four hundred.[52]

Morgan broke down all 139 systems of kinship into two "radically distinct" types: descriptive and classificatory. Semitic, Aryan, and Uralian speakers used the descriptive system, everyone else the classificatory. Perhaps predictably, Morgan thought the descriptive system—his own—more "natural"; it "follows the streams of the blood." In its purest form—in, say, Scandinavian languages or Sanskrit—a term exists for every biological relationship: mother, father, son, daughter, father's sister, mother's sister, father's brother, mother's brother, and so forth. This quickly gets bulky, so the descriptive system commonly grew simplified. For instance, in English, 'uncle' and 'aunt' came to label siblings of both father and mother. Morgan called this process 'classifying'—that is, lumping into one class relatives who shared a *type* of kinship (such as being *sisters* of *either* of a child's parents). But, however abridged, the descriptive system kept lines of descent clear.[53]

The classificatory system carried classifying so far as to obliterate the distinction between relationships of *descent* and collateral relationships. In the Malayan example, my biological father's brothers are also *my* fathers, not uncles; my mother's sister's children are *my* brothers and sisters, not cousins; when *they* grow up and have babies, *their* infants are also *my* sons and daughters. A "fundamental characteristic of the classificatory system" is that "the posterity of my brothers and sisters, and of my collateral relatives, become my posterity." The classificatory system thus erased the difference—crucial to Morgan—between lineal and collateral relatives.[54]

Morgan believed the classificatory system to have arisen in a more primitive state of society in which men and women united "in *compound marriages in a communal family.*" If (for example) several brothers shared a clutch of wives, then all brothers became equally 'father' since no one could tell which had actually sired a given child. The descriptive system, Morgan thought, developed in a later, more elevated social system in which one man had one wife. When monogamy came to prevail over earlier, promiscuous forms of sexual intercourse, the descriptive system tended to oust the classificatory system—

---

* Turanian and Uralian may need explanation. Turanian was an obsolete family, promoted by Max Müller, that grouped Turkic, Mongolic, and eastern Siberian-Manchurian languages. Uralian (now more commonly Uralic) includes Finno-Ugric languages (e.g., Finnish, Hungarian, Estonian) plus those of some reindeer-herding peoples of the Russian northwest. (Most, though not all, linguists accept these groupings.)

because the descriptive fitted more closely the new realities of reproduction. As in Tylor and Maine, the story in broadest outline tells of the progressive evolution of human societies, the basic narrative dynamic inherited from Enlightened Scots. Morgan's variant started with primitive promiscuity and ended in Victorian monogamy, as hunter-gatherers headed toward commercial civilization.[55]

Morgan's tale is not so simply told. He had other irons in this fire—to trace the ancestry of American Indians to Asia; to vindicate the unity of the human race. Those issues will wait for a moment. His methodology needs attention now.

Leaving aside details of his schema, Morgan had given anthropologists a powerful new tool: "the bastard algebra of kinship," as Bronislaw Malinowski snarkily called it in 1930. A better-mannered Robin Fox in 1967 described kinship as "the basic discipline" of anthropology, comparing it to logic in philosophy and the nude in art. Morgan's speculative reconstruction of evolution of the family had a shorter shelf life. It continued a debate begun by Johann Jakob Bachofen's *Mutterrecht* (1861) and J. F. McLennan's *Primitive Marriage* (1865). These arguments petered out soon after 1900, and anthropologists found other things to quarrel about.[56]

There remained from Morgan's *Systems of Consanguinity* three enduring legacies. The first was empirical: an agenda that preoccupied many later anthropologists. In the summary of Thomas R. Trautmann, himself a distinguished student of kinship, this "unfinished project" entailed "the global classification of kinship systems, the working-out of their historical interconnections, and the elucidation of the links between kinship institutions and the semantic patternings of the terminology of kinship." The second was theoretical: a roundabout path (see below) that led to structuralist analysis in anthropology, perhaps the single most influential approach in the discipline for most of the twentieth century. The third was neglected: the genealogical method of tracing now-lost connections that link institutions and cultural patterns with each other over time and space. This line of attack persists only in what Trautmann called "a submerged tradition within the discipline." Morgan himself delighted in showing, by likenesses in kinship structures, that the American Indians' ancestors migrated from Asia. Later anthropologists leached out the genealogy essential to Morgan's approach—stripped away the evolutionary linkages over time among kinship systems. The skeleton left behind was structural anthropology.[57]

We seem to have drifted far from philology, but that is an illusion. By remarkable scholarly detective work, Trautmann tracked comparative philology into the very heart of Morgan's kinship studies. Philology, as he noted, "is the first word with which Morgan addresses his readers."[58]

To start with motive. Morgan turned to kinship because comparative philology had failed in its onetime aspiration to trace all languages back to one or a few originals. By finding a common origin of language, philology might have vindicated the unity of the human race. Then the time revolution ballooned the biblical span of several thousand years of human life into scores or even hundreds of thousands of years. The newly bloated timescale laid waste to this ambition: no philologist could follow a language back so far. The unity of humanity mattered greatly to Morgan; and he hoped to renew the project by tracing kinship systems further back than comparative philology could track language families: "It was with special reference to the bearing which the systems of consanguinity and affinity of the several families of mankind might have upon this vital question, that the research, the results of which are contained in this volume, was undertaken."[59]

To look next at method, Morgan's kinship work borrowed heavily and decisively from philology. Philologists had long ago developed word lists as a crude tool for recording systematically the vocabulary of 'exotic' languages—used, for instance, to record Amerindian tongues. This simple instrument became the basis of Morgan's collecting. But the word list, in the form in which Morgan put it into the hands of missionaries and diplomats around the world, blossomed into much greater sophistication. As Trautmann wrote, Morgan "forged it into something that reached well beyond its original purpose." He conceived "kinship as a system of ideas, as a semantic pattern," and then devised "the research instrument to reveal it." More broadly, Morgan's method—comparing kinship systems to show their "genealogical connections"—directly adapted the idea of branching evolution from comparative philology. Comparative philology showed how human language families branched out from a single Ur-language (say, Proto-Indo-European) into more or less numerous daughter languages. While some branches withered altogether (the ancient Anatolian tongues) and others grew pretty much straight ahead (Greek), some branched out luxuriantly (all the Romance languages being twigs on the stem of Latin). This pattern Morgan applied to the ramification of kinship systems, each potentially branching out into modified successor schemes. Substitute 'kinship system' for 'language,' and Morgan's *Systems of Consanguinity* exactly mimics the pattern of comparative philology.[60]

All this sounds much like comparative method à la Maine, and so it is—but with a crucial twist. For both writers, the most fecund source of the practice was comparative philology, with Scottish stadial theory lurking in the remoter background. But in Morgan's case, comparative philology worked with more specificity. Morgan shared the social evolutionism of Tylor and Maine, the genetic approach of Maine. But he added to it branching evolution lifted directly from the Indo-European research of philologists like August Schleicher and, especially, Max Müller. Still, the commonalities of these three anthropologists perhaps today loom larger than their differences.

Together, the three men, in one decade, laid the foundations for modern Anglophone anthropology—and for a lot of anthropological practice beyond the English-speaking world. Tylor, at least as much as anyone else, marked off the territory of what came to be called cultural anthropology. Maine and Morgan pioneered the ethnological study of social organization, specifically through kinship, and went a long way toward defining the field of social anthropology. Cultural and social anthropology became the twin pillars of the ethnological side of the composite discipline of anthropology. In this genesis, philology—or philologies—played a decisive part. If today philology visibly survives only in anthropological linguistics, its wraith haunts all ethnology.

The Ghost in the Attic

So philological were the habits of anthropologists that for decades they could not shake off links to philology. James Frazer tacked back and forth between anthropology and classical philology all his long life, while younger Cambridge anthropologists pillaged the Semitic philology of Frazer's master William Robertson Smith. In Philadelphia, Daniel Brinton, the first anthropology professor in the United States, studied Amerindian cultures through Humboldtian axioms about language and mind—language, for him, giving outward evidence of internal mental processes (though not the timeless, generalized ones of Schoolcraft). Another key figure in making anthropology a coherent discipline in the United States, Alfred Kroeber, came to the subject from an early and enduring fascination with linguistics and an MA in English literature. (His daughter is the novelist Ursula Le Guin.) His anthropological menu at Berkeley always included a large helping of research in languages; linguistic studies, he said, gave him the model for understanding culture. Footprints of philology dotted writings of other anthropologists throughout the English-speaking world.[61]

For brevity, Oxford will serve as example. Among nineteen "anthropological essays" published in 1907 to toast Tylor on his seventy-fifth birthday, five arose directly from classical or biblical philology. Tylor's successor R. R. Marett helped to establish anthropology as a postgraduate diploma subject at Oxford. Marett came from classical philology (winner of the Chancellor's Prize for Latin verse, like Maine). After election as secretary to the committee for anthropology in 1907—the classicist John Myres served as the first in 1905 (and last in 1938!)—Marett organized "a course of lectures on Graeco-Roman Culture in the light of Anthropology." The lecturers all worked, like Frazer, in both classics and anthropology. Marett's main collaborator in Oxford anthropology at this period was Myres, once and future editor of *Man*. Myres mentored the first Oxford graduate awarded a diploma in anthropology, in 1908. (Barbara Freire-Marreco did fieldwork among pueblo-dwelling Indians in the American Southwest and then studied English folklore.) He gave a summer course to the Workers' Education Association, "Economics of Primitive Societies." Yet all the while he pursued classical philology. While president of the

Royal Anthropological Institute (1928–31), he published his 1927 Sather Classical Lectures as *Who Were the Greeks?* (1930). His last book was *Homer and His Critics* (1958).[62]

Such bonds show how long it can take a child to break away from home. The largest chunk of anthropology—its varieties of ethnology—modeled themselves in one way or another on humanistic philology. It is no wonder that, even when disguised as a social science, anthropology kept in touch with its siblings history and literature, other philologically grounded disciplines. It still plays with them. Amnesia about ancestry and methodological affinity does not erase elemental unities, only veils them.

13

"The Highest and Most Engaging of the
Manifestations of Human Nature"

BIBLICAL PHILOLOGY AND THE RISE
OF RELIGIOUS STUDIES AFTER 1860

As anthropologists trekked off to observe primitive religion, other heirs of
philology turned attention to the civilized sort, in such great historic cultures as China, India, and Persia. So, as the sway of Christian churches over
education and erudition waned, learned inquiries into religion broadened.
The philologists originally concerned with religion—the biblical sort—felt
their footing in this new world of knowledge shifting and uncertain.

Biblical philologists studied—and usually believed in—a divine revelation,
not human creations. Increasingly, as disciplinarity advanced, they devoted
their scholarly efforts *only* to the Bible. When the fluid diversity of philology
fragmented into specific new disciplines in the later nineteenth century, the
'divinity' of biblical philology looked odd among 'humanities.' Humanistic
study of religion, in turn, distanced itself from Christian or Jewish specificity
and commitments, widening its gaze to take in religions—or religion-like traditions—across the globe.

This final chapter will examine first the trajectory of biblical criticism in
relation to the new humanities. It will then explore how different varieties of
philology—including borrowings from biblical philology—coalesced into a
new humanistic discipline taking multiple approaches to comparative study of
'world religions.'

PART I: THE FATE OF BIBLICAL PHILOLOGY

Biblical critics faced a peculiar situation in the later nineteenth century. On
one hand, no other research—including that loosely labeled Darwinian—

touched so directly on sensitive religious, spiritual, and moral issues. No other drew so many lightning strikes. Protestant biblical philologists spoke indirectly, in the pews, to a bigger, more attentive public audience than probably any other academic enterprise. (I neglect Catholics and Jews, who had little resonance in Anglophone biblical scholarship during this period.) On the other hand, the place of biblical erudition within the ecology of knowledge grew dubious, even isolated.

So long as philologists saw themselves simply as philologists, classical and biblical studies rubbed along comfortably together, as they had for centuries. As late as the 1850s the same scholars, especially in the United Kingdom, engaged seriously in both. Benjamin Jowett's commentaries on four Pauline Epistles appeared in 1855. After *Essays and Reviews* in 1860, however, Jowett abandoned biblical criticism to concentrate on translating Plato's dialogues. In 1854, in Cambridge, Joseph Lightfoot and two colleagues founded the *Journal of Classical and Sacred Philology*. It lasted until 1859. In the later 1850s Lightfoot lectured in Trinity College on both the New Testament and classical topics. He contemplated an edition of Aeschylus's Orestean trilogy. Lightfoot did not so much consciously give up the scheme as put it into a drawer that he never opened again. After 1860 he worked exclusively on the New Testament. The pattern was common. Quarantining Bible scholarship in seminaries or divinity faculties sometimes reinforced it, especially in the United States.[1]

The rift deepened even as Anglophone biblical criticism flourished anew. Using historical-literary methods well ensconced in philology, Lightfoot convincingly dated the New Testament books to the late first century CE. This torpedoed F. C. Baur's hitherto widely accepted claim for a late second-century origin. Lightfoot thus pushed the writings back into a time when at least secondhand memories of Jesus still circulated—cutting the legs off the powerful historical skepticism of Baur and his Tübingen school. Lightfoot's meticulous studies of early Church Fathers likewise sapped Baur's thesis that the New Testament mirrored quarrels in the early church: Ignatius of Antioch knew nothing of them at the end of the first century. Lightfoot's Cambridge colleagues Brooke Westcott and F.J.A. Hort meanwhile took advantage of two ancient manuscripts recently come to light to complete in 1881 a Greek text of the New Testament.* It became de facto the new Textus Receptus—though, with manuscript discoveries ongoing, not cast in stone. Westcott and Hort restored English textual philology to the glory days of the eighteenth century.[2]

Yet, as philology morphed into 'the humanities,' this reenergized biblical philology drifted away from them—more rapidly in the United States than

---

* In 1862 Constantin Tischendorf published a fourth-century Greek manuscript of the New Testament and parts of the Old Testament, the Codex Sinaiticus. (It came from Sinai—the Orthodox monastery of St. Catherine.) A fourth-century manuscript in the Vatican Library had long been known but shielded from outside eyes. In 1857 a defective edition of this Codex Vaticanus by Cardinal Angelo Mai appeared. In 1867 Tischendorf published a better one.

United Kingdom. The Bible belonged, after all, to 'divinity', the very name distinguishing it from study of human things. True, philologists could analyze a biblical text from a nonreligious point of view, as Spinoza made clear long before. By 1900 some did. But the Bible *merited* study mainly because of its religious significance; and most Britons, Irish, and North Americans still revered it as God's word. The place of biblical philology in the changing institutional structure of universities reflected this increasingly awkward fit with other studies descended from philology. Biblical criticism gradually floated away from secularizing centers of academic research, into separate theological faculties, divinity schools, even stand-alone theological seminaries. In 1880 Americans set up a disciplinary organization, the Society for Biblical Literature and Exegesis, with its own scholarly journal. Characteristically, biblical critics in the United Kingdom (and Canada) proved reluctant to institutionalize their field, to distinguish biblical philology from general philology—slower even than classicists. But they seldom branched out into humanistic disciplines, and they wrote mostly for other specialists or for churches. Meanwhile, the religious, mostly Protestant framework of learning slowly crumbled. A growing minority of unbelieving professors questioned whether the Christian and Jewish tenets that made the Bible relevant counted as knowledge. Thus, as biblical criticism itself became discipline-like, methods that once bound it to other forms of textual philology no longer linked it to humanistic disciplines with the same ancestry.

For all these reasons, biblical philology as a coherent, evolving whole began to drop out of the story of the emergent humanities. Though vital to Christians, and impressive in their own right, New Testament studies like those of Lightfoot, Hort, and Westcott hardly affected scholarship outside biblical studies. But Bible scholarship did not become wholly irrelevant to the humanities. Instead, fragments of biblical erudition, at discrete moments, influenced a few of the new disciplines. Biblical philology powerfully shaped comparative study of religions (or 'history of religion'), and its effects on anthropology and archaeology were not negligible.

A Highly Selective Account of Biblical Philology, 1860–1910

A hasty *tour d'horizon* will situate in their context aspects of biblical studies most influential on the humanities. The first thing to note is that no revolutions shook biblical philology in the decades after 1860 like those of the eighteenth and earlier nineteenth centuries. Rather, scholars—the foremost still mostly Germans—built on ideas introduced earlier. Meanwhile, English-speaking biblical critics grew more comfortable with once radical positions. Historical criticism nonetheless remained for them a higher-risk business than for Germans.

Institutional factors illuminate both acclimation and risk. In Britain in the 1860s biblical criticism became a formal university subject, belatedly following

American precedent.[3] This 'academizing' of biblical philology raised technical sophistication but reduced contact with other forms of philology. Biblical criticism drifted closer to a distinct 'discipline' apart from the emerging humanities. More American and British biblical scholars worked as full-time, research-oriented members of university or seminary faculties. As such, they dug deeper into publications by German counterparts, came to terms with German ideas. Yet Christianity in the English-speaking world remained more traditional in theology than in Germany; and the university faculties and independent seminaries where many biblical critics taught often operated under more or less direct control of churches. These ideological and organizational constraints held biblical philologists back from straying too far into German territory—and extra-academic guardians of orthodoxy might slap them down if they did.

Yet the 'Bible wars' flaring up after *Essays and Reviews* left few scholars dead on the battlefield: testimony to the moderation of Anglophone biblical critics or their skill in keeping their heads down. Rare heresy trials did explode, memorably those of the Scot William Robertson Smith in 1878–81 and the American Charles Briggs in 1891–93. Because Lightfoot's historical criticism bolstered trust in New Testament scholarship, the Old Testament became center of the storm. Both Smith and Briggs foundered on it. In the United Kingdom, controversy petered out with the 1880s. Traditionalists still held some teaching positions, but after 1890 historical criticism ruled British biblical scholarship. In the United States, historical approaches took longer to win out—partly because the Civil War and its aftermath delayed the clash, partly because churches kept scholars more firmly in tow. Deeper historical approaches to scripture did sneak in, as alarmed Presbyterians discovered when Briggs taught moderate higher criticism at their Union Theological Seminary. (Their effort to shut him up made Briggs Episcopalian and Union autonomous.) Such incursions of German methods provoked Americans to replicate between about 1890 and 1930 the earlier British quarrels. In the United States protracted conflict over biblical interpretation got tangled up with biological evolution in the notorious fundamentalist controversy, but the Bible caused more anguish than the missing link. The series of tracts called *The Fundamentals*—which gave the row its name—centered on biblical disputes. This contest for the soul of American Protestantism reached scholarly resolution in the 1920s with the victory of historical criticism in most seminaries and divinity schools. Many fundamentalists then fled mainline churches for newly founded denominations. These groups created their own, alternative seminaries. So, on both sides of the Atlantic, conservatives held out on the margins. In the United Kingdom they produced little worthy of the name of scholarship. In the United States fundamentalists just went their own way, ignoring mainstream critics.[4]

Battles during the Bible wars raged mainly over historicity. Although the key ideas and methods were in place by 1860, later elaborations gave these a keener edge, wider ramifications. Both the Jesus stories and the Old Testament raised issues, but the Old Testament's had more academic impact outside of biblical philology. The studies most salient for other disciplines grew from the insight that multiple sources fed into early books of the Old Testament. This idea went back to Jean Astruc's observations about Genesis in 1753. By the time Hermann Hupfeld published *Die Quellen der Genesis* (*The Sources of Genesis*) a hundred years later, German philologists had identified four major textual strands that some ancient editor had woven together; and scholars had extended this 'documentary hypothesis' (as it is now called) from the Pentateuch, the five 'books of Moses,' to include Joshua—all together making the Hexateuch.[5]

This textual question transformed into a historical inquiry. The pivotal figure was Heinrich Ewald, the most influential his student Julius Wellhausen. In the five-volume *Geschichte des Volkes Israel* (*History of the People of Israel*, 1843–59), Ewald brought the methods and insights of German historical criticism to bear on the history of the Hebrews through the time of Christ. The book impressed a lot of scholars, and not only in Germany. As a result, as R. E. Clements noted, "writing such a history became a fully accepted part of the modern critical approach to the Bible."[6]

Ewald's history galvanized one of his last students at Göttingen, Julius Wellhausen. A pastor's son, Wellhausen made his scholarly name by research into the composition of the Hexateuch, which he published in the mid-1870s. From analysis of the text, he argued in detail when the four major sources were produced, how they were modified, how they were combined. Very quickly, this 'Wellhausen hypothesis' became orthodoxy among German biblical scholars and spread abroad.* For almost a century his work dominated critical understanding of the formation of the historical books of the Old Testament, and it remains the classic form of the documentary hypothesis. Then in 1878 appeared his revolutionary *Geschichte Israels* (*History of Israel*). In it, Wellhausen explored "liturgical antiquities and dominant religious ideas" in ancient Israel from a completely secular point of view. On the basis of meticulous dissection and dating of the compositional elements of the Hexateuch, he brilliantly reconstructed from these pieces a history of the evolution of Hebrew religious practices. He depicted a move from an early period of localized cults to a priestly, legalistic, temple-centered religion of Israel after the Babylonian exile. Wellhausen built his historical case out of literary materials in the Old Testament itself, filtered through nineteenth-century German intellectual axioms. These included socioevolutionary ideas about progressing from primitive to advanced and philosophic notions about moving from material to spiritual. His major technical innovation was to make explicit the implications of dating the 'priestly' strand in the Hexateuch (one of the four major sources) as most

* The Wellhausen hypothesis is sometimes called Graf-Wellhausen to recognize the earlier contribution of Karl Heinrich Graf. The hypothesis ruled for most of the twentieth century, but in the past three decades many biblical scholars have dumped it—while retaining the fundamental idea of the Hexateuch taking shape over time from multiple sources.

recent rather than earliest. But by depicting ancient Hebrews as primitive nomads who worshiped like their Middle Eastern contemporaries, he invited
other scholars to bring extrabiblical materials to bear on Israelite religion.
Among his disciples was the young Scot William Robertson Smith, who will
shortly return.[7]

Smith aside, Wellhausen's ideas took a while to persuade Anglophone biblical philologists. In 1881 A. A. Hodge and Benjamin Warfield of Princeton
Theological Seminary—hardly a scholarly backwater—published an influential essay on "Inspiration." They argued that God directly oversaw the biblical authors "in their entire work of writing, with the design and effect of rendering that writing an errorless record of the matters He designed them to
communicate." So much for Wellhausen's stitched-together, propagandizing
hodgepodge. Jewish Theological Seminary in New York was a self-consciously
modern institution. Its professor of biblical literature from 1903 until his death
in 1920 was Israel Friedlaender. He had studied in Berlin and Strasbourg with
leading German philologists, including Wellhausen. Friedlaender appreciated
newfangled evidence from Near Eastern archaeology and comparative study
of religion. Yet he disdained Wellhausen.[8]

Even in 1903 Friedlaender was becoming a relic among mainstream scholars. The first professor of Semitic languages at Johns Hopkins, German-born
and -trained Paul Haupt, supervised publication between 1893 and 1904 of a
sixteen-volume Hebrew Bible with commentary. It illustrated the documentary hypothesis by printing different sources in different colors: the so-called
Polychrome Bible. (The name echoed early modern Polyglot Bibles.) Haupt
also coedited with William Rainey Harper the learned journal *Hebraica*; it
peddled a 'reverent' version of the documentary hypothesis from its first issue
in 1884. Samuel R. Driver, Regius Professor of Hebrew at Oxford from 1882
until his death in 1914, at first sniffed suspiciously at Wellhausen's hypothesis;
but long study persuaded him. His *Introduction to the Literature of the Old
Testament* (1891) by its very caution went a long way toward naturalizing the
documentary hypothesis in British scholarship. George Foot Moore, at Andover Seminary (1883–1902) and then at Harvard (1902–28), played Driver for
the United States. Curiously, few Anglophone Jewish biblical scholars in this
period engaged higher criticism, even though it challenged the Hebrew Bible.
Still, by 1899, a writer in London's *Jewish Quarterly Review* could assert, generally, that "English biblical scholarship has assimilated during the past quarter
of a century all that is best in German work." Fifteen years later, an American
might claim the same.[9]

The Bible and the Humanities

By then, biblical philology had evolved into a discipline in its own right, often
encased in *divinity* faculties, more and more isolated from the new *humanities*. But common ancestry and common methods still supplied ground for

interaction. In a few cases cross-fertilization helped to breed a humanistic discipline.

One connection was direct—and unsurprising, given academic secularization. Christians had always learned Hebrew to enable biblical scholarship. This remained true in divinity schools and seminaries, now including a small but growing number of institutions for educating rabbis. But some Hebrew philologists pursued research from profane motives. Various of them hived off into new faculties of Semitics, where they joined scholars of Arabic, Akkadian, and related tongues. The value of cuneiform tablets for the history of ancient Hebrews and their neighbors meanwhile boosted the status of Assyriology. Thus emerged a new, or newly configured, humanistic discipline. ('Semitics' now calls itself something like Near Eastern languages and cultures.) The break with biblical philology was neither sudden nor complete. One early course offered "theological" interpretations of the Hebrew Bible alongside "philological" and "historical" ones. Semitics departments gave a scholarly home to a growing number of Jews unlikely to find academic jobs elsewhere in the humanities before World War II. Semitics seems to have played this role particularly in the United States, where both Jewish population and anti-Semitism grew rapidly in the decades around 1900. Prejudice saturated American higher education—as a rule the more elite the institution, the more anti-Semitic. Bigotry kept Jews out of humanities faculties in leading research universities. But Jews apparently 'fit' in Semitics. At least they flourished there. (Likewise, Solomon Schechter—who in 1897 brought to scholarly notice the vast medieval Hebrew manuscript horde from the Cairo Geniza—held jobs at Cambridge with Jewish labels.) Morris Jastrow of the University of Pennsylvania and Richard Gottheil of Columbia, sons of rabbis, coedited a major Semitics series. The secular-minded Jastrow's first love was Assyriology, but he published much biblical philology. Conversely, he applied Wellhausen's 'documentary' method to the Babylonian epic of Gilgamesh. Gottheil served as president of the American Society of Biblical Literature in 1902–3. Another rabbi's son, Max Margolis, pioneered Semitics at the University of California and went on to supervise the 1917 translation of the Hebrew Bible that replaced the 1853 'Leeser Bible.' From biblical philology to Semitics was a pretty obvious step. Other leaps from biblical philology to the humanities were slightly longer.[10]

One jump ended in Near Eastern archaeology and Assyriology. Chapter 7 discussed Edward Robinson's pioneering exploration of Palestine. By laying out evidence for identifying certain places with biblical locales, Robinson enabled scientific excavation. His 1841 book antedated by about a decade Henry Layard's and Henry Rawlinson's Mesopotamian digs. Their work made a splash, owing largely to Assyria's and Babylon's prominence in the Old Testament. When in 1872 news broke of the flood story in tablet 11 of the epic of Gilgamesh, devout hearts soared to think Noah's flood confirmed in cuneiform. All this boosted interest in the archaeology of ancient Israel. Swayed by the Anglican luminary Arthur Stanley and led by his protégé George Grove, elite Englishmen clubbed together in 1865 as the Palestine Exploration Fund (PEF), to promote archaeological study of the Holy Land. The PEF oozed Protestantism from every pore; but Grove talked even the Jewish leaders Sir Moses Montefiore and Baron Lionel de Rothschild into lending their names, though little else. Nearly two decades elapsed before a parallel Egypt Exploration Fund got under way—the PEF providing its model. (The PEF also inspired an American Palestine Exploration Society in 1870. Internal conflict and incompetence killed it within a decade.) Some of the same personnel got involved in both the PEF and the Egyptian fund. The pioneering Egyptologist Flinders Petrie excavated in Palestine under PEF auspices. He also trained—haphazardly—the PEF's lead excavator in the 1890s, an American called Frederick Bliss. Bliss had studied at Union Theological Seminary in the 1880s; he averred that methods he learned there for sorting out "the composite authorship of the Pentateuch" helped him to "determin[e] the comparative ages" of "a confused series of ancient walls" in Jerusalem—an "exact analogy."[11]

Biblical archaeology neither preceded nor directly inspired most Mesopotamian or Egyptian archaeology: the point is the synergy among all these digs in the Near East. The ball that Robinson got rolling encouraged the new discipline of archaeology as well as Mesopotamian philology. Proving the Old Testament historically trustworthy partly motivated the first American archaeological work in Mesopotamia in the later 1880s. A remarkable number of Assyriologists in the decades around 1900 also at least dabbled in biblical studies; some went further in their exploration. Paul Haupt moved from Göttingen to Johns Hopkins as expert in Sumerian and Akkadian language and cuneiform. There he produced the first full edition of the Gilgamesh fragments. But he devoted much time at Johns Hopkins to biblical philology. The Mesopotamian archaeologist Herman Hilprecht of the University of Pennsylvania initially moved from Erlangen to Philadelphia in 1886 in order to work for the *Sunday School Times*, and he titled his self-promoting 1903 history of Near Eastern excavations *Explorations in Bible Lands*. His student and foe, the cuneiform epigrapher Rev. Albert Clay of Yale, investigated Mesopotamian contexts of the Old Testament. George Barton wrote his 1891 Harvard dissertation on the cult of the Babylonian goddess Ishtar, published in 1913 a major book on *The Origin and Development of Babylonian Writing*—and then got fascinated by biblical archaeology. His textbook *Archaeology and the Bible* (1916) went through seven editions. For the rest of his career, he published on both Babylonians and the Bible. As Semitic studies and Near Eastern archaeology moved out of the orbit of theological scholarship into independent, secular fields, biblical scholarship supplied initial direction and momentum.[12]

One individual provides perhaps the most multifaceted, most dramatic instance of biblical philology spurring new, secular humanistic disciplines: William Robertson Smith. Smith's story is sufficiently instructive about the perils and reach of biblical philology to tell at some length.[13]

It starts with the Disruption in the Church of Scotland three years before his birth in 1846. Long-simmering tensions divided the evangelical wing of the church, holding to Calvinist orthodoxy and stricter in moral tone, from its so-called moderate wing, more liberal in theology and more relaxed in lifestyle. The strains erupted in 1843. Evangelicals bolted from the general assembly to form a new Free Church of Scotland. Smith's father became a Free Church minister. Before the Disruption unexpectedly ordained him, he had headed a school in Aberdeen.

So Willie, his eldest son, got a solid education at home and grew into a bookish lad (a trait fostered by also being a sickly one). He showed precocious brilliance in mathematics and natural science. Taking his first degree at Aberdeen University, he proceeded to the Free Church's New College in Edinburgh for theological studies. There he learned to read Hebrew skillfully. (His father reported that Willie could piece out Hebrew at the age of six but later forgot it.) Besides Hebrew, Smith learned from the biblical critic A. B. Davidson (his favorite teacher) to set aside the "reverence and solemnity" normally due the scriptures when engaged in the "intellectual" task of "ascertaining their meaning." In such work—"so far as interpretation and general formal criticism are concerned"—the critic should handle the Bible in the same way, "mainly," as other ancient texts. Davidson also lauded German biblical philologists of moderate tenor. In the Free Church this approach teetered on the edge of daring, if it did not fall off. During the summers of 1867 and 1869, Smith enrolled at Bonn and Göttingen. There he made firsthand acquaintance with German biblical philologists (and mathematicians and natural scientists). He formed ties with some. As he was finishing his studies at New College, death opened the chair of Hebrew and the Old Testament at the Free Church College in Aberdeen. Not yet twenty-four, Smith shone among applicants. It speaks to his range of learning that he had published scientific papers on mathematics and electricity. (Was he the only candidate for a biblical professorship in Scottish history to come with a testimonial from the country's foremost physicist?) In May 1870 the church's general assembly elected him by a large majority to fill the vacancy.[14]

Right away, troubling omens clouded the horizon. In his inaugural lecture Smith spoke of esteem for German "higher criticism" and of treating the Bible "as a historical record." "Our notions of the origin, the purpose, the character of the Scripture books must be drawn, not from vain traditions, but from a historical study of the books themselves." Such comments should have set off alarm bells in the Free Church—and perhaps would, had the wardens of orthodoxy not been busy dousing a different fire. Smith—like 'advanced' German philologists—had gone far toward understanding the Old Testament as the record of an ancient people much like neighboring tribes. In 1871 he wrote to a friend, John Ferguson McLennan, who had recently published much-noticed articles on worship of plants and animals by primitive peoples. Smith told him that "the Israelites, being by nature like other people at the time, had a great love for sorcery which creatures like the witch of Endor gratified," noting as well "traces of nature religion" in the Old Testament. He still felt sure that "the Old Testament religion" did not *evolve from* such crude beliefs but, in contrast, "confronted and destroyed them." And he scorned radical Germans who made the Gospels mythical. Smith's faith would hardly have reassured most Free Churchers, a highly literate, highly orthodox folk who could sniff out heresy faster than a border collie could smell a wolf.[15]

To vary the animal metaphor, Smith's German chickens came home to roost. Smith had decided that early Hebrew texts needed contextualizing in the ancient Semitic world as a whole. To this end, he spent the summer of 1872 in Göttingen studying Arabic under Paul de Lagarde. (Smith admired Lagarde's erudition, seemingly ignored his savage anti-Semitism.) Later, in 1878 and 1879, Smith traveled in Arabia. At Göttingen in 1872 he met Julius Wellhausen, just two years older. He and Smith bonded. By 1874 Smith's scholarly reputation had risen so high that the *Encyclopædia Britannica* recruited him to write several articles for the forthcoming ninth edition, including the long, general one on the Bible. His contributions showed the hold on him of approaches like Wellhausen's. In the general "Bible" article, published in 1875, Smith wrote in a self-evidently Christian tone. That would not have consoled most Free Churchers; for he went on to treat the sacred texts like any old book—or, rather, *books*, since he began by denying that "the sacred writings of Christendom" comprised a unitary word of God, as his coreligionists generally assumed. He detailed the theses of German critics but failed to discuss divine inspiration. He pointed out that Moses did not write the Pentateuch and replaced Mosaic authorship with the documentary hypothesis. He suggested that early Israelites worshipped animals. He informed readers that "Assyriologists" had recently traced "peculiarities of Hebrew poetry" to "Accadian [Akkadian] models." This kind of stuff hardly counted as radical by 1875, though it was by no means universally accepted. Any German biblical philologist would have yawned through Smith's article.[16]

Scotland was not Germany. As Smith's friend James Bryce wrote later, in Scotland "few persons had become aware of the conclusions reached by recent Biblical scholars in Continental Europe." Smith's article thus "excited alarm and displeasure" among the more conservative Free Churchers. That puts it mildly. In the newspapers several church dignitaries fainted from shock. In May 1876 Smith came under investigation. In 1878 he was formally arraigned for writings "tending to disparage the divine authority and inspired character of the books of Holy Scripture." A series of ecclesiastical trials ensued whose convolutions might have been inspired by Dickens's *Bleak House*. They dragged on and on. Amid them Smith—following up on McLennan's work a decade earlier—published an article lumping the early Chosen People with their unchosen Semitic neighbors in worshipping reptiles and mice and organizing clans around animal totems. The jig was up. In 1881, though not convicted, Smith lost his professorship in something like a plea bargain. Three hundred supporters—Free Church ministers and elders among them—gathered in Edinburgh to protest his deprivation and the insult to scholarship. Smith himself remained a believing son of the Free Church though, understandably, he gave up preaching.[17]

He now needed to put food on the table. He quickly joined the *Encyclopædia Britannica* as coeditor (becoming sole editor in 1887). The contract guaranteed him time for biblical and philological research. Soon, another opportunity beckoned south of the border. In 1882, with the Anglo-Egyptian War raging, Gladstone's government sent Edward Palmer, Lord Almoner's Professor of Arabic at Cambridge, to the Sinai Peninsula to win over Bedouin tribes. (A talented prestidigitator, Palmer had written "Legerdemain" for Smith's *Encyclopædia Britannica*.) In August he was led by a Bedouin turncoat into ambush and murdered. In 1883 Smith succeeded Palmer at Cambridge. Smith remained there, serving as university librarian from 1886 to 1889, then as Adams Professor of Arabic, until spinal tuberculosis killed him in 1894.[18]

Smith's firing from Aberdeen turned his scholarly energies decisively toward wider horizons. The new direction was forecast by his *Journal of Philology* article on animal worship, combining Arabic and Hebrew philological expertise. Until leaving Aberdeen, he published overwhelmingly in the field of biblical criticism, strictly defined. Afterwards biblical philology continued, but Smith also wrote on subjects as varied as Islamic mahdis and animal sacrifice in ancient Cyprus. His last book-length venture in biblical philology, *The Prophets of Israel*, appeared in 1882, based on lectures given during his trial. There were three later books: *Kinship and Marriage in Early Arabia* in 1885; *The Religion of the Semites* in 1889; and an Arabic grammar, published posthumously.[19]

Religion of the Semites proved Smith's most influential work. In it, he sweepingly surveyed "the common features and general type" of religious life shared among those "kindred nations, including the Arabs, the Hebrews and Phœnicians, the Aramæans, the Babylonians and Assyrians, which in ancient times occupied" the great sweep of land from the Arabian Peninsula to "the base of the mountains of Iran and Armenia." For comparative material, Smith occasionally wandered as far as Athens and Australia. But he stuck pretty closely to sources unearthed through Hebrew and Arabic philology.[20]

In interpreting these data, Smith adapted his friend Wellhausen's claim for the priority of sacrificial cult in the oldest stratum of the Hebrew scriptures. Smith knew well that he followed also in the footsteps of early modern philologists who studied ritual. John Spencer's *De legibus Hebraeorum ritualibus* (1683–85: see chapter 3) "still remains by far the most important book on the religious antiquities of the Hebrews." In early forms of religion, Smith argued, beliefs and creeds did not figure. Rather, "ritual and practical usage were, strictly speaking, the sum-total of ancient religions." People did want "a reason for their action; but in ancient religion the reason was not first formulated as a doctrine and then expressed in practice, but conversely, practice preceded doctrinal theory." Smith drew an analogy to politics. Political institutions come first. Only later do political theories develop to explain them. Likewise, myths arise to explain ritual, not the other way around. This theory, spread further by Smith's friend and disciple James Frazer, wreaked havoc in the study of myth for decades to come. Practicing the ritual, said Smith, was obligatory; believing the myth was optional. "This being so," he went on to say, "it follows that mythology ought not to take the prominent place that is too often assigned to it in the scientific study of ancient faiths."[21]

"The scientific study of ancient faiths" was a telling phrase. Smith's adaptation of biblical philology to analyze affinities *among* religions offered one method for a new humanistic discipline: the comparative study of religions.[22] Smith moved from cultural contextualization, a tool of textual philology, to analysis of what religions shared and how they differed. Shortly this legacy will get close attention.

But the method worked for analyzing not only religions but also other cultural forms—all the more obviously since Smith had himself borrowed ethnographic baggage from McLennan. Smith's friend Frazer famously applied Smith's approach in his own *Golden Bough* to remodel classical studies and to generate one type of cultural anthropology.

Smith's case shows how biblical philology, even as it left behind its disciplinary cousins among the new humanities in the later nineteenth century, nonetheless shaped a few of them. It provides a striking example of how adjusting philological methods to handle new intellectual problems produced self-consciously new fields of knowledge.

PART II: THE RISE OF COMPARATIVE RELIGIOUS STUDIES

As Smith's biblical philology broadened into comparative study of religions beyond Christianity and Judaism, so other roads led in the same direction. In roughly the third quarter of the nineteenth century, a new humanistic discipline dedicated to such inquiries took shape. Its origins stood in sharp contrast to those of disciplines like art history and classics, which Anglophone philologists created largely by reprocessing German erudition. English-speaking scholars led in inventing comparative religion.

The naming of the new discipline requires comment. Many nineteenth-century scholars called the field 'history of religions' or 'religious history.' 'Science of religion' also enjoyed currency, parallel to 'science of language' for linguistics. In the twentieth century, these terms fell out of favor in Britain, Ireland, and North America, replaced by 'religious studies' or simply 'religion.' Another term commonly heard was and is 'comparative religion.' This chapter will use this last label, because it highlights the comparative impulse central to the field from its beginnings, directly imported from philology.

But what was being compared? Here the philological origin of the discipline proved decisive. To merit close scrutiny at first, a religion had to have 'sacred' *texts* to study. (Western scholars sometimes imputed sacredness, by analogy to Bible and Qur'an, to writings not thought 'holy' by their normal readers. 'Religion' itself notoriously shares this drawback; but, absent any better general term, people in the discipline use it anyway.) Sacred texts meant writings of great age and complexity. These posed the eternal philological problems of transmission, corruption, interpretation. The experts who invented the field came from areas of scholarship focused on just such challenging documents. Heavily textual traditions like Hinduism, Buddhism, the Abrahamic faiths, and Taoism thus became the main things to compare. Greek and Roman gods were grandfathered in, without having to pass the textual test. Widely practiced 'religions' of still greater antiquity—shamanism, for instance—got scanted. So did faiths with fewer adherents and few fans among Western philologists, such as Sikhs and Jains. This picking and choosing created the 'world religions.' The phrase apparently first entered English in the 1882 Hibbert Lectures, *National Religions and Universal Religions*, by the Leiden Old Testament philologist Abraham Kuenen. The idea had bounced around longer. World religions supplied the meat of comparative religion in its formative decades. Thus, when William James published his groundbreaking *Varieties of Religious Experience* in 1902, spotlighting individual psychology, scholars of comparative religion admired but did not emulate it.[23]

Other religions might catch the philological eye, especially if deemed to bear on a world religion, but remained marginal to the new discipline. In 1867 Max Müller lauded the "patient researches of oriental scholars" into "the religious ideas of the nomads of the Arabian peninsula." But the nomads' ideas mattered because they supposedly threw light on ancient Hebrews, remote ancestors of modern Christians. As a rule, such 'barbarian' religions landed in a different disciplinary in-box altogether. Religions of tribal peoples encountered by missionaries and colonial officials fascinated some scholars and many general readers; students of Native Americans took special interest in their rituals and mythology. Religion dominated E. B. Tylor's *Primitive Culture* (1871)—and he is today called a founder of comparative religion. But he is more often remembered as an author of anthropology, and in his own day primitive religion mostly belonged to that domain. In 1893 the section of the École Pratique des Hautes Études dealing with *sciences religieuses* added teaching on "peuples non civilisés," expanding the new discipline's field of view. But English-speaking scholars did not hurry to emulate Paris. Text-free religions might, however, claim their attention when they tried to specify the nature of religion as a general phenomenon, including world religions. *Introduction to the History of Religions* (1913) by Harvard's Crawford Toy stood out in devoting itself largely to primitive religions. Toy meant thereby to reveal the "principal customs and ideas that underlie all public religion," indicating the "lines of progress" leading to "the higher religions." The series in which his book appeared planned separate volumes for each of these "higher" religions. World religions still dominate faculties of comparative religion, even if professors politely no longer mention their height.[24]

Comparative study of religions as such was nothing new; only its disciplinary form was. Early chapters of this book discussed learned curiosity about the rites of other peoples. Chapter 8 showed this interest widening in the first half of the nineteenth century in writers as different as Lydia Maria Child and Wilhelm de Wette. The record reveals persisting fascination with what other people believe, sometimes taking erudite form. It does not show a coherent, continuing scholarly discourse, in which participants recognized and communicated with each other as fellow investigators. This latter thing is what developed after 1850: a discipline of comparative religion.

Modernizing Motives

Comparative religion seems—obviously but deceptively—to owe its existence to European imperialism. Certainly, imperial ventures brought deeper, broader awareness of beliefs and practices of subject peoples. Such knowledge of other religious systems enabled emergence of the discipline. But this wealth of information had built up for centuries. Other factors turned it into a coherent scholarly field after 1850.

One was the climate of discipline formation itself. Given the template of other fields, scholars comparing religions crystallized into a new discipline, once numbers reached a critical mass.

But why did numbers grow? The indispensable wild card was the rise in the English-speaking world of an increasingly liberal Protestant theology. It explains a surge of interest, right in the middle of the nineteenth century, in non-Christian religions sharing both Christianity's transnational reach and its basis in normative texts. Radical American Unitarians such as Theodore Parker and equivalent British theists like Frances Power Cobbe (adulator of Parker) provide the limit case. Throwing off first their Calvinist heritage, then discarding the authority of the Bible, these extreme Unitarians came to believe that 'pure' Christianity consisted in the voice of God in each individual heart. Creeds and institutions were transient, love of God and of one's fellow human beings permanent; and truth thus appeared in all religions, under varied incrustations of human error.[25] Even few Unitarians went as far as Parker in denying to Christianity *any* authority beyond the moral high-mindedness of Jesus, but many liberal Protestants who believed Christianity superior nonetheless saw truth in lesser faiths.

It became important, then, to look into the relationship between Christianity and other widespread faiths. American Unitarians led this endeavor. As chapter 8 mentioned, Parker spent much time exploring Asian religions. The slightly less radical Unitarian minister Thomas Wentworth Higginson wrote in 1871, "Our true religious life begins when we discover that there is an Inner

Light, not infallible but invaluable, which 'lighteth every man that cometh into the world.'" But not every man professeth Christianity; ergo, Christianity could hardly monopolize the light: "we might say that under many forms there is but one religion, whose essential creed is the Fatherhood of God, and the Brotherhood of Man,—disguised by corruptions, symbolized by mythologies, ennobled by virtues, degraded by vices, but still the same." (Unitarians in the United States often described the essence of their faith as the Fatherhood of God and the Brotherhood of Man—to which some wag added the Neighborhood of Boston.) The Bible, Higginson logically added, is incomplete in itself. "The time will come" when "all pious books will be called sacred scriptures." It is not clear how much Higginson really knew about, say, Buddhism; probably not much, given some of his claims. But ignorance never saps optimism. "It is our happiness to live in a time when all religions are at last outgrowing their mythologies, and emancipated men are stretching out their hands to share together 'the luxury of a religion that does not degrade.'" "The great religions of the world," he averred, "share the same aspirations, and every step in the progress of each brings it nearer to all the rest."[26]

A more conservative Unitarian colleague, Rev. James Freeman Clarke, refused to boil all religions down to one. Clarke published in 1871 a book called *Ten Great Religions: An Essay in Comparative Theology*. It showed appreciable knowledge of—and sympathy for—most non-Christian religions. (Clarke said he had "made of this study a speciality" for over twenty-five years.) But these other "great religions" each expressed at best—Clarke excoriated Islam—only one important aspect of faith. Buddhism, for example, was "the Protestantism of the East." Clarke thought Christianity "adapted to take their place, not because they are false, but because they are true as far as they go." Only Christianity, "of all human religions, seems to possess the power of keeping abreast with the advancing civilization of the world." As it evolved, then, Christianity would "become the Religion of all Races." Like quite a few Unitarians in his day, Clarke believed the human race headed toward a universal creed that would one day absorb and transcend all faiths, including Christianity in its present form. Unlike more radical Unitarians, he believed Christianity alone could and would furnish the framework of this future faith.[27]

Other modernizing Protestants stepped more cautiously in a similar direction. The moderate liberal W. Boyd Carpenter, the bishop of Ripon, typified them. In his 1887 Bampton Lectures at Oxford, Carpenter compared "the three universal religions," Islam, Buddhism, and Christianity. By examining these and other faiths, Carpenter thought he could deduce the basic human psychological wants that a successful religion must satisfy. Buddhism and Islam, he conceded, had their good points. But his analysis allowed him to predict "the religion of the future." His hearers were perhaps not shocked to learn that—"changes of form" aside—it was to be Christianity, "in its essential elements."[28]

A good deal of writing comparing religions pivoted on the missionary enterprise. Liberal Protestants rejected fogyish notions like Rev. Charles Hardwick's that 'heathenism' sprang from "the lower and depraved tastes of humanity" or even from the work of the devil, best eradicated root and branch. John Henry Barrows, a liberal minister in Chicago, chaired the organizing committee of the celebrated World's Parliament of Religions at World's Columbian Exposition in Chicago in 1893. The event included some forty spokespersons for Asian religions. (It also included Roman Catholic clergy, whom Barrows, Presbyterian that he was, at first found scarier than any six-armed Hindu deity.) The experience made Barrows an advocate of interreligious understanding, convinced of the "many important truths the various Religions hold and teach in common." Barrows was no Unitarian; but, like Higginson, he invoked "divine fatherhood" and "human brotherhood." And, much like Clarke, while insisting on the superiority of Christianity, he warned against running down religions of the missionized. Protestantism must win in the end, but sensitivity to other faiths would help Protestants to convey their "blessed knowledge" in better-attuned language and so harvest pagans faster: "Though light has no fellowship with darkness, light does have fellowship with twilight." If Protestants would "bear brotherly hearts toward all who grope in a dimmer illumination," their tolerance would dial up missionary wattage.[29]

So religious purposes in comparing religions covered a wide spectrum. Motives ranged from the moderate conviction that missionary success demanded understanding and respect for non-Christian religions, to the post-Christian notion that all faiths were at bottom the same. Religion did not animate every pioneering scholar of comparative religion. But changing Protestant attitudes thrust the practice into new prominence, gave it new urgency. So, for instance, James Freeman Clarke called for a "comparative theology," borrowing its method from comparative anatomy and comparative philology. Clarke himself lacked the Asian languages needed to do more than ask for it. But heightened curiosity like his promoted a new, philologically grounded academic discipline. It aimed to classify faiths systematically and to parse their relationships, based on comparisons of religions by scholars more erudite than Clarke.[30]

Three different streams of philology flowed into the new discipline: Sanskrit studies (both comparative philology and textual philology); biblical criticism; and classical philology. Sometimes the same religious studies scholar dipped his toes in more than one of these waters. Looking closely at a couple of key figures from the early days of comparative religion will lay open its diverse philological sources.

Philological Origins: Sanskrit

Modernizing religious motives drove the first scholar to lay out a clear program for comparative religion: Friedrich Max Müller. The preface to his printed lectures on "the science of religion" linked his work to the writings of Thomas Wentworth Higginson, James Freeman Clarke, and other American Unitarians seeking the religion of the future.[31] Even before Müller's defeat in the Boden Chair election in 1860 turned him from Sanskrit philology to broader questions, he had published in 1856 an *Essay on Comparative Mythology*, based on comparing languages and foreshadowing things to come. In 1867 he devoted the first volume of his collected essays, *Chips from a German Workshop*, to "the science of religion." Then, in 1873 he published a book-length *Introduction to the Science of Religion*.

These last two volumes in effect specified the first learned methodology for comparative study of religion—professedly academic, impartial, scientific, and at least protodisciplinary. Müller fleshed out his project in later publications. Between 1888 and 1892 he delivered four courses of Gifford Lectures on Natural Religion, published as *Natural Religion*, *Physical Religion*, *Anthropological Religion*, and *Psychological Religion*. In 1897 there followed a two-volume *Science of Mythology*. But Müller spent most time in his last twenty-five years editing *The Sacred Books of the East*. This series comprised translations of canonical texts of Hinduism, Buddhism, Taoism, Confucianism, Zoroastrianism, and Islam, ultimately running to fifty volumes of 'scriptures' of the world religions. Müller referred to the suite as "my *Bibliotheca Sacra*." Thus was fulfilled Higginson's prophecy that in due time "all pious books will be called sacred scriptures." Müller planned to include the Old and New Testaments until more prudent colleagues warned him that lumping Christian scriptures with the Qur'an and the Avesta might ruffle sensibilities.[32]

A clue to Müller's deeper motives appeared in his dedication of *Essays on the Science of Religion* "to the memory of Baron Bunsen, my friend and benefactor." The reference was to Christian von Bunsen, erudite Prussian ambassador to the Court of St. James, who had befriended Müller when the young man arrived in England. They remained scholarly comrades until Bunsen's death in 1860. Bunsen devoted his intellectual life to baring the progressive divine revelation governing, as he believed, the religious histories of all races. Emerging human consciousness of God showed up most distinctly in evolution of languages. Bunsen's theories resonated with the idealism Müller had picked up from Schelling during studies in Berlin. Müller by now had abandoned anything resembling the Lutheranism of his childhood. He spoke not of the Bible as the authoritative divine revelation but instead of "the great revelations of the world," found in Sanskrit texts as well as Hebrew ones.[33]

Thus, when Müller moved beyond his Sanskrit texts, he took with him an animating idea: the belief that those texts, along with "sacred books" of all other peoples, belonged to a larger story of the progress of human religious consciousness. For Müller, this history was embedded in a still grander narrative: the development of human thought. Philology here tried to swallow cognitive psychology whole—failing, as it turned out. But in religious studies Müller's omnivorous philological ambition added to the structures of academic knowledge.

Müller directly paralleled comparative philologists with students of religion. After all, he believed the history of language *was* the history of human thinking. Just as "the Comparative Philologist" had learned to classify languages "genealogically, *i.e.* according to their real relationship," so the scholar of religion would one day classify religions: "the same division which has introduced a new and natural order into the history of languages, and has enabled us to understand the growth of human speech in a manner never dreamt of in former days, will be found applicable to a scientific study of religions." The "combined and well directed efforts of many scholars" had enabled "a comparative analysis of the languages of mankind," an achievement once thought beyond "the powers of man." Comparative analysis of religions would go the same route. Already much necessary data was at hand—in 'scriptures' of world religions, in mythologies of ancient peoples from Greeks to Celts, in "recent researches of Biblical scholars" and Egyptian archaeologists, in ethnological evidence recorded by "travellers and missionaries." More would amass. The analytic framework already existed: families of religions would naturally mirror families of languages. A scholar could, for instance—simply by following the linguistic genealogy—trace the genetic connection of the gods (and thus the religious *conceptions*) of the Indo-European family, from India to Greece to Rome to Germany. This approach produced some contorted results. Christianity, born in Judea, had to jump "from Semitic to Aryan ground, from the Jews to the Gentiles," to "develope [*sic*] its real nature and assume its world-wide importance." So much for Jews—though Müller inadvertently fed anti-Semitism rather than promoted it willfully. (He said much the same about Buddhism moving from Aryan India to 'Turanian' east Asia, without meaning to denigrate Indians.) In any case, his stress on religious conceptions proved decisive. Müller's science of religion zeroed in on ideas and creeds. Like Clarke, he sometimes called it "comparative theology."[34]

Here, bred from Müller's comparative philology, was a new thing under the academic sun: "a new science has been called into life, a science which concerns us all, and in which all who truly care for religion must sooner or later take their part—the *Science of Religion*." Müller forged his science of religion as a weapon for reform. He depicted himself fighting against "downright atheism" on one hand and narrow, superstitious Christianity on the other. Study of humankind's religious evolution would ultimately reveal the pure truths common to all faiths. But method could divorce motive. A downright atheist or a superstitious Christian could easily adopt Müller's method to carry out neutral—'scientific'—study of world religions: a procedure lifted directly from branching evolution in language families as explicated by comparative philologists.[35]

Müller was far from the only researcher to move from Indology and related fields to comparative religion. One translator who contributed to his *Sacred Books of the East*, Thomas William Rhys Davids, studied Sanskrit in Germany, went on to Pali in Ceylon (Sri Lanka), made himself into Britain's leading scholar of Buddhism, and served from 1904 to 1915 as professor of comparative religion at Manchester. John Nicol Farquhar, inspired at Oxford by both

Müller and Monier-Williams, spent years in India as a scholarly missionary-mediator between Christians and Hindus, went on to write books on Indian religion, and eventually followed Rhys Davids in the Manchester chair. Samuel Henry Kellogg, a Princeton Seminary graduate, started out teaching Presbyterian theology in India, became fluent in Hindi and conversant with Indian religions, then returned to America to publish *The Genesis and Growth of Religion* (1892) and a once standard *Handbook of Comparative Religion* (1899). His *The Light of Asia and the Light of the World* (1885) compared Christ and Buddha. The American Sanskritist E. Washburn Hopkins won a European reputation and succeeded the great William Dwight Whitney at Yale in 1895. Hopkins started his career with focused monographs on the caste system (not to mention a study of the dog in the *Ṛg Veda*); but then, in the year he moved from Bryn Mawr to Yale, he produced the first general scholarly study in English of the history of Indian religions, going on to still broader topics in *History of Religions* (1918) and *Origin and Evolution of Religion* (1923).[36]

Philological Origins: Biblical Criticism

Even more scholars came to comparative religion from biblical criticism than from Sanskrit and kindred studies; and they could take a very different—though equally philological—approach to the new discipline. Samuel Henry Kellogg, in fact, taught and published Old Testament criticism as well as writing on comparative religion. Crawford Toy appeared earlier as author of a history of religions and taught the subject at Harvard; but the bulk of his work concerned the Bible, and his appointments at Harvard after 1880 were as Hancock Professor of Hebrew and Dexter Lecturer on Biblical Literature. Two other individuals illustrate the range. The *Oxford Hexateuch* (1900), supervised by J. Estlin Carpenter, helped—second only to Samuel Driver's writings—to make Wellhausen's documentary hypothesis palatable in Britain; and Carpenter published important work on the New Testament as well. Then, having learned Pali with Rhys Davids's help, he went on to edit Pali texts, to publish *Theism in Medieval India* (1921) and *Buddhism and Christianity: A Contrast and a Parallel* (1923), and to serve in the twilight of his career as Wilde lecturer in comparative religion at Oxford. An American parallel was George Foot Moore, that conduit through whom German biblical criticism flowed into the United States. Moore went from professor of Old Testament at Andover Seminary (1883–1902) to professor of history of religion at Harvard (1902–28). There with his comparativist hand he wrote a major *History of Religions* (1913–19) and with his biblical hand *Judaism in the First Centuries of the Christian Era* (1927–30).[37]

Of all biblical philologists who turned to comparative religion, William Robertson Smith left by far the biggest mark on the field. His approach—shaped by the contextualizing practices of his Old Testament philology—stood athwart Müller's search for the evolution of religious beliefs. Ancient

Hebrews always remained the imaginative center of Smith's work, the sun around which other ancient faiths orbited. But Smith's adaptation of philology took him beyond texts. Recall that Smith insisted on the priority of ritual over doctrine: practicing a ritual was obligatory, believing a myth optional. "This being so," comparative religion ought not focus on mythology.[38] In this declaration Smith almost certainly had Max Müller in his sights. But if he shot down mythology, with what would he replace it?

The answer derived from the minute scrutiny applied to the Old Testament by his friend Wellhausen and adapted by Smith. Wellhausen had dissected the text itself to infer an evolution of Hebrew religion from polytheistic, local rites (like those of neighboring tribes mentioned in the Bible) to a priestly, monotheistic cult centered on Jerusalem. But it was ever the habit of the textual philologist to bring to bear on a text any surrounding data that might clarify its meanings. This Smith did, moving beyond Wellhausen, beyond the evidence of the Bible itself, to comprehensive investigation of ancient Semitic cultures. To Wellhausen's essentially literary analysis Smith added another step: sociological-anthropological analysis of evidence from ancient non-Jewish cultures and what he took to be parallel modern ones. (Wellhausen came to a similar conclusion and published in 1887 *Reste arabischen Heidentums* [*Remains of Arab Heathenism*], a work important to Smith's *Religion of the Semites*.) If primitive Hebrew religion resembled those of other ancient Semitic peoples, then learning about those other cults would illuminate the Old Testament. (It becomes clear why Smith so admired John Spencer's *De legibus Hebraeorum ritualibus*, linking Hebrew and Egyptian practices.) This axiom set Smith searching for scattered clues of ancient Semitic religion, wherever they might appear—in Herodotus, Pliny, Porphyry, in Ibn Hisham, Ibn Saʾd, Baladhuri, in scholarly editions and travelers' accounts of his own time. In 1883 he was excited that an "allusion by Nöldeke" had just led him to Paul de Lagarde's *Reliquiae juris ecclesiastici antiquissimae Syriace* (*Remnants of the Most Ancient Syrian Ecclesiastical Law*, 1856). There he found "many survivals of magic & fetich [*sic*] among the Syrians about 700 A. D."[39]

Smith hoped to use such sources to (in Hans Kippenberg's words) "grasp and describe the life behind the tradition." His old Edinburgh friend J. F. McLennan shaped this effort. In his dyad of articles "The Worship of Animals and Plants," McLennan proposed a new understanding of primitive religion that he called totemism. Totemism differed from the fetish-worship sketched a few years earlier by E. B. Tylor in that the totem (a kind of fetish) belonged to and unified a whole tribe. "In other words [Adam Kuper's], totemism was fetishism but given a sociological anchor in McLennan's primordial society." In his own 1880 article in the *Journal of Philology* Smith swallowed McLennan's idea whole and argued that remnants of totemism persisted among early Hebrews. He supported his thesis by analogy to pre-Islamic Arab sources.[40]

Smith thus came to think of primal religion as social glue, noting that "the fundamental conception of ancient religion is the solidarity of the gods and their worshippers as part of one organic society." Thus, "ancient faiths must be looked on as matters of institution rather than of dogma or formulated belief"—or of mythology, as Max Müller had it. Smith did not ignore values and beliefs but stressed their social origin. His theory of animal sacrifice exemplified his doctrine. The heart of the ritual was the feast after the victim's slaying. This sacrificial meal expressed "the antique ideal of religious life," not only in being "a social act and an act in which the god and his worshippers were conceived as partaking together," but also because "the very act of eating and drinking with a man was a symbol and a confirmation of fellowship and mutual social obligations." "Fellowship in religion" in the ritual meal reinforced "reciprocal social duties." Smith fortified his argument by citing contemporary Arab customs. He blandly ignored the passage of millennia not because he doubted cultural change but because modern Arab and ancient Hebrew nomads supposedly shared the same stage of social development: "independent evolution of Semitic society was arrested at an early stage."* Whether present-day Arab or ancient Israelite, primitive religion functioned primarily to create and reaffirm the existence and solidarity of the ethnos: "A man did not choose his religion or frame it for himself; it came to him as part of the general scheme of social obligations and ordinances laid upon him, as a matter of course, by his position in the family and in the nation."[41]

Modern religion differed. The "typical form of ancient religion" was "strictly tribal or national." But as "nationality and religion began to fall apart," some "advanced forms" even of paganism grew "more or less cosmopolitan"; and some gods assumed the role of "guardians of universal morality, and not merely of communal loyalty."[42] At this point, religion began to evolve into a different kind of thing. Its function as social bond grew less important; values and beliefs rose in significance. The world religions had arrived. Among them stood the highest, most universal form of religion: Christianity.

This distinction between ethnic and universal (or world) religions—hence between 'social' and 'creedal' religions (my terms, not Smith's)—did not flow solely from the logic of his scholarship. The Free Church of Scotland may have viewed Smith as sowing seeds of infidelity; but he remained a believing Christian, of a reasonably orthodox Calvinist sort. For him, Christianity supplied not social cement but gateway to salvation. The propositional truths stated in its creeds mattered vastly, and whatever bonding occurred among partakers in its own ritual meal paled into insignificance compared to the spiritual sustenance of the individual soul. Whereas "heathen religions" believed that the god literally fathered the clan, mature Hebrew religion—and still more, Christianity—conceived divine fatherhood as spiritual. In some ancient rituals "the God-man dies for his people," and such "mystical sacrifices" did pave the way for "the deepest thought in the Christian doctrine." But these "crude and ma-

---

* Denigration of Arabs was so nearly universal in Britain that Smith probably failed to notice the bizarreness of his procedure.

terialistic" rituals utterly lacked "those ethical ideas which the Christian doctrine of the atonement derives from a profounder sense of sin and divine justice." Smith drew a bright line fencing off his own faith from religions he studied comparatively.[43]

Yet not every scholar respected that line, and Smith's writings on ancient Semitic religions founded the sociological method in comparative study of religions.[44] Much of the content of Smith's work did not endure, including the totem fever that he caught from McLennan. But his basic approach to comparative religion—through the social function of religious practice—became a staple of the new discipline.

A Discipline Takes Shape

Smith's study of ancient Middle Eastern religions proved decisive as well in turning the attention of classical philologists to comparative religion, as chapter 11 showed. There is no need to discuss Frazer and the so-called Cambridge Ritualists again—only to note that Frazer and his followers mattered for more than classical studies and anthropology. They figured, too, in the ancestry of comparative religion. Their decidedly nondoctrinal conception of 'religion' as gesturing toward the inexpressible also became part of the vocabulary of the new discipline. There it joined notions derived from continental European scholars as diverse as Émile Durkheim and Max Weber. But, strikingly, the early works that shaped the field came mostly from Britain.[45]

The fact that Frazer—as molded by Smith—reappears in three chapters of this book also says something of general importance about the formation of the modern humanities. Max Müller popping up in study of linguistics as well as religion—and Smith contributing to biblical philology, comparative religion, and anthropology—repeat the same something. Philology still resisted disciplinary cages as late as the early 1900s: in a substantial sense it remained a single type of practice, addressing different topics. Thus, multiple philologies could and did feed multiple disciplines.

Comparative religion quickly put down academic roots in the United States. As early as 1854, Harvard Divinity School students heard James Freeman Clarke lecture on it; he returned in 1867 for a four-year stint. Charles Carroll Everett succeeded him in 1872, Crawford Toy in 1880. Harvard got a chair in the field in 1904 when George Moore became Frothingham Professor of the History of Religions. By 1873 the new Boston University had a professor of "comparative history of religion, comparative theology, and philosophy of religion" (who happened also to be the university's president). Under the leadership of George S. Goodspeed, an expert on the ancient Mediterranean, the University of Chicago set up a program in comparative religion not long after it opened in 1892, adding in 1894 a lecturer on comparative religion and in 1895 a docent specialized in Asian religion. The program awarded the first doctorate in 1894, a second five years later. In 1894 Morris Jastrow at the Uni-

versity of Pennsylvania began teaching the history of religions (the label preferred by his mentor C. P. Tiele of Leiden, a pioneer of the discipline). In 1910
the university authorized graduate study in the field. Comparative religion did
not implant itself widely in American colleges until after the Second World
War. But already in 1895 the *New York Times* commented on "the growing interest in this country and abroad in the historical study of religions . . . one of
the notable features in the intellectual phases of past decades." An experienced
textbook publisher (Ginn and Company) judged in the mid-1890s that the
tide had risen high enough to float a series of handbooks aimed at university
students.[46]

Oddly, in the United Kingdom, birthplace of 'the science of religion,' comparative religion took much longer to win firm footing in universities. (The
different fates of art history in the United States and United Kingdom provide
a parallel.) In 1875 Manchester New College in London did hire Estlin Carpenter to teach comparative religion along with ecclesiastical history and Hebrew, two other topics melding religion and philology. In 1896 the Oxford
archaeologist Arthur Evans encouraged founding a journal to meet "the new
popular need for a vent on such questions as Comparative Religion." The
University of Manchester created the first British chair in the subject in 1904.
By 1907, Oxford students could enroll in a seminar on "Comparative Religion"; and the next year Oxford got its first Wilde lecturer in "natural and
comparative religion," the classicist Lewis Farnell. Yet universities awarded
few, scattered positions to comparative religion before the later twentieth century. Not until 1967 did Ninian Smart found the first full-scale department,
at Lancaster—inciting a string of imitators. Yet, despite delay in blooming, a
well-defined discipline housed teaching and research by the early twentieth
century.[47]

Intellectually rather than institutionally, comparative religion appears to
have evolved through a three-stage, dialectical process over time: first, importation of methods from comparative philology in Müller's *Science of Religion*;
second, importation of methods from biblical philology in Smith's writings,
especially *Religion of the Semites*; and finally, elaboration and refinement of
Smith's approach by a few classical philologists. Appearances deceive. Smith
developed his methods not in reaction to Müller's 'science' but in response to
changes within biblical philology—initially with no thought of general comparative study of religions. And Frazer's significant interactions with Smith
occurred as Smith was working out his version of comparative religion in
preparation for delivering the lectures published as *Religion of the Semites*.

What really occurred was simpler. Comparative philology rested on the
principle that language families grew by a process of branching evolution.
When Müller adapted it to comparative study of religions, he inevitably produced a method focused on development of religions over time, with shared
elements explained by common ancestry. Unsurprisingly, too, given its basis
in word patterns, Müller's system stressed ideas rather than actions. Smith's

Old Testament philology assumed that religious practices common to neighboring Semitic tribes illuminated contemporaneous rites of their Hebrew cousins. When Smith expanded the axiom to comparative study of religions, he predictably generated a method emphasizing links across space rather than time, with shared elements explained by common modes of life. Inevitably, too, given its basis in social practices, Smith's method stressed religion as a social system.

And for all twists and turns since 1871 and 1889 in comparative religion, these two basic approaches still animate the discipline: one diachronic, the other synchronic; one intellectual, the other sociological; one inherited from comparative philology, the other from textual philology. Yet both have something in common. Both depend utterly on the comparative method nurtured in centuries of philology. Both share a genealogical understanding of history—front and center in Müller's evolutionary account, at least implicit in Smith's conviction that ancient Semites performed rituals ancestral to his own, vastly changed Christianity. Philology did not vanish. It went underground.

EPILOGUE

Y ou have come to the end of a long, winding road. The road would have wound a lot farther had I tried to do justice to every modern humanistic discipline. Perhaps musicologists, scholars of Chinese literature, and other neglected humanists will feel grateful that their fields escaped my misunderstandings. All readers should give thanks that, in disciplines I did treat, I sketched a few exemplary cases rather than attempting a full account. This book is not an encyclopedia but a history: a sustained argument about change over time, cast in the form of empirical description. I have included enough (I hope *only* enough) to represent fairly the main lines of the history of humanistic scholarship—and to make my case.

One omitted discipline, however, does need a word of explanation. Must not a history of the humanities include the oldest component, philosophy? Absolutely not. As we have seen, the modern humanities are cousins related by branching descent from common ancestors. For most of this long evolutionary history, philosophers understood *their* studies as the *opposite* of philology, rhetoric, and antiquarianism. Philosophy was logical, deductive, precise in conclusions, dismissive of change over time. Philology was interpretive, empirical, treating in probabilities, drenched in history. For much of the past two and a half millennia, starting with Plato, philosophers snickered at philology and rhetoric when not castigating them. Hostilities have cooled in recent centuries, but basic natures did not alter.[1]

Philosophy's classification as one of the humanities in modern American higher education resulted only from administrative convenience and accident of timing. For one thing, a practical problem emerged when the old curricula heavy on Greek and Latin fell apart in the later nineteenth century. How ought colleges and universities to reconfigure knowledge for purposes of teaching and research? At first uncertainty prevailed. In 1884 a Princeton professor believed it "now customary among the most advanced students of modern education to divide the area of collegiate studies into the three great departments of Science, Philosophy, Language and Literature."[2] He proved a poor forecaster. In the United States a different tripartite division became almost universal: natural sciences, social sciences, and humanities. Philosophy did not fit neatly into any of these slots (so our Princeton professor gave it its own branch). But its aims apparently seemed closer to those of literature and art history than to those of biology or political science. Ideology also mattered. The humanities came into prominence in colleges and universities just when most of these institutions were shedding their Christian ties and axioms. Yet most students, parents, and professors remained Christians. Studying literature, art, philosophy, and classics was held to build character, even to deepen the student's 'spiritual' nature. This prescription supplied an antidote to angst about the fading of real religion.[3] Such elevating 'culture studies' came to be grouped together as humanities, regardless of methodological coherence. Studying savages informed but did not edify, which helps to explain why Americans stuck anthropology with the social sciences. Ancient history—the glory that was Greece, the grandeur that was Rome*—uplifted; postclassical history seemed grubbier; and history today sometimes finds itself among social sciences, sometimes humanities, even though its own history binds it tightly to the philological tradition.

Universities in Ireland and the United Kingdom proved more flexible in chopping up knowledge and did not invariably squeeze philosophy into the humanities. Oxford and Cambridge do today assign their philosophy faculties to the humanities; but Oxford also features a famed undergraduate program joining philosophy, politics, and economics. (As to the intellectual cogency of administrative compartments, please note that Cambridge classifies divinity as a humanity. This oxymoron would have caused Isaac Newton's brain to explode, but my own University of Notre Dame also indulges it. Where else do you put theology nowadays?) Not every institution followed the Oxbridge example. The University of Edinburgh groups philosophy with psychology and linguistics. University College Dublin places philosophy among the social sciences. At Manchester, philosophy also belongs to the School of Social Sciences, where specific undergraduate degree programs link it with politics, economics, mathematics, and physics.[4] Hobnobbing with political theorists and mathematicians does make more methodological sense for the average Anglophone philosopher than hanging out with art historians. Philosophy is a guest among the humanities, and a dubious one.

Otherwise, shared background gives all the humanities a collective integrity, even if one not always acknowledged. The great German theorist Wilhelm Dilthey split the human sciences into two sorts: systematic and historical. His typology echoed the traditional divide between philosophy and philology. It makes a good jumping-off point for thinking about the nature of humanistic scholarship, for what do archaeology, art history, classics, social and cultural anthropology, history, literature, linguistics, and religious studies have in common? All descended from early modern philology and its companions antiquarianism and rhetoric—just as these early modern studies had derived from their ancient equivalents. As in other families, children do not each get an

---

* To plagiarize Edgar Allan Poe's "To Helen" (1831).

identical mix of genes. Archaeology inherits more from antiquarianism than from philology. Literary criticism owes much to rhetoric, little to philology; in literary history the pattern reverses. By now, none of this should surprise. What needs emphasis is that common methods, a common mode of knowledge, survive in all disciplines within the philological family. All are interpretative in method; all deploy comparison in making their interpretations; all are sensitive to contexts, cultural or textual or visual; all believe historical lineages of some sort essential to understanding; all think that ideas, texts, paintings, institutions, artifacts, languages are products of history, shaped by their historical contexts. William James once contended, "You can give humanistic value to almost anything by teaching it historically." Otherwise, he went on, "literature remains grammar, art a catalogue, history a list of dates."[5]

Deviations have occurred. Many linguists have shifted so far from hermeneutic method to law-like generalization that their work often looks more 'scientific' than 'humanistic.' (I can testify that their grant proposals routinely baffle peer reviewers from the—'other'?—humanities.) Anglophone literary critics at certain periods have renounced history in favor of atemporal analysis, as in the New Criticism of the 1940s and 1950s. But humanistic scholars even today share enough to make them an extended family of erudition, as much as the philologists and antiquarians of the seventeenth century.*

Why then do historians, literary scholars, archaeologists, and so forth today go their separate ways, inhabit discrete academic departments, attend different scholarly conferences, and publish in distinct journals? Any reader who has gotten this far knows the answer as well as I do.

The rise of modern academic disciplines in the nineteenth century—the invention of the modern *idea* of an academic discipline, the *principle* of disciplinarity—fractured learning. This innovation grew up alongside the modern research university. Whether the research university per se *produced* disciplinarity is a nice puzzle. I tend to think not, since some productive scholars who scorned disciplinary lines flourished within major universities around 1900 and after—William James, Charles Eliot Norton, John Linton Myres, James G. Frazer, to name a few mentioned in these pages. Sometimes colleagues tell me that 'information overload' made modern disciplinarity inevitable. But people have always had more information than they could cope with. Subconsciously or consciously they developed filters to select the information that mattered and invented tools to manage it. Early *Homo sapiens* presumably picked out data most important to survival and breeding. Renaissance scholars feared drowning in a flood of information—but responded with technologies to organize it, like Ciceronian 'memory palaces' and notetaking methods, not with hyperspecialization. Disciplines are just a new filter, and a peculiarly cramping one.[6]

---

* And, of course, humanistic methods and outlooks have in some cases migrated beyond the humanities. Consider historical sociology.

Yet how one explains where disciplines came from hardly matters right now. The *fact* that disciplinarity triumphed does. Indeed, the chapters of this book replicate the fate of humanistic erudition in the West. Philology and its allied studies—such as rhetoric and chronology—began as thickly interconnected enterprises, if not actually as a single one, and are thus properly studied together in this volume's first four chapters. Around 1800, they began to fragment. By the end of the century, the pieces stood apart from each other as independent disciplines, properly treated one by one. Professors around 1900 observed this decomposition, and it made some of them uneasy. At least a few remain a little uncomfortable. The literary historian Debora Kuller Shuger notes wryly that hardly any scholar today knows George Buchanan's influential Renaissance drama *Jephthah*: "The modern division of academic labor cannot cope with a neo-Latin play written by a Scotsman living in France." James Bryce commented in 1903 that the late Lord Acton could talk as an equal in their own fields with historians, biblical scholars, and other experts in "all of the so-called 'human subjects' " (as Bryce labeled the still novel humanities). Acton was a prodigy of knowledge in his own day. But could even the most deeply learned scholar today speak, like him, across the humanities?[7]

And yet their division into separate disciplines at times looks like sleight of hand. No sooner did humanistic disciplines emerge than cries rang out for 'interdisciplinary' cooperation among them. Institutions even emerged to this end. In 1902 a royal charter created the British Academy for the Promotion of Historical, Philosophical, and Philological Studies (soon blessedly abbreviated to British Academy), to represent humanistic scholars from the United Kingdom in an international congress of academies. In 1917 delegates from the British Academy and from the various learned societies for classics, literature, and history came together in a Council for Humanistic Studies to negotiate with counterparts from the sciences about the future shape of British education. In 1919—to cope with the same exigency of representation across borders as the founders of the British Academy—the American Council of Learned Societies was organized in the United States, bringing together scholarly associations in the humanities "and related social sciences." In both nations the reaction to the problem was the same. Need new voices in the Union Académique Internationale? Why not (one idea bruited) enlarge the Royal Society to include all areas of learning (and why not do so also in the American Association for the Advancement of Science)? Or why not set up separate academies for classicists, historians, and so forth? Neither happened. Rather, it seemed obvious to all concerned that humanists belonged together in one group. And this makes perfect sense. Interdisciplinary research and interdisciplinary graduate programs today typically bring together historians with literary specialists or classicists with cultural anthropologists—not religious studies scholars with chemists. This is not to say that political scientists and literary critics cannot fruitfully cooperate. It is only to say that the 'natural' collaborators of humanistic researchers are other humanists who share similar methods and approaches deriving from a common background.[8]

Today's humanities disciplines are not ancient, integral modes of knowledge. They are modern, artificial creations—where made-up lines pretend to divide the single sandbox in which we all play into each boy's or girl's own inviolable kingdom. It is a sham. Students of early America freely mingle history, archaeology, and anthropology; literary scholars write history, and historians study literature; a political historian of the pre–Civil War South publishes a book on American art history.[9] If the lines were real, disciplines would not need so relentlessly to police their borders within colleges and universities. Consider the processes of hiring, tenure (or the equivalent), and promotion now ubiquitous in the English-speaking world. If you are labeled 'assistant professor of art history,' a study of medieval church architecture might get you tenure. Translating Dante's *Divine Comedy* or editing John Donne's poems will get you a place in the line at your local unemployment office. Conversely, if you are 'associate professor of Italian,' translating Dante may win you a full professorship; editing Donne or studying Holbein will get you nowhere, and do not expect a salary rise. The examples are not random. I have in mind, as readers with strong memories will know, the most prolific progenitor of the humanities in the modern American university. Charles Eliot Norton did all these things. He could not today, nor any time after about 1920. The modern rules of the game demand make-believe.

This home truth bears on the ballyhooed crisis of humanistic scholarship today. Without question, the humanities now face greater flux than they have routinely endured in the past century. Some causes are scholarly. Global history challenges old-style nation-centric narratives, while indigenous traditions of history telling contest disciplinary history and disciplinary studies of art, literature, and culture. Gender studies and environmental studies now and then model a humanistic scholarship sweeping across disciplinary lines. Other unsettlements are existential. Full-throated advocates of science and technology throughout the English-speaking world—who find plenty of listeners in governments and foundations—sound as if humanistic learning bears no relevance for the future. Funding for research in the humanities has declined substantially in the past several years, as have jobs in higher education. If such trends continue, fundamental change must come in the near future. If they do not, fundamental change will only be postponed: the structures of academic knowledge always evolve. Natural scientists have in the past proved far nimbler than humanists in adapting disciplinary boundaries to emerging problems. Life scientists reorganize themselves, as research agenda develop, into units that come and go: microbiology, molecular biology, biochemistry, biophysics, biomedical informatics, neurosciences, behavioral biology. Any acolyte of the laboratory can chant a litany of cross-bred scientific programs: astrophysics, earth and planetary sciences, geophysics, biogeochemistry, biological engineering. Meanwhile, English and history departments soldier stolidly on, muskets on their shoulders. But ultimately stasis will not serve.

Sooner or later, the humanities disciplines must shift their shapes, even drastically shrink in number. The past does not prophesy the future. But perhaps some day humanistic scholarship will, once again, inhabit more wide-ranging academic divisions than it does today. If so, erudition will command a higher premium: more extensive knowledge, multiple languages will be required, to broaden the monoglot, narrowly focused scholarship increasingly common in the humanities during the past half century. Bryce's Lord Acton may serve again as one ideal, but environmental historians may provide a new one. At any rate, when the time for change comes—whatever form change takes—it will help to remember that the humanities amount to more than a set of isolated disciplines, each marooned on its own island. Modern disciplinarity masks a primal oneness. Today's multiple humanities collectively form the latest version of a millennia-long Western tradition of inquiry into language and its products—inquiry, that is, into worlds that human beings have created for themselves and expressed in words.

Philology: the love of words.

Notes

Prologue

1. "Multa novit vulpes verum echinus unum magnum." Erasmus was translating a fragment attributed to the ancient Greek poet Archilochus, but Erasmus's version seems to have stuck. The proverb owes its modern fame to Isaiah Berlin's 1953 essay *The Hedgehog and the Fox*.

2. The specific phrase *studia humanitatis* seems to have been coined by the Italian humanist Coluccio Salutato in 1374.

3. Pollock 2009, 933. My own quizzing of scores of first-year doctoral students over the past twenty years yields the same result.

4. Some, possibly most historians of knowledge would argue for a somewhat earlier triumph of natural science in the English-speaking world, but I believe this position to rest on a linguistic misunderstanding: a prematurely early restriction of 'science' to mean primarily natural science. See Turner 2002. In any case the dispute hardly matters for the influence of philology in the genesis of the modern humanities.

5. J. Turner 1993. The friend was Maurice Olender, a faculty member at the École des Hautes Études en Sciences Sociales, where I was then giving seminars. The article appeared in English in Turner 2003. The quarrel with Emerson gave Norton his faint claim on the attention of scholars today.

6. Turner 1999.

7. A partial translation of the first section by John Paul Pritchard appeared in 1968 as *On Interpretation and Criticism*.

8. Hailperin 1963.

Conventions

1. Kepler's chronological study appears in WorldCat, which notes that the book was published in Frankfurt in 1615; the full title promises that Kepler will show that "the passion, death, and resurrection of Our Lord Jesus Christ" occurred in "anno aerae nostrae vulgaris 31"—that is, in "year 31 of our common era." The title page of Muratori's *Annali* is reproduced in Hay 1988, [102].

2. Attentive readers will notice my waffling on the date of the bulk of Ireland's exit from the United Kingdom. Should it be the declaration of an Irish republic at Easter 1916, an uprising crushed by the British but in a sense parallel to the American Declaration of Independence in 1776? Should it be the unilateral creation of an Irish parliament in 1919? Should it be the creation of the Irish Free State in 1922, following the Anglo-Irish treaty of the previous year?

Chapter 1. "Cloistered Bookworms, Quarreling Endlessly in the Muses' Bird-Cage"

The quotation in this chapter's title comes from Athenaeus of Naucratis 2007-12, 1:124-25 (1.22d), quoting the satirist Timon of Phlius, who was referring to the scholars of the Alexandria Museum. The quoted words meld Douglas Olson's translation of Athenaeus, cited above, with that in Fraser 1972, 1:317. For dates and biographical information about individuals in the ancient world mentioned in this chapter, my fallback resource has been Hornblower and Spawforth 1996. In rendering names of ancient writers and places, I use the form that I judge most familiar to readers of English.

1. Sandys 2009, 1:5-6; Fraser 1972, 1:456-58; Bonner 1977, 55-56.

2. Thomas 1992, chap. 4; Robb 1994, 21; Powell 2004, 22-27; Fischer 2001, 68-133; Burkert 2004, 16-20; Hock and Joseph 1996, 84-88; Harris 1989. Famously, the Greeks' Minoan and Mycenaean predecessors also had writing systems: Linear A and Linear B, the latter used to write Mycenaean Greek, to which it was not very well adapted. Some scholars argue for a much earlier adaptation of the Phoenician alphabet (technically, a syllabary) to Greek. For the state of play according to one such scholar, see Lloyd-Jones 2005, 13-16. For a broader survey of recent scholarship on the development of Greek writing systems, see Werner 2009, 334-35.

3. Clackson and Horrocks 2007, 85-88.

4. Robins 1967, 11-12.

5. Sandys 2009, 1:91-95; Pfeiffer 1968, 12, 58-65; Robins 1967, 11, 24-30; Plato 1961, 422-74; Seuren 1998, 5-12; Law 2003, 19-23; Bruns 1992, 92-93; Law and Sluiter 1995, 14.

6. Kennedy 1994, 3-4, 6-8, 11-43; Sciappa 1999; Fuhrmann 2007, 15-41; Conley 1990, 4-13; Cole 1991, 1-68, 120-25; Vickers 1998, chaps. 2-3. The early history of rhetoric is contested, the evidence foggy; I have tried to find common ground shared by most parties. Thanks to Plato, Protagoras and Gorgias are the best-known early sophists.

7. Cole 1991, 96-97; Conley 1990, 14-20; Kennedy 1994, 43-49, 55-58; Marrou 1982, 79-91; Sciappa 1999, 163-64; Connolly 2009, 130; Grube 1995, 41.

8. Connolly 2009, 134-35; Kennedy 1980, 31-32, 34-35; Kennedy 1994, 81-84; Grube 1995, 39, 40, 44; Sciappa 1999, 168-80; Marrou 1982, 95-96, 194-205; Morgan 1998, 190-98. Eden 1997, 21, stresses the overlap of rhetoric and textual philology in method—"hermeneutical strategies"—as well as in educational program. Ironically, Isocrates suffered some disability that barred him from public oratory. Some schools that taught reading and writing to boys whose fathers could afford to pay probably existed in the sixth century; by the end of the fifth almost all polises seems to have had them; Harris 1989, 57-59, 96-102.

9. Wilson 1983, 18-19; Blum 1977, 27-29; Lamberton 1986, 10-15 and passim; Sandys 2009, 1:37; Reynolds and Wilson 1991, 1; Boardman and Hammond 1982, 412; West 1998, 95, 97-98; Thomas 1992, 119, 123-24; Davison 1962, 216-17, 219-21. For the dating and nature of written Homeric texts, see, e.g., Kahn 1983, 110; Nagy 1996 and 2002; Lesky 1963, 49-58; Burkert 2004, 47n91. (Nagy persuades me, but my point is the diversity of respectable opinions.)

10. Ford 2002, 18-19; Lewis 1974, 4, 8-9, 11-12, 34-69, 78; Gamble 1995, 44-48; Harris 1989, 84-85, 103-15, 126, 140-41; Lewis et al. 1992, 268; Casson 2001, 23-28; Cribiore 2001, chap. 3. To ancient Greeks, book—βιβλος, biblos—first meant the papyrus plant, by extension a papyrus scroll. Only later was it a 'book' in our sense—either a section of a longer work, as in the twenty-four books of the Iliad, or an independent work. But the usage familiar to modern readers is adopted here. Burkert 2004, 47, speculates that the first Greek library, of the leather scrolls that preceded papyrus, may date from the mid-seventh century.

11. Parkes 2008, 3–5; Cicero 1988, 86 [3.5.6] (and cf. Rawson 1985, 43); Hobbins 2009, 165–66; Casson 2001, 29–30; Zimmerman 1991, 4–5; Davison 1962, 218–20; Too 1998, 137; Pfeiffer 1968, 82; Blum 1977, 88–91; West 1998, 98. For generic sources of scribal error, see Parkes 2008, 63–68, and Metzger and Ehrman 2005, 250–59.

12. Fraser 1972, 1:305–35; Blum 1977, 89, 141–152; Walbank et al. 1984, 73, 170; Pfeiffer 1968, 96–104; Reynolds and Wilson 1991, 6–7; Grube 1995, 123; Casson 2001, 32–33, 35; White 2009, 281–82; Quintilian 2002, 1:54–56. To be precise, the Ptolemies founded two libraries, the so-called Great Library associated with the Museum and later a smaller but substantial collection in the temple of Serapis. All these projects appear to have formed part of an effort to Hellenize the new Egyptian domain.

13. Pfeiffer 1968, 81, 93–95; Davison 1962, 221; Laks and Most 1997, 9–37, 55–63, 81–90; Betegh 2004, 1–181; Kouremenos, Parássoglou, and Tsantsanoglou 2006; Blum 1977, 29–64, 72–73, 82–88, 99–109; Lloyd-Jones 1982, 267; Fraser 1972, 1:448–51; Sandys 2009, 1:33–37, 108–10; Walbank et al. 1984, 170–71.

14. Fraser 1972, 1:325–33, 452–53; Lesky 1963, 752–55; Casson 2001, 37–41; Blum 1977, chap. 4; Walbank et al. 1984, 171.

15. Casson 2001, 34–35.

16. Pfeiffer 1968, 105–14; Fraser 1972, 1:459, 463–65, 476–77; Montanari 1998, 1–2, 4–10; Blum 1977, 21–22, 164–68; Davison 1962, 222–25; West 1998, 95, 99; Grube 1995, 124–25, 127–29; Too 1998, 135–36; Nagy 2004, chap. 1.

17. Walbank et al. 1984, 170–71; Reynolds and Wilson 1991, 10, 13; Grube 1995, 129–31; Conte 1994, 572; Pfeiffer 1968, 212–32; Fraser 1972, 1:458–59, 462–65; Casson 2001, 43–44.

18. For a broad interpretation of this philological tradition in antiquity and the Renaissance as hermeneutics, see Eden 1997.

19. Reynolds and Wilson 1991, 10–12, 14–15, 45; Grube 1995, 125, 128; Zetzel 1984, 16; Davison 1962, 224; Fraser 1972, 1:459; Parkes 1993, pt. 1. Aristophanes's punctuation marks did not look like ours and were not meant to show the grammatical structure of the sentence—which in any case was only vaguely specified.

20. Momigliano 1990, esp. 13, 18, 30–31, 67–68; Momigliano 1960, 30–34; Burrow 2008, chaps. 1–2; Kelley 1998, 31–35, 43; Press 1982, 23–42, 121–22; Conte 1994, 214; Pfeiffer 1968, 134–35, 208–9, 246–51; Fraser 1972, 1:454–55, 460.

21. Kugel 1997, 5–10; Nigosian 2004, 19–23; Walbank et al. 1984, 171; Rajak 2009; Ackroyd and Evans 1975, 135–49, 166–68. The translation possibly went on under the patronage of Ptolemy II, who would have had his own royal reasons for wanting the law of a subject people in his Library. LaMarche 1997, 16–23, helpfully summarizes the ancient Greek translations, adding some theological special pleading. The legend of the seventy-two first appeared in the *Letter of Aristeas* in the second(?) century BCE. The numbers vary a bit in different versions of the tale, which may explain why LXX, not LXXII, became the label. Hebrew scriptures were also rendered into other Semitic tongues, notably Aramaic.

22. Blum 1977, 225; Robins 1967, 24; Grube 1995, 135; Pfeiffer 1968, 37–38, 77–78, 202–3; Fraser 1972, 1:463–66; Auroux et al. 2000–2006, 1:388–91; Law 2003, 26–31; Law and Sluiter 1995, 14–17, 62; Luhtala 2005, 7, 15–16, 27–28.

23. Pfeiffer 1968, 245, 266–72; Law 2003, 55–58, and Law and Sluiter 1995, esp. 7–11 and 13–22 for a summary of the state of play; Auroux et al. 2000–2006, 1:394–400; Robertson 2008, 4n10, 6; Morgan 1998, 153–55; Luhtala 2005, 20–23, 28–29; Fraser 1972, 1:463–70; Casson 2001, 45. The name Thrax means 'Thracian,' although Dionysius was the rare Alexandrian scholar native to Alexandria. Apparently his father's name sounded Thracian.

24. Robertson 2008, 4–5; Sandys 2009, 1:140; Rawson 1985, 42, 46–48, 69, 118–19; Pfeiffer 1968, 272–73; Bolgar 1964, 41; Press 1982, 38–39; Bonner 1977, 28–30, 189–276. The beginning of Dionysius's book, where he made his six-part distinction, is the only section of

generally accepted authenticity: Cribiore 2001, 185. It is only probable, not certain, that Tyrannion was the first to divide grammar into these four parts. His name (strictly, nickname) appears in the literature both with and without the terminal *n*, presumably because his Greek name got Latinized.

25. Astin et al. 1989, 425–26, 428–34, 438–51, 457–68, 471–76, and chap. 13; Crook, Lintott, and Rawson 1992, 696–700; Hock and Joseph 1996, 89; Grube 1995, 150; Quintilian 2002, 1:102. There is dispute whether Romans adapted their alphabet from Greek colonists in southern Italy or from the Etruscans, who in turn got theirs from Greek. First Latin poet: Lucius Livius Andronicus (ca. 280–200); first Roman historian: Quintus Fabius Pictor (ca. 254–?).

26. Grube 1995, 132; Reynolds and Wilson 1991, 20–21; Zetzel 1984, 10–11; Bonner 1977, 53–54; Rawson 1985, 51, 118, 120, 194, 234, 269–70, 319; Sandys 2009, 1:175–77; Conte 1994, 124. Rawson 1985, chap. 1, sketches the context within which Romans absorbed Greek scholarship; cf. Moatti 1997, 59–61. One version of the story has Crates visiting Rome in 168; another a few years later. Aelius owed his cognomen Stilo to ghostwriting speeches for rich Romans (*stilus* = 'pen').

27. Crook, Lintott, and Rawson 1992, 701–7; Conte 1994, 209–20; Grube 1995, 160–63; Wilamowitz 1982, 12; Rawson 1985, passim; Moatti 1997, 138–39, 143–47, 168; Bloomer 1997, chap. 2; Bonner 1977, 4, 54, 77, 118, 190, 193; Robins 1967, 47–52; Roesch 1999; Law 2003, 43–49; Kennedy 1994, 91n; Holford-Strevens 2003, 14, 183–84, 222, 270, 293; Quintilian 2002, 1:11. Varro's priority in saying that all rhetoric is divided into three parts rests on a quotation in Aulus Gellius. Moatti 1997 provides a larger context for Roman scholarship of the late republican period, framing, as it were, the detailed excavations of Rawson 1985.

28. Bonner 1977, 288; Grube 1995, 163, 165–92, 284–307; Rawson 1985, chap. 10; Quintilian 2002, 1:5–6, 22; Krostenko 2001, chap. 4; Wilamowitz 1982, 12; Kennedy 1980, chap. 5; Caplan 1954; Kennedy 1994, 117–27, 177–86, 274–75; Knappe 1996, 111–18; Kaster 1988, 275–78. Cicero wrote a great deal more about rhetoric after *De inventione*, but it was the latter that played a decisive role in the Middle Ages. Something more than half of the *Institutio oratoria* was available to medieval readers.

29. Crook, Lintott, and Rawson 1992, 714; Conte 1994, 386, 577–79, 584, 628; Robins 1967, 53; Wilamowitz 1982, 12–13; Prete [1970], 9–10; Bonner 1977, 153–54; Holford-Strevens 2003; Zetzel 1984, chap. 6; Kaster 1988, 169–97, 356–59. Some medieval MSS give Servius the praenomen Maurus or Marius and others the cognomen Honoratus (perhaps an honorific misunderstood as a name): the accuracy of all this very uncertain. Likewise, much that passed for Servius in medieval MSS did not come from his hand. The term *scholia*, a neo-Latin word coined later (singular *scholium*), derives from the Greek σχόλιον, meaning 'comment or interpretation.'

30. Luhtala 2005, chap. 5; Bolgar 1964, 37; Colish 1997, 42–44, 176; Orme 2006, 28–30, 40–42, 54, 67, 76, 88, 90, 97, 122, 205; Robins 1967, 70.

31. Bonner 1977; Marrou 1982, 274–89; Quintilian 2002, 1:5–18; Kaster 1988, 14 (quotation); Morgan 1998; Brown 1992, esp. 35–47; Watts 2006, 2–5. Roman schools needed to instill 'Romanity' into provincial boys from non-Roman backgrounds, but this imperative affected such matters as examples for declamatory practice and attention to pronunciation, rather than the structure of education. For education into 'Romanness,' see, e.g., Bloomer 1992, 13, 259; Law 2003, 83–85. In late antiquity an additional layer was added on top of rhetorical training: the philosopher's school.

32. Rawson 1985, 117–18; Grube 1995, 163–64. Eden 1997, 21, stresses the overlap between ancient grammar and ancient rhetoric in methods as well as in schooling.

33. Rawson 1985, 117; Shanzer 1986, 14–16; Shanzer 2005 (but note the caution of Moatti

1997, 305); Bolgar 1964, 35–36; e.g., John of Salisbury 1955, 11; Colish 1997, 43–44; Stahl 1965.

34. Shanzer 1986, 16, 21–28; MacMullen 1984; MacCormack 2004; Williams 2006, 12–13, 57; Watts 2006, 14–17. Colish 1997, 43, says we know nothing of Martianus's religion; along with Shanzer 1986, Hornblower and Spawforth 1996, 932, and Stahl 1965, 106, say flatly that he was pagan.

35. Williams 2006, 25–28, thinks Jerome's famous dream, in which he is condemned as a Ciceronian rather than a Christian, to be largely if not entirely a fiction.

36. MacMullen 1984, 6; Conte 1994, 603, 683; Kaster 1988, 77–78, 87–88; MacCormack 1998, 2 (quotation, in which I have silently corrected a typographical error); Browning 1995, 17–19; Kennedy 1980, 177. Auerbach 1965, chap. 1, offers a learned account of Christian adaptations of classical rhetoric, treating Augustine's *De doctrina Christiana*, pp. 33ff; cf. Penner and Vander Stichele 2009, 253–58, and McKeon 1942, 5–7. The aristocrat was Tonantius Ferreolus, praetorian prefect of Gaul: Sidonius Apollinaris 1936–65, 1:452 (II, ix); for information about Tonantius, see Stroheker 1970, 173 (no. 149 in Stroheker's prosopography). I thank the late Sabine MacCormack for steering me to Sidonius's account of Tonantius's library.

37. Robertson 2008, chap. 3; Watts 2006, 162–67, for the philosophical content of Origen's teaching. I give the commonest translation of λόγος as used in the fourth Gospel (traditionally ascribed to Jesus's disciple John). Λόγος is a protean word, meaning everything from 'word' or 'language' to 'thought' or 'reason.' The Stoics who lurked in Origen's background used λόγος to refer to the divine principle that vivifies the universe; the writer of the fourth Gospel used λόγος more specifically to mean God as creative power, incarnated in Jesus (John 1:1–3). With λόγος understood as a spiritual principle, one more easily sees how Origen came to distinguish language—the word—from the physicality of the voice.

38. Metzger 1987; Hopkins 1999, 99–100; Gamble 1985, chaps. 2–3; Ackroyd and Evans 1975, 232–308; Gamble 1995, 3. Metzger (7–8) points out that "minor fluctuations" affected the New Testament text even after canonization was more or less complete. The label Christian appeared surprisingly soon (perhaps at first used derisively). Acts 11:26 says that the followers of Jesus were first called Christians in Antioch; this would have been at most two decades after his execution. Given the variety of Jewish sects at the time, use of the tag did not necessarily imply differentiation between Christians and Jews; 'Christians' could have been understood as a Jewish subgroup, parallel to, e.g., Pharisees. As centuries passed, Christian exegetical traditions in the Greek east increasingly diverged from those in the Latin west. The Latin traditions matter much more in this book.

39. Levine 2005, 21–22, 24–44, 45–70, 74–96, 105–7, 127–76; Stroumsa 2009. The Jewish temple was also odd in having no cult statue or other representation of the deity in it. One smallish Jewish sect in the period before the temple was destroyed, the Essenes, seem to have boycotted temple worship, believing the current priests illegitimate. *Rabbi* comes from a Hebrew root meaning, in this context, 'revered.' Scholarly consensus has the rabbis originating in the sect called Pharisees.

40. Stroumsa 2009, 31–34, 63–70; Nigosian 2004, 8–16; Rajak 2009, 227–38; Grafton and Williams 2006, 83–84; Ackroyd and Evans 1975, 114–35, 143–55, 164–70; Leiman 1991, 125–35; Evans and Tov 2008, 58–63, 104–25, 127, 139–42; VanderKam 2001, 16, 21, 142–46; VanderKam 2010, 57–58, 159, 191–92. The Jews who took Jubilees as authoritative were those linked with the Dead Sea scrolls, whom most scholars believe to have been an Essene community at Qumran. James VanderKam (personal communication) points out that the status of Jubilees in the canon of the Ethiopian church is confusing but that "in no Bible

today" may be correct if "today" is underlined: thus my addition of the weasel-word "standard." I use anachronistically the common phrase 'religion of the book,' which first appears in the Qur'an. Consensus on a tripartite division of Hebrew scriptures is likely also anachronistic before the Common Era. The oldest textual witnesses known today for the Masoretic Text—the Cairo and Aleppo Codices—date from circa 895 and 925.

41. Stroumsa 1996; Ackroyd and Evans 1975, 50, 135–42, 145; Rajak 2009, chap. 9; Nigosian 2004, 20–23; Simon 1997, 52–53; Gamble 1995, 23–25; Augustine, quoted in Stroumsa 2009, 44. Aquila was from Pontus (on the south coast of the Black Sea), a region whose Hellenistic Jewish inhabitants figure in the narratives of the earliest converts to the Jesus movement from outside Palestine: Acts 2:9 and 18: 2; 1 Peter 1:1. Curiously, the Pontian Jew mentioned in Acts 18 was also called Aquila.

42. Lamberton 1986, 44–54, 78–82, 284; Gamble 1995, 23–28; Hopkins 1999, 89–90; Grant and Tracy 1984, 54–56; McKim 1998, 36–39, 58–60; Lampe 1975, 155–58, 173–77; Ackroyd and Evans 1975, 436–37; Grafton and Williams 2006, 56–68, 80–81.

43. Grafton and Williams 2006, 81–83, 86–132; McKim 1998, 54–56; Ackroyd and Evans 1975, 188–89, 455–59; Kamesar 1993, 4–28.

44. Ackroyd and Evans 1975, 510–35; Williams 2006, 81–94; Kamesar 1993, passim; Stroumsa 2009, 42–44.

45. Bickerman 1963, 37–51; Grafton and Williams 2006, 143–48; Finegan 1964, 21–147. *Synchronism* is a term of art coined in early modern chronology, not an ancient term.

46. Eusebius, *Chronicon*, trans. Robert Bedrosian, http://rbedrosian.com/eusebl.htm, accessed September 29, 2010, 1; McKitterick 2006, 10–12, 14–19; Grafton and Williams 2006, 135–43, 148–76 (quotation, 140); Finegan 1964, 147–87; Jerome, *Temporum liber*, trans. Roger Pearse et al., http://www.tertullian.org/fathers/jerome_chronicle_02_part1.htm, accessed September 29, 2010; Kelley 1998, 87–89. The first book of the *Chronicon* survives complete only in an Armenian translation, the second only in a Latin translation and updating by Jerome (from which I draw the miscellany of events cited in the text). Eusebius revised the *Chronicon* as the years passed; 310 CE is Grafton and Williams's estimated date for first completion. Limited space requires passing over Grafton and Williams's discussions of Eusebius's other innovations in use of the codex form, although they, too, bear on philology in his wake.

47. Grafton and Williams 2006, 200–203, 223–25; Press 1982, 9, 100–101, 133–34.

48. Nigosian 2004, 4; Casson 2001, chap. 8; Harris 1989, 296–97; Roberts and Skeat 1987, esp. 11–12, 15, 24, 29, 37, 42–44, 48–61; Lewis 1974, 90–94; Metzger and Ehrman 2005, 12–14; Kugel 1997, 28–30; Gamble 1995, 24–25, 49–66, 69–70; Febvre and Martin 1976, chap. 1. Romans also wrote in ink on smoothed, bleached, unwaxed wooden tablets; the wax-covered, stylus-inscribed variety seems to have been more popular. Ink flowed easily on either side of parchment; but the back side of a papyrus sheet was harder to write on than the front because of how the fibers lay.

49. Wilson 1983; Kelley 1998, 70–74; Browning 1964, esp. 5–7, 9; Davison 1962, 226–28; Herrin 2007, 119–21, 125–30; Schreiner 2008, 113–15; Reynolds and Wilson 1991, 76–77; Mergiali 1996, 49–52; Browning 1995, 23–24. Photios is far better known as a powerful and controversial Patriarch of Constantinople.

50. Conley 1990, 114–17; Kennedy 1980, 103–5, 199–203; Monfasani 1976.

51. Sandys 2009, 1:441–678. The story of the Byzantine Empire, in contrast, is in Sandys still a history of scholarship.

52. Wickham 2009, chaps. 4–9; McCormick 2001; Riché 1978; Harris 1989, 312–22. In the sixth century Constantinople reasserted imperial authority in Italy and Africa, but shakily and not for long.

53. Colish 1997, 48–50; Bolgar 1964, 35–37; Wilamowitz 1982, 15 and 15n69; Vessey 2004,

22–24, 36–42; Cassiodorus Senator 2004, 158–159 (bk. 1, 26 and 27:1); Gamble 1995, 198–202. Senator was part of his name, not an office.

54. Colish 1997, 50–51; Conte 1994, 720–21; Reynolds and Wilson 1991, 84. *Origins or Etymologies* was the best known of Isidore's several encyclopedic works.

55. Reynolds and Wilson 1991, 88–89; McKitterick 1995, 682–84; Kelley 1998, 107–11; McKitterick 2006, 19–21; Godden and Lapidge 1991, 5, 208–9, 224, 277–78; Orme 2006, 22–23; Colish 1997, 64–65; Conte 1994, 724–25; Brown 1996, 229; Campbell 1966, 160–65; Knappe 1996, 469, 472–75; Law 1997, chap. 5.

56. McKitterick 1995, chaps. 27 and 29; Law 1997, 81–86, 133, 136–44; Marrone 2003, 18–19; Reynolds and Wilson 1991, 94–106; Auerbach 1965, 112–19, 123–33; Beeson 1930; McKitterick 2006, 26–28, 38–42, 56–61; Prete [1970], 14–18; Colish 1997, 67, 69–70; Townend 1967, 98–106. On the development of scribal handwriting in the West, see Parkes 2008.

57. Haskins 1927 (the classic work on the renaissance of the twelfth century); Benson, Constable, and Lanham 1991 (a conference updating Haskins); Witt 2012, 324–29; Smalley 1964, 149–69; Stock 1983, 62–63; Luscombe 2004, 474–75; Colish 1997, 177.

58. John of Salisbury 1955, 67–68.

59. Bolgar 1964, 221–24; Rand 1929; Orme 2006, chap. 3; Kelley 1998, 118–24; Franklin 2001, 193–94; Daston and Park 2001, chaps. 1–3; Ridder-Symoens 1992, 307–16; Colish 1983, xi; Luscombe 2004, 481–82.

60. Jaeger 1994; Colish 1997, 272; Luscombe 2004, 482–86; Law 1997, 85; Hobbins 2009, 105, 111; Witt 2000, 15; Witt 2012; Kennedy 1980, 184–87; Hoskin 1999, 58; Ridder-Symoens 1992, chaps. 10 and 13.

61. Dear 1995, 24; Lohr 1974, 231–32.

62. Rabil 1988, 1:33–34; Bolgar 1964, 208 (teaching of Peter Helias); McKeon 1942, 8–10, 15–19, 21–29, 32; Witt 2012, 323–24; Kukenheim 1951, 49–50; Witt 2000, 17, 31–32, 78–79.

63. Smalley 1964, 83–105; Van Engen 1996, 34–36. Kennedy 1980, 180–94, and Conley 1990, chap. 4, show that rhetorical theory—as distinct from practical problems of preaching—was not dead in the Middle Ages but marginal to the universities and unimaginative.

64. Le Goff 1985, 51, 98; Gilson 1955, 313–14; Law 2003, 172–79; Grendler 1989, 164–65; Eco 1995, chaps. 2–3. *Grammatica speculativa* had antecedents in Carolingian efforts to link dialectic to the study of language: Law 1997, 147. On the history of speculation about the reasons for the multiplicity of human tongues, the masterwork is Borst 1957–63. On 931–52, Borst reproduces lists of human languages from different periods, showing the ongoing fascination with the problem. The earliest list was compiled by Hippolytus of Rome in 234–235 CE, the latest by Alsted in 1650.

65. Lamberton 1986, 78–82; Lampe 1975, 177–215; Grant and Tracy 1984, 54–56, 63ff., 85; Smalley 1964, 86–88; McKim 1998, 107–8.

66. Smalley 1964, 292–93 (quotation); McKim 1998, 88–89, 107–8; Van Engen 1996, 26–33.

67. Grant and Tracy 1984, 90–91; Ocker 2002; Lampe 1975, 216–19; Krey and Smith 2000, 1–4, 17 (quotation), 150–61, 170, 309–10; Smalley 1964, 329; Ridder-Symoens 1992, 95, 111, 455.

68. Hobbins 2009, 1–2, 10–11, 16, 26–27, 39–40, 49, 111–27; Jean Gerson 1389, quoted in Hobbins 2009, 1. The pope (or an antipope, during the Great Schism) resided in Avignon in what is now southern France from 1309 to 1403. Technically, Jean Gerson's office was chancellor of the cathedral of Notre Dame, but this gave him authority over the theology faculty of the university.

69. Blair 2010, 33–46. *Encyclopedia* is anachronistic; the term was not coined until the

sixteenth century; Blair 2010, 12. Medieval indexes were not commonplace and were generally separate from the work indexed.

CHAPTER 2. "A COMPLETE MASTERY OF ANTIQUITY"

The quotation in this chapter's title comes from Pattison 1875, 58, referring to Isaac Casaubon's supposed aim.

1. Rummel 1995, 36–37; Grendler 2002, 205–36, 247–48.

2. Kennedy 1980, 185–87; Mann 1996, 5–6; Witt 2012, 252–59, 291, and chaps. 10–12, passim; Grendler 1989, 114–16; Witt 2000, 8, 31–33, 35–36, 55–57, 78–80, 88–95; Grendler 2002, 432–34. City-states were able to rise to effective independence because conflict between pope and Holy Roman emperor opened a power vacuum. Scholars at present debate whether medieval Italian schooling (that is, education in Latin grammar) persisted largely unchanged into the Renaissance (Black) or changed a great deal (Grendler); See especially Black 1991 and 2001 and Grendler 1989 and 1991.

3. Weiss 1951, 5–25; Witt 2000, 17, 52–54, 65, 78, 95–112, 118; Weiss 1969, 18–19; Mann 1996, 6–7; Reynolds and Wilson 1991, 124–26. Weiss 1951, 17: "In tutte queste metriche Lovato mostra chiaramente i risultati delle sue letture nel campo della letteratura classica." On the reinvention of the birthday party as deliberate imitation of ancient Romans, see Poggio Bracciolini and Niccolò de Niccoli 1991, 161–62 and 339n2.

4. Mann 1996, 8–14; Reynolds and Wilson 1991, 128–32; Prete [1970], 18–20; Billanovich 1951, 137–78, 191–203; Grafton 1980, 282–83; Mommsen 1942, 233–41; Burke 1969, 21–24; but see Baron 1933, 8, 12–13. For how closely Petrarch's Latin matched classical Latin, see Rizzo 1988, esp. 54–55.

5. Kühlmann 1982, 288–89; Scaglione 1961, 52–70.

6. Weiss 1969, 32–33, 63–70, and passim; Petrarch to Giovanni Colonna, 1341, quoted in Mommsen 1942, 232; Stenhouse 2005, 21–22; Barkan 1999, 18–20; Grafton 2000, 228–29, 275; Herklotz 1999, 204–8, 241–43; Momigliano 1955, 73.

7. Murphy 1983, 1–19, 174–87, 207–20, 253–73; Witt 2000, 244; Pfeiffer 1976, 31–33; Poggio Bracciolini and Niccolò de' Niccoli 1991; Vickers 1998, 286–92; Kühlmann 1982, 288; Conley 1990, 111–14; Fumaroli 1999, 45–81; Kennedy 1980, chap. 10; Grendler 1989, chaps. 7–8; Rabil 1988, 1:338–41; Mack 1993, 12–13; Lorenzo Valla, quoted in Franklin 2001, 187; Dupré 1993, 109; Witt 2000, chap. 8; Grafton and Jardine 1986; Black 2001. Sankt-Gallen lies some twenty-six miles from Konstanz by road.

8. Mack 1993, 14, chaps. 2–5.

9. Fumaroli 1999, 198–200; Mack 1993, chaps. 6–14, 17; Schmidt-Biggemann 1983, 3–6, 31–52; Jardine 1994; Ong 2004, chaps. 5, 7, 8–12, 13 (sect. 1); Conley 1990, 124–33; Kennedy 1980, 208–12; Howell 1961, 178–79, 187, 189–91, 193, 199, 219, 245; Murphy 1983, 58; Miller 1961, 12, 72, 238; Morison 1936, 1:140, 146; Vickers 1998, 292–93.

10. Hankins 1994, 155; Soll 2003, 155–56; Witt 2000, 22–23, 171, 402–3; Law 2003, 232–41; Burke 2004, 19–20; Mann 1996, 11; Burke 1969, 50–54; Rabil 1988, 1:333–35; Reynolds and Wilson 1991, 142; Herklotz 1999, 204; G. W. Bowersock, "Introduction," in Valla 2007, vii; Bentley 1983, 65. Petrarch exposed a 'grant' from Julius Caesar and Nero (!) used by Rudolf IV Habsburg to support his claim that Austria was sovereign within the empire. The *Constitutum Constantini*, recording the 'donation,' was probably forged in the papal chancery in the second half of the eighth century. Dionysius the Areopagite appears in Acts 17:22–34.

11. Grafton 2009, 70–78; Pomata and Siraisi 2005, 54–55; Grafton 1990b; Grafton 1990a, passim; Whitford 2009, 50–62. Among his fictions, Annius concocted a link between No-

ah's supposedly cursed son Ham and 'depraved' Africa; this 'curse of Ham' later served American slaveholders as a biblical defense of racial slavery. The curse rests on Genesis 9:20–27. Whitford 2009 explains how the story told there got twisted.

12. Reynolds and Wilson 1991, 134–49; D'Amico 1988, 10–11; Harrison 1998, 70–88.

13. Reynolds and Wilson 1991, 134–49; Kraye 1996, 151–52; Grafton 1991, 52–72; Grafton 1980, 283–84; Scaglione 1961, 55–56; D'Amico 1988, 24–25.

14. Kraye 1996, 151; Camporeale 2000; Bentley 1983, 49; Kelley 1970, chap. 2, esp. pp. 37–39, 45–46; Tully 1988, 20–21; Burke 1969, passim.

15. Trinkaus 1995; Witt 1996, 117–18; Witt 2000, 156–61, 248–60, 270, 334–37.

16. Weiss 1969, 3.

17. Cochrane 1981, chap. 1; Quillen 2010, 380–85; James Hankins, "Introduction," in Bruni 2001–7, 1:x–xi, xvii–xviii (anticipated by Baron 1933); Hay 1988, 40–48, 55; Rudolph 2006, 4; Bouwsma 2000, 56. As Hay notes (36), Biondo drew on the "extraordinarily luxuriant" tradition of chronicle writing in later medieval Italy; and one can see Bruni's history of Florence as a humanist version of the medieval urban chronicles of Italian city-states.

18. L. P. Hartley's novel *The Go-Between* (1953) famously begins, "The past is a foreign country; they do things differently there." The first clause has slipped its origin and entered into common usage.

19. Zimmerman 1995, 5, 67 (quotation), 80–85.

20. Pfeiffer 1976, 33.

21. Trinkaus 1979, 11, 44n23; Reeve 1996, 32–34; Wilson 1992; Rabil 1988, 1:350–81; Loomis 1908, 250–52.

22. Rummel 1995, 107–9, 12–14; Hankins 1994, 154–64; James Hankins, commentary in Bruni 1987, 201–10; Schmitt 1983, 65–71; Ianziti 2002. Hankins 1994, 164, points out that by the mid-sixteenth century even Scholastics recognized the superiority of humanist methods of translation.

23. Bentley 1983, 12, 32–50, 67–68; Shuger 1994, 19; Rabil 1988, 1:335, 337–38; Hamilton 1996, 101, 104–5; Reynolds and Wilson 1991, 149–54.

24. Bentley 1983, 22; Rummel 1995, 108; Kukenheim 1951, 90; Oberman 1992, 21–23 and 22n10 (Valla's phrase); Jones 1983, 21–22; Poggio Bracciolini to Niccolò de' Niccoli, 1416, in Poggio Bracciolini and Niccolò de' Niccoli 1991, 24–25. For Andrew of St. Victor and the Franciscans see chapter 1.

25. Oberman 1992, 31–32; Horowitz 2006, 86–90, 93–98, 126–35, 160–81; Burnett 2004; Wakefield 1989, 44–45, 50–51; Price 2011, 7, 60–65, 68–74, 109–206, 213–19, 230; Law 2003, 241–50; Rummel 1995, 108; Hamilton 1996, 106; Hsia and Van Nierop 2002, 3; Jones 1983, 5–6; Grafton and Weinberg 2011, 42, 67–73, 233, 255–67 and passim; Cousturier, *De tralatione Bibliae, et novarum reprobatione interpretationum*, quoted in Rummel 1995, 113; the sneer is quoted in Bietenholz and Deutscher 1985–87, 1:352; Lefèvre d'Etaples 2009, 128–30; Bedouelle 2008. In the quotation from Wakefield (Jones's facing-page English-Latin edition, 1983, 50–51), I have altered considerably Jones's translation, bringing it closer to Wakefield's Latin. Reuchlin's Hebrew grammar was principally indebted to the grammatical and lexicographical writings of the thirteenth-century rabbi brothers David and Moses Kimhi. Reuchlin argued against burning Jewish books on grounds of both their legality and their importance to biblical learning.

26. Jones 1983, 56–66, 93–99; 190–93; Oberman 1992, 24; Plongeron 1977, 113; Morison 1936, 1:141–47.

27. Grafton and Weinberg 2011, 55; Den Boer 2002, 101–2; Breuer 1996, 81, 85.

28. Bentley 1983, 70–111; Hamilton 1996, 106–8; Rummel 1995, 94, 109–10; Burnett 2005, 428. The question of priority is tricky. *Printed* in 1514, the Polyglot's New Testament was

published six years after Erasmus's edition of 1516. Of course, the first major printed book to survive was the Gutenberg Bible, some sixty years earlier; though lovely, it was not *scholarly*.

29. Febvre and Martin 1976, 143–50, 180–215, 248–87; Burke 2004, x–xiv; Reynolds and Wilson 1991, 156–58; Hamilton 1996, 105–6; Burnett 1994, 199–202, 204; Burnett 2006, 508–13; Kenney 1974, 3, 14, 17–18, 47–51; Davies 1995, 241–51; Grafton 1980, 276–78; Trunz 1970, 147–81; D'Amico 1988, 9–10, 12. Kenney (18) goes overboard in endorsing the harsh, black-and-white, ahistorical judgment of Wilamowitz that, except for Valla and Poliziano, no humanist was a textual philologist. For an overview of the impact of printing more generally in early modern Europe—a fundamental study often judged to be overstated—see Eisenstein 1980; for a corrective see Grafton 1980.

30. Tracy 1996; Jean-Claude Margolin, "Erasmus (1467?–1536)," http://www.ibe.unesco.org/fileadmin/user_upload/archive/publications/ThinkersPdf/erasmuse.PDF, accessed November 10, 2011, 3; Bentley 1983, 34–35, 95, 112–85; Pfeiffer 1976, 88–89; Metzger and Ehrman 2005, 142–49; D'Amico 1988, 32–34; Kenney 1974, 49–51; Levine 1999, chap. 2. Valla compiled two sets of notes; Erasmus found a copy of the later, more sophisticated, set. The 'Johannine comma' is 1 John 5:7, now agreed by scholars to be a later interpolation. Erasmus was not immune to pressure, and in the third edition he restored the spurious verse, though querying the authenticity of the Greek MS that forced this concession—a MS that had, in fact, been written about 1520 with the disputed verses translated from the Latin of the Vulgate. Metzger and Ehrman 2005, 146.

31. Bentley 1978, 309–21; Hamilton 1996, 110–11; Jardine 1993, 62; Erasmus, *Ratio verae theologiae* (1519), quoted in McKim 1998, 189; Rummel 1995, 89–91. The principle of the harder reading became better known from Jean Le Clerc's statement of it in his *Ars Critica* in 1697.

32. Shuger 1994, 53.

33. D'Amico 1988, 56–57, 72–90, 112, 185–205, and passim. Beatus later wrote a biography of Erasmus.

34. Hamilton 1996, 114–15; Hamilton 2001, 61–73.

35. Rummel 1995, chap. 5 and 126–29; Pfeiffer 1976, 77; Rummel 2000, 5; Buckley 1851, 19; Reynolds and Wilson 1991, 165; Bentley 1983, 194–213; Hamilton 2001, 61–65; Price 2011, 208–11.

36. Bentley 1983, 13, 211–13; Laplanche 1986, 83–84; Hamilton 1996, 113; Pfeiffer 1976, 96; Grant and Tracy 1984, 98–99; Bouwsma 2000, 236–37.

37. Grafton and Weinberg 2011, 283–88; Grafton 1983–93, 2:413–18. Grafton notes that Scaliger's achievement was a case of independent rediscovery. The Italian Jewish scholar Azariah ben Moses de Rossi (ca. 1511–ca. 1578) had "also identified a distinctive world of Hellenistic Judaism" (2:418). Azariah's work was evidently not yet known to the wider world of learning when Scaliger published his views.

38. Harrison 1998, 92–98, 107–9, 113–14. For the lability of even the literal sense, see Yoffie 2009, 168–69, 180–201.

39. Harrison 1998, 122–33; Grafton and Weinberg 2011, 167; Dopffel 2010, 212–14; Grafton 2009, 118, 374n19 (where Kepler's original Latin is quoted); Donne 1651, 16, 32–33. Little was known about either bird migration or the moon in Morton's day; his theory was not crazy—only his citation of Jeremiah 8:7 in support of it.

40. Rummel 2000, chaps. 2, 4; Stenhouse 2005, 1–2, 5; Grafton and Weinberg 2011, 22–23, 177–80; Nuttall 2003, 124–31, 147.

41. Kelley 1998, 169–74; Grafton 2009, 102–13; Bouwsma 2000, 62; Kewes 2006, 147–67, 307–10, 314–28; McKisack 1971, 119–20; Grafton and Weinberg 2011, 189–91, 231–32. A buccaneer sailing his own course in these waters was Paolo Sarpi. A Catholic monk who had

earlier turned his scholarly guns on jurisdictional claims of the pope, Sarpi wrote a history of the Council of Trent (1619). He massively (if imperfectly) documented his new text in the Eusebian tradition, yet he structured it by the rhetorical canons of humanist history. The huge, lumbering product proved more popular among Protestants than his fellow Catholics. In seeking to let his evidence explain the developments he narrated, Sarpi was equally oddball in his generation. Cochrane 1981, 472–77.

42. Bouwsma 2000, 201, 214; Grafton and Weinberg 2011, 255; Grafton 2009, 4; Summit 2008, passim; Kewes 2006, 115–23 (quotation, 315); Dew 2009, 34. Sir Thomas Bodley himself took a broader view of the library's aims than did his keeper; Summit 2008, 216–18.

43. Kelley 1970, 112–14; Grafton 1991, 72–73.

44. Bots and Waquet 1997, 12–13, 91–95; Grafton 2009, chap. 1; Shuger 1994, 13–17; Miller 2000; Pattison 1875, 509–10; Shelford 2007; Grafton and Jardine 1986. The phrase *respublica literarum* seems first to have appeared in the fifteenth century and to have been adopted as the self-designation of the international clan of scholars around 1500.

45. Bolgar 1964, 375; Reynolds and Wilson 1991, 155–56, 165; Kenney 1974, chap. 1.

46. Herklotz 1999, 209; Reynolds and Wilson 1991, 167; Reeve 1996, 36; Bolgar 1964, 373.

47. Caspar Hofmann, *De barbarie imminente sylvvla orationis* (1578) and Johannes Woverus, *De Polymathia* (1604), quoted in Kühlmann 1982, 289 and 290. Kühlmann gives the original Latin in footnotes and his German translations in the text.

48. Kühlmann 1982, 291 and passim; Morford 1991; Bolgar 1964, 377.

49. Haskell 1993, chap. 1; Stenhouse 2005, 14, 18–19, 23–25, 28, 43, 54, 68–72; Herklotz 1999, 210–11; Woolf 2003, 142–45.

50. Stenhouse 2005, 1–6, 103–12; Beard 2003, 23–24; McCuaig 1991, 141–59. On the peculiar publication history—with two dates a year apart—of Panvinio's *Fasti*, see Stenhouse 2005, 1. Ancient writers differed on the founding date of Rome; but the Roman calendar that calculated dates *ab urbe condita* (from the founding of the city) reckoned 753 as the year.

51. Stenhouse 2005, 1–6 (quotation, 6), 103–12; Beard 2003, 23–24; McCuaig 1991, 141–59; Erasmus [1962], 33.

52. Bolgar 1964, 377; Grafton 1983–93, 2:21 (quotation), 88–89, 624–32.

53. Miller 2001; Miller 2000, 10 (quotation); Popkin 1987, 47–48; Livingstone 2008, chap. 2; Mungello 1989, 124–28; Rossi 1984, 140; Stroumsa 2010, 52.

54. Hamilton 1996, 108–9; Burnett 2005; Fück 1955, 37–95; Toomer 1996, 14–15, chap. 2; Russell 1994, 1, 3–10, 20–28, 71–96, 120–23, 128–37; Hamilton 2001, 66–70; Hamilton and Richard 2004, 11–14 and passim; Hamilton, Van den Boogert, and Westerweel 2005, 3–5; Marshall 1986, 550–52; Morison 1936, 1:142; Dew 2009, 206, 208, 218–19, 222–27. The complicated reasons why Arabic came to matter to Christian biblical scholars are summarized in Russell 1994, 3–5. The famous Jesuit mission in China made possible the Confucius edition.

55. Games 2008, chaps. 2–3, 154–60, 165–74, 177–79, chap. 7; Cook 2007.

56. Stroumsa 2010, chap. 1 (for an overview), 41, 45–47, 68–69; Burnett 1996; Pomata and Siraisi 2005, 181–82, 187; for Selden, see below; Abulafia 2008, 47, 61, 113, 130–44, 155, 222, 288, 292; MacCormack 1991, esp. chaps. 5, 6, 8.

57. Geoffrey of Monmouth 1966, 54–74 (giants, 72); Kendrick 1950, 3–17; M. Curley 1994, 14–16; Struever 1995, 11–12; MacCormack 2007, 37–38; Kliger 1952.

58. Grafton 1983–93, 2:78; Miller 2000, 8; Kelley 1970, esp. 242–300; Huppert 1970, 31–60, 75–83, 171–81; Pocock 1962, 227–28; Brockliss 1996, 607–8. For an important qualification, see Shuger 1994, 60–65.

59. De Thou, quoted in Bouwsma 2000, 2; Douglas 1951, 20; McKisack 1971, 96, 121; Quantin 2009.

60. Kendrick 1950, 143–56; Trevor-Roper 1985, 121–48; Camden 1610, 23. On chorography, see Shapiro 2000, 65–69.

61. Wormald and Wright 1958, 177; Summit 2008, 174–75; Sharpe 1979, chaps. 1–3; cf. Miller 2000, 91; McKisack 1971, 85–89; Woolf 2003, 142–43.

62. Bouwsma 2000, 56; Selden, quoted in Shapiro 2000, 41; Pocock 1967; Gasnault 1999, 5, 34–36; Neveu 1994, 175–233, esp. 209–10; Kelley 1998, 208; Barret-Kriegel 1988, 59–82. The Jesuit was the Bollandist Daniel Papenbroeck (also spelled Papebroch[e]). Shapiro's excellent, comprehensive work stresses testimony in law courts as chief source for the novel stress on 'fact.' The influence of legal proceedings conceded, textual philology, its offshoots, and related areas such as historical scholarship on law strike me as much more formative among antiquarians and historians. They would, after all, usually be more deeply immersed in scholarship than in lawsuits.

63. Eco 1995, 15, 34, 40–43, 81, 95–97; Grafton and Weinberg 2011, 92, 95–96; Olender 1989, 13–14; Olender 1994, 12–16; Borst 1957–63, passim.

64. Olender 1994, 10–12; Burke 2004, 24–25; Metcalf 1953.

65. In the background of the universal-language quest was another medieval project, with a lineage stretching back before Aristotle: the 'art of memory'; mnemonic disciplines interacted with the widely known combinatorial logic invented by Raymond Lull (ca. 1235–1316), supposed to organize all knowledge according to its real nature and, ipso facto, to generate new knowledge. For this part of the story, see Yates 1966 (chap. 8 for Lull); cf. Yates 1982; Rossi 2000, 7–20, 130–32 (chap. 2 for Lull); Eco 1995, chaps. 4, 6.

66. Eco 1995, 216–18; Knowlson 1975, 65–97; Zagorin 1998, 176–77; Fraser 1977, chap. 1.

67. Shapiro 1969, 207–23; Eco 1995, chap. 12 (quotations 238–39); Knowlson 1975, 98–106; Aarsleff 1982, 260–64; Rossi 2000, 160–65; Struever 1995, 40. A Latin translation was made but never printed; Shapiro 1969, 221.

68. Seuren 1998, 41–48; Pécharman 1995; Arens 1969, 89–90; Fraser 1977, 19–21. A modern linguist might be tempted to see in Sánchez's *Minerva* roots of the version of transformational grammar that Noam Chomsky articulated in the 1950s; she should fight the temptation. The linguistic classifications of the sixteenth century were not those of the twentieth. *La Logique, ou l'art de penser* (1662)—the 'Port-Royal Logic'—takes a closely related approach to revising Aristotelian logic; cf. Marin 1975. On the roots of Port-Royal in medieval *grammatica speculativa* and its awkward relation to subsequent linguistic theorizing, see Droixhe 1978, 14–20. The Port-Royal group has been thought Cartesian in philosophy—Noam Chomsky entitled his *Cartesian Linguistics* as tribute to the philosophical grammarians of Port-Royal—but Jan Miel has persuasively challenged that conventional view; Struever 1995, 50–60.

69. Findlen 2004, title, 33, 390; Stroumsa 2010, 28, 33, 47, 146.

70. Jon Miller, "Hugo Grotius," *Stanford Encyclopedia of Philosophy*, ed. Edward N. Zalta, http://plato.stanford.edu/archives/fall2011/entries/grotius/, accessed April 12, 2013; Knight 1925, 26–32 and chap. 12; Pfeiffer 1976, 127; Miller 2000, 89, 104–5; Nuttall 2003, 164 (Scaliger quotation); Bouwsma 2000, 18, 56; Grotius, *De jure belli ac pacis*, prolegomena, §49, quoted in Breuer 1996, 85; Shuger 1994, 11, 23, 25–47 passim; Freiday 1979, chap. 8. See Hsia and Van Nierop 2002 for Dutch tolerance and its limits.

71. Toomer 1996, 64–71 and passim; Toomer 2009, 211–50, 441–69, 471–89, 626–786.

72. Skinner 1996, esp. 230–32, 235–36; Hobbes 1968, 417–22 [chap. 33]; 2 Esdras 14: 19–48; Malcolm 2004; Popkin 1987, 48–49; Malcolm 2002, 382–431. The biblical accounts of Ezra are in Ezra 7–10 and Nehemiah 8–9. Hobbes prudently added that Moses did write everything that the Pentateuch actually says he wrote, incorporated into the text by Ezra/Esdras.

73. Israel 2001, 219–20, 222–23; Spinoza 2007, 126–29 (chap. 8; quotation, 126); E. Curley

1994, 68–81; Hazard 1967, 166; Bruns 1992, 149; Bernus 1969, 71–77. The biblical narratives that Spinoza addressed were almost entirely in the Hebrew scriptures. He avoided commenting on the New Testament—perhaps out of prudence, perhaps (as he said) because his Greek was not good enough. Spinoza inherited and transformed a debate over biblical interpretation sparked by his older friend Lodewijk (Louis) Meyer; see Preus 2001; Scholder 1990, 133–42. More broadly, a plausible link ties Spinoza to the philologically rigorous Huguenot exegetical school of Saumur, through Meyer. See the introduction to Meyer 1988, 6–7; and, for Saumur and its considerable influence, Laplanche 1986 (Laplanche briefly discusses Meyer on 588–89). Suggesting this connection is, of course, not to deny other influences such as Grotius, Hobbes, La Peyrère, and the learned rabbis whom Spinoza cites.

74. Anonymous 1968, 201–14; Hazard 1967, 167–81; Gusdorf 1988, 113–14; Bernus 1969, 77–95; Malcolm 2004, 244–45; Laplanche 1994, 72–73; Prickett 1991, 136–42. Simon did acknowledge Spinoza as a predecessor. Neveu 1994, 346, sees Simon's influence already in the representations of Jewish ceremonies "et les usages des nations du Levant" in Arnold Van Gennep's diptych *Mœurs des Israélites* and *Mœurs des chrétiens* (1681–82).

75. Woodbridge 1984; Steinmann 1960, 100–110, 138, 141–45; Israel 2001, 447–53; Prickett 1991, 142–43; Champion 1999, 43–44 (Evelyn quotation, 43), 47–58; Stroumsa 2010, 66–76. Daniel Elzevier published the Amsterdam edition in 1679, with a date of 1680 on the title page. The English version was published in late 1681. The story of suppression is complicated; the book first passed the censor and got an imprimatur, then caught the shocked attention of the powerful Bishop Bossuet. The degree of Simon's orthodoxy and of his sympathy for Protestantism remain controversial; that he did not share Spinoza's religious agenda is not.

76. Anonymous 1968, 37–39; Pitassi 1987, 23–25.

77. Pitassi 1987, xiii, 12, 13–14 (Le Clerc quotation from 1685), 46–50, [98]; Pomata and Siraisi 2005, 42; Kenney 1974, 40–44; Grafton 2007, 3–13. Le Clerc's *Ars critica* and similar theoretical works of the period were also responding to a revival of the ancient skepticism (Pyrrhonism) associated with Sextus Empiricus (ca. 160–210 CE). In its extreme form 'historical Pyrrhonism' denied that we have any solid knowledge of ancient history. The magisterial study of early modern Pyrrhonism is Popkin 2003.

78. Erasmus [1962], 75–85, 112–17. The Ciceronian allusion is in *Brutus*, sect. 75: "Atque utinam exstarent illa carmina, quae multis saeculis ante suam aetatem in epulis esse cantitata a singulis conviviis de clarorum virorum laudibus in Originibus scriptum reliquit Cato." Cicero 1939, 70. Perizonius got this theory from his teacher Theodorus Ryckius.

79. Febvre and Martin 1976, 233, 235–36, 319–21, 329–32; Israel 2001, 137, 199; Golden 1972, 56; Burke 2004, 87; Eskildsen 2004, 428n–29n; Bots and Waquet 1997, 146–48, 153. University lectures in the vernacular also began to be heard in the later seventeenth century, although Latin lectures remained the norm into the eighteenth century; Burke 2004, 77–78.

80. Feldman and Richardson 1972.

81. Fleury 1682, 5. The book first appeared in 1681. I owe this reference to Stroumsa 2010.

CHAPTER 3. "A VORACIOUS AND UNDISTINGUISHING APPETITE"

The quotation in this chapter's title comes from Edward Gibbon on Thomas Hearne, quoted in Douglas 1951, 185.

1. Sandys 2009, vol. 2, chap. 15 (on Linacre, 225–28); Golden 1972, 16–17; Shuger 1994, 16.

2. Berkhout and Gatch 1982, 8; Haugen 2011, 67–70; Junius 2004, 3–11; Graham 2000, 300–303, 336–42; Stephen W. Massil, "Immigrant Librarians in Britain: Huguenots and

Some Others," paper presented at the World Library and Information Congress, Berlin, August 1–9, 2003, http://archive.ifla.org/IV/ifla69/papers/058e-Massil.pdf, accessed September 22, 2011, 6. Junius was born in Heidelberg of a Huguenot father but brought to the Netherlands by his father and educated there.

3. Haugen 2011, 16–17; Berkhout and Gatch 1982, 7–10; Toomer 1996, 86–93, 116–26, 131–36, 145–46, 155–67, 202–10, 213–27, 229–30, 271–79 (for the coffee, see G. J. Toomer, "Pococke, Edward [the elder]," *Oxford Dictionary of National Biography*); Kilpatrick 2010, 20–23, 25–28; Fück 1955, 87–90; Miller 2001, 463–82; Fox 1954, 47–49; Assmann 1997, chap. 3; Schmidt 1994, 122–30; Brink 1986, chap. 1; Stroumsa 2010, 95–100. The doggerel came from the miscellaneous writer Tom Brown who, while an Oxford student around 1680, according to legend thus translated extempore Martial's epigram 1.32 under Fell's nose. Abu 'l-Faraj (1226–86), called in Latin Bar-Hebraeus, was a bishop (and is now a saint) of the Syriac Orthodox Church and a prolific and versatile writer. Pococke also taught Hebrew, a natural companion to Arabic.

4. Stuart Handley, "Mill, John," *Oxford Dictionary of National Biography*; Richard Bentley, *Epistola ad Joannem Millium* (1691), in Dyce 1836–38, 2:241–368; Haugen 2011, chap. 3. *Epistola ad Cl. V. Joannem Millium* (*Cl. V.* being the Latin abbreviation for Illustrious Man, an exaggerated courtesy) was first printed separately in Dyce's edition of Bentley's works, under the slightly abbreviated title given above. (Dyce's edition was truncated at three volumes: "the indifference of general readers to classical literature prevented my carrying-out the design"; Dyce 1972, 145.)

Until the publication of the excellent Haugen 2011, students of Bentley relied on two nineteenth-century biographies: the two-volume Monk 1969 (published first in 1833) and R. C. Jebb's brief 1882 volume in the English Men of Letters series (Jebb 1889). Monk is still valuable for details of Bentley's life, and Jebb has expert comments on his classical scholarship. Haugen contextualizes Bentley's work in modern understanding of the scholarly traditions of his era.

5. Haugen 2011, 76–79, chap. 3; G. P. Goold, "Introduction," in Bentley 1962, 7–24; Brink 1986, 41–49; Jebb 1889, 16; Bentley 1962, 269–80; Monk 1969, 1:14–16, 48 (Stillingfleet quotation); Levine 1991, 246. Monk says the Stillingfleet story was current in Bentley's lifetime but does not vouch for its truth. Bentley's work was brilliantly done but not at all unprecedented: Isaac Casaubon had pinpointed and emended pieces of lost Greek poems that lay embedded in Athenaeus's *Deipnosophistae* (ca. 300 CE). Bentley had for some years worked toward an edition of the extant fragments of *all* Greek poets (a project nearly lunatic in its ambition); this may help to explain the breadth of his reading.

6. Goldgar 1995, 140; Jebb 1889, 34–35; Brink 1986, 61–62; Monk 1969, 1:49–52.

7. Haugen 2011, 101–5 (quotation from Boyle's will, 101); Turner 1985, 55. For the printed version of the lectures, Newton tutored Bentley by correspondence.

8. Simonsuuri 1979, 19–26, 37–45; Levine 1991, 13–46, 122–32; De la Pryme 1870, 29 (quotation, entry for July 9, 1693). In England the quarrel also became known as the Battle of the Books, thanks to Jonathan Swift's satire by that name.

9. Levine 1991, 41–42, chap. 2, and passim; Monk 1969, 1:58–182 passim; Haugen 2011, 112; Temple 1690, 61. The affair of Bentley and his critics was as convoluted as only academic quarrels can be and involved animosity between Bentley and Christ Church, Oxford. For this see Jarvis 1995, 20–30. On the history of Phalaris and 'his' letters before Bentley, see Hinz 2001, 19–282.

10. Bentley 1699; Hinz 2001, 344–58, 371–81; Haugen 2011, 110–22; Jebb 1889, 64–68; Brink 1986, 57–58; Pfeiffer 1976, 152.

11. Haugen 2011, chap. 5; Monk 1969, 1:316; Kenney 1974, 71 (Bentley quotation); *Dunciad* 4:211–12; Jarvis 1995, 66, 161. Bentley's celebrated words appear in his note to *Odes* 3.27.15:

"Nobis & ratio & res ipsa centum codicibus potiores sunt." In 1700, Bentley acquired new duties as Master of Trinity College Cambridge—and epic wrangling with his own fellows. These delayed his edition of Horace from the intended 1702 to the actual 1712.

12. Walsh 1997, 62–75 (76–94 also recounts contemporary reactions to Bentley's edition); Haugen 2011, 219–29 (Bentley quotation, 220; Haugen quotation, 228); Levine 1991, chap. 8; *Dunciad* 4:212.

13. Myres 1958, 50–53; Brink 1986, 75–76; Jebb 1889, 148–53; Monk 1969, 2:360–67; Haugen 2011, 182–86. Today, a well-informed surmise is that digamma dropped out of the Homeric dialect before the *Iliad* and *Odyssey* were composed but that formulaic phrases persisting from earlier times affected the meter as if digammas were still present; West 1998, 101. Bentley's digamma theory first saw print in the posthumous second volume of Samuel Clarke's edition of the *Iliad* (where Clarke attributed it to Bentley) and in Bentley's own edition of *Paradise Lost*, in which he quoted Homer; Jebb 1889, 150–51. Writers about Bentley (though not his biographer Bishop Monk) tend to link his digamma theory with the never-completed edition of Homer that he began in 1732; scant remains in the Bentley Papers in the Wren Library at Trinity College (B-17.17, James Catalog 414) do show his thinking. But he apparently had worked out the idea long before. The digamma was used in Byzantine Greek for the number 6, and early modern scholars knew it as such.

14. Brink 1986, 78–79; Wolf, quoted in Wilamowitz 1982, 81; Housman 1961, 12. Because much of Bentley's classical criticism remained in unpublished notes at his death, even Wolf could not appreciate his full powers. This unedited material was more or less absorbed in the course of the nineteenth century.

15. Kenney 1974, 115.

16. Haugen 2011, 50, 80; Sandys 2009, 2:411–19; Clarke 1945, 49–50.

17. Ferreri 2007, 113–63; Simonsuuri 1979, pt. I.

18. [Blackwell] 1735, 11, 15; Feldman and Richardson 1972, 99–102; Simonsuuri 1979, 99–107; Bauman and Briggs 2003, 90–99; Blackwell cloaked his work in anonymity, concealing both his own name and the publisher's; the book is even dedicated to "The Right Honourable My Lord * * * *." (The asterisks hide his patron, Lord Lisle.) Why he indulged in this parade of secrecy is a bit baffling, but he seems to have felt that knocking so revered a figure as Homer off his pedestal might be seen as having implications for the foundations of Christianity. This seems absurd until one recalls that a century later B. G. Niebuhr's source criticism of Livy did raise exactly this alarm about the Bible. At any rate Blackwell's authorship soon became well known.

19. Simonsuuri 1979, 107; [Blackwell] 1747; Bauman and Briggs 2003, 90; Feldman and Richardson 1972, 102; Reill 1975, 273n63. His book's popularity grew to the point that in 1747 Blackwell published an English translation of the footnotes, to aid readers innocent of Greek and Latin. He also published important books on ancient mythology and Roman history.

20. Spencer 1957; Feldman and Richardson 1972, 191–92; Levine 1991, 164–65, 167–73; Carhart 2007b, 135–39; Simonsuuri 1979, 133–42; Wood 1971.

21. Wood 1971, 235, 238, 247, 257–58; Carhart 2007b, 139–43; Spencer 1957, 82–105.

22. Kelly 2009, 125–27; Hecht 1933, 15, 25; Spencer 1957, 81–82; Reill 1975, 269n6. The Georg-August-Universität Göttingen (called in academic Latin the Georgia Augusta), a scholarly innovator in the German state of Hanover, will reappear often. From 1714 to 1837, the rulers of Hanover were also the 'Hanoverian' kings of the United Kingdom. Founded by George II (opening in 1737), the university was very hospitable to English speakers.

23. Champion 1999, 43, 46, 51–61; Marshall 1994, 337–38; Prickett 1991, 143.

24. Breuer 1996, 34–36, 89; Sheehan 2005, 23–24; Legaspi 2010, 22–23; Killeen 2009, 44–46.

25. Fox 1954, chap. 5; Sheehan 2005, 45–46; Ehrman 2006, 10–11; Metzger and Ehrman 2005, 154–55; Haugen 2011, 201–2. John Fell had published in 1675 a small Greek Testament—the first printed at Oxford—that noted many variants, with their sources inadequately cited (Metzger and Ehrman 2005, 153–54). Mill took over Fell's materials in 1677, possibly because of Fell's election as bishop of Oxford in 1676.

26. Anonymous 1968, 36–39; Marshall 1994, 338–39; Golden 1972, 134–35. The fact that Le Clerc was known to be on friendly terms with several English writers (including Locke) may have exacerbated the outrage, and the anonymous translation was attributed to Locke. Le Clerc's surname was and is variously rendered le Clerc, LeClerc, and Le Clerc. My choice is arbitrary, as I have never found a reason to prefer one form over another. My very rough definition of deist here is a stab at a term that neither had nor has precise meaning. My very rough definition of *deist* here is a stab at a term that neither had nor has precise meaning.

27. Wigelsworth 2009; Sullivan 1982, 132–36; Lucci 2008, chap. 2 and 118–23; Moeller 1987, 15; Legaspi 2010, 46–47, 49; Kümmel 1973, 54; Reventlow, Sparn, and Woodbridge 1988, 60–61. The first volume of Stephen 1962 remains a lucid and entertaining survey of the Deist Controversy, if also an artifact of 'advanced' Victorian attitudes. Strictly speaking, Toland seems to have been a pantheist rather than an 'orthodox' deist believer in a creator transcending the natural world.

28. Young 1998, 171–79; Rossi 1984, 236–44; Assmann 1997, 96–102, 104–14; Condillac 2001, xxxii–xxxiii (Hans Aarsleff, "Introduction"), 117–18, 178–81.

29. Rossi 1984, 129–32; Stephen 1962, 1:213–27; Legaspi 2010, 134–35, 141–42; Assmann 1997, chap. 4.

30. Harvey 2008; Turner 2011, 8–12; Marshall 1986, 557; Hunt, Jacob, and Mijnhardt 2010; Hamilton 2011. For the Confucius edition, see chapter 2. Lafitau's book was *Moeurs des sauvages amériquains, comparées aux moeurs des premiers temps* (*Customs of American Savages Compared to Customs of the Earliest Times*); he tried to fit the aboriginal peoples into the framework of biblical history.

31. Pagden 1986, 199–208; [Blackwell 1748], 352–62; Stephen 1962, 1:222; Turner 2011, 17. In this paragraph and the next I adapt some language from Turner 2011. The gap between the scholar's Bible and the believer's Bible is both a matter of concern for some biblical critics today and the burden of excellent recent historical or historical-theological studies (Sheehan 2005, Kugel 2007, Legaspi 2010). Fretting about the effects of biblical scholarship on believers is as old as biblical philology, but the present understanding that the *character* of biblical narratives itself changed as a result of the scholarship discussed in this chapter was perhaps first fully clarified by the now classic study of Frei 1974.

32. Cicero 1979, 32 (1.8.24); Aquinas 1946, 2 (1.3); Sheehan 2006; Byrne 1989; Harrison 1990.

33. Sheehan 2005, 27–28, 32–33, 43–44, 47–48; Kenney 1974, 99; Metzger and Ehrman 2005, 155, 157–58.

34. Sheehan 2005, 46; [Bentley] 1737, 100 (quotation); Monk 1969, 1:397–401, 406; 2:123–33, 286–89; Fox 1954, chap. 8 (124–25 for possible explanations of Bentley's failure to finish); Prickett 1991, 151 (for another view of why he gave up); Sheehan 2005, 46–49; Jebb 1889, 158–71; [Bentley] 1721, [1]–[2]; Reynolds and Wilson 1991, 186–88; Ehrman 2006, 14. The Erasmian *textus receptus* was of course improved by later editors, who introduced variant readings, but was not substantially changed. Bentley got help from the Swiss philologist Johann Wettstein and the Maurists of St. Germain-des-Prés, among others. A reader can get a sense of Bentley's approach from his manuscript remains in the Wren Library at Trinity College Cambridge; see especially B17.20 (James Catalog 415); B17.19; and possibly the annotations to Codex Augiensis ("Epistolae Pauli Graece et Latine"), parallel Greek and Latin texts, the latter in ninth-century Carolingian minuscule (James Catalog no. 412).

Haugen 2011 maintains (e.g., 104–5) that Bentley engaged in "theological writing" (including his proposed New Testament edition) "solely on occasions when he might gain patronage and reward." This seems a tad harsh. The first letter in his published correspondence (1689) shows Bentley's interest in New Testament manuscripts without any "patronage and reward" in sight; Bentley 1977, 1–3.

35. McKane 1977, 445–64; Sheehan 2005, 183; Kennicott 1753, 10, 12–13; Ruderman 2000, 23, 33; Breuer 1996, 87; Prickett 1991, 151. A second volume (or "Dissertation") of *State of the Printed Hebrew Text* was published in 1759, treating, inter alia, the history of the Old Testament text and the Samaritan Pentateuch. These works were probably published in English rather than scholarly Latin because they were, in part, meant to raise funds for the project.

36. Ruderman 2000, 24, 33, 42; Kennicott 1753, 275 (quotation); Breuer 1996, 87–89; Sheehan 2005, 183. Kennicott's rejection of vowel points put him at odds with most Protestant exegetes; indeed, he may have been influenced by a Catholic scholar he knew and admired, the French philologist Charles François Houbigant (an Oratorian like Simon), who had rejected the Masoretic Text in works published before Kennicott's research was far advanced; Prickett 1991, 154–55.

37. McKane 1977, 446, 456–57; Eichhorn, in *Jenaische Zeitungen von Gelehrten Sachen* 12 (1776): 827, quoted in Sheehan 2005, 184; Ruderman 2000, chap. 1; Purvis 1968, 74; Katz 1993, 175; Eissfeldt 1965, 690–91; G[eorge]. Gregory, "The Translator's Preface," in Lowth 1787, viii. The Samaritan Pentateuch was that used by the Jewish sect called Samaritans; it differed somewhat from the rabbinic Hebrew version and was written with different letters. Kennicott's collection of variants has not outlived its usefulness; Eissfeldt 1965, 691.

38. Hepworth 1978, 15–16; Hecht 1933, 15–17; Frei 1974, 103; Robert Lowth to Rev. Joseph Spence, September 29, 1761, Robert Lowth Papers, Bodleian Library, MS Eng. lett. c. 574, ff. 82–83; Lowth to ?, n.d. (ca. 1758), Lowth Papers, MS Eng. lett. c. 573, ff. 39–40; Legaspi 2010, 107–8, 115–16. Lowth thought Michaelis a "learned, ingenious" critic but also "very bold"; and he disagreed with the German in "a great many things" (and "cannot judge" much else, "as depending on a knowledge of Arabic"). Nonetheless, Lowth thought Michaelis's "performance very well deserves to be examined & considered"; and he issued an English translation of the notes as a separate publication when printing a second edition in 1763; this second edition also included notes on variants by Kennicott. The 1787 English translation of Lowth's book was not by Lowth (then ill and nearing his death) but by George Gregory, an Anglican clergyman and miscellaneous writer. Gregory added selections from Michaelis's notes to the 1787 English translation. For Lowth's life, see Hepworth 1978.

39. Olender 1989, 49–50; Laplanche 1994, 76–78. Kugel 1998 is the masterwork on Lowth's theory of Hebrew poetry and the long tradition leading up to it.

40. Lowth 1787, passim; Kugel 1998, 12–15, 69–95, 149–56, 204–286; Legaspi 2010, 108–15; Breuer 1996, 89 (Lowth quotation); Bauman and Briggs 2003, 110–14, 116.

41. Lowth 1787, 44; Legaspi 2010, 110–11; Kugel 1998, 286; Frei 1974, 151. Witte 2007 discusses Lowth's afterlife in form-critical interpretation and biblical poetics from Herder to the present, focusing on the Book of Job.

42. Theobald 1726, ii–iii, v; Blackwall 1971, 3; Jarvis 1995, 43, 66; Kernan 1989, 160; Alderson and Henderson 1970, chap. 5. The 1721 Chaucer edition was attributed on the title page to John Urry, the first of its successive editors, perhaps responsible for most emendations. He died in 1715 and his successor as editor, Thomas Ainsworth, followed him to the grave in 1719, leaving Timothy and William Thomas to finish the job. This editorial confusion may account for the haphazard quality of the text.

43. Shakespeare 1733, 1:xxv, xxxiv, xxxix; Murphy 2003, 67–76; Walsh 1997, 126–49; Kernan 1989, 171; Kramnick 2008, 91–94. Theobald's *Shakespeare Restored* was provoked by

Alexander Pope's edition of Shakespeare that tailored the Bard's language to the taste and mind-set of modern readers.

44. Shakespeare 1733, 1:xl–xli (for some of Theobald's aesthetic criticism, see xix–xxvii); Kramnick 2008, pt. 1; Kernan 1989; Raven 2007, 7–8, 131.

45. Summit 2008, 3–4, 21–22, 101–21; Wormald and Wright 1958, 154–71; Douglas 1951, 52–53, 156; Adams 1917, 18–19, 23–25; Graham 2000, 1–5; Schwyzer 2004, 60–64; Woolf 2003, 170–71; Berkhout and Gatch 1982, ix–x, 2. The 1566 book was produced either by Matthew Parker, the archbishop of Canterbury, or more likely by his learned Latin secretary John Joscelyn. (An archbishop could afford to have the font cast, and Parker had genuine antiquarian interests even if politics were primary.) Joscelyn and Parker's son John also prepared a MS Anglo-Saxon dictionary. After Joscelyn's death in 1603, it went to the London library of Robert Cotton—founded in part precisely to preserve the pre-Conquest records dispersed from monastic libraries—which in the earlier seventeenth century was the chief center of Anglo-Saxon and other English historical studies; Graham 2000, 8–10, 84–86; Wormald and Wright 1958, 189–93; Sharpe 1979, chap. 1.

46. Douglas 1951, 53 (quotation from Henry Spelman to Abraham Wheelocke, September 28, 1638), 54–57, 61–62; Graham 2000, chap. 1; Berkhout and Gatch 1982, x, 7–9. Wheelocke later was criticized for failing to consult five of the seven extant MSS of the Anglo-Saxon Chronicle. Sir Henry Spelman, historian and antiquary, funded Wheelocke's position. King Alfred commissioned the Anglo-Saxon Chronicle around 890, but it recorded events earlier and later. Bede wrote his *Historia ecclesiastica gentis Anglorum* (*Ecclesiastical History of the English People*) in Latin, but it was translated early into Anglo-Saxon.

47. Franciscus Junius to Thomas Marshall, June 3–4, 1667, and Thomas Marshall to Franciscus Junius, January 30, 1668, in Junius 2004, 1024–28; Humfrey Wanley to George Hickes, May 30 1697, and Humfrey Wanley to George Hickes, February 5 and February 28, 1699, in Wanley 1989, 55–57, 116–20; Arthur Charlett to Humfrey Wanley, September 15, 1700, Add. MSS 70476, and Arthur Charlett to Humfrey Wanley, June 27, 1701, Add. MSS 70477, British Library. Junius himself had first printed the Gothic script of Bishop Ulfilas's translation of the Gospels in 1664–65 from the sole exemplar in Uppsala.

48. Douglas 1951, chap. 4; Levine 1991, 352–56; Woolf 2003, 161. As Douglas notes (19–20), nonjurors like Hickes played a large role, for obvious theological reasons, in the study of English ecclesiastical history, as well as in patristics and Byzantine studies. (Nonjurors are those who refused to swear the oath of allegiance to William and Mary after 1689.)

49. Levine 1991, 356–67; Douglas 1951, 87–94, 116; Berkhout and Gatch 1982, 11; Theodor Harmsen, "Hickes, George," *Oxford Dictionary of National Biography*. Printing actually began four years before the first volume was published.

50. Ashdown 1925, 128–29, 131–33; Collins 1970, 69–134, 185–87; Levine 1991, 378–79; Sutherland 1994; Arthur Charlett to Humfrey Wanley, 13 February [1711?], Add. MSS 70477, British Library; Douglas 1951, 62–64, 69. Wilkins was a Prussian (originally Wilke), who settled in England in 1685: another case of the migration of erudition out of German-speaking Europe. Not until 1896 was Smith's edition of Bede superceded.

51. Ashdown 1925, 133–36; Collins 1970, 144–53, 155–56, 161–85, 188–93; Hughes 1979, 177–82, 190–91; Levine 1991, 379; Douglas 1951, 72–76; Adams 1917, 104–8; Jefferson 1851; Thompson 1936, 241–46; Hauer 1983, 879–98; Thompson 2003, 197–98. A penciled note on the title page of the Library of Congress's copy of Jefferson's *Essay* says that Maximillian Schele de Vere, professor of modern languages at the University of Virginia (and the man who finally realized Jefferson's ambition for instruction in Old English), suggested to the university's trustees the printing of Jefferson's MS.

52. Douglas 1951, 103–5, 112–13, 234–42; Sweet 2004, 81–86. The Society of Antiquaries

got started in 1707 as an informal discussion group but temporarily foundered on politics and on the bankruptcy of the tavern where it met. In 1717 it was re-created on a more solid basis—thus my verb 'establish.' An earlier College of Antiquaries, founded in 1586, was suppressed by James I in 1614 because its debates raised awkward political questions.

53. Woolf 2003, 146–47, 149, 154–63, 175, and chap. 7; Douglas 1951, 105–8; Levine 1991, 385–87; Piggott 1989, 14–15, 18, 25 (Evelyn quotation), 27; Wormald and Wright 1958, 188–89; Dr. John Woodward to Rev. John Strype, August 1, 1707, Add. MS 6/295, Department of Manuscripts and University Archives, Cambridge University Library; Sweet 2004, 159–61, 167–70; Poole 2010, chap. 6; Haycock 2002, 121–32; Piggott 1985, 43–51, 60–66, 90–96. John Woodward is the physician famed for "Dr. Woodward's Shield" (Levine 1977)—who indeed sent a copy of the engraving of his 'ancient' shield to Strype; Dr. John Woodward to Rev, John Strype, February 3, 1706, Add. MS 6/292.

54. Woolf 2003, 180–81; Piggott 1989, 134–35; Piggott 1985, 99–107; Haycock 2002, chap. 7.

55. Piggott 1989, 136; Woolf 2003, 163, 181–82; Levine 1987, 95–96.

56. Aarsleff 1982, 4, 25–27. Dugald Stewart invented 'conjectural history' to characterize Adam Smith's stadial theory of human social evolution; it is now generically applied to the speculative reconstructions of human social, cultural, and linguistic evolution that flourished during the Scottish Enlightenment.

57. Locke 1975, 479 (book 3, chap. 9, §8); Locke 1990, 13 [§4]; Aarsleff 1982, 24. Locke was interested chiefly in the *arbitrariness* of the connection between words and ideas and therefore the need for careful definition by individual speakers; the Scottish Common Sense philosophers of the next century stressed in addition the *conventional* nature of meaning—the consensus of a language community on the meanings of words, as a prerequisite for communication—as an answer to Locke's problem; Alter 2005, 72–74. The Scottish stress on convention, of course, does not entirely rebut Locke's point that the more complex the idea, the more likely the word for it to be understood differently by different listeners.

58. Edwards 1989, 626–27; Aarsleff 1982, 45–46, 146–99; Antognazza 2009, 92–96. Aarsleff, "Introduction," in Condillac 2001, xv–xvii, sorts out what Condillac did and did not owe to Locke.

59. Probyn 1991, 141–62, 169–71, 352; Robins 1967, 153–56. For an obscure reason, the words "Language and" were dropped from the title of the second, revised edition of *Hermes* in 1765. The only full biography is Probyn 1991.

60. Locke 1975, 432–33 (book 3, chap. 5, §8); Schulenburg 1975, 3–4; Pitassi 1987, 37.

61. Probyn 1991, passim; Woolhouse 2007, passim; Kernan 1989, 62–90, 102–6; Douglas 1951, 246, 260–62.

62. *Oxford English Dictionary*, s.v. "discipline"; see, generally, Kelley 1997 and, specifically therein, Kelley's "Introduction," 1–9, and his "The Problem of Knowledge and the Concept of Discipline," 13–28; Smith 1995, 105; Roberts and Turner 2000, 85–87; Turner 2003, chap. 5. The most formally organized and professionally policed early modern disciplines—law, theology, medicine—remain today closest to their earlier dimensions: a fact probably related to the first point, about institutional walls.

CHAPTER 4. "DEEP ERUDITION INGENIOUSLY APPLIED"

The quotation in this chapter's title comes from Jones 1799a, 20, referring to Jacob Bryant (1715–1804), author of several works on ancient history, philology, and mythology, whose method Jones immediately questioned.

1. Thomas 2003, 136. These languages were all Austronesian.

2. [Kennicott 1767], 3, 14–15.

3. [Kennicott 1767], 3, 5–7, 9–10.

4. Schwab 1950, 29.

5. Kieffer 1983 (map of Indian travels, 165); Anquetil 2005, 79–170; Guido Abbattista, "Profilo Biografico di Anquetil-Duperron," in Anquetil-Duperron 1993, cv–cxxiii; Schwab 1950, 7, 20–21, 25, 32–33. Ironically, William Jones attacked the translation as a forgery. The French learned establishment leapt to Anquetil's defense; but, with his great authority in matters Persian, Jones still retarded scholarship. Waley 1952, 30–32; Kieffer 1983, 24–26; Mukherjee 1968, 38; Franklin 2011, 74. Schwab 1950, 41, says Jones later recognized "son injustice" to Anquetil—though grudgingly, according to Waley.

6. Franklin 2011, 10, 36, 71–74, 76–89; Cannon 1990, 12, 14–17, 23, 28–29, 40, 53–54, 63–64, 89, 107, 151–53, 188–89; Mukherjee 1968, 31. As a barrister, Jones did not entirely abandon orientalist scholarship; e.g., he published in 1782 a translation of seven pre-Islamic Arabic poems. The three major modern biographies—Mukherjee 1968, Cannon 1990, and Franklin 2011—have different strengths and weaknesses, and I have drawn on all three to understand Jones's life and work.

7. Franklin 2011, 161; Cannon 1990, 153; Mukherjee 1968, 74. Mukherjee, 35, notes that as early as 1771 Jones had explored the possibility of a diplomatic post in Istanbul as a way of furthering his orientalist studies.

8. Mukherjee 1968, 77–80; Trautmann 1997, 17, 28–37; Cohn 1996, 60–72; Franklin 2011, 19–20, 213–14; Sinha 2010, 300–303. See also Thomas R. Trautmann, "Wilkins, Charles," *Oxford Dictionary of National Biography.* The title was *Bhăgvăt-Gēētā* in his transliteration. A French translation of Wilkins's work appeared just two years later. Wilkins went on to translate perhaps a third of the epic of which the Bhagavad Gita forms part, the Mahābhārata, and to publish pieces of that, including the story of Śakuntalā, with which Jones became involved; see below. Other Europeans, recently Anquetil-Duperron, had learned something of Sanskrit. Schwab 1950, 35–41, recounts earlier European encounters with Sanskrit, mostly by Roman Catholic missionaries.

9. Cannon 1990, 203–4, 224–25 (quotation from Jones's opening speech); Mukherjee 1968, 83–90; Franklin 2011, 205–11, 215. Indian members were not accepted until 1829.

10. Cannon 1990, 206–7, 225, 229–30, 232; Franklin 2011, 34–35; Franklin 1995, 89. Learning Sanskrit was no easy thing for a European: there was not even a published grammar until 1790.

11. William Jones to Charles Wilkins, "Saturday noon" [1785], bound in Lord Teignmouth's *Memoirs* of Jones (London, 1804), MSS Eur C227, Asia, Pacfic, and Africa Collections, British Library; Cannon and Brine 1995, 54–60; Mukherjee 1968, 94–95; Franklin 2011, 34–36; Cannon 1990, 231–32, 285–88, 348–51. John Baillie did the actual translations for the Islamic digest.

12. Cannon 1990, 218, 232–35, 274, 310–15; Mukherjee 1968, 114–15; [Jones] 1789; [Jones] 1790; Franklin 2011, chap. 7 (Goethe quotation, 251); Schwab 1950, 32, 65–71 (Goethe quotation, 66); Germana 2009, 50–54. Jones's romanticized poems of India set the pattern followed by later Romantic poets; e.g., Southey's endless *Curse of Kehama.* I have preferred my own translation of Goethe to Franklin's. Schubert never completed the opera, but the libretto by Johann Philipp Neumann—long believed lost—was found in 2001 in a Vienna used-book store. *Österreich Journal* 212, April 2, 2002, http://www.oe-journal.at/Kurznach richten/nr020402.htm, accessed November 16, 2011.

13. Franklin 2011, chap. 6 passim; Mukherjee 1968, 101–4; Cannon and Brine 1995, 60–65, 67; Cannon 1990, 297, 302–3, 306–7, 328; McGetchin 2009, 64. Hoffmann in one of his Kreisleriana has Romantic enthusiasts describing music as the "Sanskritta der Natur"; Hoffmann 1985–2004, 1:612 (*Kreisleriana,* pt. 1, sec. 3). The first five volumes of *Asiatic Re-*

searches were published in London in 1799–1800, to catch up with the Calcutta editions; publication ceased in 1839 after the twentieth volume; Schwab 1950, 49. Von Günderode's married lover was the philologist Friedrich Creuzer, who appears later in this book.

14. Thomas R. Trautmann, "Wilkins, Charles," *Oxford Dictionary of National Biography*; Trautmann 1997, 114–17; Schwab 1950, 54–56; Cannon and Brine 1995, 131–40; Rocher and Rocher 2012, esp. 163–67, 185–88. The first European professorship of Sanskrit was founded in 1814 in Paris and occupied by Silvestre de Sacy; Schwab 1950, 54. Deist enthusiasm for Asian religions antedated Indology; see chapter 3 and App 2010. The term *Indology* seems to have been coined in the 1820s but did not become common until the late nineteenth century; Sengupta 2005, [xv]; *Oxford English Dictionary*, s.v. "Indology." I use it anachronistically for lack of an alternative to label the studies comprised in it.

15. William Jones, "On the Gods of Greece, Italy, and India, Written in 1784, and since Revised," *Asiatic Researches; or, Transactions of the Society, Instituted in Bengal, for Inquiring into the History and Antiquities, the Arts, Sciences, and Literature, of Asia* 1 (1799): 221, 239.

16. Adam Ferguson to John Macpherson, 16 February 1786, MSS Eur/F291/97, Asia, Pacfic, and Africa Collections, British Library; Cannon 1990, 94, 151, 223, 226, 251; Azad 1988, 134 (Hastings quotation); Carhart 2007b, 1. Devanāgarī, developed around 1100 CE from earlier alphabets, is used to write Sanskrit as well as modern Indian languages.

17. Cannon 1990, 241; Jones 1799a, 26.

18. Trautmann 1997, 41–61; Olender 1989; Mukherjee 1968, 95–96; Filippo Sassetti to Bernardo Davanzati, 22 January 1586, in Sassetti 1970, 501–2; Trautmann 2006, 118, 213, 213n1; Cannon 1990, 244. Among the "molte cose comuni" between Sanskrit and "la lingua d'oggi," Sassetti noted "molti de' nostri nomi, e particolarmente de' numeri 6, 7, 8 e 9, Dio, serpe, e altri assai." A French Jesuit missionary in India, Gaston-Laurent Cœurdoux, in 1767 reported to the Académie Royale des Sciences on similarities among Sanskrit, Latin, Greek, German, and Russian; this observation came perhaps closest to Jones's.

19. Cannon 1990, 243 (Jones quotation); Trautmann 1997, 38, 48, 56 (quotation).

20. Cannon 1990, 328–29; Jones 1799b; Schwab 1950, 71 (Goethe quotation, translated into French); Dowling 1986, 51.

21. Although not directly relevant to this book, it is worth mentioning that the work of early British orientalists in India helped to spark a cultural revival among erudite Indians— doubly ironic given Jones's failure to get them admitted to the Asiatick Society. See Kopf 1969.

22. Hanzeli 1969, 17, 19–20, 22, 59, 64, 72–81.

23. Gray 1999, 44–50; Lauzon 2010, chap. 3; Bailyn 2012, 294.

24. Gray 1999, 24–26, 35 (quotation); Bailyn 2012, 294.

25. Aarsleff 1982, 158–70, 176–94; O'Brien 1997, 156–61.

26. Jefferson 1972, 58–64, 100–102 (queries 6 and 11); Gray 1999, 120–21.

27. Aarsleff 1982, 84–100; Antognazza 2009, 325, 362–64; Trautmann 2006, 21–22, 31–34; Robins 1990, 87–92; Robins 1967, 169; Jefferson 1972, 100–102 (query 11); Cecere 2007, esp. 202, 204–6; Zande 2010, 424. Pallas published in 1787–89 the *Linguarum totius orbis vocabularia comparativa* [*Worldwide Comparative Vocabulary of Languages*]. Jefferson's *Notes*, completed by December 1781, were not published until 1785, in Paris.

28. Gray 1999, 112, 118–24, 127–28, 130–38; Jefferson 1972, 101 (quotation); Thomas Jefferson, word list with comments, June 13, 1791, folder 14, Historical and Literary Committee American Indian Vocabulary Collection, pt. 1, MSS 497 V85, pt. 1, and [William V. Murray], "Vocabulary of the Nanticoke Indians," n.d. [summer 1792], printed broadside with MS entries, Historical and Literary Committee American Indian Vocabulary Collection, pt. 2, MSS 497 V85, pt. 2, American Philosophical Society, Philadelphia; Wallace 1999, 130, 144–46; Thomas Jefferson to Ezra Stiles, September 1, 1786, in Jefferson 1954, 316; Harvey

2009, 78–87, 105–108. Marquis de La Fayette to George Washington, February 10, 1786, George Washington to Thomas Hutchins, August 20, 1786; Washington to Richard Butler, November 27, 1786; Richard Butler to George Washington, November 30, 1787 (including Butler's Indian vocabulary), all in *The Papers of George Washington Digital Edition*, ed. Theodore J. Crackel (Charlottesville: University of Virginia Press, Rotunda, 2007, http://rotunda.upress.virginia.edu.proxy.library.nd.edu/founders/GEWN.html, accessed November 18, 2008. In strict accuracy I should say that the space for 'mammoth' was always blank on the numerous forms that *I* examined.

29. Harvey 2009, 91–105; Gray 1999, 128–30; Barton 1798, lvi–lvii, lxxxviii, ci; Robertson 1777, 1:272. The basic idea of a land bridge was not original with Barton and Robertson. In the late sixteenth century José de Acosta speculated that the Indians had come from Asia over a land link between the continents; Pagden 1986, 194–95. In Acosta's day, only local native peoples knew of the stretch of water now called the Bering Strait.

30. *Oxford English Dictionary*, s.v. "archaeology."

31. Clarke 1945, 177–78, 182, 185, 187–89 (quotation from Richard Chandler, *Ionian Antiquities* [1769], 177); Kelly 2009, esp. chaps. 1, 3–5; Levine 1987, 97–98. The society was formally organized four years after its first meeting.

32. Kelly 2009, 111, 125–37.

33. Soros 2006, 24–25, 38, 52, 67–71, 118, 122–23, and passim; Watkin 1982, chap. 1 (quotation, 16). Revett did most of the measuring. An older view—not yet extinct—saw Stuart and Revett's expedition as "the beginning of scientific archaeology"; Clarke 1945, 175.

34. Soros 2006, 67; Gordon 2007; Parslow 1995, 19–31, 44–46, 83–84, 275–81, and passim; Dyson 2006, 15–19; Grell 1982, 33–55, 94–102, 134–39; Leppmann 1970, 175–82.

35. Kennedy 1980, 220–27.

36. Court 1992, 17–19; Crawford 1998, 4–8.

37. Crawford 1998, 2–4, 6–7, 28–29; Crawford 1997, 3, 33–34; Meikle 1945, 90–92, 94; Skinner 1979, 7–8; Miller 1997, 166; Palmer 1965, 173; Kennedy 1980, 232–39. Stevenson taught rhetoric apparently along the same lines as his pupil Hugh Blair did later, though evidence is slim. The term *belles lettres* entered widespread British usage as a result of the popular four-volume translation in 1734 of Charles Rollin's *Traite des etudes: De la maniere d'enseigner et d'etudier les Belles-Lettres*.

38. Court 2001, esp. chaps. 1–2; Moss 1996. Dissenting academies had actually taught English rhetoric before the Scots, though less influentially; Palmer 1965, 7.

39. Crawford 1998, 29–31; Palmer 1965, 2–3, 11–12; Meikle 1945, 90.

40. Blair 1783; Kames 2005.

41. Conley 1990, 223–24; Miller 1997, 2, 227–28.

42. Court 2001; Crawford 1997; Bain, quoted in Palmer 1965, 176. Histories of the origins of English as an academic discipline often have a polemical edge. For a balanced and realistic view, see Palmer 1965, appendix 1. To grasp the place of rhetoric in eighteenth-century education, it helps to recall that the study of language had long been associated with the study of logic; and in the English Dissenting academies universal grammar—an approach to language through logic—formed part of the subject matter of "polite literature" or *belles lettres*; Azad 1988, 122–23. In Scottish universities, rhetoric was taught by the professor of logic—Adam Smith's original post at Glasgow—until special chairs were created for it. Miller 1997 recognizes that Hugh Blair and his ilk aimed to teach effective writing and speaking; nonetheless, he calls them the first teachers of college English because he wants to end the privileging of literature over composition in modern English departments. But the "academic study of English literature, as we know it in schools and universities" (Palmer 1965, 1) historically *has* privileged literature over composition for as long as there have been professors of a subject labeled English (rather than rhetoric) in British and American col-

leges and universities. In this book I am interested in what English as an academic discipline is, not what it ought to be or might become in the future.

43. Conley 1990, 220; Walsh 1997, 150, 175–98; Jarvis 1995, chap. 7; Murphy 2003, 82–83; Kernan 1989, 267–82; Wellek 1941, 148–52, chap. 6; Hugh Reid, "Warton, Thomas," *Oxford Dictionary of National Biography.*

44. Gibbon 1994.

45. Momigliano 1955, 95–96, 197–99; Kelley 1998, chap. 9; Schlenke 1976, 327–28; Force 2009, 462–67; O'Brien 1997, 2–3 and passim; Ferguson 1767, 2; Hay 1977, 172–73.

46. Hay 1977, 174–75, 178–91; Burrow 2008, 314–17, 320–21; Hay 1988, 91–94; Schlenke 1976, 330; Momigliano 1955, 202–3; Hume 1770; Robertson 1769; Phillips 2000, 65–71.

47. Force 2009, 467; Gibbon 1984, 115.

48. Momigliano 1955, 199–201, 205; M. S. Phillips 1996; Levine 1999, 158–60; e.g., Gibbon 1994, 1:387n97, 1:602n67, 1:799n105, 2:175n34, 2:208n116, 2:715n67, 3:302n167, 3:666n26; Pocock 1999, 5, 16; Fumaroli 2007, 167–68; Levine 1987, 181–82, 184. For the institution of antiquarian learning that loomed largest on Gibbon's horizon, the Académie des Inscriptions et Belles-Lettres, see Raskolnikoff 1992, 48–97, 221–388.

49. Womersley, "Introduction," in Gibbon 1994, xi–xiii; Kelley 1998, 229; Momigliano 1955, 195, 207; Stuchtey and Wende 2000, 69–70; Hay 1977, 181–82; Hay 1988, 95–97; Bowersock 2009, 10–12; Levine 1999, 161, 165, 171; Levine 2004, 200–201; Burrow 2008, 341. Anthony Grafton comprehensively but concisely laid out this story (from the perspective of the footnote), in longer historical perspective and greater detail than is possible here, in Grafton 1994 and in a book to which his article led, Grafton 1997.

50. Levine 1999, 171–72; Pocock 2005, 184; Craddock 1989, 352–59.

51. Jarick 2007, 157–73, 190–219; Legaspi 2010, 135–37; Acosta 2002, 257–59; Doe 1960.

52. Sheehan 2005, 116; Reventlow, Sparn, and Woodbridge 1988, 62; for Semler, see Hornig 1961; for Michaelis, see Legaspi 2010; Rogerson 1984, 10. I omit Hermann Samuel Reimarus (1694–1768), a third traditional founder of German biblical criticism, on the ground that his influence, like that of his fellow deists in the British Isles, seems to me to have had little effect on the form and content of biblical philology, as distinct from unsettling orthodoxies.

53. Reventlow et al. 1988, 80–85; Löwenbrück 1986, 116, 118, 120, 126; Kümmel 1973, 69; Breuer 1996, 95; Legaspi 2010, 117–20; Reill 1975, 165–72, 193–94; "Parkhurst's Greek *and* English *Lexicon*," *Critical Review, or, Annals of Literature* 28 (1769): 91. Sheehan 2005, 185, led me to the *Critical Review* quotation.

54. Breuer 1996, 21, 26–28, 43–44, 99, 101–2, 117–19 (Semler quotation, 118), 122–23; Hess 2002, chap. 2 (Michaelis quotation, 67); Legaspi 2010, 97–100. In pointing out their postbiblical introduction, Levita did not intend to question the authority of the vowel points. On him and *Masoret ha-Masoret*, see Newman 2006.

55. Rogerson 1984, 17; Löwenbrück 1986, 118–20; Hepworth 1978, 16.

56. Reill 1975, 194–98; Carhart 2007b, 29–32, 45–51; Sheehan 2005, 184–99; Hess 2002, chap. 2; Legaspi 2010, 100–103, 120–21, 126–27, 140–46; Moeller 1987, 65–66 (quotation). Michaelis's substantive aim in *Mosaisches Recht*—to show (like a second Montesquieu) that Moses the wise legislator adapted his laws to the primitive state of his people and that, therefore, Mosaic law is irrelevant to moderns—is for our purposes unimportant compared to his historicizing method.

57. Kümmel 1973, 69 (quotation from Michaelis's *Einleitung*); Löwenbrück 1986, 127; Legaspi 2010, 137–39; Gusdorf 1988, 130–38. The *Einleitung* was first published in 1750, as a much smaller work, derivative from Richard Simon. The two-volume fourth edition of 1788 was really a new book.

58. Metzger and Ehrman 2005, 158–59, 161–62, 165–67; Kümmel 1973, 74–75. Griesbach called the three recensions Alexandrian, Western, and Constantinopolitan.

59. Moeller 1987, 73–74; Rogerson 1984, 17–18; Sheehan 2005, 220; Gusdorf 1988, 165; Eichhorn 1787, 7, 10, 12–16. *Litterärgeschichte* grew organically out of an earlier genre, *historia litteraria*; see, e.g., Schmidt-Biggemann 1983 and Carhart 2007a. Michaelis had similarly broad scholarly interests, even if he did not publish on quite as wide a range of subjects as Eichhorn; Moeller 1987, 60–68.

60. Anthony Grafton, Glenn W. Most, and James E. G. Zetzel, "Introduction," in Wolf 1985, 24–25; Moeller 1987, 75; Rogerson 1984, 22–27.

61. Eichhorn 1787, vi.

62. Leppmann 1970; Wangenheim 2005; Potts 1994, chap. 1; Völher 2002, 46; Butler 1935. For an important qualification to eighteenth- and early nineteenth-century German neo-Hellenism, see Reill 1975, 142–43.

63. Völher 2002, 39–54; Anonymous 1980, esp. Wolf-Harmut Friedrich, "Heyne als Philologe," 15–31.

64. Pattison 1889; Pfeiffer 1976, 174–75; August Wolf to C. G. Heyne, November 18, 1795, in Wolf 1797, 7 (quotation); Fuhrmann 1959, 216–26; Anthony Grafton, Glen W. Most, and James E. G. Zetzel, "Introduction," in Wolf 1985, 18–28; Grafton 1991, 223–42.

65. Wolf 1797, passim; Grafton, Most, and Zetzel, "Introduction," in Wolf 1985, 4, 17; Grafton 1991, 216–23; Flasher 1979; Fuhrmann 1959, 230–32. In *Darstellung der Altertums-Wissenschaft nach Begriff, Umfang, Zweck und Wert* (1807), Wolf gave a programmatic statement of the newly conceived field. His student August Boeckh influentially systematized Altertumswissenschaft in lectures published posthumously in 1877 as *Enzyklopaedie und Methodologie der philologischen Wissenschaft.*

66. Burke 2007; Miller 1970, 2:37, 40 (quotation).

67. Grafton 2009, 9; Goldgar 1995, 54–59; Thirlwall 1936, 28–29 (Porson quotation); Clarke 1937, 69. Wolf's name appears in Clarke's biography of Porson only in an allusion (109) to the eventual displacement of Porson's verbal criticism by Altertumswissenschaft.

68. Burrow 2008, 329–32; Kewes 2006, 395–97.

PART II: ON THE BRINK OF THE MODERN HUMANITIES, 1800 TO THE MID-NINETEENTH CENTURY

1. Quincy 1840, 2:323; Morison 1964, 264; Maxwell 1946, 194–95.

2. Bailyn et al. 1986, 117; Maxwell 1946, 188.

3. Dates of learned societies from the Scholarly Societies Project, University of Waterloo Library, http://www.lib.uwaterloo.ca/society/history/, accessed January 18, 2012.

CHAPTER 5. "THE SIMILARITY OF STRUCTURE WHICH PERVADES ALL LANGUAGES"

The quotation in this chapter's title comes from Smith 1812, 1:105.

1. Auroux 1990, 215–16, 228–29; Du Ponceau 1838, 5–6. The full title was *Mithridates, oder allgemeine Sprachkunde mit dem Vater Unser als Sprachprobe in beynahe fünfhundert Sprachen und Mundarten* (*Mithridates, or General Science of Language Using the Our Father as a Linguistic Test in Nearly Five Hundred Languages and Dialects*). The use of the Lord's Prayer to compare languages goes back at least to the sixteenth century, and Adelung's title echoed a similar work of that century by the Swiss scholar Konrad Gesner.

2. Robins 1967, 164.

3. Peter Stephen Du Ponceau, *Note Books on Philology*, vols. 5–6, MSS 410 D92, American Philosophical Society, Philadelphia; Humboldt's letters to John Pickering, edited by Kurt Müller-Vollmer as the appendix to Hammacher 1976, 276–315; Pickering 1887, 289, 297–305, 312, 315; Sweet 1978–80, 2:399–404.

4. Dwight 1859, 201.

5. Herder, quoted in Richards 2002, 342; Robins 1967, 151–52; Miller 1968, 21–22; H[arris] 1751, 407–8. Harris went on to add that "the *wisest* Nations, having the *most* and *best Ideas*, will consequently have the *best* and *most copious Languages*."

6. Mosse 1978, 37–38; Samuel Johnson to William Drummond, August 13, 1766, in Boswell 1791, 1:287; Trautmann 2006, 220–25; [A. G. de Gurowski], "Slavic Languages and Literature," *North American Review* 71 (1850): 330–31. On 'Mosaic ethnology,' see Trautmann 1987, passim, and especially Trautmann 1997, 42–57.

7. Ogris 1986, 73–75; Benes 2008, 119–21; Scherer 1921, 13, 16, 18.

8. Trautmann 2006; Trautmann 1997, 141; Rocher 1968 (quotation, 65, from minutes of the East India College governing committee, August 6, 1806). Rocher's article on Hamilton in the *Oxford Dictionary of National Biography* updates her biography.

9. Rocher 1968, chap. 4; Rocher 2002, 389–90; Chaudhuri 1974, 221; Schwab 1950, 86–87; Irwin 2007, 141–50; McGetchin 2003. Mill's association with the East India Company did not actually begin until 1819, Macaulay's until 1834. I cite their names as the most notorious anglicizers.

10. Schwab 1950, 64–67, 76; Marchand 2009, 58–63; Germana 2009, 118–19, 122–29, and passim; Sebastiano Timpanaro, "Friedrich Schlegel and the Beginnings of Indo-European Linguistics in Germany," trans. J. Peter Maher, in Schlegel 1977, xxii–xxiii, xxvii; Fiesel 1927, 2; McGetchin, Park, and SarDesai 2004, 119–22; Benes 2008, 74.

11. Schlegel 1977; Marchand 2009, 123; Friedrich Schlegel to Jean de Müller, May 2, 1808, quoted in Schwab 1950, 79 (Schlegel quotation); Benes 2008, 73–74, 76, 81; Schwab 1950, 80; Sengupta 2005, 15–17, 25–26, 37–38; Germana 2009, 171, 181–94; George Cornewall Lewis to Edmund Walker Head, May 13, 1836, in Lewis 1870, 53; McGetchin, Park, and SarDesai 2004, 141–48; Hoffmann 1985–2004, 1:612 (*Kreisleriana*, pt. 1, sec. 3); Jackson 1981, chaps. 3–4, 6. The oddly named Jean de Müller was the Swiss/German historian also known as Johannes von Müller.

12. Benes 2008, 74–75; Schlegel 1977, 28 ("vergleichende Grammatik"); Timpanaro, "Friedrich Schlegel and the Beginnings of Indo-European Linguistics," xxxiv. The term *comparative grammar* appeared in earlier works by J. S. Vater, but he did not use it to describe genealogical comparison; Timpanaro, xxx.

13. Benes 2008, 77–79.

14. Benes 2008, 79–83; Pedersen 1962, 254–58; Jespersen [1921]), 47–55; Marchand 2009, 62, 71, 124–26; Sengupta 2005, 29. In a second edition (1857), Bopp added Armenian. Schlegel's Romantic Indology put him sharply at odds with Bopp's linguistic approach to Sanskrit, an animosity that continued in their students; Sengupta 2005, 27–36. This division of German Indology into two schools matters little for our Anglophone story.

15. Olender 1989, 29 (Bopp quotation). The term *Indo-European* first appeared in 1814, *indogermanisch* in 1823; Robins 1967, 170.

16. McGetchin 2003, 580; Rocher 1957–58; Marchand 2009, 95; Sengupta 2005, 15–27, 36–39, 61–62.

17. Fiesel 1927, 240.

18. Jespersen [1921], 37; Pedersen 1962, 248–54; Rask 1932, 1:51 (quotation); Trautmann 2006, 219–20. This 1932 edition of Rask's selected writings contains a long introduction

(xiii-lxiii) in German by Holger Pedersen, very helpful to readers like me who can barely piece out a Danish sentence even with a trot. I adopt the translation in Robins 1967, 171.

19. Robins 1967, 171–72; Seuren 1998, 83–84; Pedersen 1962, 38–42, 258–62; Jespersen [1921], 43–46; Benes 2008, 118–19, 123–27.

20. Robins 1967, 172–73; Jespersen [1921], 38, 41–43; Scherer 1921, passim.

21. Dowling 1986, 51–53; Aarsleff 1983, 161, 164–65, 177–78, 182, 211–12, 221; [D. R. Goodwin], "The Unity of Language and of Mankind," *North American Review* 73 (1851): 163–89; Benes 2008, 212; Lewis 1862; Donaldson 1839, esp. 31–36; Donaldson 1844; Rocher 2002, 390n43. I have been unable to lay hands on a copy of the first edition (1835) of Lewis's book. But Lewis (iii–ix) said that the second edition is identical to the first, aside from correction of a few errors and updating of reference notes, and that he wrote the work in 1833. At 62n1, Lewis cites *Deutsche Grammatik*, so he was at least aware of Grimm's work on language; in several places he cites Grimm's medieval legal research. Bopp's student was Friedrich Rosen.

22. Aarsleff 1983, 137, 162, 176, 195–206; Turley 2001, 237, 241–45, 249; Winning 1838; Bosworth 1841; John Pickering, "Address at the First Annual Meeting," *Journal of the American Oriental Society* 1 (1843): 42 (quotation), 74.

23. Wilhelm von Humboldt to B. G. Neibuhr, July 8, 1820, quoted in Sweet 1978–80, 2:394. A good brief general survey of Humboldt's life and writings is online: Kurt Mueller-Vollmer, "Wilhelm von Humboldt," *Stanford Encyclopedia of Philosophy* (Fall 2011 edition), ed. Edward N. Zalta, http://plato.stanford.edu/archives/fall2011/entries/wilhelm-humboldt /, accessed February 10, 2012. The fullest biography remains Sweet 1978–80.

24. Sweet 1978–80, 2:460–73. For the book's very complicated publication history, see also Mueller-Vollmer, "Humboldt." It was not translated into English until 1957, according to WorldCat.

25. Aarsleff 1982, 343–47; Humboldt 2010, 415, 604–6; Grossman 1997; Arendt 1946, 3–4; Benes 2008, 109–10; Olender 1989, 20–26.

26. Humboldt 2010, 403–14, 463–73; Seuren 1998, 112–19; Stubbs 2002, 308; Robins 1990, 95; Robins 1967, 176. On the uncertainties and interpretations of the concept of *innere Sprachform*, see Borsche 1989. For the intellectual relation of Herder and Humboldt, see Stubbs 2002, chaps. 4–5, and Miller 1968, chap. 1.

27. Miller 1968, 29–34; Brown 1967, chap. 8.

28. Gray 1999, chap. 6; Zeisberger 1827, 25–26; Tieck 1965, 52–55; Swiggers 1998, 21; Pickering 1887, 268–69; Peter Du Ponceau to Thomas Jefferson, November 14, 1815, and Peter Du Ponceau to John Heckewelder, January 9 and July 31, 1816, in Historical Committee Letter Books, APS Archives VIII, 4a (V.3), vol. 1, 1–2, 11–12, 39, and Du Ponceau, Note Books on Philology, 8 vols., MSS 410 D92, and Du Ponceau, "Indian Vocabularies Collected September 1820," MSS 497 In2, American Philosophical Society, Philadelphia; "A Correspondence between the Rev. John Heckewelder, of Bethlehem, and Peter S. Du Ponceau, Esq.[,] Corresponding Secretary of the Historical and Literary Committee of the American Philosophical Society, respecting the Languages of the American Indians," *Transactions of the Historical and Literary Committee of the American Philosophical Society* 1 (1819): 355–56, 369; Harvey 2009, 172–207. See also the biographical sketch that begins Du Ponceau 1838. Two closely related but mutually unintelligible Lenape/Delaware languages existed: Unami and Munsee. Heckewelder probably knew Unami, given his missionary territory. The APS's full name was the American Philosophical Society Held at Philadelphia for Promoting Useful Knowledge.

29. Pickering 1887, 266, 287 (Du Ponceau quotation), 291, 296, 309–13, 316 (Pickering quotation), 378; Swiggers 1998, 23–27; Cotton 1829; Edwards 1788; Harvey 2009, 50–57, 218–23. Edwards was the son of the more famous theologian/philosopher Jonathan Ed-

wards; his little book was a missionary source only, as it were, by courtesy. The younger Edwards had become fluent in Mahican as a boy when his father worked as a missionary in western Massachusetts; he himself never evangelized Indians.

30. Sweet 1978–80, 2:403; Peter Du Ponceau to John Heckewelder, August 21, 1816, in Heckewelder 1876, 406–7 ("ingenious"); [John Pickering], "Dr. Jarvis' Discourse," *North American Review* 11 (1820): 110, 113 ("speech as a science," "neglected"); Pickering 1887, 281–83, 286–87, 291–93, 296–97, 304, 315, 321 ("barbarous languages"), 322, 334–35, 355–56; Pickering 1820; Taylor 1963, 52; Harvey 2009, 298–300; Stevens 1957, 43–45. Specialists will recognize in Pickering's talk of science the 'Baconian' principles common in his day.

31. Pickering 1887, 288–89 ("well of science"), 381–82; Swiggers 1998, 21–22, 36–40; Peter S. Du Ponceau, "Report of the Corresponding Secretary to the Committee, of His Progress in the Investigation Committed to Him of the General Character and Forms of the Languages of the American Indians," *Transactions of the Historical and Literary Committee of the American Philosophical Society* 1 (1819): esp. xxii–xxiii, xxx–xxxi (quotation), xxxviii; [John Pickering], "Du Ponceau on the Chinese System of Writing," *North American Review* 48 (1839): 272 ("highly compounded"); Du Ponceau 1838, esp. 89–91; Andresen 1990, 108; Pickering 1834. The translator was the German wife of the American biblical scholar Edward Robinson.

32. Du Ponceau 1838, 12–15; Swiggers 1998.

33. Wissler 1942, 193–94; Greene 1984, 403–7; Walls 2009, 103, 106, 114–15, 186–87; Gallatin 1836; Taylor 1963, 51; Andresen 1990, 70.

34. [Pickering], "Du Ponceau on Chinese Writing," 271; Pickering 1887, 469–70; Dunglison 1844, 41–42.

35. Donaldson 1839, 74–75.

36. Horne Tooke 1798–1805, 1:12, 51 (quotations); Aarsleff 1983, chap. 2; Smith 1984, chap. 4.

37. Aarsleff 1983, chap. 3 (81–88 for Murray); Struever 1995, 220–33; Wiseman 1836, 1:55–56; John Wordsworth to "My dear Aunt" [probably his father's sister Dorothy (Dora), not his Uncle William's wife Mary], March 1830, Add. MSS 46136/ff. 51–52, British Library ("distinguished men"). Wiseman's book was based on lectures delivered in 1835.

38. Court 1992, 68–69, 78–80; Aarsleff 1983, 211–22; Donaldson 1839, 75; Murray 1979, 134–140. One can track the decline of interest in linguistic speculation in tandem with the rise of 'scientific' study of language in Stam 1976, chaps. 9–12. The idea of an English dictionary on historical principles did not originate with the Philological Society; see J. M. Kemble to John Allen, "Tuesday Morning" ["1 May 1838" penciled in], Add. MSS 52184/ff. 188–90, British Library.

39. Smith 1984, 148–49; Edgerton 1943, 26; Wilson 1965; Conser 1993, 94–96.

40. Peabody 1849, 108, 215. Crosby 1975, chap. 2, discusses other such American speculators without recognizing them as a distinct group. This and the following paragraphs incorporate material from J. Turner 1993; fuller references will be found there.

41. Robins 1999, 23; Josiah Gibbs, "On the Natural Significancy of Articulate Sounds," *Biblical Repository*, 2nd ser., 2 (1839): 167, 171, 173; Alter 2005, 58–60; Bushnell 1849, 38–39, 42, 74 (quotations); Crosby 1975, chap. 1 and passim; Duke 1984; Conser 1993, 99–104.

42. Johnson 1947; Todd and Sonkin 1977; Hazard 1836; Hazard 1857; Crosby 1975, 53–54; Durfee 1953; Cardell 1825; Kraitsir 1846, 8–9; Trautmann 1987, 74. Kraitsir advocated the logical arrangement of sounds in the Sanskrit alphabet. Alter 2005, 57–60, comments on some of this American speculation, linking it to natural theology. Other historians of linguistics seem to have overlooked it. E.F.K. Koerner (2002, 22) believes that "an empirical, descriptive approach to linguistic analysis," rooted in study of Amerindian languages, "predominated in the United States until the mid-1960s." Bushnell, Gibbs, Johnson, Cardell,

Kraitsir, and Hazard do not even appear in the index to Andresen 1990, although students of Indian languages do. The omission may occur because historians of linguistics do not believe these speculators belong in the family tree of linguistics. Alter, in contrast, is a general American intellectual historian who happens to be writing about linguistics.

43. Dwight 1859, 257; Benjamin R. Foster, "Edward Elbridge Salisbury," *American National Biography*; Stevenson 1986, passim; Alter 2005, 18, 26–27, 34–35, 99, 114–18.

44. [Charles Hodge], "Furst's Hebrew Concordance," *Princeton Review* 1 (1839): 311–15. Catalog of Tappan's books, MS, circa 1864; Tappan, "A Course of Moral Philosophy," MS notes, n.d.; Tappan, "Preliminary Essay," MS, n.d.; all in Henry Philip Tappan Papers, Michigan Historical Collections, Bentley Library, University of Michigan. [Mrs. S. R. (Mary Lowell) Putnam], "The Significance of the Alphabet," *North American Review* 68 (1849): 160–82; Benson 1926, 754–55.

45. Turner 1985, 160–62; J. Turner 1993, 460–61; Stallo 1885, ii–iv, ix, xiv–xv; Joseph 2007, 14; Chauncey Wright, "Evolution of Self-Consciousness," *North American Review* 116 (1873): 245–310. Saussure learned of Stallo's book through his brother René, who worked in the United States.

46. Whitney, quoted in Alter 2005, 162; Alter sums up Whitney's reaction to (and against) some of these earlier American theorists at 60–61.

47. Germana 2009, chap. 5; Benes 2008, 76–77; Robins 1967, 164–65; Sweet 1978–80, 2:371–72, 392–94; Gray 1999, 144; Grimm 1984, 1.

48. *Oxford English Dictionary*, s.v. "linguistic" (Whewell quotation); [Pickering], "Du Ponceau on Chinese Writing," 271. The *OED* wrongly gives the first appearance of the word *linguistics* as 1847. Even in 1839 Pickering seemed to indicate that the word was not brand new.

CHAPTER 6. "GENUINELY NATIONAL POETRY AND PROSE"

The quotation in this chapter's title comes from Ticknor 1849, 1:5.

1. Quincy 1840, 2:265, 290–91, 323–24; Adams 1810; [Hillard et al.] 1876, 1:116–18, 120, 319–24. Ticknor accepted the job in 1816, while already studying in Göttingen, on condition that he be allowed to remain in Europe to complete his studies and to use the salary of the professorship to buy relevant books.

2. Palmer 1965, chap. 2; Court 1992, 52–59, 87, 119; Meikle 1945, 99–100; Espagne 1993, 19, 25. *New Schaff-Herzog Encyclopedia of Religious Knowledge*, vol. 12, s.v. "Vinet, Alexandre Rodolfe"; Moody and Beckett 1959, 115–16, 159; Donald Hawes, "Craik, George Lillie," *Oxford Dictionary of National Biography*; Ash et al. 1999, 211; Parrinder 1991, 67. Dale had resigned from London University in 1830.

3. Rüegg 2004, 421n85; Wiley 1979, 208, 227, 236–42; John D. Haigh, 'Kemble, John-Mitchell," *Oxford Dictionary of National Biography*.

4. Whitney 1867, 6; *Oxford English Dictionary*, s.v. "criticism"; Dryden 1677, unpaginated (2nd page of preface). Whitney's definition is actually narrower than Ernest Renan's in 1890; Renan 1995, 191–92, 253.

5. Murphy 2003, 145–52, 167–82, 188–202.

6. Isaac Ambrose Eccles to Joseph Cooper Walker, July 8, 1802, ff. 123–24, and September 13, 1802, ff. 131v–132r, folio vol., Joseph Cooper Walker Correspondence, MS 1461, Manuscript Department, Trinity College Dublin; Cunningham 2008; Sherbo 1986, chaps. 8, 11.

7. J. P. Hopson, "Dyce, Alexander," *Oxford Dictionary of National Biography* (including quotation from Hazlitt); *Encyclopædia Britannica*, 9th ed., s.v. "Dyce, Alexander."

8. Francis Child to James Halliwell, 16 January 1849 (vol. 11, letter 19) and 2 March 1849

(vol. 11, letter 18), Halliwell-Phillipps Collection, Special Collections, University of Edinburgh Library; Lowell, 1866, quoted in Haskin 2002, 179–80. (Halliwell later changed his surname to Halliwell-Phillipps.)

9. Fry 1896, 38–41, 45–47, 50–53, 61–62, 66–73, 77, 81–82, 85, 125–26, 143; Fox 2003, 94, 113, 124, 282.

10. [Child] 1848; McMurtry 1985, 71–74; Mary Ellen Brown, "Introduction," in Brown 2001, 1–2, 7–8; George Lyman Kittredge, "Professor Child," *Atlantic Monthly* 78 (1896): 740; James Orchard Halliwell to Francis Child, February 7, 1849, John Payne Collier to Francis Child, October 25, 1855, Sir Frederic Madden to Francis Child, November 16, 1855, Charles Eliot Norton to Francis Child, October 31, 1860, Alexander Ellis to Francis Child, November 22, 1868, James Russell Lowell to Francis Child, June 11, 1883 and January 17, 1884, Francis J. Child Papers, bMS Am 1922, Houghton Library, Harvard University; Haskin 2002, 174–75. Child's monograph on Chaucer was superseded in 1884 by Bernhard ten Brink's *Chaucers Sprache und Verskunst*; Utz 2002, 88.

11. Haskin 2002, 171–79 (quotations, 176). I am grateful to Professor Haskin for many years of illumination of Donne scholarship, going back to my research on Charles Eliot Norton in the 1980s and 1990s.

12. Murphy 2003, 195–201; Freeman and Freeman 2004. Collier had in 1853 detailed the supposed 'Old Corrector's' alterations in *Notes and Emendations to the Text of Shakespeare's Plays* and in 1853 published a one-volume edition of the plays incorporating these 'emendations.'

13. John-Mitchell Kemble to Jacob Grimm, January 7, 1840, in Wiley 1971, 188; Horsman 1981, chap. 4; Young 2008, chap. 2; Simmons 1990, chap. 2; Wawn 2000, chaps. 3–7.

14. Horsman 1981; Thompson 1936, 241–46, 248–49; Henneman 1892, xlvii–xlix; Trent et al. 1921, 3:478–79.

15. Birrell 1966, 110–12; Berkhout and Gatch 1982, 13–14, 153; Ackerman and Ackerman 1979, 1–43; Matthews 1999, 116–35; [Henry Wadsworth Longfellow], "Anglo-Saxon Literature," *North American Review* 47 (1838): 92.

16. Wiley 1979; Ackerman and Ackerman 1979, passim; Whewell to J. C. Hare, n.d. ["4 January 1834" penciled in], William Whewell Papers, Add. MS a.215/30, Wren Library, Trinity College Cambridge; Bruce Dickins [1940]; Gretchen P. Ackerman, "J. M. Kemble and Sir Frederic Madden: 'Conceit and Too Much Germanism?'" in Berkhout and Gatch 1982; Kemble 1833. The poems were *Beowulf*, *The Traveler's Song*, and *The Fight at Finnesburh*.

17. Kiernan 1996, 133; Kiernan 1986; Turner 1805, 398–408; Berkhout and Gatch 1982, 155; Conybeare 1826, 30–81; [Henry Wadsworth Longfellow], "Anglo-Saxon Language and Literature," *North American Review* 33 (1831): 345–47; Savage 1949; Birrell 1966, 112–14; Kemble 1833, xiv–xix; Ackerman, "Kemble and Madden," 170; Kemble 1837. Conybeare's translation and commentary is followed (82–136) by the original Anglo-Saxon of the passages earlier rendered into modern English (with Latin translation)—followed in turn (137–55) by a collation of Thorkelin's edition with the manuscript in the British Museum. In short, this edition made a real contribution to scholarship. Conybeare died before his book got through the press; his brother finished the job. Longfellow knew Turner's discussion, Thorkelin's and Grundtvig's versions, and Conybeare's selections. The preface to Kemble's 1837 edition took the odd form of a "Postscript to the Preface" of his 1833 edition, correcting his earlier mistaken views with a redacted version of his 1836 *Stammtafel*. The *Beowulf* manuscript was one of several bound together in the so-called Nowell Codex (Vitellius A. xv in the Cotton Library).

18. John O'Donovan to Myles John O'Reilly, March 9, 1831, ff. 7–8, and September 9, [1831], f. 48; "Observations and Remarks on the Book of O'Hara, an ancient Irish MS.," twenty-four-page manuscript, ff. 21–42; all in Letters to Myles John O'Reilly, relating to

O'Hara Family of County Sligo, MS 3403, Manuscripts Department, Trinity College Dublin; Breatnach 1952. Dr. Heard was not judicious and learned enough to make it into the *Dictionary of Irish Biography*, and I have been unable to identify him. I thank my colleagues Diarmuid Ó Giolláin and Mary O'Callaghan for aid with Irish language.

19. Wellek 1955–92, vol. 1, chap. 5; Charvat 1936, 86–88; Baym 1984, 271; *Knickerbocker*, quoted in Pritchard 1956, 107. Pritchard 1942 found even significant continuing influence of Aristotelian and Horatian categories of analysis in nineteenth-century American criticism.

20. G. M. Ditchfield and Sarah Brewer, "Hurd, Richard," *Oxford Dictionary of National Biography*; Waters 2004a, 2, 5–9; Waters 2004b, 415–22; Prescott 1961, passim; O'Brien 1985, esp. chap. 5.

21. Wakefield 2001; Waters 2004a, chaps. 1–2; O'Brien 1985, passim; Jane Spencer, "Inchbald, Elizabeth," *Oxford Dictionary of National Biography*; Parrinder 1991, 67.

22. Wellek 1955–92, 2:150–57, 170; Helmholtz 1907; Barfield 1971, 6; Sauer 1981, 81–100; Coleridge 1930, 1:213. The quotation refers specifically to Shakespeare's *Venus and Adonis*.

23. Staël 1813; Schlegel 1818; Schlegel 1815; Charvat 1936, 61; Prescott 1961, 1:5, 22. In noting a comment of Schlegel on Tasso, Prescott is careful to put "(F)" after his name, to distinguish Friedrich from August. René Wellek, the most authoritative historian of modern literary criticism, William Charvat, the pioneering historian of American criticism, and Michael O'Brien, the doyen of Southern intellectual history (writing with respect to Southern critics) agree that August Schlegel's lectures were the most influential German literary criticism in the English-speaking world. Wellek 1955–92, 2:36; Charvat 1936, 61–62 and passim; O'Brien 2004, 692. But, against these weighty judgments, consider the data compiled systematically in Schilling 1972.

24. Blair 1783, lecture 6.

25. Pritchard 1963, 91; Walhout 1996; Channing 1890, 295; Channing 1853, ix.

26. Prickett 1991, 66–68, 86–88, 146–47, 186–88, 210–12.

27. Anger 2005, chap. 1, esp. pp. 45–46; Matthew Arnold, "The Bishop [Colenso] and the Philosopher [Spinoza]," *Macmillan's Magazine* 39 (1863): 245 ("arithmetical") and passim; Arnold 1960–77, 3:277–80, 6:244 ("Bible-language").

28. Walhout 1996, 685–90, 692 (Allen quotation); Moses Stuart, "Are the Same Principles of Interpretation to be Applied to the Scriptures as to Other Books," *Biblical Repository* 2 (1832): 124–37 (quotation, 135).

29. Blair 1783, 2:312, 314–15; Stovall 1955, 16–35, 43–52.

30. Legaré 1845, 2:372–74, 377–79, 381, 407, 410, 415, 424, 426, 431–32, 440; O'Brien 1985, 82. The articles here cited originally appeared in the *Southern Review* in 1830 and 1831.

31. Moody and Beckett 1959, 159, 592.

32. Eichhorn 1812, [1]; Eichhorn 1796, vi–vii. The umlaut in *Littërärgeschichte* seems to have disappeared around 1800, and the doubled *t* in the twentieth century.

33. Niggl 1991, 265–66; Hart 1953; Prescott 1961, 1:9, 14. Strictly speaking, Bouterwek did not become professor until 1802, although he had lectured at the university for the preceding ten years. The full title of Dunlop's triple-decker was *The History of Fiction: Being a Critical Account of the Most Celebrated Prose Works of Fiction, from the Earliest Greek Romances to the Novels of the Present Day*.

34. Collier 1831; Wellek 1955–92, 3:92–93; Hallam 1837–39. The title page of Hallam's first volume spells out the number of each century; the titles of the remaining three volumes label the centuries with ordinal numbers; thus one commonly sees the title in that form.

35. Marsch 1975, 17–18; Niggl 1991, 265–66; Müller 1840, [1]–2; Legaré 1845, 2:299 (reprinted from *Southern Review*, February 1830).

36. Kramer 1992, 72–74; Richard Henry Wilde, "The Author to the Reader," in "The Life

and Times of Dante with Sketches of the State of Florence, and of his friends and enemies," unpublished MS, n.d., box 5, R. H. Wilde Papers, Library of Congress (capitalization sic), xvii. Thanks to Professor Michael O'Brien for supplying a photocopy of Wilde's preface.

37. [Hillard et al.] 1876, 1:76, 79–80, 95 ("amusement"), 105–7, 121–24, 127–29, 131–32, 134, chaps. 9–12, chaps. 21–25; [Hillard et al.] 1876, vol. 2, chaps. 1–9; Niggl 1991, 266n; Jaksić 2007, 84–92, 115–21; Ticknor 1849, 1:v–vii; Robert L. Gale, "George Ticknor," *American National Biography* (size of library). Ticknor not only studied with Eichhorn but socialized with and became personally attached to him. Bouterwek does not appear in [Hillard et al.] 1876—perhaps because by 1876 his name meant nothing to a New England readership—but it seems unlikely that Ticknor had no contact with him, given Ticknor's interest in literary history.

38. Ticknor 1849, passim; Jaksić 2007, chap. 2. Ticknor's own division was not by volume but by three periods, not corresponding to the volumes.

39. Jaksić 2007, chap. 3; Hart 1954, 76; Gale, "Ticknor" (publication dates of translations).

CHAPTER 7. "AN EPOCH IN HISTORICAL SCIENCE"

The quotation in this chapter's title comes from an unsigned review of *The Life and Letters of Barthold George [sic] Niebuhr, Princeton Review* 24 (1852): 705.

1. Grafton 1983.
2. Since late antiquity Christians had understood the "nascens puer"—infant boy—of Vergil's Fourth Eclogue as prophesying the birth of Jesus.
3. Grafton 1983, 179–81.
4. Sandys 2009, vol. 3, chap. 29; Claudia Ungefehr-Kortus, "Böckh-Hermann-Auseinandersetzung," in *Der Neue Pauly*, Brill Online Reference Works, http://reference works.brillonline.com/entries/der-neue-pauly/bockh-hermann-auseinandersetzung-rwg -e1305720, accessed April 13, 2012; Bravo 1968, 69–71, 85; Barthold Georg Niebuhr to Adam Moltke, August 15, 1812, in Winkworth et al. 1852, 1:350. Boeckh and Hermann had other grounds for disagreement. Boeckh (who had studied with Schleiermacher) believed the philologist needed a systematic hermeneutic theory to interpret texts properly; Hermann thought that linguistic expertise sufficed to penetrate the 'mind' of a people and thus understand their writings.
5. Walther 1993, esp. 139–48, 321–487, 500–523, 556–59; Momigliano 1982, 3, 8 (quotation); Niebuhr to "a young man who wished to devote himself to philology," summer 1822, and Niebuhr to [Dora Hensler], November 24, 1810, in Winkworth et al. 1852, 2:244 and 1:319; Pfeiffer 1976, 183–84; Momigliano 1994, 232–36. In Momigliano's comment, "modern study" is the operative term; see Moore, Morris, and Bayliss 2008, 187–218.
6. Lewis 1997; Gooch 1959, 30; Wolfhart Unte, "Karl Offried Müller," in Briggs and Calder 1990, 310–20; Feldman and Richardson 1972, 387–89; 416–18; Blok 1994; Müller, *Handbuch der Archäologie der Kunst* (*Handbook of the Archaeology of Art*, 1830); Müller, *History of the Literature of Ancient Greece* (1840).
7. August Boeckh, "Rede zur Eröffung der eilten Versammlung Deutscher Philologen, Schulmänner und Orientalisten, gehalten zu Berlin am 30. September 1850," in Boeckh 1858–71, 2:184, 189 (quotation); Boeckh 1886; Bravo 1968, 79–96. Range of years and number of semesters are from Ernst Bratuscheck's foreword to Boeckh 1886, iii. 'Encyclopedia' here carried its older meaning of a circle of knowledge (in this case, the knowledge needed to undertake philological studies at a sophisticated level) rather than an exhaustive compendium.

8. Sandys 2009, 3:393–408, 426–29; Clarke 1945, 87–88.

9. F. M. Turner 1993, 286–87; Daunton 2005, 170–71; Stray 1998, 62–63; Christopher Stray, "Key, Thomas Hewitt," and W. W. Wroth, rev. Martin D. W. Jones, "Long, George," in *Oxford Dictionary of National Biography*.

10. Horsfall 1974, 455; Stray 1998, 61–62; Dowling 1986, 54–55; Dockhorn 1950, 17–19, 22–23; B. G. Niebuhr to John Welsford Cowell, October 24 and December 22, 1826, February 1 and June 26, 1827, and February 9, 1828, printed in J. W. Donaldson to the Editor, *Journal of Classical and Sacred Philology* 4 (1859): 360–73; Niebuhr 1828–31; Connop Thirlwall to W. J. Bayne, 16 March 1821, Miscellaneous Letters, MS Eng. letters d. 111, ff. 146–47, Western Manuscripts, Bodleian Library; William Whewell to Julius Hare, n.d. ["1 July 1820" penciled in], Add. MS a.215/4, Wren Library, Trinity College Cambridge; Distad 1979, 74, 112; Gooch 1959, 22; Thirlwall 1936, 41–42, 61; Stray 2004, 299–300, 303–6; "Preface," *Philological Museum* 1 (1831): ii, iv; [Hare], "On English Orthography," *Philological Museum* 1 (1831): 640–78; Julius Hare to William Whewell, 13 December [1833?], Add. MS a.206/161, Wren Library, Trinity College Cambridge. Hare and Thirlwall translated Niebuhr's second, expanded edition (1827–28); a mediocre translation of the 1812 edition by Francis Augustus Walker was published in 1827 but immediately eclipsed by the Hare-Thirlwall version. Niebuhr's third volume, published posthumously in 1832, appeared in English translation by William Smith and Leonhard Schmitz in 1842. It is likely but not proven that Thirlwall met Niebuhr in Rome in the winter of 1818–19.

11. Dockhorn 1950, 22; Boeckh 1828; Müller 1830 (quotation, vii); Calder, Smith, and Vaio 2002, xii–xiii; G. C. Lewis to K. O. Müller, 20 August [1828] and 6 December [1828], in Calder et al. 2002, 1–3. Hare left Cambridge to take a parish in the gift of his family; Thirlwall was kicked out after he objected in print to compulsory chapel. Lewis could not write to Müller in German, and he had to ask the author to reply in Roman characters because German script (*Kurrentschrift*) baffled Lewis. The printer insisted on censoring pederasty; G. C. Lewis to K. O. Müller, 6 December [1828], in Calder et al. 2002, 4.

12. "Critical Notices," *New Monthly Magazine* 33 (1831): 158; [John Roles Fishlake], "Greek-and-German and Greek-and-English Lexicography," *Quarterly Review* 51 (1834): 144–45.

13. B. G. Niebuhr to [Amalie Behrens (his fiancée)], February 11, 1799, in Winkworth et al. 1852, 1:137–38; Isaac Ambrose Eccles to Joseph Cooper Walker, September 10 and September 13, 1802, MS 1461, folio vol./ff. 127–30 and 131v–132r, Manuscript Department, Trinity College Dublin; *Museum Criticum* 2 (1814–26): 152–54; Liddon 1893, 1:72; [Arthur P. Stanley], "Archdeacon Hare," *Quarterly Review* 97 (1855): 17; [Thomas Arnold], "Early History of Rome," *Quarterly Review* 27 (1822): 281; Calder and Schlesier 1998, 7. *The Wellesley Index to Victorian Periodicals* goes back only to 1824, but it identifies Arnold as author of a later review of Niebuhr, in which he says that "we" mentioned Niebuhr in the 1822 article: [Thomas Arnold], "Early Roman History," *Quarterly Review* 32 (1825): 67. For Milman see the citations in chapter 8.

14. Stray 2007b, 2–10; Stray 1998, 60–62; Pattison 1969, 151; Clough 1990, 25; Bristed 1852, 1:88–91; Turner 1981, 5–6, 324–38.

15. Clarke 1945, 102; Charles James Blomfield to Peter Elmsley, October 14, 1812, quoted in Horsfall 1974, 459–60; Dyce 1972, 166; [Hazlitt] 1824, 2:79; Wilamowitz 1982, 83–84; Porson 1814; Roger D. Dawe, "Richard Porson," in Briggs and Calder 1990, 376–88; Brink 1986, 102–3.

16. Stray 2007c; Wilamowitz 1982, 84; Clarke 1945, 85, 88–89, 97–99; Horsfall 1974.

17. [J. H. Monk], "Memoir of Edward Valentine Blomfield," *Museum Criticum* 2 (1814–26): 520–28; Blomfield, "Account of the Present State of Classical Literature in Germany," *Museum Criticum* 1 (1813–14): 273–78; Horsfall 1974, 468–69, 471–73.

18. *Museum Criticum* 2 (1814–26): 155–204, 329–39; Horsfall 1974, 455, 463–66, 469–70; J. H. Monk to William Whewell, 17 December 1827, Add. MS a.209/75, Wren Library, Trinity College Cambridge; Stray 2004, 290–98; Stray 2007a, 16–17. My generalizations about the *Museum Criticum* are subject to the limitation that the third issue was missing in the set I used.

19. *Classical Journal* 1 (1810): iii–iv. On Valpy's circle and the *Classical Journal*, see Clarke 1945, 85–86, 93–96, 101. The Heyne biography appeared in 19, no. 37 (1819), and 20, no. 39 (1819): 17–42. (I have seen only the second part and know of the first from it.)

20. A. E. Housman, introduction to Manilius 1937, 1:xlii; Lloyd-Jones 1982, 15; *Philological Museum* 1 (1831): 1; Clarke 1945, 100–101.

21. Donaldson 1839, 29; Brink 1986, 148–49; Lloyd-Jones 1982, 185 (Pattison quotation); Distad 1979, 74; Dockhorn 1950, 23 (Hare quotation).

22. *Philological Museum* 1 (1832): ii–iii; Wiese 1854, 76.

23. Distad 1979, 112; John William Donaldson, "On the Life and Writings of Karl Otfried Müller," in Donaldson 1858, 1:xxi–xxiv; Calder and Schlesier 1998, 14–16; Stray 1998, 100; George Cornewall Lewis to Thomas Coates, June 25, [1834], and March 6, 1835, Society for the Diffusion of Useful Knowledge Papers, Special Collections, University College London Library; George Cornewall Lewis to Friedrich Max Müller, July 4, 1834, in Calder et al. 2002, 75.

24. This paragraph rests on scanning the seven volumes of the *Classical Museum* and dipping into some of the articles.

25. Cole 2011, 175–85; Winterer 2007; George Ticknor to Stephen Higginson, May 20, 1816, in T. W. Higginson, "Göttingen and Harvard Eighty Years Ago," *Harvard Graduates' Magazine* 6 (1897–98): 8; Edward Everett to William Whewell, 26 February 1847, Add. MS a.203/111, Wren Library, Trinity College Cambridge; [Levi Frisbie], "Wells' Edition of Tacitus," *North American Review* 6 (1818): 324.

26. Handlin 1983; George Ticknor to Elisha Ticknor, November 10, 1815, quoted in Hillard et al. 1876, 1:73n.

27. Miller 1970, 2:325; [George Bancroft], "Economy of Athens," *North American Review* 32 (1831): 344–67; [Hugh Swinton Legaré], "The Public Economy of Athens," *Southern Review* no. 16 (1832): 265–326; Winterer 2002, 54–56, 78; Diehl 1978, 66–67, 104–5; Briggs 1994, 480; Collins 1914, 139–40; Donnegan 1832.

28. Joseph Cogswell to Stephen Higginson, July 13, 1817, in Higginson, "Göttingen and Harvard Eighty Years Ago," 13 ("very few"); James Russell Lowell to Charles Eliot Norton, 15 February 1889, Norton Papers, Houghton Library, Harvard University (Lowell got the story about Bancroft and German from Bancroft); Diehl 1978; George Ticknor to Elisha Ticknor, November 10, 1815, quoted in Hillard et al. 1876, 1:73n. Willard's father, a Harvard president inclined toward the natural sciences, was a foreign member of the Royal Society of Göttingen and may have introduced his son to the language. A few others in eastern Massachusetts could read German. It is impossible to say how many Americans went to study classical philology; it was housed in the faculties of philosophy, and there is no systematic way of calculating how many studied what within these faculties. From decades of poking around, I suspect the numbers were fairly small before 1850. The German language persisted in many communities, springing from German immigration; learned men from these communities helped to mediate German theology to Americans; they do not seem to have done the same vis-à-vis Altertumswissenschaft.

29. O'Brien 2004, 331; Gildersleeve 1987, 3–4. O'Brien, 331, estimates that around 1800 German had already displaced Italian as the fourth or fifth language of educated Southerners (after Latin, Greek, and French) and eventually even rivaled French.

30. Winterer 2002, 49–62; Felton 1833, v; Felton 1831, 16, 18, 20; Andrews Norton, Dexter

Lectures, 1819, esp. nos. 5 and 10, MSS, Andrews Norton Papers, Houghton Library, Harvard University; Woolsey 1862, 7–8.

31. Sears, Edwards, and Felton 1843; quotations 20, 27–28.

32. Winterer 2002, 6, 92; Paul Shorey, "Fifty Years of Classical Studies in America," *Transactions and Proceedings of the American Philological Association* 50 (1919): 35–36. Felton's 1833 version of Wolf's edition of the *Iliad*, with Felton's own notes in English to enhance student appreciation, was apparently the first American publication of a Greek text derived from German scholarship: "an exact reprint of the Leipzig edition, published by Tauchnitz in 1829" (Felton 1833, iii). Felton also edited Aristophanes's *Clouds* (1841) and *Birds* (1849), Isocrates's *Panegyricus* (1847) and Aeschylus's *Agamemnon* (1847) and translated writings of a couple of contemporary German philologists. Woolsey 1862, 10–11. Woolsey himself edited Euripides's *Alcestis* (1834), Sophocles's *Antigone* (1835) and *Electra*; Winterer 2002, 92n65, and Library of Congress catalog.

33. Winterer 2002, 84.

34. *American Journal of Philology* 23 (1902): 110; Gildersleeve 1998, 45, 67, 70–71, 86; Gildersleeve 1909, 41–42; Ward W. Briggs Jr., "*Sophrosyne*: Beginnings, 1851–1856," in Gildersleeve 1987, 4–6; Briggs and Benario 1986, 66.

35. B[asil]. L[anneau]. G[ildersleeve]., "Necessity of the Classics," *Southern Quarterly Review* 9 (1854): 157, 161–62; Gildersleeve specified the achievements of both German textual criticism and Altertumswissenschaft at 162–63.

36. Tylor 1871, 1:38.

37. Gildersleeve 1998, 47, 90 ("masters"); Dyson 2006, 53–54, 168.

38. Trigger 2006, 55–56; Grafton 2009, 138–39; Spon 1685, "Praefatio," unpaginated [1–2]; *Oxford English Dictionary*, s.v. "archaeology"; Marchand 1996, 41. Trigger (56) called Spon "the first person to use the term archaeology in its modern sense to designate the investigation of the material remains of former human societies." Spon did actually travel in Greece and Asia Minor, with an English companion, and survey antiquities—one of the vanishingly few Europeans to do so; Stoneman 1987, 61–81.

39. Trigger 2006, 57–58; Dyson 2006, chaps. 1–2 (Corneto/Tarquinia, 34–35); Michaelis 1908, 60–61; Fitton 1996, 31; Dyson 1998, 69.

40. Dyson 2006, 45–47; Trigger 2006, 60; Wilson 1964, 31; Marchand 1996, 62–64.

41. Trigger 2006, 57; Marchand 1996, 10–11, 56–58, 67–68; Welcker 1827; Michaelis 1908, 62–68, 299; Dyson 2006, 31, 35–36, 168.

42. Momigliano 1994, 310–11; Marchand 1996, 40–43 (quoting Gerhard and Jahn), 64; Michaelis 1908, 297; Trigger 2006, 62; Gaertringen 1908.

43. [Michaelis] 1879, 8–31, 47–53; Dyson 2006, 30–34, 42–44; Marchand 1996, 53–62; Ceserani 2012, 137–47, 154–58.

44. Dyson 2006, 45, 50, 53; Marchand 1996, 68.

45. Fitton 1996, 39–40; Dyson 2006, 40–41, 55–58.

46. Dyson 2006, 7–8, 66, 69–70, 135–37; Clarke 1945, 191–99; Stoneman 1987, 147–60, 168–79, 268; George Gordon, Lord Byron, "The Curse of Minerva" (1811); Fitton 1996, 51; Gell 1804, 55–56, 114–17; Allen 1999, 44–45, 47, 73, 76; Moore, Morris, and Bayliss 2008, 169–83; J. M. Wagstaff, "Leake, William Martin," *Oxford Dictionary of National Biography*; MacCormack 2010, 300–301. Elgin had originally meant only to have his crew make pictures and casts of Athenian monuments, in the spirit of Stuart and Revett; he changed his aims when he learned of the parlous situation of the antiquities.

47. Dyson 1998, 6–7, 9–10, 15–20, 22–23, 25; Charles Eliot Norton, "The First American Classical Archaeologist," *The American Journal of Archaeology and of the History of the Fine Arts* 1 (1885): 3–9. Students of American history remember Biddle as president of the Bank of the United States during Andrew Jackson's Bank War of 1832. Poinsett—diplomat, politi-

cian, avid gardener—brought back from a stint as the first United States minister to Mexico the scarlet-flowered plant now called the poinsettia.

48. Connop Thirlwall to William Whewell, 18 November 1842, Add. MS a.213/178, Wren Library, Trinity College Cambridge; Dyson 2006, 70–71, 134; Stoneman 1987, 162–64.

49. Stoneman 1987, 183–86, 188–90, 209–15; David Watkin, "Cockerell, Charles Robert," *Oxford Dictionary of National Biography*; Dyson 2006, 52; Brand 1998, 140–43. Cockerell was first to discover entasis but not first to publish. For clarity, I say the Temple of Aphaia, its modern identification; in Cockerell's day it was thought to be dedicated to Zeus Panhellenius; Dyson 2006, 134. Xanthus is the Romanized Hellenistic name (Ξάνθος) for the Lycian Arñna, present-day Kınık in Turkey's Antalya Province.

50. Stoneman 1987, 194, 198–200, 212; Dyson 2006, 136–37.

51. Dyson 2006, 137; R. C. Jebb, "Sir C. T. Newton," *Journal of Hellenic Studies* 14 (1894): xlix–l; William Cureton to Philip Bliss, n.d. [March 1840], Add. MSS 34582/ff. 5–6, Charles Newton to Philip Bliss, May 7, 1849, and May 18, 1849, Add. MSS 34582/ff. 141–44, British Library.

52. Charles Newton to Philip Bliss, 19 February 1847, Add. MSS 34582/ff. 120–23, British Library.

53. Wilson 1964, 15–19, 38–39; Wortham 1971, 49–54.

54. Wilson 1964, 31–32; Wortham 1971, 60–65, 71–74.

55. Trigger 2006, 70; Stanley Lane-Poole, rev. Elizabeth Baigent, "Rich, Claudius James," *Oxford Dictionary of National Biography*.

56. Wilson 1964, 40; Brackman 1978; Damrosch 2007, chap. 3; Jonathan Parry, "Layard, Sir Austen Henry," *Oxford Dictionary of National Biography*; Denis Wright, "Rassam, Hormuzd," *Oxford Dictionary of National Biography*.

57. Williams 1999, 89, 99, chap. 5, 190, 192–94, 221; Robinson 1841, 1:xiv.

58. Williams 1999, chap. 7, 298; Robinson 1841, 1:[v], x, 81–86; Exodus 12:37–38, 14:19–29. The book was published in Boston, New York, and London (by John Murray), and Halle (in German translation, probably by Robinson's German wife, a well-known author). Robinson returned to Palestine in 1852, resulting in a revised edition of the original work plus a supplementary volume.

59. Brand 1998, v–vi, 24–26, 33, 93–101, 125–37; Levine 1986, 7–19; Charles Newton to Philip Bliss, 5 March [1845], Charles Newton to Philip Bliss, "Easter Sunday Alfred" [1845], Add. MSS 34582/ff. 70–74, Charles Newton to Philip Bliss, January 4[?], [1846], Add. MSS 34582/ff. 88–93, printed broadside, n.d. [ca. March 1, 1845], in Philip Bliss Correspondence, Add. MSS 34576, f. 64, British Library.

60. Charles Newton to Philip Bliss, January 4[?], [1846], Add. MSS 34582/ff. 88–93, British Library; Robinson 1841, 2:620n1, 3:117n4, 3:220n5; Layard 1849, passim.

61. Fellows 1841, v, 272–78; Ezekiel 23:14–15; Charles Newton to Philip Bliss, February 19, 1847, cited above.

62. Levine 1999, 160n6; Stuchtey and Wende 2000, 74–75; Peardon 1933, 24; see also chapter 4.

63. Oleson and Brown 1976, 163 (quotation re MHS), 252–53 (quotation from petition to Massachusetts legislature requesting charter for AAS); Lawson 1998, 128; Callcott 1970, 35–36, 49; Freeman 2001, 262–63; Cheng 2008, 132–38.

64. Kenyon 1984, 89–96; Peardon 1933, 295–307 (quotation, 295); Levy 1964. For a broader European overview, see Blouin and Rosenberg 2011, 20–35.

65. Cheng 2008, chap. 2; Miller 1970, 2:145, 322.

66. Lester H. Cohen, "Foreword" in Warren 1994, 1:xvii; Warren 1994, 1:xli; Cheng 2008, 60–63; Burrow 2008, 354–65. The title of Weems's biography was *A History of the Life and Death, Virtues and Exploits, of General George Washington*.

67. [Johann Wilhelm] Loebell, "On the Character of Niebuhr as an Historian," in Winkworth et al. 1852, 2:431–32 (quotation); Christ 1982, 39–40; Momigliano 1982, 8–11.

68. Stephens 1895, 1:54–56; William Prescott, quoted in Ticknor 1873, 41; Winterer 2007; G. F. H[olmes]., "Roman History," *Southern and Western Literary Messenger and Review* 12 (1846): 507.

69. Turner 1981, chap. 5; Jenkyns 1980, 14–15, 245–46; Momigliano 1994, 1, 16; Moore, Morris, and Bayliss 2008, 249–52; Stuchtey and Wende 2000, 9; Bammel 1984, 143 (quotation).

70. Pinkerton 1794, 1:xxiv–xxv; Peardon 1933, 146, 221, 272; Birrell 1966, 115.

71. Jones 2001; P. Phillips 1996, 180–81; Peardon 1933, 277–83; Kenyon 1984, 86–89; Stuchtey and Wende 2000, 75; Shea 1969, 42, 52–56. A journal that Lingard kept in 1800 shows him reading Luigi/Ludovico Antonio Muratori (1672–1750), the great Italian antiquary and historian who worked in the style of the Maurists. Shea 1969, 16.

72. Shea 1969, 47–51; Kelley 2003, 95–96; Peter Phillips, "Lingard, John," *Oxford Dictionary of National Biography*.

73. Gardiner 1969, ix; Cheng 2008, 125–28; entries dated May 17, 1830, November 3, 1828, May 12, 1839, and December 18, 1825, in Prescott 1961, 1:65, 96, 143, 2:15; Kelley 2003, 289; Carlyle 1845, 1:24; Ticknor 1873, 90; Burrow 2008, 402–4. The victim of Carlyle's bile was Rev. Mark Noble, author of *Memoirs of the Protectoral House of Cromwell*, 2 vols. (London, 1787).

74. Levin 1959, 11, 22; Charles Eliot Norton to James Russell Lowell, May 7, 1858, James Russell Lowell Papers, Houghton Library, Harvard University ("flayed"); Herbst 1965, 101; Handlin 1984, 57–68, 100; Kelley 2003, 290–93. In referring to "exhaustive exploration of archival sources," Kelley exaggerates the considerable original research these historians did.

75. Mahon 1853, vol. 6, appendix, iv–xxv; Sparks 1852; Callcott 1970, 130–31. Lord Mahon was Philip Henry Stanhope, known better as, after 1855, the fifth Earl Stanhope.

76. Bammel 1984, 139–42; Stuchtey and Wende 2000, 123–57; Cheng 2008, 26; Christ 1982, 39.

77. Guilland 1899, 39; Loebell, "Niebuhr as an Historian," in Winkworth et al. 1852, 2:430–31, 433–35; Bammel 1984, 145, 148–50; A.J.H. Reeve, "Arnold, Thomas," *Oxford Dictionary of National Biography*; Thomas Arnold to Julius Hare, October 7, 1833, in Stanley 1846, 222; Macaulay and Grote, quoted in Gooch 1959, 22–23; Browne 1996, 127; Liddell 1855, 1:iv.

78. Callcott 1970, 10; entry dated January 1, 1826, in Prescott 1961, 1:65; "National Literature, the Exponent of National Character," *Princeton Review* 24 (1852): 209–10; Lucian Minor, "A Few Thoughts on the Death of John C. Calhoun," *Southern Literary Messenger* 16 (1850): 378; [Edgar Allan Poe], "Reminiscences of Niebuhr," *Southern Literary Messenger* 2 (1836): 125; Martha Fenton Hunter, "The Seldens of Sherwood, Chapters XIX–XXII," *Southern Literary Messenger* 16 (1850): 109; "Rome and the Romans," *Southern Quarterly Review* 6 (Oct 1844): 290; "False Views of History," *Southern Quarterly Review*, n.s., 6 (1852): 46; review of *Life and Letters of Niebuhr*, *Princeton Review* 24 (1852): 704–5; "Cimon and Pericles," *Southern Quarterly Review*, n.s., 3 (1851): 341.

79. G. F. H[olmes]., "Roman History," *Southern and Western Literary Messenger and Review* 12 (1846): 509; Thomas Arnold to Julius Hare, October 7, 1833, in Stanley 1846, 222 (quotation); Thirlwall 1936, 42; Gooch 1959, 297–98.

80. Thirlwall 1936, passim; J. W. Clark, rev. H. C. G. Matthew, "Thirlwall, (Newell) Connop," *Oxford Dictionary of National Biography*; Kelley 2003, 88, 90; Thirlwall 1835–44; Momigliano 1994, 16–18, 20; Gooch 1959, 290–91; Clarke 1962, 104–5; Clarke 1945, 102–8; Moore, Morris, and Bayliss 2008, 247–55; Thirlwall 1852. Thirlwall finished the first volume while still at Trinity College, and the introduction is dated from there.

81. Clarke 1962, 5–80.

82. Clarke 1962, 106; Turner 1981, 207–8, 229; Moore, Morris, and Bayliss 2008, 255–68, 270–73; Momigliano 1994, 18–19; Wilamowitz 1893, 1:378.

83. Calder and Trzaskoma 1996, 21, 41–42; Peardon 1933, 266–68; Momigliano 1994, 21–22; Forbes 1952.

84. Thomas Carlyle to Rev. William Jacobson, 20 January 1846, Add. MSS 34576, ff. 11–12, British Library.

85. Lewis 1855, quotations at 1:13 and 2:556–57; Momigliano 1955, 255–62; Raskolnikoff 1992, 762–77; Stuchtey and Wende 2000, 97; Dockhorn 1950, 125–26; Kemble 1876. Lewis wanted Niebuhr to apply "those tests of credibility which are consistently applied to modern history." Niebuhr, in contrast, had thought it worthwhile to probe legendary stories to learn what such fictions in literary sources can reveal about the changing shape and meanings of the legends themselves—a matter that seemed to him, formed by Altertumswissenschaft, worthy of investigation. See, e.g., his discussion of the story of Aeneas and the Trojan refugees in Latium: Niebuhr 1828–31, 1:150–67. Here is perhaps a telling difference between the real philologist, German-style, and the philologic historian, English-style.

86. "National Literature, the Exponent of National Character," *Princeton Review* 24 (1852): 209–10.

Chapter 8. "Grammatical and Exegetical Tact"

This chapter's title comes from Moses Stuart, translator's introduction to J.A.H. Tittmann, "Use of the Particle 'INA in the N. Testament," *Biblical Repository* 5 (1835): 84.

1. Hodge 1822, 28 (quotation).

2. Rogerson 1984, 52.

3. Rogerson 1992, esp. 47–61; Howard 2000, chaps. 1, 3 (quotation, 86–87).

4. Rogerson 1984, pt. 1 (esp. 139, where Rogerson sketches the distribution among universities of German scholars adhering to the different schools of biblical studies). More generally, on the shift from a 'naive' reading of the Bible as history to a 'disillusioned' historicist reading, see Frei 1974. To understand the course of German biblical criticism in its own terms, as distinct from its influence in Britain and America, would also require exploring its interactions with philosophy—especially Hegel's.

5. Neill 1964, 12–17, 19–27; Harris 1975, chap. 2 passim, chap. 12; Howard 2000, chap. 3.

6. Rogerson 1984, 158–59; Harding 1985, passim; Prickett 1991, 201–8; Giltner 1988, 7–8; James Turner, "Andrews Norton," *American National Biography*; Gutjahr 2011, 90, 99; Williams 1999, 95, 108. Stuart, Norton, and Robinson devoted their major scholarly efforts to biblical scholarship; Hodge was more of a theological generalist, especially as his career went on.

7. Turner 1999, 26.

8. M. Stuart, "Genuineness of the Gospels," *American Biblical Repository* 11 (1838): 265. Stuart was singling out Andrews Norton as one of the few.

9. Rogerson 1984, 192; Allen 1883, 68; [Hugh James Rose?], "Schleiermacher—On the Gospel of St. Luke," *British Critic, Quarterly Theological Review and Ecclesiastical Record* 2 (1827): 351; Schleiermacher 1993, ix ("candour"); [Stanley], "Archdeacon Hare," 21; Thirlwall ("in the dark"), quoted in Thirlwall 1936, 29; Hodge 1822, 43.

10. Hodge 1822, 43, 45, 48 (quotations); Gutjahr 2011, chaps. 17–19; Stewart 1990, 135–49; Liddon 1893, vol. 1, chaps. 4–5; Forrester 1989, 32–49; Edward B. Pusey to John Henry Newman, November 25, 1826 (from Berlin), in Liddon 1893, 1:102; Giltner 1988, 9–11; Peter G. Cobb, "Pusey, Edward Bouverie," *Oxford Dictionary of National Biography*. It is telling

whom Hodge studied with in Germany (from late winter 1827 through spring 1828): principally the conservative scholars Tholuck (Halle) and Hengstenberg (Berlin) and the moderate Gesenius (Halle); Hodge also visited the more radical Ewald at Göttingen, among others.

11. Pusey 1828, 135n1; Moses Stuart, "Samaritan and Hebrew Pentateuch," *North American Review* 22 (1826): 278 (quotation), 282–302.

12. Williams 1999, 171, 173–74, 185–86, 188–89, 197, 337–38; Benjamin R. Foster, "Edward Robinson," *American National Biography*.

13. C[harles]. K[ent]., "Alford, Henry, D. D.," *Encyclopædia Britannica*, 9th ed. (quotations); W. H. Fremantle, "Alford, Henry," rev. Roger T. Stearn, *Oxford Dictionary of National Biography*; Distad 1979, 112; Smart et al. 1985, 3:149–50; Metzger and Ehrman 2005, 62–64, 67–68. It was Alford's bad luck to publish before Constantin Tischendorf's edition of the complete Sinaiticus in 1862 and his much improved edition of Vaticanus in 1867.

14. Rogerson 1984, 155–56; Gerard Carruthers, "Geddes, Alexander," *Oxford Dictionary of National Biography*; Geddes 1800, 26, 35–37; Johnstone 2004, 26–28; Fuller 1984, 89–90, 104. Geddes is principally remembered by biblical scholars today for articulating the 'fragmentary hypothesis' of the composition of the Pentateuch, in opposition to the 'documentary hypothesis' developed by Eichhorn from Astruc's insight. Johnstone 2004 provides an overview of Geddes's biblical philology at 1–20. I refer to Geddes's bishop (George Hay); strictly speaking, Hay was bishop only of a see *in partibus infidelium* and in Scotland a vicar-apostolic, since the Roman Catholic hierarchy was not restored in Scotland until 1878.

15. Robert K. Forrest, "Marsh, Herbert," *Oxford Dictionary of National Biography*; Marsh 1828, 51–52. Marsh met the anglophile Michaelis while living in Germany. Forrest mentions Buckminster sending students to study with Marsh (though he calls Buckminster "John"). 'Unitarian' is slightly anachronistic; New England 'liberal' Congregationalists did not get the Unitarian label until about a decade later. For the Harvard edition of Griesbach's New Testament, see Brown 1969, 23–24.

16. O. W. Jones, "Ollivant, Alfred," *Oxford Dictionary of National Biography*; Rogerson 1984, 170–73, 192–96, and chap. 14; Grodzins 2002, 79, 133, 372–74; Brown 1969, 164–69; Ellis 1980, 1. The very orthodox Moses Stuart apparently instigated Parker's 'translation.' This is fascinating. Stuart did not hesitate to cite De Wette selectively, but he might have lost his job if he had ventured a translation himself. One almost wonders if Stuart in this case was trying to game the system.

17. Duncan 1997; George F. Moore, "An Appreciation of Professor Toy," *American Journal of Semitic Languages and Literatures* 36 (1919): 3–5; David G. Lyon, "Crawford Howell Toy," *Harvard Theological Review* 13 (1920): 7–11; Brown 1969, 164, 168 (quotations). Toy landed on his feet, moving to Harvard in 1880, as the first non-Unitarian on the divinity school faculty.

18. Stevenson 1986, 150.

19. A Society of Clergymen 1829, [iii], v; Turner 1863, 166–67; Schleiermacher 1993, v–cliv; Rose 1825, 51–54, 67 (quotation), 68–69, 80 (quotation), 82–83, 126–27, 134–35, 141–61; Rogerson 1984, 166.

20. Stuart 1827, iii–vi, 2; Giltner 1988, 33–34, chap. 4; Conser 1993, 28; Gutjahr 2011, 143–45, 275; Turner 2003, chap. 2; [Charles Hodge], "Gleanings from the German Periodicals," *Biblical Repertory and Princeton Review* 9 (1837): 198–200. For analyses of Stuart's and Hodge's attitudes toward German criticism, see Kamen 2004, 49–56, 63–70. Hodge's journal began simply as *Biblical Repertory*; its title changed several times during its century-long career. I use the form that had the longest run (1837–72).

21. Sperling 1992, 2, 8, 20, 34–39 (quotation, 37), 203; Orlinsky 1955, 374–75, 379–82;

Sussman 1995, esp. 159–60, 186–93. Isaac Wise in the United States did write on biblical history, as part of a larger history of the Jews, and attacked higher criticism.

22. Orlinsky 1955, 378–79; [Robinson] 1843; Goldman 2004, 149–50 and chap. 8; Henry Neill, "Reminiscences of Dr. Isaac Nordheimer," *New Englander and Yale Review* 33 (1874): 506–13; Williams 1999, 287; "Correspondence between Prof. M. Stuart and Dr. I. Nordheimer, on the Use and Omission of the Hebrew Article in Some Important Passages of Scripture," *American Biblical Repository*, 2nd ser., 6 (1841): 404–18.

23. Pusey 1854, 61–62; Niebuhr 1828–31, 1:25–26, 137–38; Bammel 1984, 146. Pusey also reported (62n) Heyne's fantasy that the English bishops interdicted Wolf's *Prolegomena* because it would inevitably be applied to the Bible. Pusey said he had learned of this in Göttingen in 1825.

24. Samuel Wilberforce, "Essays and Reviews," *Quarterly Review* 109 (1861): 293; Stuchtey and Wende 2000, 91; Ellis 1980, 1; Müller 1901, 278; F. D. Maurice to D. J. Vaughan, November 22, 1865, in Maurice 1884, 2:509; Thomas Arnold to Chevalier Bunsen, February 10, 1835, in Stanley 1846, 243. "Young Renan" is, of course, Ernest.

25. Milman 1900, esp. 83–85; Clements 1995, 248; Gooch 1959, 479; Forbes 1952, 34–35; [H. H. Milman], "The Turkish Empire," *Quarterly Review* 49 (1833): 287. Milman had read both Vico and Wood; see his "Origin of the Homeric Poems," *Quarterly Review* 44 (1831): 128–30, 137.

26. Milman 1900, 83–95; Arnaldo Momigliano, "G. C. Lewis, Niebuhr e la critica delle fonti," in Momigliano 1955, 254; [Milman] 1829, 3:iii–v, 1:8–9; Clements 1995, 246; H. H. Milman to John Taylor Coleridge, December 3, 1822, in Milman 1900, 77. The second and third volumes concern the Jews from the Babylonian Captivity up to modern times. High church and Tractarian elements in the Church of England, deeply suspicious of German theology, were the most furious.

27. Stanley 1870, 576, 579–80; Clements 1995, 254; [Milman] 1829, 1:4–5; Rogerson 1984, 185; Gooch 1959, 479.

28. H. H. Milman to George Ticknor, 15 April 1844, quoted in George Ticknor to Andrews Norton, n.d. [May 1844?], box 9, Andrews Norton Papers, Houghton Library, Harvard University; [Francis Bowen], "Norton *on the Genuineness of the Gospels*," *North American Review* 59 (1844): 143; Norton 1846–48, 1:3, 7–20. Thus Stuart lauded Norton's attack on the 'Protoevangelium' hypothesis: M. Stuart, "Norton on the *Genuineness of the Gospels*," *American Biblical Repository* 11 (1838): 322. Indeed, Stuart in general had high praise for Norton's book (mixed with some specific criticisms, notably of Norton's excisions from the Gospels), since in writing biblical philology Norton avoided the theological differences that separated him from Stuart; Stuart, "Norton on the *Genuineness of the Gospels*," 288–89.

I have used the second edition, Norton 1846–48, which was a fine-tuning of the first edition. The first volume is key for our purposes, the latter two comprising an extended study of Gnosticism. Norton's professed aim in devoting so much attention to Gnostics was to show that even they treated the Gospels as genuine, although the Gospels undermined their doctrine. In fact, most of what Norton had to say in the last two volumes is at best tangential to this purpose. Clearly, he grew fascinated by the task of understanding Gnosticism for its own sake.

29. Norton 1846–48, 1:xxi–lxxiii (extended footnote), 24–25, 28 (footnote).

30. Norton, Dexter Lectures, esp. nos. 5 and 10, Andrews Norton Papers, Houghton Library, Harvard University ("oriental style"); Giltner 1988, 98–99; Brown 1969, 93; Norton 1846–48, 1:lxxiii (footnote ["fabulous"]).

31. Hodge 1822, 26; [Hodge], "Neill's Lectures on Biblical History," *Biblical Repertory and Princeton Review* 18 (1846): 456–61.

32. Treloar 1998, 276–77 (Cambridge essay topic); Mark Pattison, "Present State of Theology in Germany," *Westminster and Foreign Quarterly Review* 67 (1857): 340–44.

33. Shea and Whitla 2000, 5–6, 14–18, 23–25; [Frederic Harrison], "Neo-Christianity," *Westminster and Foreign Quarterly Review* 18 (1860): 293; H[einrich]. E[wald]., "Essays and Reviews," *Göttingische gelehrte Anzeigen* 2 (1861): 1162–67; Willey 1956, 137; Lecky 1896, 1:510–11; see, more generally, Altholz 1994.

34. Shea and Whitla 2000, 8–10.

35. Willey 1956, 140; Shea and Whitla 2000, 106–23; Rogerson 1984, 209 (quotation), 217; Benjamin Jowett to Arthur Stanley, August 1858, quoted in Ellis 1980, 49 ("abominable"); Benjamin Jowett, "On the Interpretation of Scripture," in Shea and Whitla 2000, 477–536 ("great steps," 483; "any other book," 504, emphasis in the original); Altholz 1994, 141.

36. Cameron 1987, 3.

37. Shea and Whitla 2000, 479.

38. Rogerson 1984, 48; Kippenberg 2002, 17–22; Rocher 1989, 622–24; Higgins 1829; Higgins 1836; Alexander Gordon, "Higgins, Godfrey," rev. Myfanwy Lloyd, *Oxford Dictionary of National Biography*.

39. Turner 2011, 17–31.

40. Ward 1811, 1:ix, 35–36, 40, 42, 267, 304, 310, 332, 438, 599 (e.g.); Goodrich 1842, 5–6, 15 (quotations); Moffat 1852, 15–16. This paragraph is adapted from Turner 2011, 32–34.

41. Turner 2011, 34–36, 42 (quotation), 43–46; Child 1855, 1:vii–viii, x (quotations); Maurice 1847; Wheeler-Barclay 2010, 37; Masuzawa 2005, 75–77, 79, 87–95; Hardwick 1855–59, 1:v–vi; John D. Pickles, "Hardwick, Charles," *Oxford Dictionary of National Biography*. Parts of this paragraph are adapted from Turner 2011.

42. Turner 2011, 36 (quotation), 39.

PART III: THE MODERN HUMANITIES IN THE MODERN UNIVERSITY, MID-NINETEENTH TO TWENTIETH CENTURY

1. Schaff 1879, 12.

2. *Oxford English Dictionary*, s.v. "discipline"; Blair 2010.

3. Small 1991, 20–25, discusses this process in specific relation to literary studies. Small's claim (26–27) that university-based literary studies were limited to philology and textual scholarship overgeneralizes and, if one looks at an influential scholar like Edward Dowden, is patently false.

4. Roberts and Turner 2000, 83–87.

5. Roberts and Turner 2000, 75; *Oxford English Dictionary*, s.v. "humanity"; Bryce 1913, 341.

CHAPTER 9. "THIS NEWLY OPENED MINE OF SCIENTIFIC INQUIRY"

This chapter's title comes from Müller 1861–64, 1:1.

1. Biographical information in this and subsequent paragraphs comes from four sources: Van den Bosch 2002; Müller 1901; and the two biographies of Müller—one by his widow (Müller 1902), the other by a distinguished Indian man of letters (Chaudhuri 1974). Müller 1901 is the source for virtually everything known about his life in Germany (encounter with Schlegel's book, 142). Both Müller 1902 and Chaudhuri 1974 are inflected by hero worship; neither handles knowledgeably the scholarly contexts within which Müller worked. Van

den Bosch 2002 (a study of Müller's thinking in the various fields in which he worked) goes far to remedy that last deficiency, as well as providing a judicious 183-page biographical chapter. There remains room for a new, full-scale, scholarly biography of Müller. By some mysterious linguistic gravity, Max Müller's given name and surname attracted each other as his fame began to grow. Thus his wife called herself Georgina Max Müller, and their children added a hyphen, becoming the Max-Müller family.

2. For Bunsen, see Höcker 1951, esp. 99ff, and Wheeler-Barclay 1987, 73–74; for Bunsen and Müller's scholarly commonality, see Bunsen 1854 and Bunsen 1868–70; for the two emperors, see Lloyd-Jones 1982, 155. Bunsen is another important figure badly in need of a modern biography. When Müller visited Istanbul, the sultan did decorate him in a private audience, and Müller did have dinner at Dolmabahce Palace (Müller 1902, 2:300, 303), possibly source of the rumor.

3. Müller 1902, 1:235–45 (quotation, 242); Chaudhuri 1974, 220–29; Wheeler-Barclay 1987, 76–77; Mark Pattison to Jacob Bernays, 23 October 1860, in Miscellaneous Correspondence III, MS Bywater 61, ff. 4–5, Ingram Bywater Papers, Special Collections, Bodleian Library. Late in life, Monier Williams underwent one of those nominal transformations for which the English are renowned and became Monier Monier-Williams. He was far from incompetent, founded the Indian Institute Library in Oxford, and is still known for his Sanskrit-English dictionary.

4. Müller 1999, 109–11, 149. The *Essay on Comparative Mythology* appeared in *Oxford Essays* but was also published as a separate pamphlet; so it sometimes pops up in quotation marks, sometimes in italics.

5. Müller 1895a, ix; Müller to the Duke of Argyll, February 27, 1868, MS Eng d.2307, Special Collections, Bodleian Library.

6. Biographical information in this and following paragraphs from Alter 2005 (quotation, 15–16); on the orientation of Albrecht Weber and Rudolph Roth, see Sengupta 2005, 72–85. Alter's is the standard (and only) biography of Whitney. Fortunately, it is intelligent, incisive, and well informed on both technical issues of linguistics and the larger intellectual context. For the type of agnosticism shared by Whitney and similarly minded Americans in this period, see Turner 1985, pt. 2. Whitney, of course, had a mother, too, Sarah Williston; but she died when he was little.

7. Stevenson 1986; Rosenberg 1962, 382–83.

8. Whitney 1971, xxvii (Brugman quotation), 3 (Breslau, Bopp Prize).

9. Marchand 2009, 133–34, 190; Sengupta 2005, 71–72; Michael Silverstein, "Preface," vii, and "Whitney on Language," xxii, both in Whitney 1971.

10. Marchand 2009, 88 (Bunsen quotation); Neufeldt 1980, 11–12 (Müller quotations: "childish," "sparks"), 62–64; Müller, "Notes for First Lectures on Comparative Philology, Oxford, 1851," 1:1–2, 11–12 and passim, MS Eng d.2353, Special Collections, Bodleian Library; Van den Bosch 2002, 260–65.

11. Alter 2005, 40–44, 46, 49–50; W. D. Whitney, "The Cosmogonic Hymn, Rig-Veda X. 129," *Journal of the American Oriental Society* 11 (1885): cix–cxi (quotations, cxi).

12. Schleicher 1871, 1, notes that the chief task of linguistics ("glottik") is describing and arranging in correct order language families (defined by descent from a common ancestor) "according to a natural system"; Whitney, "Strictures on the Views of August Schleicher Respecting the Nature of Language and Kindred Subjects," *Transactions of the American Philological Association* 2 (1871): 35. For an overview of the turmoil after midcentury, see Auroux et al. 2000–2006, 2:1326–38. For a bird's-eye view of nineteenth-century comparative historical linguistics, see Robins 1967, chap. 7. For a thorough survey, see Auroux 1989–92, vol. 3.

13. Auroux 1989–92, 3:164–68, 241–44; Koerner 1989, 184–88; Robins 1967, 178–81; Au-

roux et al. 2000–2006, 2:1329–30. Schleicher was not the first to use a Stammbaum to represent the relationships of languages. Around 1800 an obscure French grammarian named Félix Gallet got the idea of engraving a 'family tree' for all languages. His information was woefully out of date, but his tree did effectively show the idea of branching descent, key to comparative philology; Auroux 1990, 228–29. There is no reason to think Schleicher saw Gallet's picture. Schleicher's first version was drawn as an outline sketch of a real tree; by 1861, the 'tree' had become a spare set of lines (like the evolutionary tree in *Origin of Species*), with no resemblance to an actual tree; Schleicher 1861, 7.

14. Robins 1967, 181; Bopp 1836, 1; Christy 1983, 34 ("Languages are"), 43–44; Schleicher 1871, 1 ("natural history"); Koerner 1989, 343–55, 357. Bopp 1836 reprints an article first published in 1827. The emphasis on "are" in the Schleicher quotation is my own.

15. Koerner 1989, 357–58; Christy 1983, 36–37.

16. Schleicher 1861; Koerner 1989, 360–61; Anthony 2007, 21.

17. Müller 1902, 1:239, 247–52, 257–59, 262–64, 268–70, 273–76; bibliography preceding Müller 1999.

18. Dowling 1986, 69–70; Müller 1861–64, 1:340, 342, 344–51; Van den Bosch 2002, chap. 2; Müller 1902, 1:450–53, 461, 475–76, 480–82, 495, 2:20–22, 215, 283–84; Alter 2005, 159–60, 181–92.

19. Müller 1861–64, 1:238–39, 249–55

20. Müller, "Notes for First Lectures," 1:2.

21. Müller, "Notes for First Lectures," 1:4, 2:5; Müller 1861–64, lecture 1, esp. 31–32, 36–37; Van den Bosch 2002, 218. Whewell was alert to German erudition and his distinction between physical and historical (or moral) sciences had German roots, but most English-speaking scholars, including Müller, referred to him in invoking the difference.

22. Müller, "Notes for First Lectures," 2:6, 3:6, 4:8, 5:7; Van den Bosch 2002, 207–10; Müller to the Duke of Argyll, February 24, 1868, MS Eng d.2307, and Müller, "The Simplicity of Language," MS of lecture delivered at the Royal Institution, n.d. (post 1886), 66–67 MS Eng C.2811, Special Collections, Bodleian Library.

23. Müller, "Notes for First Lectures"; Alter 2005, chap. 2 ("abominably," 51), 68, 272; Whitney, "On the Views of Biot and Weber Respecting the Relations of the Hindu and Chinese Systems of Asterisms; with an Addition, on Müller's Views Respecting the Same Subject," *Journal of the American Oriental Society* 8 (1866): 1–94, esp. 1–2, 73, 78; Ebenezer Burgess, "Translation of the Sûrya-Siddhânta, A Text-Book of Hindu Astronomy; with Notes, and an Appendix," *Journal of the American Oriental Society* 6 (1858–60): 141–498. Burgess was an American ex-missionary to India.

24. Alter 2005, 66, 68–71.

25. Alter 2005, 71–72, 74–76; Whitney 1867, 13–14, 22, 35, 68–69, 128–29, 132–34; Josiah Gibbs, "On the Natural Significancy of Articulate Sounds," *Biblical Repository*, 2nd ser., 2 (1839): 166–73; Aarsleff 1982, 299–303. Aarsleff and Alter both point out that the Dane J. N. Madvig articulated "semantic presentism" earlier than but unknown to Whitney—an apparent case of independent discovery.

26. Whitney 1867, 35–36, 38–39, 46–48, 50–55, chaps. 3–5; Turner 2002.

27. Whitney, "The Study of Hindu Grammar and the Study of Sanskrit," *American Journal of Philology* 3 (1871): 279–97.

28. Silverstein, "Whitney on Language," x–xi, xv; Alter 2005, 11–12, 17–18.

29. Silverstein, "Whitney on Language," xix–xxi; Whitney 1867, 95; Jakobson, "World Response," xxxi (Saussure quotation).

30. Alter 2005, 214, 248–53; Jakobson, "World Response," xxviii–xlii. I omit, for reasons of space, the *Junggrammatiker* or neogrammarians of Germany, whom Whitney influenced in a rather different direction. "Very 'structuralist' teaching" closely paraphrases words of

Stephen Alter, but Professor Alter asked that I not quote him lest I disguise his debt to John Joseph on this point.

31. For Marsh, Brinton, Boas, Sapir, Whorf, and Bloomfield, see the *American National Biography*. Information about Dwight and Schele De Vere must be pieced together from multiple scattered sources.

32. All of these individuals can be found in the *Oxford Dictionary of National Biography*. The original title of the *Oxford English Dictionary* was *A New English Dictionary on Historical Principles, Founded Mainly on the Materials Collected by the Philological Society*.

CHAPTER 10. "PAINSTAKING RESEARCH QUITE EQUAL TO MATHEMATICAL PHYSICS"

This chapter's title comes from Robert S. Woodward (president, Carnegie Institution of Washington) to Morgan Callaway, Jr., July 11, 1913, in Box 3V62, Morgan Callaway, Jr., Papers, Center for American History, University of Texas–Austin. Woodward was referring to Callaway's book *The Infinitive in Anglo-Saxon* (1913). I have abridged the original quotation ("your work has required a great deal of painstaking research which is quite equal to that necessary in the investigations of mathematical physics") to make it a manageable title.

1. Small 1991, 136.

2. Francis A. March, "Recollections of Language Teaching," *PMLA* 7 (1892), appendix, xx; *Catalogue of the Officers and Students of the University of Michigan: 1857–58* (Ann Arbor, 1858), 39, Bentley Historical Library, University of Michigan–Ann Arbor; Morison 1930, 66–67. At first, like Dale, White taught literature in connection with a rhetoric course, severing the two in 1861.

3. *Catalogue of Officers and Students of Baylor University, 1866–67* (Houston, 1867), 14; Vanderbilt 1986, 84; Pierson 1952, 52, 299; Solberg 1968, 109, 266–67. Illinois Industrial University became the University of Illinois. This paragraph is lifted almost verbatim from Roberts and Turner 2000, 78.

4. Palmer 1965, 50–53, 56–63; Anderson 1983, 70–72; Meikle 1945, 102; Court 1992, 123–32; notes by George J. Lumsden of David Masson's lectures on "Rhetoric and English Literature," 1881–82, Dk.4.28, Dk.4.29, Dk.4.30, and Dk.4.31, Special Collections, University of Edinburgh Library. Volume Dk.4.30 is devoted to the "*Theoretical Course* i.e. Rhetoric, Style, and the principles of Literature"; Dk.4.28 and Dk.4.29 to the "*Historical Course* i.e. History of English Literature including History of English Language"; Dk.4.31 contains some of each.

5. Palmer 1965, 70, chap. 7–8; Walter Raleigh, quoted in "University Intelligence," *Times* [of London], Wednesday, December 6, 1893, 5; Gordon 1912; Tillyard 1958, 20 (quoting Cambridge Senate, May 23, 1878 [emphasis added]), 28–33, chap. 4; on Cambridge methods, see correspondence of W. W. Skeat and A. S. Napier, in Letters to Professor A. S. Napier, MS Eng. Letters d. 79, Western Manuscripts, Bodleian Library, Oxford University. On social and institutional forces pushing Oxford and Cambridge toward incorporating English studies into the curriculum, see Baldick 1987, chap. 3. Were my subject the emergence of the humanities in university curricula rather than the development of the humanities as scholarly disciplines, I would pay attention to these 'external' forces.

6. J. M. Rigg, "Spalding, William," rev. Elizabeth Baigent, *Oxford Dictionary of National Biography*; John Hill Burton, "Life of Professor W. Spalding," in Spalding 1876, xiii–xxii; F. J. Furnivall, "Forewords" [sic], in Spalding 1876, v; Spalding 1876, 10 ("decisive test"). I borrow the title of this section of the chapter from McMurtry 1985.

7. *Catalogue of the University of Alabama, 1854–55* (Tuscaloosa: Printed by M.D.J. Slade,

1855), unpaginated, Special Collections, Hoole Library, University of Alabama; Spalding 1853, 3, 5–6.

8. Macksey 1985, 915, 917–18; "Minutes of the Second Section of the Teutonic Seminary, of the Johns Hopkins University, Dr. Wood, Director, [beginning] October 1889," bound MS volume, 27, 33, in Records of the Department of German 1889–1987, Record group 04.100, subgroup 1, series 1, box 1, and "Minutes of the Journal Meetings of the English Seminary of the Johns Hopkins University, 1895–1903," bound MS volume, in Records of the Department of English, Record group 04.130, series 4, box 1, Johns Hopkins University Archives; analysis of Browning's Rabbi Ben Ezra, MS, 1903, box 3V63, and Albert S. Cook to William L. Prather [president of University of Texas], May 19, 1900 [copy], Morgan Callaway, Jr., Papers, Center for American History, University of Texas–Austin. The judgment about teaching mostly Shakespeare is based on my survey of his papers, not of catalogs. Colleagues recalled his *favorite* teaching fields as "Victorian poetry and the history of the English language." W. J. Battle et al., "In Memoriam Morgan Callaway," undated faculty minute [1936], http://www.utexas.edu/faculty/council/2000–2001/memorials/SCANNED /callaway.pdf, accessed April 2, 2012.

9. Payne 1895, 81 (March quotation); "Lectures on English Literature By B. F. Meek, A.M., Prof. Eng. Lit. Uni. of Ala," fall term 1872, bound MS volume, 1–42, folder 7, Box 2826, Special Collections, Hoole Library, University of Alabama; Court 1992, 86; Lumsden notes of Masson lectures on "Rhetoric and English Literature," "*Historical Course*," lectures 18–21; Kitzhaber 1990, 38; Solly 1898, 233; University College *Calendar*, 1889–90, quoted in McMurtry 1985, 51; W. W. Skeat to A. S. Napier, 26 January 1891, Letters to Professor A. S. Napier, MS Eng. Letters d. 79, ff. 179–80, Western Manuscripts, Bodleian Library, Oxford University; cf. transcript of Robert S. Hyer's classes at Emory College, 1877 to 1881, Emory University transcript, April 8, 1931, TS, folder 2, box 1, SMU 94.203, Robert S. Hyer Papers, University Archives, DeGolyer Library, Southern Methodist University.

10. Solly 1898, 231–33, 260–62, 355–57; McMurtry 1985, 59–61; Treglown and Bennett 1998, 61–64; Brander Matthews, "An American Scholar: Thomas Raynesford Lounsbury," *Century Illustrated Magazine* 55, no. 4. (1898): 562–63 (quotation); Kitzhaber 1990, 39. One fact raises suspicion about Lounsbury's being first to require college students to read actual works of literature: William James Rolfe before 1850 required his Massachusetts *high school* students to read "English classics" and in 1870 published a school edition of *The Merchant of Venice*: Ernest Hunter Wright, "Furnivall and Rolfe," *New York Times Saturday Review of Books*, July 16, 1910, 303, 306.

11. [Thomas Lounsbury], "The Study of English Literature," *New Englander* 29 (1870): 582–85; Cross 1943, 112–14. Later commentators, mostly English professors largely ignorant of the long history of philology and looking through glasses tinted by present practices, have chronically misunderstood the nature of this linkage of language and literature; Graff 1987, chaps. 4–6, is a typical example.

12. [Lounsbury], "The Study of English Literature," 585–87, 589. Reading authors in chronological order was also "vital" for understanding "the history of the language" (587).

13. Corson 1899, xix. For a fuller exposition of Corson's view of literature, see Corson 1901.

14. Macksey 1985, 920; [Lounsbury], "The Study of English Literature," 590.

15. Corson 1887, viii; James Morgan Hart, "The College Course in English Literature, How It May Be Improved," *Transactions of the Modern Language Association of America* 1 (1884–85): 85 (quotation; emphasis added), 87.

16. Meikle 1945, 102; Tyler 1878; Tyler 1897; Vanderbilt 1986, chap. 6; Jones and Casady 1933, esp. 201, 204–5, 218; Dowden [1881], 7, 16–18; Lumsden notes of Masson lectures on "Rhetoric and English Literature," Historical Course; G. G. Smith, "Masson, David Mather,"

rev. Sondra Miley Cooney, *Oxford Dictionary of National Biography*; notes by W. S. Davidson '06 on Professor Stockton Axson's course on nineteenth-century English poetry, lecture 1, 1906, box 4, folder 7, and notes by Davidson on Professor George Harper's English literature course (identified in Princeton catalog as "Elizabethan Drama. Predecessors of Shakespeare"), 1904, box 21, folder 14, Lecture Notes Collection, Department of Rare Books and Special Collections, Princeton University Library; Wendell 1900 (quotation, 3).

17. W. P. Ker, "Introductory Lecture [as Quain Professor]," MS, 2 October 1889, KER 2/41; W. P. Ker, Lecture notes on Chaucer, unpaginated bound MS notebook, n.d. [1911], MS Add. 178/4; W. P. Ker, "The Literary Influence of the Middle Ages," MS, n.d., KER 2/22; Ker, untitled MS, n.d., KER 2/75, Special Collections, University College London.

18. MS notes by Margaret Low of Sir Herbert J. C. Grierson, History of English literature from the fourteenth century onward: lectures to First Ordinary class in English literature, 1925–26 session, 2 bound volumes, unpaginated, Special Collections, University of Edinburgh Library.

19. Charles Eliot Norton to Richard Grant White, April 5, 1860, Letters of Charles Eliot Norton to Richard Grant White, bMS Am 1430.1, Houghton Library, Harvard University.

20. Benzie 1983, 4–5, 16–22, 27–28, 84–89, chaps. 5–6, 274n53; Peterson 1979, xxix; [Munro] 1911, 122–35, 174–77; Corson 1896, viii.

21. Benzie 1983, 186–91; Robert Sawyer, "The New Shakspere Society, 1873–94," *Borrowers and Lenders: The Journal of Shakespeare and Appropriation* 2 (2006), http://www .borrowers.uga.edu/cocoon/borrowers/request?id=781463, accessed April 6, 2012; Dowden [1881], xv–xvi; Edward Dowden to [Alexander or George] Macmillan, May 3, 1877, ff. 23–24, Add. MSS 55029, British Library; Fleay 1876, 107–8. Fleay's metrical test was not totally unprecedented: James Spedding applied quantitative metric analysis to a Shakespeare play in "Who Wrote Shakspere's Henry VIII?" *Gentleman's Magazine*, August 1850, 121–22.

22. F. J. Furnivall to David Laing, February 1, 1868, David Laing Collection, La. IV.17, f. 3402, Special Collections, University of Edinburgh Library; Benzie 1983, passim; [Munro] 1911, 10; F. J. Furnivall to T. R. Lounsbury, October 29, 1887, quoted in Peterson 1979, xxvii.

23. Furnivall 1868, 1–2; Baker 1984; Benzie 1983, 163–78.

24. Haskin 2002; Haskin 1989; Norton, "The Text of Donne's Poems," *Studies and Notes in Philology and Literature* 5 (1896): 1–19.

25. Haskin 2002, 186. For the defects and complexities of the attribution to Lachmann of 'Lachmann's method,' see Timpanaro 2005. Norton did not "make his career" in universities: Harvard recruited him in middle age, after he had won scholarly distinction.

26. McMurtry 1985, 71–73; Cheesman and Rieuwerts 1997, 20–21; Brown 2011, 31, 36–37. Biblical philology: Child's closest friend in his Harvard class of 1846 was Charles Norton; and Child often visited the Norton house, a short walk from the college. Charles's father was the biblical scholar Andrews Norton; the final volumes of his *Genuineness of the Gospels* appeared while the two boys were in college. Andrews worked at home and, an attentive parent, talked at length with his children's friends. I am grateful to Mary Ellen Brown for indispensable advice on Child's ballad work.

27. Brown 2011, 84–87, 94, 98–99, chaps. 4–5; Hustvedt 1930, chap. 7, 208–20; N.F.S. Grundtvig to Francis Child, February 17, 1872, v. 9, f. 3, Charles Norton to Francis Child, December 30, 1872, and February 2–10, 1873, v. 12, ff. 13 and 21, Francis James Child Ballad Manuscripts, fMS Am 2349, Houghton Library, Harvard University; Cheesman and Rieuwerts 1997, 30–37; Child 1898, 1:vii–ix. Child gives the rabbi's name as Dr. Cohn. I have been unable to identify him beyond this.

28. On Thoms, see Arthur Sherbo, "Thoms, William John," *Oxford Dictionary of National Biography*. Thoms's usage is in any case the earliest citation in the *Oxford English Dictionary*.

29. W. P. Ker, "Criticism," MS, February 6 , 1889, KER 2/40, Special Collections, University College London.

30. Anonymous editor of a "leading Review," quoted in Collins 1912, 157; Treglown and Bennett 1998, 77–84; Kearney 1986, 60–67, 70–84. The attack on Gosse was so sensitive that a quarter century later Collins's biographer cloaked its victim in anonymity; Collins 1912, chap. 6.

31. Turner 2002; Moulton 1885, 1 ("organized thought"); Liddell, "Memoranda of letter of July 18, 1903 to President Eliot," folder 1, Box 2N491, Henry Bradley to Mark Harvey Liddell, July 24, 1901, folder 2, box 2N491, Charles W. Shields to Mark Harvey Liddell, March 2, 1903, folder 1, box 2N491, Mark Harvey Liddell Papers, Center for American History, University of Texas–Austin; Payne 1895, 173 (Gayle quotation). For the epistemological basis of Liddell's belief that literary study was a science, see his lecture "Browning's Paracelsus," TS with MS emendations, n.d. [1912?], box 2N511, Liddell Papers.

32. Moulton 1885, vi, 2, 25; Baldick 1987, 41; Stovall 1955, 119 (Falk quotation).

33. On this vast subject, see especially, amid a growing literature, Reuben 1996; Turpin 2011; Chadwick 1990; Turner 2003, 109–20; Roberts and Turner 2000.

34. Turner 2003, 50–68; Roberts and Turner 2000, 92–93, 107–22; Cortés 2008; Arnold 1960–77, 9:161–63.

35. William Roscoe Thayer, "Professor Charles Eliot Norton," *Twenty-Eighth Annual Report of the Dante Society* (1909), 5 ("minute," "spiritual significance"); William Roscoe Thayer, "James Russell Lowell as a Teacher: Recollections of His Last Pupil," *Scribner's Magazine* 68 (1920): 477 ("spiritual insight").

36. Thayer, "Norton," 6; Corson 1901, 57; Corson 1896, v; Corson 1867, 16; Corson 1970, v, 3; Bishop 1962, 117–18.

37. Bishop 1962, 117; Payne 1895, 9; Wendell 1893, 96.

38. Kitzhaber 1990, 38; Corson 1893; Graff 1987, 66; Kittredge 1927, 71. Histories by English professors written long after the fact (such as Graff's) sometimes posit a universal enmity between 'philologists' and 'teachers of literature' in this period. These alleged battle lines were not a feature of the nineteenth and very early twentieth centuries, but rather a projection back in time of later clashes.

39. Graff and Warner 1989, 8.

40. Edward Dowden to William McNeile Dixon, 18 May 1899, MS 2259/10, and Edward Dowden to John Todhunter, 29 March 1885, MS 3715/35, Manuscripts Department, Trinity College Dublin.

41. Payne 1895, 18, 19, 26; F. J. Furnivall to A. S. Napier, May 23, 1888, Letters to Professor A. S. Napier, MS Eng. Letters d. 79, f. 23, Western Manuscripts, Bodleian Library, Oxford University.

42. [Jay B. Hubbell], "John Hathaway McGinnis," TS, n.d. ["c. 1978" penciled in], 15, box 1, Department of English files, Dedman College, SMU 98.320, University Archives, DeGolyer Library, Southern Methodist University.

43. Mansell 1986, 280–81; George Saintsbury to David Hannay, 19 April 1896, MS ADD 203, Special Collections, University College London; Ward 1891, 5 (quotation); Turner 1999.

CHAPTER 11. "NO TENDENCY TOWARD DILETTANTISM"

This chapter's title comes from Charles Eliot Norton, "Syllabus of Lectures, 1874–75," in Notebook 1874–75, box 2, Miscellaneous Papers, Norton Papers, Houghton Library, Harvard University.

1. Marett 1908, [3].

2. T. E. Page to Editor, *Times* [of London], December 26, 1903, 8; Stray 1998, 205–10; Daunton 2005, 383.

3. Briggs, "Introduction," in Gildersleeve 1992, xxv; Clifford H. Moore, "William Watson Goodwin," *Classical Journal* 8 (1912): 2; James Hadley, "On the Nature and Theory of the Greek Accent," *Transactions of the American Philological Association* 1 (1869–70): 1–19; Briggs 1994, 245; Arthur Twining Hadley, "Biographical Memoir of James Hadley, 1821–1872," *National Academy of Sciences Biographical Memoirs* 5 (1905): 251; M. L. D'Ooge to James B. Angell, n.d. [ca. February 7, 1872], H. S. Frieze and D'Ooge to unknown (application for appropriation), n.d. [early to mid 1870s], D'Ooge to Angell, n .d. [ca. February 7, 1872], accounting of books bought by University of Michigan library from D'Ooge, n.d. [before January 3, 1873], folder labeled Greek Correspondence and Records, 1872–1878, Box 1, Department of Classical Studies records, University of Michigan Archives, Bentley Historical Library, University of Michigan–Ann Arbor. "Probably earlier": no earlier records exist, but extant correspondence gives no hint that teaching ancient art is novel. Briggs mistakenly calls Hadley's work a Latin grammar.

4. Morison 1930, 34–35. Charles W. Eliot became Harvard's president in 1869. Although Eliot and 'electives' are synonymous in potted histories of American higher education, the movement toward easing requirements and allowing students to elect courses antedated him.

5. Sihler 1930, 58–63, 68–72; quotation, 69.

6. Gonzalez Lodge to Basil L. Gildersleeve, August 20, 1899, Box 10, Basil Lanneau Gildersleeve Papers, MS 5, Series 1, Johns Hopkins University Archives; Sihler 1930, 58, 76, 90; Greek Seminary Minutes, November 21, 1877–May 29, 1879 (bound MS volume wrongly stamped November 21, 1878–May 29, 1879), 1, record group 04.040, subgroup 1, series 7, box 1, Johns Hopkins University Archives.

7. Greek Seminary Minutes, November 21, 1877–May 29, 1879 (bound MS volume wrongly stamped November 21, 1878–May 29, 1879), 1–3, 12, 65, record group 04.040, subgroup 1, series 7, box 1, Johns Hopkins University Archives; Herbert T. Archibald to Basil L. Gildersleeve, July 13, 1901 ("general culture"), Box 1, Basil Lanneau Gildersleeve Papers, MS 5, Series 1, Johns Hopkins University Archives.

8. Frank Gardner Moore, "A History of the American Philological Association," *Transactions and Proceedings of the American Philological Association* 50 (1919): 5–32 (esp. 5–6, 8, 14–15); "Proceedings," *Transactions of the American Philological Association* 1 (1869): 6.

9. Moore, "American Philological Association," 15 ("migration"), 25; A. L. Frothingham to Basil L. Gildersleeve, March 5, 1915, Box 5, Edwin A. Alderman to Basil L. Gildersleeve, March 13, 1912 ("first class"), Howard Ayers to Basil L. Gildersleeve, March 21, 1900, Box 1, Nicholas Murray Butler to Basil L. Gildersleeve, November 14, 1905, Box 2, Basil Lanneau Gildersleeve Papers, MS 5, Series 1, Johns Hopkins University Archives; J. B. Greenough, "Memoir of Frederic De Forest Allen," *Harvard Studies in Classical Philology* 9 (1898): 28; list of papers delivered at 1919 anniversary meeting: "Proceedings of the Fifty-first Annual Meeting and Semi-centennial of the American Philological Association," *Transactions and Proceedings of the American Philological Association* 50 (1919): i–lxii.

10. Ward W. Briggs Jr., "Basil L. Gildersleeve," in Briggs and Calder 1990, 103–5; B. L. Gildersleeve, "Editorial Note," *American Journal of Philology* 1 (1880): 2; Basil L. Gildersleeve to Francis G. Allinson, December 18, 1913, Basil Lanneau Gildersleeve Papers, MS 5, Series 1, Box 1, Johns Hopkins University Archives. Johns Hopkins's founding president, Daniel Coit Gilman, wanted every department to house a journal, as part of his program to make Johns Hopkins the preeminent center of research in the United States.

11. [Allan Marquand], undated [ca. 1880?] bound MS notebook labeled "Greek Mythol-

ogy" in Marquand's hand, Box 5, folder 5, Allan Marquand Papers, C0269, Special Collections, Firestone Library, Princeton University.

12. Paul Shorey, "Fifty Years of Classical Studies in America," *Transactions and Proceedings of the American Philological Association* 50 (1919): 42–43, 45 (quotation); Joseph E. Fontenrose, *Classics at Berkeley: The First Century 1869–1970* (Berkeley, Calif.: Department of Classics History Fund, 1982), http://escholarship.org/uc/item/5066c75h, accessed July 22, 2012, 2–3, 6, 15–16; "Records of the Classical Seminary of Princeton University from December 14th 1898 to 19[08]," bound MS volume, 19, 21, and typed report (tipped in) of director of Classical Seminary for 1901–2, Department of Classics vol. 2, and Minutes of the Graduate Classics Club 1911–1922, entry for March 17, 1911, Department of Classics vol. 1, Academic Department Records, University Archives, Department of Rare Books and Special Collections, Princeton University Library; E. Christian Kopff, "Paul Shorey," in Briggs and Calder 1990, 447–53.

13. Shorey, "Fifty Years," 58–60; Hermann Diels to Ulrich von Wilamowitz-Moellendorff, May 7, 1912, and Ulrich von Wilamowitz-Moellendorff to Hermann Diels, May 8, 1912, in Diels and Wilamowitz-Moellendorff 1995, 275–76; A. W. Verrall to [George?] Macmillan, May 25, 1881 and December 26, 1884, Add. MSS 55125/ff. 153–56, 178–79, British Library; John Williams White to Ingram Bywater, January 2, 1884, George M. Lane to Ingram Bywater, June 6, 1884, John Williams White to Ingram Bywater, February 22, 1886, in Miscellaneous Correspondence I, in MS Bywater 58, f. 159, f. 166, ff. 219–20, Ingram Bywater Papers, Special Collections, Bodleian Library; Charles W. Bain to B. L. Gildersleeve, May 3, 1904 (from South Carolina College), Basil Lanneau Gildersleeve Papers, MS 5, Series 1, Box 1, Johns Hopkins University Archives; Greenough, "Memoir of Allen," 31.

14. Briggs 1994, 196–97; Fontenrose, *Classics at Berkeley*, http://escholarship.org/uc/item/5066c75h, accessed July 22, 2012, 3, 13–14. Of American classicists active before the First World War, four, besides Gildersleeve, have an entry among the fifty in Briggs and Calder 1990: Tenney Frank, William Oldfather, Paul Shorey, and Lily Ross Taylor.

15. Richard Jebb, "Sir C. T. Newton," *Journal of Hellenic Studies* 14 (1894): xlix–lxiv (quotation, xlix); Marchand 1996, 87–90, 97–98.

16. Charles Newton, "On the Study of Archaeology," *Archaeological Journal* 8 (1851): 1–26 (quotations, 2).

17. Newton, "Study of Archaeology," 1–26 (quotations, 9–11, 14, 16, 19–20, 24); cf. Turner 1981, 63–65.

18. Jebb, "Newton," 1; Dyson 2006, 137–38; Stoneman 1987, 216–19; Michaelis 1908, 99; Charles Newton, "On the Sculptures from the Mausoleum at Halicarnassus," *Classical Museum* 5 (1848): 170–201, esp. 173–81; Charles Newton to Philip Bliss, 9 January 1852, Add. MSS 34582/ff. 329–30, British Library.

19. Jebb, "Newton," l–li; C. T. Newton to the Earl of Clarendon [foreign secretary], November 15, 1856, C. T. Newton to Viscount Stratford de Redcliffe [Canning, ennobled in 1852], November 18, 1856, C. T. Newton to E. Hammond [assistant foreign secretary], November 18, 1856, C. T. Newton to Viscount Stratford de Redcliffe, January 12, February 15, and April 3, 1857, C. T. Newton to the Earl of Clarendon, August 12 and 28 and October 19, 1857, Add. MSS 46889A/ff. 1, 3–4, 5–7, 26–30, 34–36, 50–55, 180–81, 222–23, British Library; Sketches and photographs from Halicarnassus, bound super-folio volume, Add. MSS 31980, British Library; Newton with Pullan 1862–63, 1:v–vii, 2:346; Dyson 2006, 138–39. A second volume describing excavations at nearby Knidos and elsewhere came out in 1863.

20. Michaelis 1908, xiv, 294.

21. Dyson 2006, 140–41; B. F. Cook, "Newton, Sir Charles Thomas," *Oxford Dictionary of National Biography*.

22. R. A. Higgins, "Wood, John Turtle," *Oxford Dictionary of National Biography*; Stone-

man 1987, 225–35; Dyson 2006, 140; Michaelis 1908, 102–4. I tracked down the history and route of the Izmir–Aydin railway through too many websites to record here.

23. Fitton 1996, 31–32; Traill 1995, 166–67, 177. Biliotti was another archaeological diplomat, British vice consul in Rhodes.

24. Winterer 2002, 157–74; Allen 2002, 42–43, 52–53, 99–100; Turner 1999, 273–75, 277–80, 286–87, 289–94, 296–99, 301, 305–6, 313–16, 320–21, 328–30, 369, and passim.

25. Turner 1999, passim; Allen 2002, 13–15, 80, and chap. 4; Dyson 1998, 54–58; Morison 1930, 44–45; "Obituary: Professor John Williams White," *Classical Review* 31 (1917): 202–3; Fontenrose, *Classics at Berkeley*, 13.

26. Turner 1999, 314–15; Dyson 1998, 46–49; quotation from Charles Eliot Norton and A. L. Frothingham, *Circular to Literary Contributors*, in American Journal of Archaeology file, box 4, AIA Archives, Boston University (emphasis added); Salomon Reinach, "Inscribed Base of an Archaic Bronze Statue from Mount Ptous," *The American Journal of Archaeology and of the History of the Fine Arts* 1 (1885): 358–60; Pedley 2012, 154–55. The AIA archives have been recataloged since my research, and the location of the cited item may have changed. The Frenchman Reinach soon became a famous archaeologist.

27. Allen 2002, 17–18, 100–102, 206 (quotation, 102); Murray and Runnels 2007, 609; Dyson 1998, 59–60, 98–100; D.J.I. Begg, "Harriet Ann Boyd Hawes," *American National Biography*.

28. Trigger 2006, 78–79.

29. Anderson 1983, esp. chaps. 1–3 and 7; Stoddart 1895; Carswell [1927], 125–28, 130–33, 135–54; Wallace 2006 (Blackie quotation, 151, Butcher quotation, 208); John Marshall to J. S. Blackie, June 2 and July 24, 1869, Thomas Kirkup to J. S. Blackie, July 11, 1870, and Robert Clark to J. S. Blackie, July 24, 1870, MS 2629, ff. 69–70, 89–91, 253–56, William Peterson to J. S. Blackie, July 5, 1875, MS 2631, ff. 309–10, Thomas Gilray to J. S. Blackie, June 23, 1876, MS 2632, ff. 86–89, and Wᵐ Keith Leask to J. S. Blackie, May 15, [18]86, MS 2636, ff. 219–22, National Library of Scotland; Turner 1981, 172–73; Jebb 1907, 225 (Jebb quotation). Scrapbooks of Blackie's correspondence, MS 2621–43, National Library of Scotland, make clear the extraordinary range of his intellectual interests.

30. Park 1902; *Scottish Jurist: Being Reports of Cases Decided in the Supreme Courts of Scotland, and in the House of Lords on Appeal from Scotland* 20 (1848): 78–98; Charles MacDouall, "A Lecture on the Study of Oriental Languages and Literature," n.d. [1847], MS 6/19, MacDouall, First lecture as professor of Latin (1849), 4–6, 7–9, 11, MS 6/14, MacDouall, "An Elaborate Essay on Greek Philosophy," MS 6/8, MacDouall, "Essay on the Origin and Development of the Greek Drama," MS 6/1, in Charles MacDouall Papers, Special Collections, Queen's University Belfast. In the Queen's University library catalog, MacDouall's books bear the prefix MacD/ in the shelf number; an Excel spreadsheet listing his books also exists in Special Collections.

31. J. P. Mahaffy to [Alexander Macmillan?], "Wednesday" [1875], Add. MS 55118/ff. 10–11, Mahaffy to [Alexander] Macmillan, October 8, 1873, Add. MS 55118/ff. 1–2, Mahaffy to [Alexander Macmillan], February 28, 1875, Add. MS 55118/ff. 8–9, British Library; Mahaffy 1871; John Pentland Mahaffy, "Brief summary of the principal stages of my life," 1919, MS notebook, 8–12, MS 11137, John Pentland Mahaffy Notebook, MSS 4980, Manuscripts Department, Trinity College Dublin; J. P. Mahaffy, "New Fragments of the *Antiope* of Euripides," *Hermathena* 8, no. 17 (1891): 38–51; Hermann Diels to Ulrich von Wilamowitz-Moellendorff, February 24, 1891, in Diels and Wilamowitz-Moellendorff 1995, 71.

32. Kenney 1974, 115; Stray 1997, 364, 367–68; Thompson 1864, 33 ("Porsonian pause"); Stray 1998, 121–24; Turner 1981, chap. 8; Page 1983, 146 (Housman quotation). Thompson was recalling his own Cambridge-formed headmaster.

33. Turner 1981, 5–6, 10–12; Brink 1986, 115; William Everett, "Catullus vs. Horace," *Har-*

vard Studies in Classical Philology 12 (1901): 7–17; J[ohn]. Conington, review of J. A. Hartung, *Aeschylos' Die Ermordung Agamemnon's*, 105–9, and "Anecdota," 96–97, both in *Journal of Classical and Sacred Philology* 1 (1854). The three editors were the biblical philologists Joseph Barber Lightfoot (1828–89) and Fenton John Anthony Hort (1828–92) and the classicist John Eyton Bickersteth Mayor (1825–1910).

34. I have omitted St. David's College (1827) in Lampeter, Wales, essentially an Anglican seminary during the nineteenth century.

35. Engel 1983; Rothblatt 1968; Green 1964, 297–306; Stray 1998, 87–88, 93–94, 109–10, 119–20, 142–46.

36. Ward 1918, 1:140–41. Whether "Curtius" was the archaeologist Ernst or his younger brother, the philologist Georg, is not clear. The reference to Balliol may seem anachronistic, since the college's stress on forming civil servants is associated with Benjamin Jowett, and Jowett was not elected Master until 1870. But his ascendancy among Balliol tutors dates from 1864.

37. Jones 2007, 43–51, 56, 87, 183–84, 229–31; Momigliano 1994, 123–24, 127–28; Nuttall 2003, chap. 2; Grafton 2009, chap. 11; Mark Pattison to Jacob Bernays, October 23, 1860, March 28, 1865, July 5, 1868, July 10, 1869, and June 18, 1870, in Miscellaneous Correspondence III, MS Bywater 61, ff. 4–6, 10, 12, 14, Ingram Bywater Papers, Special Collections, Bodleian Library.

38. Pattison to Bernays, March 28, 1865, and July 5, 1868, and Henry Nettleship to Jacob Bernays, March 21, 1877, in Miscellaneous Correspondence III, MS Bywater 61, f. 6, 10, 111–12, Ingram Bywater to Jacob Bernays, n.d. [ca. 1875], November 20 and December 6, 1875, September 7, 1876, July 30, 1877, and draft of lost letter, n.d. [late 1877 or early 1878], in "Personalia," MS Bywater 60, ff. 109–11, 113–16, 123–24, 155–56, bound MS notebook with notes on history of classical scholarship, MS Bywater 34, Ingram Bywater Papers, Special Collections, Bodleian Library; Stray 2007b, 107–14; Bollack 1998, 29, 63; Stary 1998, 217. Bywater's edition of Heraclitus strongly influenced Hermann Diels's *Fragmente der Vorsokratiker* (1903) that, revised, remains basic to its subject. Bywater anticipated Diels in providing both fragments of Heraclitus embedded in later writers and *testimonia*, secondary witnesses to his thinking.

39. Stray 1998, 151–52, 205–6; J.M.C. Toynbee and H.D.A. Major, "Gardner, Percy," rev. John Boardman, *Oxford Dictionary of National Biography*; Miyahara 2006, 39; Stray 2007b, 135–37.

40. Stray 1998, 94, 106–9, 146–49; Daunton 2005, 382–84; Stray 2007b, 10.

41. Roger D. Dawe, "R. C. Jebb," in Briggs and Calder 1990, 239–47 ("barren," 240); Hugh Lloyd-Jones, "Jebb, Sir Richard Claverhouse," in *Oxford Dictionary of National Biography*; Jebb 1907, esp. 89–92, 229n; Stray 1998, 218–21; Bobbitt 1960, 104 ("adornment"); drafts of Bywater letters to Jebb in "Personalia," MS Bywater 60, Ingram Bywater Papers, Special Collections, Bodleian Library; F. W. Thomas, "Cowell, Edward Byles," rev. J. B. Katz, in *Oxford Dictionary of National Biography*.

42. Jebb 1907, 211, 215–20, 244–49; Stray 1998, 137–39; Lloyd-Jones, "Jebb"; Ingram Bywater to Jacob Bernays, January 25, 1881, in "Personalia," MS Bywater 60, ff. 137–38, Ingram Bywater Papers, Special Collections, Bodleian Library; Daunton 2005, 171; Nigel Spivey, "Walston , Sir Charles," *Oxford Dictionary of National Biography*; Stray 2007a, 75–96; Dawes, "Jebb," 241–44 ("yardstick," 241); Maehler 2004, 28; Daunton 2005, 374–84. Waldstein had been at Cambridge since 1880 as a lecturer in classics; he changed his name to Walston during the First World War. It took a while for the British School's excavations to—so to speak—get off the ground; the earliest were incompetent.

43. James G. Frazer to George A. Macmillan, July 12, 1884, Add. MSS 55134/ff. 1–2, Brit-

ish Library; James G. Frazer to Francis Galton, March 8, 1885, Galton 243, Special Collections, University College London; Ackerman 1987, chaps. 1–3.

44. Ackerman 1987, 61–62; Frazer to John F. White, December 15, 1897, in Ackerman 2005, 102–10 (quotation); Jones 1984, 33–35. Frazer relates these details, including the small rooms in Whewell's Court, in the quoted letter to White. Smith lived in Trinity, eventually moving to better rooms, until 1885 when Christ's elected him a professorial fellow.

45. Ackerman 1987, 27, 29; Frazer 1935, 126 (quotation); Frazer 1890, 1:x; Jones 1984, 33.

46. Ackerman 1987, chap. 4 and 60–63; William Robertson Smith to John Sutherland Black, 1889, quoted in Black and Chrystal 1912, 495; James G. Frazer to Henry Jackson, October 27, 1887, Add. MS c.30.41, Wren Library, Trinity College Cambridge; James G. Frazer to George A. Macmillan, June 7, 1888, December 18, 1889, January 17, 1891, and February 22, 1894, Add. MSS 55134/ff. 8–9, 18–21, 49–50, 74–75, and April 13, 1903, Add. MSS 55136/ff. 3–4, British Library; Frazer 1890, 1:[v]; Ackerman 2002, 39–41, 47–48; Turner 1981, 119–22; MacCormack 2010; Fraser 1990, chap. 1.

47. Tylor 1871, 1:15; James G. Frazer to George A. Macmillan, November 8, 1889, Add. MSS 55134/ff. 10–13, British Library; Kippenberg 2002, 81–92; Frazer 1890, 1:ix–x.

48. James G. Frazer to George Macmillan, August 19, 1899, BL Add. 55135, quoted in Fraser 1990, 120; Jones 1984, 38–43; Robert Ackerman, "Frazer, Sir James George," *Oxford Dictionary of National Biography*; Fraser 1990, 206–12. Ackerman 1987, 226–28, reports a curious exchange with R. R. Marett in 1911, in which Frazer insisted that Smith did *not* believe that ritual preceded belief. When Marett pointed out passages in *Religion of the Semites* showing that Smith *did* so believe, Frazer could not accept plain truth. He claimed that, in stressing "the importance of *the study of* ritual [my emphasis] as compared with myth or dogma," Smith "omitted to state (what he probably assumed) that every ritual is preceded in the minds of the men who institute it by a definite train of reasoning." It is a nice (and unanswerable) question whether Frazer never understood Smith or whether, many years after his adored friend's death, he could not admit that the two fundamentally disagreed and tailored his memories accordingly. The phrase positive science can make Frazer sound like a Comtean. He was far too skeptical for that; natural science was not the last word.

49. James G. Frazer to George A. Macmillan, November 8, 1889, October 5, 1890, Add. MSS 55134/ff. 10–13, 47–48, British Library.

50. Jones 1984, 38; Turner 1981, 115–17, 121–28; Harrison 1991, 7–8; Gilbert Murray, *Ancient Greek Literature*, 272, quoted in Harrison 1991, 657; Ackerman 2002; F. M. Cornford to JGF, 21 February [1911 written on envelope], Add. MS c.56/24, Wren Library, Trinity College Cambridge; Beard 2000; Robinson 2002. For a skeptical view of the existence of a coherent group of Ritualists, see Beard 2000, 112–17. I find implausible Beard's effort to write Frazer's impact out of the story on the ground that myth, ritual, and even totemism appeared in the classical archaeology section of the Cambridge classical tripos in the late 1880s.

51. Renate Schlesier, "Jane Ellen Harrison," in Briggs and Calder 1990, 135.

52. Ulrich von Wilamowitz-Moellendorff to Gilbert Murray, 1912, quoted in William M. Calder III, review of Ackerman, *Myth and Ritual School*, in *Bryn Mawr Classical Review* 02.05.01, http://bmcr.brynmawr.edu/1991/02.05.01.html#NT1, accessed July 17, 2012; W. M. L. Hutchinson, review of Harrison, *Themis*, *Classical Review* 27 (1913): 132–34; Grene 2007, 74.

53. Stray 2003, chap. 1; Stray 1998, 248–49.

54. Bryce 1913, 341; Soffer 1994, 6–7; Dixon 1902, 185.

55. J. A. Allen, "Progress of Ornithology in the United States during the Last Century," *American Naturalist* 10 (1876): 537; "Administrative/Biographical History" in finding guide

to Papers of the Botany Department of the University of St Andrews, ms37783–ms37852, Department of Special Collections, St. Andrews University Library; Bryce 1913, 342; Kinmont 1839, Lectures 5–6. Scottish born, Kinmont studied at the universities of Aberdeen and Edinburgh, where he likely heard lectures on 'natural and civil history.'

56. Herbert B. Adams, "Is History Past Politics?" *Johns Hopkins University Studies in Historical and Political Science* 13th ser. (1895): 197.

57. Rudwick 2005, 116–18. Ussher used the Julian calendar.

58. Trautmann 1992; Grayson 1983; Van Riper 1993, 41–73; Daniel 1968, 8–12; Gräslund 1987, chaps. 3–4; W. Dreyer, "The Main Features of the Advance in the Study of Danish Archaeology," *American Anthropologist*, n.s., 10 (1908): 505–8; Trigger 2006, 121–29; Brand 1998, 35–59.

59. Gruber 1965; Trautmann 1992; Van Riper 1993, chaps. 4–6; Grayson 1983, 179–85; J. Prestwich, "Report on the Exploration of Brixham Cave, Conducted by a Committee of the Geological Society, and under the Immediate Superintendence and Record of Wm. Pengelly, Esq., F.R.S., Aided by a Local Committee; with Descriptions of the Organic Remains by G. Busk, Esq., F.R.S., and of the Flint Implements by John Evans, Esq., F.R.S. [Abstract]," *Proceedings of the Royal Society of London* 20 (1871–72): 514–24.

60. Segal 2000, 770–72; Wilson 1851, [1]–5; Lyell 1863, 11; Goldstein 2004; "The International Congress of Archaic Anthropology," *Anthropological Review* 6 (1868): 203–5. The term *pre-historic* had occasionally been used before the 1860s (first in 1832, according to the *Oxford English Dictionary*), but without the resonance it gained when *pre-history* suddenly came to encompass most of human existence. I am cribbing from the title of Samuel Noah Kramer's once famous book, *History Begins at Sumer*.

61. Trigger 2006, 171–76.

62. Hegel's exhibit A was sub-Saharan Africa. He called it "the land of childhood, which lying beyond the day of self-conscious history, is enveloped in the dark mantle of Night"; Hegel 1956, 91.

63. Burrow 2008, xiv; Samuel R. Gardiner to W.E.H. Lecky, February 8, 1882, W.E.H. Lecky Papers, MSS 1827–36/247, Manuscripts Department, Trinity College Dublin.

64. Kames 2007, 1:3; Bryce 1913, 351; F. York Powell, "To the Reader," in Langlois and Seignobos [1898], v; Charles M. Andrews to H. B. Adams, May 19, 1892, Herbert Baxter Adams Papers, MS 4, Series 1, Box 1, Johns Hopkins University Archives; Andrew C. McLaughlin, "History and Its Neighbors," p. 6, TS lecture, n.d., Andrew Cunningham McLaughlin Papers, Box 3, Folder 8, Special Collections Research Center, University of Chicago Library.

65. Langlois and Seignobos [1900], 2; Langlois and Seignobos [1898]; Lord Acton, untitled MS proposal to Syndicate [= Syndics] of Cambridge University Press, October 1896 [prior to October 21], University Archives CUP: CMH I/1–14, Department of Manuscripts and University Archives, Cambridge University Library; Wylie 1886.

66. Krieger 1977, 3; F. W. Maitland to Lord Acton, October 27, 1895, Add. MS 8119, and Richard Garnett to Lord Acton, February 3, 1900, Add. MS 8119 (1)/G972, Department of Manuscripts and University Archives, Cambridge University Library; H. B. Adams to Henry Cabot Lodge, June 2, 1872, in Adams 1982–88, 2:138–39.

67. Momigliano 1955, 367–69; J. Franklin Jameson to Albert Shaw, February 27, 1883, in Jameson 1993–2001, 2:84; John Acton to Lord Granville, May 6, 1854, in Acton 1917, 26–27; Andrew C. McLaughlin, diary of 1893–94 study in Germany, bound MS volume, entries for November 3, 1893, and January 29 and February 20, 1894, Andrew Cunningham McLaughlin Papers, Bentley Historical Library, University of Michigan–Ann Arbor; J. Franklin Jameson, diary, November 3 [1882], quoted in Jameson 1993–2001, 1:13; Jameson 1993–2001,

1:16, 269; Henry Adams to Lewis Henry Morgan, October 3, 1875, in Adams 1982–88, 2:238; J. Franklin Jameson to Joseph Dunn, February 28, 1923, cited in Jameson 1993–2001, 3:382.

68. Morison 1964, 264; Dixon 1902, 185; Soffer 1994, 55–56; Roberts and Turner 2000, 79; Levine 1986, 135–58. For Belfast and Toronto, see chapter 6.

69. Novick 1988, 31–46; Turner 2002, 753–72; Henry Adams to Lewis Henry Morgan, October 3, 1875, in Adams 1982–88, 2:238. *Civilization and Decay* propounded a cyclical law of advance and decay governing all history.

70. Iggers 1968, 80–96; Iggers and Wang 2008, 69–82; Burrow 2008, 382–86, 429–311; Adams, "Is History Past Politics?" 190–93, 198; Link 1985, 8–9; H. B. Adams to D. C. Gilman, undated draft. ["cApril1890" penciled in; fall 1890 more likely], Herbert Baxter Adams Papers, MS 4, Series 1, Box 6, Johns Hopkins University Archives; Jacobs 1968, 74–76; Goldstein 1990, 142–44; Momigliano 1994, 202–3. Adams himself published a history of the College of William and Mary (1887) and a biography of Jared Sparks (1893), neither of them political history.

71. Stuchtey and Wende 2000, 14; Burrow 2008, 383; F. J. Turner to H. B. Adams, May 17, 1891, Herbert Baxter Adams Papers, MS 4, Series 1, Box 16, Johns Hopkins University Archives; Jennifer Rutner and Roger C. Schonfeld, "Supporting the Changing Research Practices of Historians," (final report from Ithaka S+R, December 10, 2012, http://blog .historians.org/news/1847/ithaka-sr-report-changing-research-practices-among-historians, 8, accessed December 21, 2012).

72. Albert Bushnell Hart to Claude Van Tyne, December 13, 1902, Fredric L. Paxson to Claude Van Tyne, n.d. [March 1903], D. C. Munro to Claude Van Tyne, May 2, 1904, box 1, Claude Halstead Van Tyne Papers, and Andrew C. McLaughlin, autobiographical statement, n.d. [ca. 1938 or 1939], Andrew Cunningham McLaughlin Papers, Bentley Historical Library, University of Michigan–Ann Arbor; Charles K. Adams to H. B. Adams, June 2, 188?, Edward P. Allinson to H. B. Adams, May 20, 1885, Charles M. Andrews to H. B. Adams, October 8, 1900 ("strictly"), Herbert Baxter Adams Papers, MS 4, Series 1, Box 1, and J. Franklin Jameson to H. B. Adams, January 14, 1898, Adams Papers, Box 9, Johns Hopkins University Archives; Haskell 1977, 145, 168–77; Novick 1988, 48–49; Townsend 2009; Link 1985, 1–3, 7–11; J. Franklin Jameson, "The American Historical Association, 1884–1909," *American Historical Review* 15 (1909): 4–6, 11–13, 16–17, 19; Blouin and Rosenberg 2011, 36–37. McLaughlin got a law degree after his BA; he slid into teaching history at Michigan after starting as a Latin instructor. Ten of the AHA's first twenty-five presidents did not teach in a university.

73. Levine 1986, 164–68; James Bryce to H. B. Adams, June 18, 1882, June 23 [ca. 1882], August 2[7?, 1886?], October 11, 1886, Herbert Baxter Adams Papers, MS 4, Series 1, Box 3, Johns Hopkins University Archives; Kenyon 1984, 191–94; Mandell Creighton to Lord Acton, July 17, September 14, and December 23, 1885, January 24, 1887, and January 23, 1889, Add. MS 8119 (1)/C248–50, 255, 272, Lord Acton to Mandell Creighton, July 25, July 31, August 14, and December 26, 1885, and January 19, 1886, Add. MS 6871/5–10, 13–16, 27–28, 35, Department of Manuscripts and University Archives, Cambridge University Library; Lord Acton, "German Schools of History," *English Historical Review* 1 (1886): 7–42; Stuchtey and Wende 2000, 159–72.

74. Kenyon 1984, 194–95; Daunton 2005, 181–82; R. C. Jebb to Lord Acton, November 27, 1896, Add. MS 8119 (3)/J20, and F. W. Maitland to Lord Acton, 27 November [1896], Add. MS 6443/199, Department of Manuscripts and University Archives, Cambridge University Library; Ellis P. Oberholtzer to Claude Van Tyne, December 29, 1903, box 1, Claude Halstead Van Tyne Papers, Bentley Historical Library, University of Michigan–Ann Arbor.

75. Kenyon 1984, 197–98; Oleson and Voss 1979, 77; Charles M. Andrews to H. B. Adams,

November 22, 1893, Herbert Baxter Adams Papers, MS 4, Series 1, Box 1, Johns Hopkins University Archives.

76. James E. McClellan III, "George Alfred Léon Sarton," *American National Biography*; George R. Coffman, "The Mediaeval Academy of America: Historical Background and Prospect," *Speculum* 1 (1926): 5–18; Negley Harte, "The Economic History Society, 1926–2001," http://www.ehs.org.uk/ehs/AbouttheEHS/ehshistory.asp, accessed September 20, 2012.

77. J. Franklin Jameson to H. B. Adams, January 14, 1898, Herbert Baxter Adams Papers, MS 4, Series 1, Box 9, Johns Hopkins University Archives.

78. Kaufmann 2001, esp. 536 and 541.

79. Kultermann 1993, 93–94; Waetzoldt 1965, 2:70–92.

80. Kultermann 1993, 87–89, 91–92; Waetzoldt 1965, 1:287–[318], 2:29–45. For a hostile, sometimes strained, but not unperceptive account of the philological leaning of nineteenth-century German art historians, see Venturi 1964, 213–20.

81. Littlejohns 1991, 242; Schwarzer 1995, 25; Waagen 1822; Waagen 1860.

82. Waetzoldt 1965, 2:143–209; Kugler 1861; Jacob Burkhardt, "Author's Preface to Second Edition," in [Kugler and Burckhardt] 1855, vi.

83. Lyons 2005, esp. chap. 1; Dunlap 1965; Coad 1917, 271, 274; Thomas 1967, esp. 72 (Hopkins), 163–66, 176–82, 214–15, 218; Johnston 1997, esp. chaps. 6 and 7.

84. William P. Campbell, "Introduction," in Dunlap 1965, xxi; Lee Sorenson, "Jameson, Anna [Brownell], née Anna Brownell Murphy," *Dictionary of Art Historians*, http://www.dictionaryofarthistorians.org/jamesona.htm, accessed September 26, 2012.

85. Dianne Sachko Macleod, "Stephens, Frederic George," *Oxford Dictionary of National Biography*; Stephens 1875, v; Jarves 1960. Benjamin Rowland's introduction provides a helpful understanding of the context of the book.

86. Avery-Quash and Sheldon 2011, esp. chap. 2, 131–32, and chap. 5; Robertson 1978, 100–107, 109–10, 118, 135, 150, 237–40; Eastlake 1883, 1:8, 2:[3], 105.

87. Avery-Quash and Sheldon 2011, esp. chaps. 1, 3–4; Robertson 1978; Whitehead 2005, passim.

88. Eastlake 1847; Avery-Quash and Sheldon 2011, 138–40, 142–44, 151–61, 167–69. After Eastlake's death, Lady Eastlake edited chapters he had prepared for a second volume on oil painting in Italy.

89. Oleson and Voss 1979, 82. In Baltimore, America's fourth largest city in 1870, the private collection of the liquor, banking, and railroad magnate William Walters partly served the function of a civic museum. In the twentieth century, it became a genuine public museum as the Walters Art Museum.

90. Blunt 1965, esp. 135–50 (quotations 135); Panayotova 2008.

91. Mansfield 2002, 85–97; Miyahara 2006, 24–30, 32–37; David M. Wilson, "Slade, Felix," *Oxford Dictionary of National Biography*; Ruskin 1870, 12 (quotation); Wyatt 1870. At Edinburgh from 1895 a student could count two courses of art history toward an honors degree in history; Miyahara 2006, 36–37.

92. Jaffe 1983, 190–91; Smyth and Lukehart 1993, 69–70; Weir 1957, 67.

93. Smyth and Lukehart 1993, 57–62, 153–55; Leila C. Barber, J. Howard Howson, and Agnes R. Claflin, "Oliver Samuel Tonks, 1874–1953" (memorial minute), faculty meeting minutes, XIII, 433–34, box 20, Archives and Special Collections, Vassar College Libraries, http://digitallibrary.vassar.edu/fedora/repository/vassar%3A31995, accessed July 19, 2013; Hiss and Fansler 1934, 17–18.

94. The answer or answers are difficult to get at, first, because comparatively few scholars have looked into the history of the discipline and, second, because the twentieth-century art historians who did write about the origins of their field often did so with a skewed sense

of its history. Some of them conceived the 'early years' as the 1920s and 1930s, inadvertently drawing a veil over the decades when the field actually emerged in the United States. Others projected back into the past methods and preoccupations of their own graduate training as young art historians, blanking out the thinking of the founding generation. Both of these problems are well illustrated in the contributions to Smyth and Lukehart 1993. To anyone who has read the lectures, publications, or correspondence of Charles Eliot Norton, the thinking of this key figure is unrecognizable as described in intelligent essays by Agnes Mongan and Sybil Gordon Kantor.

95. Charles Eliot Norton, *The Holbein Madonna* (London? privately printed, 1872), and "Urkunden zur Geschichte des Doms von Siena," *Jarhrbücher für Kunstwissenschaft* 5 (1872): 66–90 (copies of both of these rare items are in the Harvard College Library); 1879–80 Harvard catalog, cited in Hiss and Fansler 1934, 22. Norton also assigned Viollet-le-Duc, and he continued to demand a reading knowledge of ancient Greek and modern French, but these were common abilities among Harvard students. My discussion of Norton draws heavily on Turner 1999.

96. Turner 1999, 235, 256, 260. No hard evidence seems to remain of Norton's responsibility for Moore's move into the college, but there is no other plausible candidate.

97. Even in adolescence, Charles had begun to absorb philological principles at home (where Andrews worked), from a father unusually engaged with his children's intellectual formation. Helping to edit his father's scholarly remains after his death in 1853 can only have strengthened his grasp.

98. The language of this and the preceding paragraph are adapted from Turner 1999, 258, 260 (quotations from Norton, "Syllabus of Lectures, 1874–75").

99. Smyth and Lukehart 1993, 60–61, 156–58; Turner 1999, 277, 366; Lavin 1983, 8–12, 15; Padgett 1996, 107–8; Rosasco 1996, 13, 30–41; on the 'prehistory' of the Princeton department, see Rosasco 1996, 7–14, 17–26, 30; Francis W. Kelsey to Allan Marquand, 9 September 1895, in Box 14, folder 33, Marquand Papers.

100. Rosasco 1996, 23–24; Turner 1999, 293; Prime and McClellan, 1882, 4–8.

101. Allan Marquand, "Stryzgowski and His Theory of Early Christian Art," *Harvard Theological Review* 3 (1910): 365; [Allan Marquand], "Early Christian Iconography and a School of Ivory Carvers in Provence, by E. Baldwin Smith," MS, n.d. [ca. 1918], Box 9; Robert Koldewey to Allan Marquand, April 2, 1910, in Box 14, folder 40 ("streng systematische Behandlung"); [Marquand], "Ghiberti and the Baptistry Gates," MS (draft) and TS with MS corrections, n.d., pp. 1–2, Box 9; [Marquand], "The History of Art as a University Study," MS, 1891, p. 9, Box 9; and [Marquand], "On Scientific Method in the Study of Art," MS, n.d., p. 39, Box 10, folder 22; all in Marquand Papers.

102. Schwarzer 1995, 25–28; Lee Sorensen, "Springer, Anton [Heinrich]," *Dictionary of Art Historians*,www.dictionaryofarthistorians.org, accessed October 11, 2012.

103. Hiss and Fansler 1934, 35–37, 181–97 (list); Lavin 1983, 15; Brush 2003, 15–16. I arrive at "some eight universities" by counting schools that awarded at least one PhD by 1920 (lumping Harvard and Radcliffe as a single institution) and omitting dissertations in technical archaeology. Both Yale (1832) and the University of Michigan (1858; Hiss and Fansler 1934, 8) had earlier art museums, but not for instructional purposes. In 1895 the Fogg was a building in Harvard Yard latterly known as Hunt Hall; it was torn down in the early 1970s.

104. Hiss and Fansler 1934, 181–97; Oleson and Voss 1979, 82; Holmes Smith, "Problems of the College Art Association," *Bulletin of the College Art Association* 1, no. 1 (1913): 7–8; Professor John Ankeney to Allan Marquand, November 10, 1913, in Box 12, folder 24, Marquand Papers; E. B. Smith 1912, [v]. The parent organization of the College Art Association was the Western Drawing and Manual Training Association, for which both art history and collegiate instruction were secondary.

105. Miyahara 2006, 36, 40–41; Jebb, "Newton," liv.

106. Petrie and Stokes 1872–78; Stokes 1878; Stokes 1887; C. L. Falkiner, "Stokes, Margaret M'Nair," rev. Marie-Louise Legg, *Oxford Dictionary of National Biography*; "Preface," *Journal of the Royal Society of Antiquaries of Ireland*, 5th ser., 10 (1900): vi–viii.

107. R. Langton Douglas, Director of the National Gallery of Ireland, to Thomas Patrick Bodkin, 23 November 1917, MS 6961/7, Thomas Patrick Bodkin Papers, Manuscripts Department, Trinity College Dublin; Links 1976: 311; Charles Waldstein/Walston, quoted in Hiss and Fansler 1934, 30; Mansfield 2002, 231–42; Robert Brown, "Oral History Interview with W. G. Constable, 1972 July–1973 June," Archives of American Art, Smithsonian Institution, http://www.aaa.si.edu/collections/interviews/oral-history-interview-w-g-constable-12210, accessed September 25, 2012. The *Burlington Magazine* dropped "for connoisseurs" from its title in 1948 on grounds of mustiness.

108. Miyahara 2006, 182–85 (quoting Paviere and the Royal Commission).

109. Brush 2003, 194–98; Links 1976, 311; Brown, "Interview with Constable"; Peter Kidson, "A Short History of the Courtauld Institute, 1931–2001," pp. 2–4, 2002, TS, in Archives File III, Viscount Lee of Fareham, "Draft Memorandum on the Provision of Facilities for the Study of the History of Art," 30 November 1928, TS, CIA2/2007(1)/4, Lee of Fareham, "Note on Foreign Educational Facilities," n.d. [1928], TS, CIA2/2007(1)/5, W. G. Constable to J[ames]. G[ow]. Mann, 19 July 1932, CIA 2/74, Minutes, Committee of Management, 22 June 1936, TS, CIA 3/123, Library, Courtauld Institute of Art; Constable 1954. The archives of the Courtauld Institute were on the verge of reorganization when I visited in spring 2009; the citations I give may no longer be accurate. Constable's sudden resignation apparently left the Courtauld staff in great "distress": George Hill to Electors to the Directorship of the Fitzwilliam Museum, January 22, 1937, W. G. Constable Papers, Archives of American Art, Smithsonian Institution.

110. Harold Tomlinson to W. G. Constable, February 8, 1935, W. G. Constable Papers, Archives of American Art, Smithsonian Institution. Tomlinson was secretary of the Faculty Board of Fine Arts in Cambridge.

111. Brush 2003.

112. Lee Sorenson, "Wittkower, Rudolf" and "Panofsky, Erwin," *Dictionary of Art Historians*, http://www.dictionaryofarthistorians.org, accessed October 5, 2012.

113. Clark 1974, 150–51. Clark, almost needless to say, erred in suggesting that no one cared about the correctness of emendations. I thank my colleague Dianne Phillips for leading me to this quotation.

114. "Appreciation" already appears as the parallel to "art production" in the opening manifesto of the College Art Association: Smith, "Problems of College Art Association," 6.

CHAPTER 12. "THE FIELD NATURALISTS OF HUMAN NATURE"

This chapter's title comes from Andrew Lang in [Thomas] 1907, [1], referring to students sent out from Oxford for fieldwork by E. B. Tylor.

1. Stocking 1987, 30–36; platform, http://www.ushistory.org/gop/convention_1856republicanplatform.htm, accessed October 12, 2012.

2. [Thomas] 1907, [1]–2.

3. W. P. Ker, "Culture," MS, 8 November 1896, KER 2/45, W. P. Ker Papers, Special Collections, University College London; Van Keuren 1991, 46 (Marett quotation), 48–49, 53–59; Rivière 2009, 44; Darnell 1988, 37, 75; Kuper 1988, 1–9.

4. John Wesley Powell, "The Humanities," *Forum* 10 (1890): 411 (quotation); Stocking 1987, 52; Van Keuren 1991, 54.

5. Stocking 1987, 48. The term *ethnography* was coined by a German scholar in the service of Catherine the Great; see chapter 4. Today's terminology confuses the nineteenth-century situation. Cultural anthropology now treats beliefs, values, and symbols; social anthropology focuses on social groups and institutions. The distinction is not always clear-cut. In the United States, 'cultural anthropology' typically includes social anthropology (or both fit under a newer label, 'sociocultural anthropology'). In the United Kingdom social anthropology dominates, and cultural anthropology is a smaller but distinct species. None of these subdisciplines existed before the twentieth century; all are thus treated indistinguishably in this chapter.

6. Cunnington 1975, quotations at 1, 57, 62; Levine 1986, 88–89; Wilson 1851, xxi. The publication history is complicated. The first volume, 1812, was *The Ancient History of South Wiltshire* (before the Romans); pt. 1 of vol. 2, 1819, covered pre-Roman north Wiltshire; pt. 2 of vol. 2, 1821, covered Roman Wiltshire.

7. Levine 1986, 88–89 (Marsden quote, 89); Thompson Cooper, "Marsden, John Howard," rev. H.C.G. Matthew, *Oxford Dictionary of National Biography*; Bateman 1861, [v]–vii; Margaret O'Sullivan, "Bateman, Thomas," *Oxford Dictionary of National Biography*; Penniman 1974, 56.

8. Lewis 2011, 74–92; Jefferson 1972, 97–100; Silverberg 1968, chap. 2; Harvey 2009, 151–53; Wallace 1999, 158; Trigger 2006, 159–61. Brackenridge is best known today for his satirical novel *Modern Chivalry*.

9. Ted D. Stahly, "Caleb Atwater," *American National Biography*; Lewis 2011, 92–100; "Report of the Committee . . . [to report on] the Progress and Present State of the Institution," *Archaeologia Americana: Transactions and Collections of the American Antiquarian Society* 1 (1820): 49; Atwater 1820, quotations at 107, 122, 194; Silverberg 1968, 60–75. Atwater's reports began with brief accounts of antiquities of "Indians of the present race" in the Ohio region (111) and of earlier Europeans before launching into his much longer studies of the builders of the ancient mounds. The great Mayan centers lay unknown to non-Mayans until the 1840s; otherwise they might have figured as the mound builders' destination.

10. Silverberg 1968, 109–32; Barnhart 2005, chaps. 2–4; Hinsley 1981, 35–38; Norton, "Ancient Monuments in America," *North American Review* 68 (1849): 466–96; Turner 1999, 64–65; Bieder 1986, chap. 4. Squier's *Aboriginal Monuments of the State of New York* was the second volume in the Smithsonian's "Contributions to Knowledge."

11. Bartlett 1848, 4 (quotation), 8–13; Veit 1997, 104–8. Veit has a higher opinion of Dickeson's archaeology than I have developed.

12. Ash et al. 1999, 60–80; Wilson 1851, esp. xiii–xviii, 3–4 (quotations, table of contents and xiii); Carl Berger, "Sir Daniel Wilson," *Dictionary of Canadian Biography Online*, http://www.biographi.ca, accessed October 23, 2012; Trigger 1966, 6–9; Trigger 1992, 56–57, 61–63.

13. Squier 1851, [vii]; Friedrich Ratzel, "Heckewelder, Johann Gottlieb Ernst," *Allgemeine Deutsche Biographie* 11 (1880): 214–15, http://www.deutsche-biographie.de/sfz98764.html, accessed October 19, 2012; Bieder 1986, 153 (quotation).

14. Gallatin 1836, [9]–159; Wissler 1942, 193–94; Greene 1984, 403–407; Bieder 1975, 93–94; Bieder 1986, 32–42.

15. Hinsley 1981, 20–21, 47; Bieder 1986, chap. 5; Helen Hornbeck Tanner, "Henry Rowe Schoolcraft," *American National Biography*; Schoolcraft 1839, 1:[9]–13, 18–20, 24, 26–27; Harvey 2009, 371. The Ojibwe people are also called Chippewa. Schoolcraft intended *Algic Researches* as a first installment in a three-part study—the second covering "hieroglyphics, music, and poetry," the third Indian languages as such. Parts 2 and 3 never appeared.

16. Harvey 2009, 369–71; Bieder 1975, 93–94; Bieder 1986, 13, 43–44, 175–77; list of officers and members, *Transactions of the American Ethnological Society* 2 (1848): [iii]–vi. I do

not count the well over one hundred corresponding and honorary members, doubting that Leopold von Ranke or Cardinal Wiseman longed to attend a meeting. In the early twentieth century, Franz Boas at Columbia gave the society new life; eventually it merged into the American Anthropological Association, of which it is today a section.

17. Stanton 1975, chaps 2–3 and pp. 73–76.

18. Stanton 1975; Gruber 1967, 9–11; Latham 1850, ix; Albert Gallatin, ed., "Hale's Indians of North-West America, and Vocabularies of North America, with an Introduction," *Transactions of the American Ethnological Society* 2 (1848): xxiii–130.

19. Stocking 1987, 79–80.

20. Stocking 1987, 81–87; James Belich, "Grey, Sir George," *Oxford Dictionary of National Biography*.

21. Stocking 1987, 240–45 ("authentic," 242); Penniman 1974, 53 ("centre").

22. Hinsley 1981, 28; Augstein 1999, chap. 6.

23. Smith 1991, 100–111; Zimmerman 2001, 5; Sergi 1884, [3]; Daniel G. Brinton, "The Nomenclature and Teaching of Anthropology," *American Anthropologist* 5 (1892): 264. Thus the German equivalent (founded 1869) of the Anthropological Institute of Great Britain and Ireland (founded only two years later) was the Berliner Gesellschaft für Anthropologie, Ethnologie, und Urgeschichte—Berlin Society for Anthropology, Ethnology, and Prehistory. Zimmerman obscures this distinction by anachronistically using 'anthropology' to refer to all three related fields. The German language still does not use *Anthropologie* in its English sense, while the web site of the *Deutschen Gesellschaft für Völkerkunde* translates both *Völkerkunde* and *Ethnologie* into English as anthropology, http://www.dgv-net.de /english.html, accessed November 14, 2012.

24. Mark 1988, 319–24, 332; Trigger 2006, 279–80; Haddon 1898, xvi, xviii–xix, 395–97. The Torres Strait, home to many islands and a few thousand Melanesian islanders, separates Australia and New Guinea. The 1898–99 Cambridge University Torres Straits expedition was the first time an entire expedition had been sent out from Britain for specifically anthropological research (some earlier exploring expeditions had included an anthropologist). Its considerable influence lay mainly in pioneering scholarly fieldwork and use of photography and sound recording. See Herle and Rouse 1998; Kuklick 2008, 63–64. Haddon had been there ten years earlier in his earlier incarnation as marine biologist, to study coral reefs.

25. Darnell 1988, 34–37, 50–57, 60; Brinton, "Nomenclature and Teaching," 265–68; Haddon 1898, 396. Brinton's appointment was as professor of "Archaeology and Linguistics" at the University of Pennsylvania.

26. Dieserud 1908, 2 (quotation); Sanderson 1990, chap. 3; Hinsley 1981, 133; Darnell 1998, 87–90; Trigger 1981, 74–75; Darnell 1988, 21, 135; Stocking 1995, 10–13 and chap. 4; Kuper 1988, chap. 7. The copyright date of Dieserud is 1908, but the preface is dated 1906.

27. J. W. Powell, "Sketch of Lewis H. Morgan," *Popular Science Monthly* 18 (1880): 115; Trigger 1992, 57; Brew 1968, 6–14, 125 (Eggan); Van Keuren 1991, 45, 48; Kuklick 2008, 54–60, 63–65; Stocking 1987, 247–52, 256–58; Penniman 1974, 91; Thomas R. Trautmann, "Lewis Henry Morgan," *American National Biography*; Mark 1980, 98–107; Marett 1936, 15; Darnell 1988, 37; Darnell 1998, 108; Barbara Freire-Marreco to J. L. Myres, July 5 [1909], John Linton Myres Papers, MS Myres 16, f. 82 ("wrong"), Western Manuscripts, Bodleian Library, Oxford University. Tylor became professor in 1895. The Anthropological Institute acquired the appellation 'Royal' in 1907. Following Morgan, three other anthropologists served an annual term as AAAS president before 1900: in order, Powell, Brinton, and Frederic W. Putnam. The idea that fieldwork is essential to anthropological training is often attributed to Franz Boas, but it seems to have been floating around quite generally circa 1900 because of the example of Americanist anthropologists like Alice Fletcher.

28. Darnell 1998, 246–51; *Man: A Monthly Record of Anthropological Science* 1 (1901): [i]; William Crooke to J. L. Myres, January 30, 1897, and J. L. Myres to Havelock Ellis [draft], n.d. [late November or early December 1896], Myres Papers, MS Myres 59, ff. 12–13, ff. 14–15, Western Manuscripts, Bodleian Library, Oxford University. The businessman was John Morgan Richards. His daughter, Pearl Craigie, was a popular novelist (writing as John Oliver Hobbes), which may help to explain the *Academy*'s literary turning under her father's ownership. Myres became *Man*'s first editor. His son was the great librarian of the Bodleian, Nowell Myres.

29. Gilbert Thompson, "An Indian Dance at Jemez, New Mexico," *American Anthropologist* 2 (1889): 352.

30. James G. Frazer to Henry Jackson, August 24, 1888, Add. MS c.30.46, Wren Library, Trinity College Cambridge; James G. Frazer to Francis Galton, November 24, 1907 ("collect"), Galton 243, Special Collections, University College London.

31. Physical anthropology is thus primarily a biological science but places biology in the context of human and primate behavior. Given their concern with human evolution, physical anthropologists began sometimes to call themselves biological anthropologists when the modern neo-Darwinian synthesis triumphed toward the end of the first half of the twentieth century; the DNA revolution encouraged the trend to renaming. In the same Darwinian context, they also began serious study of the primate fossil ancestors and living relatives of human beings. The names of professional organizations reflect this history. The American one, founded in 1930, is called the American Association of Physical Anthropologists (AAPA), while the very recent (1999) British equivalent is the British Association for Biological Anthropology and Osteoarchaeology. The Canadian Association for Physical Anthropology dates only from 1972 but was an offshoot of the AAPA, presumably explaining its old-fashioned name.

32. Frazer 1907, 9 (copy in Galton 243) and James G. Frazer to Francis Galton, June 1, 1888, Galton 243, Special Collections, University College London; James G. Frazer to Henry Jackson, May 31, 1888 (letter tipped into Frazer's pamphlet *Questions on the Manners, Customs, Religions, Superstitions, &c., of Uncivilized or Semi-civilized Peoples*), 289.c.85.31515, Wren Library, Trinity College Cambridge; Trautmann 1987, 81; Worster 2001, 398–99, 524; Darnell 1998, chap. 4; Darnell 1988. An anthropologist might also have gotten the idea of a questionnaire from natural historians (Kuklick 2008, 53–54); and the 1874 *Notes and Queries in Anthropology, for the Use of Travelers and Residents in Uncivilized Lands*, prepared under Tylor's supervision, seems to have been a formalization of the long tradition of seeking ethnological data from missionaries and colonial officials (Stocking 1995, 15–16); but Frazer mentioned Morgan's list specifically.

33. James G. Frazer to Henry Jackson, n.d. [1888?], Add. MS c.30.35–48, Wren Library, Trinity College Cambridge; Sanderson 1990, 16; Kuper 1988, 66–67; Macfarlane 1991, 136–41; James G. Frazer to George A. Macmillan, January 1, 1890, Add. MSS 55134/ff. 32–33, British Library. The most acute historical study of Victorian social evolutionism remains Burrow 1970; for a briefer summation, see Sanderson 1990, chap. 2.

34. Collini, Winch, and Burrow 1983, chap. 7; J. Franklin Jameson to Robert Simpson Woodward, 22 December 1906, in Jameson 1993–2001, 3:30; Freeman 1872, 3, 9; Freeman 1874, vii, 18, and more generally lecture 1. Jameson cited specifically Maine's *Ancient Law*, which he thought more valuable than any other "scientific books, excepting one or two of Darwin's," published in the period. Jameson, director of the Department of Historical Research of the Carnegie Institution, was pleading with Woodward, the Institution's president, to increase funding for "the philological sciences."

35. Müller 1861–64, 1:314; Müller 1895b, 260.

36. Macfarlane 1991, 141; Stocking 1987, 299–301; Chris Holdsworth, "Tylor, Sir Edward

446 • NOTES TO CHAPTER 12

Burnett," *Oxford Dictionary of National Biography*; Marett 1936, 14–15, 47; Tylor 1871, 1:1. On the iconic status of Tylor's sentence, see Stocking 1987, 300. The textbook, *Anthropology: An Introduction to the Study of Man and Civilization*, was also Tylor's last book.

37. Marett 1936, 11–13 and chap. 2; Holdsworth, "Tylor."

38. Kuper 1988, 79.

39. [Edward B. Tylor], "The Science of Language," *Quarterly Review* 119 (1866): 394–435 (disagreeing with Müller on origin of language, 424–25 and 428–29); Edward B. Tylor, "On the Origin of Language," *Fortnightly Review* 4 (1866): 544–559 (elaborates Tylor's own theory); Edward B. Tylor, "The Religion of Savages," *Fortnightly Review* 6 (1866): 71–86 (quotations, 81, 82, 85; explicit rejection of Müller's theory, 81); Marett 1936, chap. 6; Kuklick 2008, 115–19.

40. Kuper 1988, 81–84; Smart et al. 1985, 3:230–31 (essay by Edmund Leach); Marett 1936, chap. 6. Leach, in his haste to slay his embarrassingly simpleminded forefather, did not recognize how important it was that Tylor gave anthropology a category to organize and focus research.

41. Kuper 1988, 98.

42. Feaver 1969.

43. Jolly 2006, 557; Maine 1861, [v]; Kuper 1988, 22–23; 32–33.

44. Momigliano 1994, 237.

45. Burrow 1970, 139–41; Grant Duff 1892, 13–14; Maine 1871, 22.

46. Maine 1861, [v], 117, 119, 121–22. Maine, like William Jones, spelled Manu 'Menu.'

47. Macfarlane 1991, 100–117; Maine 1861, 122–24, 126, 170.

48. Grant Duff 1892, 3, 6; Feaver 1969, 8, 15; Burrow 1970, 157. The sources of Maine's anthropology and its motives pose very different questions. For his anti-Benthamite motives, see Feaver 1969, passim, and Kuper 1988, 17–20, 23–24, 29–31.

49. Maine 1861, 122; Burrow 1970, 148, 161–62; *Times*, quoted in Grant Duff 1892, 74. In invoking comparative philology, Maine did resemble the Darwin of 1859, who repeatedly used comparative philology to lend plausibility to his method of argument; Alter 1999.

50. Müller 1895b, 260; Stubbs 1874–78, 1:32.

51. Morgan 1870; Kuper 1988, 72–74; Hinsley 1981, 28, 133–36. At first, British anthropologists tended to look down their noses at the upstart American; Stocking 1995, 23. A reprint of *Systems of Consanguinity*, with introduction by Elisabeth Tooker, was published in 1997 by the University of Nebraska Press. (The book originally appeared in the same series, Contributions to Knowledge, inaugurated by Davis and Squier's survey of Indian mounds.) The essential work on Morgan's anthropology is Trautmann 1987, which my account follows closely.

52. Trautmann 1987, 3–6; Morgan 1868, 436–38. Morgan coined "Ganowánian" (which he also wrote as "Gänowänian," and also with no diacritical marks) from *gäno* ('arrow') and *wääno* ('bow'): "the family of the Bow and Arrow." (He does not identify the language.) Morgan 1868, 438n. Morgan 1868 can be found in the library of the Peabody Museum at Harvard; Morgan read the paper on which it is based to a meeting of the American Academy of Arts and Sciences on February 11, 1868.

53. Morgan 1868, 438; Morgan 1870, vi–vii.

54. Morgan 1868, 438–39, 445, 451; Trautmann 1987, 7–9.

55. Morgan 1868, 439 (quotation), 462–77.

56. B. Malinowski, "Kinship," *Man* 30 (1930): 19; Fox 1983, 10; Trautmann 1987, 255.

57. Trautmann 1987, 258, 262–64; Kuper 1988, 74; Fortes 1969, esp. pt. 1.

58. Trautmann 1987, 6.

59. Trautmann 1987, 6; Hinsley 1981, 28–29; Morgan 1870, v–vi; Whitney 1867, 383–84.

60. Trautmann 1987, 263; cf. Kuper 1988, 51–56.

61. For Frazer and Smith, see chapter 11; for Smith, see chapter 13; for Brinton, see Darnell 1988; for Kroeber, see Steward, Gibson, and Rowe 1961, esp. 1040, 1043, 1052, 1055.

62. [Thomas] 1907; Rivière 2009, 43–46, 59; Peter Rivière, "Marett, Robert Ranulph," *Oxford Dictionary of National Biography*; R. R. Marett to Gilbert Murray, 4 February 1908, Gilbert Murray Papers, MS Gilbert Murray 13, f. 72, Western Manuscripts, Bodleian Library, Oxford University; Marett 1908, 3–4; Barbara Freire-Marreco and J. L. Myres correspondence, MS Myres 16, J. L. Myres to Herbert Fisher, 29 March 1912, MS Myres 14, f. 26, John Linton Myres Papers, Western Manuscripts, Bodleian Library. The lecturers published in Marett's 1908 volume were Arthur J. Evans, Andrew Lang, Gilbert Murray, F. B. Jevons, J. L. Myres, and W. Warde Fowler. Myres initiated Marett into anthropology by inviting him to present a paper to the anthropological section at the 1899 meeting of the British Association. Freire-Marreco (1879–1967), later Barbara Aitken, eventually did fieldwork among Indians in both Arizona and New Mexico, informally supervised by Alice Fletcher (arranged through Myres's acquaintance with Fletcher); while in the United States she also met Adolph Bandelier and Franz Boas.

Chapter 13. "The Highest and Most Engaging of the Manifestations of Human Nature"

This chapter's title comes from Renan 1992, 15: "La religion est certainement la plus haute et la plus attachante des manifestations de la nature humaine . . ."

1. Peter Hinchliff and John Prest, "Jowett, Benjamin," *Oxford Dictionary of National Biography*; C. K. Barrett, "Lightfoot, Joseph Barber," *Oxford Dictionary of National Biography*.

2. Neill 1964, chap. 2 and 69–76; Cameron 1987, 39–41; Treloar 1998, 6–8, chap. 10, 326–30, 360–70; Noll 1991, 68–70; Metzger and Ehrman 2005, 62–64, 172–83; Smart et al. 1985, 3:150. Key to Lightfoot's achievement was his secure dating of the letters of Ignatius of Antioch and Clement of Rome to just after 100 CE; these epistles cited most books of the New Testament, showing them already in existence, while displaying no trace of an ongoing quarrel between Baur's parties—Judaizing disciples of Peter and 'gentile-izing' followers of Paul.

3. Smart et al. 1985, 3:143–44. Oxford first made biblical criticism a teaching field in 1868, when Balliol created a Semitics fellowship for T. K. Cheyne; Joanna Hawke, "Cheyne, Thomas Kelly," *Oxford Dictionary of National Biography*.

4. Noll 1991, 15–56, 71–75; Rogerson 1984, chaps. 17, 20; Shea and Whitla 2000, 7, 122; Massa 1990, chaps. 3–4 and pp. 124–25; Weber 1982, 102–110; Marsden 2006.

5. Rogerson 1984, 132–34, 257; Smart et al. 1985, 3:117.

6. Smart et al. 1985, 3:122–26 (quotation, 124); Rogerson 1984, chap. 6.

7. Rogerson 1984, 257–67; Smart et al. 1985, 128–31; Wellhausen 2001, 12 ("das Gebiet der gottesdienstlichen Antiquitäten und der herrschenden Religionsideen"). Originally meant as the first installment of a two-volume work, the work is better known under the title of its 1883 second edition, *Prolegomena zur Geschichte Israels*.

8. A. A. Hodge and B. B. Warfield, "Inspiration," *Presbyterian Review* 2 (1881): 232; Baila R. Shargel, "Israel Friedlaender," *American National Biography*; Sperling 1992, 43–44.

9. Benjamin R. Foster, "Paul Haupt," *American National Biography*; Kuklick 1996, 106; Wind 1987, 53–57; Hermann L. Strack, "The Higher Criticism, a Witness to the Credibility of the Biblical Narrative," *Hebraica* 1 (1884–85): 5–10; Rogerson 1984, 274–75, 282; Samuel A. Meier, "George Foot Moore," *American National Biography*; Sperling 1992, 18; Joseph Jacobs, "[Hastings's] Dictionary of the Bible," *Jewish Quarterly Review* 11 (1899): 349. Harper was founding president of the University of Chicago.

10. Hallote 2006, 69–70; Wechsler 1985, 339–42, 348–50, 353; Gordon 1986, 6–32 (quoted words, 15–16); Kuklick 1996, 58–59, 125, 164–66, 168–69, 171–72; Stefan C. Reif, "Schechter, Solomon," *Oxford Dictionary of National Biography*; David B. Starr, "Solomon Schechter," *American National Biography*; Sperling 1992, 44, 47–51; Harold S. Wechsler, "Morris Jastrow," Marianne Sanua, "Richard James Horatio Gottheil," and Leonard Greenspoon, "Max Leopold Margolis," *American National Biography*.

11. Damrosch 2007, 5; Burkert 2004, 21; Moscrop 2000, 46–47, 64–72; Bliss 1906, viii (quotation), 255–83; Moulton 1926–27; Hallote 2006, esp. 52–65, 91–93, 100, 103–6, 110–11. Layard found the Gilgamesh tablets in the library of Ashurbanipal in Nineveh, but they were not translated until a curator named George Smith ran across them in the British Museum in 1872. Other fragments were discovered later.

12. Kuklick 1996, 25–29, 33, 106–8, 112–13, 126–28, 164, 166, 171–72, 178, 183; Foster, "Paul Haupt"; Benjamin R. Foster, "Albert Tobias Clay" and "George Aaron Barton," *American National Biography*.

13. I take the details of Smith's life from Maier 2009 and Black and Chrystal 1912. Robertson was his mother's maiden name. He called himself Smith, not Robertson Smith, as authors often had (and still have) it.

14. Johnstone 1995, 33–34, 41–49; Beidelman 1974, 8–10; Black and Chrystal 1912, 11; Davidson 1862, vi–viii, [ix] (quotation). The physicist was Sir William Thomson, later Lord Kelvin; Black and Chrystal 1912, 118.

15. William Robertson Smith, "What History Teaches Us to Seek in the Bible," in W. Smith 1912, 233; William Robertson Smith to McLennan, ca. 1872, quoted in Black and Chrystal 1912, 144–45; William Robertson Smith to J. S. Black, June 10, 1870, William Robertson Smith Papers, Add. 7449/7476, Cambridge University Library. For a fuller explication of Smith's views of higher criticism at this time, see [Thomas Martin] Lindsay, "Pioneer and Martyr of the Higher Criticism: William Robertson Smith," *Review of the Churches* 6, no. 31 (April 14, 1894): 37–42 (copy in Smith Papers). Lindsay had been a fellow student of Smith's at New College. McLennan's articles were "The Worship of Animals and Plants," *Fortnightly Review*, n.s., 6 (1869–70): 407–27 and 562–82. Smith and McLennan came to know each other in the Edinburgh Evening Club in the later 1860s and soon became fast friends; Black and Chrystal 1912, 116.

16. W[illiam]. R[obertson]. S[mith]., "Bible," in *Encyclopædia Britannica*, 9th ed., 3:634–48; quotations from 636 and 638. Smith did mention in passing (636, in discussing the formation of the Hebrew canon) the "distinction between inspired and human writings," though a reader could not be sure whether that distinction was in his mind or the ancient Hebrews'. For the context within which Smith's article was received, see Riesen 1985, 103–6.

17. James Bryce, "William Robertson Smith," in Bryce 1903, 313; "Draft Form of Libel [indictment]," printed in Black and Chrystal 1912, 582–99 (quotation, 584); Smith, "Animal Worship and Animal Tribes among the Arabs and in the Old Testament," in W. Smith 1912, 455–83 (explicitly following up McLennan's article ten years earlier on worship of animals and plants); Black and Chrystal 1912, 571–73; Smith to "My Dear Bell," December 3, 1885. Smith Papers. In the end, Smith was not convicted of anything but, in a settlement brokered to pacify both sides, was deprived of his chair without a formal condemnation of his views.

18. Elizabeth Baigent, "Palmer, Edward Henry," *Oxford Dictionary of National Biography*.

19. "Mohammedan Mahdis," *Good Words* 25 (1884): 531, 620; "On the Sacrifice of a Sheep to the Cyrian Aphrodite: Abstract of a Paper Given before the Cambridge Philological Society on 26 January 1888," *Cambridge University Reporter*. In 1881 Smith had published *The Old Testament in the Jewish Church*, based on another lecture series given during the same period. I do not count later editions of earlier works in calling *The Prophets of Israel* Smith's

last book-length work on a biblical topic. The Arabic grammar was a revision, by Smith and M. J. de Goeje, of a grammar originally prepared by Smith's deceased Cambridge colleague William Wright—itself based on a grammar by the German orientalist Karl Paul Caspari. There is a complete list of Smith's writings in Maier 2009.

20. Smith 2000, 1 (quotation), 304–6, 323. I cite from a facsimile reprint of the second edition. Smith considerably revised and enlarged the second edition, finishing the work just before his death; and it is generally taken as standard.

21. Wellhausen 2001, passim; Smith 2000, xliv, 17–18, 20. Spencer, Smith said, thus "laid the foundations of the science of Comparative Religion"—but, alas, "his work was not followed up." The classicist G. S. Kirk complained that the indefensible theory that all myths were born from rituals "has had an astonishing vogue from the time when it was first acquired (from Robertson Smith and Frazer for the most part) by Biblical scholars, who saw that it had a certain attraction in relation to the myths and rituals of the Near East, and in particular could make theologically acceptable sense of some of the Hebrew material." Kirk 1970, 12.

22. Smith stands among the four earliest 'founders' of the field (after a "prehistory" of Hegel et al.) in Kippenberg 2002.

23. Kuenen 1882, 187; Turner 2011, 67–68, 80–81. The term appears to have been coined—as the German *Weltreligion*—by Johann Sebastian von Drey in 1827, though he meant by it Christianity (thinking specifically of Catholicism): the sole 'world religion' as opposed to the many 'national religions' (*Landesreligion*); Masuzawa 2005, chap. 3 (for Drey, see 114–16). The phrase also appeared (mostly to be criticized) in C[ornelis]. P. T[iele]., "Religions," *Encyclopædia Britannica*, 9th ed., 368. Masuzawa believes (109n) that this was the first usage in English, even though Tiele discusses his Leiden colleague Kuenen's Hibbert Lectures in this context. (At issue may be the plural; Kuenen uses the singular.) The original candidates for 'world religions' in this context were Buddhism, Christianity, and Islam.

24. Müller 1895a, xiii; Kippenberg 2002, chap. 4; Béguin et al. 1987, 24; Toy 1913, vii.

25. I allude here to Parker's most famous sermon, "A Discourse on the Transient and the Permanent in Christianity," preached in 1841.

26. Turner 2011, chap. 2; Jackson 1981, 73–79; Higginson 1876, 5, 6, 8, 33. Higginson did not identify the source of "the luxury of a religion that does not degrade." It came from a speech that Ralph Waldo Emerson delivered to the 1869 meeting of the Free Religious Association, the Boston organization that published Higginson's tract. Possibly he thought readers would recognize the line; possibly he forgot to add a footnote.

27. Clarke 1888, [vi] (unpaginated preface), 15, 29, 139.

28. Carpenter 1889, passim (quotations 78, [285], 287).

29. Hardwick 1855–59, 1:xii; Jackson 1981, chap. 5; Robert A. Schneider, "John Henry Barrows," *American National Biography*; Barrows 1904, chaps. 14–15 (quotations 255, 262–63, 280).

30. Clarke 1888; Jackson 1981, 125–26. Clarke knew French and German, and his book amounted largely to a reprocessing of European scholarship.

31. Müller 1873, ix. Müller's *Introduction to the Science of Religion* came out two years after Clarke's *Ten Great Religions*, but Müller would also have known Clarke's work because much of *Ten Great Religions* first appeared as articles in the *Atlantic Monthly* in 1868, which circulated in the United Kingdom. Clarke had also published "Comparative Theology of Heathen Religions" in 1857 in the Unitarian periodical *Christian Examiner*, a journal known to segments of the English intellectual class. Jackson 1981, 125.

32. Müller 1902, 1:483, 2:1–2, 6–12, 35, 67, 282, 374 (quotations, 1 and 7); Chaudhuri 1974, 348–56. That Müller began the modern comparative study of religion is the standard view. See, e.g., Joseph M. Kitagawa and John S. Strong, "Friedrich Max Müller and the Compara-

tive Study of Religion," in Smart et al. 1985, 3:206; Kippenberg 2002, 37; Masuzawa 2005, 2007. The first volume of Müller's *Chips* made the essentials of his approach clear in 1867.

33. Müller 1901, 276–79 (quotation, 277). Bunsen expounded his idealist view of history in Bunsen 1854. In Bunsen 1868–70, he specified in terms of linguistic families his assumption that God reveals Himself in history as well as in Scripture. The first volume treats "The Consciousness of God among the Hebrews" and "The Religious Consciousness of the Aryans of Eastern Asia, prior to the Introduction of Christianity" ("primeval," Egyptians, "Turanians," Chinese, Zoroastrians, Vedism/Brahminism/Hinduism, Buddhism). Volume 2 concerns itself with "The Religious Consciousness of the Aryans in Asia Minor and Europe Previous to the Christian Era"—devoting most space to the Greeks, but ending with a couple of chapters on the Romans, one on "the Teutons," and one on the "close of the Aryan religious belief in the ancient world, and the Aryan germ of the modern world." Volume 3 deals with "The Religious Consciousness of the Christian Aryans," from Christ himself through Schelling. Bunsen effectively turned the Jewish Jesus into an Aryan Christ, an anti-Semitic move (though apparently without vicious motives) that Müller would replicate. Arthur Stanley wrote a preface for the book.

34. Müller 1895a, xi–xiv, xix, 21–22; Müller 1873, ix, 105–6, 170–73.

35. Müller 1874, 34–35; Friedrich Max Müller to Arthur P. Stanley, 19 [month obscure] 1870, Stanley-Müller correspondence, MS Eng 2346, ff. 109–10, Western Manuscripts, Bodleian Library, Oxford.

36. [Robert Chalmers, Baron] Chalmers, "Davids, Thomas William Rhys," rev. Richard F. Gombrich, and Eric J. Sharpe, "Farquhar, John Nicol," *Oxford Dictionary of National Biography*; Paul C. Wilt, "Samuel Henry Kellogg," *American National Biography*; Franklin Edgerton, "Edward Washburn Hopkins, 1857–1932," *Journal of the American Oriental Society* 52 (1932): 311–15; Jackson 1981, 189–90. Despite the title of Baron Chalmers's article, the surname appears to have been Rhys Davids, not Davids. *The Light of Asia* part of Kellogg's title alludes to Edwin Arnold's popular 1879 verse biography of the Buddha.

37. David G. Lyon, "Crawford Howell Toy," *Harvard Theological Review* 13 (1920): 1–22; A. J. Long, "Carpenter, (Joseph) Estlin." *Oxford Dictionary of National Biography*; Meier, "Moore."

38. Smith 2000, 17–18.

39. Black and Chrystal 1912, 146; Jones 1984, passim; William Robertson Smith to [E. B.?] Tylor, April 12, 1883, William Robertson Smith Papers, Add. 7449/7476, Department of Manuscripts and University Archives, Cambridge University Library. Theodor Nöldeke (1836–1930), a leading German Semitics scholar, wrote articles for the *Encyclopædia Britannica*, edited by Smith. It is a little surprising that Smith needed Nöldeke to lead him to Lagarde's book, since Smith had studied under Lagarde. I am grateful to Mark Noll for sharpening my understanding of the methodological differences between Wellhausen and Smith.

40. Kippenberg 2002, 72; Kuper 1988, 82; William Robertson Smith, "Animal Worship and Animal Tribes among the Arabs and in the Old Testament," reprinted in W. Smith 1912, 455–83.

41. Smith 2000, 28, 32, 34 and lecture 8, passim ("view prevailed," 269). Tylor had conceived of sacrifice as a gift to the god. Smith followed Tylor insofar as thinking of vegetable offerings as gifts, but departed from him in the interpretation of animal sacrifice. Since nomadic herding preceded settled agriculture, animal sacrifice was for Smith more fundamental to ancient religion. Like most other British ethnological thinkers of his time, Smith inherited the axioms of the stadial theories of the Scottish Enlightenment though not their particular forms.

42. Smith 2000, 267–68.

43. Rogerson 1995, 146–49; Smith 2000, 41–42; Smith 1889, 393. Smith may have decided

that even his highly qualified statement of the link between ancient ritual and Christianity went too far, as he cut it when revising for the second edition.

44. Beidelman 1974. Émile Durkheim sometimes wins this plume; but Durkheim in this respect depended on Smith. In 1907 Durkheim wrote that, in 1895, "pour la première fois, je trouvai le moyen d'aborder sociologiquement l'étude de la religion. Ce fut pour moi une révélation. Ce cours de 1895 marque une ligne de démarcation dans le développement de ma pensée. . . . Il était dù tout entier aux études d'histoire religieuse que je venais d'entreprendre et nottament à la lecture des travaux de Robertson Smith et de son école." Émile Durkheim, "Deuxième lettre de M. Durkheim," *La Revue néo-scolastique* 14, no. 56 (1907): 613. "Son école" is obscure to me: Frazer? the Cambridge Ritualists? Cf. Lukes 1975, 27, 238–39, 241, 450–51, 471.

45. Experts on the subject may wonder why I do not mention Andrew Lang. Lang seems to me to matter in the history of the discipline as critic rather than creator of methods (especially as critic of Tylor and Müller). This is not to deny his influence, only to explain why he does not figure here.

46. Turner 2011, 56–63; Jackson 1981, 124; Shepard 1991, 11–13, 32–38, 80–87; Meier, "Moore," Brendan A. Rapple, "William Fairfield Warren," and Harold S. Wechsler, "Morris Jastrow," in *American National Biography*; Wind 1987, 66–69; Harper 1904, 38–39; "George Stephen Goodspeed," *Biblical World* 25 (1905): 169–72; "East Indian Faiths," *New York Times*, August 25, 1895, 23. Goodspeed is best known for his *History of the Babylonians and Assyrians* (1902). The first Haskell Lecturer on Comparative Religion at the University of Chicago was Rev. John Henry Barrows (see above); the docent was Edmund Buckley, who got his PhD at Chicago in 1894 with a thesis on "Phallicism in Japan." The 1899 PhD was awarded to Laetitia Moon Conard, with the thesis "Ideas of the Future Life Held by Algonkin Indian Tribes," which, according to the *Report*, was translated and published in 1900 in two parts in the leading French journal in the field, *Revue de l'histoire des religions*.

47. Long, "Carpenter"; Arthur J. Evans to J. L. Myres, 15 December 1896, John Linton Myres Papers, MS Myres 59, ff. 20–21, Western Manuscripts, Bodleian Library, Oxford University; Chalmers, "Davids"; Barbara Freire-Marreco [later Aitken] to J. L. Myres, 6 December [1907], Myres Papers, MS Myres 16, ff. 53–54; E. A. Barber, "Farnell, Lewis Richard," rev. R.C.T. Parker, *Oxford Dictionary of National Biography*. Freire-Marreco appears in chapter 12, on anthropology. Farnell specialized in ancient Greek cults.

EPILOGUE

1. Vickers 1998, chap. 3.
2. Th. W. Hunt, "The Place of English in the College Curriculum," *Transactions of the Modern Language Association of America* 1 (1884–85): 118.
3. Roberts and Turner 2000, pt. 2; Turner 1999, passim.
4. Information herein comes from the websites of these universities.
5. Rickman 1979, 67; William James, "The Social Value of the College-Bred: An Address Made at a Meeting of the Association of American Alumnae at Radcliffe College, November 7, 1907," *McClure's Magazine* 30 (1907–8): 420.
6. Blair 2010.
7. Albion W. Small to Herbert Baxter Adams, February 26, 1901, Herbert Baxter Adams Papers, MS 4, Series 1, Box 15, Johns Hopkins University Archives; Shuger 1994, 8; Bryce 1903, 386–87. For an earlier learned Victorian who puzzled much over the rise of specialized divisions of knowledge, see Yeo 1993.

8. "A Brief Account of the Foundation of the Academy," reproduced from *Proceedings of the British Academy* 1:vii–ix, http://www.britac.ac.uk/pubs/src/ba-history/Foundation_of _the_British_Academy.cfm, accessed March 28, 2013; Frederic J. Kenyon to A. J. Mansbridge, 28 January 1917, Council for Humanistic Studies Papers, Add. MSS 65249, British Library; *Nature*, December 6, 1917, 267–68; American Council of Learned Societies, "On Our History," http://www.acls.org/about/history/, accessed March 28, 2013.

9. I have in mind a recent study of the illustrator Howard Pyle by the Southern historian Robert E. May and his wife Jill P. May.

WORKS CITED

$\mathcal{S}$ome references are given in the notes and do not appear here. (These include online sources, general encyclopedias and dictionaries, archival material, college and university catalogs, and—except for a couple that are monographs in disguise—articles in primary-source periodicals.) In cases of reprints and translations, the year of original publication is given in parentheses. I alphabetize premodern authors by best-known name rather than strictly accurate form: Cicero, Marcus Tullius; not Tullius Cicero, Marcus. I have not made consistent the varying names of authors or publishers but have used names as given on the title page or in the publication data: you will find both Konrad Koerner and E. F. K. Koerner, the same man.

To save space I omit details a reader might expect in a fuller bibliography. Most academic publishers these days have more than one office; I give only the primary place (in rare instances, primary places) of publication. Likewise, special imprints (such as Belknap Press of Harvard University Press) are left out, except for Oxford's Clarendon Press, a distinct imprint for three centuries; and the series in which books appear (like the Loeb Classical Library) are omitted unless some special circumstance calls for their inclusion. Also for reasons of space, I usually list an individual chapter within an edited work only when I cite that chapter alone in the work; otherwise, as a rule the book is cited by editor's name, and contributors' names are omitted. I apologize to authors thus unacknowledged.

Aarsleff, Hans. 1982. *From Locke to Saussure: Essays on the Study of Language and Intellectual History*. Minneapolis: University of Minnesota Press.

Aarsleff, Hans. 1983 (1967). *The Study of Language in England, 1780–1860*. Minneapolis: University of Minnesota Press.

Abulafia, David. 2008. *The Discovery of Mankind: Atlantic Encounters in the Age of Columbus*. New Haven, Conn: Yale University Press.

Ackerman, Robert. 1987. *J. G. Frazer: His Life and Work*. Cambridge: Cambridge University Press.

Ackerman, Robert. 2002 (1991). *The Myth and Ritual School: J. G. Frazer and the Cambridge Ritualists*. New York: Routledge.

Ackerman, Robert, ed. 2005. *Selected Letters of Sir J. G. Frazer*. Oxford: Oxford University Press.

Ackerman, Robert W., and Gretchen P. Ackerman. 1979. *Sir Frederic Madden: A Biographical Sketch and Bibliography*. New York: Garland.

Ackroyd, P. R., and C. F. Evans, eds. 1975 (1970). *The Cambridge History of the Bible*. Vol. 1, *From the Beginnings to Jerome*. Cambridge: Cambridge University Press.

Acosta, Ana M. 2002. "Conjectures and Speculations: Jean Astruc, Obstetrics, and Biblical Criticism in Eighteenth-Century France." *Eighteenth-Century Studies* 35: 256–66.

Acton, John Dalberg, Baron. 1917. *Selections from the Correspondence of the First Lord Acton*, ed. John Neville Figgis and Reginald Vere Laurence. London: Longmans, Green.

Adams, John Quincy. 1810. *Lectures on Rhetoric and Oratory, Delivered to the Classes of Senior and Junior Sophisters in Harvard University*. 2 vols. Cambridge, Mass.: Hillard and Metcalf.

Adams, Eleanor N. 1917. *Old English Scholarship in England from 1566–1800*. New Haven, Conn.: Yale University Press.

Adams, Henry. 1982–88. *The Letters of Henry Adams*, ed. J. C. Levenson et al. 6 vols. Cambridge, Mass.: Harvard University Press.

Alderson, William L., and Arnold C. Henderson. 1970. *Chaucer and Augustan Scholarship*. Berkeley and Los Angeles: University of California Press.

Allen, Joseph Henry, 1883. *Our Liberal Movement in Theology: Chiefly as Shown in Recollections of the History of Unitarianism in New England*. 2nd ed. Boston: Roberts.

Allen, Susan Heuck. 1999. *Finding the Walls of Troy: Frank Calvert and Heinrich Schliemann at Hisarlik*. Berkeley and Los Angeles: University of California Press.

Allen, Susan Heuck, ed. 2002. *Excavating Our Past: Perspectives on the History of the Archaeological Institute of America*. Boston: Archaeological Institute of America.

Alter, Stephen G. 1999. *Darwinism and the Linguistic Image: Language, Race, and Natural Theology in the Nineteenth Century*. Baltimore: Johns Hopkins University Press.

Alter, Stephen G. 2005. *William Dwight Whitney and the Science of Language*. Baltimore: Johns Hopkins University Press.

Altholz, Josef L. 1994. *Anatomy of a Controversy: The Debate over "Essays and Reviews," 1860–64*. Aldershot, England: Scolar.

Anderson, R. D. 1983. *Education and Opportunity in Victorian Scotland: Schools and Universities*. Oxford: Clarendon.

Andresen, Julie Tetel. 1990. *Linguistics in America, 1769–1924: A Critical History*. London: Routledge.

Anger, Suzy. 2005. *Victorian Interpretation*. Ithaca, N.Y.: Cornell University Press.

Anonymous, ed. 1968. *Religion, érudition et critique à la fin du XVIIe siècle et au début du XVIIIe*. Paris: Presses Universitaires de France.

Anonymous, ed. 1980. *Der Vormann der Georgia Augusta: Christian Gottlob Heyne zum 250. Geburtstag: Sechs akademische Reden*. Göttingen, Germany: Vandenhoeck & Ruprecht.

Anquetil, Jacques. 2005. *Anquetil-Duperron: premier orientaliste français*. Paris: Presses de la Renaissance.

Anquetil-Duperron, Abraham-Hyacinthe. 1993 (1780–1804). *Considérations philosophiques, historiques et géographiques sur les deux mondes*, ed. Guido Abbattista. Pisa: Scuola Normale Superiore.

Anthony, David W. 2007. *The Horse, the Wheel, and Language: How Bronze-Age Riders from the Eurasian Steppes Shaped the Modern World*. Princeton, N.J.: Princeton University Press.

Antognazza, Maria Rosa. 2009. *Leibniz: An Intellectual Biography*. Cambridge: Cambridge University Press.

App, Urs. 2010. *The Birth of Orientalism*. Philadelphia: University of Pennsylvania Press.

Aquinas, Thomas. 1946 (ca. 1270). *Summa contra gentiles. Editio Leonina manualis.* Rome: Casa Editrice Marietti.

Arendt, Hannah. 1946. "Privileged Jews." *Jewish Social Studies* 8: 3–30.

Arens, Hans. 1969. *Sprachwissenschaft: Der Gang ihrer Entwicklung von der Antike bis zur Gegenwart.* 2nd ed. Freiburg: Verlag Karl Alber.

Arnold, Matthew. 1960–77. *The Complete Prose Works of Matthew Arnold,* ed. R. H. Super. 11 vols. Ann Arbor: University of Michigan Press.

Ash, Marinell, et al. 1999. *Thinking with Both Hands: Sir Daniel Wilson in the Old World and the New,* ed. Elizabeth Hulse. Toronto: University of Toronto Press.

Ashdown, Margaret. 1925. "Elizabeth Elstob, the Learned Saxonist." *Modern Language Review* 20: 125–46.

Assmann, Jan. 1997. *Moses the Egyptian: The Memory of Egypt in Western Monotheism.* Cambridge, Mass.: Harvard University Press.

Astin, A. E., et al., eds. 1989. *Rome and the Mediterranean to 133 B.C.* Cambridge Ancient History, vol. 8. Cambridge: Cambridge University Press.

Athenaeus of Naucratis. 2007–12. *The Learned Banqueters,* ed. and trans. S. Douglas Olson. 8 vols. Cambridge, Mass.: Harvard University Press.

Atwater, Caleb. 1820. "Description of the Antiquities Discovered in the State of Ohio and Other Western States." *Archaeologia Americana: Transactions and Collections of the American Antiquarian Society* 1: 105–267.

Auerbach, Erich. 1965 (1958). *Literary Language and Its Public in Late Latin Antiquity and in the Middle Ages,* trans. Ralph Manheim. New York: Pantheon.

Augstein, H. F. 1999. *James Cowles Prichard's Anthropology: Remaking the Science of Man in Early Nineteenth-Century Britain.* Amsterdam: Rodopi.

Auroux, Sylvain, ed. 1989–92. *Histoire des idées linguistiques.* 3 vols. Liège, Belgium: Mardaga.

Auroux, Sylvain. 1990. "Representation and the Place of Linguistic Change before Comparative Grammar." In *Leibniz, Humboldt, and the Origins of Comparativism,* ed. Tullio de Mauro and Lia Formigari, 213–38. Amsterdam: John Benjamins.

Auroux, Sylvain, et al., eds. 2000–2006. *History of the Language Sciences / Geschichte der Sprachwissenschaften / Histoire des sciences du langage.* 3 vols. Berlin: Walter de Gruyter.

Avery-Quash, Susanna, and Julie Sheldon. 2011. *Art for the Nation: The Eastlakes and the Victorian Art World.* London: National Gallery.

Azad, Yusef. 1988. "The Limits of University: The Study of Language in some British Universities and Academies, 1750–1800." *History of Universities* 7: 117–47.

Bailyn, Bernard, et al. 1986. *Glimpses of the Harvard Past.* Cambridge, Mass.: Harvard University Press.

Bailyn, Bernard. 2012. *The Barbarous Years: The Peopling of British North America: The Conflict of Civilizations, 1600–1675.* New York: Alfred A. Knopf.

Baker, Donald C. 1984. "Frederick James Furnivall (1825–1910)." In *Editing Chaucer: The Great Tradition,* ed. Paul G. Ruggiers, 157–69. Norman, Okla.: Pilgrim.

Baldick, Chris. 1987. *The Social Mission of English Criticism, 1848–1932.* Oxford: Clarendon.

Bammel, Ernst. 1984. "Niebuhr und England." In *Barthold Georg Niebuhr, Historiker und Staatsmann: Vorträge bei dem anläßlich seines 150. Todestages in Bonn veranstalteten Kolloquiums 10.-12. November 1981,* ed. Gerhard Wirth, 131–75. Bonn: Ludwig Röhrscheid Verlag.

Barfield, Owen. 1971. *What Coleridge Thought.* San Rafael, Calif.: Barfield.

Barkan, Leonard. 1999. *Unearthing the Past: Archaeology and Aesthetics in the Making of Renaissance Culture.* New Haven, Conn.: Yale University Press.

Barnhart, Terry A. 2005. *Ephraim George Squier and the Development of American Anthropology.* Lincoln: University of Nebraska Press.

Baron, Hans. 1933. "Das Erwachen des historischen Denkens im Humanismus des Quattrocento." *Historische Zeitschrift* 147: 5–20.

Barret-Kriegel, Blandine. 1988. *Jean Mabillon*. Paris: Presses Universitaires de France.

Barrows, Mary Eleanor. 1904. *John Henry Barrows: A Memoir*. Chicago: Fleming H. Revell.

Bartlett, John Russell. 1848. *The Progress of Ethnology, an Account of Recent Archaeological, Philological and Geographical Researches in Various Parts of the Globe, Tending to Elucidate the Physical History of Man*. New York: Bartlett and Welford.

Barton, Benjamin Smith. 1798. *New Views of the Origin of the Tribes and Nations of America*. Philadelphia: Printed, for the Author, by John Bioren.

Bateman, Thomas. 1861. *Ten Years' Diggings in Celtic and Saxon Grave Hills, in the Counties of Derby, Stafford, and York, from 1848 to 1858; with Notices of Some Former Discoveries, Hitherto Unpublished, and Remarks on the Crania and Pottery from the Mounds*. London: J. R. Smith / Derby: W. Bemrose and Sons.

Bauman, Richard, and Charles L. Briggs. 2003. *Voices of Modernity: Language Ideologies and the Politics of Inequality*. Cambridge: Cambridge University Press.

Baym, Nina. 1984. *Novels, Readers, and Reviewers: Responses to Fiction in Antebellum America*. Ithaca, N.Y.: Cornell University Press.

Beard, Mary. 2000. *The Invention of Jane Harrison*. Cambridge, Mass.: Harvard University Press.

Beard, Mary. 2003. "Picturing the Roman Triumph: Putting the *Fasti Capitolini* in Context." *Apollo*, n.s., 158, no. 497: 23–28.

Bedouelle, Guy. 2008. "Attacks on the Biblical Humanism of Jacques Lefèvre d'Etaples." In *Biblical Humanism and Scholasticism in the Age of Erasmus*, ed. Erika Rummel, 117–41. Leiden, Netherlands: Brill.

Beeson, Charles H. 1930. *Lupus of Ferrières as Scribe and Text Critic: A Study of His Autograph Copy of Cicero's "De oratore."* Cambridge, Mass.: Mediaeval Academy of America.

Béguin, Jacques, et al. 1987. *Cents ans de sciences religieuses en France*. Paris: Cerf.

Beidelman, T. O. 1974. *William Robertson Smith and the Sociological Study of Religion*. Chicago: University of Chicago Press.

Benes, Tuska. 2008. *In Babel's Shadow: Language, Philology, and the Nation in Nineteenth-Century Germany*. Detroit: Wayne State University Press.

Benson, Adolph B. 1926. "The Essays on Fredrika Bremer in the North American Review." *PMLA* 41: 747–55.

Benson, Robert L., Giles Constable, and Carol A Lanham, eds. 1991. *Renaissance and Renewal in the Twelfth Century*. Toronto: University of Toronto Press/Medieval Academy of America.

Bentley, Jerry H. 1978. "Erasmus, Jean Le Clerc, and the Principle of the Harder Reading." *Renaissance Quarterly* 31: 309–21.

Bentley, Jerry H. 1983. *Humanists and Holy Writ: New Testament Scholarship in the Renaissance*. Princeton, N.J.: Princeton University Press.

Bentley, Richard. 1699. *A Dissertation upon the Epistles of Phalaris, with an Answer to the Objections of the Honourable Charles Boyle, Esq*. London: Printed by J. H. for Henry Mortlock and John Hartley.

[Bentley, Richard.] 1721. *Dr. Bentley's Proposals for Printing a New Edition of the Greek Testament, and St. Hierom's Latin Version*. 2nd ed. London: J. Knapton.

[Bentley, Richard.] 1737. *Remarks upon a Late Discourse of Free-Thinking: In a Letter to N. N*. 7th ed. London: Printed for W. Thurlbourn.

Bentley, Richard. 1962 (1691). *Epistola ad Joannem Millium*, ed. G. P. Goold. Toronto: University of Toronto Press.

Bentley, Richard. 1977 (1842). *The Correspondence of Richard Bentley*, ed. John Wordsworth and Christopher Wordsworth. 2 vols. in 1. Hildesheim, Germany: Georg Olms Verlag.

Benzie, William. 1983. *Dr. F. J. Furnivall: Victorian Scholar Adventurer*. Norman, Okla.: Pilgrim.

Berkhout, Carl T., and Milton McC. Gatch, eds. 1982. *Anglo-Saxon Scholarship: The First Three Centuries*. Boston: G. K. Hall.

Bernus, Auguste. 1969 (1869). *Richard Simon et son "Histoire critique du Vieux Testament": la critique biblique au siècle de Louis XIV*. Geneva: Slatkine Reprints.

Betegh, Gábor. 2004. *The Derveni Papyrus: Cosmology, Theology, and Interpretation*. Cambridge: Cambridge University Press.

Bickerman, Elias. 1963. *Chronologie*. 2nd rev. ed. Leipzig: B. G. Teubner.

Bieder, Robert E. 1975. "Albert Gallatin and the Survival of Enlightenment Thought in Nineteenth-Century American Anthropology." In *Toward a Science of Man: Essays in the History of Anthropology*, ed. Timothy H. H. Thoresen, 91–98. The Hague: Mouton.

Bieder, Robert E. 1986. *Science Encounters the Indian, 1820–1880*. Norman: University of Oklahoma Press.

Bietenholz, Peter G., and Thomas B. Deutscher, eds. 1985–87. *Contemporaries of Erasmus: A Biographical Register of the Renaissance and Reformation*. 3 vols. Toronto: University of Toronto Press.

Billanovich, G[iuseppe]. 1951. "Petrarch and the Textual Tradition of Livy." *Journal of the Warburg and Courtauld Institutes* 14, nos. 3–4: 137–208.

Birrell, T. A. 1966. "The Society of Antiquaries and the Taste for Old English, 1705–1840." *Neophilologus* 50: 107–17.

Bishop, Morris. 1962. *A History of Cornell*. Ithaca, N.Y.: Cornell University Press.

Black, John Sutherland, and George Chrystal. 1912. *The Life of William Robertson Smith*. London: Adam and Charles Black.

Black, Robert. 1991. "Italian Renaissance Education: Changing Perspectives and Continuing Controversies." *Journal of the History of Ideas* 52: 315–34.

Black, Robert. 2001. *Humanism and Education in Medieval and Renaissance Italy*. Cambridge: Cambridge University Press.

Blackwall, Anthony. 1971 (1719). *An Introduction to the Classics: Containing a Short Discourse on Their Excellencies; . . .* Fasc. ed. New York: Garland.

[Blackwell, Thomas.] 1735. *An Enquiry into the Life and Writings of Homer*. London: n. p.

[Blackwell, Thomas.] 1747. *Proofs of the Enquiry into Homer's Life and Writings, Translated into English*. London: n. p.

[Blackwell, Thomas.] 1748. *Letters concerning Mythology*. London: n. p.

Blair, Hugh. 1783. *Lectures on Rhetoric and Belles Lettres*. 2 vols. London: Printed for W. Strahan; T. Cadell, in the Strand; and W. Creech, in Edinburgh.

Blair, Ann M. 2010. *Too Much to Know: Managing Scholarly Information before the Modern Age*. New Haven, Conn.: Yale University Press.

Bliss, Frederick Jones. 1906. *The Development of Palestine Exploration: Being the Ely Lectures for 1903*. London: Hodder and Stoughton.

Blok, Josine H. 1994. "Quests for a Scientific Mythology: F. Creuzer and K. O. Müller on History and Myth." *History and Theory* 33: 26–52.

Bloomer, W. Martin. 1992. *Valerius Maximus and the Rhetoric of the New Nobility*. Chapel Hill: University of North Carolina Press.

Bloomer, W. Martin. 1997. *Latinity and Literary Society at Rome*. Philadelphia: University of Pennsylvania Press.

Blouin, Francis X., Jr., and William G. Rosenberg. 2011. *Processing the Past: Contesting Authority in History and the Archives*. Oxford: Oxford University Press.

Blum, Rudolf. 1977. *Kallimachos und die Literaturverzeichnung bei den Griechen: Untersuchungen zur Geschichte der Biobibliographie.* Offprint from *Archiv für Geschichte des Buchwesens* 18, parts 1 and 2. Frankfurt am Main: Buchhändler-Vereinigung.

Blunt, Wilfrid. 1965. *Cockerell: Sydney Carlyle Cockerell, Friend of Ruskin and William Morris and Director of the Fitzwilliam Museum, Cambridge.* New York: Alfred A. Knopf.

Boardman, John, and N.G.L. Hammond, eds. 1982. *The Expansion of the Greek World, Eighth to Sixth Centuries B.C.* Cambridge Ancient History, vol. 3, part 3. Cambridge: Cambridge University Press.

Bobbitt, Mary Reed. 1960. *With Dearest Love to All: The Life and Letters of Lady Jebb.* London: Faber and Faber.

Boeckh, August. 1828. *The Public Economy of Athens in Four Books, to Which is Added a Dissertation on the Silver Mines of Laurion,* [trans. George Cornewall Lewis]. 2 vols. London: John Murray, 1828.

Boeckh, August. 1858–71. *Gesammelte kleine Schriften,* ed. Ferdinand Ascherson et al. 7 vols. Leipzig: B. G. Teubner.

Boeckh, August. 1886 (1877). *Encyklopädie und Methodologie der philologischen Wissenschaften,* ed. Ernst Bratuscheck. 2nd ed., overseen by Rudolf Klussmann. Leipzig: B. G. Teubner.

Bolgar, R. R. 1964 (1954). *The Classical Heritage and Its Beneficiaries from the Carolingian Age to the End of the Renaissance.* New York: Harper and Row.

Bollack, Jean. 1998. *Jacob Bernays: un homme entre deux mondes.* Villeneuve d'Ascq, France: Presses Universitaires du Septentrion.

Bonner, Stanley F. 1977. *Education in Ancient Rome: From the Elder Cato to the Younger Pliny.* Berkeley and Los Angeles: University of California Press.

Bopp, Franz. 1836. *Vocalismus, oder sprachvergleichende Kritiken: über J. Grimm's deutsche Grammatik und Graff's althochdeutschen Sprachschatz mit Begründung einer neuen Theorie des Ablauts.* Berlin: Nicolaischen Buchhandlung.

Borsche, Tilman. 1989. "Die innere Form der Sprache: Betrachtungen zu einem Mythos der Humboldt-Hermeneutik." In *Wilhelm von Humboldts Sprachdenken: Symposium zum 150. Todestag, Düsseldorf, 28.-30. 6. 1985,* ed. Hans-Werner Scharf, 47–65. Essen, Germany: Reimar Hobbing.

Borst, Arno. 1957–63. *Der Turmbau von Babel: Geschichte der Meinungen über Ursprung und Vielfalt der Sprachen und Völker.* 4 vols. in 6, continuously paginated. Stuttgart: Anton Hiersemann.

Boswell, James. 1791. *The Life of Samuel Johnson, LL. D.* 2 vols. London: Printed by Henry Baldwin for Charles Dilly.

Bosworth, Joseph. 1841. *The Essentials of Anglo-Saxon Grammar: With an Outline of Professor Rask [sic] and Grimm's Systems.* London: Longman, Rees, Orme, Brown, Green, and Longman.

Bots, Hans, and Françoise Waquet. 1997. *La République des lettres.* Paris: De Boeck.

Bouwsma, William J. 2000. *The Waning of the Renaissance, 1550–1640.* New Haven, Conn.: Yale University Press.

Bowersock, G. W. 2009. *From Gibbon to Auden: Essays on the Classical Tradition.* New York: Oxford University Press.

Brackman, Arnold C. 1978. *The Luck of Nineveh: In Search of the Lost Assyrian Empire.* New York: Van Nostrand Reinhold.

Brand, Vanessa, ed. 1998. *The Study of the Past in the Victorian Age.* Oxford: Oxbow.

Bravo, Benedetto. 1968. *Philologie, histoire, philosophie de l'histoire: étude sur J. G. Droysen, historien de l'antiquité.* Wroclaw: Polish Academy of Sciences.

Breatnach, R. A. 1952. "The Book of O'Hara. Leabhar Í Eadhra by Lambert McKenna" [review]. *Studies: An Irish Quarterly Review* 41: 373–75.

Breuer, Edward. 1996. *The Limits of Enlightenment: Jews, Germans, and the Eighteenth-Century Study of Scripture*. Cambridge, Mass.: Harvard University Center for Jewish Studies.

Brew, J. O., ed. 1968. *One Hundred Years of Anthropology*. Cambridge, Mass.: Harvard University Press.

Briggs, Ward W., Jr., ed. 1994. *Biographical Dictionary of North American Classicists*. Westport, Conn.: Greenwood.

Briggs, Ward W. Jr., and Herbert W. Benario, eds. 1986. *Basil Lanneau Gildersleeve: An American Classicist*. Baltimore: Johns Hopkins University Press.

Briggs, Ward W., and William M. Calder III, eds. 1990. *Classical Scholarship: A Biographical Encyclopedia*. New York: Garland.

Brink, C. O. 1986. *English Classical Scholarship: Historical Reflections on Bentley, Porson, and Housman*. Cambridge: James Clarke.

Bristed, Charles Astor. 1852. *Five Years in an English University*. 2 vols. New York: G. P. Putnam.

Brockliss, Laurence. 1996. "Curricula." In *Universities in Early Modern Europe (1500–1800)*, ed. Hilde de Ridder-Symoens, 563–620. Cambridge: Cambridge University Press.

Brown, Jerry Wayne. 1969. *The Rise of Biblical Criticism in America, 1800–1870: The New England Scholars*. Middletown, Conn.: Wesleyan University Press.

Brown, Mary Ellen, ed. 2001. *The Bedesman and the Hodbearer: The Epistolary Friendship of Francis James Child and William Walker*. Aberdeen, Scotland: Aberdeen University Press for the Elphinstone Institute.

Brown, Mary Ellen. 2011. *Child's Unfinished Masterpiece: The English and Scottish Popular Ballads*. Urbana: University of Illinois Press.

Brown, Peter. 1992. *Power and Persuasion in Late Antiquity: Towards a Christian Empire*. Madison: University of Wisconsin Press.

Brown, Peter. 1996. *The Rise of Western Christendom: Triumph and Diversity, A.D. 200–1000*. Oxford: Blackwell.

Brown, Roger Langham. 1967. *Wilhelm von Humboldt's Conception of Linguistic Relativity*. The Hague: Mouton.

Browne, Janet. 1996 (1995). *Charles Darwin: Voyaging*. Princeton, N.J.: Princeton University Press.

Browning, Robert, 1964. "Byzantine Scholarship," *Past and Present* no. 28 (July): 3–20.

Browning, Robert. 1995. "Tradition and Originality in Literary Criticism and Scholarship." In *Originality in Byzantine Literature, Art and Music*, ed. A. R. Littlewood, 17–28. Oxford: Oxbow.

Bruni, Leonardo. 1987. *The Humanism of Leonardo Bruni: Selected Texts*, ed. and trans. Gordon Griffiths, James Hankins, and David Thompson. Binghamton, N.Y.: Medieval and Renaissance Texts and Studies.

Bruni, Leonardo. 2001–7 (1416–42?). *History of the Florentine People*, ed. and trans. James Hankins. 3 vols. Cambridge, Mass.: Harvard University Press.

Bruns, Gerald L. 1992. *Hermeneutics Ancient and Modern*. New Haven, Conn.: Yale University Press.

Brush, Kathryn. 2003. *Vastly More than Brick and Mortar: Reinventing the Fogg Art Museum in the 1920s*. Cambridge, Mass.: Harvard University Art Museums / New Haven, Conn.: Yale University Press.

Bryce, James. 1903. *Studies in Contemporary Biography*. New York: Macmillan.

Bryce, James. 1913. *University and Historical Addresses: Delivered during a Residence in the United States as Ambassador of Great Britain*. New York: Macmillan.

Buckley, Theodore Alois, trans. 1851. *Canons and Decrees of the Council of Trent*. London: George Routledge.

Bunsen, Christian Charles Josias. 1854. *Outlines of the Philosophy of Universal History, Applied to Language and Religion*. 2 vols. London: Longman, Brown, Green, and Longman.

Bunsen, C.C.J., Baron. 1868–70. *God in History, or the Progress of Man's Faith in the Moral Order of the World*, trans. Susanna Winkworth. 3 vols. London: Longmans, Green.

Burke, Peter. 1969. *The Renaissance Sense of the Past*. London: Edward Arnold.

Burke, Peter. 2004. *Languages and Communities in Early Modern Europe*. Cambridge: Cambridge University Press.

Burke, Peter. 2007. "Translations into Latin in Early Modern Europe." In *Cultural Translation in Early Modern Europe*, ed. Peter Burke and R. Po-Chia Hsia, 65–80. Cambridge: Cambridge University Press.

Burkert, Walter. 2004. *Babylon, Memphis, Persepolis: Eastern Contexts of Greek Culture*. Cambridge, Mass.: Harvard University Press.

Burnett, Stephen G. 1994. "Hebrew Censorship in Hanau: A Mirror of Jewish-Christian Coexistence in Seventeenth-Century Germany." In *The Expulsion of the Jews: 1492 and After*, ed. Raymond B. Waddington and Arthur H. Williamson, 199–222. New York: Garland.

Burnett, Stephen G. 1996. *From Christian Hebraism to Jewish Studies: Johannes Buxtorf (1564–1629) and Hebrew Learning in the Seventeenth Century*. Leiden, Netherlands: Brill.

Burnett, Stephen G. 2004. "Reassessing the 'Basel-Wittenberg Conflict': Dimensions of the Reformation-Era Discussion of Hebrew Scholarship." In *Hebraica Veritas? Christian Hebraists and the Study of Judaism in Early Modern Europe*, ed. Allison P. Coudert and Jeffrey S. Shoulson, 181–201. Philadelphia: University of Pennsylvania Press.

Burnett, Stephen G. 2005. "Christian Aramaism: The Birth and Growth of Aramaic Scholarship in the Sixteenth Century." In *Seeking Out the Wisdom of the Ancients: Essays Offered to Honor Michael V. Fox on the Occasion of His Sixty-Fifth Birthday*, ed. Ronald L. Troxel, Kelvin G. Friebel and Dennis R. Magary, 421–36. Winona Lake, Ind.: Eisenbrauns.

Burnett, Stephen G. 2006. "German Jewish Printing in the Reformation Era (1530–1633)." In *Jews, Judaism, and the Reformation in Sixteenth-Century Germany*, ed. Dean Phillip Bell and Stephen G. Burnett, 503–527. Leiden, Netherlands: Brill.

Burrow, J. W. 1970 (1966). *Evolution and Society: A Study in Victorian Social Theory*. Cambridge: Cambridge University Press.

Burrow, John. 2008. *A History of Histories: Epics, Chronicles, Romances and Inquiries from Herodotus and Thucydides to the Twentieth Century*. New York: Alfred A. Knopf.

Bushnell, Horace. 1849. *God in Christ: Three Discourses Delivered at New Haven, Cambridge, and Andover, with a Preliminary Dissertation on Language*. Hartford, Conn.: Brown and Parsons.

Butler, E. M. 1935. *The Tyranny of Greece over Germany: A Study of the Influence Exercised by Greek Art and Poetry over the Great German Writers of the Eighteenth, Nineteenth, and Twentieth Centuries*. Cambridge: Cambridge University Press.

Byrne, Peter. 1989. *Natural Religion and the Nature of Religion: The Legacy of Deism*. London: Routledge.

Calder, William M., III, and Renate Schlesier, eds. 1998. *Zwischen Rationalismus und Romantik: Karl Otfried Müller und die Antike Kultur*. Hildesheim, Germany: Weidmann.

Calder, William M., III, R. Scott Smith, and John Vaio, eds. 2002. *Teaching the English Wis-*

senschaft: The Letters of Sir George Cornewall Lewis to Karl Otfried Müller (1828–1839). Hildesheim, Germany: Georg Olms Verlag.

Calder, William M., III, and Stephen Trzaskoma, eds. 1996. *George Grote Reconsidered*. Hildesheim, Germany: Weidmann.

Callcott, George H. 1970. *History in the United States, 1800–1860: Its Practice and Purpose*. Baltimore: Johns Hopkins University Press.

Camden, William. 1610. *Britain, or A Chorographicall Description of the Most Flourishing Kingdomes, England, Scotland, and Ireland, and the Ilands Adioyning, Out of the Depth of Antiquitie*, trans. Philemon Holland. London: Eliot's Court.

Cameron, Nigel M. de S. 1987. *Biblical Higher Criticism and the Defense of Infallibilism in 19th Century Britain*. Lewiston, N.Y.: Edwin Mellen.

Campbell, J. 1966. "Bede." In *Latin Historians*, ed. T. A. Dorey, 159–90. London: Routledge and Kegan Paul.

Camporeale, Salvatore I. 2000. "Rhetoric, Freedom, and the Crisis of Christian Tradition: Valla's *Oratio* on the pseudo-'Donation' of Constantine (1440)." Unpublished manuscript.

Cannon, Garland. 1990. *The Life and Mind of Oriental Jones: Sir William Jones, the Father of Modern Linguistics*. Cambridge: Cambridge University Press.

Cannon, Garland, and Kevin R. Brine, eds. 1995. *Objects of Inquiry: The Life, Contributions, and Influences of Sir William Jones (1746–1794)*. New York: New York University Press.

Caplan, Harry. 1954. "Introduction." In *Rhetorica ad Herennium*, ed. Harry Caplan, vii–xl. Cambridge, Mass.: Harvard University Press.

Cardell, William S. 1825. *Essay on Language, as Connected with the Faculties of the Mind, and as Applied to Things in Nature and Art*. New York: Charles Wiley.

Carhart, Michael C. 2007a. "Historia Literaria and Cultural History from Mylaeus to Eichhorn." In *Momigliano and Antiquarianism: Foundations of the Modern Cultural Sciences*, ed. Peter N. Miller, 184–206. Toronto: University of Toronto Press.

Carhart, Michael C. 2007b. *The Science of Culture in Enlightenment Germany*. Cambridge, Mass.: Harvard University Press.

Carlyle, Thomas. 1845. *Oliver Cromwell's Letters and Speeches, with Elucidations*. 4 vols., London: Chapman and Hall.

Carpenter, W. Boyd. 1889. *The Permanent Elements of Religion: Eight Lectures Preached before the University of Oxford in the Year 1887, on the Foundation of the Late Rev. John Bampton, M. A., Canon of Salisbury*. London: Macmillan.

Carswell, Donald. [1927]. *Brother Scots*. New York: Harcourt, Brace.

Cassiodorus Senator, Magnus Aurelius. 2004. *"Institutions of Divine and Secular Learning" and "On the Soul,"* ed. and trans. James W. Halporn. Liverpool, England: Liverpool University Press.

Casson, Lionel. 2001. *Libraries in the Ancient World*. New Haven, Conn.: Yale University Press.

Cecere, Guilia. 2007. "Russia and Its 'Orient': Ethnographic Exploration of the Russian Empire in the Age of Enlightenment." In *The Anthropology of the Enlightenment*, ed. Larry Wolff and Marco Cipolloni, 185–208. Stanford, Calif.: Stanford University Press.

Ceserani, Giovanna. 2012. *Italy's Lost Greece: Magna Graecia and the Making of Modern Archaeology*. Oxford: Oxford University Press.

Chadwick, Owen. 1990. *The Secularization of the European Mind in the Nineteenth Century*. Cambridge: Cambridge University Press.

Champion, Justin A. I. 1999. "Pere [sic] Richard Simon and English Biblical Criticism, 1680–1700." In *Everything Connects: In Conference with Richard H. Popkin: Essays in His Honor*, ed. James E. Force and David S. Katz, 43–61. Leiden, Netherlands: Brill.

Channing, William Ellery. 1853. "Dr. Channing's Essay on the Poetical Genius of Milton." In *The Poetical Works of John Milton*, vii–xiv. Halifax, England: Milner and Sowerby.

Channing, William E. 1890 (1875). *The Works of William E. Channing, D.D.* New ed. Boston: American Unitarian Association.

Charvat, William. 1936. *The Origins of American Critical Thought, 1810–1835*. Philadelphia: University of Pennsylvania Press.

Chaudhuri, Nirad C. 1974. *Scholar Extraordinary: The Life of Professor the Rt. Hon. Friedrich Max Müller*. New York: Oxford University Press.

Cheesman, Tom, and Sigrid Rieuwerts, eds. 1997. *Ballads into Books: The Legacies of Francis James Child*. Bern, Switzerland: Peter Lang.

Cheng, Eileen Ka-May. 2008. *The Plain and Noble Garb of Truth: Nationalism and Impartiality in American Historical Writing, 1784–1860*. Athens: University of Georgia Press.

[Child, Francis James, ed.] 1848. *Four Old Plays—Three Interludes: Thersytes[,] Jack Jugler[,] and Heywood[']s Pardoner and Frere: and Jocasta a Tragedy by Gascoigne and Kinwelmarsh*. Cambridge, Mass.: George Nichols.

Child, Francis James, ed. 1898. *The English and Scottish Popular Ballads*. 5 vols. Boston: Houghton, Mifflin.

Child, Lydia Maria. 1855. *The Progress of Religious Ideas, through Successive Ages*. 3 vols. New York: C. S. Francis.

Christ, Karl. 1982. *Römische Geschichte und deutsche Geschichtswissenschaft*. Munich: Verlag C. H. Beck.

Christy, Craig. 1983. *Uniformitarianism in Linguistics*. Amsterdam: John Benjamins.

Cicero, Marcus Tullius. 1939. *Brutus—Orator*, trans. G. L. Hendrickson and H. M. Hubbell. Cambridge, Mass.: Harvard University Press.

Cicero, Marcus Tullius. 1979. *De legibus*, ed. Konrat Ziegler. Freiburg: Verlag Ploetz.

Cicero, Marcus Tullius. 1988. *Epistulae ad Quintum fratrem; Epistulae ad M. Brutum*, ed. D. R. Shackleton Bailey. Stuttgart: B. G. Teubner.

Clackson, James, and Geoffrey Horrocks. 2007. *The Blackwell History of the Latin Language*. Oxford: Blackwell.

Clark, Kenneth. 1974. *Another Part of the Wood: A Self-Portrait*. London: John Murray.

Clarke, James Freeman. 1888 (1871). *Ten Great Religions: An Essay in Comparative Theology*. Boston: Houghton, Mifflin.

Clarke, M. L. 1937. *Richard Porson: A Biographical Essay*. Cambridge: Cambridge University Press.

Clarke, M. L. 1945. *Greek Studies in England, 1700–1830*. Cambridge: Cambridge University Press.

Clarke, M. L. 1962. *George Grote: A Biography*. London: Athlone Press, University of London.

Clements, R. E. 1995. "The Intellectual Background of H. H. Milman's *The History of the Jews* (1829) and Its Impact on English Biblical Scholarship." In *Biblical Studies and the Shifting of Paradigms, 1850–1914*, ed. Henning Graf Reventlow and William Farmer. Sheffield, England: Sheffield Academic Press.

Clough, Arthur Hugh. 1990. *The Oxford Diaries of Arthur Hugh Clough*, ed. Anthony Kenny. Oxford: Clarendon.

Coad, Oral Sumner. 1917. *William Dunlap: A Study of His Life and Works and of His Place in Contemporary Culture*. New York: Dunlap Society.

Cochrane, Eric. 1981. *Historians and Historiography in the Italian Renaissance*. Chicago: University of Chicago Press.

Cohn, Bernard S. 1996. *Colonialism and Its Forms of Knowledge: The British in India*. Princeton, N.J.: Princeton University Press.

Cole, Nicholas P. 2011. "America and Ancient and Modern Europe." In *Thomas Jefferson, the Classical World, and Early America*, ed. Peter S. Onuf and Nicholas P. Cole, 171–92. Charlottesville: University of Virginia Press.

Cole, Thomas. 1991. *The Origins of Rhetoric in Ancient Greece*. Baltimore: Johns Hopkins University Press.

Coleridge, Samuel Taylor. 1930. *Coleridge's Shakespearean criticism*, ed. Thomas Middleton Raysor. 2 vols. London: Constable.

Colish, Marcia L. 1983. *The Mirror of Language: A Study in the Medieval Theory of Knowledge*. 2nd rev. ed. Lincoln: University of Nebraska Press.

Colish, Marcia L. 1997. *Medieval Foundations of the Western Intellectual Tradition, 400–1400*. New Haven, Conn.: Yale University Press.

Collier, J. Payne. 1831. *History of English Dramatic Poetry to the Time of Shakespeare: and Annals of the Stage to the Restoration*. 3 vols. London: John Murray.

Collini, Stefan, Donald Winch, and John Burrow. 1983. *That Noble Science of Politics: A Study in Nineteenth-Century Intellectual History*. Cambridge: Cambridge University Press.

Collins, L. C. 1912. *Life and Memoirs of John Churton Collins*. London: John Lane/Bodley Head.

Collins, Sarah Huff. 1970. "Elizabeth Elstob: A Biography." PhD diss., Indiana University.

Collins, Varnum Lansing. 1914. *Princeton*. New York: Oxford University Press.

Condillac, Etienne Bonnot de. 2001 (1746). *Essay on the Origin of Human Knowledge*, ed. Hans Aarsleff. Cambridge: Cambridge University Press.

Conley, Thomas M. 1990. *Rhetoric in the European Tradition*. Chicago: University of Chicago Press.

Connolly, Joy, 2009. "The Politics of Rhetorical Education." In *The Cambridge Companion to Ancient Rhetoric*, ed. Erik Gunderson, 126–41. Cambridge: Cambridge University Press.

Conser, Walter H. 1993. *God and the Natural World: Religion and Science in Antebellum America*. Columbia: University of South Carolina Press.

Constable, W. G. 1954. *The Painter's Workshop*. London: Oxford University Press.

Conte, Gian Biagio. 1994 (1987). *Latin Literature: A History*, trans. Joseph B. Solodow, rev. Don Fowler and Glenn W. Most. Baltimore: Johns Hopkins University Press.

Conybeare, John Josias. 1826. *Illustrations of Anglo-Saxon Poetry*, ed. William Daniel Conybeare. London: Harding and Lepard.

Cook, Harold John. 2007. *Matters of Exchange: Commerce, Medicine, and Science in the Dutch Golden Age*. New Haven, Conn.: Yale University Press.

Corson, Hiram, ed. 1867 (1864). *An Elocutionary Manual: Consisting of Choice Selections from English and American Literature*. Philadelphia: Charles Desilver.

Corson, Hiram. 1887. *Hand-Book of Anglo-Saxon and Early English*. Rev. ed. New York: Henry Holt.

Corson, Hiram. 1893. *A Primer of English Verse: Chiefly in its Aesthetic and Organic Character*. Boston: Ginn.

Corson, Hiram, ed. 1896. *Selections from Chaucer's Canterbury Tales (Ellesmere Text)*. New York: Macmillan.

Corson, Hiram, ed. 1899. *An Introduction to the Prose and Poetical Works of John Milton*. New York: Macmillan.

Corson, Hiram. 1901 (1894). *The Aims of Literary Study*. New York: Macmillan.

Corson, Hiram. 1970 (1901). *An Introduction to the Study of Browning's Poetry*. 3rd ed. Freeport, N.Y.: Books for Libraries.

Cortés, Ángel de Jesús. 2008. "Student Idealists and the Specter of Natural Science, 1870–1910." PhD diss., University of Notre Dame.

Cotton, Josiah. 1829. *Vocabulary of the Massachusetts (or Natick) Indian Language*, ed. J[ohn]. P[ickering]. Cambridge, Mass.: E. W. Metcalf.

Court, Franklin E. 1992. *Institutionalizing English Literature: The Culture and Politics of Literary Study, 1750–1900*. Stanford, Calif.: Stanford University Press.

Court, Franklin E. 2001. *The Scottish Connection: The Rise of English Literary Study in Early America*. Syracuse, N.Y.: Syracuse University Press.

Craddock, Patricia B. 1989. *Edward Gibbon, Luminous Historian, 1772–1794*. Baltimore: Johns Hopkins University Press.

Crawford, Robert, ed. 1997. *Launch-Site for English Studies: Three Centuries of Literary Studies at the University of St. Andrews*. St. Andrews, Scotland: Verse.

Crawford, Robert, ed. 1998. *The Scottish Invention of English Literature*. Cambridge: Cambridge University Press.

Cribiore, Raffaella. 2001. *Gymnastics of the Mind: Greek Education in Hellenistic and Roman Egypt*. Princeton, N.J.: Princeton University Press.

Crook, J. A., Andrew Lintott, and Elizabeth Rawson, eds. 1992. *The Last Age of the Roman Republic, 146–43 B.C.* Cambridge Ancient History, vol. 9. Cambridge: Cambridge University Press.

Crosby, Donald A. 1975. *Horace Bushnell's Theory of Language in the Context of Other Nineteenth-Century Philosophies of Language*. The Hague: Mouton.

Cross, Wilbur L. 1943. *Connecticut Yankee: An Autobiography*. New Haven, Conn.: Yale University Press.

Cunningham, Vanessa. 2008. *Shakespeare and Garrick*. Cambridge: Cambridge University Press.

Cunnington, Robert H. 1975. *From Antiquary to Archaeologist: A Biography of William Cunnington, 1754–1810*, ed. James Dyer. Aylesbury, England: Shire.

Curley, Edwin. 1994. "Notes on a Neglected Masterpiece: Spinoza and the Science of Hermeneutics." In *Spinoza: The Enduring Questions*, ed. Graeme Hunter, 68–81. Toronto: University of Toronto Press.

Curley, Michael J. 1994. *Geoffrey of Monmouth*. New York: Twayne.

D'Amico, John F. 1988. *Theory and Practice in Renaissance Textual Criticism: Beatus Rhenanus between Conjecture and History*. Berkeley and Los Angeles: University of California Press.

Damrosch, David. 2007. *The Buried Book: The Loss and Rediscovery of the Great Epic of Gilgamesh*. New York: Henry Holt.

Daniel, Glyn. 1968. *Man Discovers His Past: A Survey of Archaeological Findings*. New York: Crowell.

Darnell, Regna. 1988. *Daniel Garrison Brinton: The "Fearless Critic" of Philadelphia*. Philadelphia: Department of Anthropology, University of Pennsylvania.

Darnell, Regna. 1998. *And Along Came Boas: Continuity and Revolution in Americanist Anthropology*. Amsterdam: John Benjamins.

Daston, Lorraine, and Katharine Park. 2001. *Wonders and the Order of Nature, 1150–1750*. New York: Zone Books.

Daunton, Martin, ed. 2005. *The Organization of Knowledge in Victorian Britain*. Oxford: Oxford University Press for the British Academy.

Davidson, A. B. 1862. *A Commentary, Grammatical and Exegetical, on the Book of Job; with a Translation*. Vol. 1 [no more published]. Edinburgh: Williams and Norgate.

Davies, Martin. 1995. "Making Sense of Pliny in the Quattrocento." *Renaissance Studies* 9: 240–57.

Davison, J. A. 1962. "The Transmission of the Text." In *A Companion to Homer*, ed. Alan J. B. Wace and Frank H. Stubbings, 215–233. New York: Macmillan.

Dear, Peter. 1995. *Discipline and Experience: The Mathematical Way in the Scientific Revolution*. Chicago: University of Chicago Press.

De la Pryme, Abraham. 1870. *The Diary of Abraham De la Pryme, the Yorkshire Antiquary*, ed. Charles Jackson. Durham, England: Surtees Society.

Den Boer, Harm. 2002. "Literature, Politics, Economy: The Spanish and Portuguese Literature of the Sephardic Jews of Amsterdam." In *The Mediterranean and the Jews: Society, Culture and Economy in Early Modern Times*, ed. Elliott Horowitz and Moises Orfali, 101–13. Ramat-Gan, Israel: Bar-Ilan University Press.

Dew, Nicholas. 2009. *Orientalism in Louis XIV's France*. Oxford: Oxford University Press.

Dickins, Bruce. [1940] (1938). *J. M. Kemble and Old English Scholarship*. Sir Israel Gollancz Memorial Lecture, British Academy. London: Humphrey Milford.

Diehl, Carl. 1978. *Americans and German Scholarship, 1770–1870*. New Haven, Conn.: Yale University Press.

Diels, Hermann, and Ulrich von Wilamowitz-Moellendorff. 1995. *"Lieber Prinz": Der Briefwechsel zwischen Hermann Diels und Ulrich von Wilamowitz-Moellendorff (1869–1921)*, ed. Maximilian Braun, William M. Calder III, and Dietrich Ehlers. Hildesheim, Germany: Weidmann.

Dieserud, Juul. 1908. *The Scope and Content of the Science of Anthropology: Historical Review, Library Classification and Select, Annotated Bibliography; with a List of the Chief Publications of Leading Anthropological Societies and Museums*. Chicago: Open Court.

Distad, N. Merrill. 1979. *Guessing at Truth: The Life of Julius Charles Hare (1795–1855)*. Shepherdstown, W.V.: Patmos.

Dixon, W. Macneile. 1902. *Trinity College, Dublin*. London: F. E. Robinson.

Dockhorn, Klaus. 1950. *Der deutsche Historismus in England: ein Beitrag zur englischen Geistesgeschichte des 19. Jahrhunderts*. Göttingen, Germany: Vandenhoeck & Ruprecht.

Doe, Janet. 1960. "Jean Astruc (1694–1766): A Biographical and Bibliographical Study." *Journal of the History of Medicine and Allied Sciences* 15: 184–97.

Donaldson, John William. 1839. *The New Cratylus, or Contributions towards a More Accurate Knowledge of the Greek Language*. Cambridge: J. and J. J. Deighton.

Donaldson, John William. 1844. *Varronianus: A Critical and Historical Introduction to the Philological Study of the Latin Language*. Cambridge: J. and J. J. Deighton.

Donaldson, John William. 1858. *A History of the Literature of Ancient Greece; from the Foundation of the Socratic Schools to the Taking of Constantinople by the Turks. Being a Continuation of K. O. Müller's Work*. 2 vols. London: John W. Parker and Son.

Donne, John. 1651. *Essayes in Divinity; by the Late Dr Donne, Dean of St Paul's. Being Several Disquisitions, Interwoven with Meditations and Prayers: Before He Entred into Holy Orders*. London: Printed by T. M. for Richard Marriot.

Donnegan, James. 1832. *A New Greek and English Lexicon; Principally on the Plan of the Greek and German Lexicon of Schneider*, rev. R. B. Patton. Boston: Hilliard, Gray.

Dopffel, Michael. 2010. "Between Biblical Literalism and Scientific Inquiry: Cotton Mather's Commentary on Jeremiah 8:7." In *Cotton Mather and Biblia Americana—America's First Bible Commentary*, ed. Reiner Smolinski and Jan Stievermann, 204–25. Tübingen, Germany: Mohr Siebeck.

Douglas, David C. 1951. *English Scholars, 1660–1730*. Rev. ed. London: Eyre and Spottiswoode.

Dowden, Edward. [1881] (1875). *Shakespere: A Critical Study of His Mind and Art*. 3rd ed. New York: Harper and Brothers.

Dowling, Linda. 1986. *Language and Decadence in the Victorian Fin de Siècle*. Princeton, N.J.: Princeton University Press.

Droixhe, Daniel. 1978. *La linguistique et l'appel de l'histoire (1600–1800): rationalisme et révolutions positivistes*. Geneva: Librairie Droz.

Dryden, John. 1677. *The State of Innocence, and Fall of Man: An Opera*. London: Printed by T. N. for Henry Herringman.

Duke, James O. 1984. *Horace Bushnell on the Vitality of Biblical Language*. Chico, Calif.: Scholars.

Duncan, Pope A. 1997. "Crawford Howell Toy (1836–1919)." In *Dictionary of Heresy Trials in American Christianity*, ed. George H. Shriver, 430–38. Westport, Conn.: Greenwood.

Dunglison, Robley. 1844. *Public Discourse in Commemoration of Peter S. Du Ponceau, LL.D., Late President of the American Philosophical Society*. Philadelphia: John C. Clark for the American Philosophical Society.

Dunlap, William. 1965 (1834). *History of the Rise and Progress of the Arts of Design in the United States*, ed. Alexander Wyckoff. New York: Benjamin Blom.

Du Ponceau, Peter S. 1838. *Mémoire sur le système grammatical des langues de quelques nations indiennes de l'Amérique du nord*. Paris: A. Pihan de la Forest.

Dupré, Louis. 1993. *Passage to Modernity: An Essay in the Hermeneutics of Nature and Culture*. New Haven, Conn.: Yale University Press.

Durfee, Harold. 1953. "Language and Religion: Horace Bushnell and Rowland Gibson Hazard." *American Quarterly* 5: 57–70.

Dwight, Benjamin. 1859. *Modern Philology: Its Discoveries, History, and Influence, with Maps, Tabular Views, and an Index*. New York: A. S. Barnes and Burr.

Dyce, Alexander, ed. 1836–38. *The Works of Richard Bentley, D.D.* 3 vols. London: F. Macpherson.

Dyce, Alexander. 1972. *The Reminiscences of Alexander Dyce*, ed. Richard J. Schrader. Columbus: Ohio State University Press.

Dyson, Stephen L. 1998. *Ancient Marbles to American Shores: Classical Archaeology in the United States*. Philadelphia: University of Pennsylvania Press.

Dyson, Stephen L. 2006. *In Pursuit of Ancient Pasts: A History of Classical Archaeology in the Nineteenth and Twentieth Centuries*. New Haven, Conn.: Yale University Press.

Eastlake, Charles Lock. 1847. *Materials for a History of Oil Painting*. London: Longman, Brown, Green, and Longman.

Eastlake, Lady [Elizabeth Rigby]. 1883. *Five Great Painters: Essays Reprinted from the Edinburgh and Quarterly Reviews*. 2 vols. London: Longmans, Green.

Eco, Umberto. 1995. *The Search for the Perfect Language*, trans. James Fentress. Oxford: Blackwell.

Eden, Kathy. 1997. *Hermeneutics and the Rhetorical Tradition: Chapters in the Ancient Legacy and Its Humanist Reception*. New Haven, Conn.: Yale University Press.

Edgerton, Franklin. 1943. "Notes on Early American Work in Linguistics." *Proceedings of the American Philosophical Society* 87: 25–34.

Edwards, Jonathan [the Younger]. 1788. *Observations on the Language of the Muhhekaneew Indians; in Which the Extent of That Language in North-America is Shewn; its Genius is Grammatically Traced: Some of its Peculiarities, and Some Instances of Analogy between That and the Hebrew Are Pointed Out*. New Haven, Conn.: Josiah Meigs.

Edwards, Jonathan. 1989 (1765 [written 1753–55?]). *Two Dissertations, I. Concerning the End for Which God Created the World. II. The Nature of True Virtue*, in *Jonathan Edwards: Ethical Writings*, ed. Paul Ramsey. New Haven, Conn.: Yale University Press.

Ehrman, Bart D. 2006 (1987). "Methodological Developments in the Analysis and Classification of New Testament Documentary Evidence." In *Studies in the Textual Criticism of the New Testament*, 9–32. Leiden, Netherlands: Brill.

Eichhorn, Johann Gottfried, 1787. *Einleitung ins Alte Testament.* First Part. 2nd rev. ed. Leipzig: Weidmans, Erban, und Reich.

Eichhorn, Johann Gottfried. 1796. *Allgemeine Geschichte der Cultur und Litteratur des neuren Europa.* Göttingen, Germany: Johann Georg Rosenbusch.

Eichhorn, Johann Gottfried. 1812. *Litterärgeschichte.* 2nd ed. Göttingen, Germany: Vandenhoek [*sic*] und Ruprecht.

Eisenstein, Elizabeth L. 1980. *The Printing Press as an Agent of Change: Communications and Cultural Transformations in Early Modern Europe.* 2 vols. Cambridge: Cambridge University Press.

Eissfeldt, Otto. 1965 (1964). *The Old Testament: An Introduction*, trans. Peter R. Ackroyd. 3rd German ed. New York: Harper and Row.

Ellis, Ieuan. 1980. *Seven against Christ: A Study of 'Essays and Reviews.'* Leiden, Netherlands: E. J. Brill.

Engel, A. J. 1983. *From Clergyman to Don: The Rise of the Academic Profession in Nineteenth-Century Oxford.* Oxford: Clarendon.

Erasmus, H. J. [1962]. *The Origins of Rome in Historiography from Petrarch to Perizonius.* Assen, Netherlands: Van Gorcum.

Eskildsen, Kasper Risbjerg. 2004. "How Germany Left the Republic of Letters," *Journal of the History of Ideas* 65: 421–32.

Espagne, Michel. 1993. *Le Paradigme de l'étranger: les chaires de littérature étrangère au XIXe siècle.* Paris: Éditions du Cerf.

Evans, Craig A., and Emanuel Tov, eds. 2008. *Exploring the Origins of the Bible: Canon Formation in Historical, Literary, and Theological Perspective.* Grand Rapids, Mich.: Baker Academic.

Feaver, George. 1969. *From Status to Contract: A Biography of Sir Henry Maine, 1822–1888.* London: Longmans, Green.

Febvre, Lucien, and Henri-Jean Martin. 1976 (1958). *The Coming of the Book: The Impact of Printing, 1450–1800*, trans. David Gerard, ed. Geoffrey Nowell-Smith and David Wooton. London: Verso.

Feldman, Burton, and Robert D. Richardson. 1972. *The Rise of Modern Mythology 1680–1860.* Bloomington: Indiana University Press.

Fellows, Charles. 1841. *An Account of Discoveries in Lycia, Being a Journal Kept during a Second Excursion in Asia Minor.* London: John Murray.

Felton, Cornelius C. 1831. *A Lecture on the Classical Learning, Delivered before the Convention of Teachers, and Other Friends of Education, Assembled to Form the American Institute of Instruction, August, 20, 1830.* Boston: Hilliard, Gray, Little and Wilkins.

Felton, C. C., ed. 1833. *The Iliad of Homer, from the Text of Wolf: with English Notes and Flaxman's Illustrative Designs.* Boston: Hilliard, Gray, and Cambridge, Mass.: Brown, Shattuck.

Ferguson, Adam. 1767. *An Essay on the History of Civil Society.* Edinburgh: Printed for A. Kincaid and J. Bell.

Ferreri, Luigi. 2007. *La questione Omerica dal cinquecento al settecento.* Rome: Edizioni di Storia e Letteratura.

Fiesel, Eva. 1927. *Die Sprachphilosophie der deutschen Romantik.* Tübingen, Germany: J.C.B. Mohr.

Findlen, Paula. ed. 2004. *Athanasius Kircher: The Last Man Who Knew Everything.* New York: Routledge.

Finegan, Jack. 1964. *Handbook of Biblical Chronology: Principles of Time Reckoning in the Ancient World and Problems of Chronology in the Bible.* Princeton, N.J.: Princeton University Press.

Fischer, Steven Roger. 2001. *A History of Writing.* London: Reaktion.

Fitton, J. Lesley. 1996. *The Discovery of the Greek Bronze Age.* Cambridge, Mass.: Harvard University Press.

Flasher, Hellmut. 1979. "Die methodisch-hermeneutischen Ansätze von Friedrich August Wolf und Friedrich Ast—Traditionelle und neue Begründungen." In *Philologie und Hermeneutik im 19. Jahrhundert: zur Geschichte und Methodologie der Geisteswissenschaften,* ed. Hellmut Flasher, Karlfried Gründer, and Axel Horstmann, 21–31. Göttingen, Germany: Vandenhoeck & Ruprecht.

Fleay, F. G. 1876. *Shakespeare Manual.* London: Macmillan.

Fleury, [Charles.] 1682. *Les moeurs des Israelites, ou l'on voit le modele d'une politique simple & sincere pour le gouvernement des etats & la reforme des moeurs.* The Hague: Adrian Moetjens.

Forbes, Duncan. 1952. *The Liberal Anglican Idea of History.* Cambridge: Cambridge University Press.

Force, Pierre. 2009. "Voltaire and the Necessity of Modern History." *Modern Intellectual History* 6: 457–84.

Ford, Andrew. 2002. *The Origins of Criticism: Literary Culture and Poetic Theory in Classical Greece.* Princeton, N.J.: Princeton University Press.

Forrester, David. 1989. *Young Doctor Pusey: A Study in Development.* London: Mowbray.

Fortes, Meyer. 1969. *Kinship and the Social Order: The Legacy of Lewis Henry Morgan.* Chicago: Aldine.

Fox, Adam. 1954. *John Mill and Richard Bentley: A Study of the Textual Criticism of the New Testament, 1675–1729.* Oxford: Basil Blackwell.

Fox, Robin. 1983 (1967). *Kinship and Marriage: An Anthropological Perspective.* Cambridge: Cambridge University Press.

Fox, Stephen. 2003. *Transatlantic: Samuel Cunard, Isambard Brunel, and the Great Atlantic Steamships.* New York: HarperCollins.

Franklin, James. 2001. *The Science of Conjecture: Evidence and Probability before Pascal.* Baltimore: Johns Hopkins University Press.

Franklin, Michael J. 1995. *Sir William Jones.* Cardiff: University of Wales Press.

Franklin, Michael J. 2011. *Orientalist Jones: Sir William Jones, Poet, Lawyer, and Linguist, 1746–1794.* Oxford: Oxford University Press.

Fraser, P. M. 1972. *Ptolemaic Alexandria.* 3 vols. Oxford: Clarendon.

Fraser, Robert. 1990. *The Making of "The Golden Bough": The Origins and Growth of an Argument.* New York: St. Martin's.

Fraser, Russell. 1977. *The Language of Adam: On the Limits and Systems of Discourse.* New York: Columbia University Press.

Frazer, J. G. 1890. *The Golden Bough: A Study in Comparative Religion.* 2 vols. London: Macmillan.

Frazer, James G. 1907. *Questions on the Customs, Beliefs, and Languages of Savages.* Cambridge: Cambridge University Press.

Freeman, Arthur, and Janet Ing Freeman. 2004. *John Payne Collier: Scholarship and Forgery in the Nineteenth Century.* 2 vols. New Haven, Conn.: Yale University Press.

Freeman, Edward A. 1872. *The Unity of History: The Rede Lecture Delivered in the Senate-House before the University of Cambridge on Friday, May 24, 1872.* London: Macmillan.

Freeman, Edward A. 1874. *Comparative Politics: Six Lectures Read before the Royal Institution in January and February, 1873.* New York: Macmillan.

Freeman, Joanne B. 2001. *Affairs of Honor: National Politics in the New Republic*. New Haven, Conn.: Yale University Press.

Frei, Hans. 1974. *The Eclipse of Biblical Narrative: A Study in Eighteenth and Nineteenth Century Hermeneutics*. New Haven, Conn.: Yale University Press.

Freiday, Dean. 1979. *The Bible—Its Criticism, Interpretation and Use—in 16th and 17th Century England*. Pittsburgh: Catholic and Quaker Studies.

Fry, Henry. 1896. *The History of North Atlantic Steam Navigation, with Some Account of Early Ships and Shipowners*. London: Sampson Low, Marston.

Fück, Johann. 1955. *Die arabischen Studien in Europa bis in den Anfang des 20. Jahrhunderts*. Leipzig: Otto Harrassowitz.

Fuhrmann, Manfred. 1959. "Friedrich August Wolf: zur 200. Wiederkehr seines Geburtstages am 15. Februar 1959." *Deutsche Vierteljahrsschrift für Literaturwissenschaft und Geistesgeschichte* 33: 187–236.

Fuhrmann, Manfred. 2007 (1995). *Die antike Rhetorik: eine Einführung*. Rev. ed. Düsseldorf: Patmos.

Fuller, Reginald C. 1984. *Alexander Geddes, 1737–1802: Pioneer of Biblical Criticism*. Sheffield, England: Almond.

Fumaroli, Marc, ed. 1999. *Histoire de la rhétorique dans l'Europe moderne, 1450–1950*. Paris: Presses Universitaires de France.

Fumaroli, Marc. 2007. "Arnaldo Momigliano et la réhabilitation des 'antiquaires': le comte de Caylus et le 'retour à l'antique' au XVIIIe siècle." In *Momigliano and Antiquarianism: Foundations of the Modern Cultural Sciences*, ed. Peter N. Miller, 154–83. Toronto: University of Toronto Press.

Furnivall, F. J. 1868. *A Temporary Preface to the Six-Text Edition of Chaucer's Canterbury Tales*. London: N. Trübner. for the Chaucer Society.

Gaertringen, F. Hiller von. 1908. *Briefwechsel über eine attische Inschrift zwischen A. Boeckh und K. O. Mueller aus dem Jahre 1835*. Leipzig: B. G. Teubner.

Gallatin, Albert. 1836. "A Synopsis of the Indian Tribes within the United States East of the Rocky Mountains, and in the British and Russian Possessions of North America." *Archaeologia Americana: Transactions and Collections of the American Antiquarian Society* 2: 1–422.

Gamble, Harry Y. 1985. *The New Testament Canon: Its Making and Meaning*. Philadelphia: Fortress.

Gamble, Harry Y. 1995. *Books and Readers in the Early Church: A History of Early Christian Texts*. New Haven, Conn.: Yale University Press.

Games, Alison. 2008. *The Web of Empire: English Cosmopolitans in an Age of Expansion, 1560–1660*. New York: Oxford University Press.

Gardiner, C. Harvey. 1969. *William Hickling Prescott: A Biography*. Austin: University of Texas Press.

Gasnault, Pierre. 1999. *L'érudition mauriste à Saint-Germain-des-Prés*. Paris: Institut d'Études Augustiniennes.

Geddes, Alexander. 1800. *Critical Remarks on the Hebrew Scriptures: Corresponding with a New Translation of the Bible*. Vol 1 [no more published]. London: Printed for the author by Davis, Wilks, and Taylor.

Gell, W[illiam]. 1804. *The Topography of Troy, and Its Vicinity; Illustrated and Explained by Drawings and Descriptions*. London: T. N. Longman and G. Rees.

Geoffrey of Monmouth. 1966 (ca. 1136). *The History of the Kings of Britain*, trans. Lewis Thorpe. Harmondsworth, England: Penguin.

Germana, Nicholas A. 2009. *The Orient of Europe: The Mythical Image of India and Competing Images of German National Identity*. Newcastle upon Tyne: Cambridge Scholars.

Gibbon, Edward. 1984 (final draft 1792–93). *Memoirs of My Life*, ed. Betty Radice. Harmondsworth, England: Penguin.

Gibbon, Edward. 1994 (1776–88). *The History of the Decline and Fall of the Roman Empire*, ed. David Womersley. 3 vols. London: Allen Lane.

Gildersleeve, Basil Lanneau. 1909. *Hellas and Hesperia: or the Vitality of Greek Studies in America*. New York: Henry Holt.

Gildersleeve, Basil Lannneau. 1987. *The Letters of Basil Lanneau Gildersleeve*, ed. Ward W. Briggs. Baltimore: Johns Hopkins University Press.

Gildersleeve, Basil Lannneau. 1992. *The Selected Classical Papers of Basil Lanneau Gildersleeve*, ed. Ward W. Briggs Jr. Atlanta: Scholars, 1992.

Gildersleeve, Basil Lanneau. 1998. *Soldier and Scholar: Basil Lanneau Gildersleeve and the Civil War*, ed. Ward W. Briggs. Charlottesville: University Press of Virginia.

Gilson, Etienne. 1955. *History of Christian Philosophy in the Middle Ages*. New York: Random House.

Giltner, John H. 1988. *Moses Stuart: The Father of Biblical Science in America*. Atlanta: Scholars.

Godden, Malcolm, and Michael Lapidge, eds. 1991. *The Cambridge Companion to Old English Literature*. Cambridge: Cambridge University Press.

Golden, Samuel A. 1972. *Jean LeClerc*. New York: Twayne.

Goldgar, Anne. 1995. *Impolite Learning: Conduct and Community in the Republic of Letters, 1680–1750*. New Haven, Conn.: Yale University Press.

Goldman, Shalom. 2004. *God's Sacred Tongue: Hebrew and the American Imagination*. Chapel Hill: University of North Carolina Press.

Goldstein, Doris S. 1990. "History at Oxford and Cambridge: Professionalization and the Influence of Ranke." In *Leopold von Ranke and the Shaping of the Historical Discipline*, ed. Georg G. Iggers and James M. Powell, 141–53. Syracuse, N.Y.: Syracuse University Press.

Goldstein, Doris. 2004. "Confronting Time: The Oxford School of History and the Non-Darwinian Revolution." *Storia della Storiografia* 45: 3–27.

Gooch, G. P. 1959 (1913). *History and Historians in the Nineteenth Century*. Boston: Beacon.

Goodrich, Charles A. 1842. *A Pictorial and Descriptive View of All Religions; Embracing the Forms of Worship Practiced by the Several Nations of the Known World, from the Earliest Records to the Present Time*. Hartford, Conn.: Sumner and Goodman.

Gordon, Alden R. 2007. "Subverting the Secret of Herculaneum: Archaeological Espionage in the Kingdom of Naples." In *Antiquity Recovered: The Legacy of Pompeii and Herculaneum*, ed. Victoria C. Gardner and Jon L. Seydl. Los Angeles: J. Paul Getty Museum.

Gordon, Cyrus H. 1986. *The Pennsylvania Tradition of Semitics: A Century of Near Eastern and Biblical Studies at the University of Pennsylvania*. Atlanta: Scholars.

Gordon, G. S., ed. 1912. *English Literature and the Classics*. Oxford: Clarendon.

Graff, Gerald. 1987. *Professing Literature: An Institutional History*. Chicago: University of Chicago Press.

Graff, Gerald, and Michael Warner, eds. 1989. *The Origins of Literary Studies in America: A Documentary Anthology*. New York: Routledge.

Grafton, Anthony T. 1980. "The Importance of Being Printed." *Journal of Interdisciplinary History* 11: 265–86.

Grafton, Anthony. 1983. "Polyhistor into Philolog: Notes on the Transformation of German Classical Scholarship, 1750–1850." *History of Universities* 3: 159–92.

Grafton, Anthony. 1983–93. *Joseph Scaliger: A Study in the History of Classical Scholarship*. 2 vols. Oxford: Clarendon.

Grafton, Anthony. 1990a. *Forgers and Critics: Creativity and Duplicity in Western Scholarship*. Princeton, N.J.: Princeton University Press.

Grafton, Anthony. 1990b. "Invention of Traditions and Traditions of Invention in Renaissance Europe: The Strange Case of Annius of Viterbo." In *The Transmission of Culture in Early Modern Europe*, ed. Grafton and Ann Blair, 8–38. Philadelphia: University of Pennsylvania Press.

Grafton, Anthony. 1991. *Defenders of the Text: The Traditions of Scholarship in an Age of Science*. Cambridge, Mass.: Harvard University Press.

Grafton, Anthony. 1994. "The Footnote from De Thou to Ranke." *History and Theory* 33, no. 4: 53–76.

Grafton, Anthony. 1997. *The Footnote: A Curious History*. Cambridge, Mass.: Harvard University Press.

Grafton, Anthony. 2000. *Leon Battista Alberti: Master Builder of the Italian Renaissance*. New York: Hill and Wang.

Grafton, Anthony. 2007. *What Was History? The Art of History in Early Modern Europe*. Cambridge: Cambridge University Press.

Grafton, Anthony. 2009. *Worlds Made by Words: Scholarship and Community in the Modern West*. Cambridge, Mass.: Harvard University Press.

Grafton, Anthony, and Lisa Jardine. 1986. *From Humanism to the Humanities: Education and the Liberal Arts in Fifteenth- and Sixteenth-Century Europe*. Cambridge, Mass.: Harvard University Press.

Grafton, Anthony, and Joanna Weinberg. 2011. *"I Have Always Loved the Holy Tongue": Isaac Casaubon, the Jews, and a Forgotten Chapter in Renaissance Scholarship*. Cambridge, Mass.: Harvard University Press.

Grafton, Anthony, and Megan Williams. 2006. *Christianity and the Transformation of the Book: Origen, Eusebius, and the Library of Caesarea*. Cambridge, Mass.: Harvard University Press.

Graham, Timothy, ed. 2000. *The Recovery of Old English: Anglo-Saxon Studies in the Sixteenth and Seventeenth Centuries*. Kalamazoo, Mich.: Medieval Institute Publications.

Grant, Robert, and David Tracy. 1984. *A Short History of the Interpretation of the Bible*. 2nd ed. Philadelphia: Fortress.

Grant Duff, M. E. 1892. *Sir Henry Maine: A Brief Memoir of His Life*. New York: Henry Holt.

Gräslund, Bo. 1987. *The Birth of Prehistoric Chronology: Dating Methods and Dating Systems in Nineteenth-Century Scandinavian Archaeology*. Cambridge: Cambridge University Press.

Gray, Edward G. 1999. *New World Babel: Languages and Nations in Early America*. Princeton, N.J.: Princeton University Press.

Grayson, Donald K. 1983. *The Establishment of Human Antiquity*. New York: Academic Press.

Green, V.H.H. 1964. *Religion at Oxford and Cambridge*. London: SCM.

Greene, John C. 1984. *American Science in the Age of Jefferson*. Ames: Iowa State University Press.

Grell, Chantal. 1982. *Herculanum et Pompéi dans les récits des voyageurs français du XVIIIe siècle*. Naples: Bibliothèque de l'Institut Français de Naples.

Grendler, Paul F. 1989. *Schooling in Renaissance Italy: Literacy and Learning, 1300–1600*. Baltimore: Johns Hopkins University Press.

Grendler, Paul F. 1991. "Reply to Robert Black." *Journal of the History of Ideas* 52: 335–37.

Grendler, Paul F. 2002. *The Universities of the Italian Renaissance*. Baltimore: Johns Hopkins University Press.

Grene, David. 2007. *Of Farming and Classics: A Memoir.* Chicago: University of Chicago Press.

Grimm, Jakob Karl Ludwig. 1984 (1851). *On the Origin of Language,* trans. Raymond A. Wiley. Leiden, Netherlands: E. J. Brill.

Grodzins, Dean. 2002. *American Heretic: Theodore Parker and Transcendentalism.* Chapel Hill: University of North Carolina Press.

Grossman, Jeffrey. 1997. "Wilhelm von Humboldt's Linguistic Ideology: The Problem of Pluralism and the Absolute Difference of National Character: Or, Where Do the Jews Fit In?" *German Studies Review* 20: 23–47.

Grube, G.M.A. 1995 (1965). *The Greek and Roman Critics.* Indianapolis: Hackett.

Gruber, Jacob W. 1965. "Brixham Cave and the Antiquity of Man." In *Context and Meaning in Cultural Anthropology,* ed. Melford E. Spiro, 373–402. New York: Free Press / London: Collier Macmillan.

Gruber, Jacob W. 1967. "Horatio Hale and the Development of American Anthropology," *Proceedings of the American Philosophical Society* 111: 5–37.

Guilland, Antoine. 1899. *L'Allemagne nouvelle et ses historiens.* Paris: Félix Alcan.

Gusdorf, Georges. 1988. *Les origines de l'herméneutique.* Paris: Éditions Payot.

Gutjahr, Paul C. 2011. *Charles Hodge: Guardian of American Orthodoxy.* New York: Oxford University Press.

Haddon, Alfred C. 1898. *The Study of Man.* New York: G. P. Putnam's Sons.

Hailperin, Herman. 1963. *Rashi and the Christian Scholars.* Pittsburgh: University of Pittsburgh Press.

Hallam, Henry. 1837–39. *Introduction to the Literature of Europe in the Fifteenth, Sixteenth and Seventeenth Centuries.* 4 vols. Paris: Baudry's European Library (vol. 1) and A. and W. Galignani. (vols. 2–4).

Hallote, Rachel. 2006. *Bible, Map, and Spade: The American Palestine Exploration Society, Frederick Jones Bliss, and the Forgotten Story of Early American Biblical Archaeology.* Piscataway, N.J.: Gorgias.

Hamilton, Alastair. 1996. "Humanists and the Bible." In *The Cambridge Companion to Renaissance Humanism,* ed. Jill Kraye, 100–17. Cambridge: Cambridge University Press.

Hamilton, Alastair. 2001. *Arab Culture and Ottoman Magnificence in Antwerp's Golden Age.* London: Arcadian Library and Oxford University Press.

Hamilton, Alastair. 2011. "All the World's Faiths," *Times Literary Supplement,* July 1, 22–23.

Hamilton, Alastair, Maurits H. van den Boogert, and Bart Westerweel, eds. 2005. *The Republic of Letters and the Levant.* Leiden, Netherlands: Brill.

Hamilton, Alastair, and Francis Richard. 2004. *André du Ryer and Oriental Studies in Seventeenth-Century France.* Oxford: Arcadian Library and Oxford University Press.

Hammacher, Klaus, ed. 1976. *Universalismus und Wissenschaft im Werk und Wirken der Brüder Humboldt.* Frankfurt am Main: Vittorio Klostermann.

Handlin, Lilian. 1983. "Harvard and Göttingen, 1815," *Proceedings of the Massachusetts Historical Society* 95: 67–87.

Handlin, Lilian. 1984. *George Bancroft: The Intellectual as Democrat.* New York: Harper and Row.

Hankins, James, 1994. "Translation Practice in the Renaissance: The Case of Leonardo Bruni." In *Méthodologie de la traduction: de l'antiquité à la Renaissance,* ed. Charles Marie Ternes and Monique Mund-Dopchie, 154–75. Luxembourg: Centre Universitaire de Luxembourg.

Hanzeli, Victor Egon. 1969. *Missionary Linguistics in New France: A Study of Seventeenth- and Eighteenth-Century Descriptions of American Indian Languages.* The Hague: Mouton.

Harding, Anthony John. 1985. *Coleridge and the Inspired Word*. Kingston and Montreal: McGill-Queen's University Press.

Hardwick, Charles. 1855–59. *Christ and Other Masters: An Historical Inquiry into Some of the Chief Parallelisms and Contrasts between Christianity and the Religious Systems of the Ancient World, with Special Reference to Prevailing Difficulties and Objections*. 4 vols. Cambridge: Macmillan.

Hardy, Grant. 1999. *Worlds of Bronze and Bamboo: Sima Qian's Conquest of History*. New York: Columbia University Press.

Harper, William R. 1904. *The Report of the President: Publications of the Members of the University*. Chicago: University of Chicago Press.

Harris, Horton. 1975. *The Tübingen School*. Oxford: Clarendon.

H[arris], J[ames]. 1751. *Hermes: or, A Philosophical Inquiry concerning Language and Universal Grammar*. London: H. Woodfall for J. Nourse and P. Vaillant.

Harris, William V. 1989. *Ancient Literacy*. Cambridge, Mass.: Harvard University Press.

Harrison, Peter. 1990. *'Religion' and the Religions in the English Enlightenment*. Cambridge: Cambridge University Press.

Harrison, Peter. 1998. *The Bible, Protestantism, and the Rise of Natural Science*. Cambridge: Cambridge University Press.

Hart, Thomas R., Jr. 1953. "Friedrich Bouterwek, a Pioneer Historian of Spanish Literature." *Comparative Literature* 5: 351–61.

Hart, Thomas R., Jr. 1954. "George Ticknor's *History of Spanish Literature*: The New England Background." *PMLA* 69: 76–88.

Harvey, David Allen. 2008. "Living Antiquity: Lafitau's *Moeurs des sauvages amériquains* and the Religious Roots of the Enlightenment Science of Man," *Proceedings of the Western Society for French History* 36: 75–92.

Harvey, Sean P. 2009. "American Languages: Indians, Ethnology, and the Empire for Liberty." PhD diss., College of William and Mary.

Haskell, Francis. 1993. *History and Its Images: Art and the Interpretation of the Past*. New Haven, Conn.: Yale University Press.

Haskell, Thomas L. 1977. *The Emergence of Professional Social Science: The American Social Science Association and the Nineteenth-Century Crisis of Authority*. Urbana: University of Illinois Press.

Haskin, Dayton. 1989. "New Historical Contexts for Appraising the Donne Revival from A. B. Grosart to Charles Eliot Norton." *ELH* 56: 869–95.

Haskin, Dayton. 2002. "No Edition Is an Island: The Place of the Nineteenth-Century American Editions within the History of Editing Donne's Poems." *Text: An Interdisciplinary Annual of Textual Studies* 14: 169–207.

• Haskins, Charles Homer, 1927. *The Renaissance of the Twelfth Century*. Cambridge, Mass.: Harvard University Press.

Hauer, Stanley R. 1983. "Thomas Jefferson and the Anglo-Saxon Language." *PMLA* 98: 879–98.

Haugen, Kristine Louise. 2011. *Richard Bentley: Poetry and Enlightenment*. Cambridge, Mass.: Harvard University Press.

Hay, Denys. 1977. *Annalists and Historians: Western Historiography from the Eighth to the Eighteenth Centuries*. London: Methuen.

Hay, Denys. 1988. *Renaissance Essays*. London: Hambledon.

Haycock, David Boyd. 2002. *William Stukeley: Science, Religion and Archaeology in Eighteenth-Century England*. Woodbridge, England: Boydell.

Hazard, Paul. 1967 (1935). *La crise de la conscience Européenne, 1680–1715*. Paris: Fayard.

Hazard, Roland Gibson. 1836. *Language: Its Connexion with the Present Condition and Future Prospects of Man.* Providence, R.I.: Marshall, Brown.

Hazard, Roland Gibson. 1857. *An Essay on Language and Other Papers.* Boston: Phillips, Sampson.

[Hazlitt, William.] 1824. *Table-Talk; or, Original Essays on Men and Manners.* 2nd ed. 2 vols. London: Printed for Henry Colburn.

Hecht, Hans. 1933. *T. Percy, R. Wood und J. D. Michaelis: ein Beitrag zur Literaturgeschichte der Genieperiode.* Stuttgart: W. Kohlhammer Verlag.

Heckewelder, John. 1876 (1819). *History, Manners, and Customs of the Indian Nations Who Once Inhabited Pennsylvania and the Neighbouring States,* ed. William C. Reichel. Rev. ed. Philadelphia: Historical Society of Pennsylvania.

Hegel, Georg Wilhelm Friedrich. 1956 (1837; trans. 1857). *The Philosophy of History,* trans. J. Sibree. New York: Dover.

Helmholtz [later Phelan], Anna Augusta. 1907. The Indebtedness of Samuel Taylor Coleridge to August Wilhelm von Schlegel. *Bulletin of the University of Wisconsin* 163: Philology and Literature Series 3, no. 4: 273–370.

Henneman, J. B. 1892. "Two Pioneers in the Historical Study of English, Thomas Jefferson and Louis F. Klipstein: A Contribution to the History of the Study of English in America." *PMLA* 7: Appendix, xliii–liii.

Hepworth, Brian. 1978. *Robert Lowth.* Boston: Twayne.

Herbst, Jurgen. 1965. *The German Historical School in American Scholarship: A Study in the Transfer of Culture.* Ithaca, N.Y.: Cornell University Press.

Herklotz, Ingo. 1999. *Cassiano Dal Pozzo und die Archäologie des 17. Jahrhunderts.* Munich: Hirmer Verlag.

Herle, Anita, and Sandra Rouse, eds. 1998. *Cambridge and the Torres Strait: Centenary Essays on the 1898 Anthropological Expedition.* Cambridge: Cambridge University Press.

Herrin, Judith. 2007. *Byzantium: The Surprising Life of a Medieval Empire.* London: Allen Lane.

Hess, Jonathan M. 2002. *Germans, Jews, and the Claims of Modernity.* New Haven, Conn.: Yale University Press.

Higgins, Godfrey. 1829. *An Apology for the Life and Character of the Celebrated Prophet of Arabia, Called Mohamed, or the Illustrious.* London: R. Hunter.

Higgins, Godfrey. 1836. *Anacalypsis, An Attempt To Draw Aside The Veil Of The Saitic Isis; or, An Inquiry into the Origin of Languages, Nations, and Religions.* 2 vols. London: Longman, Rees, Orme, Brown, Green, and Longman.

Higginson, Thomas Wentworth. 1876 (1871). *The Sympathy of Religions,* Free Religious Tracts no. 3. New ed., rev. and enlarged. Boston: Free Religious Association.

[Hillard, George S., et al.] 1876. *The Life, Letters and Journals of George Ticknor.* 2 vols. London: Sampson Low, Marston, Searle, and Rivington.

Hinsley, Curtis M., Jr. 1981. *Savages and Scientists: The Smithsonian Institution and the Development of American Anthropology, 1846–1910.* Washington, D.C.: Smithsonian Institution Press.

Hinz, Vinko. 2001. *Nunc Phalaris doctum protulit ecce caput: antike Phalarislegende und Nachleben der Phalarisbriefe.* Munich: K. G. Saur, 2001.

Hiss, Priscilla, and Roberta Fansler. 1934. *Research in Fine Arts in the Colleges and Universities of the United States.* New York: Carnegie Corporation.

Hobbes, Thomas. 1968 (1651). *Leviathan, or the Matter, Forme, and Power of a Common-Wealth, Ecclesiasticall and Civill,* ed. C. B. MacPherson. Harmondsworth, England: Penguin.

Hobbins, Daniel. 2009. *Authorship and Publicity before Print: Jean Gerson and the Transformation of Late Medieval Learning*. Philadelphia: University of Pennsylvania Press.

Hock, Hans Heinrich, and Brian D. Joseph. 1996. *Language History, Language Change, and Language Relationship: An Introduction to Historical and Comparative Linguistics*. Berlin: Mouton de Gruyter, 1996.

Höcker, Wilma. 1951. *Der Gesandte Bunsen als Vermittler zwischen Deutschland und England*. Göttingen, Germany: Musterschmidt Wissenschaftlicher Verlag.

Hodge, Charles. 1822. *A Dissertation on the Importance of Biblical Literature*. Trenton, N.J.: George Sherman.

Hoffmann, E.T.A. 1985–2004. "Des Kapellmeisters, Johannes Kreislers, Dissertatiuncula über den hohen Wert der Musik." In *Sämtliche Werke*, ed. Hartmut Steinecke and Wulf Segebrecht (6 vols.; Frankfurt am Main: Deutscher Klassiker Verlag, 1985–2004), 1: 608–14 (*Kreisleriana*, part 1).

Holford-Strevens, Leofranc. 2003. *Aulus Gellius: An Antonine Scholar and His Achievement*. Rev. ed. Oxford: Oxford University Press.

Hopkins, Keith. 1999. *A World Full of Gods: The Strange Triumph of Christianity*. New York: Free Press.

Hornblower, Simon, and Anthony Spawforth, eds. 1996. *The Oxford Classical Dictionary*. 3rd ed. Oxford: Oxford University Press.

Horne Tooke, John. 1798–1805. *ΕΠΕΑ ΠΤΕΡΟΕΝΤΑ. Or, The Diversions of Purley*. 2nd ed. 2 vols. London: Printed for the author, at J. Johnson's, No. 72, St. Paul's Church Yard. (The volumes are called "Part I" and "Part II" on the respective title pages.)

Hornig, Gottfried. 1961. *Die Anfänge der historisch-kritischen Theologie: Johann Salomo Semlers Schriftverständnis und seine Stellung zu Luther*. Göttingen, Germany: Vandenhoeck & Ruprecht.

Horowitz, Elliott. 2006. *Reckless Rites: Purim and the Legacy of Jewish Violence*. Princeton, N.J.: Princeton University Press.

Horsfall, Nicholas. 1974. "Classical Studies in England, 1810–1825." *Greek, Roman, and Byzantine Studies* 15: 449–77.

Horsman, Reginald. 1981. *Race and Manifest Destiny: The Origins of American Racial Anglo-Saxonism*. Cambridge, Mass.: Harvard University Press.

Hoskin, Michael, ed. 1999. *The Cambridge Concise History of Astronomy*. Cambridge: Cambridge University Press.

Housman, A. E. 1961. *Selected Prose*, ed. John Carter. Cambridge: Cambridge University Press.

Howard, Thomas Albert. 2000. *Religion and the Rise of Historicism: W.M.L. de Wette, Jacob Burckhardt, and the Theological Origins of Nineteenth Century Historical Consciousness*. Cambridge: Cambridge University Press.

Howell, Wilbur Samuel. 1961. *Logic and Rhetoric in England, 1500–1700*. New York: Russell and Russell.

Hsia, R. Po-Chia, and Henk van Nierop, eds. 2002. *Calvinism and Religious Toleration in the Dutch Golden Age*. Cambridge: Cambridge University Press.

Hughes, S.F.D. 1979. "Mrs. Elstob's Defense of Antiquarian Learning in Her *Rudiments of Grammar for the English-Saxon Tongue* (1715)." *Harvard Library Bulletin* 27: 172–91.

Humboldt, Wilhelm von. 2010 (1836). "Ueber die Verschiedenheit des menschlichen Sprachbaues und ihren Einfluss auf die geistige Entwicklung des Menschengeschlechts." In Wilhelm von Humboldt, *Werke*, ed. Andreas Flitner and Klaus Giel, 5 vols, 3: 368–756. Darmstadt, Germany: Wissenschaftliche Buchgesellschaft.

Hume, David. 1770 (1754–62). *The History of England, from the Invasion of Julius Caesar to the Revolution in 1688*. New ed., corrected. 8 vols. London: Printed for T. Cadell.

Hunt, Lynn, Margaret C. Jacob, and Wijnand Mijnhardt. 2010. *The Book That Changed Europe: Picart and Bernard's "Religious Ceremonies of the World."* Cambridge, Mass.: Harvard University Press.

Huppert, George. 1970. *The Idea of Perfect History: Historical Erudition and Historical Philosophy in Renaissance France.* Urbana: University of Illinois Press.

Hustvedt, Sigurd Bernhard. 1930. *Ballad Books and Ballad Men: Raids and Rescues in Britain, America, and the Scandinavian North since 1800.* Cambridge, Mass.: Harvard University Press.

Ianziti, Gary. 2002. "Leonardo Bruni and Biography: 'The Vita Aristotelis.'" *Renaissance Quarterly* 55: 805–32.

Iggers, Georg G. 1968. *The German Conception of History: The National Tradition of Historical Thought from Herder to the Present.* Middletown, Conn.: Wesleyan University Press.

Iggers, Georg G., and Q. Edward Wang. 2008. *A Global History of Modern Historiography.* Harlow, England: Pearson Education.

Irwin, Robert. 2007 (2006). *For Lust of Knowing: The Orientalists and Their Enemies.* London: Penguin.

Israel, Jonathan I. 2001. *Radical Enlightenment: Philosophy and the Making of Modernity, 1650–1750.* Oxford: Oxford University Press.

Jackson, Carl T. 1981. *The Oriental Religions and American Thought: Nineteenth-Century Explorations.* Westport, Conn.: Greenwood.

Jacobs, Wilbur R. 1968. *The Historical World of Frederick Jackson Turner, with Selections from His Correspondence.* New Haven, Conn.: Yale University Press.

Jaeger, C. Stephen. 1994. *The Envy of Angels: Cathedral Schools and Social Ideals in Medieval Europe, 950–1200.* Philadelphia: University of Pennsylvania Press.

Jaffe, Irma B. 1983. "The John Trumbull Memorial Exhibition at Yale." *Art Journal* 43: 190–93.

Jaksić, Iván. 2007. *Ven conmigo a la España lejana: los intelectuales norteamericanos ante el mundo hispano, 1820–1880.* Santiago, Chile: Fondo de Cultura Económica.

Jameson, J. Franklin. 1993–2001. *John Franklin Jameson and the Development of Humanistic Scholarship in America*, ed. Morey Rothberg et al., 3 vols. Athens: University of Georgia Press.

Jardine, Lisa. 1993. *Erasmus, Man of Letters: The Construction of Charisma in Print.* Princeton, N.J.: Princeton University Press.

Jardine, Lisa. 1994. "Ghosting the Reform of Dialectic: Erasmus and Agricola Again." In *Renaissance Rhetoric*, ed. Peter Mack, 27–45. New York: St. Martin's.

Jarick, John. 2007. *Sacred Conjectures: The Context and Legacy of Robert Lowth and Jean Astruc.* New York: T and T Clark.

Jarves, James Jackson. 1960 (1864). *The Art-Idea*, ed. Benjamin Rowland, Jr. Cambridge, Mass.: Harvard University Press.

Jarvis, Simon. 1995. *Scholars and Gentlemen: Shakespearian Textual Criticism and Representations of Scholarly Labour, 1725–1765.* Oxford: Clarendon.

Jebb, Caroline. 1907. *Life and Letters of Sir Richard Claverhouse Jebb.* Cambridge: Cambridge University Press.

Jebb, R. C. 1889 (1882). *Bentley.* London: Macmillan.

Jefferson, Thomas. 1851. *An Essay towards Facilitating Instruction in the Anglo-Saxon and Modern Dialects of the English Language. For the Use of the University of Virginia. Printed by Order of the Board of Trustees for the University of Virginia.* New York: John F. Trow.

Jefferson, Thomas. 1954. *The Papers of Thomas Jefferson*, vol. 10, ed. Julian P. Boyd et al. Princeton, N.J.: Princeton University Press.

Jefferson, Thomas. 1972 (1785). *Notes on the State of Virginia*, ed. William Peden. New York: W. W. Norton.

Jenkyns, Richard. 1980. *The Victorians and Ancient Greece*. Cambridge, Mass.: Harvard University Press.

Jespersen, Otto. N.d. [1921]. *Language: Its Nature, Development, and Origin*. New York: Henry Holt.

John of Salisbury. 1955 (ca. 1160). *The Metalogicon of John of Salisbury: A Twelfth-Century Defense of the Verbal and Logical Arts of the Trivium*, trans. Daniel D. McGarry. Berkeley and Los Angeles: University of California Press.

Johnson, Alexander Bryan. 1947 (1854). *A Treatise on Language*, ed. David Rynin. Berkeley and Los Angeles: University of California Press.

Johnston, Judith. 1997. *Anna Jameson: Victorian, Feminist, Woman of Letters*. Aldershot, England: Scolar.

Johnstone, William. ed. 1995. *William Robertson Smith: Essays in Reassessment*. Sheffield, England: Sheffield Academic.

Johnstone, William. 2004. "Introduction." In *The Bible and the Enlightenment: A Case Study—Dr. Alexander Geddes (1737–1802)*. London: T and T Clark.

Jolly, Roslyn. 2006. "Robert Louis Stevenson, Henry Maine, and the Anthropology of Comparative Law." *Journal of British Studies* 45: 556–80.

Jones, Edwin. 2001. *John Lingard and the Pursuit of Historical Truth*. Brighton, England: Sussex Academic.

Jones, G. Lloyd. 1983. *The Discovery of Hebrew in Tudor England*. Manchester: Manchester University Press.

Jones, Howard Mumford, and Thomas Edgar Casady. 1933. *The Life of Moses Coit Tyler*. Ann Arbor: University of Michigan Press.

Jones, H. S. 2007. *Intellect and Character in Victorian England: Mark Pattison and the Invention of the Don*. Cambridge: Cambridge University Press.

Jones, Robert Alun. 1984. "Robertson Smith and James Frazer on Religion: Two Traditions in British Social Anthropology." In *Functionalism Historicized: Essays on British Social Anthropology*, ed. George W. Stocking Jr., 31–58. Madison: University of Wisconsin Press.

[Jones, William.] 1789. *Sacontalá, or the Fatal Ring; An Indian Drama by Cálidás: Translated from the Original Sanscrit and Prácrit*. Calcutta: Joseph Cooper.

[Jones, William.] 1790. *Sacontalá; or, the Fatal Ring: An Indian Drama. By Cálidás. Translated from the Original Sanscrit and Prácrit*. London: Edwards.

Jones, William. 1799a. "The Third Anniversary Discourse [to the Asiatick Society], delivered 2 February, 1786." In *The Works of Sir William Jones*, ed. A[nna]. M[aria]. J[ones], 6 vols., 1:19–34. London: Printed for G. G. and J. Robinson and R. H. Evans.

Jones, William. 1799b. "The Eighth Anniversary Discourse [to the Asiatick Society], delivered 24 February, 1791." In *The Works of Sir William Jones*, ed. A[nna]. M[aria]. J[ones], 6 vols., 1:113–27. London: Printed for G. G. and J. Robinson and R. H. Evans.

Joseph, John E. 2007. "He Was an Englishman," *Times Literary Supplement*, November 16, 14.

Junius, Franciscus. 2004. *"For My Worthy Freind Mr Franciscus Junius": An Edition of the Correspondence of Francis Junius F. F. (1591–1677)*, ed. Sophie van Romburgh. Leiden, Netherlands: Brill.

Kahn, Charles H. 1983. "Philosophy and the Written Word: Some Thoughts on Heraclitus and the Early Greek Uses of Prose." In *Language and Thought in Early Greek Philosophy*, ed. Kevin Robb, 110–24. La Salle, Ill.: Monist Library of Philosophy.

Kames, Henry Home, Lord. 2005 (1785). *Elements of Criticism.* 6th ed. 2 vols. Indianapolis: Liberty Fund.

Kames, Henry Home, Lord. 2007 (1788). *Sketches of the History of Man, Considerably Enlarged by the Last Additions and Corrections of the Author,* ed. James A. Harris. 3rd ed. 3 vols. Indianapolis: Liberty Fund.

Kamesar, Adam. 1993. *Jerome, Greek Scholarship, and the Hebrew Bible: A Study of the "Quaestiones Hebraicae in Genesim."* Oxford: Clarendon.

Kamen, Michael L. 2004. "The Science of the Bible in Nineteenth-Century America: From 'Common Sense' to Controversy, 1820–1900." Ph.D. diss., University of Notre Dame.

Kaster, Robert A. 1988. *Guardians of Language: The Grammarian and Society in Late Antiquity.* Berkeley and Los Angeles: University of California Press.

Katz, David S. 1993. "Isaac Vossius and the English Biblical Critics 1670–1689." In *Scepticism and Irreligion in the Seventeenth and Eighteenth Centuries,* ed. Richard H. Popkin and Arjo Vanderjagt, 142–84. Leiden, Netherlands: Brill.

Kaufmann, Thomas DaCosta. 2001. "Antiquarianism, the History of Objects, and the History of Art before Winckelmann." *Journal of the History of Ideas* 62: 523–41.

Kearney, Anthony. 1986. *John Churton Collins: The Louse on the Locks of Literature.* Edinburgh: Scottish Academic.

Kelley, Donald R. 1970. *Foundations of Modern Historical Scholarship: Language, Law, and History in the French Renaissance.* New York: Columbia University Press.

Kelley, Donald R., ed. 1997. *History and the Disciplines: The Reclassification of Knowledge in Early Modern Europe.* Rochester, N.Y.: University of Rochester Press.

Kelley, Donald R, 1998. *Faces of History: Historical Inquiry from Herodotus to Herder.* New Haven, Conn.: Yale University Press.

Kelley, Donald R. 2003. *Fortunes of History: Historical Inquiry from Herder to Huizinga.* New Haven, Conn.: Yale University Press.

Kelly, Jason M. 2009. *The Society of Dilettanti: Archaeology and Identity in the British Enlightenment.* New Haven, Conn.: Yale University Press.

Kemble, John M. 1833. *The Anglo-Saxon Poems of Beowulf[,] The Travellers Song and The Battle of Finnes-Burh, Edited Together with a Glossary of the More Difficult Words and an Historical Preface.* London: William Pickering.

Kemble, John M. 1837. *The Anglo-Saxon Poem of Beowulf with a Copious Glossary[,] Preface and Philological Notes.* London: William Pickering.

Kemble, John M. 1876 (1849). *The Saxons in England: A History of the English Commonwealth till the Period of the Norman Conquest,* revised by Walter de Gray Birch. 2 vols. London: Bernard Quaritch.

Kendrick, T. D. 1950. *British Antiquity.* London: Methuen.

Kennedy, George A. 1980. *Classical Rhetoric and Its Christian and Secular Tradition from Ancient to Modern Times.* Chapel Hill: University of North Carolina Press.

Kennedy, George A. 1994. *A New History of Classical Rhetoric.* Princeton, N.J.: Princeton University Press.

Kenney, E. J. 1974. *The Classical Text: Aspects of Editing in the Age of the Printed Book.* Berkeley and Los Angeles: University of California Press.

Kennicott, Benjamin. 1753. *The State of the Printed Hebrew Text of the Old Testament Considered: A Dissertation in Two Parts.* Oxford: Printed at the Theatre.

[Kennicott, Benjamin.] [1767.] *A Proposal for Establishing a Professorship of the Persian Language in the University of Oxford.* N.p. [Oxford?]: n.p.

Kenyon, John. 1984. *The History Men: The Historical Profession in England since the Renaissance.* Pittsburgh: University of Pittsburgh Press.

Kernan, Alvin. 1989 (1987). *Samuel Johnson and the Impact of Print*. Princeton, N.J.: Princeton University Press.

Kewes, Paulina, ed. 2006. *The Uses of History in Early Modern England*. San Marino, Calif.: Huntington Library.

Kieffer, Jean-Luc. 1983. *Anquetil-Duperron: l'Inde en France au XVIIIe siècle*. Paris: Les Belles Lettres.

Kiernan, Kevin S. 1986. *The Thorkelin Transcripts of "Beowulf."* Copenhagen: Rosenkilde og Bagger.

Kiernan, Kevin S. 1996. *"Beowulf" and the "Beowulf" Manuscript*. Ann Arbor: University of Michigan Press.

Killeen, Kevin. 2009. *Biblical Scholarship, Science and Politics in Early Modern England: Thomas Browne and the Thorny Place of Knowledge*. Farnham, England: Ashgate.

Kilpatrick, Hilary. 2010. "Arabic Private Correspondence from Seventeenth-Century Syria: The Letters to Edward Pococke." *Bodleian Library Record* 23, no. 1: 20–40.

Kinmont, Alexander. 1839. *Twelve Lectures on the Natural History of Man, and the Rise and Progress of Philosophy*. Cincinnati, Ohio: U. P. James.

Kippenberg, Hans G. 2002 (1997). *Discovering Religious History in the Modern Age*, trans. Barbara Harshav. Princeton, N.J.: Princeton University Press.

Kirk, G. S. 1970. *Myth: Its Meaning and Functions in Ancient and Other Cultures*. Cambridge and Berkeley: Cambridge University Press and University of California Press.

Kittredge, George Lyman. 1927 (1915). *Chaucer and His Poetry: Lectures Delivered in 1914 on the Percy Turnbull Memorial Foundation in the Johns Hopkins University*. Cambridge, Mass.: Harvard University Press.

Kitzhaber, Albert R. 1990. *Rhetoric in American Colleges, 1850–1900*. Dallas: Southern Methodist University Press.

Kliger, Samuel. 1952. *The Goths in England: A Study in Seventeenth and Eighteenth Century Thought*. Cambridge, Mass.: Harvard University Press.

Kopf, David. 1969. *British Orientalism and the Bengal Renaissance: The Dynamics of Indian Modernization, 1773–1835*. Berkeley and Los Angeles: University of California Press.

Kouremenos, Theokritos, George M. Parássoglou, and Kryiakos Tsantsanoglou. 2006. *The Derveni Papyrus*. Florence, Italy: Leo S. Olschki Editore.

Knappe, Gabriele. 1996. *Traditionen der klassichen Rhetorik in angelsächsischen England*. Heidelberg: Universitätsverlag C. Winter.

Knight, W.S.M. 1925. *The Life and Works of Hugo Grotius*. London: Sweet and Maxwell.

Knowlson, James. 1975. *Universal Language Schemes in England and France, 1600–1800*. Toronto: University of Toronto Press.

Koerner, Konrad. 1989. *Practicing Linguistic Historiography*. Amsterdam: John Benjamins.

Koerner, E.F.K. 2002. *Toward a History of Americanist Linguistics*. London: Routledge.

Kraitsir, Charles. 1846. *Significance of the Alphabet*. Boston: E. P. Peabody.

Kramer, Michael P. 1992. *Imagining Language in America: From the Revolution to the Civil War*. Princeton, N.J.: Princeton University Press.

Kramnick, Jonathan Brody. 2008 (1999). *Making the English Canon: Print-Capitalism and the Cultural Past, 1700–1770*. Cambridge: Cambridge University Press.

Kraye, Jill. 1996. "Philologists and Philosophers." In *The Cambridge Companion to Renaissance Humanism*, ed. Jill Kraye, 142–60. Cambridge: Cambridge University Press.

Krey, Philip D. W., and Lesley Smith, eds. 2000. *Nicholas of Lyra: The Senses of Scripture*. Leiden, Netherlands: Brill.

Krieger, Leonard. 1977. *Ranke: The Meaning of History*. Chicago: University of Chicago Press.

Krostenko, Brian A. 2001. *Cicero, Catullus, and the Language of Social Performance*. Chicago: University of Chicago Press.

Kuenen, A[braham]. 1882. *The Hibbert Lectures, 1882: National Religions and Universal Religions: Lectures Delivered at Oxford and in London, in April and May, 1882.* London: Williams and Norgate.

Kugel, James L. 1997. *The Bible as It Was.* Cambridge, Mass.: Harvard University Press.

Kugel, James L. 1998 (1981). *The Idea of Biblical Poetry: Parallelism and Its History.* Baltimore: Johns Hopkins University Press.

Kugel, James L. 2007. *How to Read the Bible: A Guide to Scripture, Then and Now.* New York: Free Press.

Kugler, Franz. 1861. *Handbuch der Kunstgeschichte.* 4th edition, ed. Wilhelm Lübke. Stuttgart: Ebner und Seubert.

[Kugler, Franz, and Jacob Burckhardt.] 1855. *Handbook of Painting: The Italian Schools,* trans. "a Lady" [Elizabeth Eastlake], ed. Charles Eastlake. 3rd ed. London: John Murray.

Kühlmann, Wilhelm. 1982. *Gelehrtenrepublik und Fürstenstaat: Entwicklung und Kritik des deutschen Späthumanismus in der Literatur des Barockzeitalters.* Tübingen, Germany: Max Niemeyer.

Kukenheim, Louis. 1951. *Contributions à l'histoire de la grammaire greque, latine, et hébraïque à l'époque de la Renaissance.* Leiden, Netherlands: E. J. Brill.

Kuklick, Bruce. 1996. *Puritans in Babylon: The Ancient Near East and American Intellectual Life, 1880–1930.* Princeton, N.J.: Princeton University Press.

Kuklick, Henrika, ed. 2008. *A New History of Anthropology.* Malden, Mass.: Blackwell.

Kultermann, Udo. 1993. *The History of Art History.* New York: Abaris.

Kümmel, Werner Georg. 1973 (1970). *The New Testament: The History of the Investigation of Its Problems,* trans. S. McLean Gilmour and Howard C. Kee. London: SCM.

Kuper, Adam. 1988. *The Invention of Primitive Society: Transformations of an Illusion.* London: Routledge,

Laks, André, and Glenn W. Most, eds. 1997. *Studies on the Derveni Papyrus.* Oxford: Clarendon.

Lamarche, Paul, S. J. 1997. "The Septuagint: Bible of the Earliest Christians." In *The Bible in Greek Christian Antiquity,* ed. and trans. Paul M. Blowers, 15–33. Notre Dame, Ind.: University of Notre Dame Press.

Lamberton, Robert. 1986. *Homer the Theologian: Neoplatonist Allegorical Reading and the Growth of the Epic Tradition.* Berkeley and Los Angeles: University of California Press.

Lampe, G.W.H., ed. 1975 (1969). *The Cambridge History of the Bible.* Vol. 2, *The West from the Fathers to the Reformation.* Cambridge: Cambridge University Press.

Langlois, Ch[arles]-V[ictor], and Ch[arles] Seignobos. [1898]. *Introduction to the Study of History,* trans. G. G. Berry. New York: Henry Holt.

Langlois, Ch[arles]-V[ictor], and Ch[arles] Seignobos. [1900] (1897). *Introduction aux études historiques.* 4th ed. Paris: Librairie Hachette.

Laplanche, François. 1986. *L'Écriture, le sacré et l'histoire: érudits et politiques protestants devant la Bible en France au XVIIe siècle.* Amsterdam and Maarssen: APA/Holland University Press.

Laplanche, François. 1994. *La Bible en France entre mythe et critique (XVIe–XIXe siècle).* Paris: Albin Michel.

Latham, Robert Gordon. 1850. *The Natural History of the Varieties of Man.* London: John Van Voorst.

Lauzon, Matthew. 2010. *Signs of Light: French and British Theories of Linguistic Communication, 1648–1789.* Ithaca, N.Y.: Cornell University Press.

Lavin, Marilyn Aronberg. 1983. *The Eye of the Tiger: The Founding and Development of the Department of Art and Archaeology, 1883–1923, Princeton University.* Princeton, N.J.: Department of Art and Archaeology, Princeton University.

Law, Vivien. 1997. *Grammar and Grammarians in the Early Middle Ages*. London: Longman.

Law, Vivien. 2003. *The History of Linguistics in Europe from Plato to 1600*. Cambridge: Cambridge University Press.

Law, Vivien, and Ineke Sluiter, eds. 1995. *Dionysius Thrax and the "Technē grammatikē."* Münster, Germany: Nodus Publikationen.

Lawson, Russell M. 1998. *The American Plutarch: Jeremy Belknap and the Historian's Dialogue with the Past*. Westport, Conn.: Praeger.

Layard, Austen Henry. 1849. *Nineveh and Its Remains: With an Account of a Visit to the Chaldaean Christians of Kurdistan, and the Yezidis, or Devil-Worshippers; and an Enquiry into the Manners and Arts of the Ancient Assyrians*. 2 vols. London: John Murray.

Legaré, Hugh Swinton. 1845. *Writings of Hugh Swinton Legaré*, ed. Mary Swinton Legaré. 2 vols. Charleston, S.C.: Burges and James.

Legaspi, Michael C. 2010. *The Death of Scripture and the Rise of Biblical Studies*. Oxford: Oxford University Press.

Lecky, William Edward Hartpole. 1896. *Democracy and Liberty*. 2 vols. New York: Longmans, Green.

Lefèvre d'Etaples, Jacques. 2009. *Jacques Lefèvre d'Etaples and the Three Maries Debates*, ed. and trans. Sheila M. Porrer. Geneva: Droz.

Le Goff, Jacques. 1985 (1957). *Les intellectuels au Moyen Age*. Paris: Éditions du Seuil.

Leiman, Sid Z. 1991 (1976). *The Canonization of Hebrew Scripture: The Talmudic and Midrashic Evidence*. New Haven, Conn.: Connecticut Academy of Arts and Sciences.

Leppmann, Wolfgang. 1970. *Winckelmann*. New York: Alfred A. Knopf.

Lesky, Albin. 1963. *Geschichte der griechischen Literatur*. 2nd ed. Bern, Switzerland: Francke.

Levin, David. 1959. *History as Romantic Art: Bancroft, Prescott, Motley, and Parkman*. Stanford, Calif.: Stanford University Press.

Levine, Joseph M. 1977. *Dr. Woodward's Shield: History, Science, and Satire in Augustan England*. Berkeley and Los Angeles: University of California Press.

Levine, Joseph M. 1987. *Humanism and History: Origins of Modern English Historiography*. Ithaca, N.Y.: Cornell University Press.

Levine, Joseph M. 1991. *The Battle of the Books: History and Literature in the Augustan Age*. Ithaca, N.Y.: Cornell University Press.

Levine, Joseph M. 1999. *The Autonomy of History: Truth and Method from Erasmus to Gibbon*. Chicago: University of Chicago Press.

Levine, Joseph M. 2004. *Re-enacting the Past: Essays on the Evolution of Modern English Historiography*. Aldershot, England: Ashgate.

Levine, Lee I. 2005. *The Ancient Synagogue: The First Thousand Years*. 2nd ed. New Haven, Conn.: Yale University Press.

Levine, Philippa. 1986. *The Amateur and the Professional: Antiquarians, Historians and Archaeologists in Victorian England, 1838–1886*. Cambridge: Cambridge University Press.

Levy, F. J. 1964. "The Founding of the Camden Society." *Victorian Studies* 7: 295–305.

Lewis, Andrew J. 2011. *A Democracy of Facts: Natural History in the Early Republic*. Philadelphia: University of Pennsylvania Press.

Lewis, David M. 1997. "Boeckh, *Staatshaushaltung der Athener*, 1817–1967." In *Selected Papers in Greek and Near Eastern History*, ed. P. J. Rhodes, 1–6. Cambridge: Cambridge University Press.

Lewis, D. M., et al., eds. 1992. *The Fifth Century B.C.* Cambridge Ancient History, vol. 5. Cambridge: Cambridge University Press.

Lewis, George Cornewall. 1855. *An Inquiry into the Credibility of the Early Roman History*. 2 vols. London: John W. Parker and Son.

Lewis, George Cornewall. 1862 (1835). *An Essay on the Origin and Formation of the Romance Languages. Containing an Examination of M. Raynouard's Theory on the Relation of the Italian, Spanish, Provençal, and French to the Latin.* 2nd ed. London: Parker, Son, and Bourn.

Lewis, George Cornewall. 1870. *Letters of the Right Hon. Sir George Cornewall Lewis, Bart. to Various Friends,* ed. Gilbert Frankland Lewis. London: Longmans, Green.

Lewis, Naphtali. 1974. *Papyrus in Classical Antiquity.* Oxford: Clarendon.

Liddell, Henry G. 1855. *A History of Rome from the Earliest Times to the Establishment of the Empire.* 2 vols. London: John Murray.

Liddon, Henry Parry. 1893. *Life of Edward Bouverie Pusey.* 4 vols. London: Longmans, Green.

Link, Arthur S. 1985. "The American Historical Association, 1884–1984: Retrospect and Prospect." *American Historical Review* 90: 1–17.

Links, J. G. 1976. "W. G. Constable." *Burlington Magazine* 118: 311–12.

Littlejohns, Richard. 1991. "Fruhromantische Kunstauffassung und wissenschaftliche Kunstgeschichte." In *Die deutsche literarische Romantik und die Wissenschaften,* ed. Nicholas Saul, 234–49. Munich: Iudicium Verlag.

Livingstone, David N. 2008. *Adam's Ancestors: Race, Religion, and the Politics of Human Origins.* Baltimore: Johns Hopkins University Press.

Lloyd-Jones, Hugh. 1982. *Blood for the Ghosts: Classical Influences in the Nineteenth and Twentieth Centuries.* Baltimore: Johns Hopkins University Press.

Lloyd-Jones, Hugh. 2005. *The Further Academic Papers of Sir Hugh Lloyd-Jones.* Oxford: Oxford University Press.

Locke, John. 1975 (1700). *An Essay concerning Human Understanding,* ed. Peter H. Nidditch. 4th ed. Oxford: Clarendon.

Locke, John. 1990. "Draft A." In *Drafts for the Essay concerning Human Understanding and Other Philosophical Writings,* ed. Peter H. Nidditch and G.A.J. Rogers, 1–86. Oxford: Clarendon.

Lohr, C. H. 1974. "Renaissance Latin Aristotle Commentaries: Authors A–B." *Studies in the Renaissance* 21: 228–89.

Loomis, Louise Ropes. 1908. "The Greek Renaissance in Italy." *American Historical Review* 13: 246–58.

Löwenbrück, Anna-Ruth. 1986. "Johann David Michaelis et les débuts de la critique biblique." In *Le siècle des Lumières et la Bible,* ed. Yvon Belavel and Dominique Bourel, 113–28. Paris; Beauchesne.

Lowth, Robert. 1787. *Lectures on the Sacred Poetry of the Hebrews.* 2 vols. London: J. Johnson.

Lucci, Diego. 2008. *Scripture and Deism: The Biblical Criticism of the Eighteenth-Century British Deists.* Bern, Switzerland: Peter Lang.

Luhtala, Anneli. 2005. *Grammar and Philosophy in Late Antiquity: A Study of Priscian's Sources.* Amsterdam: John Benjamins.

Lukes, Steven. 1975 (1973). *Emile Durkheim, His Life and Work: A Historical and Critical Study.* New York: Peregrine.

Luscombe, David. 2004. "Thought and Learning." In *The New Cambridge Medieval History c. 1024–c. 1198,* ed. David Luscombe and Jonathan Riley-Smith, 461–98. New Cambridge Medieval History, vol. 4, part 1. Cambridge: Cambridge University Press.

Lyell, Charles. 1863. *The Geological Evidences of the Antiquity of Man, with Remarks on Theories of the Origin of Species by Variation.* 2nd American ed. Philadelphia: George W. Childs.

Lyons, Maura. 2005. *William Dunlap and the Construction of an American Art History*. Amherst: University of Massachusetts Press.

MacCormack, Sabine. 1991. *Religion in the Andes: Vision and Imagination in Early Colonial Peru*. Princeton, N.J.: Princeton University Press.

MacCormack, Sabine. 1998. *The Shadows of Poetry: Vergil in the Mind of Augustine*. Berkeley and Los Angeles: University of California Press.

MacCormack, Sabine. 2004. "Creation according to Genesis in the Late Roman Latin West: Interpretations in Prose and Verse." Paper presented to the seminar "The Christian Scriptures and the Transmission of Culture in Late Antiquity and Early Modernity," Hebrew University of Jerusalem.

MacCormack, Sabine. 2007. *On the Wings of Time: Rome, the Incas, Spain, and Peru*. Princeton, N.J.: Princeton University Press.

MacCormack, Sabine. 2010. "Pausanias and His Commentator Sir James George Frazer." *Classical Receptions Journal* 2: 287–313.

MacDonald, Dennis R. 2000. *The Homeric Epics and the Gospel of Mark*. New Haven, Conn.: Yale University Press.

MacDonald, Dennis R. 2003. *Does the New Testament Imitate Homer? Four Cases from the Acts of the Apostles*. New Haven, Conn.: Yale University Press.

Macfarlane, Alan D. J. 1991. "Some Contributions of Maine to History and Anthropology." In *The Victorian Achievement of Sir Henry Maine: A Centennial Reappraisal*, ed. Alan Diamond, 111–42. Cambridge: Cambridge University Press.

Mack, Peter. 1993. *Renaissance Argument: Valla and Agricola in the Traditions of Rhetoric and Dialectic*. Leiden, Netherlands: E. J. Brill.

Macksey, Richard. 1985. "Border Line: One Hundred Years of Scholarship." *MLN* 100: 913–21.

MacMullen, Ramsay. 1984. *Christianizing the Roman Empire (A.D. 100–400)*. New Haven, Conn.: Yale University Press.

Maehler, H., ed. 2004. *Bacchylides: A Selection*. Cambridge: Cambridge University Press.

Mahaffy, John P. 1871. *Prolegomena to Ancient History*. London: Longmans, Green.

Mahon, Lord [Philip Henry Stanhope, Viscount]. 1853 (1836–53). *History of England from the Peace of Utrecht to the Peace of Versailles, 1713–1783*. 3rd ed. 7 vols. Boston: Little, Brown.

Maier, Bernhard. 2009. *William Robertson Smith: His Life, His Work, and His Times*. Tübingen, Germany: Mohr Siebeck.

Maine, Henry Sumner. 1861. *Ancient Law: Its Connection with the Early History of Society, and Its Relation to Modern Ideas*. London: John Murray.

Maine, Henry Sumner. 1871. *Village-Communities in the East and West: Six Lectures Delivered at Oxford*. London: John Murray.

Malcolm, Noel. 2002. *Aspects of Hobbes*. Oxford: Clarendon.

Malcolm, Noel. 2004. "Leviathan, the Pentateuch, and the Origins of Modern Biblical Criticism." In *Leviathan after 350 Years*, ed. Tom Sorell and Luc Foisneau, 241–64. Oxford: Oxford University Press.

Manilius, Marcus. 1937 (1903). *M. Manilii Astronomicon*, ed. A. E. Housman. 5 vols. Cambridge: Cambridge University Press.

Mann, Nicholas, 1996. "The Origins of Humanism." In *The Cambridge Companion to Renaissance Humanism*, ed. Jill Kraye, 1–19. Cambridge: Cambridge University Press.

Mansell, Darrel. 1986. "Matthew Arnold's 'The Study of Poetry' in Its Original Context." *Modern Philology* 83: 279–85.

Mansfield, Elizabeth, ed. 2002. *Art History and Its Institutions: Foundations of a Discipline*. London: Routledge.

Marchand, Suzanne L. 1996. *Down from Olympus: Archaeology and Philhellenism in Germany, 1750–1970*. Princeton, N.J.: Princeton University Press.

Marchand, Suzanne L. 2009. *German Orientalism in the Age of Empire: Religion, Race, and Scholarship*. Washington: German Historical Institute, and New York: Cambridge University Press.

Marett, R. R., ed. 1908. *Anthropology and the Classics: Six Lectures Delivered before the University of Oxford*. Oxford: Clarendon.

Marett, R. R. 1936. *Tylor*. New York: John Wiley and Sons.

Marin, Louis. 1975. *La critique du discours: sur la "Logique de Port-Royal" et les "Pensées" de Pascal*. Paris: Éditions de Minuit.

Mark, Joan. 1980. *Four Anthropologists: An American Science in its Early Years*. New York: Science History.

Mark, Joan. 1988. *A Stranger in Her Native Land: Alice Fletcher and the American Indians*. Lincoln: University of Nebraska Press.

Marrone, Steven P. 2003. "Medieval Philosophy in Context." In *The Cambridge Companion to Medieval Philosophy*, ed. A. S. McGrade, 10–50. Cambridge: Cambridge University Press.

Marrou, H. I. 1982 (1948). *A History of Education in Antiquity*, trans. George Lamb. Madison: University of Wisconsin Press.

Marsch, Edgar, ed. 1975. *Über Literaturgeschichtsschreibung: die historisierende Methode des 19. Jahrhunderts in Programm und Kritik*. Darmstadt, Germany: Wissenschaftliche Buchgesellschaft.

Marsden, George. 2006 (1980). *Fundamentalism and American Culture*. 2nd ed. New York: Oxford University Press.

Marsh, Herbert. 1828. *Lectures on the Criticism and Interpretation of the Bible, with Two Preliminary Lectures on Theological Study and Theological Arrangement*. New ed., rev. and corrected. Cambridge: J. Smith, Printer to the University.

Marshall, John. 1994. *John Locke: Resistance, Religion and Responsibility*. Cambridge: Cambridge University Press.

Marshall, P. J. 1986. "Oriental Studies." In *The Eighteenth Century*, ed. L. S. Sutherland and L. G. Mitchell, vol. 5, *The History of the University of Oxford*, ed. T. H. Aston, 551–63. Oxford: Clarendon, 1986.

Massa, Mark Stephen. 1990. *Charles Augustus Briggs and the Crisis of Historical Criticism*. Minneapolis: Fortress.

Masuzawa, Tomoko. 2005. *The Invention of World Religions: Or, How European Universalism Was Preserved in the Language of Pluralism*. Chicago: University of Chicago Press.

Maurice, Frederick, ed. 1884. *The Life of Frederick Denison Maurice Chiefly Told in His Own Letters*. 2 vols. London: Macmillan.

Maurice, Frederick Denison. 1847. *The Religions of the World and Their Relations to Christianity, Considered in Eight Lectures Founded by the Right Hon. Robert Boyle*. London: John W. Parker.

Maxwell, Constantia. 1946. *A History of Trinity College Dublin, 1591–1892*. Dublin: University Press, Trinity College.

McCormick, Michael. 2001. *Origins of the European Economy: Communications and Commerce, A.D. 300–900*. Cambridge: Cambridge University Press.

McCuaig, William. 1991. "The Fasti Capitolini and the Study of Roman Chronology in the Sixteenth Century." *Athenaeum* 79: 141–59.

McGetchin, Douglas T. 2003. "Wilting Florists: The Turbulent Early Decades of the Société Asiatique, 1822–1860," *Journal of the History of Ideas* 64: 565–80.

McGetchin, Douglas T. 2009. *Indology, Indomania, and Orientalism: Ancient India's Rebirth in Modern Germany*. Madison, N.J.: Fairleigh Dickinson University Press.

McGetchin, Douglas T., Peter K. J. Park, and Damodar SarDesai, eds. 2004. *Sanskrit and 'Orientalism': Indology and Comparative Linguistics in Germany, 1750-1958*. New Delhi: Manohar.

McKane, William. 1977. "Benjamin Kennicott: An Eighteenth-Century Researcher." *Journal of Theological Studies* 28: 445-64.

McKeon, Richard. 1942. "Rhetoric in the Middle Ages." *Speculum* 17: 1-31.

McKim, Donald K. 1998. *Historical Handbook of Major Biblical Interpreters*. Downers Grove, Ill.: InterVarsity.

McKisack, May. 1971. *Medieval History in the Tudor Age*. Oxford: Clarendon.

McKitterick, Rosamond, ed. 1995. *The New Cambridge Medieval History c. 700-c. 900*. New Cambridge Medieval History, vol. 2. Cambridge: Cambridge University Press.

McKitterick, Rosamond. 2006. *Perceptions of the Past in the Early Middle Ages*. Notre Dame, Ind.: University of Notre Dame Press.

McMurtry, Jo. 1985. *English Language, English Literature: The Creation of an Academic Discipline*. London: Mansell.

Meikle, H. W. 1945. "The Chair of Rhetoric and Belles-Lettres in the University of Edinburgh." *University of Edinburgh Journal* 13: 89-103.

Mergiali, Sophia. 1996. *L'enseignement et les lettrés pendant l'époque des Paléologues (1261-1453)*. Athens: Hetaireia tōn Philōn tou Laou, Kentron Ereunēs Vyzantiou [Society of the Friends of the People, Center for Byzantine Studies].

Metcalf, George J. 1953. "Abraham Mylius on Historical Linguistics." *PMLA* 68: 535-54.

Metzger, Bruce M. 1987. *The Canon of the New Testament: Its Origin, Development, and Significance*. Oxford: Clarendon.

Metzger, Bruce M. and Bart D. Ehrman. 2005. *The Text of the New Testament: Its Transmission, Corruption, and Restoration*. 4th ed. New York: Oxford University Press.

Meyer, Louis. 1988 (1666). *La philosophie interprète de l'Écriture Sainte [Philosophia S. Scripturae Interpres]*, trans. and ed. Jacqueline Lagrée and Pierre-François Moreau. Paris: Intertextes Éditeur.

[Michaelis, Adolf Theodor Friedrich.] 1879. *Geschichte des deutschen Archäologischen Instituts 1829-1879*. Berlin: A. Asher.

Michaelis, A. 1908. *A Century of Archaeological Discoveries*, trans. Bettina Kahnweiler. London: John Murray.

Miller, Perry. 1961 (1953). *The New England Mind: From Colony to Province*. Boston: Beacon.

Miller, Peter N. 2000. *Peiresc's Europe: Learning and Virtue in the Seventeenth Century*. New Haven, Conn.: Yale University Press.

Miller, Peter N. 2001. "The 'Antiquarianization' of Biblical Scholarship and the London Polyglot Bible (1653-57)." *Journal of the History of Ideas* 62: 463-82.

Miller, Robert L. 1968. *The Linguistic Relativity Principle and Humboldtian Ethnolinguistics: A History and Appraisal*. The Hague: Mouton.

Miller, Samuel. 1970 (1803). *A Brief Retrospect of the Eighteenth Century*. 2 vols. New York: Burt Franklin.

Miller, Thomas P. 1997. *The Formation of College English: Rhetoric and Belles Lettres in the British Cultural Provinces*. Pittsburgh: University of Pittsburgh Press.

Milman, Arthur. 1900. *Henry Hart Milman, D.D., Dean of St. Paul's: A Biographical Sketch*. London: John Murray.

[Milman, Henry Hart.] 1829. *The History of the Jews*. 3 vols. London: John Murray.

Miyahara, Katsura. 2006. "'An Un-English Activity?' The Development of Art History Education after Ruskin and before the Courtauld." PhD diss., Cambridge University.

Moatti, Claudia. 1997. *La raison de Rome: naissance de l'esprit critique à la fin de la République*. Paris: Éditions du Seuil.

Moeller, Bernd, ed. 1987. *Theologie in Göttingen: eine Vorlesungsreihe*. Göttingen, Germany: Vandenhoeck & Ruprecht.

Moffat, James C. 1852. *Biblical Criticism as an Object of Popular Interest: An Address Delivered at the Opening of the Third Session of the Cincinnati Theological Seminary of the Presbyterian Church*. Cincinnati, Ohio: John D. Thorpe.

Momigliano, Arnaldo. 1955. *[Primo] Contributo alla storia degli studi classici*. Rome: Edizioni di Storia e Letteratura.

Momigliano, Arnaldo. 1960. *Secondo contributo alla storia degli studi classici*. Rome: Edizioni di Storia e Letteratura.

Momigliano, Arnaldo. 1982. "Niebuhr and the Agrarian Problems of Rome." *History and Theory* 21, no. 4, Beiheft 21: 3–15.

Momigliano, Arnaldo. 1990. *The Classical Foundations of Modern Historiography*. Berkeley and Los Angeles: University of California Press.

Momigliano, Arnaldo. 1994. *Studies on Modern Scholarship*, ed. G. W. Bowersock and T. J. Cornell. Berkeley and Los Angeles: University of California Press.

Mommsen, Theodore E. 1942. "Petrarch's Conception of the 'Dark Ages.'" *Speculum* 17: 226–42.

Monfasani, John. 1976. *George of Trebizond: A Biography and a Study of His Rhetoric and Logic*. Leiden, Netherlands: E. J. Brill.

Monk, James Henry. 1969 (1833). *The Life of Richard Bentley, D.D.* 2nd ed. 2 vols. Osnabruck, Germany: Biblio Verlag.

Montanari, Franco. 1998. "Zenodotus, Aristarchus and the *Ekdosis* of Homer." In *Editing Texts / Texte edieren*, ed. Glenn W. Most, 1–21. Göttingen, Germany: Vandenhoeck and Ruprecht.

Moody, T. W., and J. C. Beckett. 1959. *Queen's, Belfast, 1845–1949: The History of a University*. 2 vols, continuously paginated. London: Faber and Faber.

Moore, James, Ian Macgregor Morris, and Andrew J. Bayliss, eds. 2008. *Reinventing History: The Enlightenment Origins of Ancient History*. London: Centre for Metropolitan History, Institute of Historical Research, School of Advanced Study, University of London.

Morford, Mark, 1991. *Stoics and Neostoics: Rubens and the Circle of Lipsius*. Princeton, N.J.: Princeton University Press.

Morgan, Lewis H. 1868. *A Conjectural Solution of the Origin of the Classificatory System of Relationship*. Cambridge, Mass.: Welch, Bigelow. Reprinted from *Proceedings of the American Academy of Arts and Sciences* 7 (1868): 436–77.

Morgan, Lewis H. 1870. *Systems of Consanguinity and Affinity of the Human Family*. Washington, D.C.: Smithsonian Institution.

Morgan, Teresa. 1998. *Literate Education in the Hellenistic and Roman Worlds*. Cambridge: Cambridge University Press.

Morison, Samuel Eliot, ed. 1930. *The Development of Harvard University since the Inauguration of President Eliot, 1869–1929*. Cambridge, Mass.: Harvard University Press.

Morison, Samuel Eliot. 1936. *Harvard College in the Seventeenth Century*. 2 vols. Cambridge, Mass.: Harvard University Press.

Morison, Samuel Eliot. 1964 (1936). *Three Centuries of Harvard, 1636–1936*. Cambridge, Mass.: Harvard University Press.

Moscrop, John James. 2000. *Measuring Jerusalem: The Palestine Exploration Fund and British Interests in the Holy Land*. London: Leicester University Press.

Moss, Jean Dietz. 1996. " 'Discordant Consensus': Old and New Rhetoric at Trinity College, Dublin," *Rhetorica* 14: 383–441.

Mosse, George L. 1978. *Toward the Final Solution: A History of European Racism*. New York: Howard Fertig.

Moulton, Richard G. 1885. *Shakespeare as a Dramatic Artist: A Popular Illustration of the Principles of Scientific Criticism*. Oxford: Clarendon.

Moulton, Warren J. 1926–27. "The American Palestine Exploration Society." *Annual of the American Schools of Oriental Research* 8: 55–78.

Mukherjee, S. N. 1968. *Sir William Jones: A Study in Eighteenth-Century Attitudes to India*. Cambridge: Cambridge University Press.

Müller, F. Max. 1873. *Introduction to the Science of Religion: Four Lectures Delivered at the Royal Institution*. London: Longmans, Green.

Müller, F. Max. 1874. *On Missions: A Lecture Delivered in Westminster Abbey, on December 3, 1873*. New York: Scribner, Armstrong.

Müller, F. Max. 1895a (1867). *Essays on the Science of Religion*. Chips from a German Workshop vol. 1. New York: Charles Scribner's Sons.

Müller, F. Max. 1895b (1869). *Essays on Mythology, Traditions, and Customs*. Chips from a German Workshop vol. 2. New York: Charles Scribner's Sons.

Müller, F. Max. 1901. *My Autobiography: A Fragment*. London: Longmans, Green.

Müller, Friedrich Max. 1902. *The Life and Letters of the Right Honourable Friedrich Max Müller, ed. by His Wife* [Georgina Adelaide Müller]. 2 vols. London: Longmans, Green.

Müller, Friedrich Max. 1999 (1849). "Comparative Philology of the Indo-European Languages in Its Bearing on the Early Civilization of Mankind." In *The Prix Volney: Contributions to Comparative Indo-European, African and Chinese Linguistics: Max Müller and Steinthal*, ed. Joan Leopold, 109–206. Prix Volney Essay Series, vol. 3 Dordrecht, Netherlands: Kluwer Academic.

Müller, [Friedrich] Max. 1861–64. *Lectures on the Science of Language Delivered at the Royal Institution of Great Britain*. 2 vols. London: Longman, Green, Longman, and Roberts [and Green, 1864]. (Strictly, vol. 2 is "Second Series," but it is common and convenient to treat this title as a two-volume work—as it appears in Müller's collected works.)

Müller, C. O. [Karl Otfried]. 1830. *The History and Antiquities of the Doric Race*, trans. Henry Tufnell and George Cornewall Lewis. 2 vols. London: John Murray.

Müller, K. O. 1840. *History of the Literature of Ancient Greece*, trans. [George Cornewall Lewis]. Vol. 1. London: Baldwin and Cradock. (For continuation, see Donaldson 1858.)

Müller, C. O. [Karl Otfried]. 1844. *Introduction to a Scientific System of Mythology*, trans. John Leitch. London: Longman and Co.

Müller, C. O. [Karl Otfried]. 1847. *Ancient Art and Its Remains; or a Manual of the Archæology of Art*, trans. John Leitch. London: A. Fullarton and Co.

Mungello, D. E. 1989 (1985). *Curious Land: Jesuit Accommodation and the Origins of Sinology*. Honolulu: University of Hawaii Press.

[Munro, John, ed.] 1911. *Frederick James Furnivall: A Volume of Personal Record*. London: Henry Frowde/Oxford University Press.

Murphy, Andrew. 2003. *Shakespeare in Print: A History and Chronology of Shakespeare Publishing*. Cambridge: Cambridge University Press.

Murphy, James J. 1983. *Renaissance Eloquence: Studies in the Theory and Practice of Renaissance Rhetoric*. Berkeley and Los Angeles: University of California Press.

Murray, K. M. Elisabeth. 1979 (1977). *Caught in the Web of Words: James Murray and the Oxford English Dictionary*. Oxford: Oxford University Press.

Murray, Priscilla M., and Curtis N. Runnels. 2007. "Harold North Fowler and the Beginnings of American Study Tours in Greece." *Hesperia* 76: 597–626.

Myres, John L. 1958. *Homer and His Critics*. London: Routledge and Kegan Paul.

Nagy, Gregory. 1996. *Homeric Questions*. Austin: University of Texas Press.

Nagy, Gregory. 2002. *Plato's Rhapsody and Homer's Music: The Poetics of the Panathenaic Festival in Classical Athens*. Washington, D.C.: Center for Hellenic Studies, and Athens: Foundation of the Hellenic World.

Nagy, Gregory. 2004. *Homer's Text and Language*. Urbana: University of Illinois Press.

Neill, Stephen. 1964. *The Interpretation of the New Testament, 1861–1961*. London: Oxford University Press.

Neufeldt, Ronald W. 1980. *Max Müller and the Rg Veda: A Study of Its Role in His Work and Thought*. Columbia, Mo.: South Asia Books.

Neveu, Bruno. 1994. *Érudition et religion aux XVIIe et XVIIIe siècles*. Paris: Albin Michel.

Newman, Zelda Kahan. 2006. "Elye Levita: A Man and His Book on the Cusp of Modernity," *Shofar: An Interdisciplinary Journal of Jewish Studies* 24, no. 4: 90–109.

Newton, C. T., with R. P. Pullan. 1862–63. *A History of Discoveries at Halicarnassus, Cnidus, and Branchidae*. 2 vols. London: Day and Son.

Niebuhr, B. G. 1828–31. *The History of Rome*, trans. Julius Charles Hare and Connop Thirlwall. 2 vols. Cambridge and London: Printed by John Smith in Cambridge for John Taylor, Bookseller and Publisher to the University of London.

Niggl, Günter. 1991. "Die Anfänge der romantischen Literaturgeschichtsschreibung: Friedrich und August Wilhelm Schlegel." In *Die deutsche literarische Romantik und die Wissenschaften*, ed. Nicholas Saul, 265–81. Munich: Iudicium Verlag.

Nigosian, S. A. 2004. *From Ancient Writings to Sacred Texts: The Old Testament and Apocrypha*. Baltimore: Johns Hopkins University Press.

Noll, Mark A. 1991. *Between Faith and Criticism: Evangelicals, Scholarship, and the Bible in America*. 2nd ed. Grand Rapids, Mich.: Baker Book House.

Norton, Andrews. 1846–48 (1837–44). *The Evidences of the Genuineness of the Gospels*. 2nd ed. 3 vols. Cambridge, Mass.: John Owen and George Nichols.

Novick, Peter. 1988. *That Noble Dream: The "Objectivity Question" and the American Historical Profession*. Cambridge: Cambridge University Press.

Nuttall, A. D. 2003. *Dead from the Waist Down: Scholars and Scholarship in Literature and the Popular Imagination*. New Haven, Conn.: Yale University Press.

Oberman, Heiko A. 1992. "Discovery of Hebrew and Discrimination against the Jews: The *Veritas Hebraica* as Double-Edged Sword in Renaissance and Reformation." In *Germania Illustrata: Essays on Early Modern Germany Presented to Gerald Strauss*, ed. Andrew C. Fix and Susan C. Karant-Nunn, 19–34. Kirksville, Mo.: Sixteenth Century Journal Publishers.

O'Brien, Karen. 1997. *Narratives of Enlightenment: Cosmopolitan History from Voltaire to Gibbon*. Cambridge: Cambridge University Press.

O'Brien, Michael. 1985. *A Character of Hugh Legaré*. Knoxville: University of Tennessee Press.

O'Brien, Michael. 2004. *Conjectures of Order: Intellectual Life and the American South, 1810–1860*. Chapel Hill: University of North Carolina Press.

Ocker, Christopher. 2002. *Biblical Poetics before Humanism and Reformation*. Cambridge: Cambridge University Press.

Ogris, Werner. 1986. "Jacob Grimm und die Rechtsgeschichte." In *Jacob und Wilhelm Grimm: Vorträge und Ansprachen in den Veranstaltungen der Akademie der Wissenschaften und der Georg-August-Universität in Göttingen anläßlich der 200. Wiederkehr ihrer Geburtstage*. Göttingen, Germany: Vandenhoeck & Ruprecht.

Olender, Maurice. 1989. *Les langues du Paradis: Aryens et Sémites, un couple providentiel*. Paris: Gallimard/Le Seuil.

Olender, Maurice. 1994. "Europe, or How to Escape Babel." *History and Theory*, theme issue 33: 5–25.

Oleson, Alexandra, and Sanborn C. Brown, eds. 1976. *The Pursuit of Knowledge in the Early American Republic: American Scientific and Learned Societies from Colonial Times to the Civil War*. Baltimore: Johns Hopkins University Press.

Oleson, Alexandra, and John Voss, eds. 1979. *The Organization of Knowledge in Modern America*. Baltimore: Johns Hopkins University Press.

Ong, Walter J. 2004 (1958). *Ramus, Method, and the Decay of Dialogue: From the Art of Discourse to the Art of Reason*. Chicago: University of Chicago Press.

Orlinsky, Harry M. 1955. "Jewish Biblical Scholarship in America." *Jewish Quarterly Review*, n.s., 45 (1955): 374–412.

Orme, Nicholas. 2006. *Medieval Schools: From Roman Britain to Renaissance England*. New Haven, Conn.: Yale University Press.

Padgett, J. Michael. 1996. "The Collections of Ancient Art: The Early Years," *Record of the Art Museum, Princeton University* 55: 107–24.

Pagden, Anthony. 1986 (1982). *The Fall of Natural Man: The American Indian and the Origins of Comparative Ethnology*. Cambridge: Cambridge University Press.

Page, Norman. 1983. *A. E. Housman: A Critical Biography*. New York: Schocken.

Palmer, D. J. 1965. *The Rise of English Studies: An Account of the Study of English Language and Literature from its Origins to the Making of the Oxford English School*. Oxford: Oxford University Press.

Panayotova, Stella. 2008. *I Turned It into a Palace: Sydney Cockerell and the Fitzwilliam Museum*. Cambridge: Fitzwilliam Museum.

Park, John. 1902. "Charles MacDouall, LL.D." In *Belfast Literary Society, 1801–1901: Historical Sketch with Memoirs of Some Distinguished Members* (Belfast: M'Caw, Stevenson and Orr), 130–31.

Parkes, M. B. 1993. *Pause and Effect: An Introduction to the History of Punctuation in the West*. Berkeley and Los Angeles: University of California Press.

Parkes, M. B. 2008. *Their Hands before Our Eyes: A Closer Look at Scribes*. Aldershot, England: Ashgate.

Parrinder, Patrick, 1991. *Authors and Authority: English and American Criticism, 1750–1990*. New York: Columbia University Press.

Parslow, Christopher Charles. 1995. *Rediscovering Antiquity: Karl Weber and the Excavation of Herculaneum, Pompeii, and Stabiae*. Cambridge: Cambridge University Press.

Pattison, Mark. 1875. *Isaac Casaubon, 1559–1614*. London: Longmans, Green.

Pattison, Mark. 1889. "F. A. Wolf." In *Essays by the Late Mark Pattison, Sometime Rector of Lincoln College*, ed. Henry Nettleship, 2 vols., 1:337–414. Oxford: Clarendon.

Pattison, Mark. 1969 (1885). *Memoirs*. Fontwell, England: Centaur.

Payne, William Morton, ed. 1895. *English in American Universities*. Boston: D. C. Heath.

Peabody, Elizabeth Palmer, ed. 1849. *Aesthetic Papers*. New York: G. P. Putnam.

Peardon, Thomas Preston. 1933. *The Transition in English Historical Writing, 1760–1830*. New York: Columbia University Press.

Pécharman, Martine. 1995. "La signification dans la philosophie du langage d'Antoine Arnauld." In *Antoine Arnauld: philosophie du langage et de la connaissance*, ed. Jean-Claude Pariente, 65–98. Paris: Librairie Philosophique J. Vrin.

Pedersen, Holger. 1962 (1931). *The Discovery of Language: Linguistic Science in the Nineteenth Century*, trans. John Webster Spargo. Bloomington, Ind.: Indiana University Press.

Pedley, John Griffiths. 2012. *The Life and Work of Francis Willey Kelsey: Archaeology, Antiquity, and the Arts*. Ann Arbor: University of Michigan Press.

Penner, Todd, and Caroline Vander Stichele. 2009. "Rhetorical Practice and Performance in Early Christianity." In *The Cambridge Companion to Ancient Rhetoric*, ed. Erik Gunderson, 245–60. Cambridge: Cambridge University Press.

Penniman, T. K. 1974 (1965). *A Hundred Years of Anthropology*. 3rd ed. New York: William Morrow.

Peterson, William, ed. 1979. *Browning's Trumpeter: The Correspondence of Robert Browning and Frederick J. Furnivall, 1872–1889*. Washington, D.C.: Decatur House.

Petrie, George, and Margaret Stokes. 1872–78. *Christian Inscriptions in the Irish Language*. 2 vols. Dublin: Royal Historical and Archaeological Association of Ireland.

Pfeiffer, Rudolf. 1968. *History of Classical Scholarship: From the Beginnings to the End of the Hellenistic Age*. Oxford: Clarendon.

Pfeiffer, Rudolf. 1976. *History of Classical Scholarship from 1300 to 1850*. Oxford: Clarendon.

Phillips, Mark Salber. 1996. "Reconsiderations on History and Antiquarianism: Arnaldo Momigliano and the Historiography of Eighteenth-Century Britain." *Journal of the History of Ideas* 57: 297–316.

Phillips, Mark Salber. 2000. *Society and Sentiment: Genres of Historical Writing in Britain, 1740–1820*. Princeton, N.J.: Princeton University Press.

Phillips, Peter. 1996. "John Lingard and the Anglo-Saxon Church." *Recusant History* 23: 178–98.

Pickering, John. 1820. *An Essay on a Uniform Orthography for the Indian Languages of North America*. Cambridge, Mass.: Hilliard and Metcalf.

Pickering, John. 1834. *Ueber die indianischen Sprachen Amerikas*, trans. Talvj [Therese Albertine Louise von Jacob]. Leipzig: Friedr[ich]. Christ[ian]. Wilh[elm]. Voegl.

Pickering, Mary Orne. 1887. *Life of John Pickering*. Boston: Privately printed.

Pierson, George Wilson. 1952. *Yale College: An Educational History, 1871–1921*. New Haven, Conn.: Yale University Press.

Piggott, Stuart. 1985. *William Stukeley: An Eighteenth-Century Antiquary*. Rev. ed. New York: Thames and Hudson.

Piggott, Stuart. 1989. *Ancient Britons and the Antiquarian Imagination: Ideas from the Renaissance to the Regency*. New York: Thames and Hudson.

Pinkerton, John. 1794. *An Enquiry into the History of Scotland Preceding the Reign of Malcom III. or the Year 1056*. 2 vols. London: John Nichols.

Pitassi, Maria Cristina. 1987. *Entre croire et savoir: Le problème de la méthode critique chez Jean Le Clerc*. Leiden, Netherlands: E. J. Brill.

Plato. 1961. *The Collected Dialogues of Plato including the Letters*, ed. Edith Hamilton and Huntington Cairns. Princeton, N.J.: Princeton University Press.

Plongeron, Bernard. 1977. "Du modèle jésuite au modèle oratorien dans les collèges français à la fin du XVIIIᵉ siècle." In *Église et enseignement: actes du Colloque du Xe anniversaire de l'Institut d'histoire du christianisme de l'Université Libre de Bruxelles, 22–23 avril 1976*, ed. Jean Préaux, 89–136. Brussels: Éditions de l'Université de Bruxelles.

Pocock, J.G.A. 1962. "The Origins of Study of the Past: A Comparative Approach." *Comparative Studies in Society and History* 4, no. 2: 209–46.

Pocock, J.G.A. 1967 (1957). *The Ancient Constitution and the Feudal Law: A Study of English Historical Thought in the Seventeenth Century*. New York: W. W. Norton.

Pocock, J.G.A. 1999. *Barbarism and Religion*, vol. 2, *Narratives of Civil Government*. Cambridge: Cambridge University Press.

Pocock, J.G.A. 2005. *Barbarism and Religion*, vol. 4, *Barbarians, Savages and Empires*. Cambridge: Cambridge University Press.

Poggio Bracciolini and Niccolò Niccoli 1991 (1974). *Two Renaissance Book Hunters: The*

Letters of Poggius Bracciolini to Nicolaus de Niccolis, trans. and ed. Phyllis Walter Goodhart Gordan. New York: Columbia University Press.

Pollock, Sheldon, 2009. "Future Philology? The Fate of a Soft Science in a Hard World." *Critical Inquiry* 35: 931–61.

Pomata, Gianna, and Nancy G. Siraisi, eds. 2005. *Historia: Empiricism and Erudition in Early Modern Europe*. Cambridge, Mass.: MIT Press.

Poole, William. 2010. *John Aubrey and the Advancement of Learning*. Oxford: Bodleian Library.

Popkin, Richard H. 1987. *Isaac La Peyrère (1596–1676): His Life, Work and Influence*. Leiden, Netherlands: E. J. Brill.

Popkin, Richard H. 2003. *The History of Scepticism: From Savonarola to Bayle*. Oxford: Oxford University Press.

Porson, Richard. 1814. *Adversaria: notae et emendationes in poetas Graecos*, ed. James Henry Monk and Charles James Blomfield. Rev. ed. Leipzig: Johann August Gottlieb Weigel.

Potts, Alex. 1994. *Flesh and the Ideal: Winckelmann and the Origins of Art History*. New Haven, Conn.: Yale University Press.

Powell, Barry B. 2004. *Homer*. Oxford: Blackwell.

Prescott, William Hickling. 1961. *The Literary Memoranda of William Hickling Prescott*, ed. C. Harvey Gardiner. 2 vols. Norman: University of Oklahoma Press.

Press, Gerald A. 1982. *The Development of the Idea of History in Antiquity*. Montreal and Kingston: McGill-Queen's University Press.

Prete, Sesto. [1970]. *Observations on the History of Textual Criticism in the Medieval and Renaissance Periods*. Collegeville, Minn.: St. John's University Press.

Preus, J. Samuel. 2001. *Spinoza and the Irrelevance of Biblical Authority*. Cambridge: Cambridge University Press.

Price, David H. 2011. *Johannes Reuchlin and the Campaign to Destroy Jewish Books*. New York: Oxford University Press.

Prickett, Stephen, ed. 1991. *Reading the Text: Biblical Criticism and Literary Theory*. Oxford: Basil Blackwell.

Prime, William C., and George B. McClellan. 1882. *Suggestions on the Establishment of a Department of Art Instruction at the College of New Jersey*. Trenton, N.J.: W. S. Sharp Printing Company.

Pritchard, John Paul. 1942. *Return to the Fountains: Some Classical Sources of American Criticism*. Durham, N.C.: Duke University Press.

Pritchard, John Paul. 1956. *Criticism in America: An Account of the Development of Critical Techniques from the Early Period of the Republic to the Middle Years of the Twentieth Century*. Norman: University of Oklahoma Press.

Pritchard, John Paul. 1963. *Literary Wise Men of Gotham: Criticism in New York, 1815–1860*. Baton Rouge: Louisiana State University Press

Probyn, Clive T. 1991. *The Sociable Humanist: The Life and Works of James Harris, 1709–1780: Provincial and Metropolitan Culture in Eighteenth-century England*. Oxford: Clarendon.

Purvis, James D. 1968. *The Samaritan Pentateuch and the Origin of the Samaritan Sect*. Cambridge, Mass.: Harvard University Press.

Pusey, E. B. 1828. *An Historical Enquiry into the Probable Causes of the Rationalist Character Lately Predominant in the Theology of Germany*. London: Printed for C. & J. Rivington.

Pusey, E. B. 1854. *Collegiate and Professorial Teaching and Discipline, in Answer to Professor Vaughan's Strictures, Chiefly as to the Charges against the Colleges of France and Germany*. Oxford and London: John Henry Parker and Messrs. Rivingtons.

Quantin, Jean-Louis. 2009. *The Church of England and Christian Antiquity: The Construction of a Confessional Identity in the 17th Century*. Oxford: Oxford University Press.

Quillen, Carol. 2010. "The Uses of the Past in Quattrocento Florence: A Reading of Leonardo Bruni's Dialogues." *Journal of the History of Ideas* 71: 363–85.

Quincy, Josiah. 1840. *The History of Harvard University*. 2 vols. Cambridge: John Owen.

Quintilian. 2002. *The Orator's Education*, ed. D. A. Russell. 5 vols. Cambridge, Mass.: Harvard University Press.

Rabil, Albert, ed. 1988. *Renaissance Humanism: Foundations, Forms, and Legacy*. 3 vols. Philadelphia: University of Pennsylvania Press.

Rajak, Tessa. 2009. *Translation and Survival: The Greek Bible of the Ancient Jewish Diaspora*. Oxford: Oxford University Press.

Rand, Edward Kennard. 1929. "The Classics in the Thirteenth Century," *Speculum* 4: 249–269.

Rask, Rasmus. 1932 (1818). *Undersøgelse om det gamle nordiske eller islandske sprogs oprindelse*, in Rask, *Ausgewählte Abhandlungen*, ed. Louis Hjelmslev. 3 vols. Copenhagen: Levin og Munksgaard.

Raskolnikoff, Mouza. 1992. *Histoire romaine et critique historique dans l'Europe des Lumières: la naissance de l'hypercritique dans l'historiographie de la Rome antique*. Rome: École Française de Rome.

Raven, James. 2007. *The Business of Books: Booksellers and the English Book Trade, 1450–1850*. New Haven, Conn.: Yale University Press.

Rawson, Elizabeth. 1985. *Intellectual Life in the Late Roman Republic*. Baltimore: Johns Hopkins University Press.

Reeve, Michael D. 1996. "Classical Scholarship." In *The Cambridge Companion to Humanism*, ed. Jill Kraye, 20–46. Cambridge: Cambridge University Press.

Reill, Peter Hanns. 1975. *The German Enlightenment and the Rise of Historicism*. Berkeley and Los Angeles: University of California Press.

Renan, Ernest. 1992 (1857). *Études d'histoire religieuse*. Paris: Gallimard.

Renan, Ernest. 1995 (1890). *L'Avenir de la science*, ed. Annie Petit. Paris: Flammarion.

Reuben, Julie A. 1996. *The Making of the Modern University: Intellectual Transformation and the Marginalization of Morality*. Chicago: University of Chicago Press.

Reventlow, Henning Graf, Walter Sparn, and John Woodbridge, eds. 1988. *Historische Kritik und biblischer Kanon in der deutschen Aufklärung*. Wiesbaden, Germany: In Kommission bei Otto Harrassowitz.

Reynolds, L. D., and N. G. Wilson. 1991. *Scribes and Scholars: A Guide to the Transmission of Greek and Latin Literature*. 3rd ed. Oxford: Clarendon.

Richards, Robert J. 2002. *The Romantic Conception of Life: Science and Philosophy in the Age of Goethe*. Chicago: University of Chicago Press.

Riché, Pierre. 1978 (1962). *Education and Culture in the Barbarian West from the Sixth through the Eighth Century*, trans. John J. Contreni. Columbia: University of South Carolina Press.

Rickman, H. P. 1979. *Wilhelm Dilthey: Pioneer of the Human Studies*. Berkeley and Los Angeles: University of California Press.

Ridder-Symoens, Hilde de, ed. 1992. *Universities in the Middle Ages*. Cambridge: Cambridge University Press.

Riesen, Richard Allan. 1985. *Criticism and Faith in Late Victorian Scotland: A. B. Davidson, William Robertson Smith, and George Adam Smith*. Lanham, Md.: University Press of America.

Rivière, Peter. 2009 (2007). "The Formative Years: The Committee for Anthropology 1905–

38." In *A History of Oxford Anthropology*, ed. Peter Rivière, 43–61. New York: Berghahn.

Rizzo, Silvia. 1988. "Il latino del Petrarca nelle *Familiari*." In *The Uses of Greek and Latin: Historical Essays*, ed. A. C. Dionisotti, Anthony Grafton, and Jill Kraye, 41–56. London: Warburg Institute.

Robb, Kevin. 1994. *Literacy and Paideia in Ancient Greece*. New York: Oxford University Press.

Roberts, Colin H., and T. C. Skeat. 1987. *The Birth of the Codex*. London: Oxford University Press for the British Academy.

Roberts, Jon H., and James Turner. 2000. *The Sacred and the Secular University*. Princeton, N.J.: Princeton University Press.

Robertson, David. 1978. *Sir Charles Eastlake and the Victorian Art World*. Princeton, N.J.: Princeton University Press.

Robertson, David, 2008. *Word and Meaning in Ancient Alexandria: Theories of Language from Philo to Plotinus*. Aldershot, England: Ashgate.

Robertson, William. 1769. *The History of the Reign of the Emperor Charles V., with a View of the Progress of Society in Europe, from the Subversion of the Roman Empire, to the Beginning of the Sixteenth Century*. 3 vols. London: W. and W. Strahan.

Robertson, William. 1777. *History of America*. 2 vols. London: W. Strahan and T. Cadell / Edinburgh: J. Balfour.

Robins, R. H. 1967. *A Short History of Linguistics*. Bloomington: Indiana University Press.

Robins, Robert H. 1990. "Leibniz and Wilhelm von Humboldt and the History of Comparative Linguistics." In *Leibniz, Humboldt, and the Origins of Comparativism*, ed. Tullio de Mauro and Lia Formigari, 86–102. Amsterdam: John Benjamins.

Robins, Robert Henry. 1999. "Du Ponceau and General and Amerindian Linguistics." In *The Prix Volney: Early Nineteenth-Century Contributions to General and Amerindian Linguistics: Du Ponceau and Rafinesque*, ed. Joan Leopold. Dordrecht, Netherlands: Kluwer Academic.

Robinson, Annabel. 2002. *The Life and Work of Jane Ellen Harrison*. Oxford: Oxford University Press.

Robinson, Edward. 1841. *Biblical Researches in Palestine, Mount Sinai and Arabia Petraea: A Journal of Travels in the Year 1838, by E. Robinson and E. Smith. Undertaken in Reference to Biblical Geography*. 3 vols. Boston: Crocker and Brewster.

[Robinson, Edward.] 1843. "Nordheimer." In *Bibliotheca Sacra: or Tracts and Essays on Topics Connected with Biblical Literature and Theology*, ed. Edward Robinson, 379–90. New York: Wiley and Putnam.

Rocher, Ludo. 1957–58. "Les philologues classiques et les débuts de la grammaire comparée." *Revue de l'Université de Bruxelles* 10: 251–86.

Rocher, Ludo. 1989. "Vans Kennedy (1784–1846), a Preliminary Bio-Bibliography." *Journal of the American Oriental Society* 109 (1989): 621–25.

Rocher, Rosane. 1968. *Alexander Hamilton (1762–1824): A Chapter in the Early History of Sanskrit Philology*. New Haven, Conn.: American Oriental Society.

Rocher, Rosane. 2002. "Sanskrit for Civil Servants, 1806–1818." *Journal of the American Oriental Society* 122: 381–90.

Rocher, Rosane, and Ludo Rocher. 2012. *The Making of Western Indology: Henry Thomas Colebrooke and the East India Company*. London: Routledge.

Roesch, Sophie. 1999. "Le rapport de *res* et *verbum* dans le *De lingua latina* de Varron." In *Conceptions latines du sens et de la signification*, ed. Marc Baratin and Claude Moussy, 65–80. Paris: Presses de l'Université de Paris-Sorbonne.

Rogerson, J. W. 1984. *Old Testament Criticism in the Nineteenth Century: England and Germany*. London: Society for Promoting Christian Knowledge.

Rogerson, John W. 1992. *W. M. L. de Wette, Founder of Modern Biblical Criticism: An Intellectual Biography*. Sheffield, England: Sheffield Academic.

Rogerson, J. W. 1995. *The Bible and Criticism in Victorian Britain: Profiles of F. D. Maurice and William Robertson Smith*. Sheffield, England: Sheffield Academic.

Rosasco, Betsy. 1996. "The Teaching of Art and the Museum Tradition: Joseph Henry to Allan Marquand." *Record of the Art Museum, Princeton University* 55: 7–52.

Rose, Hugh James. 1825. *The State of the Protestant Religion in Germany: in a Series of Discourses Preached before the University of Cambridge*. Cambridge: J. Deighton and Sons.

Rosenberg, Ralph P. 1962. "Eugene Schuyler's Doctor of Philosophy Degree: A Theory concerning the Dissertation." *Journal of Higher Education* 33: 381–86.

Rossi, Paolo. 1984 (1979). *The Dark Abyss of Time: The History of the Earth and the History of Nations from Hooke to Vico*, trans. Lydia G. Cochrane. Chicago: University of Chicago Press.

Rossi, Paolo. 2000 (1983). *Logic and the Art of Memory: The Quest for a Universal Language*, trans. Stephen Clucas. Chicago: University of Chicago Press.

Rothblatt, Sheldon. 1968. *Revolution of the Dons: Cambridge and Society in Victorian England*. London: Faber.

Ruderman, David B. 2000. *Jewish Enlightenment in an English Key*. Princeton, N.J.: Princeton University Press.

Rudolph, Conrad, ed. 2006. *A Companion to Medieval Art: Romanesque and Gothic in Northern Europe*. Oxford: Blackwell.

Rudwick, Martin J. S. 2005. *Bursting the Limits of Time: The Reconstruction of Geohistory in the Age of Revolution*. Chicago: University of Chicago Press.

Rüegg, Walter, ed. 2004. *Universities in the Nineteenth and Early Twentieth Centuries (1800–1945)*. Cambridge: Cambridge University Press.

Rummel, Erika. 1995. *The Humanist-Scholastic Debate in the Renaissance and Reformation*. Cambridge, Mass.: Harvard University Press.

Rummel, Erika. 2000. *The Confessionalization of Humanism in Reformation Germany*. Oxford: Oxford University Press.

Ruskin, John. 1870. *Lectures on Art, Delivered before the University of Oxford in Hilary Term, 1870*. New York: John Wiley and Son.

Russell, G. A., ed. 1994. *The 'Arabick' Interest of the Natural Philosophers in Seventeenth-Century England*. Leiden, Netherlands: E. J. Brill.

Sanderson, Stephen K. 1990. *Social Evolutionism: A Critical History*. Cambridge, Mass.: Blackwell.

Sandys, John Edwin. 2009 (1921). *A History of Classical Scholarship*. 3rd ed. 3 vols. Mansfield Centre, Conn.: Martino.

Sassetti, Filippo. 1970. *Lettere da vari paesi 1570–1588 di Filippo Sassetti*, ed. Vanni Bramanti. Milan: Longanesi.

Sauer, Thomas G. 1981. *A. W. Schlegel's Shakespearean Criticism in England, 1811–1846*. Bonn: Bouvier Verlag Herbert Grundmann.

Savage, David J. 1949. "Grundtvig: A Stimulus to Old English Scholarship." In *Philologica: The Malone Anniversary Studies*, ed. Thomas A. Kirby and Henry Bosley Woolf, 275–80. Baltimore: Johns Hopkins University Press.

Scaglione, Aldo. 1961. "The Humanist as Scholar and Politian's Conception of the Grammaticus." *Studies in the Renaissance*, 8: 49–70.

[Schaff, Philip], ed. 1879. *Anglo-American Bible Revision*. Philadelphia: American Sunday-School Union.

Scherer, Wilhelm. 1921 (1885). *Jacob Grimm*. 2nd ed. Berlin: Dom Verlag.

Schilling, Hanna-Beate. 1972. "The Role of the Brothers Schlegel in American Literary Criticism as Found in Selected Periodicals, 1812–1833: A Critical Bibliography," *American Literature* 43: 563–79.

Schlegel, August Wilhelm. 1815. *A Course of Lectures on Dramatic Art and Literature, by Augustus William Schlegel*, trans. John Black. London: Baldwin, Cradock and Joy.

Schlegel, Friedrich. 1818. *Lectures on the History of Literature, Ancient and Modern. From the German of Frederick Schlegel* [trans. John Gibson Lockhart]. 2 vols. Edinburgh: William Blackwood / London: Baldwin, Cradock, and Joy.

Schlegel, Friedrich. 1977 (1808). *Über die Sprache und die Weisheit der Indier: ein Beitrag zur Begründung der Altertumskunde*, ed. E.F.K. Koerner. Amsterdam: John Benjamins.

Schleicher, August. 1861. *Compendium der vergleichenden Grammatik der indogermanischen Sprachen*. Weimar, Germany: Hermann Böhlau.

Schleicher, August. 1871. *Compendium der vergleichenden Grammatik der indogermanischen Sprachen*. 3rd ed. Weimar, Germany: Hermann Böhlau.

Schleiermacher, Friedrich. 1993 (1825). *Luke: A Critical Study: Translation, with an Introduction by Connop Thirlwall, with Further Essays, Emendations and Other Apparatus by Terence N. Tice*. Lewiston, N.Y.: Edwin Mellon.

Schlenke, Manfred. 1976. "Anfänge einer wissenschaftlichen Geschichtsschreibung in Großbritannien im 18. Jahrhundert." In *Historische Forschung im 18. Jahrhundert: Organisation, Zielsetzung, Ergebnisse*, ed. Karl Hammer and Jürgen Voss, 314–33. Bonn: Ludwig Röhrscheid Verlag.

Schmidt, Francis. 1994. "Des inepties tolérable: la raison des rites de John Spencer (1685) à W. Robertson Smith (1889)." *Archives de science sociale des religions* 85: 121–36.

Schmidt-Biggemann, Wilhelm. 1983. *Topica universalis: Eine Modellgeschichte humanistischer und barocker Wissenschaft*. Hamburg: Felix Meiner Verlag.

Schmitt, Charles B. 1983. *Aristotle and the Renaissance*. Cambridge, Mass.: Harvard University Press for Oberlin College.

Scholder, Klaus. 1990 (1966). *The Birth of Modern Critical Theology: Origins and Problems of Biblical Criticism in the Seventeenth Century*. London: SCM / Philadelphia: Trinity Press International.

Schoolcraft, Henry Rowe. 1839. *Algic Researches, Comprising Inquiries Respecting the Mental Characteristics of the North American Indians. First Series, Indian Tales and Legends.* 2 vols. in 1. New York: Harper and Brothers.

Schreiner, Peter. 2008. *Byzanz 565–1453*. 3rd ed. Munich: R. Oldenbourg.

Schulenburg, Sigrid von der. 1975. *Leibniz als Sprachforscher*. Frankfurt am Main: Vittorio Klostermann.

Schwab, Raymond. 1950. *La Renaissance orientale*. Paris: Payot.

Schwarzer, Mitchell. 1995. "Origins of the Art History Survey Text." *Art Journal* 54, no. 3: 24–29.

Schwyzer, Philip. 2004. *Literature, Nationalism and Memory in Early Modern England and Wales*. Cambridge: Cambridge University Press.

Sciappa, Edward. 1999. *The Beginnings of Rhetorical Theory in Classical Greece*. New Haven, Conn.: Yale University Press.

Sears, Barnas, B. B. Edwards, and C. C. Felton. 1843. *Classical Studies. Essays on Ancient Literature and Art. With the Biography and Correspondence of Eminent Philologists*. Boston: Gould, Kendall, and Lincoln.

Segal, Daniel A. 2000. " 'Western Civ' and the Staging of History in American Higher Education," *American Historical Review* 105: 770–805.

Sengupta, Indra. 2005. *From Salon to Discipline: State, University and Indology in Germany, 1821–1914*. Würzburg, Germany: Ergon Verlag.

Sergi, Giuseppe. 1884. *Antropologia biologica*. Milan: Fratelli Dumolard Editori.

Seuren, Pieter A. M. 1998. *Western Linguistics: An Historical Introduction*. Oxford: Blackwell.

Shakespeare, William. 1733. *The Works of Shakespeare. Collated with the Oldest Copies, and Corrected; with Notes, Explanatory, and Critical*, ed. Lewis Theobald. 7 vols. London: Printed for A. Bettesworth et al.

Shanzer, Danuta. 1986. *A Philosophical and Literary Commentary on Martianus Capella's "De Nuptiis Philologiae et Mercurii" Book 1*. Berkeley and Los Angeles: University of California Press.

Shanzer, Danuta R. 2005. "Augustine's Disciplines: *Silent diutius Musae Varronis?*" In *Augustine and the Disciplines: From Cassiciacum to "Confessions,"* ed. Karla Pollman and Mark Vessey, 69–112. Oxford: Oxford University Press.

Shapiro, Barbara J. 1969. *John Wilkins, 1614–1672: An Intellectual Biography*. Berkeley and Los Angeles: University of California Press.

Shapiro, Barbara J. 2000. *A Culture of Fact: England, 1550–1720*. Ithaca, N.Y.: Cornell University Press.

Sharpe, Kevin. 1979. *Sir Robert Cotton, 1586–1631: History and Politics in Early Modern England*. Oxford: Oxford University Press.

Shea, Donald F. 1969. *The English Ranke: John Lingard*. New York: Humanities Press.

Shea, Victor, and William Whitla, eds. 2000. *Essays and Reviews: The 1860 Text and Its Reading*. Charlottesville: University Press of Virginia.

Sheehan, Jonathan. 2005. *The Enlightenment Bible: Translation, Scholarship, Culture*. Princeton, N.J.: Princeton University Press.

Sheehan, Jonathan. 2006. "Sacred and Profane: Idolatry, Antiquarianism, and the Politics of Distinction in the Seventeenth Century." *Past and Present* 192: 35–66.

Shelford, April G. 2007. *Transforming the Republic of Letters: Pierre-Daniel Huet and European Intellectual Life, 1650–1720*. Rochester, N.Y.: University of Rochester Press.

Shepard, Robert S. 1991. *God's People in the Ivory Tower: Religion in the Early American University*. New York: Carlson.

Sherbo, Arthur. 1986. *The Birth of Shakespeare Studies: Commentators from Rowe (1709) to Boswell-Malone (1821)*. East Lansing, Mich.: Colleagues.

Shuger, Debora Kuller. 1994. *The Renaissance Bible: Scholarship, Sacrifice, and Subjectivity*. Berkeley and Los Angeles: University of California Press.

Sidonius Apollinaris. 1936–65. *Poems and Letters*, ed. W. B. Anderson. 2 vols. Cambridge, Mass.: Harvard University Press.

Sihler, Ernest G. 1930. *From Maumee to Thames and Tiber: The Life-Story of an American Classical Scholar*. New York: New York University Press.

Silverberg, Robert. 1968. *Mound Builders of Ancient America: The Archaeology of a Myth*. Greenwich, Conn.: New York Graphic Society.

Simmons, Clare A. 1990. *Reversing the Conquest: History and Myth in Nineteenth-Century British Literature*. New Brunswick, N.J.: Rutgers University Press.

Simon, Marcel. 1997. "The Bible in the Earliest Controversies between Jews and Christians." In *The Bible in Greek Christian Antiquity*, ed. and trans. Paul M. Blowers, 49–68. Notre Dame, Ind.: University of Notre Dame Press.

Simonsuuri, Kirsti. 1979. *Homer's Original Genius: Eighteenth-Century Notions of the Early Greek Epic*. Cambridge: Cambridge University Press.

Sinha, Mishka. 2010. "Corrigibility, Allegory, Universality: A History of the Gita's Transnational Reception, 1785–1945." *Modern Intellectual History* 7: 297–317.

Skinner, Andrew S. 1979. *A System of Social Science: Papers Relating to Adam Smith*. Oxford: Clarendon.

Skinner, Quentin. 1996. *Reason and Rhetoric in the Philosophy of Hobbes*. Cambridge: Cambridge University Press.

Small, Ian. 1991. *Conditions for Criticism: Authority, Knowledge, and Literature in the Late Nineteenth Century*. Oxford: Clarendon.

Smalley, Beryl. 1964 (1952). *The Study of the Bible in the Middle Ages*. Notre Dame, Ind.: University of Notre Dame Press.

Smart, Ninian, et al. eds. 1985. *Nineteenth Century Religious Thought in the West*. 3 vols. Cambridge: Cambridge University Press.

Smith, E. Baldwin. 1912. *The Study of the History of Art in the Colleges and Universities of the United States*. N.p. [Princeton, N.J.]: n.p.

Smith, Olivia. 1984. *The Politics of Language, 1791–1819*. Oxford: Clarendon.

Smith, Roger. 1995. "The Language of Human Nature." In *Inventing Human Science: Eighteenth-Century Domains*, ed. Christopher Fox, Roy Porter, and Robert Wokler, 88–111. Berkeley and Los Angeles: University of California Press.

Smith, Samuel Stanhope. 1812. *The Lectures, Corrected and Improved, Which Have Been Delivered for a Series of Years, in the College of New Jersey; on the Subjects of Moral and Political Philosophy*. 2 vols. Trenton, N.J.: Daniel Fenton.

Smith, William Robertson. 1912. *Lectures and Essays of William Robertson Smith*, ed. John Sutherland Black and George Chrystal. London: Adam and Charles Black.

Smith, W. Robertson. 1889. *Lectures on the Religion of the Semites. First Series: The Fundamental Institutions*. Edinburgh: Adam and Charles Black.

Smith, William Robertson. 2000 (1894). *Religion of the Semites*. New Brunswick, N.J.: Transaction. (Title abbreviated from original *Lectures on the Religion of the Semites*.)

Smith, Woodruff D. 1991. *Politics and the Sciences of Culture in Germany, 1840–1920*. New York: Oxford University Press.

Smyth, Craig Hugh, and Peter M. Lukehart, eds. 1993. *The Early Years of Art History in the United States: Notes and Essays on Departments, Teaching, and Scholars*. Princeton, N.J.: Department of Art and Archaeology, Princeton University.

A Society of Clergymen 1829. *Essays and Dissertations in Biblical Literature*. Vol. 1 [apparently no more published]. New York: G. and C. and H. Carvill.

Soffer, Reba N. 1994. *Discipline and Power: The University, History, and the Making of an English Elite, 1870–1930* Stanford, Calif.: Stanford University Press.

Solberg, Winton U. 1968. *The University of Illinois, 1867–1894: An Intellectual and Cultural History*. Urbana: University of Illinois Press.

Soll, Jacob. 2003. "Introduction: The Uses of Historical Evidence in Early Modern Europe." *Journal of the History of Ideas* 64: 149–57.

Solly, Henry Shaen. 1898. *The Life of Henry Morley, LL.D*. London: Edward Arnold.

Soros, Susan Weber, ed. 2006. *James "Athenian" Stuart, 1713–1788: The Rediscovery of Antiquity*. New Haven, Conn.: Yale University Press.

Spalding, William. 1853. *The History of English Literature; with an Outline of the Origin and Growth of the English Language: Illustrated by Extracts. For the Use of Schools and of Private Students*. New York: D. Appleton.

Spalding, William. 1876 (1833). *A Letter on Shakspere's Authorship of "The Two Noble Kinsmen"; and on the Characteristics of Shakspere's Style and the Secret of His Supremacy*. London: N. Trübner for the New Shakspere Society.

Sparks, Jared. 1852. *A Reply to the Strictures of Lord Mahon and Others, on the Mode of Editing the Writings of Washington*. London: Trübner / Boston: James Munroe.

Spencer, T.J.B. 1957. "Robert Wood and the Problem of Troy in the Eighteenth Century." *Journal of the Warburg and Courtauld Institutes* 20: 75–105.

Sperling, S. David. 1992. *Students of the Covenant: A History of Jewish Biblical Scholarship in North America.* Atlanta: Scholars.

Spinoza, Benedict de. 2007 (1670). *Theological-Political Treatise*, ed. Jonathan Israel, trans. Michael Silverthorne and Israel. Cambridge: Cambridge University Press.

Spon, Jacques [Jacobus Sponius]. 1685. *Miscellanea eruditae antiquitatis* [etc.]. Lyon, France: Thomas Amaulry.

Squier, E. G. 1851. *The Serpent Symbol, and the Worship of the Reciprocal Principles of Nature in America.* New York: George P. Putnam.

Staël, Germaine de. 1813. *Germany; by the Baroness Staël Holstein. Translated from the French.* 3 vols. London: John Murray.

Stahl, William H. 1965. "To a Better Understanding of Martianus Capella." *Speculum* 40: 102–15.

Stallo, J. B. 1885 (1884). *The Concepts and Theories of Modern Physics*, 2nd ed. New York: D. Appleton.

Stam, James H. 1976. *Inquiries into the Origin of Language: The Fate of a Question.* New York: Harper and Row.

Stanley, Arthur Penrhyn. 1846. *The Life and Correspondence of Thomas Arnold, D.D.* 2nd American ed. 2 vols. in 1. New York: D. Appleton.

Stanley, Arthur Penrhyn. 1870. *Essays Chiefly on Questions of Church and State from 1850 to 1870.* London: John Murray.

Stanton, William. 1975. *The Great United States Exploring Expedition of 1838–1842.* Berkeley and Los Angeles: University of California Press.

Steinmann, Jean. 1960. *Richard Simon et les origines de l'exégèse biblique.* Paris: Desclée de Brouwer.

Stenhouse, William. 2005. *Reading Inscriptions and Writing Ancient History: Historical Scholarship in the Late Renaissance.* London: Institute of Classical Studies, School of Advanced Study, University of London.

Stephen, Leslie. 1962 (1876). *History of English Thought in the Eighteenth Century.* 2 vols. New York: Harcourt, Brace and World.

Stephens, F. G. 1875. *Flemish and French Pictures: With Notes concerning the Painters and Their Works.* London: Sampson Low, Marston, Low, and Searle.

Stephens, W.R.W. 1895. *The Life and Letters of Edward A. Freeman.* 2 vols. London: Macmillan.

Stevens, Cj [*sic*]. 1957. "The Rediscovery of the Indian Languages: A Survey." *American Speech* 32: 43–48.

Stevenson, Louise L. 1986. *Scholarly Means to Evangelical Ends: The New Haven Scholars and the Transformation of Higher Learning in America, 1830–1890.* Baltimore: Johns Hopkins University Press.

Steward, Julian H., Ann J. Gibson, and John H. Rowe. 1961. "Alfred Louis Kroeber, 1876–1960." *American Anthropologist*, n.s., 63: 1038–87.

Stewart, John William. 1990. "The Tethered Theology: Biblical Criticism, Common Sense Philosophy, and the Princeton Theologians, 1812–1860." PhD diss., University of Michigan.

Stock, Brian. 1983. *The Implications of Literacy: Written Language and Models of Interpretation in the Eleventh and Twelfth Centuries.* Princeton, N.J.: Princeton University Press.

Stocking, George W., Jr. 1987. *Victorian Anthropology.* New York: Free Press.

Stocking, George W., Jr. 1995. *After Tylor: British Social Anthropology, 1888–1951.* Madison: University of Wisconsin Press.

Stoddart, Anna M. 1895. *John Stuart Blackie.* 2 vols. Edinburgh: W. Blackwood.

Stokes, Margaret. 1878. *Early Christian Architecture in Ireland.* London: George Bell and Sons.

Stokes, Margaret. 1887. *Early Christian Art in Ireland.* 2 vols. in 1. London: Chapman and Hall for the Committee of Council on Education.

Stoneman, Richard. 1987. *Land of Lost Gods: The Search for Classical Greece.* Norman: University of Oklahoma Press.

Stovall, Floyd, ed. 1955. *The Development of American Literary Criticism.* Chapel Hill: University of North Carolina Press.

Stray, Christopher. 1997. "'Thucydides or Grote?' Classical Disputes and Disputed Classics in Nineteenth-Century Cambridge." *Transactions of the American Philological Association* 127: 363–71.

Stray, Christopher. 1998. *Classics Transformed: Schools, Universities, and Society in England, 1830–1960.* Oxford: Clarendon.

Stray, Christopher, ed. 2003. *The Classical Association: The First Century, 1903–2003.* Oxford: Oxford University Press for the Classical Association.

Stray, Christopher. 2004. "From One Museum to Another: The *Museum Criticum* (1813–26) and the *Philological Museum* (1831–33)." *Victorian Periodicals Review* 37 (2004): 289–314.

Stray, Christopher, ed. 2007a. *Classical Books: Scholarship and Publishing in Britain since 1800.* London: Institute of Classical Studies, School of Advanced Study, University of London.

Stray, Christopher, ed. 2007b. *Oxford Classics: Teaching and Learning, 1800–2000.* London: Duckworth.

Stray, Christopher. 2007c. "The Rise and Fall of Porsoniasm," *Cambridge Classical Journal* 53: 40–71.

Stroheker, Karl Friedrich. 1970 (1948). *Der senatorische Adel im spätantiken Gallien.* Darmstadt, Germany: Wissenschaftliche Buchgesellschaft.

Stroumsa, Guy G. 1996. "From Anti-Judaism to Antisemitism in Early Christianity?" In *Contra Judaeos: Ancient and Medieval Polemics between Christians and Jews*, ed. Ora Limor and Guy G. Stroumsa, 1–26. Tübingen, Germany: J.C.B. Mohr [Paul Siebeck].

Stroumsa, Guy G. 2009 (2005). *The End of Sacrifice: Religious Transformations in Late Antiquity*, trans. Susan Emanuel. Chicago: University of Chicago Press.

Stroumsa, Guy G. 2010. *A New Science: The Discovery of Religion in the Age of Reason.* Cambridge, Mass.: Harvard University Press.

Struever, Nancy, ed. 1995. *Language and the History of Thought.* Rochester, N.Y.: University of Rochester Press.

Stuart, Moses. 1827 (1814). *Elements of Interpretation, Translated from the Latin of J. A. Ernesti and Accompanied by Notes, with an Appendix Containing Extracts from Morus[,] Beck[,] and Keil.* 3rd ed. [corrected printing]. Andover, Mass.: Mark Newman.

Stubbs, Elsina. 2002. *Wilhelm von Humboldt's Philosophy of Language, Its Sources and Its Influence.* Lewiston, N.Y.: Edwin Mellen.

Stubbs, William. 1874–78. *The Constitutional History of England in its Origin and Development.* 3 vols. Oxford: Clarendon.

Stuchtey, Benedikt, and Peter Wende, eds. 2000. *British and German Historiography, 1750–1950: Traditions, Perceptions, and Transfers.* Oxford: Oxford University Press for the German Historical Institute London.

Sullivan, Robert E. 1982. *John Toland and the Deist Controversy: A Study in Adaptations.* Cambridge, Mass.: Harvard University Press.

Summit, Jennifer. 2008. *Memory's Library: Medieval Books in Early Modern England*. Chicago: University of Chicago Press.

Sussman, Lance J. 1995. *Isaac Leeser and the Making of American Judaism*. Detroit: Wayne State University Press.

Sutherland, Kathryn. 1994. "Editing for a New Century: Elizabeth Elstob's Anglo-Saxon Manifesto and Aelfric's St. Gregory Homily." In *The Editing of Old English: Papers from the 1990 Manchester Conference*, ed. D. G. Scragg and Paul E. Szarmach, 213–37. Woodbridge, England: D. S. Brewer.

Sweet, Paul R. 1978–80. *Wilhelm von Humboldt: A Biography*. 2 vols. Columbus: Ohio State University Press.

Sweet, Rosemary. 2004. *Antiquaries: The Discovery of the Past in Eighteenth-Century Britain*. London: Hambledon and London.

Swiggers, Pierre. 1998. "Americanist Linguistics and the Origin of Linguistic Typology: Peter Stephen Du Ponceau's 'Comparative Science of Language.'" *Proceedings of the American Philosophical Society* 142: 18–46.

Taylor, Allan R. 1963. "The Classification of the Caddoan Languages," *Proceedings of the American Philosophical Society* 107: 51–59.

Temple, William. 1690. *Miscellanea, the Second Part, in Four Essays*. 2nd ed. London: Printed by J. R. for Ri. and Ra. Simpson.

Theobald, [Lewis]. 1726. *Shakespeare Restored: or, A Specimen of the Many Errors, as Well Committed, as Unamended, by Mr. Pope in His Late Edition of This Poet*. London: Printed for R. Francklin, et al.

Thirlwall, Connop. 1835–44. *A History of Greece*. 8 vols. London: Longman, et al. [name varies] and John Taylor.

Thirlwall, Connop. 1852. *Histoire des origines de la Grèce ancienne*, trans. Adolphe Joanne. Paris: Paulin et Le Chevalier.

Thirlwall, John Connop, Jr. 1936. *Connop Thirlwall: Historian and Theologian*. London: Society for Promoting Christian Knowledge.

Thomas, Clara. 1967. *Love and Work Enough: The Life of Anna Jameson*. Toronto: University of Toronto Press.

Thomas, Nicholas. 2003. *Cook: The Extraordinary Voyages of Captain James Cook*. New York: Walker.

[Thomas, Northcote W.] 1907. *Anthropological Essays Presented to Edward Burnett Tylor in Honour of His 75th Birthday Oct. 2 1907*. Oxford: Clarendon.

Thomas, Rosalind. 1992. *Literacy and Orality in Ancient Greece*. Cambridge: Cambridge University Press.

Thompson, C. R. 1936. "The Study of Anglo-Saxon in America." *English Studies* 18: 241–53.

Thompson, D'Arcy W. 1864. *Day Dreams of a Schoolmaster*. 2nd ed. Edinburgh: Edmonston and Douglas.

Thompson, Peter. 2003. "Judicious Neology: The Imperative of Paternalism in Thomas Jefferson's Linguistic Studies." *Early American Studies* 1: 187–224.

Ticknor, George. 1849. *History of Spanish Literature*. 3 vols. New York: Harper and Brothers.

Ticknor, George. 1873 (1864). *Life of William Hickling Prescott*. Philadelphia: J. B. Lippincott.

Tieck, William A. 1965. "In Search of Peter Stephen Du Ponceau." *Pennsylvania Magazine of History and Biography* 89: 52–67, 69–78.

Tillyard, E.M.W. 1958. *The Muse Unchained: An Intimate Account of the Revolution in English Studies at Cambridge*. London: Bowes and Bowes.

Timpanaro, Sebastiano. 2005 (1981). *The Genesis of Lachmann's Method*, ed. and trans. Glenn W. Most. Chicago: University of Chicago Press.

Todd, Charles L., and Robert Sonkin. 1977. *Alexander Bryan Johnson: Philosophical Banker*. Syracuse, N.Y.: Syracuse University Press.

Too, Yun Lee. 1998. *The Idea of Ancient Literary Criticism*. Oxford: Clarendon.

Toomer, G. J. 1996. *Eastern Wisedome [sic] and Learning: The Study of Arabic in Seventeenth-Century England*. Oxford: Clarendon.

Toomer, G. J. 2009. *John Selden: A Life in Scholarship*. 2 vols., continuously paginated. Oxford: Oxford University Press.

Townend, G. B. 1967. "Suetonius and His Influence." In *Latin Biography*, ed. T. A. Dorey, 79–111. New York: Basic Books.

Townsend, Robert B. 2009. "The Social Shape of the AHA, 1884–1945." *Perspectives on History* 47, no. 9: 36–40.

Toy, Crawford Howell. 1913. *Introduction to the History of Religions*. Boston: Ginn.

Tracy, James D. 1996. *Erasmus of the Low Countries*. Berkeley and Los Angeles: University of California Press.

Traill, David A. 1995. *Schliemann of Troy: Treasure and Deceit*. New York: St. Martin's.

Trautmann, Thomas R. 1987. *Lewis Henry Morgan and the Invention of Kinship*. Berkeley and Los Angeles: University of California Press.

Trautmann, Thomas R. 1992. "The Revolution in Ethnological Time." *Man*, n.s., 27: 379–97.

Trautmann, Thomas R. 1997. *Aryans and British India*. Berkeley and Los Angeles: University of California Press.

Trautmann, Thomas R. 2006. *Languages and Nations: The Dravidian Proof in Colonial Madras*. Berkeley and Los Angeles: University of California Press.

Treglown, Jeremy, and Bridget Bennett, eds. 1998. *Grub Street and the Ivory Tower: Literary Journalism and Literary Scholarship from Fielding to the Internet*. Oxford: Clarendon.

Treloar, Geoffrey R. 1998. *Lightfoot the Historian: The Nature and Role of History in the Life and Thought of J. B. Lightfoot (1828–1889) as Churchman and Scholar*. Tübingen, Germany: Mohr Siebeck.

Trent, William Peterfield, et al., eds. 1921. *The Cambridge History of American Literature*. 4 vols. New York: G. P. Putnam's Sons.

Trevor-Roper, Hugh. 1985. *Renaissance Essays*. Chicago: University of Chicago Press.

Trigger, Bruce G. 1966. "Sir Daniel Wilson: Canada's First Anthropologist." *Anthropologica*, n.s., 8: 3–28.

Trigger, Bruce G. 1981. "Giants and Pygmies: The Professionalization of Canadian Archaeology." In *Toward a History of Archaeology*, ed. Glyn Daniel, 69–84. London: Thames and Hudson.

Trigger, Bruce G. 1992. "Daniel Wilson and the Scottish Enlightenment." *Proceedings of the Society of Antiquaries of Scotland* 122: 55–75.

Trigger, Bruce G. 2006. *A History of Archaeological Thought*. 2nd ed. Cambridge: Cambridge University Press.

Trinkaus, Charles. 1979. *The Poet as Philosopher: Petrarch and the Formation of Renaissance Consciousness*. New Haven, Conn.: Yale University Press.

Trinkaus, Charles. 1995 (1970). *In Our Image and Likeness: Humanity and Divinity in Italian Humanist Thought*. 2 vols. in one. Notre Dame, Ind.: University of Notre Dame Press.

Trunz, Erich. 1970. "Der deutsche Späthumanismus um 1600 als Standeskultur." In *Deutsche Barockforschung: Dokumentation einer Epoche*, ed. Richard Alewyn, 4th ed., 147–81. Cologne: Kiepenheuer und Witsch.

Tully, James. 1988. "The Pen Is a Mighty Sword." In *Meaning and Context: Quentin Skinner and His Critics*, ed. James Tully, 7–25. Princeton, N.J.: Princeton University Press.

Turley, Richard Marggraf, 2001. "Nationalism and the Reception of Jacob Grimm's *Deutsche Grammatik* by English-Speaking Audiences." *German Life and Letters* 54: 234–52.

Turner, Frank M. 1981. *The Greek Heritage in Victorian Britain*. New Haven, Conn.: Yale University Press.

Turner, Frank M. 1993. *Contesting Cultural Authority: Essays in Victorian Intellectual Life*. Cambridge: Cambridge University Press.

Turner, James. 1985. *Without God, without Creed: The Origins of Unbelief in America*. Baltimore: Johns Hopkins University Press.

Turner, James. 1993. "Religion et langage dans l'Amérique du XIXe siècle. Le cas étrange de Andrews Norton." *Revue de l'histoire des religions* 210, no. 4: 431–62.

Turner, James. 1999. *The Liberal Education of Charles Eliot Norton*. Baltimore: Johns Hopkins University Press.

Turner, James. 2002. "Le concept de science dans l'Amérique du XIXe siècle." *Annales: histoire, sciences sociales* 57, no. 3: 753–72.

Turner, James. 2003. *Language, Religion, Knowledge: Past and Present*. Notre Dame, Ind.: University of Notre Dame Press.

Turner, James. 2011. *Religion Enters the Academy: The Origins of the Scholarly Study of Religion in America*. Athens: University of Georgia Press.

Turner, Samuel. 1863. *Autobiography of the Rev. Samuel H. Turner, D.D., Late Professor of Biblical Learning and the Interpretation of Scripture in the General Theological Seminary of the Protestant Episcopal Church in the United States of America*. New York: A.D.F. Randolph.

Turner, Sharon. 1805. *The History of the Manners, Landed Property, Government, Laws, Poetry, Literature, Religion, and Language of the Anglo-Saxons*. London: Longman, Hurst, Rees, and Orme.

Turpin, Andrea Lindsay. 2011. "Gender, Religion, and Moral Vision in the American Academy, 1837–1917." PhD diss., University of Notre Dame.

Tyler, Moses Coit. 1878. *A History of American Literature, 1607–1765*. 2 vols. New York: G. P. Putnam's Sons.

Tyler, Moses Coit. 1897. *The Literary History of the American Revolution, 1763–1783*. 2 vols. New York: G. P. Putnam's Sons.

Tylor, Edward B. 1871. *Primitive Culture: Researches into the Development of Mythology, Philosophy, Religion, Art, and Custom*. 2 vols. London: John Murray.

Utz, Richard. 2002. *Chaucer and the Discourse of German Philology: A History of Reception and an Annotated Bibliography of Studies, 1793–1948*. Turnhout, Belgium: Brepols.

Valla, Lorenzo. 2007. *On the Donation of Constantine*, ed. and trans. G. W. Bowersock. Cambridge, Mass.: Harvard University Press.

Van den Bosch, Lourens P. 2002. *Friedrich Max Müller: A Life Devoted to the Humanities*. Leiden, Netherlands: Brill.

Vanderbilt, Kermit. 1986. *American Literature and the Academy: The Roots, Growth, and Maturity of a Profession*. Philadelphia: University of Pennsylvania Press.

VanderKam, James C. 2001. *The Book of Jubilees*. Sheffield, England: Sheffield Academic.

VanderKam, James C. 2010. *The Dead Sea Scrolls Today*. 2nd ed. Grand Rapids, Mich.: Wm. B. Eerdmanns.

Van Engen, John. 1996. "Studying Scripture in the Early University." In *Neue Richtungen in der hoch- und spatmittelalterlichen Bibelexegese*, ed. Robert E. Lerner, 17–38. Munich: R. Oldenbourg.

Van Keuren, David K. 1991. "From Natural History to Social Science: Disciplinary Development and Redefinition in British Anthropology, 1860–1910." In *The Estate of Social Knowledge*, ed. JoAnne Brown and David K. Van Keuren, 45–66. Baltimore: Johns Hopkins University Press.

Van Riper, A. Bowdoin. 1993. *Men among the Mammoths: Victorian Science and the Discovery of Human Prehistory*. Chicago: University of Chicago Press.

Veit, Richard. 1997. "A Case of Archaeological Amnesia: A Contextual Biography of Montroville Wilson Dickeson (1810–1882), Early American Archaeologist." *Archaeology of Eastern North America* 25: 97–123.

Venturi, Lionello. 1964 (1936). *History of Art Criticism*, trans. Charles Marriott. Rev. ed. New York: E. P. Dutton.

Vessey, Mark. 2004. "Introduction." In Magnus Aurelius Cassiodorus Senator, *"Institutions of Divine and Secular Learning" and "On the Soul,"* ed. and trans. James W. Halporn, 3–101. Liverpool, England: Liverpool University Press.

Vickers, Brian. 1998. *In Defence of Rhetoric*. Oxford: Clarendon.

Vöhler, Martin. 2002. "Christian Gottlob Heyne und das Studium des Altertums in Deutschland." In *Disciplining Classics—Altertumswissenschaft als Beruf*, ed. Glenn W. Most, 39–54. Göttingen, Germany: Vandenhoeck & Ruprecht.

Waagen, Gustav Friedrich. 1822. *Ueber Hubert und Johann van Eyck*. Breslau, Germany: Josef Max.

Waagen, [Gustav Friedrich ("Dr. Waagen")]. 1860. *Handbook of Painting. The German, Flemish, and Dutch Schools. Based on the Handbook of Kugler. Enlarged and for the Most Part Re-Written*. 2 vols. London: John Murray.

Waetzoldt, Wilhelm. 1965. *Deutsche Kunsthistoriker*. 2nd ed. 2 vols. in 1 (separately paginated). Berlin: Verlag Bruno Hessling.

Wakefield, Dick. 2001. *Anna Letitia Barbauld*. London: Centaur.

Wakefield, Robert. 1989 (1524). *On the Three Languages*, ed. and trans. G. Lloyd Jones. Binghamton, N.Y.: Medieval and Renaissance Texts and Studies.

Walbank, F. W., et al., eds. 1984. *The Hellenistic World*. Cambridge Ancient History vol. 7, part 1. Cambridge: Cambridge University Press.

Waley, Arthur. 1952. "Anquetil-Duperron and Sir William Jones." *History Today* 2, no. 1: 23–33.

Walhout, M. D. 1996. "The Hermeneutical Turn in American Critical Theory, 1830–1860." *Journal of the History of Ideas* 57: 683–703.

Wallace, Anthony F. C. 1999. *Jefferson and the Indians: The Tragic Fate of the First Americans*. Cambridge, Mass.: Harvard University Press.

Wallace, Stuart, 2006. *John Stuart Blackie: Scottish Scholar and Patriot*. Edinburgh: Edinburgh University Press.

Walls, Laura Dassow. 2009. *The Passage to Cosmos: Alexander von Humboldt and the Shaping of America*. Chicago: University of Chicago Press.

Walsh, Marcus. 1997. *Shakespeare, Milton, and Eighteenth-Century Literary Editing: The Beginnings of Interpretative Scholarship*. Cambridge: Cambridge University Press.

Walther, Gerrit. 1993. *Niebuhrs Forschung*. Stuttgart: Franz Steiner Verlag.

Wangenheim, Wolfgang von. 2005. *Der verworfene Stein: Winckelmanns Leben*. Berlin: Matthes und Seitz.

Wanley, Humfrey. 1989. *Letters of Humfrey Wanley, Palaeographer, Anglo-Saxonist, Librarian, 1672–1726*, ed. P. L. Heyworth. Oxford: Clarendon.

Ward, Mrs. Humphry [Mary Augusta]. 1918. *A Writer's Recollections*. 2 vols. New York: Harper and Brothers.

Ward, Thomas Humphry. 1891 (1880). "Preface." In *The English Poets*, ed. Thomas Humphry Ward, 1:v–vii. London: Macmillan.

Ward, W[illiam]. 1811. *Account of the Writings, Religion, and Manners, of the Hindoos: Including Translations from Their Principal Works*. 4 vols. Serampore, India: Mission.

Warren, Mercy Otis. 1994 (1805). *History of the Rise, Progress, and Termination of the American Revolution interspersed with Biographical, Political and Moral Observations*. 2 vols. Indianapolis: Liberty Fund.

Waters, Mary A. 2004a. *British Women Writers and the Profession of Literary Criticism, 1789–1832*. Houndmills, England: Palgrave Macmillan.

Waters, Mary A. 2004b. "'The First of a New Genus': Mary Wollstonecraft as a Literary Critic and Mentor to Mary Hays." *Eighteenth-Century Studies* 37: 415–34.

Watkin, David. 1982. *Athenian Stuart: Pioneer of the Greek Revival*. London: George Allen and Unwin.

Watts, Edward J. 2006. *City and School in Late Antique Athens and Alexandria*. Berkeley and Los Angeles: University of California Press.

Wawn, Andrew. 2000. *The Vikings and the Victorians: Inventing the Old North in Nineteenth-Century Britain*. Woodbridge, England: D. S. Brewer.

Weber, Timothy P. 1982. "The Two-Edged Sword: The Fundamentalist Use of the Bible." In *The Bible in America: Essays in Cultural History*, ed. Nathan O. Hatch and Mark A. Noll, 101–20. New York: Oxford University Press.

Wechsler, Harold S. 1985. "Pulpit or Professoriate: The Case of Morris Jastrow." *American Jewish History* 74: 338–55.

Weir, John Ferguson. 1957. *The Recollections of John Ferguson Weir, Director of the Yale School of the Fine Arts, 1869–1913*, ed. Theodore Sizer. New York and New Haven, Conn.: New-York Historical Society and Associates in Fine Arts at Yale University.

Weiss, Roberto. 1951. "Lovato Lovati (1241–1309)." *Italian Studies* 6: 3–28.

Weiss, Roberto. 1969. *The Renaissance Discovery of Classical Antiquity*. Oxford: Basil Blackwell.

Welcker, F. G. 1827. *Das akademische Kunstmuseum zu Bonn*. Bonn: E. Weber.

Wellek, René. 1941. *The Rise of English Literary History*. Chapel Hill: University of North Carolina Press.

Wellek, René. 1955–92. *A History of Modern Criticism, 1750–1950*. 8 vols. New Haven, Conn.: Yale University Press.

Wellhausen, Julius. 2001 (1927). *Prolegomena zur Geschichte Israels*. 6th ed. Berlin: De Gruyter.

Wendell, Barrett. 1893. *Stelligeri and Other Essays concerning America*. New York: Charles Scribner's Sons.

Wendell, Barrett. 1900. *A Literary History of America*. New York: Charles Scribner's Sons.

Werner, Shirley. 2009. "Literacy Studies in Classics: The Last Twenty Years." In *Ancient Literacies: The Culture of Reading in Greece and Rome*, ed. William A. Johnson and Holt N. Parker, 333–82. Oxford: Oxford University Press.

West, Martin L. 1998. "The Textual Criticism and Editing of Homer." In *Editing Texts / Texte edieren*, ed. Glenn W. Most, 94–110. Göttingen, Germany: Vandenhoeck and Ruprecht.

Wheeler-Barclay, Marjorie. 1987. "The Science of Religion in Britain, 1860–1915." PhD diss., Northwestern University.

Wheeler-Barclay, Marjorie. 2010. *The Science of Religion in Britain, 1860–1915*. Charlottesville: University of Virginia Press.

White, Peter. 2009. "Bookshops in the Literary Culture of Rome." In *Ancient Literacies: The Culture of Reading in Greece and Rome*, ed. William A. Johnson and Holt N. Parker, 268–87. Oxford: Oxford University Press.

Whitehead, Christopher. 2005. *The Public Art Museum in Nineteenth Century Britain: The Development of the National Gallery*. Aldershot, England: Ashgate.

Whitford, David M. 2009. *The Curse of Ham in the Early Modern Era: The Bible and the Justifications for Slavery*. Farnham, England: Ashgate.

Whitney, William Dwight. 1867. *Language and the Study of Language: Twelve Lectures on the Principles of Linguistic Science*. New York: Charles Scribner.

Whitney, William Dwight. 1971. *Whitney on Language: Selected Writings of William Dwight Whitney*, ed. Michael Silverstein. Cambridge, Mass.: MIT Press.

Wickham, Chris. 2009. *The Inheritance of Rome: A History of Europe from 400 to 1000*. New York: Viking.

Wiese, L[udwig Adolf]. 1854. *German Letters on English Education*, trans. W. D. Arnold. London: Longman, Brown, Green, and Longman.

Wigelsworth, Jeffrey R. 2009. *Deism in Enlightenment England: Theology, Politics, and Newtonian Public Science*. Manchester, England: Manchester University Press.

Wilamowitz-Moellendorff, Ulrich von. 1893. *Aristoteles und Athen*. 2 vols. Berlin: Weidmannsche Buchhandlung. (Cited as Wilamowitz 1893.)

Wilamowitz-Moellendorff, Ulrich von. 1982 (1921). *History of Classical Scholarship*, trans. Alan Harris. Baltimore: Johns Hopkins University Press. (Cited as Wilamowitz 1982.)

Wiley, Raymond A., ed. 1971. *John Mitchell Kemble and Jakob Grimm: A Correspondence 1831–52*. Leiden, Netherlands: E. J. Brill.

Wiley, Raymond A. 1979. "Anglo-Saxon Kemble: The Life and Works of John Mitchell Kemble 1807–1857: Philologist, Historian, Archaeologist." *Anglo-Saxon Studies in Archaeology and History* 1: 165–273.

Willey, Basil. 1956. *More Nineteenth Century Studies: A Group of Honest Doubters*. New York: Columbia University Press.

Williams, Jay. 1999. *The Times and Life of Edward Robinson: Connecticut Yankee in King Solomon's Court*. Atlanta: Society of Biblical Literature.

Williams, Megan Hale. 2006. *The Monk and the Book: Jerome and the Making of Christian Scholarship*. Chicago: University of Chicago Press.

Wilson, Daniel. 1851. *The Archaeology and Prehistoric Annals of Scotland*. Edinburgh: Sutherland and Knox / London: Simpkin, Marshall, and Co., and J. H. Parker.

Wilson, John A. 1964. *Signs and Wonders upon Pharaoh: A History of American Egyptology*. Chicago: University of Chicago Press.

Wilson, John B. 1965. "Grimm's Law and the Brahmins," *New England Quarterly* 38: 234–39.

Wilson, N. G. 1983. *Scholars of Byzantium*. Baltimore: Johns Hopkins University Press.

Wilson, N. G. 1992. *From Byzantium to Italy: Greek Studies in the Italian Renaissance*. Baltimore: Johns Hopkins University Press.

Wind, James P. 1987. *The Bible and the University: The Messianic Vision of William Rainey Harper*. Atlanta: Scholars.

Winkworth, Susanna, et al. 1852. *The Life and Letters of Barthold George [sic] Niebuhr, and Selections from His Minor Writings*. 2nd ed. 3 vols. London: Chapman and Hall. (Winkworth appears on title page as "editor and translator," but she altered so much of the German edition that she functioned as coauthor.)

Winning, William Balfour. 1838. *A Manual of Comparative Philology, in Which the Affinity of the Indo-European Languages is Illustrated, and Applied to the Primeval History of Europe, Italy, and Rome*. London: J. G. & F. Rivington.

Winterer, Caroline. 2002. *The Culture of Classicism: Ancient Greece and Rome in American Intellectual Life, 1780–1910*. Baltimore: Johns Hopkins University Press.

Winterer, Caroline. 2007. *The Mirror of Antiquity: American Women and the Classical Tradition, 1750–1900*. Ithaca, N.Y.: Cornell University Press.

Wiseman, Nicholas Patrick. 1836. *Twelve Lectures on the Connexion between Science and Revealed Religion*. 2 vols. London: Joseph Booker.

Wissler, Clark. 1942. "The American Indian and the American Philosophical Society." *Proceedings of the American Philosophical Society* 86: 189–204.

Witt, Ronald G. 1996. "The *Crisis [of the Early Italian Renaissance]* after Forty Years," *American Historical Review* 101: 110–18.

Witt, Ronald G. 2000. *In the Footsteps of the Ancients: The Origins of Humanism from Lovato to Bruni*. Leiden, Netherlands: Brill.

Witt, Ronald G. 2012. *The Two Latin Cultures and the Foundation of Renaissance Humanism in Medieval Italy*. Cambridge: Cambridge University Press.

Witte, Markus. 2007. "Die literarische Gattung des Buches Hiob: Robert Lowth und seine Erben." In *Sacred Conjectures: The Context and Legacy of Robert Lowth and Jean Astruc*, ed. John Jarick, 93–123. New York: T and T Clark.

Wolf, F. A. 1797. *Briefe an Herrn Hofrath Heyne von Professor Wolf: Eine Beilage zu den neuesten Untersuchungen über den Homer*. Berlin: G. C. Nauk.

Wolf, F. A. 1985 (1795). *Prolegomena to Homer*, ed. and trans. Anthony Grafton, Glenn W. Most, and James E. G. Zetzel. Princeton, N.J.: Princeton University Press.

Wood, Robert. 1971 (1775). *An Essay on the Original Genius and Writings of Homer: with a Comparative View of the Ancient and Present State of the Troade*. New York: Garland.

Woodbridge, John D. 1984. "Richard Simon's Reaction to Spinoza's 'Tractatus Theologico-Politicus.'" In *Spinoza in der Frühzeit seiner Religiösen Wirkung*, ed. Karlfried Gründer and Wilhelm Schmidt-Biggemann, 201–26. Heidelberg: Verlag Lambert Schneider.

Woolf, Daniel. 2003. *The Social Circulation of the Past: English Historical Culture, 1500–1700*. Oxford: Oxford University Press.

Woolhouse, Roger. 2007. *Locke: A Biography*. New York: Cambridge University Press.

Woolsey, Theodore D. 1862. *Eulogy of Cornelius Conway Felton, LL.D., &c., One of the Regents of the Smithsonian Institution. Prepared at the Request of the Board. May 1862*. Washington, D.C.: Smithsonian Institution.

Wormald, Francis, and C. E. Wright. 1958. *The English Library before 1700: Studies in Its History*. London: Athlone.

Worster, Donald. 2001. *A River Running West: The Life of John Wesley Powell*. New York: Oxford University Press.

Wortham, John David. 1971. *The Genesis of British Egyptology, 1549–1906*. Norman: University of Oklahoma Press.

Wyatt, M. Digby. 1870. *Fine Art, a Sketch of Its History, Theory, Practice, and Application to Industry: Being a Course of Lectures Delivered at Cambridge in 1870*. London: Macmillan.

Wylie, J. A. 1886. *History of the Scottish Nation*, vol. 1, *Pre-Historic, Druidic, Roman, and Early Christian Scotland*. London: Hamilton, Adams.

Yates, Frances. 1966. *The Art of Memory*. Chicago: University of Chicago Press.

Yates, Frances. 1982. *Lull and Bruno*. London: Routledge and Kegan Paul.

Yeo, Richard. 1993. *Defining Science: William Whewell, Natural Knowledge, and Public Debate in Early Victorian Britain*. Cambridge: Cambridge University Press.

Yoffie, Adina Miriam. 2009. "Biblical Literalism and Scholarship in Protestant Northern Europe, 1630–1700." PhD diss., Harvard University.

Young, B. W. 1998. *Religion and Enlightenment in Eighteenth-Century England: Theological Debate from Locke to Burke*. Oxford: Clarendon, 1998.

Young, Robert J. C. 2008. *The Idea of English Ethnicity*. Oxford: Blackwell.

Zagorin, Perez. 1998. *Francis Bacon*. Princeton, N.J.: Princeton University Press.

Zande, Johan van der. 2010. "Statistik and History in the German Enlightenment." *Journal of the History of Ideas* 71: 411–32.

Zeisberger, David. 1827. *Grammar of the Language of the Lenni Lenape or Delaware Indians. Translated from the German Manuscript of the Author by Peter Stephen Du Ponceau. With a Preface and Notes by the Translator.* Philadelphia: James Kay Jr.

Zetzel, James E. G. 1984 (1980). *Latin Textual Criticism in Antiquity.* Salem, N.H.: Ayer.

Zimmerman, Andrew. 2001. *Anthropology and Antihumanism in Imperial Germany.* Chicago: University of Chicago Press.

Zimmerman, Bernhard. 1991 (1986). *Greek Tragedy: An Introduction*, trans. Thomas Marier. Baltimore: Johns Hopkins University Press.

Zimmerman, T. C. Price. 1995. *Paolo Giovo: The Historian and the Crisis of Sixteenth-Century Italy.* Princeton, N.J.: Princeton University Press

INDEX

Celtic, 97, 98
Celtic philology, 156–57
Celts, 334
Ceylon, 194
Chaldeans, 109
Chambers, E. K., 265
Chambers, Robert, 141
Champollion, Jean-François, 188, 193, 196
Channing, William Ellery, 160
Charlemagne, 27, 38
Charles IV, Emperor, 36
Charles V, Emperor, 39
Charles VIII, King of France, 39
charters, 81, 83, 84, 109. *See also* diplomatics
Chartres, cathedral school at, 27–28
Chaucer, Geoffrey, 8, 80, 108, 151, 257, 258, 259,
    260, 262–63, 265, 267, 403n42; *Book of the
    Duchess*, 271; *Canterbury Tales*, 232, 264; and
    Child, 153, 264; and Junius, 82; as newer clas-
    sic, 84; *Troilus and Criseyde*, 264
Chaucer Society, 263, 264
Cherokee language, 138
Chicago, University of, 280, 286, 303, 305, 308,
    322, 378, 451n46
Child, Francis J., 152–53, 154, 183, 264, 265–67,
    268, 415n10, 431n26; *The English and Scottish
    Popular Ballads*, 153, 266–67
Child, Lydia Maria, 370; *Progress of Religious
    Ideas*, 229
China, 2, 176, 247, 357; character and nationality
    of, 246; chronology of, 52; gods of, 96; Jesuit
    mission to, 75; missionary reports about, 95;
    rituals of, 53; and Ussher's timeline of human
    history, 301; and Voltaire, 109
Chinese, 1, 52, 58, 135, 139, 234, 288
Chomsky, Noam, 398n68
Christian Hebraists, 41, 47, 52
Christianity, 18–25, 53, 63; and archaeology, 188;
    and Bede, 26; and Bible, 73; and Child, 229;
    and Clarke, 371; and classical antiquity, 168–
    69; and comparative religions, 370, 371, 374;
    and Confucian writings, 75; and De Wette,
    227; and doctrine of Trinity, 43; early English,
    202; and ecclesiastical history, 47; and Euse-
    bius, 23; and Frazer, 294; and H. Adams, 228;
    and Hardwick, 229; and Italian humanists, 38;
    and Jewish scriptures, 19; and Jews/Judaism,
    19–20, 21, 47; and Maurice, 229; and J. Mi-
    chaelis, 113; and Milman, 220; and F. M. Mül-
    ler, 237–38, 374; and paganism, 21, 22, 38; and
    Parker, 229; and Semler, 113; and Septuagint,
    20, 21; and Simon, 73; and W. R. Smith, 377–

78; and textual corruption, 73–74; and Valla,
    35; and W. D. Whitney, 239
Christians, 4, 210, 391n38; and Bible, 7; and co-
    dices, 24; and Hebrew texts, 43; and W. von
    Humboldt, 135; and Jews, 13, 41
Christians, early: and Bible, 19–20, 24; and Jew-
    ish and Gentile factions, 74; and myth, 212;
    and pagans, 18–19, 168; and rabbinic tradi-
    tions and Jewish rituals, 61; and Septuagint,
    13
Christ's College, Aberdeen, 365, 367
Christy, Henry, 346–47
chronicles, 28, 38, 109
Chronicles and Memorials of Great Britain and
    Ireland during the Middle Ages (Rolls Series),
    199, 304
chronology, 63, 126, 298, 304, 384; and Alexan-
    drian scholars, 11–12; Aztec, 170; and Bede, 26;
    and Bentley, 70; and Bible (Mosaic chronol-
    ogy), 26, 51–52, 220, 224, 300, 301, 328, 345;
    and Biondo, 38–39; and Boeckh, 170; and
    Bruni, 38–39; and Carolingian Renaissance,
    27; and Constable, 325; and Cornelius Nepos,
    16; as discipline, 232; and Eratosthenes, 11; and
    Eusebius of Caesarea, 23; and Fasti Capitolini,
    51; of Gospels, 116; Hellenistic and Roman,
    22–23; and humanism, 51, 63; of Indian his-
    tory, 95; and medieval monasteries, 32; and
    Middle Ages, 28; and oriental studies, 52; and
    Origen, 22; and Roman grammar, 17; and Jo-
    seph Scaliger, 51, 95; and Simon, 61; synchro-
    nisms in, 22, 23
Chrysoloras, Manuel, 40
Chthonic ritual, 296
Church Fathers, 32, 38, 55, 73, 358
Church of England, 54, 81, 88, 106, 174, 216–17,
    220, 225
Church of Scotland, 288; Disruption in, 365
Cicero, Marcus Tullius, 8, 18, 27, 31, 36, 44, 80,
    169, 399n78; *De inventione*, 16, 390n28; *Insti-
    tutio oratoria*, 390n28; and Italian humanism,
    38, 39; and Middle Ages, 28; and Middleton,
    75; and natural religion, 76; and Perizonius,
    62; *Pro Archia*, 34; *Rhetorica ad Herennium*,
    16; in Scottish universities, 106; *Tusculan Dis-
    putations*, 39
Cincinnati Art Museum, 316
Cincinnati Theological Seminary, 228
Circleville, Ohio, 332
civilization, 95, 97, 135, 167, 168, 274, 302, 328,
    345
Clarendon, Edward Hyde, 1st Earl of, 304

Göttingen (*cont.*)
American students at, 180; art history at, 312, 317; and Blackie, 287; and Gildersleeve, 183; library of, 179; and W. R. Smith, 365, 366
Gower, John, 260, 262–63, 267
Graevius, Joannes, 67
Graff, Gerald, 271, 430n11
Grafton, Anthony, 23, 51
Grammaire générale et raisonnée, 58
grammar, 63, 64; at Alexandria, 13–14; and ancient philology, 4, 13; Anglo-Saxon, 82, 84, 134, 155; and Aristarchus, 13–14; and Bacon, 57; and Bede, 26; and Bernard of Chartres, 27, 28; and Bopp, 132; and Carolingian Renaissance, 27; and Cassiodorus, 26; classical, 36n; and classical authors in Middle Ages, 28; comparative, 98, 99, 130, 131, 132, 138, 139, 231–32, 245, 254, 411n12; descriptive, 249; and Dionysius Thrax, 14; and Greeks, 2, 3; and Grimm, 132; Hebrew, 41; and humanism, 63; and W. von Humboldt, 134, 135; and language families, 130; and liberal arts, 18; and literary studies, 148, 260; and Lowth, 88; and medieval education, 35; and medieval trivium, 28; and mental processes, 58; of modern languages, 124; and Origen, 21; and Pergamum, 13, 14; Persian, 93; and Petrarch, 34; and *philología*, 14; and polymathy, 50; and Quintilian, 35; and Remmius Palaemon, 16; and rhetoric, 13; and Roman education, 14; and Roman elite, 17; and Romans, 16; Sanskrit, 128; and Joseph Scaliger, 59; and Scholasticism, 28, 29, 30, 57; and Scottish rhetoric, 107; and twelfth-century renaissance, 27; and Tyrannion, 14; universal, 57–58, 87; and Valla, 35; and Varro, 17; vernacular, 36n; and western Middle Ages, 25
grammatica speculativa, 30, 32, 57, 87, 393n64, 398n68
Greater Panathenaea, 7, 8
Greece, ancient, 52, 63; and Age of Goethe, 169; and *American Journal of Philology*, 279; and American Philological Association, 279; archaeology of, 188, 196, 281, 284; and art history, 311; and Boeckh, 171; canons of beauty and value from, 169; civilization of, 51, 181; and classics as modern discipline, 275; culture of, 168; and democracy, 6; education in, 2, 7; evolution of sculpture and painting in, 310; and Felton, 181; German historians of, 207; and Grote, 206; historians of, 12; history of, 168, 200, 205–7, 206; holistic approach to,

299, 300; and Italian humanism, 39; and Jebb, 293; and language, 1–2; and literacy, 4; and MacDouall, 288; and C. E. Norton, 319; as primitive, 274, 275; religion and mythology of, 8, 53, 96, 116, 172, 184, 186, 227, 369; social history of, 288; and Winckelmann, 117; and Wolf, 119
Greek, 1, 3, 10, 47, 231, 290; accents in, 12, 276; alphabet of, 4, 7, 15, 70; and American higher educational curriculum, 276–77; and American Philological Association, 278; American teaching of, 179, 181; Attic dialect of, 4, 24; Attic-Ionic dialect family of, 70; and Bentley, 69, 70–71, 90; and Blackie, 287; and British universities, 171; and Christianity, 19; and *collegium trilinguae*, 41–42; and common ancestral language, 98; as common language (*koiné*) of Hellenistic world, 4, 5; and Complutensian Polyglot Bible, 42; and Cousturier, 41; curriculum centered on, 233; de-emphasis in education on, 381; development of, 354; dictionaries of, 49; and digamma, 70, 401n13; and Donaldson, 133; in eastern Roman Empire, 24; and English literary studies, 255, 256; and Erasmus, 43, 45; and Gildersleeve, 280; grammar of, 14; and Halhed, 98; and higher education curriculum in United Kingdom, 298; and humanism, 63; and human mind, 246; and Indo-European, 244; and Jews, 13, 46; and Jones, 97; and MacDouall, 288; medieval and Renaissance knowledge of, 40; and medieval biblical scholarship, 31; modern student composition in, 176, 177; and Newton, 192; and Northern humanism, 40; and Poliziano, 37; and Quarrel of the Ancients and Moderns, 68; and Rask, 132; regional dialects of, 5; and Rosetta Stone, 188; and Scholasticism vs. humanism, 40; speakers of, 4; teaching of, xii, 49; and undergraduate education, 168. *See also* Bible, New Testament: Greek
Greek literature, 126, 164; and American classical philology, 181, 182; and Bentley, 67; and Boeckh, 170; and Bywater, 292; Callimachus's survey of, 10; and Christianity, 168; and classics as modern discipline, 275; and Gildersleeve, 183; medieval translation into Latin, 32; and K. O. Müller, 170; and J. C. Scaliger, 186; and Welcker, 184; and Winckelmann, 117
Greek Orthodox Church, 40
Greek Revival, 104, 190
Greeks, ancient, 5–14; architecture of, 185; art of, 185, 186, 187; and Boeckh, 170; as closer to